A writer is not so much someone who has something to say as he is someone who has found a process that will bring about new things he would not have thought of if he had not started to say them.   – William Stafford

Writing and rewriting are a constant search for what it is one is saying.
                                                                – John Updike

. . . I think best with a pencil in my hand. . . .   –Anne Morrow Lindbergh

You can write any time people will leave you alone and not interrupt you.
                                                            – Ernest Hemingway

I have to write every day because, the way I work, the writing generates the writing.   – E. L. Doctorow

My first draft usually has only a few elements worth keeping. I have to find what they are and build from them and throw out what doesn't work, or what simply is not alive.   – Susan Sontag

SHORT THIRD EDITION

The St. Martin's Guide to Writing

RISE B. AXELROD

California State University,

San Bernardino

CHARLES R. COOPER

University of California,

San Diego

ST. MARTIN'S PRESS

New York

Senior Editor: Mark Gallaher
Editor: Marilyn Moller
Project Editor: Denise Quirk
Development Associate: Kristin Bowen
Production Supervisor: Alan Fischer
Text and Cover Design: Anna Post George

Library of Congress Catalog Card Number: 89-63883
Copyright © 1991 by St. Martin's Press, Inc.

For information, write:
St. Martin's Press, Inc.
175 Fifth Avenue
New York, NY 10010

ISBN: 0-312-03494-6

ACKNOWLEDGMENTS

Margot Adler. From *Drawing Down the Moon,* by Margot Adler. Copyright © 1979 by Margot
Adler. Reprinted by permission of Viking Penguin, a division of Penguin Books USA Inc.

American Heritage definition of "brave." Copyright © 1985 by Houghton Mifflin Company.
Reprinted by permission from *The American Heritage Dictionary, Second College Edition.*

Maya Angelou. From *I Know Why the Caged Bird Sings* by Maya Angelou. Copyright © 1969
by Maya Angelou. Reprinted by permission of Random House, Inc.

David Ansen. "Searing, Nervy and Very Honest." From *Newsweek,* July 3, 1989, and © 1989,
Newsweek, Inc. All rights reserved.

David Attenborough. From *Life on Earth,* Little, Brown and Company, 1987. Copyright ©
1979 by David Attenborough Productions, Ltd.

*Acknowledgments and copyrights are continued at the back of the book on pages 583–85, which
constitute an extension of the copyright page.*

To the Instructor

When we first wrote *The St. Martin's Guide to Writing,* we tried to take the best that has been thought and said in the field of rhetoric and composition and turn it to practical use. We saw the *Guide* as continuing the classical tradition of treating rhetoric very seriously indeed, not just as a matter of producing correct, effective prose but as one of thinking, reading, and writing intelligently. To the best insights from that tradition, we added what we believed to be the most promising developments in the New Rhetoric.

We have been tremendously gratified by the enthusiastic reception of the first two editions of *The St. Martin's Guide,* and in this third edition, we continue in our efforts to bring new ideas and pedagogy into the composition classroom. But our basic goals remain unchanged. We aim to teach students how to use the composing process as a means of discovering, developing, and presenting their ideas. We seek to give them the skills and information they need to analyze different writing situations so that they can respond thoughtfully and creatively to the intellectual and rhetorical demands of any situation in which they find themselves. Finally, we hope to inspire students with the desire to examine with a critical eye their own ideas in the context of the heterogeneous and often conflicting values and beliefs current in society.

AN OVERVIEW OF THE BOOK

As a rhetoric and reader, *The St. Martin's Guide* can serve as a comprehensive introduction to discursive practice. It comprises several parts:

Part I. Writing Activities presents nine different essay assignments, all reflecting actual writing situations that students may encounter both in and out of college, kinds of discourse that they should learn to read critically and to write intelligently. Among the types of essays included are autobiography, explanation, position paper, proposal, and literary interpretation.

You may choose among these chapters and teach them in any sequence you wish, though they are sequenced here to move students from writing based on personal experience and observation to academic types of writing calling for the analysis and synthesis of ideas and information derived from a variety of sources.

Each chapter follows the same organizational plan:

- several brief scenarios identifying the kind of discourse covered in the chapter and suggesting the range of occasions when such writing is done
- an activity *for group inquiry* that gets students working with the kind of discourse
- a set of readings accompanied by a critical apparatus designed to help students explore pertinent readerly and writerly questions
- a summary of the purpose and audience and the features basic to writing of this kind
- a flexible guide to writing that escorts students through all the stages of the composing process
- a look at one writer at work showing some aspect of the process of writing the student essay in that chapter

Part II. Writing Strategies looks at a wide range of essential writers' strategies: invention; paragraphing and coherence; logic and reasoning; and the familiar modes of presenting information, like narrating, defining, and classifying. Examples and exercises are almost all taken from contemporary nonfiction, and many exercises deal with reading selections appearing in Part I. This cross-referencing between Parts I and II facilitates teaching writing strategies in the context of purpose and audience.

Part III. Research Strategies discusses both field and library research and includes thorough guidelines for using and documenting sources, with detailed examples of the MLA and APA documentation styles. The part concludes with a sample student research paper.

Part IV. Writing under Pressure treats a special kind of academic writing: essay examinations, showing students how to analyze different kinds of exam questions and offering strategies for writing answers. The chapter is illustrated with actual questions from courses throughout the disciplines, plus two sample student essays.

Noteworthy Features

The St. Martin's Guide to Writing has several features that distinguish it from other college rhetorics. Chief among these are the practical guides to writing, the integration of modes and aims, and the integration of reading and writing.

Practical Guides to Writing. We do not merely talk about the composing process; rather, we offer practical, flexible guides that escort students through the entire process, from invention through revision and self-evaluation. Thus, this book is more than just a rhetoric that students will refer to occasionally. It is a guidebook that will help them to write. Commonsensical and easy to follow, these writing guides teach students to assess a rhetorical situation, identify the kinds of information they will need, ask probing questions and find answers, and organize their writing to achieve their purpose most effectively.

Systematic Integration of Reading and Writing. Because we see a close relationship between the abilities to read critically and to write intelligently, *The St. Martin's Guide* combines reading instruction with writing instruction. Each chapter in Part I introduces one kind of discourse, which students are led to consider both as readers and as writers. Readings are followed by questions that make students aware of how they as readers respond and at the same time help them understand the decisions writers make. Students are then challenged to apply these insights to their own writing as they imagine their prospective readers, set goals, and write and revise their drafts.

Integration of Modes and Aims. This book treats the traditional modes of writing as writing strategies to be used to achieve particular purposes. Unlike many current rhetorics, we do not distinguish writing by its modes but rather by its aims. Hence, while we focus on craft in our discussion of the modes in Part II, we emphasize the integration of modes with aims through exercises analyzing how the modes are used strategically in the essays in Part I.

New to This Edition

We had the benefit of much helpful advice from instructors and students across the nation who had used the earlier editions. They helped us to see what worked well and what needed improvement, and they provided valuable suggestions for specific changes and additions.

More than half the readings are new. In addition to seeking selections that would capture the interest and imagination of college students throughout the nation and that would illustrate a range of discursive practices, we also looked for readings that would have some *thematic unity.* The theme we chose is difference. Nearly *one-half of the readings deal with issues of gender, ethnicity and culture,* followed by questions For Discussion that prompt students to give serious consideration to the network of cultural values and beliefs that characterize our relations with one another.

Also new is a series of activities to promote group discussion and inquiry. At the start of each of the writing chapters is an exercise For Group Inquiry that invites students to try out some of the thinking and planning they'll be doing for the kind of writing covered in that chapter. Then, following each reading comes a new question For Discussion, designed to provoke thoughtful response about the social and political dimensions of the reading. Finally, in the Guide to Writing is another exercise For Group Inquiry that gets students to discuss their work in progress with one another. All of these materials have been class-tested, and all include questions and prompts to guide students to work productively together.

Our book is now accompanied by *three new ancillaries,* all innovative and—we think—exciting ones. We hope you'll find them useful.

The St. Martin's MindWriter/Descant, an invention and revision software program. The award-winning Daedalus Group has developed a computer software program to complement *The St. Martin's Guide to Writing.* Designed to be used together with the writing guides, the program includes materials for invention, drafting, critical reading, and revision. Available in IBM and Macintosh versions, this software is complementary to instructors, who can make copies for students.

A Guide to Evaluating Student Writing, by Charles Cooper. This practical booklet offers advice on evaluating student writing and holding conferences, detailed guides for responding to the writing assignments in *The St. Martin's Guide,* and a collection of important journal articles on evaluation.

The Great American Bologna Festival and other student essays, edited by Elizabeth Rankin, University of North Dakota. We've always valued the use of student writing in the composition class. Now we can offer you a collection of essays written by students throughout the nation using *The St. Martin's Guide.* It is a charming, regional collection that celebrates the writing our students are doing. The collection includes whimsical essays, like that about a Michigan bologna festival, as well as gripping personal stories, such as one about a family's escape from Afghanistan, and serious academic efforts such as a proposal about topsoil erosion in Iowa.

For Courses with Diverse Emphases

The St. Martin's Guide is designed to be used in courses with diverse emphases. Courses focusing on *the writing process,* for example, might rely most heavily on the writing guides and the Writer at Work sections of Part I, whereas those focusing on *critical reading* have thirty-five complete essays, each accompanied by questions and commentary to help students read analytically, as well as guidelines to reading with a critical eye. Courses concerned with *writing in academic disciplines* will find academic assignments for explaining concepts, causal analysis, arguing for a position, and interpreting literature; lists of resources for research in various disciplines in the library research chapter; and a chapter on taking essay exams, with example questions from diverse disciplines. Instructors wishing to use *group-learning* methods have available two inquiry activities in each writing chapter; discussion questions suitable for small-group work after each reading; and a section in each writing guide on getting (and giving) critical comments.

Detailed teaching suggestions and course plans for these and other courses can be found in the Instructor's Resource Manual. Whatever approach is taken, we hope our book will provide an exciting and innovative course of study for your students.

ACKNOWLEDGMENTS

We owe a great deal to others. The history of rhetoric reaches back to Greece in the fifth century B.C., and among our predecessors are teachers and scholars—Aristotle, Quintilian, and Cicero in classical times; Erasmus from the early Renaissance; the eighteenth-century Scottsmen George Campbell and Hugh Blair; and Henry Day, the author of the most distinguished American rhetoric of the nineteenth century—who believed that rhetoric instruction was of great intellectual, social, and ethical importance. They considered rhetoric to be a study of thinking, speaking, and writing intelligently and responsibly. From this humanistic tradition comes our belief that students must learn to write well to realize their potential as thinkers, and as citizens.

And we owe a great deal to our contemporaries. Any list of debts will necessarily be incomplete, but we would be remiss in failing to acknowledge how much we have learned from Arthur Applebee, Walter Beale, James Berlin, James Britton, Ann Brown, Kenneth Burke, Wallace Chafe, Francis Christensen, Robert Connors, Robert de Beaugrande, Jacques Derrida, Peter Elbow, Janet Emig, Jeanne Fahnestock, Lester Faigley, Stanley Fish, Linda Flower, Michel Foucault, Anne Gere, Sidney Greenbaum, Joseph Grimes, M.A.K. Halliday, Ruqaiya Hasan, John Hayes, George Hillocks, James Kinneavy, William Labov, Richard Larson, Richard Lloyd-Jones, Ann Matsuhashi, John Mellon, James Moffett, James Murphy, Donald Murray, Lee Odell, Chaim Perelman, Anthony Petrosky, Richard Rieke, D. Gordon Rohman, Mike Rose, Robert Scholes, John Schultz, Marie Secor, Mina Shaughnessy, Malcolm Sillars, Frank Smith, William Strong, Barbara Tomlinson, Stephen Toulmin, Tuen van Dijk, John Warnock, Eliot Wigginton, Joseph Williams, Ross Wintercrowd, Stephen Witte, and Richard Young.

We must also acknowledge immeasurable lessons learned from all the writers, professional and student alike, whose works we read in search of selections and examples for this text. The clarity and grace found in much current nonfiction prose have repeatedly astounded us. To all the writers represented in this text we owe a great debt—together, they have set a high standard indeed for all writers. Our aim has been not to contradict their practice by anything we recommend to students in this book.

With this third edition, our debt is even greater to the staff, instructors, and students in the Third College Writing Program at the University of California at San Diego. Since 1979 this book has been developed very gradually in courses there, with instructors and students helping us to discover what worked and what did not. We appreciate their candor and support. The first and second editions have served as the main text in this program, and we are indebted to all of the fifty or so instructors who have used it and provided helpful criticism and advice. Special and notable contributions have been made by James Degan, Kate Gardner, Keith Grant-Davie, Kristin Hawkinson, Karen Hollis, Sherrie Inness, Du-Hyoung Kang, Gesa Kirsch, Mary Jane Lind, Susan MacDonald, Michael A. Pemberton, Steven Storla, M.A. Syverson, Evelyn Torres, Wendy Wagreich, and Pamela Wright. Once again, we owe an enormous debt to Phyllis Campbell and Rebekah Kessab, who have continued to eliminate the sort of administrative fuss and bother that discourages teachers and writers. And we would like to express special thanks to our students, for generous and willing feedback.

We would also like to thank friends, colleagues, and students at California State University, San Bernardino, and the University of California at Riverside for their continuing advice and support. In particular, we would like to thank Steven Axelrod, Larry Barkley, Kim Devlin, Stephanie Kay, Kathryn O'Rourke, and Dian Pizurie.

Many instructors across the nation helped us to improve the book by responding to a detailed questionnaire about the second edition. For their perceptive comments and valuable suggestions, we thank Julia M. Allen, University of California at Irvine; Laura S. Armesto, Barry University; Constance Balides, University of Wisconsin—Milwaukee; Richard Bullock, Wright State University; Vicki Byard, Purdue University; Jo-Anne Cappeluti, Fullerton University; Christine Cetrulo, University of Kentucky; Ruth E. Chapin, University of Portland; Dr. Wilfred O. Dietrich, Blinn College; Paul D. Farkas, Metropolitan State College; Carolyn E. Foster, Clemson University; Kate Gadbow, Montana State University; Irene F. Gale, University of South Florida; Jerome Goodman, Mohawk Valley Community College; Christopher Gould, University of North Carolina at Wilmington; Kathleen Gould, University of North Carolina at Wilmington; Peter J. Hager, University of Texas at El Paso; Judith I. Hall, Monroe Community College; Jon Harned, University of Houston; Jeane Harris, Arkansas State University; Carol Hewer, Cerro Coso Community College; Connie Hosler, University of Cincinnati; Karen Kappen, Allan Hancock College; Deepika Karle, Bowling Green State University; David M. Kvernes, Southern Illinois University; Elizabeth Larsen, West Chester University; Teresa A. Layden, George Washington University; Harriet Linkin, New Mexico State University; David Mair, University of Oklahoma; Lisa J. McClure, Southern Illinois University; Lee McKenzie, Weber State University; G. Douglas Meyers, University of Texas at El Paso; Michael Miller, Longview Community College; Rosemary Olds, Des Moines Area Community College; Don C. Perkins, University of Wisconsin—Milwaukee; Joseph Powell, Central Washington University; Elizabeth Rankin, University of North Dakota; Birgit L. Scherer, Southern Illinois University; Leora Schermerhorn, Seminole Community College; Linda S. Schwartz, Coastal Carolina College; Michael T. Sita, Pima County Community College; David Smit, Kansas State University; Sheryl Stevenson, University of Akron; Jack Troutner, Bowling Green State University; Irwin Weiser, Purdue University; Stephen Wilhoit, University of Dayton; Willie T. Williams, Florida A and M University; James Wilson, Trinidad State Junior College; and Richard Zbaracki, Iowa State University.

For reviewing new readings we thank Vicki Byard, Purdue University; Jo-Anne Cappeluti, Fullerton College; Marvin Diogenes, University of Arizona; Kathleen Gould, University of North Carolina at Wilmington; Peter

J. Hager, University of Texas at El Paso; Judith I. Hall, Monroe Community College; Maurice Hunt, Baylor University; David M. Kvernes, Southern Illinois University; Joseph Powell, Central Washington University; and Richard Zbaracki, Iowa State University.

And we'd like to give special thanks to the following students for reading and carefully evaluating the new readings: Brian Bigler, Iowa State University; Melinda Blessing, Purdue University; Carlos Gallego, University of Arizona; Krista Hanson, Central Washington University; Scott Lewis Hutchins, University of North Carolina at Wilmington; Walter Lynch, Baylor University; Debra Terry, Monroe Community College; Joel Whitley, Iowa State University; and Joel Zizik, University of Texas at El Paso.

We also wish to thank colleagues who helped us to shape and create the exciting supplementary materials that now accompany *The St. Martin's Guide to Writing*. For insightful reviews of *The Guide to Evaluating Student Writing*, we thank Leon Coburn, University of Nevada at Las Vegas; David Mair, University of Oklahoma; and Lucy Schultz, University of Cincinnati. For their expert and innovative work on *The St. Martin's MindWriter/Descant* software, we thank the Daedalus Group, and especially Wayne Butler and Paul Taylor. For the new appendix on writing with a word processor, we thank John M. Slatin, also of the Daedalus Group.

And we thank the many instructors across the nation who shared with us their students' essays, enabling us to publish *The Great American Bologna Festival and other student essays,* a companion volume celebrating the work done using *The St. Martin's Guide*. Space will not permit us to list the names of everyone who contributed papers, but we would like to acknowledge the many splendid essays received from colleagues at the University of Arizona, Blinn College, Bowling Green State University, University of California at Riverside, University of California at San Diego, University of Cincinnati, Eastern Michigan University, University of Idaho, Iowa State University, University of Kentucky, University of New Hampshire, University of North Carolina at Wilmington, University of North Dakota, University of Oklahoma, Purdue University, Southern Illinois University, Seminole Community College, University of South Carolina, Trinidad State Junior College, and Wright State University. And we wish in particular to thank Libby Rankin, University of North Dakota, who chose and arranged the essays for this collection. Her choices and her commentaries reveal a remarkable teacher and sensitive reader, and we're fortunate indeed that the collection she's edited will accompany our book.

We are particularly grateful to two professional librarians who helped us with the chapter on library research. Anne Skillion, from the New York Public Library, provided a thoughtful review of the second edition chapter and made many specific suggestions for extending the chapter to cover the new electronic forms of information retrieval. Jean Smith, from the University of California at San Diego, contributed some innovative new materials to help students find useful sources in the various academic disciplines. Having worked for some years now with students doing library research for the assignments in *The St. Martin's Guide,* she has contributed some valuable lists of sources, most notably ones for researching controversial issues and current trends.

We want to express our most sincere appreciation to the staff at St. Martin's Press, whose patience and hard work has made this book possible. We are especially indebted to Mark Gallaher, Senior Editor, and to Marilyn Moller, who has so generously given her time, imagination, skill, and friendship; without her, there would have been no third edition. Thanks also to John Elliott and Denise Quirk, for their skillful editing; to Kim Richardson, for her expert work on the software; and to Kristin Bowen for her thoughtful assistance on many, many matters, large and small.

Finally, we wish to thank our families: Rise Axelrod's husband, Steven; son, Jeremiah; and mother, Edna Borenstein; and Charles Cooper's wife, Mary Anne; daughters, Susanna and Laura; and son, Vincent. "I scarcely know where to begin," wrote Emily Dickinson, "but love is always a safe place."

A Brief Contents

Contents

GUIDE TO WRITING

THE WRITING ASSIGNMENT 116

INVENTION AND RESEARCH 117

Choosing a Subject / For Group Inquiry / Exploring Your Preconceptions / Planning Your Project / Posing Some Preliminary Questions / Finding a Tentative Theme

PLANNING AND DRAFTING 121

Seeing What You Have / Setting Goals / Outlining / Drafting

GETTING CRITICAL COMMENTS 125

Reading with a Critical Eye

REVISING AND EDITING 127

Identifying Problems / Solving the Problems / Editing and Proofreading

LEARNING FROM YOUR OWN WRITING PROCESS 129

A WRITER AT WORK

THE INTERVIEW NOTES AND REPORT 130

5   Explaining Concepts   136

For Group Inquiry

PURPOSE AND AUDIENCE 157

BASIC FEATURES OF EXPLANATORY ESSAYS 157

A Well-focused Subject / A Main Point or Thesis / An Appeal to Readers' Interests / A Logical Plan / Clear Definitions / Appropriate Writing Strategies / Careful Use of Sources

GUIDE TO WRITING

THE WRITING ASSIGNMENT 160

INVENTION AND RESEARCH 161

Finding a Concept / Exploring the Concept / Focusing on One Aspect of the Concept / Researching Your Subject / Testing Your Choice / For Group Inquiry / Establishing a Main Point / Considering Explanatory Strategies

PLANNING AND DRAFTING 165

Seeing What You Have / Setting Goals / Outlining / Drafting

GETTING CRITICAL COMMENTS 167

Reading with a Critical Eye

REVISING AND EDITING 169

Identifying Problems / Solving the Problems / Editing and Proofreading

GUIDE TO WRITING

THE WRITING ASSIGNMENT 239

INVENTION AND RESEARCH 239
Choosing a Problem / Analyzing and Defining the Problem / Identifying Your Readers / Finding a Tentative Solution / Defending Your Solution / Testing Your Choice / For Group Inquiry / Offering Reasons for Your Proposal / Considering Alternative Solutions / Doing Research

PLANNING AND DRAFTING 244
Seeing What You Have / Setting Goals / Outlining / Drafting

GETTING CRITICAL COMMENTS 247
Reading with a Critical Eye

REVISING AND EDITING 249
Identifying Problems / Solving the Problems / Editing and Proofreading

LEARNING FROM YOUR OWN WRITING PROCESS 252

A WRITER AT WORK

STRENGTHENING THE ARGUMENT 252

8   *Making Evaluations*   *256*

For Group Inquiry

PURPOSE AND AUDIENCE 274

BASIC FEATURES OF EVALUATIONS 274
A Clearly Defined Subject / A Clear, Balanced Judgment / A Convincing Argument / Pointed Comparisons

GUIDE TO WRITING

THE WRITING ASSIGNMENT 277

INVENTION AND RESEARCH 277
Choosing a Subject / Exploring Your Subject / Analyzing Your Readers / Developing an Argumentative Strategy / Testing Your Choice / For Group Inquiry

PLANNING AND DRAFTING 281
Seeing What You Have / Setting Goals / Outlining / Drafting

GETTING CRITICAL COMMENTS 283
Reading with a Critical Eye

REVISING AND EDITING 285
Identifying Problems / Solving the Problems / Editing and Proofreading

PART TWO

Writing Strategies

11   *Invention and Inquiry*   *382*

15 Defining   440

16 Classifying   452

17 Comparing and Contrasting   462

18 Arguing   468

PART THREE

Research Strategies

PART FOUR

Writing under Pressure

SHORT THIRD EDITION

The St. Martin's Guide to Writing

Why is writing important? Does it always take a lot of time and hard work? Can computer word processing make it any easier? Is it necessarily solitary work? Is it possible to *learn* how to write well? Is good writing worth the effort? If you have just opened this book and are about to begin a writing course, you may be asking yourself questions like these. If so, read on. This book has some of the answers.

Writing makes a special contribution to the way people think. When we write, we compose meanings. We put together facts and ideas and make something new, whether in a letter home, in a college essay, or in a report at work. When we write, we create an intricate web of meaning in which sentences have special relationships to each other. Some sentences are general and some specific; some expand a point and others qualify it; some define and others illustrate. These sentences, moreover, are concerned in a still larger set of relationships, with every sentence related in some way to every other. By controlling these complex relationships, we as writers can forge new meanings.

> I think best with a pencil in my hand.   —Anne Morrow Lindbergh

Writing contributes uniquely to the way we learn. When we take notes in class or as we read, writing enables us to sort out information and to highlight what is important. Taking notes helps us to remember what we are learning and yields a written record that we can review later for tests or essays. Outlining or summarizing new information provides an overview of the subject and also fosters close analysis of it. Annotating as we read with underlining and marginal comments involves us in conversation—even debate—with the author. Thus, writing helps us to learn more effectively and to think more critically.

And because we as writers are always composing new meanings, writing helps us to find and establish our own information and ideas. It allows us to bring together and connect new and old ideas. By enabling us to clarify and deepen our understanding of new concepts, writing helps us relate them to other ideas. Thus, writing tests, clarifies, and extends our understanding of the world.

> I am never as clear about any matter as when I am just finished writing about it.   —James van Allen

Introduction 1

Writing contributes to personal development. As we write we become more potent thinkers and active learners, and we come eventually to a better understanding of ourselves by recording, exploring, and telling about our personal experiences and our innermost thoughts.

> Writing is a form of therapy. —Roald Dahl

Besides contributing to the way we think and learn, *writing helps us connect to others*, to communicate. The impulse to write can be as urgent as the need to converse with someone sitting across the table in a restaurant or to respond to a provocative comment in a classroom discussion. Sometimes we want readers to know what we know; we want to share something new. Sometimes we want to influence our readers' decisions, actions, or beliefs. We may even want to irritate or outrage readers. Or we may want to amuse or flatter them. Writing allows us to communicate in all of these ways.

> I think writing is really a process of communication. —Shirley Anne Williams
>
> Writing is a political instrument . . . a way to describe and control [your] circumstances. —James Baldwin

Good writing makes a special contribution to success in college and on the job. Students who write confidently and well learn more and earn better grades, for a student's writing is often the only basis an instructor has for an evaluation. Your first job may not require you to write, but later advancement often depends on skill in writing letters, memos, reports, and proposals. The United States is now an "information" society, one in which the ability to organize and synthesize information and to write intelligently and effectively is even more important than it was in the past. Writing may seem difficult, even threatening. Knowing *how* it works, however, can make writing less an obstacle, more an opportunity.

> Learning to write well takes time and much effort, but it can be done.
>
> —Margaret Mead

EXERCISE 1.1

Make a list of the uses you have made of writing *outside* school in the last four weeks. Then make a second list of the uses you have made of writing in school during the same period. Include everything from notes, lists, and letters to applications, essays, and poems. Include both writing you were required to do and writing you chose to do.

What can you conclude about the uses you make of writing? How does your writing outside school differ from your writing in school? Do you feel the same about all the writing you do? Which kind do you find most useful? Which do you most enjoy? Why? Summarize your conclusions.

HOW WRITING WORKS

What do we know about the process of writing? Research and published interviews with writers as well as our own experience as writers reveal a great deal about the process.

Perhaps the most important point to remember is this: writing is a skill that anyone can learn. Greatness as a writer may be a dream that only a few of us will pursue, but we can all learn to write well enough to handle any writing situation we encounter in college or on the job.

Many a writer spends time writing about the experience of writing. Sometimes we express our feelings about writing by comparing it with something else, often using simile and metaphor.

> Writing is building sand castles.   –A student
>
> I work as a writer . . . on the principle of refining low-grade ore.   –James Dickey
>
> Writing is like jumping into a freezing lake and slowly coming to the surface.
> –A student

The metaphors and similes writers typically use portray writing, not surprisingly, as a process—sometimes time-consuming, like refining ore; invigorating, like jumping into a lake; or simply fun, like building sand castles—but a process nevertheless. That writing is a process is the most important point you will learn in this course.

EXERCISE 1.2

How would you describe writing? Think of a metaphor (writing is _____) or a simile (writing is like _____) that best expresses your view of writing.

Not only is writing a process, but it is a process of discovery—one that makes discovery possible. Few writers begin with a complete understanding of their subject. They gather facts and ideas, start writing, and let the writing lead them to understanding. They will be making significant discoveries as they write.

> Writing, like life itself, is a voyage of discovery.   –Henry Miller
>
> I don't see writing as a communication of something already discovered, as "truths" already known. Rather, I see writing as a job of experiment. It's like any discovery job; you don't know what's going to happen until you try it.
> –William Stafford

No matter that the process of writing can seem messy and meandering, writers learn to trust it. In fact, writers are likely to depend on the act of writing to lead them to new ideas and insights. Writing gives form to thought. When we write something down, we can examine it from one angle and then another, studying its many facets as we would a diamond. Many writers claim they write to discover what they think.

> I write entirely to find out what I'm thinking, what I'm looking at, what I see and what it means.   —Joan Didion
>
> How do I know what I think until I see what I say.   —E. M. Forster

Once started, the process of writing continues even when writers are away from their desks. Always alert for ideas, they keep journals and notebooks ready for new thoughts and discoveries. Consciously or unconsciously, they continue to work at their writing.

> I never quite know when I'm not writing.   —James Thurber

Seasoned writers accept the fact that writing takes time and hard work.

> I believe in miracles in every area of life *except* writing. Experience has shown me that there are no miracles in writing. The only thing that produces good writing is hard work.   —Isaac Bashevis Singer

The hard work in writing comes in thinking things out. Writers may have promising ideas, but until they have written them down and tried to develop them, they cannot know if their ideas make sense and are worthwhile.

> You have to work problems out for yourself on paper. Put the stuff down and read it—to see if it works.   —Joyce Cary

The same thing applies to planning. Like the discovery of ideas, plans also need to be refined during the process of writing.

> You are always going back and forth between the outline and the writing, bringing them closer together, or just throwing out the outline and making a new one.   —Annie Dillard

Sometimes the hardest part of writing is getting started, just writing that first sentence. It may be reassuring to know what agony this first sentence sometimes causes even highly acclaimed writers.

> I suffer always from fear of putting down that first line. It is amazing the terrors, the magics, the prayers, the straightening shyness that assails one.   —John Steinbeck

Most writers know they will solve problems if they can just get started and keep on going. Consequently, they employ various strategies to keep the writing flowing, particularly during early drafting. Since almost all writers revise their first drafts, they need not worry about getting it right the first time. They know that agonizing indecision is unproductive.

> There may be some reason to question the whole idea of fineness and care in writing. Maybe something can get into sloppy writing that would elude careful

writing. I'm not terribly careful myself, actually. I write fairly rapidly if I get going. . . . In trying to treat words as chisel strokes, you run the risk of losing the quality of utterance, the rhythm of utterance, the happiness.   –John Updike

Experienced writers know that strong writing does not always emerge in a first draft. They write, and they revise.

Occasionally you can hit it right the first time. More often, you don't.
                                                                              –John Dos Passos

My first draft usually has only a few elements worth keeping. I have to find what those are and build from them and throw out what doesn't work.   –Susan Sontag

Revising can be seen as an opportunity to gain an entirely new perspective on a topic. It can mean moving paragraphs around, rewriting whole sections, or adding substantial new material.

Writing *is* rewriting   –Donald Murray

What makes me happy is rewriting. . . . It's like cleaning house, getting rid of all the junk, getting things in the right order, tightening things up.   –Ellen Goodman

I have never thought of myself as a good writer. Anyone who wants reassurance of that should read one of my first drafts. But I'm one of the world's great revisers.   –James Michener

I rewrote the ending of *A Farewell to Arms*, the last page of it, thirty-nine times before I was satisfied.   –Ernest Hemingway

Most writers actively seek critical comments from friends and colleagues. Playwrights, poets, and novelists attend writers' workshops, where their drafts can be read and critiqued by other writers. Researchers, engineers, and business executives almost always write collaboratively, in teams. Contrary to the familiar image of the solitary writer, alone at a lamp in a carrel, writing is very often a social activity.

For excellence, the presence of others is always required.   –Hannah Arendt

Even professional writers sometimes find drafting frustrating. Most of them establish routines and rituals to make the process familiar and comfortable, setting a time and finding a quiet place to write away from interruptions.

I prefer to get up very early in the morning and work.   –Katherine Anne Porter

The desk is in the room, near the bed, with a good light, [I write] midnight till dawn. . . .   –Jack Kerouac

In spite of the time it takes, the inevitable delays, and the hard work, writing brings great personal fulfillment and pride. Many writers write in order to earn a living. They struggle, but they also celebrate, and they find great satisfaction in the process as well as the result of writing.

Well, it's a beautiful feeling, even it it's hard work.   —Anne Sexton

There is much more to say about how writing works. Most important, writing is something you can master. You can learn about your own writing process and develop new skills to make the process easier to control. You can accept the fact that writing requires planning and rewriting, and give yourself the time you need to draft and revise your essays. You can expand your repertoire of writing strategies and learn what is expected of the particular kinds of writing you need to do. This book will help you to do all these things.

EXERCISE 1.3

Describe your own writing habits. How do you go about writing in the classroom, library, or study hall? What conditions make it easy or hard for you to write? How do you plan and organize? Do you write first drafts slowly or quickly? Do you revise on your own or only at the request of your teacher? What kind of revisions do you usually make?

Do you do things differently when you write at home? Where do you write at home? At what time of day or night? With music? TV? Food? With a pencil, at a typewriter, or on a word processor? What helps you to get started? To sustain the writing until you finish?

Do you regularly involve anyone else in your writing? Do you discuss your ideas or show your drafts to friends or parents?

ABOUT THIS BOOK

This book is divided into several major sections:

Part I offers writing assignments, with detailed writing guides, for composing several important kinds of nonfiction prose: autobiography, firsthand biography, profile, explanation, position paper, proposal, evaluation, causal analysis, and literary interpretation. Each chapter invites you to read carefully the work of published writers and college students and then to write an essay of your own.

Parts II through IV provide strategies for writing, revising, and research. They also provide guidelines for writing research papers and essay exams, and for using sources.

As you work on the writing assignment in each chapter in Part I, you will engage in a process of inventing, drafting, and revising. You will also read several essays of the type that you yourself are writing. In each chapter you will find discussion of the purpose, audience, and basic features of that kind of writing. Most important, you will find a Guide to Writing, with detailed guidelines that will lead you through the process of writing an essay of your own. Each Guide includes help in invention and research, planning and drafting, getting critical comments, and revising and editing.

Invention and Research

The Guide to Writing in each chapter begins with invention activities designed to help you

- find a topic
- analyze your readers
- discover what you already know about the topic
- research it further
- develop your ideas

Invention means determining your purpose and audience, gathering information, searching your memory, generating ideas, making decisions—and it is a basic ongoing preoccupation for all writers. Invention is necessary to produce any writing of any type or length. As writers, we cannot choose *whether* to invent; we can only decide *how* to invent.

Invention can be especially productive when it is systematic—and when it is written down. Not only does it focus your attention on your purpose and audience, but it then helps you to identify and solve any special rhetorical problems. Exploring your topic fully *before* actually sitting down to draft can free you from the responsibility of composing coherent and grammatical prose and paragraphs and thus allow you to write more freely about your topic—turning writing into a mode of discovery.

Don't think and then write it down. Think on paper.   −Harvey Kemelman

The invention activities at the beginning of each Guide to Writing ask you to think and write about your topic systematically. They may result in quite a bit of writing. The activities include exploratory writing, the making of lists and charts, the trying out of arguments and explanations, and the stating and clarifying of your purpose or thesis. You may choose to complete all the invention activities, or you may select only those that seem especially appropriate to your topic. Even if you do all the activities, you will usually not need more than two hours to complete them. However, the easiest and most productive way to complete the invention activities is to do only one or two each day for several days, thus allowing your mind the longest possible time to do its work on your topic. Completing all the activities gives you the advantage of fully exploring your topic before you attempt a draft.

The invention activities may also be useful when you revise. As a result of your own evaluation of your draft or comments from your instructor or

NOT
KNOWING
WANTS
WRONG

classmates, you may discover problems that the invention activities will help you to solve. They can help you make small changes or major reorganizations; they can even be useful for drafting entirely new sections.

Invention work, then, may help you at several stages in the writing of an essay: while exploring your topic, while drafting, and while revising. The special advantage of the invention activities in each essay assignment chapter is that they focus on the issues of that particular kind of writing.

Chapter 11 provides a catalog of general invention strategies. Unlike the focused invention activities in the guides to writing, each strategy in the invention catalog may be used to generate many different kinds of writing. Because the catalog strategies are so adaptable, they are valuable tools to have in your repertoire and complement the more specialized invention activities offered in Chapters 2–10.

EXERCISE 1.4

Think of a topic you might enjoy writing about. It can be *anything*—soccer, Spike Lee, your grandmother, the unification of Germany, whatever. Then, to familiarize yourself with some of the strategies you might use to generate material about your subject, turn to Chapter 11. Look over the chapter, and select one invention strategy. Take five or ten minutes to try out the strategy, writing about your chosen topic.

Planning and Drafting

Once a period of invention is completed, you should review what you have learned about your topic and start to plan your essay. The Guides to Writing will help you to do this, from setting goals to organizing your ideas and information to achieve those goals. Whereas planning requires you to put your ideas into a coherent, purposeful order appropriate to your readers, drafting challenges you to find the words that will be understandable and interesting for those readers.

Invention continues as you draft, for you will make further discoveries about your topic as you work. But drafting requires you to shift your focus from generating new ideas and gathering further information to forging new and meaningful relations among your ideas and information. The Guide to Writing in each chapter offers specific as well as general advice on planning and drafting an essay. As you begin your first draft, you should try to keep in mind a number of helpful and practical points, many of which have assisted professional writers as they begin drafting.

Choose the Best Time and Place. You can write a draft any time and any place, as you probably already know. Writing gets done under the most surprising conditions. However, drafting is likely to go smoothly if you choose a time and place ideally suited for sustained and thoughtful work. The experience of writers (reported mainly in interviews) suggests that you need a place where you can concentrate for a few hours without repeated interruptions. Many writers find one place where they write best, and they return to that place whenever they have to write. Try to find such a place for yourself.

Make Revision Easy.   Write on only one side of the page. Leave wide margins. Write on every other line or triple-space your typing. Laying your draft out on the page this way invites changes, additions, cutting, and rearranging when you revise.

Set Reasonable Goals.   Divide the task into manageable bits. Set yourself the goal of writing one section or paragraph at a time. A goal of completing a long essay may be so intimidating that it keeps you from starting. Just aim for a small part of the essay at a time.

Lower Your Expectations.   Be satisfied with less than perfect writing. Remember, you are working on a draft that you will revise. Approach the draft as an experiment or an exercise, and do not take it too seriously. Try things out. Follow digressions. Later, you can always go back and cross out a sentence or a section. And do not be critical about your writing; save the criticism until you've gotten some distance from your draft.

Do Easy Parts First.   Try not to agonize over the first sentence. Just write. Do not try to write a perfect first sentence or a perfect opening paragraph. If you have trouble with the introduction, write an anecdote or example or assertion first, if that seems easier. If you have a lot of information, start with the part you understand best. If you get stuck at a difficult spot, skip over it and go on to an easier part. Just getting started can be difficult, but doing the simple parts first may ease this difficulty. If you put off getting started, your work will be rushed and late. Your ideas will not grow and change, and you will thus shut off your chances for important new insights about your topic. By starting late, you will increase your fear of writing; but by starting early with an easy part, you will find writing easier and more enjoyable. You will also do your best work.

Guess at Words, Spelling, Facts.   If you cannot think of just the right word, or if you have forgotten an important fact, just keep on drafting. You can search out the fact or find the elusive word later. If you cannot remember how to spell a word, guess and keep going. Later, you can look it up in a dictionary. Inexperienced writers lose large amounts of time puzzling over a word or spelling or trying to recall a specific fact. Sometimes they become completely blocked.

Write Quickly.   If you have reasonable goals, have not set your expectations too high, and are doing the easy parts first, then you should be able to draft quickly. Say what you want to say and move on. Review your notes, make a plan, and then put your notes aside. You can always refer to them later if you need an exact quote or fact. Now and then, of course, you will want to reread what you have written, but do not reread obsessively. Return to drafting new material as soon as possible. Avoid editing or revising during this stage. You need not have everything exactly right in the draft. If you want to delete a phrase or sentence, draw a line through it rather than erasing, in case you want to use the phrase or sentence later. Add new material above the line or in the margins.

Take Short Breaks—and Reward Yourself! Drafting can be hard work, and you may need to take a break to refresh yourself. But be careful not to wander off for too long or you may lose momentum. Set small goals and reward yourself regularly. That makes it easier to stay at the task of drafting.

Reading with a Critical Eye

After you have finished drafting your essay, you may want to show it to someone else for comments and advice on how to improve it. Experienced writers very often seek advice from others. A business executive might show the draft of a report to a colleague, while a poet might read a poem-in-progress at a writers' workshop.

To evaluate a draft, you need to read with a critical eye. You must be both positive and skeptical—positive in that you are trying to identify what is workable and promising in the draft, skeptical in that you need to question every assumption and decision that has been made.

The Guide to Writing in each chapter in Part I includes a section on reading a draft with a critical eye, which will help you to discover the possibilities and shortcomings in a draft. These guides to critical reading focus on the special requirements of each kind of writing in Part I. Here is some general advice on reading any draft critically.

Make a Record of Your Reading. While talking over your impressions of a draft may be pleasurable and useful, you can be most helpful by putting your ideas on paper. When you write down your comments and suggestions—either on the draft or on another piece of paper—you leave a record that can be used later when it is time to revise.

Read First for an Overall Impression. On first reading, do not be distracted by errors of spelling, punctuation, or word choice. Look at big issues. Look for clear focus, strong direction of movement, forcefulness of argument, novelty and quality of ideas. What seems particularly good? What problems do you see? If the essay is meant to entertain, note what seems entertaining, and why. If it is meant to persuade, indicate what was persuasive and what was not. The purpose of this first reading is to express your initial reaction. It need not be analytical or detailed. All you need to say is how the draft struck you: What you think it was trying to do and how well it did it. Write just a few sentences expressing your initial reaction.

Read Again to Analyze the Draft.   Whereas the initial reading considers the whole draft, the second reading focuses on the individual parts. This reading brings to bear what you know about the type of writing and what you already know about the subject. You may question, for example, the appropriateness of a particular argument or type of evidence. Or you may be able to think of a fact or example that contradicts the writer's conclusion.

In reading the draft at this level, you must shift your attention from one aspect of the essay to another. Consider how well the opening paragraphs introduce the essay and prepare the reader to understand and accept it. Attend to subtle shifts in tone as well as more obvious writing strategies. If there is narrative, notice whether it is complete, pointed, and well paced. If there is explanation, decide whether it is clear, organized, and comprehensive. If there is argument, indicate whether it is logical, well supported, and convincing.

As you analyze, you are evaluating as well as describing, but a critical reading should not be merely an occasion for criticizing the draft. A good critical reader helps a writer see how each part works and how all the parts work together. By describing what you see, you help the draft to be seen more objectively, a perspective that is necessary for thoughtful revising.

Offer Advice, but Do Not Rewrite.   As a critical reader, you may be tempted to rewrite the draft—to change a word here, correct an error there, add your ideas everywhere. Resist the impulse. Your role is to read carefully, to point out what you think is or is not working, to make suggestions and ask questions. Leave the revising to the writer.

In turn, the writer has a responsibility to listen to your comments but is under no obligation to do as you suggest. Then why go to all the trouble, you might ask. There are at least two reasons, and you can probably think of others. First, when you read someone else's writing critically, you learn more about writing—about the decisions writers make, how a thoughtful reader reads, and the constraints of particular kinds of writing. Second, you play an instrumental role in constructing a text. As a critical reader, you embody for the writer the abstraction called "audience." By sharing your reaction and analysis with the writer, you complete the circuit of communication.

Revising

Even productive invention and smooth drafting rarely result in the essay a writer has imagined. Experienced writers are not surprised or disappointed when this happens, however. They expect to revise a draft—unless an imminent deadline precludes revising. They know that revising will move them closer to the essay they really want to write. As they read their drafts thoughtfully and critically—and perhaps, as well, reflect on critical readings of their drafts from others—they see many opportunities for improvement. They may notice misspelled words or garbled sentences; most important, however, they discover ways to delete, move, rephrase, and add material in order to say what they want to say more clearly and thoughtfully. Some general advice on revising follows.

View the Draft Objectively. In order to know what to revise, you must read your draft objectively, to see what it actually says instead of what you intended it to say. If you have the time, put the draft aside for a day or two. When you read it again, outline or summarize it. Getting another reader to describe the draft can also help you to view it more objectively.

Reconsider Your Purpose and Audience. Ask yourself what you are trying to accomplish with this essay. Does your purpose still seem appropriate for these particular readers? Decide how you could modify the essay to make it more effective. Consider each problem and possible solution in light of your overall writing strategy.

Revise in Stages. Do not try to do everything at once. Begin by looking at the whole and then move to an analysis of the parts. Focus initially on identifying problems; consider possible solutions only after you have a general understanding of how the draft fails to achieve its purpose.

Look at Big Problems First. Identify major problems that keep the draft from achieving its purpose. Does the essay have a clear focus, a strong direction of movement, a consistent and appropriate tone? Is the thesis explicit enough? Is it supported as well as asserted? Are the ideas interesting and developed? Does the essay have all the features that readers will expect?

Focus Next on Clarity and Coherence. Consider the beginning. How well does it prepare readers for the essay? Does it adequately forecast the essay's development and thesis? Look at each section of the essay in turn. Do the paragraphs proceed in a logical order? Are there appropriate transitions to help readers follow from one point to the next? Are generalizations firmly and explicitly connected to specific details, examples, or supporting evidence?

Save Stylistic Changes and Grammatical Corrections for Last. Do not focus on word choice or sentence structure until you are generally satisfied with what you have written. Then go through the essay, carefully considering your style and diction. Focus primarily on key terms to be sure they are appropriate and well defined.

Editing

Once you have finished revising, you then want to edit carefully to make sure that every word, phrase, and sentence is clear and correct. Using language and punctuation correctly is an essential part of good writing. Errors will distract readers and lessen your credibility as a writer.

The essay assignment chapters are designed to encourage you to turn your attention to editing only *after* you have planned and worked out a revision. Too much editing too early in the writing process can limit, even block, invention and drafting. The writing you do for the predrafting invention exercises and the first draft itself should be quick and exploratory. Your main goal is to discover ways to put information together and to find out what you have to say. Worrying obsessively about spelling, punctuation, or precisely the right word at the beginning of the writing process would be the wrong use of your attention and energy.

Writing with a Computer

Computers are extraordinarily useful tools for writers, and if you have access to one you might want to use this course as an occasion to accustom yourself to writing with a computer. This book includes complementary software, the *St. Martin's MindWriter/Descant Software* (available for both IBM and Macintosh) that provides electronic versions of the Writing Guides in Chapters 2–10. These materials will help you work with a computer during all the stages of the writing process: inventing; planning and drafting; reading critically; and revising and editing. In addition, you will find an appendix at the back of the book, Writing with a Word Processor, which provides practical guidelines and suggestions for writing with computers generally and for using the *St. Martin's MindWriter/Descant Software*.

Learning from Writing

At the end of each Part I chapter is an opportunity to reflect on what you learned from the process of writing the essay. You can reread everything you have written from beginning to end and reflect on discoveries you made and problems you solved. You can analyze changes you made when you revised the draft and explain how those changes strengthened the revision. You can decide what was hardest and what was easiest about this particular kind of writing. You can compare your process in writing this essay to the process you used in writing another kind of essay.

These and other reflections can lead you to a deeper understanding of how writing works and why it is important. They can be a valuable record of what you are learning in this course.

EXERCISE 1.5

Write a brief account of your strengths and weaknesses as a writer. What are your goals for this course? What improvements do you hope to make in your writing?

Writing Activities

■ A scientist writes a book about a discovery she and several colleagues made, one that revolutionized scientific knowledge in her field. In the chapter describing how the discovery was made, she tells the dramatic story of the race between her research team and a rival group at another university. Her team had nearly solved the problem when they heard a rumor that the other researchers had made a breakthrough. She confesses that she actually broke down and cried, imagining the Nobel Prize being awarded to her rivals. The rumor turned out to be false, and her team did indeed get credit for the discovery. She admits how jealous and frustrated she felt, commenting with self-irony on her feelings. Scientists, she concludes, are only human. They may strive for objectivity and disinterestedness but can never really escape their own egotism.

■ In her autobiography, a black writer recalls her high school graduation from an all-black school in rural Arkansas in 1940. She writes about how very proud she felt until a white superintendent of schools made a condescending and insulting speech. Describing his speech and the self-hatred it inspired in her, she remembers thinking that she alone was suffering until she heard the restrained applause and recognized the proud defiance in everyone's eyes. Thus the incident, in many ways so grim, actually renewed her sense of racial pride.

■ Asked to recall a significant early childhood memory for a psychology class, a student writes about a fishing trip he took when he was nine. He reflects that the trip was significant because it was the first he ever took alone with his father and that it heralded a new stage in their relationship. He remembers wanting to go fishing but being afraid that he would do something wrong like getting seasick or losing the rod and disappointing his dad. He

relates how they awoke before dawn and drove to the boat, how he soon found his sea legs and learned to bait the hook by himself. He focuses the essay on one particular incident—his attempt to land a big fish. He writes that his first impulse was to panic and try to hand the rod to his father, but his dad insisted that he could handle it. During a struggle that seemed to last an hour but probably took only ten minutes, his dad sat beside him, offering advice and encouragement. Afterward, his dad said how proud he was and took his picture with the fish, a five-pound bass.

■ For her freshman English class, a student writes about some surprising events that occurred when she was preparing to send her high school newspaper to the printer. She and other staff writers had been working late for two consecutive nights. When the editor expressed irritation at how slowly she was working, she became furious with him. Then when she got home and tried to fall asleep, she had hallucinations that he was actually trying to harm her, that he was in her room approaching her bed. She writes about how astounded she was to realize later that she had hallucinated. In her essay she reflects on the way this experience gave her some understanding about uncontrollable mental events and how it increased her sympathy for other people who experience them.

■ A student in a sociology class studying friendship patterns writes a personal essay about the time in junior high when a girls' gang tried to enlist her. Though she didn't know any of the gang members, she guessed they wanted her because they heard she was taking karate lessons. She describes how frightened she was when they demanded to meet with her after school and then how relieved she felt after they decided she wasn't tough enough. As she writes about this incident, she is able to chuckle at her actions and feelings at the time.

Why do people write about incidents from their lives? Perhaps because telling familiar stories is sometimes fun, perhaps because it can be instructive. Examining the forces that shaped our lives can teach us something about ourselves. Reflecting on the past, in other words, can help us to understand the present and prepare for the future.

Another reason for writing about our experiences—and for reading about other people's—is to broaden our understanding of others. We come to discover that people living in different times and places share many of the same feelings, thoughts, and values. But we also learn how difference—in gender, ethnicity, and class, for example—affects our lives and our interactions with others.

In writing about our lives, in effect, we construct an image of ourselves, a "self" which we present to others. What we present depends on our rhetorical situation: who we are writing to (our audience) and why (our purpose). We obviously are *not* exactly the same in every situation, and don't necessarily want others to respond to us in the same way all the time. Based on our purpose in writing to a particular audience, we make choices on how to present ourselves, sometimes taking risks and at other times playing it safe.

The scenarios that open this chapter suggest some of the complex rhetorical situations we encounter when writing about our experiences. The scientist in the first scenario, for example, reveals having feelings about her work that are not usually associated with the cool, disinterested practice of science. Making public this kind of personal disclosure is risky for her because she knows that some readers will look down on her for "getting emotional"; they might even take her experience as evidence that women are not fit to be scientists. We can only conjecture about why she decided to present herself this way: perhaps she wanted to challenge her stodgier readers' assumptions about scientists' objectivity, or maybe she just wanted to give nonscientists a behind-the-scenes glimpse of the competitive world of scientific research.

The point to remember is that based on their purpose and audience, all writers make choices about how they present themselves. Writing about personal experiences involves fashioning our self in words much as a novelist constructs a character. As readers, we come to "know" the people we read about by the way they are described as well as by their actions, words, thoughts, and feelings.

As you work through this chapter, you will learn to present yourself purposefully by telling the story of your experience. You will learn to organize and pace the action to create dramatic tension; to describe scenes and people to make the story vivid and specific; to convey through words and images the event's significance to make the story meaningful.

Storytelling, you will discover, is an essential strategy in both academic and professional writing. Not only are some essays organized narratively like stories, but even those organized in other ways often include the brief, "telling" stories we call anecdotes as illustrations or for the main ideas.

In college, you may well have occasion to write about some of your personal experiences for your courses. Consider, for example, the following typical assignments:

■ *For a psychology course:* Erik Erikson observed that "young people . . . are sometimes preoccupied with what they appear to be in the eyes of others as compared with what they feel they are." Test this idea against your own adolescent experience. Recount a single event when you cared tremendously about what your peers thought about you. How did their judgment influence your behavior and your sense of self?

■ *For a sociology course:* Case studies of victimization have shown that victims tend to become distrustful and socially isolated. If you have had the unfortunate experience of being a victim, write briefly about what happened and how it has affected your social interactions.

■ *For a political science course:* Voter apathy is known to be a widespread problem, but not much is known about the origins of voting behavior. Recall the first time you became interested in an election, and tell about the incident in some detail. Looking back on the incident, what did it teach you about the political process?

■ *For a linguistics course:* Many linguists argue that grammar and word choice are social constructs, that "appropriateness" always depends on some context. Recall an occasion when you used language that others considered inappropriate or offensive. What did you say or write, and how did you know your language had gone over prescribed boundaries?

The kind of writing you will read and practice in this chapter will not only be worthwhile in and of itself, but will also prepare you for work in your other college courses. Following are several examples of writing about remembered events. All tell lively, engaging stories, ones that should give you ideas for writing that you yourself could do.

For Group Inquiry

The scenarios that open this chapter suggest some occasions for writing about events from one's life. Imagine that you have been asked to write about some childhood experience. Think of an event or incident that might "say something" about your life. It can be something startling, amusing, sad, exciting, whatever. The only requirement is for it to seem important to you now and for you to remember it well enough to tell about it.

Get together with two or three other students, and "try out" your stories on one another. You can be brief—three or four minutes each will do. After each story is told, go around the group for each member to say something about what the incident told (or suggested) about its author. Does everyone "hear" the same thing? Then, as a group, discuss the rhetorical situation of telling about a remembered event by considering the following points:

- Why did you choose the incident you did?
- How did the audience—that is, the group—affect your choice?
- What exactly did you want the others to learn from your story?
- Are you surprised by what they said they learned about you?
- What have you learned about telling stories purposefully by working in a group that you might not have by working alone?

Readings

Annie Dillard won the Pulitzer Prize for her very first book, *Pilgrim at Tinker Creek*, reflections on her close observation of an actual creek. In that book, she admits to being "no scientist," merely "a wanderer with a background in theology and a penchant for quirky facts." She has since written many other books, including collections of poetry, essays, and literary theory, as well as her autobiography, *An American Childhood*, from which this selection is taken.

In "Handed My Own Life," we see the early stirrings of Dillard's life-long enthusiasm for learning and fascination with nature. As you read her story, think about why she wrote it. What do you think she wanted to tell readers about herself? What impression do you have of Annie Dillard from reading the story?

HANDED MY OWN LIFE
ANNIE DILLARD

After I read *The Field Book of Ponds and Streams* several times, I longed for a 1 microscope. Everybody needed a microscope. Detectives used microscopes, both for the FBI and at Scotland Yard. Although usually I had to save my tiny allowance for things I wanted, that year for Christmas my parents gave me a microscope kit.

In a dark basement corner, on a white enamel table, I set up the microscope kit. 2 I supplied a chair, a lamp, a batch of jars, a candle, and a pile of library books. The microscope kit supplied a blunt black three-speed microscope, a booklet, a scalpel, a dropper, an ingenious device for cutting thin segments of fragile tissue, a pile of clean slides and cover slips, and a dandy array of corked test tubes.

One of the test tubes contained "hay infusion." Hay infusion was a wee brown 3 chip of grass blade. You added water to it, and after a week it became a jungle in a drop, full of one-celled animals. This did not work for me. All I saw in the microscope after a week was a wet chip of dried grass, much enlarged.

Another test tube contained "diatomaceous earth." This was, I believed, an 4 actual pinch of the white cliffs of Dover. On my palm it was an airy, friable chalk. The booklet said it was composed of the silicaceous bodies of diatoms—one-celled creatures that lived in, as it were, small glass jewelry boxes with fitted lids. Diatoms, I read, come in a variety of transparent geometrical shapes. Broken and dead and dug out of geological deposits, they made chalk, and a fine abrasive used in silver polish and toothpaste. What I saw in the microscope must have been the fine abrasive—grit enlarged. It was years before I saw a recognizable, whole diatom. The kit's diatomaceous earth was a bust.

All that winter I played with the microscope. I prepared slides from things at 5 hand, as the books suggested. I looked at the transparent membrane inside an onion's skin and saw the cells. I looked at a section of cork and saw the cells, and at scrapings from the inside of my cheek, ditto. I looked at my blood and saw not much; I looked at my urine and saw long iridescent crystals, for the drop had dried.

All this was very well, but I wanted to see the wildlife I had read about. I wanted 6 especially to see the famous amoeba, who had eluded me. He was supposed to live in the hay infusion, but I hadn't found him there. He lived outside in warm ponds and streams, too, but I lived in Pittsburgh, and it had been a cold winter.

Finally late that spring I saw an amoeba. The week before, I had gathered puddle 7 water from Frick Park; it had been festering in a jar in the basement. This June night after dinner I figured I had waited long enough. In the basement at my microscope table I spread a scummy drop of Frick Park puddle water on a slide, peeked in, and lo, there was the famous amoeba. He was as blobby and grainy as his picture; I would have known him anywhere.

Before I had watched him at all, I ran upstairs. My parents were still at table, 8 drinking coffee. They, too, could see the famous amoeba. I told them, bursting, that he was all set up, that they should hurry before his water dried. It was the chance of a lifetime.

Father had stretched out his long legs and was tilting back in his chair. Mother 9 sat with her knees crossed, in blue slacks, smoking a Chesterfield. The dessert dishes were still on the table. My sisters were nowhere in evidence. It was a warm evening; the big dining-room windows gave onto blooming rhododendrons.

Mother regarded me warmly. She gave me to understand that she was glad I 10 had found what I had been looking for, but that she and Father were happy to sit with their coffee, and would not be coming down.

She did not say, but I understood at once, that they had their pursuits (coffee?) 11 and I had mine. She did not say, but I began to understand then, that you do what you do out of your private passion for the thing itself.

I had essentially been handed my own life. In subsequent years my parents would 12 praise my drawings and poems, and supply me with books, art supplies, and sports equipment, and listen to my troubles and enthusiasms, and supervise my hours, and discuss and inform, but they would not get involved with my detective work, nor hear about my reading, nor inquire about my homework or term papers or exams, nor visit the salamanders I caught, nor listen to me play the piano, nor attend my field hockey games, nor fuss over my insect collection with me, or my poetry collection or stamp collection or rock collection. My days and nights were my own to plan and fill.

■   ■   ■

When I left the dining room that evening and started down the dark basement 13 stairs, I had a life, I sat to my wonderful amoeba, and there he was, rolling his grains more slowly now, extending an arc of his edge for a foot and drawing himself along by that foot, and absorbing it again and rolling on. I gave him some more pond water.

I had hit pay dirt. For all I knew, there were paramecia, too, in that pond water, 14 or daphniae, or stentors, or any of the many other creatures I had read about and never seen: volvox, the spherical algal colony; euglena with its one red eye; the elusive, glassy diatom; hydra, rotifers, water bears, worms. Anything was possible. The sky was the limit.

For Discussion

Are you surprised by Dillard's reaction to her parents' lack of interest in her discovery of the elusive amoeba? Would you have felt differently—confused? neglected? angry? astonished? Why do you think she is so accepting of her parents' unenthusiastic response? To what extent do you rely on the approval or involvement of others to motivate your own learning and inquiry? Discuss these questions, and then consider the experience of working with a group. How do you think collaborative work of this sort contributes to your learning?

For Analysis

For a discussion of dominant impression, see pp. 428–29.

1.   Writing about remembered events often features description of people and places. Look closely at the scene described in paragraphs 8–11. What dominant impression do you get of Dillard's parents from this description? Which words and phrases contribute most memorably to this impression?

2.   Dillard's word choice ranges widely from sophisticated words like *ingenious* and *eluded* to childish words like *dandy, scummy,* and *blobby.* She also uses some technical terms: *diatomaceous, friable,* and *silicaceous,* for instance. What impression do you get of her as a child from her use of words such as these?

3.   Here are some of the verbs Dillard uses in paragraph 7: *saw, had gathered, had been festering, figured, spread, was, would have known. Saw, figured, spread,* and *was* are simple past tense verbs. The other verbs are different. Without

knowing their technical names, you can learn something important about writing about remembered events by examining these verbs closely. Skim the essay, underlining all the verbs that are not in the simple past tense. What do these different verb tenses allow Dillard to do as she tells her story?

4.   Look back at paragraph 5 and notice that the third sentence establishes a pattern that is followed with variations throughout the rest of the paragraph. What point is Dillard making in the paragraph? How does repeating this particular sentence pattern help her to make that point? How does she vary the pattern, and what effect do you think this variation has?

For Your
Own Writing

Think of some occasions when you recall learning something important or making a significant discovery. List them. Then, choose one occasion that you would be interested in writing about for readers who don't know you. What would you want them to learn about you from reading your essay?

Commentary

"Handed My Own Life" illustrates two basic features of writing about remembered events: a well-told story and an indication of its autobiographical significance. Good storytelling attracts readers' interest and makes us want to read on to find out what happened. Autobiographical significance gives a story its meaning. If the story didn't interest us, we wouldn't read it; if it didn't have significance, we would find it pointless.

Dillard attracts our interest in the first paragraph by presenting a self with which we can readily identify. Even if we've never wanted a microscope, we've all *longed for, needed, wanted* something as badly as she wants the microscope. We wonder what she'll do with it. Curiosity spurs our interest. Once she gets on the track of the elusive amoeba, we wonder whether she'll find it.

In addition to arousing our curiosity, a story also has to have a point: it has to lead somewhere. What starts out as a simple story about a child's enthusiasm for a new toy takes a surprising turn. She not only discovers the amoeba, but also discovers something important about herself and her relationship with her parents. This discovery gives the event its significance. To be significant, an event needn't be earthshaking. Dillard's surely isn't. Her experience is significant because it taught her something she can generalize and apply to other situations: "that you do what you do out of your private passion for the thing itself" and not for the approval of others.

Notice that Dillard is somewhat vague in what she tells about her feelings at the time of the incident. She doesn't really tell us how she felt at the time, but only what she thought after some reflection. In paragraph 11, she writes that she "began to understand then," yet she doesn't say how long it took to understand fully what this event meant. Sometimes it takes a good deal of time and reflection before we gain the emotional distance necessary for understanding—and that is another reason why people write about remembered events. Writing gives us the opportunity to reflect on our experiences and, in hindsight, to figure out why they mean so much to us.

■   ■   ■

Tobias Wolff is probably best known for his short stories and for a novel, *The Barracks Thief,* for which he won the 1985 PEN/Faulkner award. "On Being a Real Westerner" comes from Wolff's autobiography, *A Boy's Life.* Reflecting on his writing process, Wolff has said that it is "part memory, part invention. I can no longer tell where one ends and the other begins. The very act of writing has transformed the original experience into another experience, more 'real' to me than what I started with."

The story Wolff tells here is based on an actual eperience. As you read, notice how his storytelling skills make this event come to life on the page.

**ON BEING
A REAL
WESTERNER**
TOBIAS WOLFF

Just after Easter Roy gave me the Winchester .22 rifle I'd learned to shoot with. 1 It was a light, pump-action, beautifully balanced piece with a walnut stock black from all its oilings. Roy had carried it when he was a boy and it was still as good as new. Better than new. The action was silky from long use, and the wood of a quality no longer to be found.

The gift did not come as a surprise. Roy was stingy, and slow to take a hint, but 2 I'd put him under siege. I had my heart set on that rifle. A weapon was the first condition of self-sufficiency, and of being a real Westerner, and of all acceptable employment—trapping, riding herd, soldiering, law enforcement, and outlawry. I needed that rifle, for itself and for the way it completed me when I held it.

My mother said I couldn't have it. Absolutely not. Roy took the rifle back but 3 promised me he'd bring her around. He could not imagine anyone refusing him anything and treated the refusals he did encounter as perverse and insincere. Normally mute, he became at these times a relentless whiner. He would follow my mother from room to room, emitting one ceaseless note of complaint that was pitched perfectly to jelly her nerves and bring her to a state where she would agree to anything to make it stop.

After a few days of this my mother caved in. She said I could have the rifle if, 4 and only if, I promised never to take it out or even touch it except when she and Roy were with me. Okay, I said. Sure. Naturally. But even then she wasn't satisfied. She plain didn't like the fact of me owning a rifle. Roy said he had owned several rifles by the time he was my age, but this did not reassure her. She didn't think I could be trusted with it. Roy said now was the time to find out.

For a week or so I kept my promises. But now that the weather had turned 5 warm Roy was usually off somewhere and eventually, in the dead hours after school when I found myself alone in the apartment, I decided that there couldn't be any harm in taking the rifle out to clean it. Only to clean it, nothing more. I was sure it would be enough just to break it down, oil it, rub linseed into the stock, polish the octagonal barrel and then hold it up to the light to confirm the perfection of the bore. But it wasn't enough. From cleaning the rifle I went to marching around the apartment with it, and then to striking brave poses in front of the mirror. Roy had saved one of his army uniforms and I sometimes dressed up in this, together with martial-looking articles of hunting gear: fur trooper's hat, camouflage coat, boots that reached nearly to my knees.

The camouflage coat made me feel like a sniper, and before long I began to act 6 like one. I set up a nest on the couch by the front window. I drew the shades to darken the apartment, and took up my position. Nudging the shade aside with the rifle barrel, I followed people in my sights as they walked or drove along the street. At first I made shooting sounds—kyoo! kyoo! Then I started cocking the hammer and letting it snap down.

Roy stored his ammunition in a metal box he kept hidden in the closet. As with 7 everything else hidden in the apartment, I knew exactly where to find it. There was a layer of loose .22 rounds on the bottom of the box under shells of bigger caliber, dropped there by the handful the way men drop pennies on their dressers at night. I took some and put them in a hiding place of my own. With these I started loading up the rifle. Hammer cocked, a round in the chamber, finger resting lightly on the trigger, I drew a bead on whoever walked by—women pushing strollers, children, garbage collectors laughing and calling to each other, anyone—and as they passed under my window I sometimes had to bite my lip to keep from laughing in the ecstasy of my power over them, and at their absurd and innocent belief that they were safe.

But over time the innocence I laughed at began to irritate me. It was a peculiar 8 kind of irritation. I saw it years later in men I served with, and felt it myself, when unarmed Vietnamese civilians talked back to us while we were herding them around. Power can be enjoyed only when it is recognized and feared. Fearlessness in those without power is maddening to those who have it.

One afternoon I pulled the trigger. I had been aiming at two old people, a man 9 and a woman, who walked so slowly that by the time they turned the corner at the bottom of the hill my little store of self-control was exhausted. I had to shoot. I looked up and down the street. It was empty. Nothing moved but a pair of squirrels chasing each other back and forth on the telephone wires. I followed one in my sights. Finally it stopped for a moment and I fired. The squirrel dropped straight into the road. I pulled back into the shadows and waited for something to happen, sure that someone must have heard the shot or seen the squirrel fall. But the sound that was so loud to me probably seemed to our neighbors no more than the bang of a cupboard slammed shut. After a while I sneaked a glance into the street. The squirrel hadn't moved. It looked like a scarf someone had dropped.

When my mother got home from work I told her there was a dead squirrel in 10 the street. Like me, she was an animal lover. She took a cellophane bag off a loaf of bread and we went outside and looked at the squirrel. "Poor little thing," she said. She stuck her hand in the wrapper and picked up the squirrel, then pulled the bag inside out away from her hand. We buried it behind our building under a cross made of popsicle sticks, and I blubbered the whole time.

I blubbered again in bed that night. At last I got out of bed and knelt down and 11 did an imitation of somebody praying, and then I did an imitation of somebody receiving divine reassurance and inspiration. I stopped crying. I smiled to myself and forced a feeling of warmth into my chest. Then I climbed back in bed and looked up at the ceiling with a blissful expression until I went to sleep.

For several days I stayed away from the apartment at times when I knew I'd be 12
alone there.

Though I avoided the apartment, I could not shake the idea that sooner or later 13
I would get the rifle out again. All my images of myself as I wished to be were
images of myself armed. Because I did not know who I was, any image of myself,
no matter how grotesque, had power over me. This much I understand now. But
the man can give no help to the boy, not in this matter nor in those that follow.
The boy moves always out of reach.

For Discussion

What does this story seem to be saying about identity and role playing? Why
do you think Wolff takes so much delight in dressing up as a soldier? What
connection do you see between his playing soldier and his desire to be a
"real Westerner"?

What roles do you recall playing when you were a child? Why do you
think soldiers and cowboys are idealized masculine roles in our society? What
qualities of character do they represent? What are the feminine roles our
society values most? If possible, consider these questions together with two
or three other students, preferably including both men and women in the
group.

How do you feel about these gender-related roles? Do they embody ideals
that you hold for yourself? Looking back at the essay, do you think Wolff
calls these stereotypical roles into question, or do you think he is basically
uncritical of them?

For Analysis

1.   What seems to be the significance of this story? What does Wolff learn
from this particular incident? Where does he state the point most explicitly?
Do you think this point can be generalized to apply to other situations and
people? How does it apply to your own experience?

2.   Successful narratives present a sequence of actions that build tension
toward a high point or climax. This narrative is organized like a staircase,
with each step up intensifying the suspense. To analyze this story's dramatic
structure, first find the climax. Then, starting with the first paragraph, number each new step. What effect does this progression of steps have on you
as one reader? Compare your response to that of your classmates. Did you
all point to the same steps? If not, how can you account for the difference?

3.   Look at the opening paragraphs. What purpose do they serve? If the
essay opened instead with the second sentence of paragraph 5 ("In the dead
hours after school . . ."), what would be lost or gained?

4.   In paragraphs 7–13, Wolff describes his reactions at the time to what
he was doing. Which of these remembered feelings and thoughts help you
to understand what he was experiencing at the time? What impression do
they give you of the young Wolff?

Usually, we can at some point look back at even the most disturbing experience with some emotional distance. Where do you see evidence of the adult writer's perspective? What does he seem to think about his younger self?

For Your Own Writing

In this essay, Wolff tells us he was on a power trip, experiencing what he calls the "ecstasy of my power" (paragraph 7). This ecstasy comes from the power he has to inflict harm on others. Can you recall any instances when you were in a position to exercise power over another person? What did you do? How did you feel? Think also of times when you were subject to someone else's power. How did you feel in that position? If you were to write about one of these instances, what point would you want to convey to your readers?

Commentary

This is a gripping story. One factor that makes it so dramatic is the topic. Putting a child together with a rifle immediately alerts readers to the possibility that something dreadful could happen. Thus the potential for suspense is great. But what makes the story so effective is Wolff's masterful use of two writing strategies: narration and description.

Good storytelling hinges on tension, usually on the reader's concern for the main character and anxiety about what will happen to him or her. If the tension slackens, if irrelevant details are introduced or the action meanders pointlessly, readers lose interest. Wolff instills tension in his narrative by pacing the action very carefully. He begins his story with a leisurely pace, summarizing his efforts to get Roy to give him the rifle and Roy's efforts to get Wolff's mother to let him have it. Once he gets the rifle, the pace picks up as the narrative moves with increasing speed from one incident to the next until finally the gun is fired and the squirrel drops.

Wolff uses another pacing technique when he gives a close-up of the action by showing concrete movements and gestures. In paragraph 7, for example, he builds suspense by focusing in on each minute action: "Hammer cocked, a round in the chamber, finger resting lightly on the trigger, I drew a bead on whoever walked by—women pushing strollers, children, garbage collectors laughing and calling to each other, anyone. . . ."

For more on specific narrative action, turn to pp. 422–23.

This specific narrative action also contributes to the vividness of the writing. Wolff uses it together with the descriptive techniques of naming, detailing, and comparing to help readers visualize key parts of the scene. He carefully names important objects and their parts. For instance, it's not just any gun, but a Winchester .22. He adds many details (italicized in our example) to further describe the rifle: "It was a *light, pump-action, beautifully balanced* piece with a *walnut* stock *black* from all its oilings." Finally, he uses comparison in the form of metaphor and simile to further enliven his description: "the action was silky," the dead squirrel "looked like a scarf someone had dropped."

■   ■   ■

Al Young has written novels, poetry, essays, and screenplays for Richard Pryor and Bill Cosby. He is copublisher, with Ishmael Reed, of the multi-cultural literary journal *Quilt*.

This selection, from *A World Unsuspected: Portraits of Southern Childhood* (ed. Alex Harris), recalls an event that took place when Young was visiting his grandfather's farm in Mississippi. Even though the incident occurred more than forty years ago, Young describes the scene, people, and his feelings as if it happened only yesterday. As you read, consider the significance of his title, "Unripened Light." How does it help you to understand the story?

UNRIPENED LIGHT

AL YOUNG

By the time we reached the low field, which took forever, my little legs were 1 tired. I wanted to sit down someplace and catch back all the breath I'd lost trying to keep up with the others. It was Jesse Earl's tough, country savvy that I aspired to; that's how I wanted to be. I was a little boy craving to be looked upon as a big boy capable of holding my own and doing my share.

When Papa saw me panting and looking for someplace to plop, he bent down 2 and, looking me right in the eye, said, "Wha'cha know, Skip?"

"OK," I told him. 3

"Well," he said, "this here's the low field, and them's the watermelons over 4 yonder. What say we go look at 'em?"

We walked down the rows of melons, we barefoot kids and grand old work- 5 booted Papa. To me the watermelons looked like magic itself as they sparkled on their bellies in the dirt, still connected to their source by vines. I didn't yet know about umbilical cords and childbirth, and yet I distinctly recall the whole feel of that warm morning vibrant with sunlight. Toeing and stepping around what looked like millions of melons—baby ones, mother ones, daddy ones, and great big grandpa and grandma ones—I began to get it. It was the first time I'd ever begun to become aware in an adult kind of way how connected up everything was to everything else.

There we stopped and fooled around for a moment, looking at ants crawl totally 6 unfelt across our happy, callused feet. Inez and Jesse Earl stalled and stooped around for the longest while before they got Papa to cut off a melon they could carry.

When it came my turn to pick one, I fell to my knees over a round, compact, 7 greenbacked, yellowbellied baby of a melon. Right away I saw it was the only one I could possibly carry all the way back to the house. But I pointed instead at a bigger, long-headed melon I thought looked more like the size and kind the big people were choosing.

Papa snapped open his pocketknife and said, "Why don't you try it out first 8 before I snip it?"

Jesse Earl and Inez looked at each other and laughed. 9

"Dog, Skippy," Jesse Earl groaned. "How you gon tote some'n that big?" 10

I got up and lifted the watermelon. Deep down I knew good and well it was 11 more than I could comfortably carry, but when I saw Papa take off his straw hat to fan his face, keeping his eyes on me all the while I was trying to prove my secret point, I decided then and there that, come what may, I was going to heft that thing from the low field and tote it the whole quarter mile—a good quarter mile—home.

Already I could picture myself arriving at the back door, the back steps where 12 chickens roamed and cats and kittens hung out; where Mama was going to come rushing out of the kitchen, wiping her hands on her apron, to say, "I declare. Skippy! You mean you toted that melon all the way from down there all by yourself?"

"Yes'm," I'd say.   13

And Papa would tell her: "Ain't he some'n, this little boy of Mary's?"   14

While Inez and Jesse Earl held their melons to their chests, Papa squatted and   15
sliced mine free from its vine, then stepped back to see what would happen.

"You gon be all right, Skippy?"   16

"I'm OK," I grunted, wobbling a little on my legs and arching my back to make   17
sure the melon was balanced smack up against my belly for the long march. Papa
grabbed a huge watermelon for himself and carried it under one arm, which tickled
me. "We better get on back," he said, "Mama'll be waitin with dinner, and we can
slice one of these for desert."

Whatever we talked about walking back to the house swept clean past me. I   18
was straining and struggling to keep up with everybody else. Maybe nothing was
said at all. Papa wasn't the most talkative of men, even when he was feeling good.
The truth, though, is that all three of us kids were concentrating with all our might
on keeping those watermelons aloft.

Papa was the main one whose OK I wanted. That's because I'd been hearing so   19
much about him from the rest of the family that to me he seemed like a monarch
of some kind; a patriarch certainly. I was too young, of course, to know what a
successful man he was, with all those lovely daughters and handsome sons, all of
them loquacious; to say nothing of his respected standing in the community. All I
remember about the walk back is how hard I had to work to keep my simple feet
moving and the sun out of my eyes.

We'd got as far as inside the front gate, the place where I could feel relieved   20
because the back porch was only a few more steps past the well, around the big
black iron clothes-washing pot and the honeysuckle bushes that looked out from
the side of the house onto the vast and seemingly borderless cottonfield.

OK, OK, OK, OK, OK, OK, OK kept running through my hard little head, spurring   21
me along, grunt upon grunt.

And then—with Papa, Inez, and Jesse Earl staring right at me, as if at some   22
galaxy through an oversized telescope—the weight of it all finally caught up and
overwhelmed me.

"Uh-uhhh, look out!" I myself hollered. And in the same breath I came back   23
with: "OK, OK, OK!!!" The meaning of *OK* by then had shattered, and each dinky
shard and broken piece of it seemed to mean something different. I didn't understand any of them. All I knew was that it sounded OK to say OK right when I was
about to fumble everything, just when the watermelon could no longer stand the
tortured care and attention I'd been giving it, just when it must've been feeling its
loneliest for the vine and all the other brother/sister melons it'd just been severed
from back there in the low field.

The thing, I swear, just slipped and squirmed and worked its way free from my   24
hands and, *zoop!*, went splattering to the ground. The moment it happened I could
smell its cool sweetness begin to spread through the sunny air and blend with the
sugary fragrance of honeysuckle. And right away the bees began buzzing around
the seeded red flesh and green and white rind of it as watermelon fragments whizzed
everywhichway.

"*Uh-uhhhhh!*" ·   25

Whether it was Inez or Jesse Earl who groaned that final uh-uhhh I still can't say 26
at this bend in time, but I've never forgotten what Papa said; it was something that
was going to affect me deeply for a long time to come.

"Mmmm-*mmmm*," he hummed deep down in his throat, surveying the wreck- 27
age with one hand in his overalls pocket and the other fastened around his own
totable melon. I wanted to vanish on the spot and slip off to that part of the barn
where they stacked hay and where it was possible, or so I thought then, to turn
myself into pure straw simply by wishing.

Papa set his watermelon down and jammed both hands into the pockets of his 28
faded blue hitch-em-ups.

I gazed up at the permanent, wet half-moon circles of dark sweat in his workshirt 29
armpits and made a connection I wouldn't be able to take apart and understand,
not even halfway, until forty more years had passed.

"You see," Papa said to the sky that morning, but in reality declaring himself to 30
everyone and everything that lay within reach of his vibrant voice. "This boy of Mary's
will never amount to the salt in his bread."

I did the only thing a four-year-old could do under the circumstances: burst into 31
tears.

In later years I would continue to do everything I could think of to win Papa's 32
approval, but eventually I had to accept his being the habitual grump he was.

For Discussion

"It was Jesse Earl's tough, country savvy that I aspired to; that's how I wanted
to be. I was a little boy craving to be looked upon as a big boy capable of
holding my own and doing my share." Thus does Young explain why this
seemingly trivial incident became so significant. Carrying the watermelon
was a symbolic test to show himself—and his grandfather—how grown-up
he was.

Have you ever turned a relatively unimportant incident into a symbolic
test of this sort? For instance, have you ever been in a game where you felt
that you had to score the winning goal? Did you ever feel that life wouldn't
be worth living if you didn't get into a particular club or school?

Discuss the importance events like these carry. Try recalling similar experiences you've each had. What do you think you were trying to prove to
yourself? How important was winning the approval or admiration of others?
What happens when someone fails a test like this, as Young does here? How
does failing contribute to its significance?

For Analysis

1. Most readers are surprised by Papa's reaction when the boy drops the
watermelon. What impression did you have of Papa up till that point? To
answer this question, reread the essay slowly, underlining the words and
phrases used to describe Papa. Which words seem to represent the little boy's
remembered feelings and thoughts, and which suggest the adult writer's
perspective?

2. Dialogue plays an important role in this narrative. What do you learn
about the characters from what they say and the way they say it?

For more on naming, detailing, and comparing turn to pp. 429–34.

3. Young uses the descriptive strategies of naming, detailing, and comparing. Skim the essay, looking for at least one example of each strategy. How do these strategies help bring the scene to life?

4. In paragraphs 12–14, Young uses a flashforward, a narrative technique you are probably familiar with from film: What is a flashforward? What does it enable Young to accomplish in this essay?

For Your Own Writing

Can you think of some events that turned out to be significant turning points in your life? Choose one that you would feel comfortable writing about for this class. In addition to telling about what happened, how could you convey its significance to your readers? Consider, first of all, whether they are likely to have had any comparable experiences.

Commentary

"Unripened Light" illustrates the importance that dialogue can have in writing about remembered events. Dialogue gives a story immediacy and vividness, allowing the writer to show rather than tell. Young's dialogue reveals the boy's relationship with Papa without any intruding commentary from the narrator. Since it is unlikely that Young could have remembered the exact words that were spoken so many years earlier, he must have reconstructed at least some of the dialogue. Even writers who can remember precisely what was said usually select only the most memorable and relevant parts; most also take poetic license occasionally and invent dialogue to make a point more emphatic or graphic.

There are basically two ways to present dialogue: quoting and summarizing. Young uses the first method, direct quotation: "You see," Papa said . . . "This boy of Mary's will never amount to the salt in his bread." Annie Dillard, in contrast, uses the second method, summarizing her own words: "They, too, could see the famous amoeba, I told them, bursting, that he was all set up, that they should hurry before his water dried. It was the chance of a lifetime." In general, dialogue that is vivid and memorable, and that tells us something about the speaker, is best quoted directly. See the difference, for instance, if Young had summarized the above dialogue, saying instead that the boy would "never amount to anything at all."

■   ■   ■

Jean Brandt wrote this essay as a freshman. It tells about something she did when she was thirteen. Reflecting on how she felt at the time, Brandt writes: "I was afraid, embarrassed, worried, mad." As you read, look for places where these tumultuous and contradictory remembered feelings are expressed.

CALLING HOME
JEAN BRANDT

As we all piled into the car, I knew it was going to be a fabulous day. My   1
grandmother was visiting for the holidays; and she and I, along with my older brother and sister, Louis and Susan, were setting off for a day of last-minute Christmas

shopping. On the way to the mall we sang Christmas carols, chattered, and laughed. With Christmas only two days away, we were caught up with holiday spirit. I felt light-headed and full of joy. I loved shopping—especially at Christmas.

The shopping center was swarming with frantic last-minute shoppers like our- 2 selves. We went first to the General Store, my favorite. It carried mostly knickknacks and other useless items which nobody needs but buys anyway. I was thirteen years old at the time, and things like buttons and calendars and posters would catch my fancy. This day was no different. The object of my desire was a 75-cent Snoopy button. Snoopy was the latest. If you owned anything with the Peanuts on it, you were ''in.'' But since I was supposed to be shopping for gifts for other people and not myself, I couldn't decide what to do. I went in search of my sister for her opinion. I pushed my way through throngs of people to the back of the store where I found Susan. I asked her if she thought I should buy the button. She said it was cute and if I wanted it to go ahead and buy it.

When I got back to the Snoopy section, I took one look at the lines at the 3 cashiers and knew I didn't want to wait thirty minutes to buy an item worth less than one dollar. I walked back to the basket where I found the button and was about to drop it when suddenly, instead, I took a quick glance around, assured myself no one could see, and slipped the button into the pocket of my sweatshirt. I hesitated for a moment, but once the item was in my pocket, there was no turning back. I had never before stolen anything; but what was done was done. A few seconds later my sister appeared and asked, ''So, did you decide to buy the button?''

''No, I guess not.'' I hoped my voice didn't quaver. As we headed for the en- 4 trance, my heart began to race. I just had to get out of that store. Only a few more yards to go and I'd be safe. As we crossed the threshold, I heaved a sigh of relief. I was home free. I thought about how sly I had been and I felt proud of my accomplishment.

An unexpected tap on my shoulder startled me. I whirled around to find a middle- 5 aged man, dressed in street clothes, flashing some type of badge and politely asking me to empty my pockets. Where did this man come from? How did he know? I was so sure that no one had seen me! On the verge of panicking, I told myself that all I had to do was give this man his button back, say I was sorry, and go on my way. After all, it was only a 75-cent item.

Next thing I knew he was talking about calling the police and having me arrested 6 and thrown in jail, as if he had just nabbed a professional thief instead of a terrified kid. I couldn't believe what he was saying.

''Jean, what's going on?''   7

The sound of my sister's voice eased the pressure a bit. She always managed to 8 get me out of trouble. She would come through this time too.

''Excuse me. Are you a relative of this young girl?''   9

''Yes, I'm her sister. What's the problem?''   10

''Well, I just caught her shoplifting and I'm afraid I'll have to call the police.''   11

''What did she take?''   12

''This button.''   13

''A button? You are having a thirteen-year-old arrested for stealing a button?''   14

''I'm sorry, but she broke the law.''   15

The man led us through the store and into an office, where we waited for the 16 police officers to arrive. Susan had found my grandmother and brother who, still shocked, didn't say a word. The thought of going to jail terrified me, not because of jail itself, but because of the encounter with my parents afterward. Not more than ten minutes later two officers arrived and placed me under arrest. They said that I was to be taken to the station alone. Then they handcuffed me and led me out of the store. I felt alone and scared. I had counted on my sister being with me, but now I had to muster up the courage to face this ordeal all by myself.

As the officers led me through the mall, I sensed a hundred pairs of eyes staring 17 at me. My face flushed and I broke out in a sweat. Now everyone knew I was a criminal. In their eyes I was a juvenile delinquent, and thank God the cops were getting me off the streets. The worse part was thinking my grandmother might be having the same thoughts. The humiliation at that moment was overwhelming. I felt like Hester Prynne being put on public display for everyone to ridicule.

That short walk through the mall seemed to take hours. But once we reached 18 the squad car, time raced by. I was read my rights and questioned. We were at the police station within minutes. Everything happened so fast I didn't have a chance to feel remorse for my crime. Instead, I viewed what was happening to me as if it were a movie. Being searched, although embarrassing, somehow seemed to be exciting. All the movies and television programs I had seen were actually coming to life. This is what it was really like. But why were criminals always portrayed as frightened and regretful? I was having fun. I thought I had nothing to fear—until I was allowed my one phone call. I was trembling as I dialed home. I didn't know what I was going to say to my parents, especially my mother.

"Hi, Dad, this is Jean."   19

"We've been waiting for you to call."   20

"Did Susie tell you what happened?"   21

"Yeah, but we haven't told your mother. I think you should tell her what you 22 did and where you are."

"You mean she doesn't even know where I am?"   23

"No, I want you to explain it to her."   24

There was a pause as he called my mother to the phone. For the first time that 25 night I was close to tears. I wished I had never stolen that stupid pin. I wanted to give the phone to one of the officers because I was too ashamed to tell my mother the truth, but I had no choice.

"Jean, where are you?"   26

"I'm, umm, in jail."   27

"Why? What for?"   28

"Shoplifting."   29

"Oh no, Jean. Why? Why did you do it?"   30

"I don't know. No reason. I just did it."   31

"I don't understand. What did you take? Why did you do it? You had plenty of 32 money with you."

"I know but I just did it. I can't explain why. Mom, I'm sorry."   33

"I'm afraid sorry isn't enough. I'm horribly disappointed in you."   34

Long after we got off the phone, while I sat in an empty jail cell, waiting for my 35 parents to pick me up, I could still distinctly hear the disappointment and hurt in my mother's voice. I cried. The tears weren't for me but for her and the pain I had put her through. I felt like a terrible human being. I would rather have stayed in jail than confront my mom right then. I dreaded each passing minute that brought our encounter closer. When the officer came to release me, I hesitated, actually not wanting to leave. We went to the front desk, where I had to sign a form to retrieve my belongings. I saw my parents a few yards away and my heart raced. A large knot formed in my stomach. I fought back the tears.

Not a word was spoken as we walked to the car. Slowly I sank into the back seat anticipating the scolding. Expecting harsh tones, I was relieved to hear almost the opposite from my father. 36

"I'm not going to punish you and I'll tell you why. Although I think what you did was wrong, I think what the police did was more wrong. There's no excuse for locking a thirteen-year-old behind bars. That doesn't mean I condone what you did, but I think you've been punished enough already." 37

As I looked from my father's eyes to my mother's, I knew this ordeal was over. Although it would never be forgotten, the incident was not mentioned again. 38

For Discussion

Brandt writes here about taking responsibility for her actions. Do you think she ultimately accepts responsibility for what she has done, or does she transfer some of the blame to others? If you have already read the essay in this chapter by Tobias Wolff, you might compare his story to Brandt's. Both of them break social rules. She gets caught, whereas he gets away with it.

Discuss what our society teaches us about breaking rules. What rules seem more bendable than others? How are people rewarded for confessing to their crimes? Why should accepting responsibility for what you have done change anything?

For Analysis

1. Reread the essay, paying particular attention to the way Brandt uses dialogue. What do you learn about her from what she says and how she says it? What do you learn about her relationships, particularly with her father and mother?

2. Reread the essay, looking for examples of the descriptive strategies of naming, detailing, and comparing. How well does Brandt use these strategies? Give at least one example of each as support for your evaluation.

3. The story begins and ends in a car, with the two car rides framing the story. Framing is a narrative device of echoing something from the beginning in the ending; what effect does this device have on your reading of the story?

4. The Writer at Work section on pp. 49–55 includes some of Brandt's invention notes and her complete first draft. These materials show how her focus shifted gradually from the act itself to her parents' reactions to it. In her final revision, printed above, the confrontation with her parents takes on an importance equal to the actual arrest. Read over all these materials, and comment on this shift in focus. Why do you think Brandt decided to stress her confrontation with her parents? How does this confrontation contribute to your understanding of the event's significance?

For more on sequencing narrative action, turn to pp. 416–20.

For Your Own Writing

Can you think of a few occasions when you did something uncharacteristic? Perhaps you acted on impulse or took a chance you wouldn't ordinarily take.

It doesn't have to be something reckless, dangerous, or illegal; it could be something quite harmless, even pleasant. Think of one occasion you might like to write about. What would you want your readers to recognize about you on the basis of reading your story?

Commentary

Sometimes it is difficult not to sentimentalize about the past or to whitewash your own behavior. It takes courage to present yourself in a bad light, as Brandt does when she lets us see her commit a crime and be arrested for it. But Brandt knows that readers of autobiography recognize and applaud honest self-disclosure. She doesn't give excuses, but simply admits that she stole the button because she didn't want to wait in a long line.

We form our impression of Brandt in part from what she does, but also from how she represents herself in her writing. Her remembered feelings and thoughts give us a sense of the kind of person she was at the time of the event. We see that initially she was childish and irresponsible, but that the experience chastened and matured her. Notice that she openly confesses her feelings at the time, saying that she felt "sly" and even "proud" of her "accomplishment," but that later, when she had to talk to her mother, she began to feel guilt and shame: "For the first time that night I was close to tears. I wanted to give the phone to one of the officers because I was too ashamed to tell my mother the truth. . . ."

These remembered feelings are important in that they let us understand and perhaps emphathize with the writer. Reading about events like Brandt's leads us to reflect on our own crimes and misdemeanors, successes and failures, needs and frustrations, disappointments and embarrassments. We all know these feelings, of course, which is why we are especially curious about how others handle them.

PURPOSE AND AUDIENCE

Writers have various reasons for writing about their experiences. Reminiscing makes it possible to relive moments of pleasure and pain, but it also helps them to gain insight, to learn who they are now by examining who they used to be and the forces that shaped them. Reflecting on the past can lead to significant self-discovery.

Writing about personal experience is public, not private. The autobiographer writes to be read and is therefore as much concerned with self-presentation as with self-discovery. In this way, personal writing is necessarily persuasive, for all writers want to influence the way readers think of them. They present themselves to readers in the way they want to be perceived. The rest they keep hidden, though readers can often see between the lines.

We read about others' experiences for much the same reason that we write about our own—to connect with others. There is much to be said about how we live our lives—about the decisions we face, the delights we share, and the fate that awaits us all. Reading autobiography can validate our sense of ourselves, particularly when we see our own experience reflected in another's life. Reading about others' lives can also challenge our complacency and help us appreciate other points of view. Not only can autobiography lead us to greater self-awareness by validating or challenging us, it can also enlarge our sympathies by awakening our humanity. When we read about others' lives, we empathize with another person's values and feelings and thus break the shell of our own egotism and isolation.

BASIC FEATURES OF ESSAYS ABOUT REMEMBERED EVENTS

Essays about remembered events share certain basic features. They tell life stories and vividly portray the scenes and people inhabiting them. They invest these stories with autobiographical significance. And finally, they appeal to the experiences of their readers. Although the essays describe the writers' own experiences, readers relate to them because they are really concerned with human experience in general.

A Well-told Story

Writing about remembered events means first of all telling an interesting story. Whatever else the writer may attempt to do, he or she must shape the experience into a story that is entertaining and memorable. This is done primarily by building suspense. As readers, we may sense disaster, shudder in anticipation of a troubling disclosure, or look forward to a humorous turn of events. The important point is that the writer makes us want to know what will happen. We wonder whether Annie Dillard will ever find the elusive amoeba and if Tobias Wolff will shoot the rifle, whether Al Young will make it home with the watermelon and if Jean Brandt will get caught for shoplifting.

In addition to telling a suspenseful story, good writers work to create tension in their narratives. *Tension* draws readers into a story, making us nervous about what might happen. Three techniques for heightening tension are specific narrative action, sentence rhythm, and dialogue. Tension rises when Wolff shows specific narrative action, giving a detailed close-up of his play with the rifle. Sentence rhythm creates emphasis when Dillard repeats the same sentence pattern over and over again, making us wonder if anything will ever come of her search for the amoeba. And dialogue conveys the immediacy and drama of personal interactions, when Brandt re-creates her conversations with her parents. By drawing us into the action, these techniques contribute to our involvement in the story as readers. One moment we're distant observers, far from the action; the next, we're thrown right into it, with the participants.

For more on tension, narrative action, dialogue, and sentence rhythm, see pp. 420–25.

**A Vivid
Presentation
of Significant
Scenes and People**

Scenes and people play an important role in most writing about remembered events. As in fiction, the scene provides a setting for the event. Instead of giving a generalized impression, skillful writers actually re-create the scene and let us hear the people. Vividness and specificity make the event—and the writing—memorable. Carefully selected details leave readers with some dominant impression of the whole tableau.

By moving in close, a writer can name specific objects in a scene: a table, a microscope, a blade of grass in the Dillard piece; a shopping center, some knickknacks, and a button in Brandt's essay. Good writers also provide details about the named objects. Dillard characterizes the table as "white enamel," the microscope as "blunt black three-speed," the blade of grass as "a wee brown chip." Brandt specifies that the shopping center was "swarming with frantic last-minute shoppers" and the coveted button was a "75-cent Snoopy button." Finally, simile and metaphor draw comparisons with other familiar things, helping readers to "see" the point and hence to better understand it. Brandt uses simile in her reference to *The Scarlet Letter* when she says she felt "like Hester Prynne being put on public display."

*The descriptive strategies
of naming, detailing, and
comparing are discussed
further on pp. 429–34.*

For presenting important people, writers can choose from a variety of strategies, including physical description, action, and dialogue. They can give details of the person's appearance, as Dillard does for her mother: sitting "with her knees crossed, in blue slacks, smoking a Chesterfield" or as Young does for his grandfather: hands "jammed . . . into the pockets of his faded blue hitch-em-ups." With a few carefully chosen details, both writers also capture something of each person's mood.

Skilled writers show people in action. Wolff, for example, shows his mother's precise movements: "She took a cellophane bag off a loaf of bread and we went outside and looked at the squirrel. 'Poor little thing,' she said. She stuck her hand in the wrapper and picked up the squirrel, then pulled the bag inside out away from her hand."

Writers can also present people through dialogue, letting us infer from their own words what the people are like and how they feel about one another. Young's grandfather, for example, reveals something about his own character when he declares, "This boy of Mary's will never amount to the salt in his bread." Brandt's mother comes across as stern and disapproving when she says she's "afraid sorry isn't enough" and that she's "horribly disappointed" in her daughter.

**An Indication of
the Significance**

In essays about remembered events, we not only expect a well-told story with vivid details, but we also expect the story to have a point. Sometimes the event's meaning is merely implied, but often it will be stated explicitly. There are two ways a writer can communicate this significance: by *showing* us that the event was important or by *telling* us directly what it meant. Most writers do both.

Showing is the heartbeat of an essay about a remembered event, for the event must be dramatized if readers are to appreciate its importance and understand the writer's feelings about it. Seeing the important scenes and people from the writer's point of view naturally leads readers to identify with the writer. Indeed, we can well imagine what that "unexpected tap on [the] shoulder" must have felt like for Brandt and how Dillard felt running upstairs to tell her parents about her great discovery.

Telling also contributes mightily to a reader's understanding, and so most writers explain something about the event's meaning and importance. They may tell us how they felt at the time, or how they feel now as they look back on the experience. Often writers do both, recalling their past feelings and thoughts and reflecting on the past from their present perspective. Wolff, for example, tells us some of his remembered feelings when he recalls feeling "like a sniper," and delighting in the "ecstasy" of power. He also tells us what he thinks about the experience in retrospect: "because I did not know who I was, any image of myself, no matter how grotesque, had power over me. This much I understand now." What Dillard tells us is a combination of what she "began to understand" at the time and what she came to realize as she got older: "that you do what you do out of your private passion for the thing itself."

Telling is the main way that writers interpret the event for readers, but skillful writers are careful not to append these reflections artificially, like a moral tagged on to a fable. They also try not to simplify or moralize, for most readers are skeptical of writing that is sentimental or self-serving. Readers expect an honest voice, one that may not reveal everything but that tries to be truthful in what it does disclose. We may not be able to identify with Wolff's compulsive need for a gun, but we have to admire his openness.

Young's story benefits from his avoidance of sentimentality in the same way. Notice that he neither presents himself pathetically nor makes his grandfather into an ogre. We can, as a result, readily sympathize with him for trying to be a big boy but also recognize, along with his grandfather, how foolish he was to choose such a huge watermelon. His grandfather may have been unkind in his response, but Young admits to having given him reason for annoyance. Just as they try to make their stories meaningful, good writers strive for honesty in their self-disclosure.

Guide to Writing

THE WRITING ASSIGNMENT

Write an essay about a significant event in your life. Choose an event that will be engaging for readers and that will, at the same time, tell them something about you. Tell your story dramatically and vividly, giving a clear indication of its autobiographical significance.

INVENTION

The following invention activities are designed to help you choose an appropriate event, recall specific details, test your choice to be sure you can write about it successfully, and define its autobiographical significance.

Choosing an Event to Write About

Finding an event to write about requires some patience and reflection. Take time to sit quietly and let your mind go. Think in terms of specific experiences you still remember as well as of specific years or other time periods.

Listing Events. List some events you might write about, making the list as long as you can. Following are some kinds of significant personal experiences that may give you some ideas. Try to recall at least one event in each category, more if at all possible.

- Any "first," such as when you first realized you had a special skill, ambition, or problem; when you first felt needed or rejected; when you first became aware of some kind of altruism or injustice

- Any memorably difficult situation: when you had to make a tough choice, when someone you admired let you down (or you let someone else down), when you struggled to learn or understand something

- Any occasion when things did not turn out as expected: when you expected to be praised but were criticized, when you were convinced you would fail but succeeded

- Any incident which challenged your basic values or beliefs

- Any humorous event, one you still laugh about, perhaps one that seemed awkward or embarrassing at the time

- Any event that shaped you in a particular way, making you perhaps independent, proud, insecure, fearful, courageous, ambitious

- Any incident charged with strong emotions such as love, fear, anger, embarrassment, guilt, frustration, hurt, pride, happiness, joy

Focusing on key periods of time is another way of looking for events to write about. Go back in five-year increments: one-to-five years ago, six-to-ten years ago, ten-to-fifteen, and so on. Try to recall at least one event from each period, more if you can.

Choosing a Significant Event. Look over your list, and choose two or three promising events. These events can be common or unusual, humorous or serious, recent or distant, but consider them carefully in light of these questions:

- Can I recall specific details about the action, scene, and people?
- Will I be able to tell what happened from beginning to end?

- As a fragment of my life story, does this event reveal anything important about me?
- Will I feel comfortable writing about it?
- Will it arouse readers' curiosity and interest?

Decide on one event to write about. Not everything needs to be clear to you at this point, but choose an event you feel drawn to explore further, one you expect will make a good story and lead you to insights about yourself.

Recalling Specific Sensory Details

Sensory details are the specific sights, sounds, and smells of the story you want to tell. The following activities will help you recall physical features of the scene and precise sensory details of these features.

Sights. Imagine your event as if it were a photograph or videotape. Take notes about what you "see": What time is it? Describe the lighting or the weather. If you are indoors, describe the room. If you are outdoors, what do you see around you? If you are on the move, what flashes by?

Now list specific objects that you see. If you were planning to write about a water-skiing incident, for example, you might list the skis, the rope, the boat, the water thrown up by your skis, other boats, and so on. Exclude people from your list.

Choose at least three items from your list, and write for about five minutes on each one. Try to remember and record specific visual details: size, shape, color, texture. Consider them from various perspectives: from a back view, a front view, a top view. Look at them both from a distance and up close. Think also in terms of simile (as when Wolff describes the dead squirrel as looking "like a scarf someone had dropped") and metaphor (as when Dillard describes the drop of water becoming "a jungle . . . full of one-celled animals).

Sounds. What sounds do you "hear" as you study the picture? Are there voices? animal sounds? horns honking? Is it quiet or noisy? Try simile and metaphor here too (remember Wolff comparing the sound of the rifle shot to "the bang of a cupboard slammed shut").

Smells, Tastes, Textures. As you picture your event, what do you smell? Is there any element you can taste? Study some of the objects in your picture, and describe some of the textures or surfaces of anything you can touch— are they soft or hard? smooth or rough?

Recalling Key People

Try to remember significant people in the event—what they looked like, what they did, what they or you said.

Listing People. List all the people who played more than a casual role in the event. You may have only one or two people to list, or you may have several.

Describing Key People. Choose one or more persons from your list who played a central role in the event. Try to select people who were important in making the event a significant one in your life. Take around five minutes to describe each person in writing—their appearance, their actions, and their significance in the event.

Re-creating Conversations.   Think about what was said: Can you recall any telling or unusual comments or choice of words? Do you remember any particular voices or accents? Try to reconstruct a conversation between one or more of these persons and yourself. Set it up as a dialogue, as Jean Brandt does on pp. 49–50.

You may not remember exactly what was said, but you can compose a dialogue that will probably reflect accurately your relationship with that person. Try for a conversational dialogue—no speeches, just a quick, informal exchange. Make an effort to extend the conversation to around ten comments by each person. Be expansive now; you can edit it later.

Finally, try to focus your thoughts about the key people in a sentence or two about your relationship with each of them and the role that he or she played in the event.

Sketching Out the Story

Take about five minutes to outline the main events. In brief phrases indicate what happened, focusing on what you and others did.

Testing Your Choice

Pause now to be sure you've chosen an event you will be able to write about successfully by asking yourself these questions:

- Am I still interested in this event? Do I feel drawn to explore its significance in my life and to tell others about it?

- Have I been able to recall enough details to describe it vividly?

- Do I recall enough about other people who were involved with this event?

If you cannot answer these questions affirmatively and confidently, you may want to find a different event to write about. If you must do so, return to your original list of events for other possible subjects.

For Group Inquiry

You might find it useful to get together in a group with two or three other students and run your chosen topics by one another. Assess the group's interest in the event you wish to write about, and invite their advice about whether it sounds promising. Does it seem likely to lead to an essay they would care to read? Your purpose is to decide whether you have chosen a good event to write about and thus to be able to proceed confidently to develop your essay.

Exploring the
Significance

Following are some questions designed to help you better understand the
meaning the event holds in your life.

(Recalling Your Feelings at the Time.) Try to remember your feelings during
the event and immediately thereafter. Spend about ten minutes jotting down
notes about your response, using these questions to stimulate your memory:

- What was my first response to the event? What did I think? How did I
  feel? What did I do?
- How did I show my feelings?
- What did I want those present to think of me, and why?
- What did I think of myself at the time?
- Did I talk to anyone during or just after the event? What did I say?
- How long did these initial feelings last?
- What were the immediate consequences of the event for me personally?

Stop a moment to focus your thoughts. In two or three sentences try to
articulate what your first response to the event seems to disclose about the
event's original importance.

(Exploring Your Present Perspective.) Next think about your present perspective
on the event—your current feelings as well as any thoughts or insights you
may have. Write for ten minutes about your present perspective, using these
questions to get you started:

- How do I feel now about the way I acted at the time of the event? Was
  my response appropriate? Why, or why not?
- Looking back, how do I feel about this event? Do I understand it dif-
  ferently now than I did then?
- What do my actions at the time of the event say about the kind of person
  I was then? In what ways am I different now? How would I respond to
  the same event if it occurred today?
- How would I summarize my current feelings?
- Are my feelings settled, or do they still seem to be changing? Am I sure
  of my feelings about the event, or am I ambivalent?

In two or three sentences explain what your present perspective reveals about
you or about the event's importance in your life.

Defining the Significance. In a sentence or two, state the significance of the
event. What importance does it hold for you? What does it tell you about
yourself?

PLANNING AND DRAFTING

The next activities are designed to help you to use your invention writing to set goals, to organize your narrative, and to write a first draft.

Seeing What You Have

You have now done a lot of thinking and writing about elements basic to an essay about a remembered event: your feelings, the autobiographical significance, specific sensory details, dialogue. Before going any further, reread everything you've written so far to see what you have. As you read through your invention materials, be on the lookout for surprising details or new insights. Watch for meaningful patterns and relationships. Highlight any such promising material by underlining or by making notes in the margin. Guided by the questions that follow, you should now be able to decide whether you have enough material to write an essay and whether you understand the autobiographical significance well enough.

- Will I be able to make any meaningful statements about my experience? What will they be? Can I find them in the invention writing?
- Do I have enough descriptive details to recreate the scene and people? What will be the dominant impression of my description and how will it reinforce the event's significance?
- Do I understand the autobiographical significance of the event well enough to feel confident writing about it?

If you do not see interesting details, connections, or patterns in your invention writing, you are not likely to write a good draft. Starting over is no fun, but there is no sense in starting to draft a composition if you do not feel confident about your topic.

If your invention writing looks thin but promising, there are several ways you may be able to fill it out. Try composing other conversations, recalling additional sensory details, thinking more about your own reactions to the event, elaborating on significant people, describing other people who were there.

Setting Goals

Before starting to draft, you should set goals to guide further invention and planning. Some of these goals concern the piece as a whole, such as holding readers' interest with a compelling story, satisfying their curiosity with meaningful self-disclosure, maintaining a good pace in the narrative, or framing the story in a satisfying way. Other goals have to do with smaller issues, such as including memorable sensory details, creating vivid images, or making dialogue sound like real conversation. You will be making dozens of decisions—and solving dozens of problems—as you work your way through a draft; these decisions and solutions are determined by the goals you set.

Following are some questions that can help you set goals before you start drafting. You may also want to return to them as you work, to help keep your goals in focus.

Your Readers

■ Will the event be familiar to my readers? How much can I assume they will know about such events? If they know little, how can I help them understand what happened? If they are familiar with such events, how can I convey the uniqueness of my experience?

■ How can I help readers to see the significance the event has for me? Shall I discuss the personal significance directly? Or shall I present it indirectly?

■ How can I get readers to connect to my experience and to reflect on their own lives?

■ How do I want to present myself? Should I be apologetic? proud? hurt? something else?

The Beginning

■ How shall I begin? What can I do in the opening sentences that will capture my readers' interest? Should I begin with the main event, integrating essential background information as I tell the story? Should I establish the setting and situation right away, as Young and Brandt do? Should I first present myself, as Dillard does? Or should I provide the complete context for the event, as Wolff does?

Telling the Story

■ What is the climax, or high point, of the story? For Wolff, it is shooting the squirrel and for Young, dropping the watermelon. For Dillard, it first seems as if finding the amoeba is the climax, but it turns out that her second discovery—that she can be independent of her parents—is even more significant.

■ How can I build tension and suspense leading to the climax? Can I show specific narrative action, as Wolff and Young do? Should I use sentence rhythm, as Dillard does? Or dialogue, as Brandt and Young do?

■ Should I tell the story chronologically, as Dillard, Wolff, and Brandt do? Or use flashback or flashforward as Young does?

The Ending

■ How should the essay end? Should I continue the story to the end, or should I end reflecting on the meaning of the experience?

■ What do I want the ending to accomplish? Do I want to frame the essay by referring to the beginning? Would it be good to jolt the reader with something unexpected?

Outlining

See Chapter 13 for information on structuring the narrative.

An essay about a remembered event should be first of all a good story. The way you organize this story will depend on what happened, what significance it had for you, who your readers will be, and what impression you want to give them. As you draft and revise, you will discover the most appropriate organization for your story. For now, start to plan this organization by listing the main incidents in the order that they took place. Then list them in the order in which you think they should be presented in your story.

Drafting

You may want to review the general drafting advice on pp. 8–11.

Start writing your essay, trying to maintain a focus on what took place in the event. Strive to paint a memorable picture of the scene and of any important people involved. Try also to describe the event in such a way as to say something about yourself and the event's significance in your life. If you feel stuck at any point in drafting the essay, try returning to the writing activities in the Invention section of this chapter.

GETTING CRITICAL COMMENTS

Now is the time to try to get a good critical reading. All writers find it helpful to have someone else read and comment on their drafts, and your instructor may schedule such a reading as part of your coursework. Otherwise, you can ask a classmate, friend, or family member to read it over. If your campus has a writing center, you might ask a tutor there to read and comment on your draft. The guidelines in this section are designed to be used by *anyone* reviewing an essay about a remembered event. (If you are unable to have someone else read over your draft, turn ahead to the revision section on pp. 46–48, which includes guidelines for reading your own draft with a critical eye.)

In order to provide focused, helpful comments, your reader must know your intended audience and purpose. Briefly write out this information at the top of your draft:

Audience. Who are your readers?

Purpose. What do you want your readers to learn about you from reading about this event?

Reading with a Critical Eye

Reading a draft critically means reading it more than once, first to get a general impression and then to analyze its basic features.

Reading for a First Impression.   Read first to enjoy the story and get a sense of its significance. As you read, try to notice any words or passages that contribute to your first impression, weak ones as well as strong ones. A good way of highlighting noteworthy language is to use the pointings system.

Pointings

■ Draw a straight line under any words or images that impress you as especially effective: strong verbs, specific details, memorable phrases, striking images.

■ Draw a wavy line under any words or images that seem flat, stale, or vague. Also put a wavy line under any words or phrases that you consider unnecessary or repetitious.

■ Look for pairs or groups of sentences that you think should be combined. Put brackets [ ] around these sentences.

■ Look for sentences that are garbled, overloaded, or awkward. Put parentheses ( ) around these sentences. Put them around any sentence that seems even slightly questionable; don't worry about whether or not you're certain about your judgment. The writer needs to know that you, as one reader, had even the slightest problem understanding a sentence.

After you've finished reading the draft, briefly give your impressions: How engaging is the story? Does the event seem truly significant? What in the draft do you think would especially interest the intended readers?

See pp. 35–37 to review the basic features.

Reading to Analyze.   Read then to focus on the basic features of writing about a remembered event.

Is the Story Told Well?

Identify the climax, and focus on how the narrative builds up to it. Note any places where the tension slackens and readers could lose interest in the outcome. Point to any sentences that seem boring or repetitious. Note any places where the story seems particularly vague or general.

Are Scenes and People Presented Vividly?

Indicate any scenes or people that seem nondescript or vague. Specify where adding dialogue might help to dramatize a scene, and where any existing dialogue rambles pointlessly. Comment on the effectiveness of any similes or metaphors. Are key scenes and people described enough to give a dominant impression?

Is the Autobiographical Significance Clear?

Summarize the incident's significance: What does it say about its author? Specify any reflections on the past that need more explanation. Is the writing overly sentimental? Does the self-disclosure seem manipulative of readers' sympathy?

Is the Organization Effective?

Consider the *overall plan* for the essay, perhaps by outlining it briefly. Point to any places where the sequence of action isn't clear or where the narrative seems to meander pointlessly. Look to see if description or other information disrupts the flow of the narrative.

Look at the *beginning*. If it is less than inviting or raises the wrong expectations, say so. Point to any other passages that might serve as a better opening.

Look at the *ending*. Indicate whether it leaves the story unresolved or whether the resolution is too pat and simplistic. Point to any other passages that would work better as endings for the essay.

What Final Thoughts Do You Have?

Which part needs the most work? What do you find most satisfying about this draft?

REVISING AND EDITING

This section will help you to identify problems in your draft and to revise and edit to solve them.

Identifying Problems

To identify problems in your draft, you need to read it objectively, analyze its basic features, and study any comments you've received from others.

Getting an Overview.   Consider the draft as a whole, trying to see it objectively. It may help to do so in two steps:

Reread. If at all possible, put the draft aside for a day or two before rereading it. When you do, start by reconsidering your purpose. Then read the draft straight through, trying to see it as your intended readers will.

Outline. Make a scratch outline to get an overview of the essay's development. This outline can be sketchy—words and phrases instead of complete sentences—but it should identify the basic features as they appear.

Charting a Plan for Revision.   You may want to make a chart like the one below to keep track of any problems you need to solve. The left-hand column lists the basic features of writing about remembered events. As you analyze your draft and study any comments you've gotten from others, note the problems you want to solve in the right-hand column.

Basic Features	*Problems to Solve*
The story	
Presentation of scenes and people	
Autobiographical significance	
Organization	

Analyzing the Basic Features of Your Draft. Turn now to the questions for analyzing a draft on pp. 45–46. Using these questions as guidelines, identify problems in your draft. Note things to solve on the preceding chart.

Studying Critical Comments. Review any comments you've received from other readers, and add to the chart any points that need attention. Try not to react too defensively to these comments; by letting you see how others respond to your draft, they provide invaluable information about how you might improve it.

Solving the Problems

Having identified problems, you now need to figure out solutions and—most important of all—to carry them out. Basically, you have three ways of finding solutions: (1) review your invention and planning notes for additional information and ideas; (2) do further invention to answer questions your readers raised; and (3) look back at the readings in this chapter to see how other writers have solved similar problems.

Following are suggestions to get you started solving some of the problems common to writing about remembered events. For now, focus on solving those issues identified on your chart. Avoid tinkering with sentence-level problems at this time; that will come later when you edit.

The Story

- If the climax is hard to identify, look to find the high point of the narrative. Be sure that the story has a climax, that it leads somewhere and doesn't just go on without a destination.
- Where the tension slackens, check to be sure that every action leads to the climax. Try intensifying the pace—either by adding specific details about movements and gestures, varying the sentence rhythm, or substituting lively quoted dialogue for summarized dialogue.
- If some sentences are boring or repetitious, try varying them in terms of pattern and length. If they all begin with a subject, for instance, see if adding an introductory phrase to one helps. Or, if they are all approximately the same length, try combining some to vary rhythm.

Presentation of Scenes and People

- If any scenes or people seem nondescript, try naming things more specifically and adding sensory details so that readers can see, touch, smell, taste, and hear aspects of the scene. Add similes and metaphors. Choose words that are concrete rather than abstract, specific rather than general.
- If any dialogue rambles pointlessly, liven it up with faster repartee or shorter, more pointed statements. Eliminate any unnecessary dialogue. Check the way it is introduced to see that it is not all "he said." Be more descriptive: "he cried out" or "she declared."

■ If any description fails to create a unified dominant impression, review the details in light of the impression you want to make. Omit extraneous ones.

Autobiographical Significance

■ If the event's significance doesn't come across clearly, you may need to state it more explicitly. Review any invention notes you took for insightful reflections or pointed images you could add. Reconsider the incident's significance now that you have written extensively about it. To establish greater emotional distance, look at the experience as if it were someone else's. What insight or advice could you offer?

■ If reflections on the past are unclear, try elaborating somewhat on your present thoughts and feelings about the experience. What did you learn from the incident?

■ If the writing seems sentimental or manipulative, you may need to re-examine the point you wish to make by writing about your subject. You do not have to disclose your every thought, but you should strive to be as honest as you can about what you do disclose.

Organization

■ If the story is hard to follow, restructure it so that the action unfolds clearly. Fill in any gaps. Eliminate unnecessary digressions.

■ If description or other information disrupts the flow of the narrative, try integrating it more smoothly by adding transitions. If that doesn't help, consider taking it out or moving it.

■ If the beginning is weak, see if there's a better place to start. Review the draft and your notes for an image, a bit of dialogue, or a remembered feeling that might catch readers' attention or arouse their curiosity.

■ If the ending doesn't work, see if there's a better place to end—a memorable image, perhaps, or a provocative question. Look to see if you can frame the essay by referring back to something in the beginning.

Editing and Proofreading

As you've been working on your draft so far, you've probably corrected some obvious errors, but grammar and style have not been a priority. Now is the time to check carefully for errors in usage, punctuation, and mechanics, and also to consider matters of style. You may find that studying your draft in separate passes—first for paragraphs, then for sentences, and finally for words—will help you to recognize any problems.

Once you have edited your draft and produced a final copy, proofread it carefully to be sure there are no typos, misspellings, or other mistakes.

LEARNING FROM YOUR OWN WRITING PROCESS

Your instructor may ask you to evaluate what you have learned in writing this essay. If so, begin by reviewing quickly the notes from your invention and planning. How successful was this part of your writing process? What major discoveries did you make during invention? Were there obstacles in drafting that your invention work did not help you overcome?

Next, reread your draft, any written analysis of it, and your revision. What did you discover about the event as you were drafting? How did other readers' comments help you improve the draft? What changes did you make between draft and revision? If you had more time, is there anything you would still like to improve? What are you most pleased with in your revision?

A Writer at Work

FROM INVENTION TO DRAFT TO REVISION

This section looks at the writing process that Jean Brandt followed in composing her essay, "Calling Home." You will see some of her invention writing and her complete first draft, which you can then compare to the final draft, printed on pp. 30–33.

Invention

Brandt's invention produced about nine handwritten pages, but it took her only two hours, spread out over four days. Here is a selection of her invention writings. She began by choosing an event and then recalling specific sensory details of the scene and the other people involved. She writes two dialogues, one with her sister Sue and the other with her father. Following is the one with her sister.

Re-creating a Conversation

SUE: Jean, why did you do it?

ME: I don't know. I guess I didn't want to wait in that long line, Sue, what am I going to tell Mom and Dad?

SUE: Don't worry about that yet, the detective might not really call the police.

ME: I can't believe I was stupid enough to take it.

SUE: I know. I've been there before. Now when he comes back try crying and act like you're really upset. Tell

```
him how sorry you are and that it was the first time you
ever stole something but make sure you cry. It got me
off the hook once.
```

```
ME: I don't think I can force myself to cry. I'm not
really that upset. I don't think the shock's worn off.
I'm more worried about Mom.
```

```
SUE: Who knows? Maybe she won't have to find out.
```

```
ME: God, I hope not. Hey, where's Louie and Grandma?
Grandma doesn't know about this, does she?
```

```
SUE: No, I sort of told Lou what was going on so he's
just taking Grandma around shopping.
```

```
ME: Isn't she wondering where we are?
```

```
SUE: I told him to tell her we would meet them in an
hour.
```

```
ME: How am I ever going to face her? Mom and Dad might
possibly understand or at least get over it, but
Grandma? This is gonna kill her.
```

```
SUE: Don't worry about that right now. Here comes the
detective. Now try to look like you're sorry. Try to
cry.
```

This dialogue helps Brandt recall an important conversation with her sister. Dialogues are an especially useful form of invention for they enable writers to remember their feelings and thoughts.

Brandt writes this dialogue quickly, trying to capture the language of excited talk, keeping the exchanges brief. She includes a version of this dialogue in her second draft but excludes it from her revision. The dialogue with her father does not appear in any of her drafts. Even though she eventually decides to feature other completely different conversations, these invention dialogues enable her to evaluate how various conversations would work in her essay.

Next, we see her first attempts to bring the autobiographical significance of the event into focus as she explores her remembered feelings and present perspective. She begins by listing eight possible events to write about. After some reflection, she chooses to write about the time she was arrested for shoplifting. Then she attempts to focus her thoughts about the significance of the event:

```
Being arrested for shoplifting was significant because
it changed some of my basic attitudes. Since that night
I've never again considered stealing anything. This
event would reveal how my attitude toward the law and
other people has changed from disrespectful to very re-
spectful.
```

Brandt begins by stating tentatively that the importance of the event was the lesson it taught her. Reading this statement might lead us to expect a moralistic story of how someone learned something the hard way. As we look at the subsequent invention activities and watch the draft develop, however, we will see how her memories of her relations with other people in the incident considerably change this potentially simplistic beginning.

Recalling Remembered Feelings

```
    I was scared, humiliated, and confused. I was terrified
    when I realized what was happening. I can still see the
manager and his badge and remember what I felt when I
knew who he was. I just couldn't believe it. I didn't
want to run. I felt there wasn't anything I could do--I
was afraid, embarrassed, worried, mad that it happened.
I didn't show my feelings at all. I tried to look very
calm on the outside, but inside I was extremely nervous.
The nervousness might have come through in my voice a
little. I wanted the people around me to think I was
tough and that I could handle the situation. I was
really disappointed with myself. Getting arrested made
me realize how wrong my actions were. I felt very
ashamed. Afterward I had to talk to my father about it.
I didn't say much of anything except that I was wrong
and I was sorry. The immediate consequence was being
taken to jail and then later having to call my parents
and tell them what happened. I hated to call my parents.
That was the hardest part. I remember how much I dreaded
that. My mom was really hurt.
```

Brandt's exploration of her first reaction is quite successful. Naming specific feelings, she focuses on the difference between what she felt and how she acted. She remembers her humiliation at being arrested as well as the terrible moment when she had to tell her parents. As we will see, this concern with her parents' reaction, more than her own humiliation, becomes the most important theme in her essay.

In exploring her first response to the event, Brandt writes quickly, noting down memories as they come to mind. Next, she rereads this first exploration and attempts to state briefly what the incident really reveals about her:

```
    I think it reveals that I was not a hard-core criminal.
    I was trying to live up to Robin Files's (supposedly my
    best girlfriend) expectations, even though I actually
    knew that what I was doing was wrong.
```

After longer pieces of exploratory writing, stopping to focus her thoughts like this helps Brandt see the point of what she has just written. Specifically, it helps her to connect diverse invention writings to her main concern: discovering the autobiographical significance of the event. Thus does she reflect on what her remembered feelings of the event reveal about the kind of person she was at the time: not a hard-core criminal. She identifies a friend, who will disappear from the writing after one brief mention. Next she looks at her present perspective on the event.

Exploring Present Perspective

```
At first I was ashamed to tell anyone that I had been
arrested. It was as if I couldn't admit it myself. Now
I'm glad it happened, because who knows where I'd be now
if I hadn't been caught. I still don't tell many people
about it. Never before have I written about it. I think
my response was appropriate. If I'd broken down and
cried, it wouldn't have helped me any, so it's better
that I reacted calmly. My actions and responses show
that I was trying to be tough. I thought that that was
the way to gain respectability. If I were to get ar-
rested now (of course it wouldn't be for shoplifting), I
think I'd react the same way because it doesn't do any
good to get emotional. My current feelings are ones of
appreciation. I feel lucky because I was set straight
early. Now I can look back on it and laugh, but at the
same time know how serious it was. I am emotionally dis-
tant now because I can view the event objectively rather
than subjectively. My feelings are settled now. I don't
get upset thinking about it. I don't feel angry at the
manager or the police. I think I was more upset about my
parents than about what was happening to me. After the
first part of it was over I mainly worried about what my
parents would think.
```

Writing about her present perspective confirms that Brandt has emotional distance from the event. She finds that she can laugh about it even after probing her feelings seriously. Reassessing her reaction at the time, she decides she acted reasonably. She is obviously pleased to recall that she did not lose control. Then, once again, Brandt tries to summarize the autobiographical disclosures she makes by exploring her present perspective on the event.

```
My present perspective shows that I'm a reasonable per-
son. I can admit when I'm wrong and accept the punish-
ment that was due me. I find that I can be concerned
about others even when I'm in trouble.
```

Next Brandt reflects on what she has written in order to articulate the autobiographical significance of the event.

Defining the Event's Autobiographical Significance

> The event was important because it entirely changed one
> aspect of my character. I will be disclosing that I was
> once a thief, and I think many of my readers will be
> able to identify with my story, even though they won't
> admit it.

After the first set of invention work, completed in about forty-five minutes on two separate days, Brandt is confident she has chosen an event with personal significance. She knows what she will be disclosing about herself and feels comfortable doing it—now that she knows she has sufficient emotional distance. In her brief focusing statements she begins by moralizing ("my attitude . . . changed") and blaming others (Robin Files) but concludes by acknowledging what she did. She is now prepared to disclose it to readers ("I was once a thief"). Also, she thinks readers will like her story because she suspects many of them will recall doing something illegal and feeling guilty about it, even if they never got caught.

The First Draft

The day after completing the invention writing, Brandt writes her first draft. It takes her about an hour.

Her draft is handwritten and contains few erasures or other changes, indicating that she writes steadily, probably letting the writing lead her where it will. She knows this will not be her only draft.

Before you read the first draft, reread the final draft, "Calling Home," in the Readings section of this chapter. Then as you read the first draft, consider what part it was to play in the total writing process.

> It was two days before Christmas and my older sister   1
> and brother, my grandmother, and I were rushing around
> doing last-minute shopping. After going to a few stores we
> decided to go to Lakewood Center shopping mall. It was
> packed with other frantic shoppers like ourselves from one
> end to the other. The first store we went to (the first
> and last for me) was the General Store. The General Store
> is your typical gift shop. They mainly have the cutesy
> knick-knacks, posters, frames and that sort. The store is
> decorated to resemble an old-time western general store
> but the appearance doesn't quite come off.
>
> We were all browsing around and I saw a basket of   2
> buttons so I went to see what the different ones were. One
> of the first ones I noticed was a Snoopy button. I'm not
> sure what it said on it, something funny I'm sure and be-
> sides I was in love with anything Snoopy when I was 13. I
> took it out of the basket and showed it to my sister and
> she said "Why don't you buy it?" I thought about it but

the lines at the cashiers were outrageous and I didn't
think it was worth it for a 75 cent item. Instead I figured just take it and I did. I thought I was so sly about
it. I casually slipped it into my pocket and assumed I was
home free since no one pounced on me. Everyone was ready
to leave this shop so we made our way through the crowds
to the entrance.

My grandmother and sister were ahead of my brother and   3
I. They were almost to the entrance of May Co. and we were
about 5 to 10 yards behind when I felt this tap on my
shoulder. I turned around already terror struck, and this
man was flashing some kind of badge in my face. It happened so fast I didn't know what was going on. Louie finally noticed I wasn't with him and came back for me. Jack
explained I was being arrested for shoplifting and if my
parents were here then Louie should go find them. Louie
ran to get Susie and told her about it but kept it from
Grandma. By the time Sue got back to the General Store I
was in the back office and Jack was calling the police. I
was a little scared but not really. It was sort of exciting. My sister was telling me to try and cry but I
couldn't. About 20 minutes later two cops came and handcuffed me, led me through the mall outside to the police
car. I was kind of embarrassed when they took me through
the mall in front of all those people.

When they got me in the car they began questioning me,   4
while driving me to the police station. Questions just to
fill out the report--age, sex, address, color of eyes,
etc.

Then when they were finished they began talking about   5
Jack and what a nuisance he was. I gathered that Jack had
every single person who shoplifted, no matter what their
age, arrested. The police were getting really fed up with
it because it was a nuisance for them to have to come way
out to the mall for something as petty as that. To hear
the police talk about my "crime" that way felt good because it was like what I did wasn't really so bad. It made
me feel a bit relieved. When we walked into the station I
remember the desk sergeant joking with the arresting officers about "well we got another one of Jack's hardened
criminals." Again, I felt my crime lacked any seriousness
at all. Next they handcuffed me to a table and questioned
me further and then I had to phone my mom. That was the
worst. I never was so humiliated in my life. Hearing the

disappointment in her voice was worse punishment than the
cops could ever give me.

This first draft establishes the main narrative line of events. About a third of
it is devoted to the store manager, an emphasis which disappears by the final
draft. What is to have prominence in the final draft—Brandt's feelings about
telling her parents and her conversations with them—appears here only in a
few lines at the very end. But its mention suggests its eventual importance,
and we are reminded of its prominence in Brandt's invention writing.

Brandt writes a second draft for another student to read critically. In this
draft, she includes dialogues with her sister and with the policemen. She also
provides more information about her actions as she considered buying the
Snoopy button and then decided to steal it instead. She includes visual details
of the manager's office. This draft is not much different in emphasis from
the first draft, however, still ending with a long section about the policemen
and the station. The parents are mentioned briefly only at the very end.

The reader tells Brandt how much he likes her story and admires her
honesty. However, he does not encourage her to develop the dramatic possibilities in calling her parents and meeting them afterward. In fact, he encourages her to keep the dialogue with the policemen about the manager
and to include what the manager said to the police.

Brandt's revision shows that she does not take her reader's advice. She
reduces the role of the police officers, eliminating any dialogue with them.
She greatly expands the role of her parents: The last third of the paper is
now focused on her remembered feelings about calling them and seeing them
afterward. In dramatic importance the phone call home now equals the arrest.
Remembering Brandt's earliest invention writings, we can see that she was
headed toward this conclusion all along . . . but she needed invention, three
drafts, a critical reading, and about a week to get there.

■ Invited by a sports magazine to write an article about the person who most influenced him, a professional football player writes about his high school football coach. He admits that his coach had such a powerful influence that he still finds himself doing things to win his approval and admiration, even though he never was able to please him in high school. He relates several anecdotes to show how the coach deliberately tried to humiliate him: challenging him to an arm-wrestling match and laughing at him when he lost, and making him do so many pushups and run so many laps that he collapsed in exhaustion.

■ A novelist writes in her autobiography about an aunt who was notorious for lying. She describes some of her aunt's most fantastic lies and the hilarious trouble they caused. Most members of the family found the woman's behavior annoying and embarrassing, but the writer acknowledges having secretly sympathized with her. As she describes her aunt, the writer points out the resemblance between them: not only does she look like her aunt, but she too has a vivid imagination and likes to embellish reality.

■ For his political science class, a college junior writes a term paper about his internship as a campaign worker for an unsuccessful candidate. In one part of the paper he focuses on the candidate, whom he came to know and to admire. He describes the woman's energy and ambition, her broad understanding of issues and attention to detail. The student writes about the anger and bitterness he felt when she lost and his amazement that the candidate seemed genuinely philosophical about her defeat.

■ Upon learning that one of her former law professors is to be honored for service to the community, an attorney decides to write an article about him for her law school alumni magazine. She criticizes him for the hard treatment he gave her, the first black woman to attend the school, illustrating her point with a few anecdotes. But she also admits that she now realizes that although he often seemed unfair, he prepared her for the competitive world of law better than any of her other teachers did.

Remembering People 3

■ For a composition class, a student writes about an old friend who had once been like a sister to her. Along with anecdotes demonstrating how very close they were, she reconstructs a conversation they had that she's never forgotten. In it they talked about their hopes for the future, specifically about going away to college together and eventually opening a small business. But the friend got married instead, and they have since grown apart. Reflecting on her friend and on what happened to their friendship, the writer describes the feelings of betrayal she has harbored but realizes that they really are unfair. The friendship just took its natural course.

As these scenarios suggest, there may be many occasions for writing about a person you have known. Whatever the occasion, your writing should present the person's physical features, mannerisms, and characteristic way of thinking and talking. When you write about someone else, you will also make clear your own feelings and attitudes. In expressing your view of another person, after all, you reveal the values and character traits you admire.

Your aim will usually be not only to portray the person as an individual but also to indicate how the person has been significant in your life. You may, like the football player and the attorney, decide to write about someone who was once in a position of authority over you. Or you may, like the composition student, choose to describe a peer. The person you select may have been a passing acquaintance, like the unsuccessful candidate, or someone you knew for a long time, like the overly imaginative aunt. The possibilities are endless.

Essays about remembered people tap our natural curiosity about other people—what they are like, how they lead their lives, how they relate to others. Such essays lead us to reflect on our own lives and on the human condition in general, enabling us to know ourselves better and to empathize with others.

You can more readily understand the focus of this chapter if you consider four familiar ways of writing about people: researched biography, reportage, memoir, and autobiography. In researched biography, the writer relies on published documents. If the subject of the biography is still living, the biographer might also interview people who know or knew the subject. In reportage, the writer relies on interviews and observation to profile some interesting person he or she has very likely never met before. In memoir, the writer presents an important person he or she once knew well. Writers of memoirs rely on memory and often also on their personal journals and correspondence. Though memoirists may reflect on their own lives, they nearly always keep the focus on others. They write more like historians than like autobiographers. In autobiography, writers explore frankly the significance to themselves of their relationships with others. Autobiographers write incidentally about others in order to learn more about themselves, and they reveal as much about themselves as about their subjects.

Writing about other people and their significance in your life is not a typical academic writing assignment, but you are likely to encounter it in one or more college courses nevertheless. Here are some typical assignments requiring this kind of writing:

- *For a theater workshop:* Write a monologue recreating the speech and behavior of a significant person in your life. Rehearse and revise the monologue with another workshop member before presenting it in class.

- *For an education class:* Write about a teacher who was unusually effective, focusing on qualities that seem to have contributed to his or her effectiveness. To move beyond generalities, relate at least three specific occasions that show this teacher's effectiveness. What, exactly, did the teacher do, and what did you learn?

- *For a history class focusing on American ethnic groups:* Describe an older family member through whom you have best come to understand your ethnic roots. How does this person embody the ethnic characteristics you most admire—or most dislike?

- *For a philosophy class:* What would constitute living a life according to Aristotle's Golden Mean? Describe a person you know who comes close to accomplishing this goal.

For Group Inquiry

The scenarios that open this chapter suggest some occasions for writing about people important in one's life. Imagine that you have been asked to write about someone who had a significant effect on your childhood. The person can be either another child or someone older, someone you still know or someone who long ago passed out of your life. The only requirements are that your relationship seems important to you now and that you remember the person well enough to tell about him or her.

Get together with two or three other students, and briefly tell one another about the subjects you have each chosen. Allow around thirty minutes to work together—fifteen to discuss your subjects, and then fifteen to consider the rhetorical situation. Take two or three minutes each to describe your person. Mention some unique characteristics, and tell about something he or she once did. After telling about your subject, ask the other members of the group for their impressions of him or her.

Then, as a group, consider the rhetorical situation of telling about a remembered person:

- What problems did you each encounter choosing and telling about someone? How did the audience—that is, the group—affect your choice?

■ Did everyone in the group have the same impression of each subject? Were any of you surprised by any of the impressions?

■ What did you each learn about yourself from telling about someone else?

Readings

Maya Angelou, a poet as well as an autobiographer, has also worked as an actress, singer, dancer, songwriter, editor, and administrator of the Southern Christian Leadership Conference. She holds an endowed professorship at Wake Forest University. She has said of her writing: "I speak to the black experience, but I am always talking about the human condition."

Angelou grew up during the 1930s in the small Arkansas town of Stamps, where she lived with her brother Bailey; her grandmother, the "Momma" mentioned in this selection; and her Uncle Willie. Momma and Willie operated a small grocery store. In this selection, from *I Know Why the Caged Bird Sings* (1970), Angelou writes about her memories of her uncle, from her perspective as an adult of forty. As you read, notice how she describes him and selects specific anecdotes to reveal their relationship.

UNCLE WILLIE
MAYA ANGELOU

When Bailey was six and I a year younger, we used to rattle off the times tables   1
with the speed I was later to see Chinese children in San Francisco employ on their abacuses. Our summer-gray pot-bellied stove bloomed rosy red during winter, and became a severe disciplinarian threat if we were so foolish as to indulge in making mistakes.

Uncle Willie used to sit, like a giant black Z (he had been crippled as a child),   2
and hear us testify to the Lafayette County Training Schools' abilities. His face pulled down on the left side, as if a pulley had been attached to his lower teeth, and his left hand was only a mite bigger than Bailey's, but on the second mistake or on the third hesitation his big overgrown right hand would catch one of us behind the collar, and in the same moment would thrust the culprit toward the dull red heater, which throbbed like a devil's toothache. We were never burned, although once I might have been when I was so terrified I tried to jump onto the stove to remove the possibility of its remaining a threat. Like most children, I thought if I could face the worst danger voluntarily, and *triumph*, I would forever have power over it. But in my case of sacrificial effort I was thwarted. Uncle Willie held tight to my dress and I only got close enough to smell the clean dry scent of hot iron. We learned the

times tables without understanding their grand principle, simply because we had the capacity and no alternative.

The tragedy of lameness seems so unfair to children that they are embarrassed 3
in its presence. And they, most recently off nature's mold, sense that they have only narrowly missed being another of her jokes. In relief at the narrow escape, they vent their emotions in impatience and criticism of the unlucky cripple.

Momma related times without end, and without any show of emotion, how 4
Uncle Willie had been dropped when he was three years old by a woman who was minding him. She seemed to hold no rancor against the baby-sitter, nor for her just God who allowed the accident. She felt it necessary to explain over and over again to those who knew the story by heart that he wasn't ''born that way.''

In our society, where two-legged, two-armed strong Black men were able at 5
best to eke out only the necessities of life, Uncle Willie, with his starched shirts, shined shoes and shelves full of food, was the whipping boy and butt of jokes of the underemployed and underpaid. Fate not only disabled him but laid a double-tiered barrier in his path. He was also proud and sensitive. Therefore he couldn't pretend that he wasn't crippled, nor could he deceive himself that people were not repelled by his defect.

Only once in all the years of trying not to watch him, I saw him pretend to 6
himself and others that he wasn't lame.

Coming home from school one day, I saw a dark car in our front yard. I rushed 7
in to find a strange man and woman (Uncle Willie said later they were schoolteachers from Little Rock) drinking Dr. Pepper in the cool of the Store. I sensed a wrongness around me, like an alarm clock that had gone off without being set.

I knew it couldn't be the strangers. Not frequently, but often enough, travelers 8
pulled off the main road to buy tobacco or soft drinks in the only Negro store in Stamps. When I looked at Uncle Willie, I knew what was pulling my mind's coattails. He was standing erect behind the counter, not leaning forward or resting on the small shelf that had been built for him. Erect. His eyes seemed to hold me with a mixture of threats and appeal.

I dutifully greeted the strangers and roamed my eyes around for his walking 9
stick. It was nowhere to be seen. He said, ''Uh . . . this this . . . this . . . uh, my niece. She's . . . uh . . . just come from school.'' Then to the couple — ''You know . . . how, uh, children are . . . th-th-these days . . . they play all d-d-day at school and c-c-can't wait to get home and pl-play some more.''

The people smiled, very friendly.   10

He added, ''Go on out and pl-play, Sister.''   11

The lady laughed in a soft Arkansas voice and said, ''Well, you know, Mr. John- 12
son, they say, you're only a child once. Have you children of your own?''

Uncle Willie looked at me with an impatience I hadn't seen in his face even when 13
he took thirty minutes to loop the laces over his high-topped shoes. ''I . . . I thought I told you to go . . . go outside and play.''

Before I left I saw him lean back on the shelves of Garret Snuff, Prince Albert 14
and Spark Plug chewing tobacco.

''No, ma'am . . . no ch-children and no wife.'' He tried a laugh. ''I have an old 15
m-m-mother and my brother's t-two children to l-look after.''

I didn't mind his using us to make himself look good. In fact, I would have 16
pretended to be his daughter if he wanted me to. Not only did I not feel any loyalty

to my own father, I figured that if I had been Uncle Willie's child I would have received much better treatment.

The couple left after a few minutes, and from the back of the house I watched 17 the red car scare chickens, raise dust and disappear toward Magnolia.

Uncle Willie was making his way down the long shadowed aisle between the 18 shelves and the counter—hand over hand, like a man climbing out of a dream. I stayed quiet and watched him lurch from one side, bumping to the other, until he reached the coal-oil tank. He put his hand behind that dark recess and took his cane in the strong fist and shifted his weight on the wooden support. He thought he had pulled it off.

I'll never know why it was important to him that the couple (he said later that 19 he'd never seen them before) would take a picture of a whole Mr. Johnson back to Little Rock.

He must have tired of being crippled, as prisoners tire of penitentiary bars and 20 the guilty tire of blame. The high-topped shoes and the cane, his uncontrollable muscles and thick tongue, and the looks he suffered of either contempt or pity had simply worn him out, and for one afternoon, one part of an afternoon, he wanted no part of them.

I understood and felt closer to him at that moment than ever before or since.   21

For Discussion

As Angelou says, Uncle Willie "couldn't pretend that he wasn't crippled, nor could he deceive himself that people were not repelled by his defect." Why are people often repelled by difference and disadvantage? How do we learn what to feel in the presence of people of unusual appearance or of different gender, ethnicity, or social class? Consider your earliest feelings about people who were different from you. How do you assess those feelings now? How do you manage your current encounters with difference or disadvantage?

For Analysis

1.   Angelou lived with Uncle Willie for years. Here she singles out just two anecdotes to disclose something about their relationship; one toward the end of paragraph 2 and another in paragraphs 6–18. What does each illustrate about their relationship? What is the relation of the first anecdote to the second?

For more on specific narrative action, see pp. 422–23.

2.   One way autobiographers present people memorably is through specific narrative action—showing a person moving or gesturing or in specific postures. Analyze the long anecdote in paragraphs 6–18, underlining each instance of specific narrative action. How do the actions contribute to this portrait of Uncle Willie?

For more on dialogue, see pp. 423–25

3.   What role does dialogue play in Angelou's essay? What do we learn about Uncle Willie from what he says and the way he says it?

4.   Angelou tells us something about Uncle Willie in both paragraph 18 and paragraph 20, yet the two are quite different. What did she choose to do in each paragraph? How are the two paragraphs related?

For Your
Own Writing

Consider writing a portrait of an adult outside your immediate family who has significantly influenced your life. You might write about a grandparent, aunt or uncle, teacher, or coach. How would you engage readers' interest and disclose the person's significance in your life? What details would you include? What anecdotes might you relate?

Commentary

We know that Uncle Willie was a very significant person in Angelou's life, yet she never tells us that directly. Instead, she shows us his significance through specific anecdotes, remembered feelings, and reflection. She might have begun the essay by stating her main point, announcing just how Uncle Willie was important to her. She chooses a much more engaging and effective strategy, however: she tells a story about how Uncle Willie forced her and her brother to memorize the multiplication tables. Learning about Uncle Willie's actions and her reactions at the time and reading her brief reflection (at the end of paragraph 2) on these sometimes-terrifying arithmetic lessons, we begin right away to understand their relationship.

This was not an easy relationship, but relationships with parents or guardians or mentors rarely are. We have mixed feelings about people we love, and autobiographers explore these feelings frankly. Angelou tells us that Uncle Willie was proud, sensitive, and relatively prosperous. He and Momma provided a home for her, and he cared about her education. Yet Angelou is not at all sentimental about him. She admits that he sometimes scared her and that she did not always feel close to him. Had she been his child, she believed, he would have treated her better. Clearly he was not a perfect guardian, and she tells us so.

As a writer, you can learn still more about writing about remembered people by considering carefully how Angelou describes Uncle Willie. Notice how she describes his posture, face, hands; his shined high-top shoes, starched shirts, and cane. She describes objects in the scene with the same precision: the stove is "summer-gray" and in winter "rosy red." Uncle Willie leans back on shelves of "Garret Snuff, Prince Albert [smoking tobacco] and Spark Plug chewing tobacco." Coming home from school, Angelou finds not a couple from out of town drinking a bottled drink, but a schoolteacher couple from Little Rock drinking Dr. Pepper.

For more on naming and detailing, see pp. 429–32.

Throughout her essay Angelou relies on inventive similes and metaphors to present people, scenes, and feelings. Uncle Willie sits "like a giant black Z" and makes his way down the aisle "like a man climbing out of a dream." When Angelou enters the store, she senses something wrong, "like an alarm clock that had gone off without being set." These comparisons enable Angelou to understand her feelings more fully and to present them to us more concretely. Similes and metaphors are not mere decoration; they enable the reader to see and to understand.

For more on simile and metaphor, see pp. 432–33.

■   ■   ■

Gerald Haslam is a professor of English at Sonoma State University in California known for his advocacy of western literature. He has published several short story collections, including *Okies: Selected Stories* (1973) and *Hawk Flights: Visions of the West* (1983). This essay, from *California Childhood* (1988), is about his great-grandmother, called here Grandma. As you read, notice how he relies on specific anecdotes and reconstructed conversations to present a subject from his childhood.

GRANDMA

GERALD HASLAM

"Expectoran su sangre!" exclaimed Great-grandma when I showed her the small 1 horned toad I had removed from my breast pocket. I turned toward my mother, who translated: "They spit blood."

"De los ojos," Grandma added. "From their eyes," mother explained, herself 2 uncomfortable in the presence of the small beast.

I grinned, "Awwwwww."   3

But my Great-grandmother did not smile. *"Son muy toxicos,"*[1] she nodded with 4 finality. Mother moved back an involuntary step, her hands suddenly busy at her breast. "Put that thing down," she ordered.

"His name's John," I said.   5

"Put John down and not in your pocket, either," my mother nearly shouted. 6 "Those things are very poisonous. Didn't you understand what Grandma said?"

I shook my head.   7

"Well . . ." mother looked from one of us to the other—spanning four gener- 8 ations of California, standing three feet apart—and said, "of course you didn't. Please take him back where you got him, and be careful. We'll all feel better when you do." The tone of her voice told me that the discussion had ended, so I released the little reptile where I'd captured him.

I later learned that my Great-grandmother—whom we simply called 9 "Grandma"—had been moving from house to house within the family, trying to find a place she'd accept. She hated the city, and most of the aunts and uncles lived in Los Angeles. Our house in Oildale was much closer to the open country where she'd dwelled all her life. She had wanted to come to our place right away because she had raised my mother from a baby when my own grandmother died. But the old lady seemed unimpressed with Daddy, whom she called *"ese gringo."*

In truth, we had more room, and my dad made more money in the oil patch 10 than almost anyone else in the family. Since my mother was the closest to Grandma, our place was the logical one for her, but Ese Gringo didn't see it that way, I guess, at least not at first. Finally, after much debate, he relented.

In any case, one windy afternoon, my Uncle Manuel and Aunt Toni drove up 11 and deposited four-and-a-half feet of bewigged, bejeweled Spanish spitfire: a square, pale face topped by a tightly-curled black wig that hid a bald head—her hair having been lost to typhoid nearly sixty years before—her small white hands veined with rivers of blue. She walked with a prancing bounce that made her appear half her age, and she barked orders in Spanish from the moment she emerged from

[1]They're very poisonous.

Manuel and Toni's car. Later, just before they left, I heard Uncle Manuel tell my dad, "Good luck, Charlie. That old lady's dynamite." Daddy only grunted.

She had been with us only two days when I tried to impress her with my horned   12
toad. In fact, nothing I did seemed to impress her, and she referred to me as *el malcriado*,[2] causing my mother to shake her head. Mom explained to me that Grandma was just old and lonely for Grandpa and uncomfortable in town. Mom told me that Grandma had lived over half a century in the country, away from the noise, away from clutter, away from people. She refused to accompany my mother on shopping trips, or anywhere else. She even refused to climb into a car, and I wondered how Uncle Manuel had managed to load her up in order to bring her to us.

She disliked sidewalks and roads, dancing across them when she had to, then   13
appearing to wipe her feet on earth or grass. Things too civilized simply did not please her. A brother of hers had been killed in the great San Francisco earthquake and that had been the end of her tolerance of cities. Until my Great-grandfather died, they lived on a small rancho near Arroyo Cantua, north of Coalinga. Grandpa, who had come north from Sonora as a youth to work as a *vaquero*,[3] had bred horses and cattle, and cowboyed for other ranchers, scraping together enough of a living to raise eleven children.

He had been, until the time of his death, a lean, dark-skinned man with wide   14
shoulders, a large nose, and a sweeping handlebar mustache that was white when I knew him. His Indian blood darkened all his progeny so that not even I was as fair-skinned as my Great-grandmother, Ese Gringo for a father or not.

As it turned out, I didn't really understand very much about Grandma at all. She   15
was old, of course, yet in many ways my parents treated her as though she were younger than me, walking her to the bathroom at night and bringing her presents from the store. In other ways — drinking wine at dinner, for example — she was granted adult privileges. Even Daddy didn't drink wine except on special occasions. After Grandma moved in, though, he began to occasionally join her for a glass, sometimes even sitting with her on the porch for a premeal sip.

She held court on our front porch, often gazing toward the desert hills east of   16
us or across the street at kids playing on the lot. Occasionally, she would rise, cross the yard and sidewalk and street, skip over them, sometimes stumbling on the curb, and wipe her feet on the lot's sandy soil, then she would slowly circle the boundary between the open middle and the brushy sides, searching for something, it appeared. I never figured out what.

One afternoon I returned from school and saw Grandma perched on the porch   17
as usual, so I started to walk around the house to avoid her sharp, mostly incomprehensible, tongue. She had already spotted me. "*Venga aqui!*"[4] she ordered, and I understood.

I approached the porch and noticed that Grandma was vigorously chewing some-   18
thing. She held a small white bag in one hand. Saying "*Qué deseas tomar?*"[5] she

---

[2]the brat
[3]cowboy
[4]Come here!
[5]What do you want to take?

withdrew a large orange gumdrop from the bag and began slowly chewing it in her toothless mouth, smacking loudly as she did so. I stood below her for a moment trying to remember the word for candy. Then it came to me: *"Dulce,"* I said.

Still chewing, Grandma replied, *"Mande?"*   19

Knowing she wanted a complete sentence, I again struggled, then came up with   20 *"Deseo dulce."*

She measured me for a moment, before answering in nearly perfect English,   21 "Oh, so you wan' some candy. Go to the store an' buy some."

I don't know if it was the shock of hearing her speak English for the first time,   22 or the way she had denied me a piece of candy, but I suddenly felt tears warm my cheeks and I sprinted into the house and found Mom, who stood at the kitchen sink. "Grandma just talked English," I burst between light sobs.

"What's wrong?" she asked as she reached out to stroke my head.   23

"Grandma can talk English," I repeated.   24

"Of course she can," Mom answered. "What's wrong?"   25

I wasn't sure what was wrong, but after considering, I told Mom that Grandma   26 had teased me. No sooner had I said that than the old woman appeared at the door and hiked her skirt. Attached to one of her petticoats by safety pins were several small tobacco sacks, the white cloth kind that closed with yellow drawstrings. She carefully unhooked one and opened it, withdrawing a dollar, then handed the money to me. *"Para su dulce,"*[6] she said. Then, to my mother, she asked, "Why does he bawl like a motherless calf?"

"It's nothing," Mother replied.   27

"Do not weep, little one," the old lady comforted me, "Jesus and the Virgin love 28 you." She smiled and patted my head. To my mother she said as though just realizing it, "Your baby?"

Somehow that day changed everything. I wasn't afraid of my great-grandmother   29 any longer and, once I began spending time with her on the porch, I realized that my father had also begun directing increased attention to the old woman. Almost every evening Ese Gringo was sharing wine with Grandma. They talked out there, but I never did hear a real two-way conversation between them. Usually Grandma rattled on and Daddy nodded. She'd chuckle and pat his hand and he might grin, even grunt a word or two, before she'd begin talking again. Once I saw my mother standing by the front window watching them together, a smile playing across her face.

No more did I sneak around the house to avoid Grandma after school. Instead,   30 she waited for me and discussed my efforts in class gravely, telling mother that I was a bright boy, *"muy inteligente,"* and that I should be sent to the nuns who would train me. I would make a fine priest. When Ese Gringo heard that, he smiled and said, "He'd make a fair-to-middlin' Holy Roller preacher, too." Even Mom had to chuckle, and my great-grandmother shook her finger at Ese Gringo. "Oh you debil, Sharlie!" she cackled.

Frequently, I would accompany Grandma to the lot where she would explain   31 that no fodder could grow there. Poor pasture or not, the lot was at least unpaved, and Grandma greeted even the tiniest new cactus or flowering weed with joy. "Look

[6]For your candy

how beautiful,'' she would croon. ''In all this ugliness, it lives.'' Oildale was my home and it didn't look especially ugly to me, so I could only grin and wonder.

Because she liked the lot and things that grew there, I showed her the horned 32 toad when I captured it a second time. I was determined to keep it, although I did not discuss my plans with anyone. I also wanted to hear more about the bloody eyes, so I thrust the small animal nearly into her face one afternoon. She did not flinch. *''Ola señor sangre de ojos,''*[7] she said with a mischievous grin. *''Qué tal?''*[8] It took me a moment to catch on.

''You were kidding before,'' I accused.   33

''Of course,'' she acknowledged, still grinning.   34

''But why?''   35

''Because the little beast belongs with his own kind in his own place, not in your 36 pocket. Give him his freedom, my son.''

I had other plans for the horned toad, but I was clever enough not to cross 37 Grandma. ''Yes, Ma'am,'' I replied. That night I placed the reptile in a flower bed cornered by a brick wall Ese Gringo had built the previous summer. It was a spot rich with insects for the toad to eat, and the little wall, only a foot high, must have seemed massive to so squat an animal.

Nonetheless, the next morning when I searched for the horned toad it was gone. 38 I had no time to explore the yard for it, so I trudged off to school, my belly troubled. How could it have escaped? Classes meant little to me that day. I thought only of my lost pet — I had changed his name to Juan, the same as my Great-grandfather — and where I might find him.

I shortened my conversation with Grandma that afternoon so I could search for 39 Juan. ''What do you seek?'' the old woman asked me as I poked through flower beds beneath the porch. ''Praying mantises,'' I improvised, and she merely nodded, surveying me. But I had eyes only for my lost pet, and I continued pushing through branches and brushing aside leaves. No luck.

Finally, I gave in and turned toward the lot. I found my horned toad nearly across 40 the street, crushed. It had been heading for the miniature desert and had almost made it when an automobile's tire had run over it. One notion immediately swept me: if I had left it on its lot, it would still be alive. I stood rooted there in the street, tears slicking my cheeks, and a car honked its horn as it passed, the driver shouting at me.

Grandma joined me, and stroked my back. ''The poor little beast,'' was all she 41 said, then she bent slowly and scooped up what remained of the horned toad and led me out of the street. ''We must return him to his own place,'' she explained, and we trooped, my eyes still clouded, toward the back of the vacant lot. Carefully, I dug a hole with a piece of wood. Grandma placed Juan in it and covered him. We said an Our Father and a Hail Mary, then Grandma walked me back to the house. ''Your little Juan is safe with God, my son,'' she comforted. We kept the horned toad's death a secret, and we visited his small grave frequently.

Grandma fell just before school ended and summer vacation began. As was her 42

[7]Hello mister bloody eyes
[8]What's up?

habit, she had walked alone to the vacant lot but this time, on her way back, she tripped over the curb and broke her hip. That following week, when Daddy brought her home from the hospital, she seemed to have shrunken. She sat hunched in a wheelchair on the porch, gazing with faded eyes toward the hills or at the lot, speaking rarely. She still sipped wine every evening with Daddy and even I could tell how concerned he was about her. It got to where he'd look in on her before leaving for work every morning and again at night before turning in. And if Daddy was home, Grandma always wanted him to push her chair when she needed moving, calling, "Sharlie!" until he arrived.

I was tugged from sleep on the night she died by voices drumming through the 43 walls into darkness. I couldn't understand them, but was immediately frightened by the uncommon sounds of words in the night. I struggled from bed and walked into the living room just as Daddy closed the front door and a car pulled away.

Mom was sobbing softly on the couch and Daddy walked to her, stroked her 44 head, then noticed me. "Come here, son," he gently ordered.

I walked to him and, uncharacteristically, he put an arm around me. "What's 45 wrong?" I asked, near tears myself. Mom looked up, but before she could speak, Daddy said, "Grandma died." Then he sighed heavily and stood there with his arms around his weeping wife and son.

The next day my Uncle Manuel and Uncle Arnulfo, plus Aunt Chintia, arrived 46 and over food they discussed with my mother where Grandma should be interred. They argued that it would be too expensive to transport her body home and, besides, they could more easily visit her grave if she was buried in Bakersfield. "They have such a nice, manicured grounds at Greenlawn," Aunt Chintia pointed out. Just when it seemed they had agreed, I could remain silent no longer, "But Grandma has to go home," I burst. "She has to! It's the only thing she really wanted. We can't leave her in the city."

Uncle Arnulfo, who was on the edge, snapped to Mother that I belonged with 47 the other children, not interrupting adult conversation. Mom quietly agreed, but I refused. My father walked into the room then. "What's wrong?" he asked.

"They're going to bury Grandma in Bakersfield, Daddy. Don't let 'em, please." 48
"Well, son . . ." 49
"When my horny toad got killed and she helped me to bury it, she said we had 50 to return him to his place."

"Your horny toad?" Mother asked. 51
"He got squished and me and Grandma buried him in the lot. She said we had 52 to take him back to his place. Honest she did."

No one spoke for a moment, then my father, Ese Gringo, who stood against the 53 sink, responded: "That's right . . ." he paused, then added, "We'll bury her." I saw a weary smile cross my mother's face. "If she wanted to go back to the ranch then that's where we have to take her," Daddy said.

I hugged him and he, right in front of everyone, hugged back. 54
No one argued. It seemed, suddenly, as though they had all wanted to do exactly 55 what I had begged for. Grown-ups baffled me. Late that week the entire family, hundreds it seemed, gathered at the little Catholic church in Coalinga for mass, then drove out to Arroyo Cantua and buried Grandma next to Grandpa. She rests there today.

For Discussion

Haslam's family seems to have assumed that Grandma should live with one of them (she "had been moving from house to house within the family, trying to find a place she'd accept"). Discuss the ways each of your families has accommodated its older members. If elderly relatives have lived with your immediate family, what role did they take and how, specifically, did their presence influence your family? What did you learn from this experience? What thoughts do you have about the care and housing of elderly people in our society?

For Analysis

1.   What role does dialogue play in revealing the relationship between Grandma and the young Haslam? List and analyze each conversation between the two of them, deciding what it contributes to the essay.

For more on naming and detailing, see pp. 429–32.

2.   Analyze the way Haslam names things, gives details, and shows specific actions to present Grandma. Underline each instance of these strategies, focusing on paragraphs 1–11 and 17–27. What do they contribute to the portrait?

3.   As in Maya Angelou's portrait of Uncle Willie, anecdotes play a central role in Haslam's portrait of Grandma. In the margin, mark off each anecdote. Then describe it briefly, and note what it tells us about Grandma.

4.   Study the way Haslam uses dashes in this essay. Underline each use of dashes, and consider what the enclosed material adds to each sentence. Is it the same kind of material in each sentence? If not, how does it differ? Can you reach any conclusions about what the dash contributes to autobiographical writing?

For Your
Own Writing

Recall some of the adults who influenced your early childhood years and then, for whatever reason, passed out of your life. Consider neighbors, parents of friends, teachers, camp counselors, or relatives. Choose one you might write about, and decide who your readers might be. How would you describe this person for those readers? What anecdotes would you present?

Commentary

Like Maya Angelou, Haslam writes about childhood memories, as do many writers. Some book-length autobiographies focus solely on incidents and people remembered from childhood, and nearly all include some episodes from this early period. When writing about a person significant in your childhood, you are more likely to be able to treat the relationship with adequate emotional distance, which seems to come only with the passage of time. Emotional distance allows you to understand an important relationship more fully and to present it in a more balanced way, thus assuring readers that you are characterizing the person frankly and exploring the relationship honestly. Readers are predictably skeptical of relationships of unambivalent feelings, relationships that seem based on the writer's slavish devotion to or unqualified resentment of a one-dimensional person, because they recognize such writing immediately as sentimental, self-serving, or unrealistic. Emotional distance permits humor, irony, ambivalence, and contradictions. It makes autobiography art, rather than confession, enabling both writer and reader to accept the relationship and to learn from it.

Haslam's essay, like Angelou's, illustrates the importance of anecdotes in writing about people important to the writer's life. Anecdotes enable a writer to show a relationship through specifics rather than tell about it in general statements. Livened by dialogue, sensory details, and specific actions, anecdotes can create a vivid, memorable portrait. The anecdotes must be to the point, of course, selected to reveal something significant about the person's character or about his or her relationship with the writer.

Anecdotes make particularly effective openings, for they are easier and more engaging than general statements. Haslam's essay opens with an anecdote—and ends with one as well.

Haslam's essay allows us to analyze closely a special kind of sentence relied on by nearly all contemporary professional writers, especially writers of autobiography: the cumulative sentence, in which phrases follow a main clause but do not modify a specific word in the clause. Here are examples from paragraphs 38–40:

> . . . so I trudged off to school, *my belly troubled.*
> I stood rooted there in the street, *tears slicking my cheeks,* . . .
> . . . and a car honked its horn as it passed, *the driver shouting at me.*

Autobiographers also often conclude a sentence with a word or phrase that modifies a specific word in a main clause. Here are two examples from paragraphs 39 and 40:

> . . . and she merely nodded, *surveying me.*
> I found my horned toad nearly across the street, *crushed.*

In the first sentence *surveying* modifies *she,* and in the second *crushed* modifies *horned toad.*

Sentences like these provide efficiency, rhythmic variety, compression of narrative action, and dramatic emphasis. They are more efficient simply because they save words. Imagining each cumulative element as a full sentence, you can readily see how at least one more word would be required. The sentences provide rhythmic variety by allowing a writer to avoid a string of predictable brief subject-plus-verb sentences (*I stood rooted there in the street. Tears slicked my cheeks. A car honked its horn as it passed. The driver shouted at me.*). Most important, such sentences compress action by linking two or more actions in the same clause, a device that provides greater immediacy (*car honked/driver shouting, she nodded/surveying me*); and they provide dramatic emphasis by holding off and singling out key elements (*crushed*).

■   ■   ■

Forrest Carter (1927–1979) was orphaned as a child and raised in the Tennessee hill country by his father's parents, who were Cherokee Indians. Carter attended school for only six months, and learned to read and write from fireside reading with his grandparents. He worked as a ranch hand until 1975, when his first novel, *Gone to Texas,* was published and made into a movie of the same title by Clint Eastwood.

This selection comes from his autobiography, *The Education of Little Tree* (1976), written in his late forties. As you read, study the way Carter presents his grandparents' friend Willow John and shows their relationship. Notice how he keeps his narrative close to informal speech, occasionally using nonstandard dialect forms like *set* for *sat, taken to* for *began,* or *give* for *gave.*

WILLOW JOHN
FORREST CARTER

He always stood back in the trees, away from the people and the church. He 1
was older than Granpa but he was as tall; full Cherokee with white plaited hair
hanging below his shoulders, and a flat-brimmed hat pulled low to his eyes . . . like
the eyes were private. When he looked at you, you knew why.

The eyes were black, open wounds; not angry wounds, but dead wounds that 2
lay bare, without life. You couldn't tell if the eyes were dim, or if Willow John was
looking past you into a dimness far away. Once, in later years, an Apache showed
me a picture of an old man. It was Gookhla-yeh, Geronimo. He had the eyes of
Willow John.

Willow John was over eighty. Granpa said that long ago, Willow John had gone 3
to the Nations. He had walked the mountains, and would not ride in a car or train.
He was gone three years and came back; but he would not talk of it. He would only
say there was no Nation.

And so we always walked to him, standing back in the trees. Granpa and Willow 4
John put their arms around each other and held each other for a long time; two
tall, old men with big hats—and they didn't say anything. Then Granma would come,
and Willow John would stoop and they would hold each other for a long time.

Willow John lived past the church, far back in the mountains; and so, the church 5
being about halfway between us, it was the place they could meet.

Maybe children know. I told Willow John that there was going to be lots of 6
Cherokees before too long. I told him I was going to be a Cherokee; that Granma
said I was natural-born to the mountains and had the feeling of the trees. Willow
John touched my shoulder and his eyes showed a far back twinkle. Grandma said it
was the first time he had looked like that in many years.

We would not go into the church until everybody else was in. We always sat on 7
the back row; Willow John, then Granma, me, and Granpa set next to the aisle.
Granma held Willow John's hand during church, and Granpa put his arm across the
bench back and laid his hand on Granma's shoulder. I taken to holding Granma's
other hand and putting a hand on Granpa's leg. This way I was not left out, though
my feet always went to sleep as they stuck straight out over the seat rim.

Once, after we taken our seats, I found a long knife laying where I set. It was 8
as long as Granpa's and had a deer skin sheath that was fringed. Granma said Willow
John gave it to me. That is the way Indians give gifts. They do not present it unless

they don't mean it and are doing it for a reason. They leave it for you to find. You would not get the gift if you didn't deserve it, and so it is foolish to thank somebody for something you deserve, or make a show of it. Which is reasonable.

I give Willow John a nickel and a bullfrog. The Sunday I brought it, Willow John 9 had hung his coat on a tree while he waited for us, and so I slipped the bullfrog and the nickel into his pocket. It was a big bullfrog I had caught in the spring branch and had fed bugs until he was practical a giant.

Willow John put on his coat and went into church. The preacher called for 10 everybody to bow their heads. It was quiet so that you could hear people breathing. The preacher said, "Lord . . ." and then the bullfrog said, "LARRRRRRRRUPP!" deep and loud. Everybody jumped and one man run out of the church. A feller hollered, "God almightly!" and a woman screamed, "Praise the Lord!"

Willow John jumped too. He reached his hand in his pocket, but he didn't take 11 out the frog. He looked over at me and the twinkle come again to his eyes; this time not so far back. Then he smiled! The smile broke across his face, wider and wider—and he laughed! A deep, booming laugh that made everybody look at him. He didn't pay any attention to them atall. I was scared, but I laughed too. Tears commenced to water in his eyes and roll down the creases and wrinkles of his face. Willow John cried.

Everybody got quiet. The preacher stood with his mouth open and watched. 12 Willow John paid no attention to anybody. He didn't make a sound, but his chest heaved and his shoulders shook, and he cried a long time. People looked away, but Willow John and Granpa and Granma looked straight ahead.

The preacher had a hard time getting started again. He didn't mention the frog. 13 He had tried once before to preach a sermon regarding Willow John, but Willow John never paid him any attention. He always looked straight before him, like the preacher wasn't there. The sermon had been on paying proper respect to the Lord's house. Willow John would not bow his head for prayers and he wouldn't take off his hat.

Granpa never commented on it. And so I thought on it, over the years. I figured 14 it was Willow John's way of saying what he had to say. His people were broken and lost, scattered from these mountains that was their home and lived upon by the preacher and others there in the church. He couldn't fight, and so he wore his hat.

Maybe when the preacher said, "Lord . . ." and the frog said, 15 "LARRRRRRRRUPP!" the frog was answering for Willow John. And so he cried. It broke some of the bitterness. After that, Willow John's eyes always twinkled and showed little black lights when he looked at me.

At the time I was sorry, but later I was glad I give Willow John the frog.   16

Every Sunday, after church, we went into the trees near the clearing and spread 17 our dinner. Willow John always brought game in a sack. It would be quail, or venison, or fish. Granma brought corn bread and vegetable fixings. We ate there in the shade of big elms and talked.

Willow John would say the deer was moving farther back to high ground in the 18 mountains. Granpa would say the fish baskets yielded such and so. Granma would tell Willow John to bring her his mending.

As the sun tilted and hazed the afternoon, we would get ready to leave. Granpa 19 and Granma would each hug Willow John, and he would touch my shoulder with his hand, shy.

Then we would leave, walking across the clearing toward our cutoff trail. I would   20
turn to watch Willow John. He never looked back. He walked, arms not swinging
but straight by his sides, in a long, loping awkward step. Always looking to neither
side; misplaced somehow—touching this fringe of the white man's civilization. He
would disappear into the trees, following no trail that I could see, and I would hurry
to catch up with Granpa and Granma. It was lonesome, walking the cutoff trail back
home in the dusk of Sunday evenings, and we did not talk.

For Discussion

Carter says that Willow John is "misplaced somehow." Discuss what it means
to be misplaced in America. Who is misplaced, and why? Who is misplaced
in your own community or college, and why? When have you felt misplaced?

For Analysis

1. Analyze Carter's strategies for presenting Willow John in paragraphs 1,
2, and 20. Underline all instances where he names things, gives details, and
shows specific action. What general impression do these instances create?

2. Reread paragraphs 9–12 and then paragraphs 13–15. How are these
two sections different? How are they related? What does each contribute to
the essay?

3. Experienced writers often "frame" a piece of writing by referring at the
end to something mentioned at the beginning. How does Carter frame his
essay?

4. Reread the beginnings and endings of the Angelou, Haslam, and Carter
essays. Describe each beginning and ending briefly. What can you conclude
from these examples about options for opening and closing essays about
remembered people?

**For Your
Own Writing**

Consider writing about a family friend who was important in your life. How
would you present this person to your readers? What anecdotes could you
tell that would show the special qualities of this person?

Commentary

Like Angelou and Haslam, Carter makes strategic use of specific anecdotes
that show us what a person is like. Besides these one-time incidents, he
depicts familiar recurring activities in his subject's life, summarizing them in
a general way without pausing to focus on an anecdote. You can see this
strategy at work in the concluding paragraphs (16–20) of the essay. There
we see a summary of typical activities after church: a picnic under the trees,
conversation, leave-taking, the walk home.

■   ■   ■

Jan Gray was a college freshman when she wrote the next selection, which
portrays her father, a man toward whom she has ambivalent but mostly
hostile feelings. As you read, notice how Gray uses description to convey
these feelings.

FATHER

JAN GRAY

My father's hands are grotesque. He suffers from psoriasis, a chronic skin disease 1
that covers his massive, thick hands with scaly, reddish patches that periodically flake
off, sending tiny pieces of dead skin sailing to the ground. In addition, his fingers
are permanently stained a dull yellow from years of chain smoking. The thought of
those swollen, discolored, scaly hands touching me, whether it be out of love or
anger, sends chills up my spine.

By nature, he is a disorderly, unkempt person. The numerous cigarette burns, 2
food stains, and ashes on his clothes show how little he cares about his appearance.
He has a dreadful habit of running his hands through his greasy hair and scratching
his scalp, causing dandruff to drift downward onto his bulky shoulders. He is grossly
overweight, and his pullover shirts never quite cover his protruding paunch. When
he eats, he shovels the food into his mouth as if he hasn't eaten for days, bread
crumbs and food scraps settling in his untrimmed beard.

Last year, he abruptly left town. Naturally, his apartment was a shambles, and I 3
offered to clean it so that my mother wouldn't have to pay the cleaning fee. I arrived
early in the morning anticipating a couple hours of vacuuming and dusting and
scrubbing. The minute I opened the door, however, I realized my task was monu-
mental: Old yellowed newspapers and magazines were strewn throughout the living
room; moldy and rotten food covered the kitchen counter; cigarette butts and ashes
were everywhere. The pungent aroma of stale beer seemed to fill the entire apartment.

As I made my way through the debris toward the bedroom, I tried to deny that 4
the man who lived here was my father. The bedroom was even worse than the front
rooms, with cigarette burns in the carpet and empty bottles, dirty dishes, and smelly
laundry scattered everywhere. Looking around his bedroom, I recalled an incident
that had occurred only a few months before in my bedroom.

I was calling home to tell my mother I would be eating dinner at a girlfriend's 5
house. To my surprise, my father answered the phone. I was taken aback to hear
his voice because my parents had been divorced for some time and he was seldom
at our house. In fact, I didn't even see him very often.

"Hello?" he answered in his deep, scratchy voice. 6

"Oh, umm, hi Dad. Is Mom home?" 7

"What can I do for you?" he asked, sounding a bit too cheerful. 8

"Well, I just wanted to ask Mom if I could stay for dinner here." 9

"I don't think that's a very good idea, dear." I could sense an abrupt change in 10
the tone of his voice. "Your room is a mess, and if you're not home in ten minutes
to straighten it up, I'll really give you something to clean." Click.

Pedalling home as fast as I could, I had a distinct image of my enraged father. I 11
could see his face redden, his body begin to tremble slightly, and his hands gesture
nervously in the air. Though he was not prone to physical violence and always
appeared calm on the outside, I knew he was really seething inside. The incessant
motion of those hands was all too vivid to me as I neared home.

My heart was racing as I turned the knob to the front door and headed for my 12
bedroom. When I opened my bedroom door, I stopped in horror. The dresser drawers
were pulled out, and clothes were scattered across the floor. Everything on top of
the dresser—a perfume tray, a couple of baskets of hair clips and earrings, and an
assortment of pictures—had been strewn about. The dresser itself was tilted on its
side, supported by the bed frame. As I stepped in and closed the door behind me,

tears welled up in my eyes. I hated my father so much at that moment. Who the hell did he think he was to waltz into my life every few months like this?

I was slowly piecing my room together when he knocked on the door. I choked 13 back the tears, wanting to show as little emotion as possible, and quietly murmured, "Come in." He stood in the doorway, one hand leaning against the door jamb, a cigarette dangling from the other, flicking ashes on the carpet, very smug in his handling of the situation.

"I want you to know I did this for your own good. I think it's time you started 14 taking a little responsibility around this house. Now, to show you there are no hard feelings, I'll help you set the dresser back up."

"No thank you," I said quietly, on the verge of tears again. "I'd rather do it 15 myself. Please, just leave me alone!"

He gave me one last look that seemed to say, "I offered. I'm the good guy. If 16 you refuse, that's your problem." Then he turned and walked away. I was stunned at how he could be so violent one moment and so nonchalant the next.

As I sat in his bedroom reflecting on what he had done to my room, I felt the 17 utmost disgust for this man. There seemed to be no hope he would break his filthy habits. I could come in and clean his room, but only he could clean up the mess he had made of his life. But I felt pity for him, too. After all, he is my father—am I not supposed to feel some responsibility for him and to love and honor him?

For Discussion

Jan Gray admits that her disgust for her father is mingled with pity. What is there about parent-child relationships that results in these or other ambivalent feelings? Why can we—at all times, in every situation—not simply love loving parents and hate hateful parents? How can you account for the occasional feelings of irritation, disappointment, disaffection, and distance that we all have, even with the best of parents? What are the implications of this ambivalence for writing about one of your parents?

For Analysis

1. What does the anecdote in paragraphs 5–16 convey about Gray's father and her relationship with him?

2. How does Gray use dialogue to reveal her father's character? Notice her father's choice of words and her description of his tone and posture.

For more on naming and detailing, see p. 429–32.

3. Look again at the way Gray describes the disorder in her father's apartment and her own room (paragraphs 3, 4, and 12). How does she make these scenes so vivid? What things does she name, and what details does she give? ·

4. What seems to you the significance of these descriptions of disorder? Why does Gray describe the disorder in such detail? What does it add to your understanding of her relationship with her father?

For Your Own Writing

Imagine writing about someone with whom you had a serious conflict. Whom would you write about? How would you present this person? What overall impression of this person and of you would you like your readers to get from this essay?

Commentary

Although description of place often plays a minimal role in essays about remembered people, it can be an important feature, as it is in this essay. Gray needs to describe her room and her father's apartment to show how destructive her father could be and how out of control his life was. She compiles long lists of things she sees, using specific names and sensory details to describe them vividly.

PURPOSE AND AUDIENCE

Writers of essays about remembered people generally have several purposes in mind. Perhaps the most prominent is better understanding the subject and his or her importance in the writer's life—analyzing and reaching conclusions about a significant personal relationship. Another purpose can be self-presentation, leading readers to see the writer in a particular way. Still another purpose can be entertaining readers with a vivid portrait of an unusual or engaging subject.

For several reasons, writing about remembered people requires careful attention to one's audience. Unless the writer selects and organizes vivid details so that readers can easily imagine persons and scenes, the portrait will seem flat and lifeless. The writer must also shape and pace anecdotes to hold readers' attention. In addition, the writer hopes that no matter how unusual the subject, readers will recognize in the portrait a significant human relationship and will find themselves reflecting on people who have been important in their own lives.

BASIC FEATURES OF ESSAYS ABOUT REMEMBERED PEOPLE

Successful essays about remembered people offer a vivid portrait of their subject, give detailed presentations of anecdotes and scenes, and reveal the subject's significance to the writer.

A Vivid Portrait

At the center of an essay about a remembered person is a vivid portrait. Writers rely on dialogue and the full range of descriptive strategies—naming, detailing, comparing—to present a person to their readers.

In presenting Uncle Willie, Maya Angelou names many features of his appearance, singling out his posture, hands, face, and clothing. Through concrete visual details and comparisons, she helps us imagine his face "pulled down on the left side, as if a pulley had been attached to his lower teeth." She also helps us to see his specific movements as he makes his way down an aisle "hand over hand, like a man climbing out of a dream."

Gerald Haslam portrays Grandma as "four-and-a-half feet of bewigged, bejeweled Spanish spitfire: a square, pale face topped by a tightly curled black wig . . . her small hands veined with rivers of blue." Forrest Carter

For more on naming, detailing, and comparing, see pp. 429–34.

shows Willow John "with white plaited hair hanging below his shoulders, and a flat-brimmed hat pulled low to his eyes." At first, Willow John's eyes were "black, open wounds . . . dead wounds that lay bare, without life," but later they "always twinkled and showed little black lights." Carter also enables us to imagine Willow John's posture and movements: "He walked, arms not swinging but straight by his sides, in a long, loping awkward step. Always looking to neither side. . . ."

Besides the array of strategies for visual presentation of their subjects, autobiographers consistently let us hear their subjects speak so that we can infer what they are like. All the readings in this chapter include some dialogue. Angelou employs it to present a stuttering Uncle Willie, and Gray gives it prominence in the confrontation with her unpredictable, threatening father. Haslam reveals a bilingual, sharp-tongued Grandma; and Carter shows the startling and comic verbal reactions of churchgoers to the bullfrog's croak. Portraits that center on dramatized anecdotes (Angelou, Haslam, Gray) are more likely to include dialogue than those that feature recurring activities and extended reflection (Carter).

For more on dialogue, see pp. 423–25.

Detailed Anecdotes and Scenes

In portraying a significant relationship, a writer almost always needs to tell anecdotes and to describe their scenes. Anecdotes—short, pointed stories about specific incidents—reveal the subject's character and dramatize the writer's relationship with him or her.

More than half of Angelou's portrait of Uncle Willie is taken up by anecdotes. In the first, Uncle Willie stops her just short of burning herself during her recitation of the multiplication tables. The second demonstrates the possibilities of an extended, dramatic anecdote in essays about remembered people. It begins (paragraph 6) with a general statement of what the anecdote will reveal: "Only once in all the years of trying not to watch him, I saw him pretend to himself and others that he wasn't lame." It ends (paragraph 20) with a return to this general idea: a conjecture about Uncle Willie's feelings abut his lameness and his motives for deceiving the Little Rock couple. Within these "framing" elements, the anecdote includes tension, variation in pacing, specific narrative action, dialogue, and remembered feelings and present perspective. Angelou also describes parts of the scene in each anecdote. The stove warming the arithmetic lesson is a "dull red heater, which throbbed like a devil's toothache."

For more on these narrative strategies, see Chapter 13.

Like Angelou, Gray centers her portrait of her father on a single extended anecdote, the time her father trashed her room. She skillfully creates suspense as she pedals home and enters her bedroom, tension as her father opens the door and the two engage in a confrontation that is physically uneventful and yet emotionally trying for her. Gray presents the scene by pointing to the details of her chaotic room and showing us her father leaning against the doorjamb, flicking cigarette ashes.

Indication of
the Person's
Significance

Portrait writers choose as their subjects people they consider significant—those they have loved or feared, those who have influenced them, those they have tried to impress—and they try to make clear exactly what that significance is. Whether or not they state this significance directly, they convey it through anecdotes, descriptions of recurring activities, vivid details—or all of these. For example, Haslam never tells us directly that he loved and revered Grandma, though he does say at one point, "I wasn't afraid of my great-grandmother any longer." Instead he shows us through anecdotes, recurring interactions with him and other family members, and Grandma's comments that she had earned his trust and that he had come to love her.

Angelou's relationship with Uncle Willie is highly ambivalent, like Gray's with her father. Neither tries to force a neat resolution, reducing deep and contradictory feelings to simple love or hate. They acknowledge ambivalence and accept it. In many portraits, in fact, the significance seems to lie in just this realization about the inevitable complexity of close relationships. Similarly, good writers avoid sentimentalizing the relationship, neither damning nor idealizing their subject. Gray comes close to damning her father, but stops just short of it by admitting her feelings of pity and responsibility. Angelou sympathizes with Uncle Willie's shame about his lameness and stuttering, but she does not present him as a long-suffering saint.

Having some emotional distance from their subjects helps writers to avoid sentimentality and probe the true significance of the relationship. Emotional distance often comes with the passage of time, but it can also be developed through sustained reflection. In fact, writing about people can actually help you gain emotional distance from them, as we can see in the Writer at Work section at the end of this chapter. There Gray sorts out some of her feelings and gains some emotional distance from her father and insight into their relationship, a process of struggle that she explores frankly in her essay.

Guide to Writing

THE WRITING ASSIGNMENT

Write an essay about a person who has been important in your life. Strive to present a vivid portrait of this person, one that will let your readers see his or her character and the significance to you of the relationship.

INVENTION

The following activities will help you choose a subject, define his or her significance for you, characterize your relationship, and describe the person.

Choosing a Person
to Write About

You may already have a person in mind. Even if you do, however, you will want to consider other people in order to choose the best possible subject. The following activities will help you make the choice.

Make a list of people you could write about, such as relatives, teachers, coaches, employers, friends, neighbors, and others. Make your list as complete as you can, including people you knew for a long time and those you knew briefly, people you knew long ago and those you knew recently, people you liked and those you disliked. Following are some categories of significant people that may give you ideas:

■ Anyone who had authority over you or for whom you felt responsible

■ Anyone who helped you in difficulty or made life difficult for you

■ Anyone whose advice or actions influenced you

■ Anyone who taught you something important about yourself

■ Anyone who ever inspired strong emotions in you—admiration, envy, disapproval, fascination

■ Anyone whose behavior or values led you to question your own

■ Anyone who really surprised or disappointed you

■ Anyone who cared for you or supported you

Look over your list of possible subjects and choose a person you believe you can describe vividly and whose significance in your life you are eager to explore. It should be a person who interests you enough to interest your readers. You may find that your choice is easy to make, or you may have several subjects that seem equally attractive. Make the best decision you can for now. If the subject does not work out, you can try a different subject later.

Describing
the Person

The following activities will help you recall specific information you can use to describe the person. If you complete them thoughtfully, you will have a wealth of remembered detail to draw on in drafting your essay. Even after you start drafting, these lists are a good place to capture fleeting memories that can be incorporated later as you need them.

Physical Features.   Try to visualize the person clearly. With this image in mind, list physical features you remember, putting one item on each line. Then describe each feature in words or brief phrases, such as "cheeks—round, bright red spots in middle." You might start at the top, with the person's hair and face, and work down to the feet. Or you might start with the person's general build, then move in close for specific details.

Next, think about the person's way of dressing, including jewelry, hats, or other accessories. List these items, one item on a line, including the purpose or occasion if necessary. Then describe the items in words or brief phrases.

Behavior.   Think about the way the person moved and acted and about his or her special interests or particular activities. Again, make a list as extensive as possible, considering the following points and putting one item on a line.

- Any specific gestures or habits you remember
- Activities or interests typical of the person
- Ways you recall him or her "in action": walking, running, driving a car, sitting at the kitchen table
- What you observed when the person expressed a mood or emotion: anger, sadness, joy. What expressions or actions showed you what the person was feeling?

Now go back and describe each item more fully in words or brief phrases if necessary.

Speech.   Think about times you observed the person in conversation. What can you remember about the way he or she speaks? List now:

- Any memorable phrases or expressions
- Tone of voice and the manner of speech
- The first thing you remember the person ever saying to you
- The most memorable thing you recall him or her saying

Reconstruct one or more brief conversations between the person and yourself or someone else. Set each conversation up as a dialogue, with each person's words starting a new line.

Anecdotes.   Can you recall any important events or incidents associated with your subject? Is he or she associated in your mind with a particular location, certain objects or activities, a particular time in your life, or another person? List these items, one per line.

Think of some anecdotes about specific incidents or events that stand out in your mind. Briefly list as many anecdotes as you can remember, one per line. Next to each one, put a number from 1 to 3, indicating how much that anecdote tells about the person or about your relationship to the person (1 = very telling, 2 = somewhat telling, 3 = not especially telling).

Choose one particularly telling anecdote from your list and write about it for ten minutes, describing what happened in a way that will interest a reader. Try to illuminate the person's character and make clear his or her significance to you. Give as much detail as you can remember, including dialogue if you remember it as important to the anecdote.

Testing Your Choice

Now that you have chosen a person to write about and spent some time describing him or her, you should decide tentatively whether your choice is a good one. Write for no more than five minutes about the person, including any details, events, or ideas that come to mind. Your purpose is simply to discover whether memories begin flowing easily or not. If your initial memories seem promising, then you have probably made a good choice. To confirm it further, you might talk about your choice with someone else.

If at any point you lose confidence in your choice, however, return to your list to consider another subject.

For Group Inquiry

At this point you might find it useful to get together in a group with two or three other students and run your chosen topics by one another. Assess the group's interest in the person you wish to write about, and invite their advice about whether he or she sounds promising. Does the subject seem likely to lead to an essay they would care to read? Your purpose is to determine whether you have chosen a good subject to write about and thus to be able to proceed confidently to develop your essay.

Defining the Person's Significance

Now you should consider what significance the person has had in your life. The following activities can help you discover this significance and find a way to share it with your readers.

Recalling Remembered Feelings and Thoughts.   Call to mind your earliest memories of the person. Take about ten minutes to put your thoughts in writing, using the following questions to stimulate your memory:

If you have always known this person:

- What are my earliest memories of him or her?
- What was our relationship like initially?
- What did we do together? How did we talk to each other?
- In the early part of our relationship, how did we influence each other?

If you met this person at a specific time in your life:

- What do I remember about our first meeting—place, time, occasion, particular incidents, other people, words exchanged?
- Had I heard of this person before our first meeting? If so, what did I expect him or her to be like?
- What was my initial impression?
- How did I act when we met? What impression, if any, was I trying to make?
- Did I talk about the person to anyone soon after we met? What did I say?

Now stop to focus your thoughts. In a couple of sentences, indicate how important the person was to you early in your relationship.

Exploring Your Present Perspective.   Think about how you feel now in reflecting on your relationship with this person. Try to articulate your insights about his or her importance in your life. Take about ten minutes to put your thoughts on paper, using these questions as a guide:

- Would I have wanted the person to act differently toward me? How?
- How do I feel about the way I acted toward the person? Would I have behaved any differently had I known then what I know now? How?
- Looking back at our relationship, do I understand it any differently now than I did at the time?
- Were my feelings toward the person ambivalent? In what way? How would I describe my current feelings? Do I have enough emotional distance to write about this person and our relationship?

Now focus your thoughts about your present perspective. In two or three sentences, describe your present perspective on the person.

Generalizing.   Reflect on what you know about this person: analyze, explain, evaluate. Try to make some generalizations about him or her. Make as many general statements as you can about the person's values, attitudes, or conduct. Include anything you think might help readers understand him or her as a person.

PLANNING AND DRAFTING

This section will help you see what you have accomplished up to this point in your assignment, and determine what you need to explore more fully, as well as guide you in the next stages of the writing process.

Seeing What You Have

You have now produced a lot of writing focused on the basic features of a portrait: descriptions of the person's appearance and behavior, recollections of anecdotes and dialogue, analysis of his or her significance to you. Before going on to plan and draft your essay, reread what you have already written. Look for patterns: evidence of growth or deterioration, harmony or tension, consistency or contradiction in the person or in the relationship. See if you make any new discoveries or gain fresh insight. Jot down your ideas in the margins, and underline or star any promising material. Then ask yourself the following questions:

- Do I remember enough specific details about the person? Will I be able to describe him or her vividly?
- Do I understand how the person was significant to me? Have I been able to state it clearly?

- Do my anecdotes and dialogues capture the person's character and portray our relationship effectively?
- Relationships tend to be complex. Will I be able to avoid sentimentality, oversimplifications, or stereotyping?

If your invention writing seems too general or superficial, or if it has not led you to a clear understanding of the significance the person holds in your life, then you may well have difficulty writing a coherent, developed draft. It may be that the person you have chosen is not a good subject after all. The person may not really be important enough to you; conversely, you may not yet have enough emotional distance to write about him or her. As frustrating as it is to start over, it is far better to do so now than later.

If your invention writing looks thin but promising, you may be able to fill it out by thinking more about your relationship with the person, probing your feelings more deeply, adding descriptive details, recalling other important anecdotes, reconstructing additional conversations.

Setting Goals

Before actually beginning to draft, most writers set goals for themselves: things to consider and problems to solve. These can include overall goals— keeping readers' interest alive, satisfying any curiosity about the person's significance, creating a vivid portrait of that person. Other goals involve smaller issues—selecting rich visual details, creating realistic dialogue, finding fresh images, connecting paragraphs to one another. All these goals, large and small, guide the decisions you will make as you draft and revise. Following are some questions that should help you in setting goals:

Your Readers

- Are my readers likely to know someone like this person? If so, how can I help them imagine this particular person?
- Will my readers be surprised by this person or by our relationship? Might they disapprove of either? If so, how can I break through their prejudices to get them to see the person as I do?
- How can I help readers see the significance this person has for me?
- How can I get readers to empathize with the person? How can I lead them to reflect on their own lives and our common human experience?

The Beginning

- How can the first sentence capture my readers' attention? Should I begin as Carter and Gray do, with an image of the person? With an anecdote, as Angelou and Haslam do? Should I first present myself, or should I focus immediately on my subject?
- On what note should I open? What tone should I adopt—casual, distant, confiding, mournful, angry, sarcastic?

■ Should I provide a context, as Carter and Gray do, or jump right into the action, as Angelou and Haslam do? Should I let readers *see* the person right away? Or should I *tell* them about him or her first?

Presenting the Person

■ Which descriptive details best present the person?

■ What direct statements should I make to characterize the person? What values, attitudes, conduct, or character traits should I emphasize?

■ To help my readers understand my relationship with this person, what can I show them in our conversations and experience together?

■ What insights or feelings do I need to discuss explicitly so my readers will see the person's significance in my life?

The Ending

■ What do I want the ending to accomplish? Should it sum things up? Fix an image in readers' minds? Provide a sense of completion? Open up new possibilities?

■ How shall I end? With reflection? With a statement of the person's significance? With speculation about my subject's feelings, as Angelou does? With an image of the person, as Carter does? With the person's words? With an anecdote, as Haslam does?

■ Shall I frame the essay by having the ending echo the beginning, as Haslam and Carter do?

Outlining

After you have set goals to guide your drafting, you might find it useful to make a rough outline of your essay, indicating a tentative sequence for the main points you will cover. Note briefly how you plan to begin; list in order possible anecdotes, descriptions, conversations, or reflections; and note how you might end. As you draft, do not be alarmed if you find yourself diverging from your outline; you may well be discovering a better way to organize your essay.

Drafting

You may want to review the general drafting advice on pp. 9–11.

Start drafting your essay, keeping in mind the goals you have set for it. As you write, try to describe your subject in a way that makes clear his or her importance in your life. If you get stuck while drafting, try exploring the problem using the writing activities in the invention section of this chapter.

GETTING CRITICAL COMMENTS

Now is the time for your draft to get a good critical reading. Your instructor may arrange such a reading as part of your course work; otherwise, you can ask a classmate, friend, or family member to read it over. You could also seek comments from your campus writing center. The guidelines in this section can be used by *anyone* reviewing an essay about a remembered person. (If you are unable to have someone else read over your draft, turn ahead to the Revision section on pp. 86–88, where you'll find guidelines for reading your own draft critically.)

In order to provide focused, helpful comments, your reader must know your intended audience and purpose. Briefly write out this information at the top of your draft, answering the following questions:

Audience. Who are your readers? How do you expect them to respond to your essay?

Purpose. What impression do you want readers to have of your subject? What do you want them to see about his or her significance in your life?

Reading with a Critical Eye

The following guidelines can be useful for approaching a draft with a well-focused, questioning eye.

Reading for a First Impression.   Begin by reading the draft straight through to get a general impression. Read for enjoyment, ignoring spelling, punctuation, and usage errors for now. Try to imagine the person and to understand his or her significance for the writer. An easy way of highlighting noteworthy features is to use the pointings system, following the steps below:

Pointings

- Draw a straight line under any words or phrases that seem especially effective: strong verbs, memorable details, striking images.
- Draw a wavy line under any words or images that impress you as flat, stale, or vague. Also put a wavy line under any words or phrases that seem unnecessary or repetitious.
- Look for pairs or groups of sentences that you think should be combined. Put brackets [ ] around these sentences.
- Look for sentences that are confusing, overloaded, or awkward. Put parentheses ( ) around these sentences. Put them around any sentence that seems even slightly questionable; don't worry now about whether your judgment is correct. The writer needs to know that you, as one reader, had even the slightest difficulty understanding a sentence.

When you have finished this first quick reading, in just a few sentences give your overall impression. Summarize the person's signficance as you understand it. If you have any insights about the person or the relationship that are not reflected in the draft, share your thoughts.

See pp. 75–77 to review the basic features.

Reading to Analyze.   Next, read to focus on the features basic to writing about a remembered person.

Is the Person Described Vividly?

Strong descriptive writing is specific and detailed. Note any places where you would like greater specificity or more detail. Point out any particularly effective descriptions as well as any that seem to contradict the overall impression the rest of the essay gives about the person.

Is there too much telling about the person's character and conduct through general statements rather than showing these through anecdotes, dialogue, and description? Look for and point out vague or unnecessary statements as well as those that need illustration. Also indicate any statements that seem to be contradicted by the overall impression created by anecdotes or dialogues. Point out any particularly revealing statements, ones that help you understand the person's character or significance.

Are the Anecdotes Effective?

Review the anecdotes, noting any that are particularly effective in portraying the person or the relationship as well as any that seem unnecessary or confusing. Is each anecdote dramatic and well paced, or could any use more specific narrative action to show people moving, gesturing, talking? Is there anything else you think might be well illustrated by anecdote?

Then review the dialogues, pointing out any particularly effective ones as well as ones that sound artificial or stilted, that move too slowly, or that seem undramatic.

Is the Autobiographical Significance Clear?

What did you learn about the writer from reading this essay? Does the essay sentimentalize the person or the relationship? State the person's significance, and suggest ways of indicating this significance more precisely. Perhaps it is overstated, understated, or unclear. Assess whether all details and anecdotes contribute to showing the significance.

Is the Organization Effective?

Look at the *beginning*. Now that you have thought some about the essay, do you consider the beginning effective? Did it capture your interest and set up the right expectations? Point out any other passages that might make a better beginning, and explain why.

Look at the *ending*. Is it satisfying? Does it repeat what you already know? Does it oversimplify or reduce the meaning of the relationship to a platitude? Look to see if the essay might end at an earlier point. Does it frame the essay by referring back to the beginning—and if not, can you suggest a way it might? Try to suggest a different ending.

Consider the *overall plan*, perhaps by making a scratch outline. Decide whether the essay might be strengthened by shifting parts around, perhaps changing the order of anecdotes or moving the description of the person. Point out spots where your reading momentum slows.

What Final Thoughts Do You Have about This Draft?

What effect did the essay have on you personally? How did it lead you to reflect on your own life or on human nature generally? What is its strongest part? What about it is most memorable? What is most in need of further work?

REVISING AND EDITING

Following are some guidelines to help you identify and solve problems as you revise your draft.

Identifying Problems

To identify problems in your draft, you need to read it objectively, analyze its basic features, and study any comments you've received from others.

Getting an Overview.   Consider your draft as a whole, trying to see it objectively. It may help to do so in two simple steps:

Reread. If at all possible, put the draft aside for a day or two before rereading it. When you do, start by reconsidering your purpose. Then read the draft straight through, trying to see it as your intended readers will.

Outline. Make a scratch outline to get an overview of the essay's development. This outline can be sketchy—words and phrases instead of complete sentences—but it should identify the basic features as they appear.

Charting a Plan for Revision.   A chart like the one below may help you to keep track of any problems you need to solve. The left-hand column lists the basic features of writing about remembered people. As you analyze your draft and study any comments you've gotten from others, note the problems you want to solve in the right-hand column.

Basic Features   *Problems to Solve*

Presentation
of the subject

Anecdotes and scenes

Autobiographical
significance

Organization

Analyzing the Basic Features of Your Draft.   Turn now to the questions for analyzing a draft on pp. 84–85 and above. Using them as guidelines, identify problems in your draft. Put anything you need to solve on the chart above.

Studying Critical Comments.   Review any comments you've received, referring to the draft on each point to see what led readers to make particular comments. Try not to react defensively. Ideally, these comments will help you to see your draft for what it is (rather than what you hoped it would be) and to identify specific problems. Do not make changes yet, however. At this stage, your goal is to discover how readers see your draft and to begin to recognize both its possibilities and its problems.

Solving the Problems

Having identified problems in your draft, you now need to figure out solutions and—most important of all—to carry them out. Basically, you have three ways to turn: (1) review your invention and planning notes for other information and ideas you can add to the draft; (2) do additional invention to answer specific questions you or other readers have; and (3) look back at the readings in this chapter to see how other writers have solved similar problems.

Following are some suggestions on how you might respond to some of the problems common to writing about remembered people.

Presentation of the Subject

- If more visual detail is needed, try naming things more specifically and adding sensory detail to bring your subject to life. Choose concrete and specific words rather than abstract and general ones. Drawing comparisons, perhaps with similes and metaphors, can tell readers a good deal about your subject. Review your invention notes for details to add.

- Eliminate any details that seem irrelevant to the dominant impression you wish to give about your subject and your relationship.

- For additional dialogue, review your notes on your subject's speech patterns for memorable phrases or expressions. Try reconstructing a conversation between the two of you for words that might "say something" about your subject. Review the dialogues in the essays by Angelou, Haslam, or Gray for ideas.

- Eliminate any dialogue that does not contribute to the dominant impression you want to give.

Anecdotes and Scenes

- If any of the anecdotes seem dull, try adding more specific narrative details to show movements and gestures.

- Eliminate any anecdotes that do not contribute to the point you're trying to make.

- If the essay could use more anecdotes, look over your notes for any incidents worth telling about. Think of incidents that might help to characterize your subject as well as the relationship between the two of you.

- If you need to elaborate on a scene, try naming specific objects and providing more sensory detail to help readers see, hear, smell, and otherwise experience the scene.

Autobiographical Significance

- To clarify the significance this person has had in your life, try to think of dialogue or anecdotes that might show readers more about your relationship. Take out details that do not help to show its significance. Look back to any notes you made on your feelings about your subject.
- If your portrait is too sentimental, reexamine the point you wish to make about your subject. Be honest!

Organization

- If the beginning is weak, see if there is a better place in your draft to begin. Look for engaging dialogue, or an intriguing anecdote, or colorful description. The idea is to find something that will capture readers' attention.
- If the essay has any slow spots, perhaps you've described something too thoroughly or gotten side-tracked telling an anecdote. See if you can speed things along by eliminating some detail.
- If the ending is flat, review your draft to see if there's a better place to end. Or try ending with a question, to leave readers with something to ponder. See if there's something in your opening that could be referred to again in your ending, thus framing the essay.

Editing and Proofreading

Although you may have already corrected some obvious errors, errors were not your first priority in the rewriting you did up to this point. Now, however, you must find and correct any errors of mechanics, usage, punctuation, and spelling before preparing and submitting a final draft. When you have finished this editing and produced a final copy, you must proofread and make further corrections if necessary before handing in your essay.

LEARNING FROM YOUR OWN WRITING PROCESS

If you are asked to write about your experience composing this essay, begin by reviewing all your notes and drafts. Look especially closely at the exploration of the person's significance you did in your invention writing and for any difficulties you had in gaining adequate emotional distance.

Next, discuss the changes you made from draft to revision. What seemed to work in the draft and what needed revising? How did others' analysis of the draft help you to see its problems? What other changes would you make if you had the opportunity? What pleases you most about your essay?

A Writer at Work

REVISING A DRAFT AFTER A CRITICAL READING

In this section we will look at the way Jan Gray's essay about her father evolved from draft to revision. Included here are her first draft and a written critique of it by one of her classmates. Read them, and then turn back to reread her final draft, "Father," printed earlier in this chapter.

The First Draft

Gray drafted her essay after spending a couple of hours on the invention and planning activities. She had no difficulty choosing a subject, since she had such strong feelings about and vivid memories of her father. She wrote the draft quickly in one sitting, not worrying about punctuation or usage. Though she wrote in pencil, her draft appears here typed and marked up with the pointings from the critical reading.

My father is a large intelligent, overpowering man. 1
He's well-respected in the food-processing trade for his
clever but shrewd business tactics but I find his manipulative qualities a reflection of the maturity that he
lacks (For as long as I can remember he's always had to be
in control, decision-maker of the family and what he said
was law.) There was no compromising with this man and for
that reason I've always feared him.

When I was little and he used to still live with us, 2
everytime he came home from work I avoided him as best I
could. If he came in the kitchen I went in the livingroom
and if he came into the livingroom I went upstairs to my
bedroom just to avoid any confrontation.

Family trips were the worst. (There was nowhere to go, 3
I was locked up with him in a camper or motel for 1 week,
2 weeks or however long the vacation lasted) I remember
one trip in particular. It was the summer after my 12th
Birthday and the whole family (5 kids, 2 adults and one
dog) were going to go "out west" for a month. (We trav-
elled through Wyoming, North and South Dakota, Colorado
and other neighboring states were on the agenda.) My
father is the type who thinks he enjoys these family out-
ings because as a loyal husband and father that's what he
should do. Going to the state parks and the wilderness was
more like a business trip than a vacation. He had made the
agenda so no matter what we were to stick to it. That

meant at every road sign like Yellowstone Nat'l Park we
had to stop, one or more of the kids would get out stand
by the sign and he'd take a picture just so he could say
we've been there. Get in and get out as quick as possible
was his motto to cover as much ground in as little time as
he could. I hated having to take those pictures because it
seemed so senseless--who cares about the dumb signs anyway? But dad is a very impatient man and any sign of non
conformity was sure to put him in a rage. Not a physical
violence, no, my father never did get violent but you always knew when he was boiling up inside. I could sense it
in the tone of his voice and the reddish glaze that would
cover his eyes. He would always stay very calm yet he was
ready to explode. He never physically hurt anyone of us
kids--sure we've all been spanked before but only when we
were younger. Although he constrained himself from in-
flicting harm on people he didn't hold back from damaging
objects.

I remember one time I was calling my mother from a   4
girlfriend's house to ask if I could stay over for dinner
when my father unexpectedly answered the phone. "Hello?"
he said, in his usually gruffy manner.

"Oh, hi dad. Is Mom around?"   5

"What can I do for you?"   6

"Well, I just wanted to ask her if I could eat dinner   7
over here at Shana's."

"I don't think that's a very good idea. Your room is a   8
shambles and if your not home in 10 minutes I'm really
going to make a mess for you to clean up." Click.

I was in shock. I hadn't expected him to be there be-   9
cause at this time my parents were divorced but I knew he
was serious so I jumped on my bike and pedalled home as
fast as I could. I know I was there within ten minutes but
apparently he didn't think so. I walked in the front door
and headed straight for my room. When I opened my bedroom
door I couldn't believe what I saw. My dresser drawers
were all pulled out and clothes strewn about the room, the
dresser was lying on its side and everything on top of the
dresser had been cast aside in a fit of anger. I closed my
door and tears began to well up in my eyes. I hated him so
much at the moment. All those years of fear suddenly
turned to anger and resentment. Who the hell was this man
to do this when he didn't even live in the house anymore?
I was slowly piecing my room back together when he knocked

on the door. <u>I choked back the tears</u> because I didn't want
him to know that his little outrage had gotten to me and
quietly said, "Come in."

He opened the door and <u>stood in the doorway one arm</u>   10
<u>leaning on the door jamb and a cigarette with ashes fall-</u>
<u>ing on the carpet dangling from his other hand.</u>

"I want you to know I did this for your own good" He   11
said. "I think its time you started taking a little responsibility around this house. Now let me help you put
the dresser back up."

"No thanks. I'd rather do it myself."   12

"Aw, come on. Let's not have any hard feelings now."   13

"Please, I said. I'd rather do it myself so would you   14
please leave me alone." By this time I was shaking and on
the verge of breaking out in tears. He gave me <u>one last</u>
<u>look that seemed to say, "I offered, I did the right</u>
<u>thing, I'm the good guy and she refused me so now it's her</u>
<u>problem" and he walked out.</u>

I was so upset that he could be so violent one moment   15
and then turn around and patronize me by offering to help
clean up what he had done. That one incident revealed his
whole character to me.

<u>My father is a spiteful, manipulative, condescending,</u>   16
<u>malicious man and from that day on I knew I would never</u>
<u>understand him or want to.</u>

Gray opens her draft with a series of direct statements describing her father's
character and stating her feelings about him. The second paragraph illustrates
what we were told in the first. Paragraph 3 also serves as illustration, showing
her father's domination over the family and concluding with a physical description and a suggestion of his potential for violence.

In paragraphs 4 to 15, Gray relates an anecdote. Though long, it is fast-
paced and dramatic. She uses dialogue to show us her father's character and
description to let us visualize the damage he did to her room. Then she ends
as she began—with a series of statements explicitly disclosing her feelings.

Critical Comments

A classmate named Tom Schwartz read Gray's draft. He first read it through
once and quickly wrote down his general impression. Following the critical
reading guide, Schwartz then reread the draft to analyze its features closely.
It took him a little more than half an hour to complete a full written critique,
which appears below. Each point corresponds to a step in Reading with a
Critical Eye earlier in this chapter.

FIRST IMPRESSION: Your dad sure seems crazy. I can see
he's impossible to live with. Because he's your dad he's

naturally significant. You say you hate him and you call
him a lot of names. But you also say he thought of himself
as a loyal father. Was there anytime he was ok?

Is the Person Described Vividly?

I can't picture him. What did he look like? I like the description of your messed up room. I'd like even more detail, like what clothes were thrown around and where. Did
he break anything when he tipped the dresser? Was the
whole room a wreck or just the dresser? Oh yeah, the detail of his cigarette ashes falling on the carpet is
great. He's the one who's making the mess, not you.

You make a lot of statements. Most need illustration. I
don't get it about there being no compromising with him.
What do you expect him to do? My dad is pretty strict too.
But he doesn't wreck my room.

Are the Anecdotes Effective?

I don't get the vacation. Was it a birthday trip? Didn't
you go to Yellowstone? Or did you just take pictures of
signs? Sounds weird. The room anecdote is the best. It's
really dramatic. The dialogue works as a frame I think.
He had some nerve offering to help pick up the dresser.
How smug and self-satisfied. Patronizing is right. Great
anecdote.

Is the Organization Effective?

The beginning doesn't lead one to expect the room anecdote. The stuff about his business seems out of place.
You're writing about your relationship with him not about
his business. I don't have any suggestions.

The ending may be going too far now that I think of it.
Also, even though you say you don't want to understand
him, here you are writing about him. Maybe there's more to
it than you're admitting. You could end with the paragraph
before. The anecdote sure does reveal his character.

Is the Autobiographical Significance Clear?

I just said you might have more feelings than you're admitting. You certainly have every reason to hate him. You
say he never really hit you. But he certainly was violent,
like you said.

I'm not sure why you wrote about your dad. Maybe you
just feel strongly about him and need to figure him out.

Maybe because he's colorful--unusual, unpredictable, not
like other fathers, even divorced ones. I think he was a
great choice for an essay. You disclose a lot of unpleasant stuff about your family. You certainly seem honest.

Final Thoughts

I guess it makes me feel lucky my dad and I get along. I
don't know what I'd do if he was like your dad. I still
wonder if your dad was all that bad. He must have some
good sides.

This critique helped Gray a great deal in revising her draft. Reread her
revision now to see what she changed; you will see that many of her changes
were suggested by Schwartz.

In writing about what she learned from writing this essay, Gray remarked:
"Tom's criticism helped me a lot. He warned me against making too many
statements without illustrating them. He said I needed more showing and
less telling. He also questioned the vacation anecdote. I guess it didn't have
much of a point. And the incident with my room seemed to work so well I
decided to add the part about my dad's apartment."

Gray realized that the heart of her essay was in the anecdote about her
room. She also saw, from Schwartz's comments, that the opening paragraphs
weren't working. Responding to his request for more physical description
of her father, Gray returned to the invention activity in which she listed
important details about the person's appearance. From this exploration, she
came up with the detailed description of her father that now opens the essay.
As she was describing her father, she remembered the incident of cleaning
his apartment and decided to use the description of his filthy apartment to
frame the description of her own ransacked room.

Perhaps Schwartz's greatest contribution, however, was to help Gray reexamine the real significance her father held in her life. Specifically, Schwartz
made her realize that her feelings were more complicated than she let on in
her first draft. In writing about what she learned, Gray concluded, "The
feelings I wanted to express didn't come across. I had a hard time writing
the paper because I held back on a lot of things. I'm pretty ambivalent in
my feelings toward my father right now." Gray discovered she could distance
herself emotionally and at the same time disclose her feelings by showing
her father, his room, and the confrontation over her room. Gray's portrait
of her father turned out to be somewhat more sympathetic than her comments about him, expressing some ambivalence—pity as well as fury.

■ A college student decides to profile a local radio station for the campus newspaper. In several visits to the station, she observes its inner workings and interviews the manager, technicians, and disc jockeys. Her profile shows how the disc jockeys, who make a living by being outrageous, are nonetheless engaged in very routine day-to-day work.

■ A journalist assigned to write about a Nobel Prize–winning scientist decides to profile a day in her life. He spends a couple of days observing her at home and at work, and interviews colleagues, students, and family, as well as the scientist herself. Her daily life, he learns, is very much like that of other working mothers—a constant effort to balance the demands of her career against the needs of her family. He presents this theme in his essay by alternating details about the scientist's career with those about her daily life.

■ A student in an art history class writes a profile of a local artist recently commissioned to paint outdoor murals for the city. The student visits the artist's studio and talks with him about the process of painting murals. The artist invites the student to spend the following day as part of a team of local art students and neighborhood volunteers working on the mural under the artist's direction. This firsthand experience helps the student describe the process of mural painting almost from an insider's point of view.

■ A student in a sociology class profiles a controversial urban renewal project. After studying newspaper reports for the names of opponents and supporters of the project, she interviews several of them. Then she tours the site with the project manager. Her essay alternates description of the renovation with analysis of the controversy.

Writing Profiles   4

■ **For a writing workshop, a student profiles his college library's rare book room. In the essay, he narrates his adventure into this unfamiliar territory, whose existence he had hardly been aware of. Expecting shelf after shelf of leather-bound first editions, he is surprised to find manuscript drafts, letters, diaries, and dogeared annotated books (including some cheap paperback editions) from famous authors' libraries.**

Magazines and newspapers are filled with profiles. Unlike conventional news stories, which report current events, profiles tell about people, places, and activities in our communities. Some profiles take us behind the scenes of familiar places, giving us a glimpse of their inner workings. Others introduce us to the exotic—peculiar hobbies, unusual professions, bizarre personalities. Still others probe the social, political, and moral significance of our institutions. At the heart of most profiles are vivid details and surprising insights that can capture readers' curiosity.

Because profiles share many features with autobiography, such as narrative, anecdote, description, and dialogue, you may use some of the strategies learned in writing about a remembered event (Chapter 2) or person (Chapter 3). Yet profiles differ significantly from autobiography. Whereas autobiography reflects on remembered personal experience, a profile synthesizes and presents newly acquired information. In writing a profile, you practice the field research methods of observing, interviewing, and notetaking commonly used by investigative reporters, social scientists, and naturalists. You also learn to analyze data and organize it creatively so that it is both informative and interesting to readers. In these ways, the profile is related both to personal writing deriving from memory and reflection and to explanatory and argumentative writing based on inquiry and deliberation.

Profiles are, in fact, familiar forms of reading and writing assignments in various college courses. Here are some typical college profile assignments:

■ *For a business course:* Report on the organizational structure of a particular place of business, first visiting the business and interviewing employees at various levels.

■ *For an education course:* Observe a class where students are learning cooperatively, taking careful notes about what the teacher and students say and do. Based on what you know about cooperative learning principles, decide how effective the teacher has been in applying them. Write a report on your conclusions, supporting them with specific details from your observations.

■ *For an anthropology course:* In "Deep Play: Notes on the Balinese Cock-fight," Clifford Geertz argues that the anthropologist, in order to acquire deep insights into a culture, should study everyday experiences as if they were printed texts. Geertz's own "close reading" of the Balinese cockfight, for example, provides insights into Balinese status hierarchy and self-regard. Closely observe some instance of play or leisure in our culture and write an essay presenting your own "close reading" of this cultural text. Some possibilities for observation might be a Little League game, a beauty contest, a fraternity party, a company picnic.

The scope of the profile you write may be large or small, depending on your assignment and your subject. You could attend a single event such as a parade or a convention and write up your observations of the place, people, and activity. Or you might conduct an interview with a person who has an unusual hobby or occupation and write up a profile based on your interview notes. If you have the time to do more extensive research, you might write a full-blown profile based on several observations and interviews with various people. Whatever the scope of your project, the readings that follow will introduce you to the many possibilities of profile writing and the Guide to Writing will help you research and plan your essay.

For Group Inquiry

The scenarios that open this chapter suggest some occasions for writing profiles. Imagine that you have been assigned to write a profile of a person, place, or activity on your campus or in your community. Think of subjects that you would like to know more about, and make a list of as many of them as you can. Consider local personalities (a flamboyant store owner, perhaps, or a distinguished teacher); places on campus (a dean's office, or an experimental laboratory); and activities in the community (the airport control tower, or a recycling center).

Then get together with two or three other students, and read your lists of subjects to one another. Ask the others to tell you which item on your list is most interesting to them and to quickly jot down any questions they have about it. After you've all read your lists and gotten responses, discuss the following questions:

■ Were you surprised by which item on your list the other members of the group found most interesting? Why?

■ Were you surprised by any of the questions they had about this subject? Why?

■ How would these questions influence your approach to the subject and your profile?

Readings

Gretel Ehrlich is a cattle rancher in Wyoming. She is also a writer—of fiction, poetry, and essays. The following essay comes from *The Solace of Open Spaces* (1985). In it she profiles the saddle bronc event at the National Rodeo Finals in Oklahoma City. In saddle bronc riding, the rider has to stay on a wildly bucking horse for at least eight seconds, holding on to nothing but the reins. Ehrlich's firsthand knowledge of ranching gives her a special perspective on and appreciation of rodeo. In addition, her training and experience as a documentary filmmaker give her writing a highly visual quality. As you read, notice the abundant visual detail and the cameralike movement of her description.

SADDLE BRONC RIDING AT THE NATIONAL FINALS
GRETEL EHRLICH

Rodeo is the wild child of ranch work and embodies some of what ranching is all about. Horsemanship—not gunslinging—was the pride of western men, and the chivalrous ethics they formulated, known as the western code, became the ground rules for every human game. Two great partnerships are celebrated in this Oklahoma arena: the indispensable one between man and animal that any rancher or cowboy takes on, enduring the joys and punishments of the alliance; and the one between man and man, cowboy and cowboy. 1

The National Finals run ten nights. Every contestant rides every night, so it is easy to follow their progress and setbacks. One evening we abandoned our rooftop seats and sat behind the chutes to watch the saddle broncs ride. Behind the chutes two cowboys are rubbing rosin—part of their staying power—behind the saddle swells and on their Easter-egg-colored chaps which are pink, blue, and light green with white fringe. Up above, standing on the chute rungs, the stock contractors direct horse traffic: "Velvet Drums" in chute #3, "Angel Sings" in #5, "Rusty" in #1. Rick Smith, Monty Henson, Bobby Berger, Brad Gjermudson, Mel Coleman, and friends climb the chutes. From where I'm sitting, it looks like a field hospital with five separate operating theaters, the cowboys, like surgeons, bent over their patients with sweaty brows and looks of concern. Horses are being haltered; cowboys are measuring out the long, braided reins, saddles are set: one cowboy pulls up on the swells again and again, repositioning his hornless saddle until it sits just right. When the chute boss nods to him and says, "Pull 'em up, boys," the ground crew tightens front and back cinches on the first horse to go, but very slowly so he won't panic in the chute as the cowboy eases himself down over the saddle, not sitting on it, just hovering there. "Okay, you're on." The chute boss nods to him again. Now he sits on the saddle, taking the rein in one hand, holding the top of the chute with the other. He flips the loose bottoms of his chaps over his shins, puts a foot in each stirrup, takes a breath, and nods. The chute gate swings open releasing a flood—not of water, but of flesh, groans, legs kicking. The horse lunges up and out in the first big jump 2 like a wave breaking whose crest the cowboy rides, "marking out the horse," spurs well above the bronc's shoulders. In that first second under the lights, he finds what will be the rhythm of the ride. Once again he "charges the point," his legs pumping forward, then so far back his heels touch behind the cantle. For a moment he looks as though he were kneeling on air, then he's stretched out again, his whole body taut but released, free hand waving in back of his head like a palm frond, reinholding hand thrust forward: *"En garde!"* he seems to be saying, but he's airborne; he looks like a wing that has sprouted suddenly from the horse's broad back. Eight seconds. The whistle blows. He's covered the horse. Now two gentlemen dressed in white chaps and satin shirts gallop beside the bucking horse. The cowboy hands the rein to one and grabs the waist of the other—the flank strap on the bronc has been undone, so all three horses move at a run—and the pickup man from whom the cowboy is now dangling slows almost to a stop, letting him slide to his feet on the ground.

Rick Smith from Wyoming rides, looking pale and nervous in his white shirt. He's 3 bucked off and so are the brash Monty "Hawkeye" Henson, and Butch Knowles, and Bud Pauley, but with such grace and aplomb, there is no shame. Bobby Berger, an Oklahoma cowboy, wins the go-round with a score of 83.

By the end of the evening we're tired, but in no way as exhausted as these 4 young men who have ridden night after night. "I've never been so sore and had so much fun in my life," one first-time bull rider exclaims breathlessly. When the performance is over we walk across the street to the chic lobby of a hotel chock full of cowboys. Wives hurry through the crowd with freshly ironed shirts for tomorrow's ride, ropers carry their rope bags with them into the coffee shop, which is now filled with contestants, eating mild midnight suppers of scrambled eggs, their numbers hanging crookedly on their backs, their faces powdered with dust, and looking at this late hour prematurely old.

In the rough stock events such as the one we watched tonight, there is no victory 5 over the horse or bull. The point of the match is not conquest but communion: the rhythm of two beings becoming one. Rodeo is not a sport of opposition; there is no scrimmage line here. No one bears malice—neither the animals, the stock contractors, nor the contestants; no one wants to get hurt. In this match of equal talents, it is only acceptance, surrender, respect, and spiritedness that make for the midair union of cowboy and horse.

For Discussion

In the final paragraph, Ehrlich contrasts what she calls sports of "communion" ("acceptance, surrender, respect, and spiritedness") with sports of "opposition" ("victory," "conquest," "scrimmage line," "malice"). List some sports that could fit into these categories, and then discuss whether this way of classifying sports makes sense.

For Analysis

For more about scratch outlining, see pp. 384–87.

1.   To see how Ehrlich has organized her observations at the rodeo, make a scratch outline of the essay: a simple list of the different scenes she shows us and the vantage points—above or below, close up or far away—from which she describes them. From analyzing the essay's organization, what do you think she assumes her readers know and feel about bronc riding?

For more about vantage point, see pp. 438–39.

2.   What do you think is Ehrlich's purpose in writing this essay? What does she want her readers to learn about bronc riding from reading her profile? What have you learned?

3.   Instead of referring generally to horses and riders, Ehrlich provides specific names in paragraphs 2 and 3. Look closely at these names and decide what you learn from them and whether they are necessary.

4.   Mark Twain once wrote: "The difference between the *almost right* word and the *right* word is really a large matter—'tis the difference between the lightning bug and the lightning. After that, of course, that exceedingly important brick, the *exact* word. . . ." Reread Ehrlich's profile, noting any words that seem to you *right* or *exact*. Select two or three of these words and explain why you think Ehrlich chose them.

For Your Own Writing

What sports, musical, or theatrical events could you observe during the next week or two? Which one do you think would make the most interesting profile? What new or unusual perspective might you bring to it?

Commentary

Ehrlich clearly likes rodeo and admires cowboys, and she hopes we will value them too. She wants us to see an event vividly and to share in her pleasure at experiencing it. But she also has a point to make about rodeos, a point about their larger meaning and significance. In the opening paragraph, she tells us that rodeo celebrates the two ranching partnerships—between cowboy and animal, and among cowboys. In the last paragraph, she asserts that rodeo fosters this sense of partnership—she calls it a "communion." The partnerships are a "match of equal talents" in which there is no conquest, opposition, or malice. Everything in her profile reveals or dramatizes this theme; indeed, the theme controls her selection and organization of scenes and details.

Discovering a controlling theme—an angle, interpretation, surprising insight, point, incongruity—will be an important part of your writing process as you work on a profile. You do not need to have a controlling theme in mind when you begin; in fact, most writers discover a theme later as they reflect on their notes, draft the profile, or discuss the draft with others. Though the theme may emerge late in the process, it is essential. Without it, and without a good understanding of your readers' expectations and knowledge, focusing and organizing your profile and choosing relevant anecdotes or details are difficult if not impossible.

Besides a controlling theme, description and narration are centrally important in profiles. The more you know about describing and narrating, the more confidently and successfully you can write profiles.

Ehrlich names many objects and people: rosin, chaps, horses, reins, stirrups, cantle, whistle, pickup man, and more. To help us imagine the scene as she saw it, she also provides many details. The cowboys' chaps are "Easter-egg-colored"—"pink, blue, and light green with white fringe." Reins are "long" and "braided"; saddles are "horn-less." The pickup men wear white chaps and satin shirts. Both horses and men have specific names.

Ehrlich also makes good use of comparisons to help us envision the scene. When she says that the horse chutes look like a "field hospital with five separate operating theaters, the cowboys, like surgeons, bent over their patients with sweaty brows and looks of concern," we understand how serious and professional the cowboys are. Once the action starts, Ehrlich describes a horse bucking "like a wave breaking whose crest the cowboy rides." The bronc-riding cowboy "looks as though he were kneeling on air" or "like a wing that has sprouted suddenly from the horse's broad back." These comparisons are surprising and pleasing—and informative. They reveal that Ehrlich is watching the bronc riding as though she has never seen it before, trying to see it freshly so that she can report it to us vividly, enabling us to see it as she does.

For more about naming, detailing, and comparing, see pp. 429–34.

In the long second paragraph, Ehrlich relies on narrative strategies to give the story conflict—between the cowboy and the horse—and suspense— we are curious to know what will happen to the cowboy as the horse lunges out of the chute. The pace of the narrative seems quick during the early preparations in the chutes but then slows to dramatize the ride. To slow the pace and increase the tension and drama, Ehrlich depicts specific actions with strong, active verbs: "the ground crew *tightens* front and back cinches," "the chute gate *swings* open," and "the horse *lunges up*."

■   ■   ■

"**S**oup," the next selection, is an unsigned profile that initially appeared in the "Goings On About Town" section of the *New Yorker* magazine (January 1989). The *New Yorker* regularly features brief, anonymous profiles like this one, whose subject is the fast-talking owner/chef of a takeout restaurant specializing in soup. As you read, notice the prominence given to dialogue.

SOUP
THE NEW YORKER

When Albert Yeganeh says "Soup is my lifeblood," he means it. And when he says "I am extremely hard to please," he means that, too. Working like a demon alchemist in a tiny storefront kitchen at 259-A West Fifty-fifth Street, Mr. Yeganeh creates anywhere from eight to seventeen soups every weekday. His concoctions are so popular that a wait of half an hour at the lunchtime peak is not uncommon, although there are strict rules for conduct in line. But more on that later. 1

"I am psychologically kind of a health freak," Mr. Yeganeh said the other day, in a lisping staccato of Armenian origin. "And I know that soup is the greatest meal in the world. It's very good for your digestive system. And I use only the best, the freshest ingredients. I am a perfectionist. When I make a clam soup, I use three different kinds of clams. Every other place uses canned clams. I'm called crazy. I am not crazy. People don't realize why I get so upset. It's because if the soup is not perfect and I'm still selling it, it's a torture. It's *my* soup, and that's why I'm so upset. 2

First you clean and then you cook. I don't believe that ninety-nine per cent of the restaurants in New York know how to clean a tomato. I tell my crew to wash the parsley *eight* times. If they wash it five or six times, I scare them. I tell them they'll go to jail if there is sand in the parsley. One time, I found a mushroom on the floor, and I fired the guy who left it here." He spread his arms, and added, "This place is the only one like it in . . . in . . . the whole earth! One day, I hope to learn something from the other places, but so far I haven't. For example, the other day I went to a very fancy restaurant and had borscht. I had to send it back. It was *junk*. I could see all the chemicals in it. I never use chemicals. Last weekend, I had lobster bisque in Brooklyn, a very well-known place. It was *junk*. When I make a lobster bisque, I use a whole lobster. You know, I never advertise. I don't have to. All the big-shot chefs and the kings of the hotels come here to see what *I'm* doing."

As you approach Mr. Yeganeh's Soup Kitchen International from a distance, the 3 first thing you notice about it is the awning, which proclaims "Homemade Hot, Cold, Diet Soups." The second thing you notice is an aroma so delicious that it makes you want to take a bite out of the air. The third thing you notice, in front of the kitchen, is an electric signboard that flashes, say, "Today's Soups . . . Chicken Vegetable . . . Mexican Beef Chili . . . Cream of Watercress . . . Italian Sausage . . . Clam Bisque . . . Beef Barley . . . Due to Cold Weather . . . For Most Efficient and Fastest Service the Line Must . . . Be Kept Moving . . . Please . . . Have Your Money . . . Ready . . . Pick the Soup of Your Choice . . . Move to Your Extreme . . . Left After Ordering."

"I am not prejudiced against color or religion," Mr. Yeganeh told us, and he 4 jabbed an index finger at the flashing sign. "Whoever follows that I treat very well. My regular customers don't say anything. They are very intelligent and well educated. They know I'm just trying to move the line. The New York cop is very smart—he sees everything but says nothing. But the young girl who wants to stop and tell you how nice you look and hold everyone up—*yah*!" He made a guillotining motion with his hand. "I tell you, I hate to work with the public. They treat me like a slave. My philosophy is: The customer is always wrong and I'm always right. I raised my prices to try to get rid of some of these people, but it didn't work."

The other day, Mr. Yeganeh was dressed in chefs' whites with orange smears 5 across his chest, which may have been some of the carrot soup cooking in a huge pot on a little stove in one corner. A three-foot-long handheld mixer from France sat on the sink, looking like an overgrown gardening tool. Mr. Yeganeh spoke to two young helpers in a twisted Armenian-Spanish barrage, then said to us, "I have no overhead, no trained waitresses, and I have the cashier here." He pointed to himself theatrically. Beside the doorway, a glass case with fresh green celery, red and yellow peppers, and purple eggplant was topped by five big gray soup urns. According to a piece of cardboard taped to the door, you can buy Mr. Yeganeh's soups in three sizes, costing from four to fifteen dollars. The order of any well-behaved customer is accompanied by little waxpaper packets of bread, fresh vegetables (such as scallions and radishes), fresh fruit (such as cherries or an orange), a chocolate mint, and a plastic spoon. No coffee, tea, or other drinks are served.

"I get my recipes from books and theories and my own taste," Mr. Yeganeh 6 said. "At home, I have several hundreds of books. When I do research, I find that I don't know anything. Like cabbage is a cancer fighter, and some fish is good for your heart but some is bad. Every day, I should have one sweet, one spicy, one cream, one vegetable soup—and they *must* change, they should always taste a little different." He added that he wasn't sure how extensive his repertoire was, but that it probably includes at least eighty soups, among them African peanut butter, Greek moussaka, hamburger, Reuben, B.L.T., asparagus and caviar, Japanese shrimp miso, chicken chili, Irish corned beef and cabbage, Swiss chocolate, French calf's brain, Korean beef ball, Italian shrimp and eggplant Parmesan, buffalo, ham and egg, short rib, Russian beef Stroganoff, turkey cacciatore, and Indian mulligatawny. "The chicken and the seafood are an addiction, and when I have French garlic soup I let people have only one small container each," he said. "The doctors and nurses love that one."

A lunch line of thirty people stretched down the block from Mr. Yeganeh's 7 doorway. Behind a construction worker was a man in expensive leather, who was in front of a woman in a fur hat. Few people spoke. Most had their money out and their orders ready.

At the front of the line, a woman in a brown coat couldn't decide which soup 8 to get and started to complain about the prices.

"You talk too much, dear," Mr. Yeganeh said, and motioned to her to move to 9 the left. "Next!"

"Just don't talk. Do what he says," a man huddled in a blue parka warned.   10

"He's downright rude," said a blond woman in a blue coat. "Even abusive. But 11 you can't deny it, his soup is the best."

For Discussion

Most people agree that the quality of American products and services has declined in recent years, particularly in relation to those in other countries, such as Japan. An enormously popular book urges American business executives to *Search for Excellence,* claiming that profit will follow. Albert Yeganeh is a prime example of this philosophy.

Discuss your experiences as workers on the job and in school. How much do you care about the quality of your work? How have your work values been shaped by the situations in which you've worked? On the job, for example, what kinds of attitudes encourage—or discourage—high-quality work? In school, what has inspired you to do your best work? If you agree that the quality of American products and services is a problem, what do you think can or ought to be done about it?

For Analysis

1.   What do you learn about Yeganeh from what he says and how he says it? Instead of quoting him, the writer could have paraphrased the quoted material. (For example, at the beginning of paragraph 2, the writer might have written: "Mr. Yeganeh said that he believed soup to be good for the digestive system. He claimed that he always used only fresh ingredients in his soups.") What do the quotations add to the essay? How would the essay be different if the writer had quoted less and paraphrased more?

2.   Review the lengthy list in paragraph 6. How does this list add to what you know about Yeganeh and his restaurant? Why might the writer have chosen to list these particular soups?

For more about dominant impression, see pp. 428–29.

3.   In addition to profiling a person, this essay shows us his place of business. Reread the essay, underlining the words and details that present the restaurant itself. What is the dominant impression made by this descriptive language?

4.   The only explicit opinion the writer expresses is in paragraph 3: "The second thing you notice is an aroma so delicious that it makes you want to take a bite out of the air." Nevertheless, most readers do form an opinion of Yeganeh and his restaurant. What opinion, if any, did you form? Review the essay to determine what might have led you to this judgment.

For Your Own Writing

List several unusual people or places on campus or in your community that you could profile. Which of these would be most interesting to you? Why? What seems special about him, her, or it?

Commentary

"Soup" illustrates some of the problems writers face in organizing a profile. For activities, such as the saddle bronc riding depicted in the previous selection, the profile can basically follow a chronological organization from the beginning to the end of the event. For profiles of people and places, however, there is usually no inherent organization. The writer imposes order by grouping bits of information and juxtaposing them in a way that seems to make sense. This kind of organization is called *analogical,* as distinct from chronological.

"Soup" is a good example of an analogical organization. It begins by focusing on Yeganeh, thus letting readers know that what is special about the place is its eccentric owner. The focus remains on Yeganeh through the second paragraph, but the third takes us outside the restaurant and shows us what we would see and smell. In the fourth paragraph, the focus returns to Yeganeh with a nice transition connecting the flashing electric sign described in paragraph 3 to Yeganeh's comments on the behavior of his customers. Paragraph 5 again shifts the focus—to a "behind the scenes" look at the soup kitchen. The numerous sensory details provide a vivid description of how the kitchen operates. Although paragraphs 7–11 return to the exterior of the restaurant, the focus is now on the customers waiting in line. By concluding with the grudging compliment of a disgruntled customer, the profile leaves readers with the impression that even though Yeganeh may be "downright rude," his soup *is* "the best."

■   ■   ■

David **Noonan,** the freelance journalist who wrote the following selection, started with a sure-fire subject, guaranteed to intrigue readers: a team of brain surgeons as they perform a complicated operation. His profile provides a direct look at something very few of us are likely ever to see—the human brain. He had to handle this subject with some delicacy, however, so as not to make readers uncomfortable with overly explicit description or excessive technical terminology. Think about your own responses as you read this piece, which was published in *Esquire* in 1983. Are you uneasy with any of the graphic detail or overwhelmed by the terminology?

INSIDE THE BRAIN
DAVID NOONAN

The patient lies naked and unconscious in the center of the cool, tiled room. His 1 head is shaved, his eyes and nose taped shut. His mouth bulges with the respirator that is breathing for him. Clear plastic tubes carry anesthetic into him and urine out of him. Belly up under the bright lights he looks large and helpless, exposed. He is not dreaming; he is too far under for that. The depth of his obliviousness is accentuated by the urgent activity going on all around him. Nurses and technicians move in and out of the room preparing the instruments of surgery. At his head, two doctors are discussing the approach they will use in the operation. As they talk they trace possible incisions across his scalp with their fingers.

It is a Monday morning. Directed by Dr. Stein, Abe Steinberger is going after a 2 large tumor compressing the brainstem, a case that he describes as "a textbook beauty." It is a rare operation, a suboccipital craniectomy, supracerebellar infratentorial approach. That is, into the back of the head and over the cerebellum, under the tentorium to the brainstem and the tumor. Stein has done the operation more than fifty times, more than any other surgeon in the United States.

Many neurosurgeons consider brainstem tumors of this type inoperable because 3 of their location and treat them instead with radiation. "It's where you live," says Steinberger. Breathing, heartbeat, and consciousness itself are some of the functions connected with this primary part of the brain. Literally and figuratively, it is the core of the organ, and operating on it is always very risky. . . .

The human skull was not designed for easy opening. It takes drills and saws and 4 simple force to breach it. It is a formidable container, and its thickness testifies to the value of its contents. Opening the skull is one of the first things apprentice brain surgeons get to do on their own. It is sometimes called cabinet work, and on this case Steinberger is being assisted in the opening by Bob Solomon.

The patient has been clamped into a sitting position. Before the first incision is 5 made he is rolled under the raised instrument table and he disappears beneath sterile green drapes and towels. The only part of him left exposed is the back of his head, which is orange from the sterilizing agent painted on it. Using a special marker, Steinberger draws the pattern of the opening on the patient's head in blue. Then the first cut is made into the scalp, and a thin line of bright-red blood appears.

The operation takes place within what is called the sterile field, a small germfree 6 zone created and vigilantly patrolled by the scrub nurses. The sterile field extends out and around from the surgical opening and up over the instrument table. Once robed and gloved, the doctors are considered sterile from the neck to the waist and from the hands up the arms to just below the shoulders. The time the doctors must spend scrubbing their hands has been cut from ten minutes to five, but this obsessive routine is still the most striking of the doctor's preparations. Leaning over the trough-like stainless-steel sink with their masks in place and their arms lathered to the elbow, the surgeons carefully attend to each finger with the brush and work their way up each arm. It is the final pause, the last thing they do before they enter the operating room and go to work. Many at NI are markedly quiet while they scrub; they spend the familiar minutes running through the operation one more time. When they finish and their hands are too clean for anything but surgery they turn off the water with knee controls and back through the OR door, their dripping hands held high before them. They dry off with sterile towels, step into long-sleeved robes, and then plunge their hands down into their thin surgical gloves, which are held for them by the scrub nurse. The gloves snap as the nurse releases them around the doctors' wrists. Unnaturally smooth and defined, the gloved hands of the neurosurgeons are now ready; they can touch the living human brain.

''Drill the hell out of it,'' Steinberger says to Solomon. The scalp has been re-   7
tracted and the skull exposed. Solomon presses the large stainless-steel power drill against the bone and hits the trigger. The bit turns slowly, biting into the white skull. Shavings drop from the hole onto the drape and then to the floor. The drill stops automatically when it is through the bone. The hole is about a half inch in diameter. Solomon drills four holes in a diamond pattern. The skull at the back of the head is ridged and bumpy. There is a faint odor of burning bone.

The drilling is graphic and jarring. The drill and the head do not go together;   8
they collide and shock the eye. The tool is too big; its scale and shape are inappropriate to the delicate idea of neurosurgery. It should be hanging on the wall of a garage. After the power drill, a hand drill is used to refine the holes in the skull. It is a sterilized stainless-steel version of a handyman's tool. It is called a perforator, and as Solomon calmly turns it, more shavings hit the floor. Then, using powerful plierlike tools called Leksell rongeurs, the doctors proceed to bite away at the skull, snapping and crunching bone to turn the four small holes into a single opening about three inches in diameter. This is a *craniectomy*; the hole in the skull will always be there, protected by the many layers of scalp muscle at the back of the head. In a *craniotomy* a flap of bone is preserved to cover the opening in the skull.

After the scalp and the skull, the next layer protecting the brain is the dura. A   9
thin, tough, leathery membrane that encases the brain, the dura (derived from the Latin for *hard*) is dark pink, almost red. It is rich with blood vessels and nerves (when you have a headache, it's the dura that aches), and now it can be seen stretching across the expanse of the opening, pulsing lightly. The outline of the cerebellum bulging against the dura is clear. With a crease in the middle, the dura-sheathed cerebellum looks oddly like a tiny pair of buttocks. The resemblance prompts a moment's joking. ''Her firm young cerebellum,'' somebody says. . . .

The dura is carefully opened and sewn back out of the way. An hour and fifteen   10
minutes after the drilling began, the brain is exposed.

The brain exposed. It happens every day on the tenth floor, three, four, and five   11
times a day, day after day, week in and week out, month after month. The brain exposed. Light falls on its gleaming surface for the first time. It beats lightly, steadily. It is pink and gray, the brain, and the cerebellar cortex is covered with tiny blood vessels, in a web. In some openings you can see the curve of the brain, its roundness. It does not look strong, it looks very soft, soft enough to push your finger through. When you see it for the first time you almost expect sparks, tiny sparks arcing across the surface, blinking lights, the crackle of an idea. You stare down at it and it gives nothing back, reveals nothing, gives no hint of how it works. As soon as they see it

the doctors begin the search for landmarks. They start talking to each other, describing what they both can see, narrating the anatomy.

In the operating room the eyes bear much of the burden of communication. 12 With their surgical masks and caps in place, the doctors and nurses resort to exaggerated stares and squints and flying eyebrows to emphasize what they are saying. After more than two decades in the operating room, Dr. Stein has developed this talent for nonverbal punctuation to a fine art. His clear blue eyes narrow now in concentration as he listens to Abe explain what he wants to do next. They discuss how to go about retracting the cerebellum. "Okay, Abe," Stein says quietly. "Nice and easy now."

The cerebellum (the word means *little brain*) is one of the most complicated parts 13 of the brain. It is involved in the processing of sensory information of all kinds as well as balance and motor control, but in this case it is simply in the way. With the dura gone the cerebellum bulges out of the back of the head; it can be seen from across the room, protruding into space, striated and strange-looking.

When the cerebellum is retracted, the microscope is rolled into place and the 14 operation really begins. It is a two-man scope, with a cable running to a TV monitor and a videotape machine. Sitting side by side, looking through the scope into the head, Steinberger and Stein go looking for the tumor.

It is a long and tedious process, working your way into the center of the human 15 brain. The joke about the slip of the scalpel that wiped out fifteen years of piano lessons is no joke. Every seen and unseen piece of tissue does something, has some function, though it may well be a mystery to the surgeon. In order to spend hour after hour at the microscope, manipulating their instruments in an area no bigger than the inside of a juice can, neurosurgeons must develop an awesome capacity for sustained concentration.

After two hours of talking their way through the glowing red geography of the 16 inner brain, Stein and Steinberger come upon the tumor. "Holy Toledo, look at that," exclaims Steinberger. The tumor stands out from the tissue around it, purple and mean-looking. It is the end of order in a very small, orderly place. It does not belong. They pause a moment, and Abe gives a quick tour of the opening. "That's tumor, that's the brainstem, and that's the third ventricle," he says. "And that over there, that's memory."

A doctor from the pathology department shows up for a piece of the tumor. It 17 will be analyzed quickly while the operation is under way so the surgeons will know what they are dealing with. The type of tumor plays an important part in decisions about how much to take out, what risks to take in the attempt to get it all. A more detailed tissue analysis will be made later.

It turns out to be a brainstem glioma, an invasive intrinsic tumor actually growing 18 up out of the brainstem. It is malignant. They get a lot of it but it will grow back. With radiation the patient could live fifteen years or even longer, and he will be told so. Abe Steinberger, in fact, will tell him. More than six hours after the first incision, the operation ends.

When the operation is over it is pointed out to Steinberger that he is the same 19 age as the patient. "Really?" he says. "It's funny, I always think of the patients as being older than me."

How they think of the patients is at the center of the residents' approach to 20 neurosurgery. It is a sensitive subject, and they have all given it a lot of thought.

They know well the classic preconceived notion of the surgeon as a cold and arrogant technician. "You think like a surgeon" is a medical-school insult. Beyond that, the residents actually know a lot of surgeons, and though they say most of them don't fit the stereotype, they also say that there are some who really do bring it to life.

In many ways the mechanics of surgery itself create a distance between the surgeon and the patient. A man with a tumor is a case, a collection of symptoms. He is transformed into a series of X rays, CAT scans, and angiograms. He becomes his tumor, is even referred to by his affliction. "We've got a beautiful meningioma coming in tomorrow," a doctor will say. Once in the operating room the patient disappears beneath the drapes and is reduced to a small red hole. Though it is truly the ultimate intimacy, neurosurgery can be starkly impersonal. 21

"The goal of surgery is to get as busy as you can doing good cases and making people *better* by operating on them," says Phil Cogen. "That automatically cuts down the time you spend with patients." Though this frustrates Cogen, who has dreams and nightmares about his patients "all the time," he also knows there is a high emotional price to pay for getting too close. "One of the things you learn to do as a surgeon in any field is disassociate yourself from the person you're operating on. I never looked under the drapes at the patient until my third year in neurosurgery, when it was too late to back out." 22

While Cogen prides himself on not having a "surgical personality," Abe Steinberger believes that his skills are best put to use in the operating room and doesn't worry too much about the problems of patient relations. "I sympathize with the patients," he says. "I feel very bad when they're sick and I feel great when they're better. But what I want to do is operate. I want to get in there and do it." 23

For Discussion

In paragraph 22, surgeon Cogen says, "One of the things you learn to do . . . is disassociate yourself from the person you're operating on." Discuss this phenomenon of specialists in the helping professions (such as doctors, teachers, counselors) disassociating themselves from their clients, treating them impersonally, even coldly. Have you ever been treated impersonally by a helping professional? What happened? How did you feel?

Are there certain situations when professionals *should* treat clients impersonally? In what situations would such treatment always be inappropriate? What conclusions can you reach about the relations between helping professionals and their clients?

For Analysis

For a discussion of narrative pace, see pp. 421–25.

1. The operation actually lasts six hours. To see how Noonan translates clock time into narrative time with its special qualities of pacing, tension, and drama, make a scratch outline of the essay. Where does the pace quicken and where does it slow? Which events receive the most and which the least narrative space in the essay? What advantages and disadvantages do you see in Noonan's narrative pacing and structure?

2. Noonan quotes both Dr. Stein and Dr. Steinberger, letting us hear what they say during the operation (paragraphs 3, 7, 12, and 16). What do these

quotations add to the essay? How might the essay have been different had Noonan paraphrased rather than quoted?

3.   Look at paragraphs 1 and 2. Either one could well have opened the essay. What would have been gained and what would have been lost if Noonan had begun his essay with paragraph 2?

4.   The features of an elegant, readable style include active verbs, few -*ion* nouns or long strings of prepositional phrases, the right words, and no more words than necessary, as well as a variety of sentence structures and lengths. Skim Noonan's essay, noting these stylistic features or their absence. What seem to be the strengths and weaknesses of his style?

For Your Own Writing

If you were asked to profile a highly skilled specialist at work, what specialty would you choose? What kind of information would you need to write such a profile? Where would you get it?

Commentary

Some profiles, like Noonan's, require the writer to research the subject in order to understand it well. Although most of his information obviously comes from observing and interviewing, he must also have done some reading to familiarize himself with surgical terminology and procedures.

Just as important as the actual information a writer provides is the way he or she arranges and presents it. Information must be organized in a way appropriate to the audience as well as to the content itself. It must be both accessible to readers and focused on some main point or theme. Noonan focuses on the drama of the operation. He was clearly struck by the incongruity between the intimate action of probing a human brain and the impersonal way this probing was done. Profile writers often use such an incongruity—as the theme of their profile.

Noonan uses narration to structure his profile. Instead of just telling us how brain surgery is done, he shows us the procedures firsthand. He presents us with an actual patient ("belly up under the bright lights"), and takes us through an actual operation—preparing the patient and the surgical instruments, drilling the skull, searching through the brain for the tumor.

One way Noonan creates tension and drama is by varying the pace of the narrative, slowing it here and quickening it there, closing in and moving back, telescoping or collapsing time as fits his purpose. Take a close look at the craniectomy (paragraphs 7–9) to see how Noonan varies the pace. He begins dramatically by quoting Dr. Steinberger ("Drill the hell out of it"), then sets the stage by telling us that the scalp has already been retracted and the skull exposed. With a series of active present-tense verbs and present participles, Noonan re-creates the actual drilling for us. But he only shows us the drilling of one hole; he summarizes the drilling of the other three. He also interrupts the narrative to reflect on his own thoughts and feelings. When he returns to narrating, we see Dr. Solomon calmly turning the perforator as "more shavings hit the floor" and hear the snapping and crunching of bone as an opening is made between the holes.

Not only does Noonan pace his narrative for dramatic effect, but he also paces the flow of information. Readers are willing to be informed by a profile, but they are not prepared to find information presented as though they were reading an encyclopedia. By controlling the amount of information he presents, Noonan maintains a brisk pace that keeps his readers informed as well as entertained. He inserts bits of information into the narrative, as in paragraph 8 when he tells us that a hand drill is used after the power drill and how a craniotomy differs from a craniectomy. Sometimes the information takes only a second to read and is subordinated in a clause or a brief sentence. At other times, it seems to suspend the narrative altogether, as when Noonan explains the idea of a sterile field and describes the scrubbing-up process in paragraph 6.

Defining concisely and explaining clearly are essential to success in writing profiles. However, the definitions and explanations must not divert readers' attention for too long a time from the details of a scene or the drama of an activity. If you profile a technical or little-known specialty, you will need to define terms, tools, and procedures likely to be unfamiliar to your readers.

For a discussion of strategies of defining, see Chapter 15.

By examining Noonan's sentences closely, you can learn much that will help you in your own profile writing. For example, he occasionally opens sentences with modifying phrases called participial phrases:

> "*Using a special marker,* Steinberger draws the pattern of the opening on the patient's head in blue." (paragraph 5)
>
> "*Sitting side by side, looking through the scope into the head,* Steinberger and Stein go looking for the tumor." (paragraph 14)
>
> "*Once robed and gloved,* the doctors are considered sterile from the neck to the waist and from the hands up the arms to just below the shoulders." (paragraph 6)
>
> "*Directed by Dr. Stein,* Abe Steinberger is going after a large tumor compressing the brain stem. . . ." (paragraph 2)

As sentence openers, participial phrases are efficient and readable. They reduce the number of separate sentences needed, provide pleasing variety in sentence patterns, and are easy for readers to follow.

■   ■   ■

Brian Cable wrote the following selection when he was a college freshman. Profiling a mortuary, Cable treats it with both seriousness and humor. He lets readers know his feelings as he presents information about the mortuary and the people working there. Notice in particular the way Cable uses his visit to the mortuary as an occasion to reflect on death.

THE LAST STOP
BRIAN CABLE

Let us endeavor so to live that when we come to die even the undertaker will be sorry. —Mark Twain

Death is a subject largely ignored by the living. We don't discuss it much, not as children (when Grandpa dies, he is said to be "going away"), not as adults, not even as senior citizens. Throughout our lives, death remains intensely private. The death of a loved one can be very painful, partly because of the sense of loss, but also because someone else's mortality reminds us all too vividly of our own. 1

Thus did I notice more than a few people avert their eyes as they walked past the dusty-pink building that houses the Goodbody Mortuaries. It looked a bit like a church—tall, with gothic arches and stained glass—and somewhat like an apartment complex—low, with many windows stamped out of red brick. 2

It wasn't at all what I had expected. I thought it would be more like Forest Lawn, serene with lush green lawns and meticulously groomed gardens, a place set apart from the hustle of day-to-day life. Here instead was an odd pink structure set in the middle of a business district. On top of the Goodbody Mortuaries sign was a large electric clock. What the hell, I thought, mortuaries are concerned with time too. 3

I was apprehensive as I climbed the stone steps to the entrance. I feared rejection or, worse, an invitation to come and stay. The door was massive, yet it swung open easily on well-oiled hinges. "Come in," said the sign. "We're always open." Inside was a cool and quiet reception room. Curtains were drawn against the outside glare, cutting the light down to a soft glow. 4

I found the funeral director in the main lobby, adjacent to the reception room. Like most people, I had preconceptions about what an undertaker looked like. Mr. Deaver fulfilled my expectations entirely. Tall and thin, he even had beady eyes and a bony face. A low, slanted forehead gave way to a beaked nose. His skin, scrubbed of all color, contrasted sharply with his jet black hair. He was wearing a starched white shirt, grey pants, and black shoes. Indeed, he looked like death on two legs. 5

He proved an amiable sort, however, and was easy to talk to. As funeral director, Mr. Deaver ("call me Howard") was responsible for a wide range of services. Goodbody Mortuaries, upon notification of someone's death, will remove the remains from the hospital or home. They then prepare the body for viewing, whereupon features distorted by illness or accident are restored to their natural condition. The body is embalmed and then placed in a casket selected by the family of the deceased. Services are held in one of three chapels at the mortuary, and afterward the casket is placed in a "visitation room," where family and friends can pay their last respects. Goodbody also makes arrangements for the purchase of a burial site and transports the body there for burial. 6

All this information Howard related in a well-practiced, professional manner. It was obvious he was used to explaining the specifics of his profession. We sat alone in the lobby. His desk was bone clean, no pencils or paper, nothing—just a telephone. He did all his paperwork at home; as it turned out, he and his wife lived right upstairs. The phone rang. As he listened, he bit his lips and squeezed his adam's apple somewhat nervously. 7

"I think we'll be able to get him in by Friday. No, no, the family wants him cremated." 8

His tone was that of a broker conferring on the Dow Jones. Directly behind him 9
was a sign announcing ''Visa and Mastercharge Welcome Here.'' It was tacked to
the wall, right next to a crucifix.

''Some people have the idea that we are bereavement specialists, that we can 10
handle the emotional problems which follow a death: Only a trained therapist can
do that. We provide services for the dead, not counseling for the living.''

Physical comfort was the one thing they did provide for the living. The lobby was 11
modestly but comfortably furnished. There were several couches, in colors ranging
from earth brown to pastel blue, and a coffee table in front of each one. On one
table lay some magazines and a vase of flowers. Another supported an aquarium.
Paintings of pastoral scenes hung on every wall. The lobby looked more or less like
that of an old hotel. Nothing seemed to match, but it had a homey, lived-in look.

''The last time the Goodbodies decorated was in '59, I believe. It still makes 12
people feel welcome.''

And so ''Goodbody'' was not a name made up to attract customers, but the 13
owners' family name. The Goodbody family started the business way back in 1915.
Today, they do over five hundred services a year.

''We're in *Ripley's Believe It or Not*, along with another funeral home whose 14
owners' names are Baggit and Sackit,'' Howard told me, without cracking a smile.

I followed him through an arched doorway into a chapel which smelled musty 15
and old. The only illumination came from sunlight filtered through a stained glass
ceiling. Ahead of us lay a casket. I could see that it contained a man dressed in a
black suit. Wooden benches ran on either side of an aisle that led to the body. I got
no closer. From the red roses across the dead man's chest, it was apparent that
services had already been held.

''It was a large service,'' remarked Howard. ''Look at that casket—a beautiful 16
work of craftsmanship.''

I guess it was. Death may be the great leveler, but one's coffin quickly reestab- 17
lishes one's status.

We passed into a bright, fluorescent-lit ''display room.'' Inside were thirty coffins, 18
lids open, patiently awaiting inspection. Like new cars on the showroom floor, they
gleamed with high-glossy finishes.

''We have models for every price range.''   19

Indeed, there was a wide variety. They came in all colors and various materials. 20
Some were little more than cloth-covered cardboard boxes, other were made of
wood, and a few were made of steel, copper, or bronze. Prices started at $400 and
averaged about $1,800. Howard motioned toward the center of the room: ''The
top of the line.''

This was a solid bronze casket, its seams electronically welded to resist corrosion. 21
Moisture-proof and air-tight, it could be hermetically sealed off from all outside
elements. Its handles were plated with 14kt. gold. The price: a cool $5,000.

A proper funeral remains a measure of respect for the deceased. But it is ex- 22
pensive. In the United States the amount spent annually on funerals is about two
billion dollars. Among ceremonial expenditures, funerals are second only to wed-
dings. As a result, practices are changing. Howard has been in this business for forty
years. He remembers a time when everyone was buried. Nowadays, with burials
costing $2,000 a shot, people often opt instead for cremation—as Howard put it,

"a cheap, quick, and easy means of disposal." In some areas of the country, the cremation rate is now over 60 percent. Observing this trend, one might wonder whether burials are becoming obsolete. Do burials serve an important role in society?

For Tim, Goodbody's licensed mortician, the answer is very definitely yes. Burials 23 will remain in common practice, according to the slender embalmer with the disarming smile, because they allow family and friends to view the deceased. Painful as it may be, such an experience brings home the finality of death. "Something deep within us demands a confrontation with death," Tim explained. "A last look assures us that the person we loved is, indeed, gone forever."

Apparently, we also need to be assured that the body will be laid to rest in 24 comfort and peace. The average casket, with its inner-spring mattress and pleated satin lining, is surprisingly roomy and luxurious. Perhaps such an air of comfort makes it easier for the family to give up their loved one. In addition, the burial site fixes the deceased in the survivors' memory, like a new address. Cremation provides none of these comforts.

Tim started out as a clerk in a funeral home, but then studied to become a 25 mortician. "It was a profession I could live with," he told me with a sly grin. Mortuary science might be described as a cross between pre-med and cosmetology, with courses in anatomy and embalming as well as in restorative art.

Tim let me see the preparation, or embalming, room, a white-walled chamber 26 about the size of an operating room. Against the wall was a large sink with elbow taps and a draining board. In the center of the room stood a table with equipment for preparing the arterial embalming fluid, which consists primarily of formaldehyde, a preservative, and phenol, a disinfectant. This mixture sanitizes and also gives better color to the skin. Facial features can then be "set" to achieve a restful expression. Missing eyes, ears, and even noses can be replaced.

I asked Tim if his job ever depressed him. He bridled at the question: "No, it 27 doesn't depress me at all. I do what I can for people, and take satisfaction in enabling relatives to see their loved ones as they were in life." He said that he felt people were becoming more aware of the public service his profession provides. Grade-school classes now visit funeral homes as often as they do police stations and museums. The mortician is no longer regarded as a minister of death.

Before leaving, I wanted to see a body up close. I thought I could be indifferent 28 after all I had seen and heard, but I wasn't sure. Cautiously, I reached out and touched the skin. It felt cold and firm, not unlike clay. As I walked out, I felt glad to have satisfied my curiosity about dead bodies, but all too happy to let someone else handle them.

For Discussion   "Death," Cable announces in the opening sentence, "is a subject largely ignored by the living. We don't discuss it much, not as children (when Grandpa dies, he is said to be 'going away'), not as adults, not even as senior citizens." Discuss the various ways that your families deal with death. Is the subject of death "largely ignored"? What euphemisms (like "going away") does your family use?

For Analysis   1.   How does the opening quotation from Mark Twain shape your expectations as a reader?

2.   In this essay, Cable plays with two stereotypical preconceptions: the vulturelike undertaker (paragraphs 5 and 6) and the Forest Lawn–style funeral home (paragraph 3). How does the information presented in the rest of the profile confirm or deny these preconceptions?

3.   Look again at paragraphs 18–21, where Cable describes the various caskets. What impression does this description give? How does it contrast with the preceding scene in the chapel (paragraph 15)?

4.   The Writer at Work section on pp. 130–34 presents Cable's interview notes and the preliminary report he prepared from them. Read over these materials, and comment on how Cable integrated quotations from the interviews and sensory details from his observations into his essay. What does his choice of quotations reveal about his impression of Howard and Tim? What does his use of sensory details tell you about the effect the mortuary had on him? How do the quotations and sensory details shape your reaction to the essay?

For Your Own Writing

Think of a place or activity about which you have strong preconceptions, and imagine writing a profile about it. What would you choose to tell about? What preconceptions do you hold? How might you use your preconceptions to capture readers' attention?

Commentary

Cable puts himself into the scene that he profiles. We accompany him on his tour of the mortuary, listen in on the interviews with Howard and Tim, and are made privy to his reflections—the feelings and thoughts he has about what he is seeing and hearing. In each of the other profiles in this chapter, the writer remains outside the scene, a more-or-less disembodied eye through which we see the people and place. Whereas the pronoun *I* (or *we* in Erhlich's case) is rare or nonexistent in the other profiles, it is an essential part of Cable's rhetorical strategy. Ehrlich uses the first-person pronoun basically to orient readers to the scene. The *New Yorker* writer and Noonan both use the second-person pronoun *you* sparingly for the same purpose. But Cable uses *I* repeatedly. Similarly, he uses shared preconceptions to establish common ground with his readers, conveying the theme by contrasting these expectations with the discoveries he makes during his visits to the mortuary.

PURPOSE AND AUDIENCE

A profile writer's primary purpose is to inform readers. Whether profiling people (a restaurant owner), places (a mortuary), or activities (saddle bronc riding or brain surgery), the writer must meet readers' expectations of interesting material presented in a lively and entertaining manner. Although a reader might learn as much about saddle bronc riding from an encyclopedia entry as from Ehrlich's profile, reading the profile is sure to be more enjoyable.

Readers of profiles expect to be surprised by such unusual subjects. If the subject is a familiar one, they expect it to be presented from an unusual perspective. When writing a profile, you will have an immediate advantage if your subject is a place, activity, or person that is likely to surprise and intrigue your readers. Even if it is very familiar, however, you can still delight your readers by presenting it in a way they had never before considered.

A profile writer has one further concern: to be sensitive to readers' knowledge of a subject. Since readers must imagine the subject profiled and understand the new information offered about it, the writer must take extreme care in assessing what readers are likely to have seen and to know. For a profile about saddle bronc riding, the decisions of a writer whose readers have never seen a rodeo will be very different from those of a writer whose readers have often sat near the chutes in rodeo arenas watching the sport. Given Ehrlich's care in presenting specific action and vivid details, she appears to be addressing readers who have never before seen a rodeo.

Profile writers must also consider whether readers know all the terms they want to use. Since profiles involve information, they inevitably require definitions and illustrations. For example, Noonan carefully defines many terms: *craniectomy, craniotomy, supracerebellar infratentorial approach, Leksell rongeurs, dura, cerebellum*, and *brainstem glioma*. However, he does not bother to define other technical terms like *angiogram* and *meningioma*. Since profile writers are not writing technical manuals or textbooks, they can choose to define only those terms necessary for readers to follow what is going on. Some concepts or activities will require extended illustrations, as when Noonan describes in detail what is involved in "opening the brain" or scrubbing up before entering the operating room.

For a discussion of sentence-definition strategies, see pp. 444–45.

BASIC FEATURES OF PROFILES

Successful profiles have intriguing, well-focused subjects; center on a controlling theme; are presented vividly; and proceed at an informative, entertaining pace.

An Intriguing, Well-focused Subject

The subject of a profile is typically a specific person, place, or activity. In this chapter, the *New Yorker* writer shows us Albert Yeganeh, soup cook extraordinaire; Brian Cable describes a particular place, the Goodbody Mortuary; David Noonan and Gretel Ehrlich both present activities, brain surgery and saddle bronc riding. Although they focus on a person, place, or activity, all of these profiles contain all three elements: certain people performing a certain activity at a particular place.

Skilled profile writers make even the most mundane subjects interesting by presenting them in a new light. They may simply take a close look at a subject usually taken for granted, as Cable does when he examines a mortuary. Or they may surprise readers with a subject they had never thought of, as the *New Yorker* writer does in portraying a fanatical soup cook. Whatever they examine, they bring attention to the uniqueness of the subject, showing what is remarkable about it.

A Controlling Theme

Profiles thus nearly always center on a theme that reveals something surprising, either in the subject or in the writer's response to it. Noonan, for instance, points out a somewhat startling discrepancy between the impersonality of neurosurgery and the extraordinary intimacy of such an operation. The *New Yorker* writer contrasts Yeganeh's perfectionism with our preconceptions about fast-food restaurants. Cable's thematic focus is his personal realization about how Americans seem to capitalize on death almost as a way of coping with it. Ehrlich presents rodeo as an expression of Western life and values. This focus, or controlling theme, makes profiles something more than mere descriptive exercises or writeups of observations. Profiles interpret their subjects, and they reveal the writer's attitude and point of view. The theme provides the point, a reason for the writer to be writing to particular readers. Along with awareness of purpose and readers, this theme guides all the writer's decisions about how to organize the material and present it vividly and memorably.

A Vivid Presentation

Profiles particularize their subjects—one night at the rodeo, an actual operation, a fast-talking restaurant owner, the Goodbody Mortuary—rather than generalize about them. Because profile writers are interested more in presenting individual cases than in making generalizations, they present their subjects vividly and in detail.

Successful profile writers master the writing strategies of description, often using sensory imagery and figurative language. The profiles in this chapter, for example, evoke the senses of sight (a "dusty-pink building" that "looked a bit like a church—tall, with gothic arches and stained glass—and somewhat like an apartment complex—low, with many windows stamped out of red brick"); touch ("a thin, tough, leathery membrane"); smell ("a faint odor of burning bone"); and hearing ("The chute gate swings open releasing a flood—not of water, but of flesh, groans, legs kicking"). Similes ("Working like a demon alchemist") and metaphors ("Rodeo is the wild child of ranch work") also abound.

For more on using sensory description, see pp. 434–37.

Profile writers often describe people in graphic detail ("The patient lies naked and unconscious in the center of the cool, tiled room. His head is shaved, his eyes and nose taped shut. His mouth bulges with the respirator that is breathing for him"). They reveal personal habits and characteristic poses ("As he listened, he bit his lips and squeezed his adam's apple some-what nervously"). They also use dialogue to suggest speakers' characters:

> He spread his arms and added, "This place is the only one like it in . . . in . . . the whole earth! One day, I hope to learn something from the other places, but so far I haven't."

Narration may be even more important, for it is used by many writers to organize their essays. Some profiles even read like stories, with tension and suspense building to a dramatic climax. Noonan's essay has two climaxes, first when the brain is exposed and second when the tumor is discovered. The climax of Cable's narrative occurs at the end when he touches a corpse. Both writers pace their narratives carefully to develop and sustain tension and drama.

The narrative strategies of conflict and pace are discussed on pp. 420–25.

An Informative, Entertaining Pace

Successful profile writers know that if they are to keep their readers' attention, they must entertain as well as inform. It is for this reason that they tell their stories dramatically and describe people and places vividly. They also pace the flow of information carefully.

Profiles present a great deal of factual detail about their subject. Noonan, for instance, tells us about the brain's parts (dura, cerebellum, brainstem), about surgical procedures (preparation of the patient and the surgeons, the difference between craniectomy and craniotomy), as well as about the attitudes of surgeons toward brain surgery. But this information is woven into the essay in bits and pieces—conveyed in dialogue, interspersed throughout the narrative, given in the description—rather than presented in one large chunk.

Parceling out information in this way increases the chances of comprehension because it allows readers to master one part of the information before going on to the next. Perhaps even more important, pacing the information injects a degree of surprise and thus makes readers curious to know what will come next. Varying the pacing of information may, in fact, help keep readers reading.

Guide to Writing

THE WRITING ASSIGNMENT

Write an essay about an intriguing person, place, or activity in your community. With the advice of your instructor, you may have several options in completing this assignment: a brief profile of an event, place, or activity observed once or twice; a brief profile of an individual based on one or two interviews; or a longer, more fully developed profile of a person, place, or activity based on several observational visits and interviews. Observe your subject closely, and then present what you have learned in a way that both informs and entertains readers.

INVENTION AND RESEARCH

Preparing to write a profile involves several activities: choosing a subject, exploring your preconceptions of it, planning your project, posing some preliminary questions, and finding a theme or focus for your profile.

Choosing a Subject

When you choose a subject, you consider various possibilities, select a promising one, and check that particular subject's accessibility.

Listing Possibilities. You may already have a subject in mind for your profile. But it might be advisable to take a few minutes now to consider some other possible subjects. The more possibilities you consider, the more confident you can be about your choice.

Before you list possible subjects, consider realistically the time you have available and the scope of the observing and interviewing you will be able to accomplish. Whether you have a week to plan and write up one observational visit or interview or a month to develop a full profile will determine what kinds of subjects will be appropriate for you. Consult with your instructor if you need help defining the scope of your writing project.

Following are several ideas you might use as starting points for your list of subjects. Try to extend your list to ten or twelve possibilities. Consider every subject you can think of, even the unlikeliest. Begin your list with subjects you are already familiar with but would like to know more about. Then add unfamiliar subjects—people or places or activities you find fascinating or bizarre or perhaps even forbidding. Take risks. People like to read about the unusual.

People

- Anyone with an unusual job or hobby—a private detective, chimney-sweep, beekeeper, classic-car owner, dog trainer
- A beauty contestant or weight-lifting contestant
- A television celebrity, newspaper editor, radio disc jockey
- A prominent local personality—parent of the year, labor organizer, political activist, consumer advocate
- A campus personality—ombudsman, coach, distinguished teacher

Places

- A weight-reduction clinic, tanning salon, body-building gym, health spa
- Small claims court, juvenile court, consumer fraud office
- A used-car lot, old movie house, used-book store, antique shop, auction hall, flower show, farmers' market
- A hospital emergency room, hospice, birthing center, psychiatric unit
- The campus dining commons; a local diner; the oldest, biggest, quickest, or most expensive restaurant in town
- The campus radio station, computer center, agricultural research facility, student center, faculty club, museum, newspaper office, health center
- A book, newspaper, or magazine publisher; florist shop, nursery, or greenhouse; pawnshop; boatyard; automobile restorer or wrecking yard
- A recycling center; fire station; airport control tower; theater, opera, or symphony office; refugee center; orphanage; convent or monastery

Activities

- A citizens' volunteer program—voter registration, public television auction, meals-on-wheels project
- An unusual sports event—a marathon, frisbee tournament, chess match
- Folk dancing, roller skating, rock climbing, poetry reading

Making a Choice.   Look over your list and select a subject that you find personally fascinating, something you want to know more about. It should also be a subject that you think you can make interesting to readers.

If you choose a subject with which you are familiar, it is a good idea to study it in an unfamiliar setting. Let us say you are a rock climber and decide to profile rock climbing. Do not rely on your own knowledge and authority. Seek out other rock-climbing enthusiasts and even some critics of the sport to get a more objective view of the subject. When research is predictable for the writer, it will probably lead to dull and uninspired writing. Most writers report greatest satisfaction and best results when they profile unfamiliar activities.

Stop now to focus your thoughts. In a sentence or two, identify the subject you have chosen and explain why you think it is a good choice for you and for your readers.

Checking on Accessibility.   Having chosen a subject, make sure you will be able to observe it. Find out who might be able to give you information, and make some preliminary phone calls. Explain that you need information for a school research project. You will be surprised how helpful people can be when they have the time. If you are unable to contact knowledgeable people or get access to the place you need to observe, you may not be able to write on this subject. Therefore, try to make initial contact now.

For Group Inquiry

You might find it useful to get together in a group with two or three other students and run your chosen topics by one another. Assess the group's interest in the person, place, or activity you wish to write about, and invite their advice about whether it sounds promising. Does it seem likely to lead to a profile they would care to read? Your purpose is to decide whether you have chosen a good subject to write about and thus to be able to proceed confidently to develop your profile.

Exploring Your Preconceptions

Before you begin observing or interviewing, you should explore your initial thoughts and feelings about your subject. Take about ten minutes to jot down your thoughts, using the following questions as a guide:

- What do I already know about this subject?
  How would I define or describe it?
  What are its chief qualities or parts?
  Do I associate anyone or anything with it?
  What is its purpose or function?
  How does it compare with other, similar subjects?
- What is my attitude toward this subject?
  Why do I consider this subject intriguing? What about it interests me?
  Do I like it? Respect it? Understand it?
- What do I expect to discover as I observe the subject?
  What would surprise me about it?
  Do I anticipate any troubling discoveries?
  Might I find anything amusing in it?
  Are there likely to be any notable incongruities—for example, between what the people are trying to do and what they are actually doing?
- How do my preconceptions compare with other people's?
  What makes my point of view unique?
  What attitudes about this subject do I share with other people?

Planning Your Project

Whatever the scope of your project—single observation, interview with follow-up, or repeated observations and interviews—you will want to get the most out of your time with your subject. Chapter 19 offers guidance in observing and interviewing, and will give you an idea of how much time will be required to plan, carry out, and write up an observation or interview.

Take time now to consult Chapter 19 and to write out a tentative research schedule. Figure out first the amount of time you have to complete your essay; then decide what visits you will need to make, whom you will need to interview, and what library work you might want to do. Estimate the time necessary for each. You might put your plan on a chart like the following one:

Date	Time Needed	Purpose	Preparation
10/23	1 hour	observe	bring map and directions, pad of paper
10/25	1½ hour	library research	bring reference, notebook, change for copy machine
10/26	45 minutes	interview	read brochure and prepare questions
10/30	2 hours	observe and interview	prepare questions, confirm appointment, bring pad

This plan will probably need to be modified once you actually begin work, but it is a good idea to keep some sort of schedule in writing.

If you are developing a full profile, your first goal is to get your bearings. Some writers begin by observing; others start with an interview. Many read up on the subject before doing anything else, to get a sense of its main elements. You may also want to read about other subjects similar to the one you have chosen. Save your notes.

Posing Some Preliminary Questions

Before launching your observations and interviews, try writing some questions for which you would like to find answers. These questions will provide orientation and focus for your visits. As you work, you will find answers to many of these questions. Add to this list as new questions occur to you, and delete any that come to seem irrelevant.

Each subject invites its own special questions, and every writer has his or her own particular concerns. Following are some questions one student posed for a profile of a campus rape-crisis center:

- Is rape a special problem on college campuses? On this campus? Why?
- Are most of the rapes on campus committed by unknown assailants? Or are they date rapes, committed by "friends"?
- Who provides information about the occurrence of rape on the campus, and how is this information made public?
- How is the center funded and operated?
- How well qualified are the people working in the center? What do they actually do? Do they counsel victims? Teach women how to defend themselves?
- How does the center publicize its services or contact rape victims to offer assistance? How many women actually use it?
- Do the police do anything to prevent rape on campus?

Finding a Tentative Theme

When you have completed your visits, you must decide on a tentative theme for your profile. To help you review your project, complete the following activities, both at one sitting, one right after the other.

Write a Narrative of Your Visits and Research.   Write nonstop for about fifteen minutes, telling the story of your project—what you did first, what happened next, where you went, who you met. Do not consult your notes, but try to include everything you recall. Do not worry if details are omitted or events are out of order.

Write an Analysis of Your Project.   Without reading over your narrative, immediately begin writing an analysis. Write nonstop for about ten minutes, trying to answer as many of the following questions as you can:

- What was the most important thing I learned? Why does it seem so important?
- If I could find out the answer to one more question, what would be the question? Why is this question so crucial?
- Were there any incongruities, surprises, or contradictions? If so, what do they tell me about the subject?
- What is the mood of the place? How do people seem to feel there?
- What is most memorable about the people I observed and talked to?
- What visual or other sensory impression is most memorable about the place I observed? What experiences can I associate with this sensory impression?
- What is most striking about the activity I observed? What is likely to be most surprising or interesting to readers?
- What about this subject says something larger about our lives and times?
- What generalization or judgment do these personal reactions lead me to?

Take a few moments to reflect on what you have discovered. Then, in a sentence or two, state what now seems to you to be a promising theme or focus for your profile. What do you want readers to see as they read your profile? What do you want them to remember later about your subject?

PLANNING AND DRAFTING

As preparation for drafting, you need to review your invention or research notes to see what you have, set goals for yourself, and organize your profile.

Seeing What You Have

You may now have a great deal of material—notes from visits, interviews, or reading; some idea of your preconceptions; a list of questions, perhaps with some answers; and both a narrative and an analysis of your project. You should also have a tentative theme or focus. Read over to see what you have. Your aim is to digest all the information you have gathered; to pick out the promising facts, details, anecdotes, and quotation; and to see how well your tentative theme focuses all the material you plan to include in the essay.

As you sort through your material, look at it in some of the following ways. They may help you clarify your theme or find an even better one.

- Contrast your preconceptions with your findings.
- Juxtapose your preliminary questions against answers you have found.
- Compare what different people say about the subject.
- Look for discrepancies between people's words and their behavior.
- Compare your reactions with those of the people directly involved.
- Consider the place's appearance in light of the activity that occurs there.
- Juxtapose bits of information, looking for contrasts or incongruities.
- Examine your subject as an anthropologist or archaeologist might, looking for artifacts that would explain its role in the society at large.

Setting Goals

The following questions will help to establish goals for your first draft. Consider each one briefly now, and return to them as necessary as you draft.

Your Readers

- Are my readers likely to be at all familiar with my subject? If not, what details do I need to provide to help them visualize it?
- If my readers are familiar with my subject, how can I present it to them in a new and engaging way? What information do I have that is likely to be new or entertaining to them?
- Is there anything I can say about this subject that will lead readers to reflect on their own lives and values?

The Beginning

The opening is especially important role in a profile. Because readers are unlikely to have any particular reason to read a profile, the writer must arouse their curiosity and interest. The best beginnings are surprising and specific, the worst are abstract. Here are some strategies you might consider:

- Should I open with a striking image or vivid scene, as Noonan does?
- Should I begin with a statement of the central theme, as Ehrlich does?
- Should I start with an intriguing epigraph, as Cable does?
- Do I have an amazing fact that would catch readers' attention?
- Is there an anecdote that captures the essence of the subject?
- Should I open with a question, perhaps one answered in the essay?
- Do I have any dialogue that would serve as a good beginning?

The General Organization

Profile writers basically use two methods of organizing their material: they arrange it either chronologically in a narrative or analogically by grouping related materials.

If I organize my material chronologically, as Noonan does:

- How can I make the narrative dramatic and intense?
- What information should I integrate into the narrative?
- What information will I need to suspend the narrative for? How can I minimize the disruption and resume the dramatic pace?
- What information should I quote and what should I summarize?
- How can I set the scene vividly?

If I organize my material analogically, as the New Yorker *writer does:*

- How can I group my material in a way that best presents the subject, informs readers, and yet holds their interest?
- How can I sequence the groupings to bring out comparisons, similarities, contrasts, or incongruities in my material?
- Can readers make connections between groupings, or do I need clearer transitions?
- At what point(s) should I describe the subject? How can I make any descriptions true and vivid?

The Ending

- Should I try to frame the essay by repeating an image or phrase from the beginning or by completing an action begun earlier in the profile?
- Would it be good to end by restating the theme, as Ehrlich does?
- Should I end with a telling image, anecdote, or bit of dialogue?

Outlining

If you plan to arrange your material chronologically, plot the key events on a timeline. Star the event you consider the high point or climax.

If you plan to arrange your material analogically, by grouping related information, you might use clustering or outlining strategies to get a graphic view of the interconnections. Both these strategies will help you to divide and group your information. After classifying your material, you might list the items in the order in which you plan to present them.

For more on clustering, see p. 383.

The following outlines illustrate the differences between chronological and analogical organization. The first is a *chronological outline* of Ehrlich's profile on saddle bronc riding:

horsemanship and partnerships: what ranching is all about

sit behind the chutes

cowboys prepare to ride

one complete ride

other riders named

walk across the street to hotel

observe scene in coffee shop

the point of rodeo

If Ehrlich had wanted to emphasize the scene in the arena, the variety of activities, and the actors and equipment—rather than the drama of individual events—she might have made observations that could be grouped as follows in an *analogical outline*:

one complete ride (an opening for dramatic effect, but narrated more briefly than in the actual profile)

panorama of rodeo arena

cowboys (dress, manner, names, hometowns)

chute boss, stock contractors, announcer, clown

saddle bronc riding (animals, equipment, rules)

calf roping (animals, equipment, rules)

steer wrestling (animals, equipment, rules)

bull riding (animals, equipment, rules)

social scene at hotel

point of rodeo

The organization you choose will reflect the possibilities in your material and in your theme, purpose, and readers. At this point, your decision must be tentative. As you begin drafting, you will almost certainly discover new ways of organizing your material. Once you have a first draft, you and others may see ways to reorganize the material to achieve your purpose better with your particular readers.

Drafting

Start drafting your essay. By now, of course, you are not starting from scratch. If you have followed this guide, you will already have done a great deal of invention and planning. Some of this material may even fit right into your draft with little alteration.

Be careful not to get stuck trying to write the perfect beginning. Start anywhere. The time to perfect your beginning is at the revision stage.

Once you are actually writing, try not to be interrupted. Should you find you need to make additional visits for further observations and interviews, do so after you have completed a first draft.

Before actually beginning to write, you might look at the general advice on drafting on pp. 9–11.

GETTING CRITICAL COMMENTS

Now is the time for your draft to get a good critical reading. Your instructor may arrange such a reading as part of your course work; otherwise, you can ask a classmate, friend, or family member to read it over. If your campus has a writing center, you might ask a tutor there to read and comment on your draft. The guidelines that follow can be used by *anyone* reviewing a profile. (If you are unable to have someone else read over your draft, turn ahead to the Revision section on pp. 127–29, which provides guidelines for reading your own draft critically.)

In order to provide focused, helpful comments, any readers must know your intended purpose and audience. Take time now to reconsider these two elements, jotting down the following information at the top of your draft.

> *Purpose.* What impression of your subject do you want to give readers?
>
> *Audience.* Who are your readers? What do you assume they already know about your subject? How have you planned to engage and hold their interest?

Reading with a Critical Eye

Reading a draft critically means reading it more than once, first to get a general impression and then to analyze its basic features.

Reading for a First Impression.   Read quickly through the draft first to get an overall impression. As you read, try to notice passages that contribute to your first impression. A good way of highlighting noteworthy features of the writing is to use the pointings system. Pointings are quick and easy to do, and they can provide helpful information for revision.

Pointings

- Draw a straight line under any words or details that impress you as especially effective: strong verbs, memorable phrases, striking images.
- Draw a wavy line under any words or images that seem flat, stale, or vague. Also put the wavy line under any words or phrases that you consider unnecessary or repetitious.
- Look for pairs or groups of sentences that you think should be combined. Put brackets [ ] around these sentences.
- Look for sentences that are garbled, overloaded, or awkward. Put parentheses ( ) around these sentences. Mark any sentence that seems even slightly questionable; don't worry now about whether you're certain about your judgment. Point to anything that you, as one reader, had even the slightest hesitation understanding.

After you've finished reading the draft, note down your immediate reaction. What do you consider most interesting in the essay? State the theme, and indicate whether or not it is well focused. Is the profile adequately informative? Can you see any holes or gaps? Did it hold your interest?

*See pp. 114–16 to
review the basic features.*
Reading to Analyze.   Read now to focus on the basic features of a profile.

Is the Subject Intriguing and Well-focused?

Indicate whether the profile contains enough details to identify the subject as a specific person, place, or event. Comment on the effectiveness of descriptive details used to show the subject's uniqueness. Point out any places where vague or general statements fail to hold your interest in the subject.

Is the Controlling Theme Clear?

Profiles must have a controlling theme, an angle or point that may be explicit (stated in the essay) or implicit (suggested by the details). Often, the theme involves some unexpected element or incongruity, either in the subject itself or in the writer's response to it. Identify what you think the theme may be; then look for information or description that may distract readers from it. Suggest ways to strengthen the thematic focus, perhaps through additional dialogue, visual details, or comparisons and contrasts.

Is the Presentation Vivid?

Profiles must present their subjects in specific details rather than general statements. Look at the description of objects, scenes, and people. Point out vivid and specific descriptions as well as places where readers would need further naming and detailing in order to imagine what the writer is talking about. Also point out any seemingly unnecessary or exaggerated description.

Consider the use of specific narrative action—moving, gesturing, talking. Suggest ways to strengthen any sections of specific action, and point out any other places where it might be appropriate.

Is Information Presented in an Entertaining Way That Is Easy to Follow?

Profile readers expect to be informed as well as entertained, but they expect the information load to be manageable. Point out any places where you felt bogged down or overwhelmed with information or where information was not clearly presented or was inadequate. If necessary, look for ways to reduce or add information or to break up long blocks of information with description of scenes or people or narration of events.

Skim the essay for definitions, and indicate whether any seem unnecessary or unclear. Also point out any other terms that need defining.

Is the Organization Effective?

If the profile is organized chronologically, point out any places where the narrative seems to drag as well as any where it seems most dramatic and intense. Identify the climax or high point of the narrative.

If the profile is organized by grouping related material, look to see whether any grouping presents too little or too much material and whether groupings might be sequenced differently or connected more clearly.

Reread the *beginning*, and decide whether it is effective. Did it capture your attention? Is there any quotation, fact, or anecdote elsewhere in the draft that might make a better opening?

Look again at the *ending*. Indicate whether it leaves you waiting for more, if it seems too abrupt, or if it oversimplifies the material. Suggest another ending, possibly by moving a passage or quotation from elsewhere in the essay.

What Final Thoughts Do You Have?

What is the strongest part of this draft? What about the draft is most memorable? What in the draft is weak, most in need of further work?

REVISING AND EDITING

Following are some guidelines to help you identify problems in your own draft, and to revise and edit to solve them.

Identifying Problems

To identify problems in your draft, you need to read it objectively, analyze its basic features, and study any comments you've received from others.

Getting an Overview.   Consider the draft as a whole, trying to see it objectively. It may help to do so in two steps:

Reread. If at all possible, put the draft aside for a day or two before rereading it. When you do, start by considering your purpose. Then read the draft straight through, looking mainly for its basic message.

Outline. Make a scratch outline of the draft that identifies the stages of your presentation of your subject.

Charting a Plan for Revision.   A good way to start plotting out your revision course is with a two-column list like the one that follows. The left-hand column lists the basic features of profiles; the right-hand column lists any problems you or other readers identified with that feature.

Basic Features	*Problems to Solve*
Choice of subject	
Controlling theme	
Presentation of the subject	
Information flow	
Organization	

Analyzing Basic Features.   Turn now to the analysis questions on pp. 126–27. Analyze your draft following these guidelines, adding any specific problems to your chart of problems to solve.

Studying Critical Comments.   Review any comments you've received from other readers, and add to the chart any points that need attention. Try not to react too defensively to these comments; by letting you see how others respond to your draft, they provide invaluable information about both its possibilities and its problems.

Solving the Problems

Having identified problems in your draft, you now need to figure out solutions and to carry them out. Basically, you have three ways to turn: (1) review your observation or interview notes for other information and ideas; (2) do additional observations or interviews to answer questions you or other readers raised; and (3) look back at the readings in this chapter to see how other writers have solved similar problems. Following are some suggestions to get you started solving some of the problems common to profiles.

The Subject

- If the subject does not seem intriguing or remarkable, add specific descriptive details to help readers see why it is noteworthy.
- If any of your statements about your subject seem too general, revise them to focus on specific characteristics.

Controlling Theme

- If readers had difficulty describing the theme, clarify it. Try stating the theme more explicitly or eliminating any dialogue, description, anecdote, or factual detail that does not contribute to or that seems to contradict the point you are trying to make.
- If your readers suggested focusing on something different, decide whether another theme would be more appropriate. If so, rework your draft to make the new theme clear.

Presentation of the Subject

- If the subject does not seem vivid, add specific words and details so that readers can better imagine it. Look for places where you can include more sensory details—sights, sounds, smells, textures.

Information Flow

- If readers felt bogged down by information at any point, move, condense, or eliminate some of it. Put some of the information in phrases instead of separate sentences. Eliminate any unnecessary definitions.

■ If the readers could not understand something, add more information or definitions. Make sure these fit smoothly into your essay and do not interrupt readers' attention to your main points.

Organization

■ If your essay is organized chronologically and seems to drag or ramble, find the climax, or high point, and try to heighten the suspense leading up to that point. Add drama through specific narrative action, showing details of movements and gestures. Summarize activity to speed the story along.

■ If you organized analogically or topically and readers found the profile disorganized, try rearranging topics to see if another order makes more sense. Look at the outlines you have made to get ideas.

■ If the opening fails to engage readers' attention, consider alternatives. Think of questions you could open with, or look for an engaging image or dialogue later in the essay to move to the beginning. Go back to your observation or interview notes for other ideas.

■ If the ending seems weak, consider ending at an earlier point or moving something more striking to the end.

■ If at any point in your essay readers felt transitions between stages in the narrative or between ideas were confusing or too abrupt, add appropriate phrasing or revise sentences to make transitions clearer or smoother.

Editing and Proofreading   Although you may have already corrected some obvious errors, they were not your first priority in the revising you did up to this point. Now, however, you must find and correct any errors of mechanics, usage, punctuation, and spelling before preparing and submitting a final draft. When you have done this editing and produced the final copy, proofread and make corrections before turning in your essay.

LEARNING FROM YOUR OWN WRITING PROCESS

If you are asked to write about your experience writing this essay, begin by reviewing your invention and planning materials. Note how you came to select your subject and how you then defined your theme. Point out any special problems you encountered in gathering information.

Then reread your first draft. What major problems did you encounter in this draft, and how did you solve them? Look over any critical reviews of your draft, and then reread your revision. What worked well in the first draft, and what needed reworking? What changes did you make, and how do you feel about them now? What other changes would you still like to make?

A Writer at Work

THE INTERVIEW NOTES AND REPORT

Most profile writers take notes when interviewing people. Later they may summarize their notes in a short report. In this section you will see some of the interview notes and a report Brian Cable prepared for his profile of a mortuary, printed earlier in this chapter.

Cable toured the mortuary and conducted two interviews—with the funeral director and the mortician. Before each interview he wrote out a few questions at the top of a sheet of paper and then divided it into two columns; he then used the left-hand column for descriptive details and personal impressions, the right-hand column for the information he got directly from the person he was interviewing. Below are Cable's notes and report for his interview with the funeral director, Howard Deaver.

Cable used the questions as a guide for the interview and then took brief notes during it. He did not concern himself too much with note-taking because he planned to spend a half-hour directly afterward to complete his notes. He kept his attention fixed on Deaver, trying to keep the interview comfortable and conversational and noting down just enough to jog his memory and to catch anything especially quotable. The typescript of Cable's interview notes follows.

The Interview

QUESTIONS

1. How do families of deceased view the mortuary business?
2. How is the concept of death approached?
3. How did you get into this business?

DESCRIPTIVE DETAILS &
PERSONAL IMPRESSIONS   INFORMATION

weird looking   "Call me Howard"
tall   How things work: Notification, pick
long fingers   up body at home or hospital, prepare
big ears   for viewing, restore distorted fea-
low, sloping forehead   tures--accident or illness, embalm,
Like stereotype--   casket--family selects, chapel
skin colorless   services (3 in bldg.), visitation
                            room--pay respects, family &
                            friends.

                            Can't answer questions about death--
                            "Not bereavement specialists. Don't

DESCRIPTIVE DETAILS & PERSONAL IMPRESSIONS	INFORMATION
	handle emotional problems. Only a trained therapist can do that."
	"We provide services for dead, not counseling for the living." (great quote)
	Concept of death has changed in last 40 yrs (how long he's been in the business)
	Funeral cost $500-600, now $2000
plays with lips blinks plays with Adam's apple desk empty--phone, no paper or pen	Phone call (interruption) "I think we'll be able to get him in on Friday. No, no, the family wants him cremated." Ask about Neptune Society--cremation Cremation "Cheap, quick, easy means of disposal."
angry disdainful of the Neptune Soc.	Recent phenomenon. Neptune Society-- erroneous claim to be only one. "We've offered them since the be- ginning. It's only now it's come into vogue." Trend now back towards burial. Cremation still popular in sophis- ticated areas 60% in Marin and Florida
	Ask about paperwork--does it up- stairs, lives there with wife Nancy
musty, old stained glass sunlight filtered	Tour around (happy to show me around) Chapel--Large service just done, Italian.
man in black suit roses wooden benches	"Not a religious institution--A business." casket--"beautiful craftsmanship"-- admires, expensive
contrast brightness fluorescent lights plexiglass stands	Display room--caskets about 30 of them Loves to talk about caskets "models in every price range"

DESCRIPTIVE DETAILS &
PERSONAL IMPRESSIONS   INFORMATION

                         glossy (like cars in a showroom)
                         cardboard box, steel, copper, bronze
                         $400 up to $1800. Top of line:
                         bronze, electronically welded, no
                         corrosion--$5000

Cable's notes include many descriptive details of Deaver as well as of various rooms in the mortuary. Though most entries are short and sketchy, much of the language will find its way into the essay. In describing Deaver, for example, Cable notes he fits the stereotype of the cadaverous undertaker, a fact Cable will make much of in his essay.

He puts quotation marks around Deaver's actual words, some of them complete sentences, others only fragments. We will see how he fills these quotes in when he writes up the interview. In only a few instances does he take down more than he can use. Even though profile writers want good quotes, they should not quote things they can better put in their own words. Direct quotation has a dual function in a profile—both to provide information and to capture the mood or character of the person speaking.

As you can see, Deaver was not able to answer Cable's questions about the families of the deceased and their attitudes toward death or mortuaries. The gap between the questions and Deaver's responses led Cable to recognize some of his own misperceptions about mortuaries—namely, that they serve the living by helping them adjust to the death of their loved ones. This misperception becomes an important theme of his essay.

After filling in his notes following the interview, Cable took some time to reflect on what he had learned. Here are some of his thoughts:

I was surprised how much Deaver looked like the under-
takers in scary movies. Even though he couldn't answer
any of my questions, he was friendly enough. It's obviously a business for him (he loves to talk about caskets and to point out all their features, like a car
dealer kicking a tire). Best quote: "We offer services
to the dead, not counseling to the living." I have to
arrange an interview with the mortician.

Writing up an account of the interview a short time afterward helped Cable to fill in more details and to reflect further on what he had learned. His report shows him already beginning to organize the information he had gained from his interview with Deaver.

A Report   I. His physical appearance.
on the Interview   Tall, skinny with beady blue eyes embedded in his bony
                 face. I was shocked to see him. He looked like the under-

takers in scary movies. His skin was white and colorless, from lack of sunshine. He has a long nose and a low sloping forehead. He was wearing a clean white shirt. A most unusual man--have you ever seen those Ames Home Loan commercials? But he was friendly, and happy to talk to me. "Would I answer some questions? Sure."

II. What people want from a mortuary.

A. Well first of all, he couldn't answer my question as to how families cope with the loss of a loved one. "You'd have to talk to a psychologist about that," he said. He did tell me how the concept of death has changed over the last ten or so years.

B. He has been in the business for forty years. (forty years?!!?) One look at him and you'd be convinced he'd been there at least that long. He told me that in the old times everyone was buried. Embalmed, put in a casket, and paid final homage before being shipped underground forever and ever. Nowadays, many people choose to be cremated instead. Hence comes the success of the Neptune Society and those like it. They specialize in cremation. You can have your ashes dumped anywhere. "Not that we don't offer cremation services. We've offered them since the beginning," he added with a look of disdain. It's just that they've become so popular recently because they offer a "quick, easy, and efficient means of disposal." Cheap too--I think it is a reflection of a "no nonsense" society. The Neptune Society has become so successful because they claim to be the only ones to offer cremations as an alternative to expensive burial. "We've offered it all along. It's just only now come into vogue."

Sophisticated areas (I felt "progressive" would be more accurate) like Marin County have a cremation rate of over 60 percent. The phone rang. "Excuse me," he said. As he talked on the phone, I noticed how he played with his lips, pursing and squeezing them. He was blinking all the time too. Yet he wasn't a schitzo or anything like that. I meant to ask him how he got into this business, but I forgot. I did find out his name and title. Mr. Deaver, general manager of Goodbody Mortuaries (no kidding, that's the real name). He lived on the premises upstairs with his wife. I doubt if he ever left the place.

III. It's a business!

Some people have the idea that mortuaries offer counseling and peace of mind--a place where everyone is sympathetic and ready to offer advice. "In some mortuaries, this is true. But by and large this is a business. We offer services to the dead, not counseling to the living." I too had expected to feel an awestruck respect for the dead upon entering the building. I had also expected green lawns, ponds with ducks, fountains, flowers, peacefulness--you know, a "Forest Lawn" type deal. But it was only a tall, Catholic-looking building. "Mortuaries do not sell plots for burial," he was saying. "Cemeteries do that, after we embalm the body and select a casket. We're not a religious institution." He seemed hung up on caskets--though maybe he was just trying to impress upon me the differences between caskets. "Oh, they're very important. A good casket is a sign of respect. Sometimes if the family doesn't have enough money, we rent them a nice one. People pay for what they get just like any other business." I wonder when you have to return the casket you rent?

I wanted to take a look around. He was happy to give me a tour. We visited several chapels and visiting rooms--places where the deceased "lie in state" to be "visited" by family and friends. I saw an old lady in a "fairly decent casket," as Mr. Deaver called it. Again I was impressed by the simple businesslike nature of it all. Oh yes, the rooms were elaborately decorated, with lots of shrines and stained glass, but these things were for the customers' benefit. "Sometimes we have up to eight or nine corpses here at one time, sometimes none. We have to have enough rooms to accommodate." Simple enough, yet I never realized how much (trouble?) people were after they died. So much money, time, and effort go into their funerals.

As I prepared to leave, he gave me his card. He'd be happy to see me again, or maybe I could talk to someone else. I said I would arrange to call for an appointment with the mortician. I shook his hand. His fingers were long, and his skin was warm.

Writing up the interview thus helped Cable probe his subject more deeply. It also helped him to develop a witty voice for his essay. Cable's interview and report are quite informal, because later he intends to integrate it into his full profile of the mortuary.

■ A business reporter for a newspaper writes an article about virtual reality. She describes the lifelike, three-dimensional experience created by wearing gloves and video goggles wired to a computer. To help readers understand this new concept, she contrasts it with television. For investors, she describes which corporations have shown an interest in the commercial possibilities of virtual reality.

■ In a textbook for introductory linguistics, a college professor discusses syntactic development, tracing children's gradual control of sentences, from the earliest two-word sentences through all basic sentence patterns. After reviewing the research on syntactic development, he divides the information into stages of development and describes what children do within each stage, including brief transcripts of monologues and conversations to illustrate each stage of development. He also discusses the work of key researchers and cites their major publications. Because he is writing for beginning students of linguistics, he carefully defines all special linguistic terms.

■ For a presentation at the annual convention of the American Medical Association, an anesthesiologist writes a report on the "awareness during surgery" concept. He presents evidence that patients under anesthesia, as in hypnosis, can hear; and he also reviews research demonstrating that they can perceive and carry out instructions that speed their recovery. He describes briefly how he applies the concept in his own work: how he prepares patients before surgery, what he tells them under anesthesia, and how their recovery goes.

■ A high school math teacher writes an article for a journal read by other math teachers about the nature of functions and graphs and the learning and teaching of them. Pointing out that the organizing power of functions and graphs is increasingly recognized as important for math learning, he reviews recent research on the tasks required in learning functions and graphs and describes their algebraic, tabular, and graphic representations.

Explaining Concepts 5

■ As part of a group assignment, a ninth-grader at a summer biology camp in the Sierra Nevada reads about the condition of mammals at birth. She discovers the distinction between infant mammals that are *altricial* (born nude and helpless within a protective nest) and those that are *precocial* (born well formed with eyes open and ears erect). In her part of the group report, she develops this contrast point by point, giving many examples of specific mammals but focusing in detail on altricial mice and precocial porcupines. Domestic cats, she points out, are an intermediate example—born with some fur, but with eyes and ears closed.

Explanatory writing serves a limited but very important purpose: to inform readers. In general, it does not feature its writers' experiences or feeings, as autobiography (Chapters 2 and 3) does. Successful explanatory writing confidently and efficiently presents information—the writing job, in fact, required most every day in virtually every profession. It may be based on first-hand observation (Chapter 4) but always moves beyond description of specific objects and scenes to explanation of general concepts and ideas. Since it deals almost exclusively with established information, explanatory writing tends not to argue for its points. While often inviting, even engaging, it does not aspire to be more than it is: a way for readers to find out about a particular subject. Much of what we find in newspapers, encyclopedias, instruction manuals, reference books, and research reports is explanatory writing.

This chapter focuses on one important kind of explanatory writing: that which explains a concept to readers. The readings all explain some concept—"parthenogenesis," "patriarchy," "individualism," and "schizophrenia." Learning to explain a concept is especially important to you as a college student: it will help you to read textbooks, which themselves exist to explain concepts; it will prepare you to write a common type of exam and assignment; and it will acquaint you with the basic strategies—definition, classification, comparison, process narration—common to all types of explanatory writing.

The term *concept* refers to a major idea or principle. Every field has its concepts: physics has "atom," psychiatry has "schizophrenia," literature has "irony," writing has "invention," music has "harmony," and mathematics has "probability." You can see from this brief list that concepts are central to the understanding of virtually every subject. Indeed, much of human knowledge is made possible by concepts. Our brains evolved to do conceptual work—to create concepts, communicate them, and use them to think.

Above all, explanatory writing should be interesting to readers. We read explanations either out of curiosity or out of necessity. But even when we are self-motivated, bad writing can turn us off. Explanatory writing goes wrong when the flow of new information is either too fast or too slow for its readers, when the information is over their heads or too far below, or when the writing is too abstract or just plain dull.

In your college courses you will frequently be asked to explain or apply concepts. Following are some typical assignments:

- *For an educational methods course:* Do the textbooks in your area of teaching interest engage in "gender stereotyping"? Choose one textbook, and analyze it carefully to discover what roles are suggested for each sex and whether one sex is overrepresented in text, pictures, or learning activities. Report your conclusions to the class.

- *For a chemistry course:* In your own words, explain the "law of definite proportions" and show its importance to the field of chemistry.

- *For a government course:* Choose one emerging democracy in eastern Europe, research it, and report on its progress in establishing a representative democratic government. Consider carefully its present arrangements for "political parties," "majority rule," "minority rights," and "popular consent."

- *For an English course:* Many works of literature depict "scapegoat" figures. Select two written works and two films, and discuss how their authors and directors present and analyze the social conflicts that lead to the creation of scapegoats.

For Group Inquiry

With two or three other students, try explaining a familiar concept. Some possible concepts might include the following:

romance	conservation of natural	a balanced diet
ambition	resources	aerobic exercise
creativity	job satisfaction	maturity
friendship	racism	a sense of community
success	vegetarianism	civil rights
irony		

Once you have chosen a concept, think about what others in the group are likely to know about it and how you can inform them about it in two or three minutes. Consider how you will define the concept and what other strategies you might use—description, comparison, and so on—to explain it in an interesting, memorable way. In turn, explain your concepts to one another. After each explanation, the other members should tell the speaker one or two things they learned about the concept.

Once you have all explained your concepts, discuss as a group what you learned from the experience:

- What most surprised you?
- What strategies did you find yourselves using to present your concepts?

Readings

David Quammen is both a novelist and a prolific science writer. His essays have been published in many magazines, including *Outside,* a nature magazine for which he writes a column called "Natural Acts." As you read this selection, first written for *Outside* and later published in *Natural Acts: A Sidelong View of Science and Nature* (1985), notice how Quammen engages readers' attention while presenting an important biological concept.

IS SEX NECESSARY?

DAVID QUAMMEN

Birds do it, bees do it, goes the tune. But the songsters, as usual, would mislead 1 us with drastic oversimplifications. The full truth happens to be more eccentrically nonlibidinous: Sometimes they *don't* do it, those very creatures, and get the same results anyway. Bees of all species, for instance, are notable to geneticists precisely for their ability to produce offspring while doing *without.* Likewise at least one variety of bird—the Beltsville Small White turkey, a domestic dinner-table model out of Beltsville, Maryland—has achieved scientific renown for a similar feat. What we are talking about here is celibate motherhood, procreation without copulation, a phenomenon that goes by the technical name *parthenogenesis.* Translated from the Greek roots: virgin birth.

And you don't have to be Catholic to believe in this one. 2

Miraculous as it may seem, parthenogenesis is actually rather common through- 3 out nature, practiced regularly or intermittently by at least some species within almost every group of animals except (for reasons still unknown) dragonflies and mammals. Reproduction by virgin females has been discovered among reptiles, birds, fishes, amphibians, crustaceans, mollusks, ticks, the jellyfish clan, flatworms, roundworms, segmented worms; and among insects (notwithstanding those unrelentingly sexy dragonflies) it is especially favored. The order Hymenoptera, including all bees and wasps, is uniformly parthenogenetic in the manner by which males are produced: Every male honeybee is born without any genetic contribution from a father. Among the beetles, there are thirty-five different forms of parthenogenetic weevil. The African weaver ant employs parthenogenesis, as do twenty-three species of fruit fly and at least one kind of roach. The gall midge *Miastor* is notorious for the exceptionally bizarre and grisly scenario that allows its fatherless young to see daylight: *Miastor* daughters cannibalize the mother from inside, with ruthless impatience, until her hollowed-out skin splits open like the door of an overcrowded nursery. But the foremost practitioners of virgin birth—their elaborate and versatile proficiency unmatched in the animal kingdom—are undoubtedly the aphids.

Now no sensible reader of even this can be expected, I realize, to care faintly 4 about aphid biology *qua* aphid biology. That's just asking too much. But there's a larger rationale for dragging you aphid-ward. The life cycle of these little nebbishy sap-sucking insects, the very same that infest rose bushes and house plants, not only exemplifies *how* parthenogenetic reproduction is done; it also very clearly shows *why.*

First the biographical facts. A typical aphid, which feeds entirely on plant juices 5
tapped off from the vascular system of young leaves, spends winter dormant and
protected, as an egg. The egg is attached near a bud site on the new growth of a
poplar tree. In March, when the tree sap has begun to rise and the buds have begun
to burgeon, an aphid hatchling appears, plugging its sharp snout (like a mosquito's)
into the tree's tenderest plumbing. This solitary individual aphid will be, necessarily,
a wingless female. If she is lucky, she will become sole founder of a vast aphid
population. Having sucked enough poplar sap to reach maturity, she produces—by
live birth now, and without benefit of a mate—daughters identical to herself. These
wingless daughters also plug into the tree's flow of sap, and they also produce
further wingless daughters, until sometime in late May, when that particular branch
of that particular tree can support no more thirsty aphids. Suddenly there is a change:
The next generation of daughters are born with wings. They fly off in search of a
better situation.

One such aviatrix lands on an herbaceous plant—say a young climbing bean in 6
some human's garden—and the pattern repeats. She plugs into the sap ducts on
the underside of a new leaf, commences feasting destructively, and delivers by parthenogenesis a great brood of wingless daughters. The daughters beget more daughters, those daughters beget still more, and so on, until the poor bean plant is en-
crusted with a solid mob of these fat little elbowing greedy sisters. Then again, neatly
triggered by the crowded conditions, a generation of daughters are born with wings.
Away they fly, looking for prospects, and one of them lights on, say, a sugar beet.
(The switch from bean to beet is fine, because our species of typical aphid is not
inordinately choosy.) The sugar beet before long is covered, sucked upon mercilessly,
victimized by a horde of mothers and nieces and granddaughters. Still not a single
male aphid has appeared anywhere in the chain.

The lurching from one plant to another continues; the alternation between wing- 7
less and winged daughters continues. But in September, with fresh tender plant
growth increasingly hard to find, there is another change.

Flying daughters are born who have a different destiny: They wing back to the 8
poplar tree, where they give birth to a crop of wingless females that are unlike any
so far. These latest girls know the meaning of sex! Meanwhile, at long last, the
starving survivors back on that final bedraggled sugar beet have brought forth a
generation of males. The males have wings. They take to the air in quest of poplar
trees and first love. *Et voilà*. The mated females lay eggs that will wait out the winter
near bud sites on that poplar tree, and the circle is thus completed. One single aphid
hatchling—call her the *fundatrix*—in this way can give rise in the course of a year,
from her own ovaries exclusively, to roughly a zillion aphids.

Well and good, you say. A zillion aphids. But what is the point of it? 9

The point, for aphids as for most other parthenogenetic animals, is (1) excep- 10
tionally fast reproduction that allows (2) maximal exploitation of temporary resource
abundance and unstable environmental conditions, while (3) facilitating the successful colonization of unfamiliar habitats. In other words the aphid, like the gall
midge and the weaver ant and the rest of their fellow parthenogens, is by its evolved
character a galloping opportunist.

This is a term of science, not of abuse. Population ecologists make an illuminating 11
distinction between what they label *equilibrium* and *opportunistic* species. According

to William Birky and John Gilbert, from a paper in the journal *American Zoologist*: "Equilibrium species, exemplified by many vertebrates, maintain relatively constant population sizes, in part by being adapted to reproduce, at least slowly, in most of the environmental conditions which they meet. Opportunistic species, on the other hand, show extreme population fluctuations; they are adapted to reproduce only in a relatively narrow range of conditions, but make up for this by reproducing extremely rapidly in favorable circumstances. At least in some cases, opportunistic organisms can also be categorized as colonizing organisms." Birky and Gilbert also emphasize that "The potential for rapid reproduction is the essential evolutionary ticket for entry into the opportunistic life style."

And parthenogenesis, in turn, is the greatest time-saving gimmick in the history 12 of animal reproduction. No hours or days are wasted while a female looks for a mate; no minutes lost to the act of mating itself. The female aphid attains sexual maturity and, bang, she becomes automatically pregnant. No waiting, no courtship, no fooling around. She delivers her brood of daughters, they grow to puberty and, zap, another generation immediately. If humans worked as fast, Jane Fonda today would be a great-grandmother. The time saved to parthenogenetic species may seem trivial, but it is not. It adds up dizzyingly: In the same time taken by a sexually reproducing insect to complete three generations for a total of 1,200 offspring, an aphid (assuming the *same* time required for each female to mature, and the *same* number of progeny in each litter), squandering no time on courtship or sex, will progress through six generations for an extended family of 318,000,000.

Even this isn't speedy enough for some restless opportunists. That matricidal gall 13 midge *Miastor,* whose larvae feed on fleeting eruptions of fungus under the bark of trees, has developed a startling way to cut further time from the cycle of procreation. Far from waiting for a mate, *Miastor* does not even wait for maturity. When food is abundant, it is the *larva,* not the adult female fly, who is eaten alive from inside by her own daughters. And as those voracious daughters burst free of the husk that was their mother, each of them already contains further larval daughters taking shape ominously within its own ovaries. While the food lasts, while opportunity endures, no *Miastor* female can live to adulthood without dying of motherhood.

The implicit principle behind all this nonsexual reproduction, all this hurry, is 14 simple: Don't argue with success. Don't tamper with a genetic blueprint that works. Unmated female aphids, and gall midges, pass on their own gene patterns virtually unaltered (except for the occasional mutation) to their daughters. Sexual reproduction, on the other hand, constitutes, by its essence, genetic tampering. The whole purpose of joining sperm with egg is to shuffle the genes of both parents and come up with a new combination that might perhaps be more advantageous. Give the kid something neither Mom nor Pop ever had. Parthenogenetic species, during their hurried phases at least, dispense with this genetic shuffle. They stick stubbornly to the gene pattern that seems to be working. They produce (with certain complicated exceptions) natural clones of themselves.

But what they gain thereby in reproductive rate, in great explosions of popula- 15 tion, they give up in flexibility. They minimize their genetic options. They lessen their chances of adapting to unforeseen changes of circumstance.

Which is why more than one biologist has drawn the same conclusion as 16 M. J. D. White: "Parthenogenetic forms seem to be frequently successful in the

particular ecological niche which they occupy, but sooner or later the inherent disadvantages of their genetic system must be expected to lead to a lack of adaptability,
followed by eventual extinction, or perhaps in some cases by a return to sexuality."

So it *is* necessary, at least intermittently (once a year, for the aphids, whether   17
they need it or not), this thing called sex. As of course you and I knew it must be.
Otherwise surely, by now, we mammals and dragonflies would have come up with
something more dignified.

For Discussion

We all have reason to care about developments in science, medicine, and
health. Surveys reveal, however, that few Americans leave school with much
scientific knowledge. Consequently, writers like David Quammen play an
important role in explaining scientific concepts as well as medical and health
findings to newspaper and magazine readers. Discuss your own education in
science. What kinds of reading, lab activities, and teaching do you remember?
How do you feel as a student of science—competent, stimulated, bored,
overwhelmed? Does your experience suggest any explanations for the fact
that so few students major in science? Do you try to keep up with scientific
developments by regularly reading newspaper and magazine articles on science? Do you find you know enough to understand what you're reading?

For Analysis

1.   Did you find Quammen's essay easy or hard to read? Point to specific
sections, and try to explain why they seemed easy or hard to you. As a writer,
what can you conclude from this essay about making unfamiliar information
accessible to readers?

2.   Readers are always influenced by the tone of an essay, which reveals the
writer's attitude toward the subject and readers. How would you describe
Quammen's tone? What specific words create that tone? How were you, as
one reader, affected by the tone of this essay?

*For an example of a
scratch outline, see
pp. 384–87.*

3.   Analyze Quammen's plan for this essay by making a scratch outline.
Given his purpose and readers, what advantages or disadvantages do you see
in the way he's organized his information?

4.   Consider ways Quammen helps readers follow his essay. What cues does
he provide? Underline all the cueing devices you find in his essay: forecasting
statements, topic sentences, transitional words and phrases, summaries. How
do these cues help to keep you, as one reader, oriented? Point to two or
three especially effective cues.

*For information about
cueing, see Chapter 12.*

**For Your
Own Writing**

What science or health concepts do you think you could, with a little reviewing, explain? Consider the science or health courses you've taken in the
last year or two, and think of concepts they covered. Choose one concept,
and consider how you would go about writing an explanatory essay on it
for a particular group of readers. The readers may already know something
about the concept, or they may be totally unfamiliar with it.

Commentary

This reading illustrates the role of a main point, or thesis, in essays explaining concepts. Since Quammen cannot say everything that is known about parthenogenesis, he must select certain information, guided by the point he wants to make. This point focuses readers' attention and makes clear the writer's purpose.

Quammen's point seems to be that parthenogenesis is far more common than readers might have guessed and that it is so widespread because it has certain advantages. He announces his point early, at the beginning of paragraph 3: "Miraculous as it may seem, parthenogenesis is rather common throughout nature, practiced regularly or intermittently by at least some species within almost every group of animals except (for reasons still unknown) dragonflies and mammals."

Quammen does several things to engage and maintain readers' interest in his subject. His title is provocative, and he begins by quoting familiar and humorous lyrics of a popular song—"Birds do it, bees do it"—and then immediately gives examples of bees and birds that *don't* always do it. At the end of the first paragraph, he defines parthenogenesis in human sexual terms (ones sure to be familiar to readers). He concludes the essay by framing it in the same terms, appealing to readers' awareness of both the serious and the humorous aspects of sex. Another way he maintains readers' interests is by using everyday language and images ("a solid mob of these fat little elbowing greedy sisters"). He occasionally addresses the reader directly ("dragging you aphid-ward," "well and good, you say") and seems to make a point of explaining insect parthenogenesis in human terms ("no waiting, no courtship, no fooling around"). He even translates scientific principles into truisms: "Don't argue with success." He simplifies but does not trivialize.

Writers explaining concepts must not only engage readers' interest but also be quite careful about how they introduce and pace information. They must be sure not to introduce too much information too soon or to pack in the information so densely that readers lose interest. After a light start, Quammen lists in the relatively long paragraph 3 the groups of animals practicing parthenogenesis and details its "bizarre and grisly" form in the gall midge *Miastor*. This paragraph offers comprehensive, substantive information. Before offering another such substantive paragraph, however, Quammen pauses (in paragraph 4) to address readers directly, acknowledging that they may not "care faintly about aphid biology," and explaining why the next paragraphs must detail substantively the particular form of aphid parthenogenesis. In paragraphs 9 and 10 he pauses again to tell readers the point of the aphid example. The remainder of the essay continues this pattern of informing and pausing. You can see that Quammen recognizes and accommodates the limits on readers' tolerance for new information, especially on a subject about which they are not experts.

■   ■   ■

Steven Mintz and Susan Kellogg teach at the University of Houston. He is a professor of history, and she is an anthropoligist. This selection comes from their book *Domestic Revolution: A Social History of American Life* (1988), which is of interest mainly to historians and students in college history courses. As you read, notice how Mintz and Kellogg define the concept of patriarchy in seventeenth-century Puritan life.

**PATRIARCHY IN
PURITAN FAMILY
LIFE**
STEVEN MINTZ
AND SUSAN KELLOGG

Puritans organized their family around the unquestioned principle of patriarchy.   1
Fathers represented their households in the public realms of politics and social leadership; they owned the bulk of personal property; and law and church doctrine
made it the duty of wives, children, and servants to submit to the father's authority.
The colonies of Connecticut, Massachusetts, and New Hampshire went so far as to
enact statutes calling for the death of children who cursed or struck their fathers
(Greven 72–99, Bailyn 104, Demos 63).

Patriarchal authority in the Puritan family ultimately rested on the father's control   2
of landed property or craft skills. Puritan children were dependent upon their father's
support in order to marry and set up independent households. Since Puritan fathers
were permitted wide discretion in how they would distribute their property, it was
important that children show a degree of deference to their father's wishes. The
timing and manner in which fathers conveyed property to the next generation ex-
erted a profound influence upon where children decided to live and when and whom
they decided to marry. In many cases fathers settled sons on plots surrounding the
parental homestead, with title not to be surrendered until after their deaths. In other
instances fathers conveyed land or other property when their sons became adults or
were married. Not uncommonly such wills or deeds contained carefully worded
provisions ensuring that the son would guarantee the parent lifetime support. One
deed, for example, provided that a son would lose his inheritance if his parents could
not walk freely through the house to go outdoors (Wells 57, 58).

Such practices kept children economically dependent for years, delayed marriage,   3
and encouraged sons to remain near their fathers during their lifetimes. In Andover,
Massachusetts, only a quarter of the second-generation sons actually owned the
land they farmed before their fathers died. Not until the fourth generation in mid-
eighteenth-century Andover had this pattern noticeably disappeared. In Plymouth,
Massachusetts, and Windsor, Connecticut, fathers gave land to children on marriage.
Among Quaker families in Pennsylvania, fathers who were unable to locate land for
sons in the same town bought land in nearby communities. In order to replicate their
parents' style of life, sons had to wait to inherit property from their fathers. In most
cases ownership and control of land reinforced the authority of fathers over their
children (Adams and Kasakoff 33).

A corollary to the Puritan assumption of patriarchy was a commitment to female   4
submission within the home. Even by the conservative standards of the time, the
roles assigned to women by Puritan theology were narrowly circumscribed. The
premise guiding Puritan theory was given pointed expression by the poet Milton:
"God's universal law gave to man despotic power / Over his female in due awe."

Women were not permitted to vote or prophesy or question church doctrine. The ideal woman was a figure of "modesty" and "delicacy," kept ignorant of the financial affairs of her family. Her social roles were limited to wife, mother, mistress of the household, seamstress, wet nurse, and midwife. Although there was no doubt that she was legally subordinate to her husband, she had limited legal rights and protections (Koehler).

Puritan doctrine did provide wives with certain safeguards. Husbands who re- 5 fused to support or cohabit with their wives were subject to legal penalties. Wives, in theory, could sue for separation or divorce on grounds of a husband's impotence, cruelty, abandonment, bigamy, adultery, or failure to provide, but divorce was generally unavailable, and desertion was such a risky venture that only the most desperate women took it as an option. Colonial statutes also prohibited a husband from striking his wife, "unless it be in his own defense." Before marriage single women had the right to conduct business, own property, and represent themselves in court. Upon marriage, however, the basic legal assumption was that of "coverture" — that a woman's legal identity was absorbed in her husband's. Spouses were nevertheless allowed to establish antenuptial or postnuptial agreements, permitting a wife to retain control over her property (Gunderson and Gampel, 114–134).

For both Puritan women and men, marriage stood out as one of the central 6 events in life. Despite their reputation as sexually repressed, pleasure-hating bigots, the Puritans did not believe that celibacy was a condition morally superior to marriage. The only thing that Saint Paul might have said in favor of marriage was that it is "better to marry than to burn," but the Puritans extolled marriage as a sacrament and a social duty. John Cotton put the point bluntly: "They are a sort of Blasphemers then who dispise and decry" [women as a necessary evil,] "for they are a necessary Good; such as it was not good that man should be without (Morgan 26–64).

For the Puritans love was not a prerequisite for marriage. They believed that the 7 choice of a marriage partner should be guided by rational considerations of property, religious piety, and family interest, not by physical attraction, personal feelings, or romantic love. Affection, in their view, would develop after marriage. This attitude reflected a recognition of the essential economic functions of the colonial family. Marriage was a partnership to which both bride and groom were expected to bring skills and resources. A prospective bride was expected to contribute a dowry (usually in the form of money or household goods) worth half of what the bridegroom brought to the marriage. Artisans tended to choose wives from families that practiced the same trade precisely because these women would be best able to assist them in their work. In New England the overwhelming majority of men and women married — and many remarried rapidly after the death of a spouse — because it was physically and economically difficult to live alone (Morgan 55–59, 81–86, 151).

According to Puritan doctrine, a wife was to be her husband's help-mate, not 8 his equal. Her role was "to guid the house &c. not guid the Husband." The Puritans believed that a wife should be submissive to her husband's commands and should exhibit toward him an attitude of "reverence," by which they meant a proper mixture of fear and awe; not "a slavish Fear, which is nourished with hatred or aversion; but a noble and generous Fear, which proceeds from Love" (Morgan 43–47, Koehler 136–37).

The actual relations between Puritan spouses were more complicated than reli- 9 gious dogma would suggest. It was not unusual to find mutual love and tenderness in Puritan marriages. In their letters Puritan husbands and wives frequently referred to each other in terms suggesting profound love for each other, such as "my good wife . . . my sweet wife" or "my most sweet Husband." Similarly, the poems of Anne Bradstreet refer to a love toward her husband that seems deeply romantic: "To my Dear and loving Husband / I prise thy love more than whole Mines of gold." It is also not difficult, however, to find evidence of marriages that failed to live up to the Puritan ideal of domestic harmony and wifely submissiveness. In 1686, a Boston spinster, Comfort Wilkins, publicly spoke out about the "Tears, and Jars, and Discontents, and Jealousies" that marred many Puritan marriages (Morgan 47–54, 59–64, 161–62; Koehler 136–65).

Puritan court records further reveal that wife abuse is not a recent development. 10 Between 1630 and 1699, at least 128 men were tried for abusing their wives. In one case a resident of Maine kicked and beat his wife with a club when she refused to feed a pig; in another case an Ipswich man poured poison into his wife's broth in an attempt to kill her. The punishments for wife abuse were mild, usually amounting only to a fine, a lashing, a public admonition, or supervision by a town-appointed guardian. Two colonists, however, did lose their lives for murdering their wives (Koehler 137–42).

Even in cases of abuse, Puritan authorities commanded wives to be submissive 11 and obedient. They were told not to resist or strike their husbands but to try to reform their spouses' behavior. Some women refused to conform to this rigid standard. At least thirty-two seventeenth-century Puritan women deserted their husbands and set up separate residences, despite such risks as loss of their dower rights and possible criminal charges of adultery or theft. Another eight women were brought to court for refusing to have sexual relations with their husbands over extended periods. Seventy-six New England women petitioned for divorce or separation, usually on grounds of desertion, adultery, or bigamy (Koehler 142–46, 152–56).

Women who refused to obey Puritan injunctions about wifely obedience were 12 subject to harsh punishment. Two hundred seventy-eight New England women were brought to court for heaping abuse on their husbands, which was punishable by fines or whippings. Joan Miller of Taunton, Massachusetts, was punished "for beating and reviling her husband and egging her children to healp her, biding them knock him in the head." One wife was punished for striking her husband with a pot of cider, another for scratching and kicking her spouse, and a third for insulting her husband by claiming he was "no man." How widespread these deviations from Puritan ideals were, we do not know (Koehler 142–46).

Works Cited

Adams, John W., and Alice B. Kasakoff. "Migration and the Family in Colonial England: The View from Genealogies." *Journal of Family History* 9 (1984): 24–43.

Bailyn, Bernard. *Education in the Forming of American Society: Needs and Opportunities for Study.* Chapel Hill: Institute of Early American History and Culture, Williamsburg, and U of North Carolina P, 1960.

Demos, John. *Entertaining Satan: Witchcraft and the Culture of Early New England.* New York: Oxford UP, 1982.

Greven, Philip J., Jr. *Four Generations: Population, Land, and Family in Colonial Andover, Massachusetts.* Ithaca: Cornell UP, 1970.

Gunderson, John R., and Gwen V. Gampel. "Married Women's Legal Status in Eighteenth-Century New York and Virginia," *William and Mary Quarterly,* 3rd ser. 39 (1982): 114–134.

Koehler, Lyle. *A Search for Power: The Weaker Sex in Seventeenth-Century New England.* Urbana: U of Illinois P, 1980.

Morgan, Edmund. *The Puritan Family: Essays on Religion and Domestic Relations in Seventeenth-Century New England.* Boston: Trustees of the Public Library, 1944.

Wells, Robert V. *Revolutions in Americans' Lives.* Westport: Greenwood, 1982.

For Discussion

Mintz and Kellogg describe marriage in Puritan times as "guided by rational considerations of property, religious piety, and family interest," with both bride and groom bringing skills and resources to contribute to the "essential economic functions" of the colonial family. Is this economic basis for marriage entirely outdated or does it still influence marital arrangements today? Might marriage-age Americans from different social classes and ethnic groups feel this influence differently? What conclusions can you reach about the basis for American marriages today?

For Analysis

For information about summarizing, see pp. 532–33.

1.   Definition is central to essays that explain concepts. Mintz and Kellogg define "patriarchy" in a general way in paragraph 1, and they continue throughout the essay to refine this definition. Reread the essay, underlining anything that adds to this definition. (Underline only statements, not examples.) Then write a brief summary, defining patriarchy. What can you conclude about the function of definition in explanatory writing?

2.   Along with definition, examples play a central role in explaining concepts. To analyze Mintz and Kellogg's use of examples, carefully reread paragraphs 9–11. Put a check in the margin by each example, and a second check by the examples that seem the most concrete or the least abstract. Then underline the generalizations, those sentences remaining after you have noted all the examples. What can you conclude about the role of examples and generalizations in explaining concepts?

3.   The information about patriarchy in this essay comes from many sources. From these sources, the authors have selected and organized certain information to make a point about patriarchy. What do you think is their point?

4.   Did you find this selection easy or hard to read? Were some parts easier than others? Which parts? Was this selection easier or harder to read than David Quammen's essay? From comparing these two readings, what can you conclude about ways of making unfamiliar information accessible to readers? Support your conclusion by pointing to specific parts of both essays.

For Your
Own Writing

Consider explaining a concept related to marriage and families: adoption, alimony, child abuse, child support, the custody of children, divorce, the extended family, the feminization of poverty, interracial marriage, matriarchy, paternity leave. Your explanation could in part contrast current American practices with those in earlier times or other countries. What sources might you need to consult? Who would your readers be, and what could you assume they already know about the concept? Your goal would be to add to what they already know.

Commentary

This selection illustrates the importance of balance in explaining concepts. Mintz and Kellogg report in paragraph 4 that "female submission within the home" was a notable feature of Puritan patriarchy, but then in paragraph 5 they note that wives had "certain safeguards" in Puritan marriages. For example, they could retain control of property acquired before marriage and sue for separation or divorce (though they rarely did). Husbands were prohibited from striking their wives, except in self-defense. Clearly, Mintz and Kellogg take pains to balance their discussion of the implications of patriarchy. They are very careful to avoid distorting the historical record.

Again, in paragraph 9, after a section describing the subordinate position of wives in Puritan religious doctrine, Mintz and Kellogg report that "the actual relations between Puritan spouses were more complicated than religious dogma would suggest." They then quote letters revealing "profound love," and they also quote a woman of the times pointing out that many marriages failed to fulfill the Puritan ideal.

Also worth noting is their use of sources and their method of citing sources. They rely on eight sources, and you may have noticed that their in-text citations of these always occur at the ends of paragraphs. In their book they justify this practice on the grounds that they did not want to clutter their text with citations. Your instructor, however, may expect you to follow the more conventional practice of citing each source where it is used.

MLA style is illustrated in Chapter 21.

Mintz and Kellogg use the citation style of the Modern Language Association (MLA), a style preferred by researchers in the humanities and arts (literature, history, philosophy, art history, music).

■   ■   ■

The authors of the next essay are sociologists. Robert N. Bellah, the author of several books, including *The New Religious Consciousness,* teaches at the University of California at Berkeley; his colleagues teach at other American universities. This selection comes from their book, *Habits of the Heart: Individualism and Commitment in American Life* (1985). As you read it, notice how they define American individualism by first describing the mythic version, in cowboy and detective fiction, and then contrasting it with a real version, in Abraham Lincoln. What seems to be the point of this contrast?

**AMERICAN
INDIVIDUALISM**
ROBERT N. BELLAH
RICHARD MADSEN
WILLAM M. SULLIVAN
ANN SWIDLER
STEPHEN M. TIPTON

A deep and continuing theme in American literature is the hero who must leave 1
society, alone or with one or a few others, in order to realize the moral good in the
wilderness, at sea, or on the margins of settled society. Sometimes the withdrawal
involves a contribution to society, as in James Fenimore Cooper's *The Deerslayer.*
Sometimes the new marginal community realizes ethical ends impossible in the larger
society, as in the interracial harmony between Huckleberry Finn and Jim. Sometimes
the flight from society is simply mad and ends in general disaster, as in *Moby Dick.*
When it is not in and through society but in flight from it that the good is to be
realized, as in the case of Melville's Ahab, the line between ethical heroism and
madness vanishes, and the destructive potentiality of a completely asocial individualism is revealed.

America is also the inventor of that most mythic individual hero, the cowboy, 2
who again and again saves a society he can never completely fit into. The cowboy
has a special talent—he can shoot straighter and faster than other men—and a
special sense of justice. But these characteristics make him so unique that he can
never fully belong to society. His destiny is to defend society without ever really
joining it. He rides off alone into the sunset like Shane, or like the Lone Ranger
moves on accompanied only by his Indian companion. But the cowboy's importance
is not that he is isolated or antisocial. Rather, his significance lies in his unique,
individual virtue and special skill and it is because of those qualities that society needs
and welcomes him. Shane, after all, starts as a real outsider, but ends up with the
gratitude of the community and the love of a woman and a boy. And while the
Lone Ranger never settles down and marries the local schoolteacher, he always leaves
with the affection and gratitude of the people he has helped. It is as if the myth
says you can be a truly good person, worthy of admiration and love, only if you
resist fully joining the group. But sometimes the tension leads to an irreparable break.
Will Kane, the hero of *High Noon,* abandoned by the cowardly townspeople, saves
them from an unrestrained killer, but then throws his sheriff's badge in the dust and
goes off into the desert with his bride. One is left wondering where they will go,
for there is no longer any link with any town.

The connection of moral courage and lonely individualism is even tighter for that 3
other, more modern American hero, the hard-boiled detective. From Sam Spade to
Serpico, the detective is a loner. He is often unsuccessful in conventional terms,
working out of a shabby office where the phone never rings. Wily, tough, smart, he
is nonetheless unappreciated. But his marginality is also his strength. When a bit of
business finally comes their way, Philip Marlowe, Lew Archer, and Travis McGee are
tenacious. They pursue justice and help the unprotected even when it threatens to
unravel the fabric of society itself. Indeed, what is remarkable about the American
detective story is less its hero than its image of crime. When the detective begins his
quest, it appears to be an isolated incident. But as it develops, the case turns out to
be linked to the powerful and privileged of the community. Society, particularly "high
society," is corrupt to the core. It is this boring into the center of society to find it
rotten that constitutes the fundamental drama of the American detective story. It is
not a personal but a social mystery that the detective must unravel.

To seek justice in a corrupt society, the American detective must be tough, and 4
above all, he must be a loner. He lives outside the normal bourgeois pattern of career
and family. As his investigations begin to lead him beyond the initial crime to the
glamorous and powerful center of the society, its leaders make attempts to buy off

the detective, to corrupt him with money, power, or sex. This counterpoint to the gradual unravelling of the crime is the battle the detective wages for his own integrity, in the end rejecting the money of the powerful and spurning (sometimes jailing or killing) the beautiful woman who has tried to seduce him. The hard-boiled detective, who may long for love and success, for a place in society, is finally driven to stand alone, resisting the blandishments of society, to pursue a lonely crusade for justice. Sometimes, as in the film *Chinatown,* corruption is so powerful and so total that the honest detective no longer has a place to stand and the message is one of unrelieved cynicism.

Both the cowboy and the hard-boiled detective tell us something important about 5 American individualism. The cowboy, like the detective, can be valuable to society only because he is a completely autonomous individual who stands outside it. To serve society, one must be able to stand alone, not needing others, not depending on their judgment, and not submitting to their wishes. Yet this individualism is not selfishness. Indeed, it is a kind of heroic selflessness. One accepts the necessity of remaining alone in order to serve the values of the group. And this obligation to aloneness is an important key to the American moral imagination. Yet it is part of the profound ambiguity of the mythology of American individualism that its moral heroism is always just a step away from despair. For an Ahab, and occasionally for a cowboy or a detective, there is no return to society, no moral redemption. The hero's lonely quest for moral excellence ends in absolute nihilism.[1]

If we may turn from the mythical heroes of fiction to a mythic, but historically 6 real, hero, Abraham Lincoln, we may begin to see what is necessary if the nihilistic alternative is to be avoided. In many respects, Lincoln conforms perfectly to the archetype of the lonely, individualistic hero. He was a self-made man, never comfortable with the eastern upper classes. His dual moral commitment to the preservation of the Union and the belief that "all men are created equal" roused the hostility of abolitionists and Southern sympathizers alike. In the war years, he was more and more isolated, misunderstood by Congress and cabinet, and unhappy at home. In the face of almost universal mistrust, he nonetheless completed his self-appointed task of bringing the nation through its most devastating war, preaching reconciliation as he did so, only to be brought down by an assassin's bullet. What saved Lincoln from nihilism was the larger whole for which he felt it was important to live and worthwhile to die. No one understood better the meaning of the Republic and of the freedom and equality that it only very imperfectly embodies. But it was not only civic republicanism that gave his life value. Reinhold Niebuhr has said that Lincoln's biblical understanding of the Civil War was deeper than that of any contemporary theologian. The great symbols of death and rebirth that Lincoln invoked to give meaning to the sacrifice of those who died at Gettysburg, in a war he knew to be senseless and evil, came to redeem his own senseless death at the hand of an assassin. It is through his identification with a community and a tradition that Lincoln became the deeply and typically Amerian individual that he was.

Notes

1. On individualism in nineteenth-century American literature see D. H. Lawrence, *Studies in Classic American Literature* (1923; Garden City, N.Y.: Doubleday, Anchor Books, 1951). On the image of the cowboy see Will Wright, *Sixguns and Society: A*

[1]the belief that all values are meaningless and that existence is senseless

Structural Study of the Western (Berkeley and Los Angeles: University of California Press, 1975). On cowboys and detectives see John G. Cawelti, *Adventure, Mystery, and Romance: Formula Stories as Art and Popular Culture* (Chicago: University of Chicago Press, 1976).

2. On the hero's avoidance of women and society see Leslie Fiedler, *Love and Death in the American Novel* (New York: Stein and Day, 1966), and Ann Swidler, "Love and Adulthood in American Culture," in *Themes of Work and Love in Adulthood*, ed. Neil J. Smelser and Erik H. Erikson (Cambridge, Mass.: Harvard University Press, 1980), pp. 120–47.

3. The best book on Lincoln's meaning for American public life is Harry V. Jaffa, *Crisis of the House Divided: An Interpretation of the Lincoln-Douglas Debates* (Garden City, N.Y.: Doubleday, 1959). Reinhold Niebuhr's remarks appear in his essay "The Religion of Abraham Lincoln," in *Lincoln and the Gettysburg Address*, ed. Allan Nevins (Urbana, Ill.: University of Illinois Press, 1964), p. 72.

For Discussion

The authors believe that too many Americans hold a concept of individualism that values isolation, and that leads potentially to despair and nihilism. They advocate an alternative to nihilism that values commitment to community and tradition. Why do so many Americans seem to feel an "obligation to aloneness"? Do you think that Americans undervalue community and tradition? Why do you think so? How much commitment do you feel to a community or tradition? To the United States as a community of citizens?

For Analysis

1. Unlike the Quammen essay, this one does not offer any initial definition of the concept. Instead, working from various examples of fictional and real heroes, it gradually builds a definition of "American individualism." Trace this incremental definition—keeping in mind that it includes both mythical and real individualism—by underlining general statements, phrases or sentences, that contribute to it. You might begin with "must leave society" in paragraph 1. Then summarize these statements in order to understand the concept of "American individualism."

2. What do you take to be the point of this essay's explanation about American individualism?

3. Analyze the examples in paragraphs 2 and 3. Why do you think the authors use so many examples (three cowboys and five detectives)? In paragraph 2, what does each example contribute? How are the examples presented differently in paragraphs 2 and 3? Given the essay's point, what advantages do you see in his use of examples?

4. Make a scratch outline of the plan this essay follows. Then examine the first sentence in each paragraph closely to see how it cues readers to the plan. Specifically, how does each sentence connect previous information with what follows and reiterate the subject of the essay?

For Your Own Writing

Bellah and his coauthors find examples in movies of the concept of "mythic individualism." Think of movies you've seen—recent ones as well as older ones. What ideas do they represent? For example:

1. What do war films suggest about concepts like masculinity, heroism, patriotism, or male bonding?

2. What do teen films suggest about the generation gap, adolescent rebelliousness, or community?

3. What do romantic comedies suggest about gender roles, friendship and marriage, or sexual politics?

Commentary

This selection illustrates the importance of comparison and contrast in explaining concepts. In the opening paragraph, destructive Ahab is contrasted with ethical Huck Finn and Jim. In the second paragraph, Shane and the Lone Ranger are contrasted with Will Kane. Paragraphs 2, 3, and 4 compare detectives and cowboys, and paragraph 5 interprets and summarizes this comparison. Finally, paragraph 6 contrasts Ahab and the most asocial cowboys and detectives with Abraham Lincoln. We might call Bellah's basic strategy definition by contrast. Such a strategy seems essential to thinking about concepts and to understanding them, as well as to writing about them.

For more about comparison and contrast, see Chapter 17.

The essay also makes use of another strategy often found with comparison and contrast: classification. It is easy to imagine the authors considering several cowboys for paragraph 2. The three they chose seem representative of three different kinds of cowboy heroes; that is, they created a three-part classification based on this difference and then assigned to each part a cowboy most readers would recognize. Classifying enables writers to reorganize information in ways that contribute to their main point.

For more on classifying, see Chapter 16.

The authors of this piece do not cite any specific sources, but an appendix to the book the essay comes from lists the many articles and books that provide the research base for it.

■   ■   ■

Veronica Murayama wrote this essay as a college freshman. In it she defines a psychiatric concept, the debilitating mental illness called schizophrenia. Since this illness has been exhaustively studied and so much has been written about it, Murayama had to find a manageable focus for her essay. As you read, consider how she made this choice. Notice, too, how she seeks to engage your interest in the concept.

SCHIZOPHRENIA: WHAT IT LOOKS LIKE, HOW IT FEELS
VERONICA MURAYAMA

Some mental illnesses, like depression, are more common than schizophrenia, but few are more severe. A schizophrenic has delusions and hallucinations, behaves in bizarre ways, talks incoherently, expresses little feeling or else feelings inappropriate to the situation, and is incapable of normal social interactions. Because these symptoms are so severe, about half the hospitalized mentally ill in America are schizophrenics. Only 1 percent of Americans (between 2 and 3 million) are schizophrenic, and yet they occupy about one-fourth of the available beds in our hospitals ("Schizophrenic," 1987, p. 1533). Up to 40 percent of the homeless may be schizophrenic (King, 1989, p. 97).

Schizophrenia has been recognized for centuries, and as early as the seventeenth 2
century its main symptoms, course of development, and outcome were described.
The term "schizophrenia," first used in 1908, refers to the disconnection or splitting
of the mind that seems basic to all the various forms of the disease. It strikes both
men and women, usually during adolescence or early adulthood, and is found all
over the world. Treatment may include chemotherapy, electroconvulsive therapy,
psychotherapy, and counseling. Hospitalization is ordinarily required, but usually not
for more than a few months. It seems that about a third of patients recover completely and the rest can eventually have "a reasonable life adjustment," but some
effect of the illness nearly always remains, most commonly lack of feeling and reduced drive or ambition ("Schizophrenic," 1987, pp. 1533, 1537–1539). Schizophrenia hits adolescents especially hard, and the effect on their families can be
disastrous.

Though much is known about schizophrenia and treatment is reasonably effec- 3
tive, specialists still argue about its causes. For example, various researchers blame
an unsatisfactory family life in which one or both parents suffer from some form of
mental illness (Lidz, 1973), some combination of genetic inheritance and family life
("Schizophrenic," 1987, p. 1534; "Schizophrenia," 1987, p. 192), or "an early de-
velopmental neuropathological process" that results in reduced size of certain brain
areas (Suddath, Cristison, Torrey, Casanova, & Weinberger, 1990, p. 793). What is
known and agreed on, however, is what schizophrenia looks like to an observer and
what it feels like to a sufferer, and these are what I want to focus on in this essay.
I have always believed that when people have knowledge about any type of human
suffering, they are more likely to be sympathetic with the sufferer. Schizophrenic
symptoms are not attractive, but they are easy to understand. The medical manuals
classify them approximately as follows: bizarre delusions, prominent hallucinations,
confusion about identity, unconnected speech, inappropriate affect, disturbances in
psychomotor behavior, impaired interpersonal functioning, and reduced drive.

Schizophrenics themselves experience the disease to a large extent as delusional 4
thinking. For example, one woman said, "If I see a phone, I can talk on it without
picking it up, immediately, anywhere in the world. But I don't abuse it. I'm authorized
by AT&T. In the Yukon. And RCA" (Shane, 1987). It is common for schizophrenics
to have delusions that they are being persecuted—that people are spying on them,
spreading false stories about them, or planning to harm them. Events, objects, or
people may be given special threatening significance, as when a patient believes a
television commentator is making fun of him. Other delusions are very likely: "the
belief or experience that one's thoughts, as they occur, are broadcast from one's
head to the external world so that others can hear them; that thoughts that are not
one's own are inserted into one's mind; that thoughts have been removed from
one's head; or that one's feelings, impulses, thoughts, or actions are not one's own,
but are imposed by some external force" ("Schizophrenia," 1987, p. 188). Sometimes delusions are grandiose, as when a patient thinks that he is the Messiah and
will save the world or that she is the center of a conspiracy. A woman patient wrote,
"I want a revolution, a great uprising to spread over the entire world and overthrow
the whole social order. . . . Not for the love of adventure! No, no! Call it unsatisfied
urge to action, if you like, indomitable ambition" (cited in Lidz, 1973, p. 134).

Related to delusions are hallucinations, which are very common in schizophrenics. 5
Usually they hear voices coming from inside or outside the head, making insulting
remarks, commenting on behavior, or giving commands that can sometimes be

dangerous to others. Sometimes they hear sounds like humming, whistling, or machinery.

These false ideas and imaginary sensations leave schizophrenics confused about 6 their identities. Feeling ruled by forces outside themselves, they lack normal feelings of individuality and uniqueness. One patient wrote, "I look at my arms and they aren't mine. They move without my direction. Somebody else moves them. . . . I have no control. I don't live in me. The outside and I are all the same" (cited in Mendel, 1974, p. 111).

Besides revealing their delusions and hallucinations, schizophrenics' speech is 7 often rambling and unconnected. It may shift rapidly from one topic to another that is seemingly completely unrelated or only loosely related, and the speaker does not show any awareness of the lack of connection. One patient, a man, said, "I have always believed in the good of mankind but I know I am not a woman because I have an Adam's apple" ("Schizophrenic," 1987). Sometimes the topics are so un-related that the patient's speech becomes incoherent and incomprehensible. Even when it is connected, schizophrenic speech can sometimes contain very little infor-mation because it is vague, abstract, or repetitive.

Schizophrenics also present themselves in recognizable ways, referred to as "in- 8 appropriate affect." Their voices are often monotonous and their faces expression-less. They may express little if any emotion, and their emotional responses do not seem varied. On the other hand, their responses may seem completely inappropriate to the situation, or there may be unpredictable outbursts of anger.

Another visible feature of schizophrenia is disturbed psychomotor behavior. The 9 most severely ill may move around very little or sit rigidly and resist being moved. Here is what one patient felt: "When I was acting so stiff and wasn't talking I had the feeling that if I moved the whole world might collapse. . . . I don't know why, but I seemed like I was the center of everything and everything depended on my not moving" (cited in Mendel, 1974, p. 108). Patients may take up strange postures or engage in rocking or pacing. At the other extreme, they may move excitedly and apparently purposelessly. Unfortunately, violent behavior is possible as well. One manual points out that "grotesque violence, with self-mutilation (often of sexual organs) or murderous attacks, may occur. Matricide [killing one's mother], the rarest form of murder, is most often perpetrated by schizophrenics, as is filicide [killing one's brother or sister]. . . . The risk of suicide is increased in all stages of schizo-phrenic illness" ("Schizophrenic," 1987, p. 1535). One woman patient wrote, "Death is the greatest happiness in life, if not the only one. Without hope of the end, life would be unendurable" (cited in Mendel, 1974, p. 137).

Even if violence does not occur, it is not surprising that the speech and behavioral 10 symptoms I have described are almost invariably accompanied by—and contribute to—impaired interpersonal functioning. Once schizophrenics become obsessed with delusions, hallucinations, and illogical ideas, they are often too distracted and cen-tered on themselves to interact with other people. Such patients are notable for their emotional detachment even from family members or friends they were previously close to. They also withdraw from all other social interactions, dropping out of school or leaving jobs. They simply cannot face the outside world. Some schizophrenics behave quite differently, however, at least during some phases of the illness. They "cling to other people, intrude upon strangers, and fail to recognize that excessive closeness makes people uncomfortable and likely to pull away" ("Schizophrenia," 1987, p. 189).

Along with social impairment comes loss of drive or ambition. Schizophrenics 11 typically have difficulty in initiating actions, making decisions, or following through with plans, and their work and other responsibilities often suffer severely as a result.

It is important to know that doctors, counselors, and psychoanalysts do not easily 12 label someone schizophrenic. They do not do so unless many of the symptoms I have described are present and unmistakable. Since depression has some of the same symptoms as schizophrenia and the treatment of the two is quite different, doctors have to be especially careful not to confuse them. We have come a long way from the time when schizophrenics were considered dangerous lunatics and were locked away without treatment, sometimes for life. Doctors now recognize the illness and can counsel both patients and families and prescribe drugs that have proven effective. The problem today is that so many of the homeless are believed to be schizophrenic, and it seems unlikely that many of them ever receive treatment.

References

King, K. (1989, November). Lost brother. *Life,* pp. 94–98.

Lidz, Theodore. (1973). *The origin and treatment of schizophrenic disorders.* New York: Basic.

Mendel, W. M. (1974). A phenomenological theory of schizophrenia. In A. Burton, J. Lopez-Ibor, & W. M. Mendel, *Schizophrenia as a life style* (pp. 106–155). New York: Springer.

Schizophrenia. (1987). *Diagnostic and statistical manual of mental disorders* (3rd. ed.) (pp. 187–198). Washington, DC: American Psychiatric Association.

Schizophrenic disorders. (1987). *The Merck manual of diagnosis and therapy* (15th ed.). (pp. 1532–1539). Rahway, NJ: Merck and Company.

Shane, S. (1987, July 28). Relatives bear demoralizing task of patient care. [Baltimore] *Sun,* p. 14.

Suddath, R. L., Cristison, G. W., Torrey, E. F., Casanova, M. F., & Weinberger, D. R. (1990). Anatomical abnormalities in the brains of monozygotic twins discordant for schizophrenia. *The New England Journal of Medicine, 322,* 791–793.

For Discussion

Murayama's essay demonstrates that schizophrenia is a diagnosable medical problem. It is only one of many mental illnesses, perhaps the most widespread being depression, which afflicts 15 percent of Americans. People with mental illness need help because their suffering is acute and the costs to their families and to society are great, yet mental health funds are often the first to be cut in times of budget constraints. How would you explain the neglect of mental health resources? What community resources for the mentally ill are you aware of?

For Analysis

1.   How, in paragraph 1, does Murayama seek to engage readers' interest in her topic? Compare her strategy with Quammen's on pp. 139–42. In what ways do their beginnings seem appropriate or inappropriate for their subject?

2.   How does Murayama frame her essay? (Framing means referring at the end to something mentioned at the beginning.) Compare her frame with Quammen's. What advantages do you see in framing an explanatory essay?

3.   Examine the list of references at the end of the essay. What generalizations can you make about the sources? Then look at the citations within the essay. How does Murayama use her sources? Where does she quote directly, and to what effect?

4.   Do you find this essay's organization logical and easy to follow? Support your answer with specific examples from the essay.

5.   In the Writer at Work discussion at the end of this chapter you will find all of the sources for paragraph 9. With the help of the Commentary below, analyze the relation between her paragraph and the sources. What conclusions can you reach about her use of sources? Notice where she quotes, paraphrases, or summarizes. How might you have used the sources differently?

Turn to pp. 173–74 to see how Murayama surveyed sources and found a focus for her essay.

For Your Own Writing

If you found Murayama's essay especially informative, you might want to consider writing an essay that would let you learn about another type of mental illness, such as hypochondriasis, mood disorders, or autism. The two manuals Murayama cites catalog many such illnesses. Like her, you would also want to look for current research and popular articles on your topic.

Commentary

Not only does Murayama try in her introduction to engage readers' interest in her topic, but she also provides an extended context for her focus on the symptoms of schizophrenia. Assuming her readers know little about her topic, she provides a broad orientation, giving information about its history, causes, and treatment. She does not extend this context too far, however: at the end of paragraph 3 she announces her focus.

This announcement also forecasts the plan of the essay. A forecast identifies the main topics or ideas in an essay, usually in the sequence in which they will be discussed. The list of schizophrenic symptoms Murayama gives lays out her topics and their sequence and also identifies the key terms she will rely on throughout the essay. Readers seeking information benefit from such an obvious cue as forecasting because it enables them to predict what is coming.

It is also worth noting some of the ways Murayama incorporates quoted material into her own sentences:

She uses a dialogue cue, like *he said* or *she wrote*:
One patient, *a man, said,* "I have always believed in the good of mankind. . . ." (paragraph 4)
One *woman patient wrote,* "Death is the greatest happiness in life. . . ." (paragraph 8)

She uses a colon:

Here is what one patient felt: "When I was acting so stiff and wasn't talking . . ." (paragraph 8)

She uses a noun clause with *that*:

One manual points out *that* "grotesque violence . . . may occur." (paragraph 8)

For more on quoting sources, see pp. 526–32.

PURPOSE AND AUDIENCE

Explanatory writing has unquestionable value. Though it often seeks to engage readers' interests, it gives prominence to the facts about its subject. It aims at readers' intellects rather than their imaginations, determined to instruct rather than entertain.

To set out to teach readers about a concept is no small undertaking. To succeed, you must know the concept so well that you can explain it simply, without jargon or other confusing language. You must be authoritative without showing off or talking down.

You must also know your readers. Primarily, you must understand what they already know about the concept in order to decide which facts will be truly new to them. You will want to define unfamiliar words and pace the information carefully so that your readers are neither bored nor overwhelmed.

BASIC FEATURES OF EXPLANATORY ESSAYS

Essays explaining concepts display certain basic features: a well-focused subject, a point or thesis, an appeal to readers' interests, a logical plan, clear definitions, writing strategies appropriate to the essay's point and to the kind of information it presents, and careful use of sources.

A Well-focused Subject

The primary purpose for explaining a concept is to inform readers, but writers of explanatory essays cannot possibly hope to say everything there is to say about a concept, nor would they want to. Instead, they must make choices about what to include, what to emphasize, and what to omit. Most writers focus on one aspect of the concept. Veronica Murayama, for example, focuses on the symptoms of schizophrenia.

A Main Point or Thesis

In explaining a concept, all writers make some point about the concept. The point, or thesis, asserts something significant or interesting about the concept. For example, Murayama makes the point in her essay that the more readers know about mental illness, the more likely they are to be understanding of those who suffer from it.

An Appeal to Readers' Interests

In explaining concepts, good writers usually try to appeal directly to their readers' interests. They may put this appeal right at the beginning, as David Quammen does by contrasting parthenogenesis with human sexuality. Bellah and his colleagues refer to fictional cowboys and detectives readers can be expected to recognize. Though Mintz and Kellogg do not overtly appeal to readers' interests, they no doubt assume that all readers of a book like theirs are interested in issues of power and authority within families.

A Logical Plan

Explanations must follow a clear path to keep readers on track. For organizing explanations and cueing readers, experienced writers rely on many strategies. They divide the information in such a way that it supports the main point and then alert readers to these divisions with forecasting statements, topic sentences, transitions, and summaries. In addition, they may try to frame the essay for readers by relating the ending to the beginning. We have seen these features repeatedly in the readings in this chapter. For example, Quammen frames his essay with references to human sexuality. His extended examples support his point that parthenogenesis is widespread and highly functional, and he summarizes the point at the end of his longest example, about aphids.

Good writers never forget that readers need clear signals. Because the writer already knows the information and is aware of how it is organized, it can be difficult for him or her to see it the way someone reading the essay for the first time would. That is precisely how it must be seen, however, to be sure that the essay includes all the signals the reader will need.

For more on cueing readers, see Chapter 12.

Clear Definitions

Essays explaining concepts depend on clear definitions. In order to relate information clearly, a writer must be sensitive to the readers' knowledge; any terms that are likely to be unfamiliar or misunderstood must be explicitly defined. Mintz and Kellogg, for example, define *coverture* (paragraph 5) and *reverence* (paragraph 8). In a sense, the essays in this chapter are extended definitions of concepts, and all the authors offer relatively concise, clear definitions of their concepts at some point in their essays. Bellah stresses the paradox in the definition of American individualism: "One accepts the necessity of remaining alone in order to serve the values of the group." Quammen offers a definition of parthenogenesis in paragraph 1: "What we are talking about here is celibate motherhood, procreation without copulation."

See Chapter 15 for further discussion of definitions.

Appropriate Writing Strategies

Many writing strategies are useful for presenting information. The strategies a writer uses are determined by the point he or she wishes to make and the kind of information available to work with. Following are some of the writing strategies that are particularly useful in explaining concepts.

Classification and Division.   One way of presenting information is to sort it into groups and discuss them one by one. Murayama, for example, uses the classification of schizophrenic symptoms found in medical manuals as a way of organizing her description of the disease. She lists the symptoms at the end of paragraph 3 and then discusses each one in turn. Bellah and his colleagues take the concept of the hero and use division two different ways. First, they discuss two types of heroes: the cowboy and the detective. Then they divide heroes another way: fictional heroes and historically real heroes.

For more about classification and division, see Chapter 16.

Process Narration.   Many concepts involve processes that unfold over time, like the geologic scale, or over both time and space, like bird migration, which could be illustrated by telling a story of a typical bird's migration between Canada and Mexico. Process narration involves some of the basic storytelling strategies required in autobiography or fiction: narrative time signals, sentence rhythm, summarizing action, and transitions showing temporal relationship. For example, Quammen narrates the life cycle of the aphid, a temporal process unfolding over about seven months. Throughout, he gives us time signals like "in March," "in late May," "suddenly there is a change," "away they fly," "in September," "meanwhile, at long last," and so on.

For further illustration of these narrative strategies, see Chapter 13.

Comparison and Contrast.   This strategy is especially useful for explaining concepts because it helps readers to understand something new by showing how it is similar to or different from things they already know. Every essayist in this chapter makes use of contrast. Quammen contrasts asexual and sexual reproduction, Mintz and Kellogg contrast the statuses of husband and wife in the Puritan family, and Murayama contrasts schizophrenics who withdraw from others with those who cling and intrude. The Bellah selection relies on several comparisons and contrasts: in the opening paragraph the authors contrast fictional protagonists (Deerslayer, Huck and Jim, Ahab) prominent in American literature; in paragraphs 2 and 3, they compare two types of "mythic individual hero," the cowboy and the detective; and in the final paragraph they contrast the mythic hero with a real hero, Abraham Lincoln.

For more about comparison and contrast, see Chapter 17.

Cause and Effect.   Still another useful strategy for explaining a concept may be to report its causes or effects. Mintz and Kellogg explain the effects on children's lives of the Puritan father's control of land, and Bellah and colleagues report other scholars' speculations about the nihilistic results of the lonely mythic hero's quest. (The authors' notes indicate they are reporting other speculations than their own.)

Notice that most explanatory writing either reports established causes or effects of the subject or reports others' speculated causes or effects. They usually do not speculate about possible causes or effects themselves.

Careful Use of Sources

Explaining concepts nearly always draws on information from many different sources. Writers often draw on their own experience and observation, but they almost always do additional research into what others have said about their subject. Referring to sources, particularly to expert ones, always lends authority to an explanation.

How writers treat sources depends on the writing situation. Certain formal situations, such as college assignments or scholarly papers, have prescribed rules for citing and documenting sources. Students and scholars are expected to cite their sources formally because their readers judge their writing in part by what they've read and how they've used their reading. In Chapter 21, two different ways of citing sources are presented: the Modern Language Association (MLA) style, used chiefly in the humanities, and the American Psychological Association (APA) style, used by many social and natural scientists. Both of these styles call for parenthetical citations within the essay that are keyed to a list of works cited at the end. Mintz and Kellogg follow MLA style, whereas Murayama follows APA style. Ask your instructor which style you should follow.

On more informal writing occasions—newspaper and magazine articles, for example—readers do not expect writers to include page references or publication information, but they do expect them to identify their sources in some way; this is often done casually within the text of the article.

Sources should be used with the greatest care. Since you nearly always find more sources on a concept than you can use, you must evaluate them carefully, choosing those that are the most reputable and current and that provide the best support for the point you want to make about the concept. For example, Murayama examined twelve sources before deciding to focus on the symptoms of schizophrenia. Consequently, she set aside those sources concerned with the history, causes, or treatment of schizophrenia.

For more on evaluating sources, see pp. 522–24.

See pp. 526–32 for helpful advice on paraphrasing, summarizing, and quoting.

Experienced writers make judicious decisions about when to paraphrase, summarize, or quote their sources. (Summary reduces and rewords information, while paraphrase retains and rewords information.) They take special care to integrate quotations smoothly into their own texts, deliberately varying the way they do it.

Guide to Writing

THE WRITING ASSIGNMENT

Write an essay that explains a concept. Choose a concept that interests you and that you want to study further. Consider carefully what your readers already know about it and how your essay might add to what they know.

INVENTION AND RESEARCH

The following guidelines will help you to find a concept, understand it fully, select a focus appropriate for your readers, research the focus in depth, and devise strategies for presenting what you've discovered in a way that will be truly informative for your particular readers.

Finding a Concept   Even if you already have a concept in mind, completing the following notes will help you to be certain of your choice.

Consider first the concepts in the suggestions For Your Own Writing on pp. 142, 148, 151–52, and 156.

Listing Concepts.   List as many concepts as you can. The longer your list, the more likely you are to find just the right concept to write about. And should your first choice not work out, you will have a ready list of alternatives. Include concepts you already know something about as well as some you know only slightly and would like to research further.

Your courses provide many concepts you will want to consider. Following are typical concepts from several academic and other subjects. Your class notes or textbooks will suggest many others.

- *Literature:* hero, antihero, picaresque, the absurd, pastoral, realism
- *Philosophy:* existentialism, nihilism, logical positivism, determinism
- *Business management:* autonomous work group, quality circle, cybernetic control system, management by objectives, zero-based budgeting, benchmarking
- *Psychology:* Hawthorne effect, assimilation/accommodation, social cognition, moratorium, intelligence, divergent/convergent thinking, operant conditioning, short-term memory, tip-of-the-tongue phenomenon
- *Government:* majority rule, minority rights, federalism, popular consent, exclusionary rule, political party, political machine, interest group, political action committee
- *Biology:* photosynthesis, morphogenesis, ecosystem, electron transport, plasmolysis, phagocytosis, homozygosity, diffusion
- *Art:* cubism, composition, Dadaism, surrealism, expressionism
- *Math:* Mobius transformation, boundedness, null space, eigenvalue, complex numbers, integral exponent, rational exponent, polynomial, factoring, Rolle's theorem, continuity, derivative, indefinite integral
- *Physical sciences:* matter, mass, weight, energy, atomic theory, law of definite proportions, osmotic pressure, first law of thermodynamics, entropy, free energy
- *Public health:* alcoholism, winter depression, vaccination, drug abuse, contraception, lead poisoning, prenatal care
- *Environmental studies:* acid rain, recycling, ozone depletion, sewage treatment, groundwater contamination

■ *Sports:* double play, bunt, squeeze play, hit and run (baseball); power play (hockey); nickel defense, wishbone offense, onside kick, shotgun offense (football); serve and volley offense (tennis); setup (volleyball); pick and roll, inside game (basketball).

Choosing a Concept.   Now look over your list and select one concept to explore. Pick a concept that interests you, one you feel eager to learn more about. Consider also whether it might interest others. You may know very little about the concept now, but the guidelines that follow will help you research it and to understand it fully.

Exploring the Concept

Discovering What You Already Know.   Now is the time to get a quick overview of your concept—to find out about its issues and controversies, the people involved, the schools of thought. Start with what you know, go to the library, perhaps consult an expert. Take a few minutes to write down whatever you know about the concept you have chosen and why you find it interesting and worth knowing about. Write quickly, without planning or organizing. Feel free to write in phrases or lists as well as in sentences. You might also want to make drawings or charts. Ask questions.

Gathering Information.   Check any materials you already have at hand that explain your concept. If you are considering a concept from one of your academic courses, you will find an explanation in your textbook or lecture notes. You may also find useful material in your lecture notes.

To acquire a comprehensive, up-to-date understanding of your concept and to write authoritatively about it, you will almost certainly want to go beyond familiar material. For example, if you research an academic concept, you will want to know how experts besides your textbook writer and instructor define and illustrate the concept. It will be especially important to know about current research or perspectives on the concept. For this information you can go to the library.

Chapter 20 provides a search strategy and specific sources for pursuing your concept.

Consulting an Expert.   Is there someone very knowledgeable about your concept who might be helpful? If you are writing about a concept related to public health, for example, a doctor at the campus health service might be someone to consult. Not only could an expert answer questions, but he or she might also direct you to important or influential articles or books.

Focusing on One Aspect of the Concept

Once you have done some research on your concept, you need to choose a focus for your essay. Since more is known about most concepts than you can include in an essay and since concepts can be approached from so many perspectives—history, definition, significance, recent research—you must have a focus in order to produce a worthwhile piece of writing. Murayama, for example, focuses her essay about schizophrenia on its symptoms. By limiting your essay to one aspect of your concept, you can avoid a common mistake: trying to explain superficially and hurriedly everything that is known about a concept.

Analyzing Your Readers.   To decide on a focus, you must first identify and analyze your readers, because the focus must reflect both your special interest in the concept and what you think is likely to be your readers' knowledge of and interest in it. Even if you are writing only for your instructor, you must be aware of his or her knowledge of your concept.

Take around ten minutes to describe your readers in writing. Think carefully about the following questions as you write:

- Who are my readers? How diverse a group are they?
- In what kind of publication might my essay appear?
- How much are my readers likely to know about this concept?
- Why might they want to learn about this concept?
- What aspects of the concept might be especially informative and interesting to them?
- How can I engage and hold their interest?

Choosing a Focus.   With your interests and your readers' interests in mind, choose a focus and write a few sentences justifying its appropriateness.

Researching Your Subject

Return to the material you read to get an overview of your concept, and with your focus in mind, select relevant material. In addition, seek out new material. Keep a careful record of all promising sources, including essential information for citing these sources. Check with your instructor about whether you should follow the Modern Language Association (MLA) or the American Psychological Association (APA) style of acknowledging sources. In this chapter, the Mintz and Kellogg essay follows MLA style, and the Murayama essay follows APA style.

For MLA and APA guidelines, see pp. 533–43.

Consider photocopying your most promising sources. Doing so may save you return trips to the library should your essay take an unpredictable turn or should you realize you need more on a particular point.

Testing Your Choice

Pause now to test whether you have chosen a workable concept and focused it appropriately. As painful as it may be to consider, starting fresh with a new concept would be better than continuing with an unworkable one. The following questions can help you test your choice:

- Do I still have a strong personal interest in my concept?
- Have I discovered a focus for writing about this concept?

- Have I located more than enough information for an essay with such a focus?
- Will readers have interest in this aspect of my subject? Do I see possibilities for engaging and holding their interest in it?

If you cannot answer all of these questions affirmatively, you should consider refocusing your subject or selecting another concept to write about.

For Group Inquiry

At this point it might be a good idea to get some response to your subject. Get together in a group with two or three other students. One by one, announce your concepts and intended readers, and then explain what in particular you plan to focus on and what your main point will be. Ask the group whether your plan sounds interesting: would they care to read about your subject? Ask them what, if anything, they already know about your subject. Feedback of this kind can help you to know whether your topic is a good one and how much explaining you'll need to do.

Establishing a Main Point

Besides a focus, which limits your topic, your essay needs a main point or thesis. The point in an essay explaining a concept can be stated or implied. You'll recall that Quammen's implied point seems to be that parthenogenesis is far more common in nature than most people realize and that Murayama's stated point is that knowledge about mental illness makes people more sympathetic with sufferers.

Probing the Significance of Your Concept.   Begin by reviewing your invention notes and research materials. With your own interest and your readers' expectations in mind, write for several minutes, answering these questions:

- What makes this aspect of this concept interesting to me?
- What is most important about it?
- What is most surprising or unusual in the information?
- Why should my readers bother to read about it?
- What significance might it have for their lives?

Stating a Point.   When you have finished writing, read over what you have written, and write one or two sentences that sum up the point you want to get across to your readers. What do you want to tell them about your concept?

Considering Explanatory Strategies

Before you move on to plan and draft your essay, consider some possible ways of presenting the information you have. Following are some questions that can help you to determine which writing strategies might prove useful. Answer each one with a sentence or two.

- What terms are used to name the concept, and what do they mean? (definition, Chapter 15)
- How is it like or unlike related concepts? (comparison and contrast, Chapter 17)
- How can this concept be divided into parts? (classification and division, Chapter 16)
- How does it happen or how do you do it? (process narration, Chapter 13)
- What are its known causes or effects? (causes and effect, Chapter 9)

PLANNING AND DRAFTING

Here are some guidelines to help you to get the most out of your invention notes, to decide on some specific goals for your essay, and to write a first draft.

Seeing What You Have

Reread everything you have written so far. This is a critically important time for reflection and evaluation. Before beginning the actual draft, you must decide whether your subject is worthwhile and whether you have sufficient information for a successful essay.

It may help as you read to annotate your invention writings. Look for details that will support your point and appeal to your readers. Underline or circle key words, phrases, or sentences; make marginal notes. Your goal here is to identify the important elements in what you have written so far.

Be realistic. If at this point your notes do not look promising, you may want to refocus your concept or select a different concept to write about. If your notes seem thin but promising, you should probably do further research to find more information before continuing.

Setting Goals

Successful writers are always looking beyond the next sentence to larger goals. Indeed, the next sentence is easier to write if you keep larger goals in mind. The following questions can help you set these goals. Consider each one now and then return to them as necessary while you write.

Your Readers

- How much are my readers likely to know about this concept? How can I build on their knowledge?
- What new information can I present to them?
- How much information will be enough and how much will be too much?
- How can I organize my essay so that my readers can follow it easily?
- What tone would be most appropriate? Would an informal tone like Quammen's or a formal one like Bellah's be more appropriate?

The Beginning

- How shall I begin? Should I open with a provocative quotation, as Quammen does? Should I begin with a general statement about the concept, as the other writers in this chapter do? With a surprising fact? With a question? What kind of opening would be most likely to capture my readers' attention?

- Should I assert my point immediately, or should I first set the context?

- How can I best forecast the plan my explanation will follow? Should I offer a detailed forecast? Or is a brief description sufficient?

The Ending

- How shall I end? Should I restate my point?

- Should I relate the ending to the beginning, as Quammen does, so as to frame the essay?

Writing Strategies

- To what extent do I need to define my terms? Can I rely on brief sentence definitions or will I need to write extended definitions?

- Should I include any tables, charts, or graphs?

- Do I need to include any particular examples?

- Are there any comparisons or contrasts that help readers to understand the information?

- Should I include any anecdotes?

- Do I need to explain any processes or describe any historical events?

Outlining

See pp. 384–87 for more on outlining.

Give some thought now to organization. Many writers find it helpful to outline their material before actually beginning to write. Whatever outlining you do before you begin drafting, consider it only tentative. Never be a slave to an outline. As you draft, you will usually see some ways to improve on your original plan. Be ready to revise your outline, to shift parts around, to drop or add parts. Consider the following questions as you plan:

- How should I divide the information?

- What order will best serve my purpose and point?

- What kinds of transitions will I need between the main parts of my essay?

Drafting

You may want to review the drafting advice on pp. 9–11.

Begin drafting your essay, keeping your mind on your main point. Remember also the needs and expectations of your readers; organize and define and explain with them in mind. Your goal is to increase their understanding of your concept.

GETTING CRITICAL COMMENTS

Now is the time to try to get a good critical reading. All writers find it helpful to have someone else read and comment on their drafts, and your instructor may schedule such a reading as part of your coursework. If not, you can ask a classmate, friend, or family member to read it over. If your campus has a writing center, you might ask a tutor there to read and comment on your draft. The guidelines that follow are designed to be used by *anyone* reviewing an explanatory essay. (If you are unable to have someone else read over your draft, turn ahead to the Revision section on pp. 169–72, which gives guidelines for reading your own draft with a critical eye.)

In order to provide focused, helpful comments, your reader must know your intended audience and purpose. Briefly write out this information at the top of your draft:

Audience. Who are your readers?

Purpose. What do you want to tell your readers about the concept?

Reading with a Critical Eye

Reading a draft critically means reading it more than once, first to get a general impression and then to analyze its basic features.

Reading for a First Impression.   Read first to learn about the concept and get a sense of its significance. As you read, try to notice any words or passages that contribute to your first impression, weak ones as well as strong ones. A good way of highlighting noteworthy language is to use the pointings system.

Pointings

- Draw a straight line under any words or images that impress you as especially effective: strong verbs, specific details, memorable phrases, striking images.
- Draw a wavy line under any words or images that seem flat, stale, or vague. Also put a wavy line under any words or phrases that you consider unnecessary or repetitious.
- Look for pairs or groups of sentences that you think should be combined. Put brackets [ ] around these sentences.
- Look for sentences that are garbled, overloaded, or awkward. Put parentheses ( ) around these sentences. Put them around any sentence that seems even slightly questionable; don't worry about whether or not you're certain about your judgment. The writer needs to know that you, as one reader, had even the slightest problem understanding a sentence.

After you've finished reading the draft, briefly give your impressions. Is the concept well focused and clearly explained? Did you find the essay informative and easy to read? What in the draft do you think would especially interest the intended readers?

See pp. 157–60 to review the basic features.

Reading to Analyze.   Now reread to focus on the basic features of writing an explanatory essay.

Is the Concept Appropriately Focused?

What aspect of the concept does the essay focus on? Given the concept, does the focus seem too broad or too narrow? Can you think of another focus that would make the essay more successful?

Is the Point Well Made?

Identify the point the essay makes about the concept. Is it stated directly or implied? If the essay doesn't seem to make a point (stated or implied), can you think of one that would declare the significance of the information?

Is the Content Appropriate for Its Intended Readers?

Does it tell them all they are likely to want to know about this concept? Is there additional information that should be included? Are there questions about the concept that readers are likely to have and that have not been answered? Is there information that seems superfluous? Will the information seem predictable or bland?

Is the Organization Effective?

Look at the way the essay is organized, outlining it briefly. Is the information logically divided? Can you think of a better way to divide it? Consider also the order—can you think of a better way of sequencing the information?

Look at the *beginning*. Does it pull you into the essay and make you want to continue? Does it adequately forecast the direction of the essay? Can you think of a better way to begin?

Find the obvious *transitions* in the draft. Are they helpful? If not, can you improve any of them? Look for additional places where transitions would be helpful.

Look at the *ending*. Is it effective? Does it frame the essay by referring back to something at the beginning? Should it? Can you think of a better way to end? Imagine someone with limited time reading this essay. This reader wants—and needs—to proceed at an even, quick pace, with as little effort as possible. Where might this draft slow a reader down?

Are Definitions Clear?

Examine the definitions. Are any likely to be unclear to readers? Is everything defined that needs to be?

Are Writing Strategies Appropriately Used?

Besides definition, what writing strategies are used and how effective are they? Examine each recognizable use of process narration, comparison and contrast, cause and effect, or classification and division, and identify any that seem unclear, incomplete, or otherwise ineffective. Can you think of ways to improve these? Are there other places where a strategy would enable readers to comprehend the concept more fully?

Are Sources Carefully Used?

If sources have been used, begin by reviewing the list of sources cited. Given the purpose, readers, and focus of the essay, does the list seem balanced and are the selections appropriate? Are there concerns or questions readers knowledgeable about the concept might raise? Then consider the use of sources within the text of the essay. Should there be more (or fewer) source citations? Where? Are there places where summary or paraphrase would be preferable to quoted material or vice versa? Note any places where quoted material is awkwardly inserted into the text. How could these areas be smoothed out?

What Final Thoughts Do You Have?

Which part needs the most work? What do you think the intended readers will find most informative or memorable?

REVISING AND EDITING

This section will help you to identify problems in your draft and to revise and edit to solve them.

Identifying Problems

To identify problems in your draft, you need to get an overview of it, analyze its basic features, and study any comments from other readers.

Getting an Overview.   First consider the draft as a whole, trying to see it objectively. It may help to do so in two steps:

Reread. If possible, put the draft aside for a day or two before rereading it. When you go back to it, start by reconsidering your audience and purpose. Then read the draft straight through, trying to see it as your intended readers will.

Outline. Make a scratch outline to get an overview of the essay's development. This outline can be sketchy—words and phrases instead of complete sentences—but it should identify the basic features as they appear.

Charting a Plan for Revision.   You may want to make a chart like the following one to keep track of any problems you need to solve. The left-hand column lists the basic features of explanatory writing. As you analyze your draft and study any comments you've gotten from others, note the problems you want to solve in the right-hand column.

Basic Features	*Problems to Solve*
Concept	
Main Point	
Appeal to Readers	
Organization	
Definitions	
Writing Strategies	
Sources	

Analyzing the Basic Features of Your Draft.   Turn now to the questions for analyzing a draft on pp. 168–69. Using these as guidelines, identify problems in your draft. Note anything you need to solve on the preceding chart.

Studying Critical Comments.   Review any comments you've received from other readers, and add to the chart any points that need attention. Try not to react too defensively to these comments; by letting you see how others respond to your draft, they provide invaluable information about how you might improve it.

Solving the Problems

Having identified problems, you now need to figure out solutions and to carry them out. Basically, you have three ways of finding solutions: (1) review your invention and planning notes and sources for additional information and ideas; (2) do further invention to answer questions your readers raised; and (3) look back at the readings in this chapter to see how other writers have solved similar problems.

Following are suggestions to get you started solving some of the problems common to explanatory essays. For now, focus on solving those issues identified on your chart. Avoid tinkering with sentence-level problems; that will come later when you edit.

The Focus

- If the focus is too broad, consider limiting it further so you can treat it in more depth. If readers were less than interested in the aspect you focused on, consider focusing on some other aspect of the concept.

- If the focus is too narrow, you may have isolated too minor an aspect. Go back to your invention and look for other larger or more significant aspects.

The Point

- If the point is not obvious, make it clear somewhere in the essay.

- If the point lacks significance, reconsider the importance or implications of your material. Review your sources for suggestions of significance. Consider what readers would find surprising or important in your material.

Appeal to Readers

- If the content seems incomplete, review your invention writing and sources for further information to satisfy your readers' needs or answer their concerns and questions.
- If any of the content seems superfluous, eliminate it.
- If the content seems predictable or bland, search for novel or surprising information to add.

Organization

- If the essay does not unfold logically and smoothly, reorganize it so that it is easy to follow. Try constructing an alternative outline. Add transitions or summaries to help keep readers on track.
- If the beginning is weak, try making your focus and point obvious immediately, forecasting the plan of your essay, or opening with an unusual piece of information that would catch readers' interest.
- If the ending is inconclusive, consider restating your point there or moving important information to the end. Try summarizing highlights of the essay or framing it by referring back to something in the beginning. Or you might reflect on the future of the concept or assert its usefulness.

Definitions

- If your concept is not clearly defined, add a concise definition early in your essay. Consider adding a brief midpoint summary that defines the concept or repeating the definition in your conclusion. Remove any information that blurs readers' understanding of the concept.
- If other key terms are inadequately defined, supply clear definitions, searching your sources or checking a dictionary if necessary.

Writing Strategies

- If the content seems thin or the definition of the concept blurred, consider whether any other writing strategies would improve the presentation.
- Try comparing or contrasting the concept with a related one, preferably one more familiar to readers.
- See whether you could divide or classify the information in a way that would make it easier to explain (and understand).
- Try explaining its known causes or effects.
- See whether adding examples will enliven or clarify your explanation.
- Would it help to tell more about how the concept works?

Use of Sources

■ If sources are inadequate, return to the library to find additional ones. Consider dropping weak or less reliable sources. Ensure that your sources cover your focus in a comprehensive, balanced way.

■ If you rely too much either on quoting or on summarizing and paraphrasing, change some of your quotations to summaries or paraphrases, or vice versa.

■ If quoted material is not smoothly integrated into your own text, revise to make it so.

■ If there are discrepancies in your in-text citations or list of sources, check citation styles in Chapter 21. Be sure that all of the citations exactly follow the style you are using.

Editing and Proofreading

As you've been working on your draft so far, you've probably corrected some obvious errors, but grammar and style have not been a priority. Now is the time to check carefully for errors in usage, punctuation, and mechanics, and also to consider matters of style. You may find that studying your draft in separate passes—first for paragraphs, then for sentences, and finally for words—will help you to recognize any problems.

Once you have edited your draft and produced a final copy, proofread it carefully to be sure there are no typos, misspellings, or other mistakes.

LEARNING FROM YOUR OWN WRITING PROCESS

Your instructor may ask you to evaluate what you have learned in writing this essay. If so, begin by reviewing quickly the notes from your invention and planning. How successful was this part of your writing process? What major discoveries did you make during invention? Were there obstacles in drafting that your invention work did not help you overcome?

Next, reread your draft, any written analysis of it, and your revision. What did you discover about the concept as you were drafting? How did other readers' comments help you improve the draft? What changes did you make between draft and revision? If you had more time, is there anything you would still like to improve? What are you most pleased with in your revision?

A Writer at Work

USING SOURCES

This section describes how Veronica Murayama searched for sources and integrated them into one part of her essay on schizophrenia, which appears on pp. 152–55.

Finding Sources   Following directions in the Invention and Research section of this chapter, Murayama went to the library to see what she could find readily on schizophrenia. She wanted a quick orientation to the concept so that she could decide on a focus for her essay and for further research. This initial search led her right away to two books and four current articles:

Schizophrenia as a Life Style, 1974
The Origin and Treatment of Schizophrenic Disorders, 1973
"Drug Gains FDA Approval," *Science News*
"Drugs among Young Schizophrenics," *Science News*
"Seeking Source of Schizophrenia," *USA Today*
"Relatives Bear Demoralizing Task of Patient Care," [Baltimore] *Sun*

She read the articles, skimmed the books, and then talked to a reference librarian. When Murayama explained the assignment—emphasizing her need for an overview—and showed the materials she had already collected, the librarian recommended that she check two basic references on mental illness, the first relied on by medical doctors, the second by psychotherapists and other mental health counselors:

The Merck Manual of Diagnosis and Therapy
Diagnostic and Statistical Manual of Mental Disorders

After reading closely the materials on schizophrenia in these two sources, she decided that given the information in all her sources she had enough material on these topics:

the history of the description and treatment of schizophrenia
its effects on families of schizophrenics
the current debate about its causes
the current preferred treatment of it
current research on it
its symptoms

She was drawn both to the debate about causes and to symptoms, but when she discussed these alternatives with a small group in her writing class, she recognized that the others, like herself before she began her research, knew so little about schizophrenia that they would be most engaged and informed by a description of the illness itself—what it looks like to a therapist diagnosing it and what it feels like to a patient experiencing it.

When she met with her instructor, he pointed out that she should seek out recent reports in a respected medical journal such as *The New England Journal of Medicine.* In that journal she found the research report demonstrating that certain areas of schizophrenics' brains appear to be smaller than the same areas in brains of those not suffering from the illness. This interesting research finding appears as one clause in paragraph 3 in her essay.

Now she reread the sources that provided information about the symptoms of schizophrenia. The basic information she needed was in the two reference manuals. Her quotes from patients came mainly from one of the books, *Schizophrenia as a Life Style*. She did not use or cite the *Science News* and *USA Today* articles.

Murayama's search for sources was far from comprehensive, but it was certainly adequate for a brief essay. She wisely stopped searching when she felt she had the information she needed. It turned out that she used only a small part of her information on symptoms.

Integrating Sources

Two paragraphs from Murayama's essay illustrate a sound strategy for integrating sources into your essay, relying on them fully—as you nearly always must do in explanatory writing—and yet making them your own. Here is paragraph 10 from Murayama's essay (the sentences are numbered for ease of reference):

(1) Even if violence does not occur, it is not surprising that the speech and behavioral symptoms I have described are almost always accompanied by—and contribute to—impaired interpersonal functioning. (2) Once schizophrenics become obsessed with delusions, hallucinations, and illogical ideas, they are often too distracted and centered on themselves to interact with other people. (3) Such patients are notable for their emotional detachment even from family members or friends they were previously close to. (4) They also withdraw from all other social interactions, dropping out of school or leaving jobs. (5) They simply cannot face the outside world. (6) Some schizophrenics behave quite differently, however, at least during some phases of the illness. (7) They "cling to other people, intrude upon strangers, and fail to recognize that excessive closeness makes other people uncomfortable and likely to pull away" ("Schizophrenia," 1987, p. 189). (8) Along with social impairment comes loss of drive or ambition. (9) Schizophrenics typically have difficulty in initiating actions, making decisions, or following through with plans, and their work and other responsibilities often suffer severely as a result.

All of the information in Murayama's paragraph comes from the following brief sections of the *Diagnostic and Statistical Manual of Mental Disorders*.

Volition. The characteristic disturbances in volition are most readily observed in the residual phase. There is nearly always some disturbance in self-initiated, goal-directed activity, which may grossly impair work or other role functioning. This may take the form of inadequate interest, drive, or ability to follow a course of action to its logical conclusion. Marked ambivalence regarding alternative courses of action can lead to near-cessation of goal-directed activity.

Impaired interpersonal functioning and relationship to the external world. Difficulty in interpersonal relationships is almost invariably present. Often this takes the form of social withdrawal and emotional detachment. When the person is severely preoccupied with egocentric and illogical ideas and fantasies and distorts or excludes the external world, the condition has been referred to as "autism."

Some with the disorder, during a phase of the illness, cling to other people, intrude upon strangers, and fail to recognize that excessive closeness makes other people uncomfortable and likely to pull away.

Comparing the source and Murayama's paragraph 10, we can see that her first sentence introduces the name of the symptom, which she borrows in part from the symptom name in the source. Sentence 2 paraphrases the source. Sentences 3 through 5 are her own elaborations of the material in the source basically giving concrete examples of the more abstract discussion in the original source. Sentence 6 again paraphrases the source. Then, finally, she quotes the source. Following the quotation, in sentences 8 and 9 she summarizes the information in the source paragraph labeled *Volition*.

■ For a sociology class, a student writes a term paper on surrogate mothering. She first learned about the subject from television news but feels that she needs more information in order to write a paper on it. In the library, she finds several newspaper and magazine articles that help her better understand the pros and cons of the issue. In her paper, she presents the strongest arguments on each side but concludes that, from a sociological perspective, surrogate mothering is bad because it exploits poor women by creating a class of professional breeders.

■ A college journalism student writes an editorial for the campus newspaper condemning the practice of hazing fraternity pledges. He acknowledges that most hazing is harmless but argues that hazing can get out of hand and even be lethal. He refers specifically to two incidents reported in the national news in which students died as a result of hazing. In one case, the student died of alcohol poisoning after drinking too much liquor; in the other, the student had a heart attack after running the track many times. To show that the potential for similar tragedy exists on his own campus, the writer recounts hazing anecdotes told to him by several students. He concludes with a plea to the fraternities on campus to curtail their hazing practices before someone gets seriously hurt or killed.

■ After reading that a Florida judge has banned the sale of an album by the rap group 2 Live Crew on the grounds that its lyrics are obscene, a concerned citizen writes a letter to the editor of her local newspaper. The writer points out that according to the standards set by the U.S. Supreme Court in a 1973 case, something can be declared obscene only if it is "patently offensive; appeals to the prurient interest; and lacks serious literary, artistic, political, or scientific value." Although she acknowledges that some listeners may be offended by its sexually explicit lyrics, the writer argues that the album does have artistic value and therefore should not be censored.

■ For a political science class, a student is assigned to write an essay either supporting or opposing the right of public employees to strike. Having no strong opinion on the issue herself, she discusses it with her mother, a nurse in a county hospital, and her uncle, a fire fighter. Her mother feels that public employees like hospital workers and teachers should have the right to strike, but that police officers and fire fighters should not because public safety would be endangered. Her uncle disagrees, arguing that allowing hospital workers to strike would jeopardize public safety as much as allowing fire fighters to strike. He insists that the central issue is not public safety, but individual rights. In her essay, the student supports the right of

Taking a Position   6

public employees to strike but argues that a system of arbitration should be used where a strike might jeopardize public safety.

■ A committee made up of business and community leaders investigates the issue of regulating urban growth. They prepare a report for the City Council in which they explain the controversy, summarize the arguments for and against regulation, and argue their own opinion that growth should be unregulated. The reasons they give for their conclusion are that supply and demand will regulate development without governmental interference, that landowners should be permitted to sell their property to the highest bidder, and that developers are guided by the needs of the market and thus serve the people.

Taking a position is the first of four chapters on argumentative writing. When you argue a point, your aim is not primarily to express yourself, as it is in Chapters 2 and 3. Nor is it basically to inform readers, as it is in Chapters 4 and 5. You seek not only to express your opinion and to inform others about the issue, but more important, to persuade them to adopt your position or at least to consider your argument seriously.

Although we may feel very strongly about our opinions, there is seldom a simple right or wrong answer in controversies. Opinions depend to some extent on facts, but they also depend on less objective factors like values and beliefs. To be convincing, an argument must not only present logical reasons backed by solid evidence, but must also be based on shared values and beliefs. The opening scenario on the issue of censoring 2 Live Crew's album provides a good example, for its argument rests on establishing the importance of a basic American value—freedom of artistic expression—and on demonstrating that the album does in fact have artistic merit.

Writing a position paper, therefore, is intellectually challenging. It requires you to look critically at your own thinking and to understand others' points of view. You must be able to separate opinion from fact, to reason logically, to marshal supporting evidence, and to recognize the values and beliefs underlying your own and others' opinions.

The strongest arguments, you will see, appeal to your readers in several ways. They appeal to logic by making a sound, well-reasoned, and well-supported argument. They appeal to emotion by making the reader share the writer's concern about the issue. They appeal to the reader's ethical sense by establishing the writer as fair and reasonable, and by basing the argument on a common set of values and beliefs.

As citizens in a democracy, we have a special duty to inform ourselves about current issues, to weigh thoughtfully the pros and cons of these issues, and to participate in the public debate over them. Some current issues we might be expected to take a position on include whether the Food and Drug Administration should make available to AIDS patients drugs that have not yet been fully tested, whether more public housing should be built for the homeless, whether experiments on animals should be more tightly controlled or banned altogether. In your future occupations, you may have many occasions to take a position. Educators, for example, argue over admissions standards and course requirements; business executives debate marketing strategies and investment decisions; health care providers argue over treatment options and hospital policies.

In your college courses, you will frequently be asked to take positions and support them with appropriate evidence. Consider, for instance, some typical assignments:

- *For an American history course:* Does the Monroe Doctrine justify the American invasions of Grenada and Panama?
- *For an economics course:* David M. Gordon claims in "Class and the Economics of Crime" that "ghetto crime is committed by people responding quite reasonably to the structure of economic opportunities available to them." Write an essay agreeing or disagreeing with this statement.
- *For a sociology course:* "Organized crime is inevitable as long as drug use is illegal." Drawing on course readings, agree or disagree with this position.
- *For a health sciences course:* Summarize the debate over aerial malathion spraying to control the Mediterranean fruit fly and take a position, arguing for or against it. Make clear your reasons for taking one side or the other.

For Group Inquiry

Get together with another student, and choose an issue that has two clearly opposing positions. You don't have to be authorities on the issue, but you should be familiar with some of the arguments that are usually raised on each side. Then decide which of you will argue which side. The side you take doesn't have to be the one you prefer; in fact, taking the opposing position can help you think through your own.

Spend five minutes considering the various reasons you could put forth in support of your position. Choose the single best reason and develop a brief argument to convince the other person why this reason should change his or her mind.

Take around twenty minutes to debate the issue. For each side, follow three steps: one person argues for his or her claim, the other person refutes that claim, and finally the first responds to the refutation.

After the debate, spend some time discussing this argument process by considering the following questions:

- On what basis did you each choose the reasons you put forth?
- Knowing now how it can be refuted, would you still choose the same reason? Would you argue for it any differently?

■ How did the other person's refutation or argument alter your view of the issue of your understanding of him or her?

Readings

Kristin A. Goss wrote the following editorial for *The Harvard Crimson* when she was a student at Harvard University. In March 1986, *The Crimson* staff decided not to run the following advertisement:

> *Playboy*'s photographer is now on campus. *Playboy* photographer David Chan is now interviewing students for *Playboy*'s "Women of the Ivy League" pictorial. To qualify, you must be a female student 18 years of age or older, registered full- or part-time at any Ivy League college. Call now for more information and to schedule an interview.

The decision not to run the ad led to considerable debate. *The Crimson* published several articles on the controversy, including this one by Goss.

Before reading her essay, think for a moment about the controversy. What do you suppose is at issue? What reasons might *The Crimson* have had for deciding not to publish the *Playboy* announcement?

TAKING A STAND AGAINST SEXISM

KRISTIN A. GOSS

The Crimson's decision not to run *Playboy*'s advertisement recruiting Harvard 1 women for its October "Women of the Ivy League" issue was both the very most and the very least the newspaper could do to fight the institutionalized exploitation of women.

Those who claim the staff endeavored to "censor" *Playboy,* or to protect Harvard 2 women from themselves, miss the point of the majority's intentions, just as they did seven years ago when *The Crimson* rejected the same ad.

The question is clearly not one of hiding information or of paternalism, but of 3 refusing to support, either tacitly or overtly, a publication whose *raison d'être* is the objectification of women and the exploitation of womankind. It is a question of integrity.

Playboy editors must not expect us—a group of undergraduates who are our- 4 selves either morally repulsed by the pornography racket or in the very least respectful of such feelings of collective degradation in our peers—to aid and abet their objectionable cause.

They should also not expect us to keep silent, as they attempt to make sex objects 5 out of our classmates by offering five times as much money to those who take their clothes off as to those who remain clothed. This is not sexuality; it is sexism.

Those who say *The Crimson* singlehandedly stifled *Playboy*'s message have no 6 argument. *Playboy* could have spent the same amount of money that running an ad in *The Crimson* would cost to make somewhere in the neighborhood of 10,000 photocopied posters, which would have effectively reached every undergraduate, professor and administrator on this campus, and then some. It could have run an advertisement on WHRB. It did run one in the *Independent* and in the *Boston Herald*.

The Crimson's rejection of the ad clearly did not compromise *Playboy*'s right to 7 freedom of expression. The newspaper has not as an institution prevented *Playboy* photographer David Chan from coming to campus.

Nor has it implied that Harvard women cannot decide for themselves whether 8 to pose before him; they can and will make a proper, reasoned decision in either case.

Nor has *The Crimson* censored *Playboy*; the newspaper is in fact on record as 9 supporting pornography's First Amendment right to exist.

The newspaper staff has used its editorial discretion to state that its toleration 10 of pornography—by default, because the alternative would be worse—does not preclude protest. It has expressed the view held by many of its editors that while *Playboy* and other forms of institutionalized sexism may be "socially acceptable," they should not be so.

Social acceptability is a function of which group controls society and to what 11 extent minority voices can influence the spectrum of opinion. Just as racist ads of 50 years ago were socially acceptable to a white-dominated society, so are sexist ads today threatening to females who, despite the women's liberation movement, still have a long way to go to gain equality.

Any woman who has walked down the street and been verbally harassed; and 12 any woman who has feared rape while walking alone in her own neighborhood at night—I might add there is not one female who has not—knows that fighting the image of woman-as-object, woman-as-silenced-victim, woman-as-sex-organ remains among her most urgent tasks.

Sexism is most dangerous when it's subtle, when it is so deeply embedded in a 13 culture that it becomes socially acceptable, as *Playboy* has. And so, you speak out, you yell, you rant and you rave when you recognize this subtle destruction. There is no other way to jar society out of its passive acceptance of the objectification of women, even though in this society it happens to be legal.

In not running the ad, *The Crimson* has taken that initiative. Seven years from 14 now, when *Playboy* again decides to try its luck with a whole new batch of Ivy League women, we can only hope all Ivy League newspapers will decide not to extend their helping hands. It is both the most and the least they can do.

For Discussion

Goss states one of her basic assumptions in the opening paragraph when she refers to "the institutionalized exploitation of women." The term *institutionalized* suggests that this exploitation is cultural, part of the way our society operates. Do you agree? In your view, does our society exploit women? If so, how and why? If you don't think so, how would you refute those who do?

For Analysis

1. Because the essay was published in *The Crimson*, we know that Goss was writing specifically for her fellow Harvard students. What assumptions do you think she makes about her audience? Specifically, what values does she assume they share with her?

2.   Goss's argument depends on certain terms like *censorship, pornography,* and *sexism.* How does she define these terms? How would you define them?

3.   How would you describe the tone of this essay? (Tone reveals the writer's attitude toward the audience and the subject, and usually affects readers' willingness to accept the writer's argument.) Point to word choices that illustrate this tone. How does it affect your acceptance of Goss's argument?

4.   Study the opening and closing paragraphs to see how Goss frames the essay (echoes something from the beginning at the end). What purpose does framing appear to serve in this particular essay? How effective or ineffective does this strategy seem?

For Your Own Writing

Make a list of issues that are currently being debated on campus, at work, or in the community. Choose one that you have strong feelings about. Why do you hold the position you do? Why do you think others feel differently? Given what you know about others' views on this issue, on what basis do you think you and they could agree?

Commentary

Because they are addressing readers with whom they may disagree, writers of position papers must carefully consider their readers' knowledge, values, and assumptions in order to find areas of common ground. The argumentative strategy they employ will reflect their purpose as well as their expectations about their audience.

Goss's ultimate purpose seems to be to inspire readers to take up the fight against sexism. She apparently assumes that her readers oppose sexism and that if she can enlighten them, they will eventually reject *Playboy*'s subtle form of sexism. To succeed, however, she must first defend *The Crimson* against charges of censoring *Playboy* because, she seems to assume, her audience dislikes censorship even more than sexism.

We can see this strategy at work in the way Goss expresses her position in her thesis statement. Her thesis, that the decision not to run the *Playboy* announcement "was both the very most and the very least the newspaper could do to fight the institutionalized exploitation of women," makes clear her position. The decision, she asserts, is "the very most" *The Crimson* can do because newspapers are limited in what they can do. They can express opinion through editorials (as Goss tries to do with her essay), or they can refuse to sell advertising space. At the same time, Goss admits, the decision was "the very least" that the newspaper could do because its action does very little to alleviate sexism. It is a symbolic action and can therefore be successful only to the extent that it raises people's consciousness and inspires them to take action themselves.

By placing her thesis in the opening paragraph, Goss follows the conventions of editorial writing, conventions that also lead to her reliance on short, one- or two-sentence paragraphs. But her decision on where to place the thesis also reflects her special purpose and audience. Because she is writing to Harvard students who already know something about *The Crimson*'s controversial decision, she must state her position emphatically at the outset. It would not do for her to begin, for example, with an extended description of the issue. Her readers already know the issue. Identifying the issue is necessary, but it can be done (as Goss shows) in the thesis statement.

Goss's writing strategy also determines how she deals with counterarguments, arguments made by those with opposing views. She refers to two counterarguments: that *The Crimson*'s decision is an act of censorship, and that it is paternalistic toward Harvard women. Both charges are important, but Goss apparently decided to focus on the former, possibly because it appeals to the same liberal attitudes she hopes to arouse with her sexism argument. She offers several reasons to refute it.

For more on counterarguments, see pp. 480–86.

Finally, as we look at the way Goss justifies *The Crimson*'s action, we see further evidence of her strategy. To defend the decision, she must establish that *Playboy* is sexist and that, moreover, its brand of sexism is particularly pernicious because it has become so ingrained that people cannot even see it is objectionable. This strategy leads her to define and classify *Playboy*'s brand of sexism. It also leads her to compare *Playboy*'s ads to the racist ads that were acceptable fifty years ago but are now seen are repugnant. This analogy is calculated to have a powerful effect on readers who consider themselves enlightened and would not want to be compared to racists.

When you plan and write a position paper, you will also want to develop an argumentative strategy that reflects thoughtful consideration of your purpose and audience. How you decide to present your thesis, acknowledge counterarguments, and support your position will all depend on this strategy.

■   ■   ■

Suzan Shown Harjo, is the president and executive director of the Morning Star Foundation and trustee of the National Museum of the American Indian. She is the former executive director of the National Congress of American Indians. She writes here about an issue that affects her personally as an American Indian of Cheyenne and Creek heritage. "Last Rites for Indian Dead" first appeared in the *Los Angeles Times* on September 16, 1989.

Before reading the essay, recollect what you know about the way American Indians have been treated historically. As you read, notice how Harjo reminds readers of this historical context. How does it influence your responsiveness to her argument?

**LAST RITES
FOR INDIAN DEAD**
SUZAN SHOWN
HARJO

What if museums, universities and government agencies could put your dead   1
relatives on display or keep them in boxes to be cut up and otherwise studied? What if you believed that the spirits of the dead could not rest until their human remains were placed in a sacred area?

The ordinary American would say there ought to be a law—and there is, for ordinary Americans. The problem for American Indians is that there are too many laws of the kind that make us the archeological property of the United States and too few of the kind that protect us from such insults.

Some of my own Cheyenne relatives' skulls are in the Smithsonian Institution today, along with those of at least 4,500 other Indian people who were violated in the 1800s by the U.S. Army for an "Indian Crania Study." It wasn't enough that these unarmed Cheyenne people were mowed down by the cavalry at the infamous Sand Creek massacre; many were decapitated and their heads shipped to Washington as freight. (The Army Medical Museum's collection is now in the Smithsonian.) Some had been exhumed only hours after being buried. Imagine their grieving families' reaction on finding their loved ones disinterred and headless.

Some targets of the Army's study were killed in noncombat situations and beheaded immediately. The officer's account of the decapitation of the Apache chief Mangas Coloradas in 1863 shows the pseudoscientific nature of the exercise. "I weighed the brain and measured the skull," the good doctor wrote, "and found that while the skull was smaller, the brain was larger than that of Daniel Webster."

These journal accounts exist in excruciating detail, yet missing are any records of overall comparisons, conclusions or final reports of the Army study. Since it is unlike the Army not to leave a paper trail, one must wonder about the motive for its collection.

The total Indian body count in the Smithsonian collection is more than 19,000, and it is not the largest in the country. It is not inconceivable that the 1.5 million of us living today are outnumbered by our dead stored in museums, educational institutions, federal agencies, state historical societies and private collections. The Indian people are further dehumanized by being exhibited alongside the mastodons and dinosaurs and other extinct creatures.

Where we have buried our dead in peace, more often than not the sites have been desecrated. For more than 200 years, relic-hunting has been a popular pursuit. Lately, the market in Indian artifacts has brought this abhorrent activity to a fever pitch in some areas. And when scavengers come upon Indian burial sites, everything found becomes fair game, including sacred burial offerings, teeth and skeletal remains.

One unusually well-publicized example of Indian grave desecration occurred two years ago in a western Kentucky field known as Slack Farm, the site of an Indian village five centuries ago. Ten men—one with a business card stating "Have Shovel, Will Travel"—paid the landowner $10,000 to lease digging rights between planting seasons. They dug extensively on the 40-acre farm, rummaging through an estimated 650 graves, collecting burial goods, tools and ceremonial items. Skeletons were strewn about like litter.

What motivates people to do something like this? Financial gain is the first answer. Indian relic-collecting has become a multimillion-dollar industry. The price tag on a bead necklace can easily top $1,000; rare pieces fetch tens of thousands.

And it is not just collectors of the macabre who pay for skeletal remains. Scientists say that these deceased Indians are needed for research that someday could benefit the health and welfare of living Indians. But just how many dead Indians must they examine? Nineteen thousand?

There is doubt as to whether permanent curation of our dead really benefits Indians. Dr. Emery A. Johnson, former assistant Surgeon General, recently observed,

"I am not aware of any current medical diagnostic or treatment procedure that has been derived from research on such skeletal remains. Nor am I aware of any during the 34 years that I have been involved in American Indian . . . health care."

Indian remains are still being collected for racial biological studies. While the 12 intentions may be honorable, the ethics of using human remains this way without the full consent of relatives must be questioned.

Some relief for Indian people has come on the state level. Almost half of the 13 states, including California, have passed laws protecting Indian burial sites and restricting the sale of Indian bones, burial offerings and other sacred items. Rep. Charles E. Bennett (D-Fla.) and Sen. John McCain (R-Ariz.) have introduced bills that are a good start in invoking the federal government's protection. However, no legislation has attacked the problem head-on by imposing stiff penalties at the marketplace, or by changing laws that make dead Indians the nation's property.

Some universities—notably Stanford, Nebraska, Minnesota and Seattle—have 14 returned, or agreed to return, Indian human remains; it is fitting that institutions of higher education should lead the way.

Congress is now deciding what to do with the government's extensive collection 15 of Indian human remains and associated funerary objects. The secretary of the Smithsonian, Robert McC. Adams, has been valiantly attempting to apply modern ethics to yesterday's excesses. This week, he announced that the Smithsonian would conduct an inventory and return all Indian skeletal remains that could be identified with specific tribes or living kin.

But there remains a reluctance generally among collectors of Indian remains to 16 take action of a scope that would have a quantitative impact and a healing quality. If they will not act on their own—and it is highly unlikely that they will—then Congress must act.

The country must recognize that the bodies of dead American Indian people are 17 not artifacts to be bought and sold as collector's items. It is not appropriate to store tens of thousands of our ancestors for possible future research. They are our family. They deserve to be returned to their sacred burial grounds and given a chance to rest.

The plunder of our people's graves has gone on too long. Let us rebury our dead 18 and remove this shameful past from America's future.

For Discussion

In noting that the secretary of the Smithsonian is applying "modern ethics to yesterday's excesses," Harjo seems to assume that a society shares a common set of values and that these values may change over time. Consider these assumptions. In the nineteenth century, what were our society's values and its attitudes toward the American Indian and other racial or ethnic minorities? How are our "modern ethics" similar or different? Give an example of today's values and attitudes toward people of color.

For Analysis

1. The essay begins by posing two questions. As a reader, how do you react to being asked these questions? How do you think Harjo wants you to react? Does this seem to you a good way to begin a position paper? Why or why not?

For more on making a
scratch outline, see pp.
384–87.

2.   To get a sense of how this argument is organized, make a scratch outline. Given her readers and purpose, what advantages or disadvantages do you see in Harjo's organization?

3.   What evidence does Harjo offer to support her claim that collecting American Indian bodies in the first place was pointless, if not malicious, and that keeping them today is unjustified? How convincing do you find this part of her argument (paragraphs 3–5 and 10–12)?

4.   Why do you think Harjo includes paragraphs 13–15? How do they support her argument?

**For Your
Own Writing**

Think of an issue about which you feel strongly, and identify your position. What arguments would you make to convince readers to agree with you? What role, if any, should your feelings play in the argument?

Commentary

Word choice is important in all writing, but it plays a crucial role in a position paper. This is especially true when the issue is highly emotional and the writer is personally involved, as is the case in this essay. Harjo argues rationally by supporting her statements with evidence, but she also consciously chooses words that express her outrage and arouse comparable feelings in us as readers. She moves us through her use of vivid images, challenges us with rhetorical questions, startles us with horrifying statistics, and upsets our complacency that things have changed with a shocking statement by a respected authority. Such appeals to emotion are no substitute for appeals to reason, but they can support and strengthen an argument.

A good example of how Harjo uses vivid language to move readers is the metaphor "mowed down," which creates a memorable image emphasizing the helplessness of the "unarmed Cheyenne people" during the Sand Creek massacre (paragraph 3). Another example is her description of a relic hunter "rummaging through" graves in a Kentucky field and leaving skeletons "strewn about like litter" (paragraph 8). These images express her feelings indirectly. She expresses them even more directly when she calls laws that make Indian remains "archeological property" an insult (paragraph 2).

Harjo uses rhetorical questions to establish a common bond of shared values and beliefs with readers. She opens her essay with two rhetorical questions and includes two others in paragraphs 9 and 10. Although writers generally know how a reasonable reader would normally answer such questions, they often supply the answers anyway, as Harjo does, to emphasize the point.

Harjo cites statistics and authorities as evidence supporting her argument, and it is worth noting that she uses the evidence not only to substantiate her claim but also to sustain our outrage. We cannot avoid asking ourselves whether as many as 4,500 skulls were really needed for a "crania study." Similarly, we have to be startled by the number of Indian skeletons still kept in museums and in private collections. The idea that they might outnumber the 1.5 million living American Indians is simply astounding. To refute the government's argument that these remains are needed for scientific research, Harjo quotes an authority, a former government official with no personal stake in the controversy. His words carry a lot of weight and are especially disturbing because they indicate that things have not really changed in the last hundred years.

For a discussion of using statistics and authorities, see pp. 473–76.

■   ■   ■

Rachel Richardson Smith, the author of the next selection, takes up an issue—abortion—that has been debated nationally for some time. In fact, few issues excite more impassioned argument than abortion. Writing in the "My Turn" section of *Newsweek,* Smith, a theology student and mother, exhibits a keen awareness of the issue's complexity.

Before reading her essay, recall what you already know about this issue. What does each side claim? What are their chief arguments? Which arguments do you find most convincing?

ABORTION, RIGHT AND WRONG
RACHEL RICHARDSON SMITH

I cannot bring myself to say I am in favor of abortion. I don't want anyone to have one. I want people to use contraceptives and for those contraceptives to be foolproof. I want people to be responsible for their actions, mature in their decisions. I want children to be loved, wanted, well cared for. 1

I cannot bring myself to say I am against choice. I want women who are young, poor, single or all three to be able to direct the course of their lives. I want women who have had all the children they want or can afford or their bodies can withstand to be able to decide their future. I want women who are in bad marriages or destructive relationships to avoid being trapped by pregnancy. 2

So in these days when thousands rally in opposition to legalized abortion, when facilities providing abortions are bombed, when the president speaks glowingly of the growing momentum behind the anti-abortion movement, I find myself increasingly alienated from the pro-life groups. 3

At the same time, I am overwhelmed with mail from pro-choice groups. They, too, are mobilizing their forces, growing articulate in support of their cause, and they want my support. I am not sure I can give it. 4

I find myself in the awkward position of being both anti-abortion and pro-choice. Neither group seems to be completely right—or wrong. It is not that I think abortion is wrong for me but acceptable for someone else. The question is far more complex than that. 5

Part of my problem is that what I think and how I feel about this issue are two entirely different matters. I know that unwanted children are often neglected, even abandoned. I know that many of those seeking abortions are children themselves. I know that making abortion illegal will not stop all women from having them. 6

I also know from experience the crisis an unplanned pregnancy can cause. Yet I have felt the joy of giving birth, the delight that comes from feeling a baby's skin 7 against my own. I know how hard it is to parent a child and how deeply satisfying it can be. My children sometimes provoke me and cause me endless frustration, but I can still look at them with tenderness and wonder at the miracle of it all. The lessons of my own experience produce conflicting emotions. Theory collides with reality.

It concerns me that both groups present themselves in absolutes. They are committed and they want me to commit. They do not recognize the gray area where I seem to be languishing. Each group has the right answer—the only answer. 8

Yet I am uncomfortable in either camp. I have nothing in common with the pro-lifers. I am horrified by their scare tactics, their pictures of well-formed fetuses tossed in a metal pan, their cruel slogans. I cannot condone their flagrant misuse of Scripture and unforgiving spirit. There is a meanness about their position that causes them to pass judgment on the lives of women in a way I could never do. 9

The pro-life groups, with their fundamentalist religious attitudes, have a fear and an abhorrence of sex, especially premarital sex. In their view abortion only compounds the sexual sin. What I find incomprehensible is that even as they are opposed to abortion they are also opposed to alternative solutions. They are squeamish about sex education in the schools. They don't want teens to have contraceptives without parental consent. They offer little aid or sympathy to unwed mothers. They are the vigilant guardians of a narrow morality. 10

I wonder how abortion got to be the greatest of all sins? What about poverty, ignorance, hunger, weaponry? 11

The only thing the anti-abortion groups seem to have right is that abortion is indeed the taking of human life. I simply cannot escape this one glaring fact. Call it what you will—fertilized egg, embryo, fetus. What we have here is human life. If it were just a mass of tissue there would be no debate. So I agree that abortion ends a life. But the anti-abortionists are wrong to call it murder. 12

The sad truth is that homicide is not always against the law. Our society does not categorically recognize the sanctity of human life. There are a number of legal and apparently socially acceptable ways to take human life. "Justifiable" homicide includes the death penalty, war, killing in self-defense. It seems to me that as a society we need to come to grips with our own ambiguity concerning the value of human life. If we are to value and protect unborn life so stringently, why do we not also value and protect life already born? 13

Why can't we see abortion for the human tragedy it is? No woman plans for her life to turn out that way. Even the most effective contraceptives are no guarantee against pregnancy. Loneliness, ignorance, immaturity can lead to decisions (or lack of decisions) that may result in untimely pregnancy. People make mistakes. 14

What many people seem to misunderstand is that no woman wants to have an abortion. Circumstances demand it; women do it. No woman reacts to abortion with joy. Relief, yes. But also ambivalence, grief, despair, guilt. 15

The pro-choice groups do not seem to acknowledge that abortion is not a perfect answer. What goes unsaid is that when a woman has an abortion she loses more than an unwanted pregnancy. Often she loses her self-respect. No woman can forget a pregnancy no matter how it ends. 16

Why can we not view abortion as one of those anguished decisions in which human beings struggle to do the best they can in trying circumstances? Why is abortion viewed so coldly and factually on the one hand and so judgmentally on the 17 other? Why is it not akin to the same painful experience families must sometimes make to allow a loved one to die?

I wonder how we can begin to change the context in which we think about 18 abortion. How can we begin to think about it redemptively? What is it in the trauma of loss of life—be it loved or unloved, born or unborn—from which we can learn? There is much I have yet to resolve. Even as I refuse to pass judgments on other women's lives, I weep for the children who might have been. I suspect I am not alone.

For Discussion

Smith makes a rather startling assertion in paragraph 13 when she writes, "Our society does not categorically recognize the sanctity of human life." Not only are there "legal and apparently socially acceptable ways to take human life," but we do not consistently "value and protect life already born." The author of the preceding essay, Suzan Shown Harjo, would agree that at least in relation to American Indians, this nation has taken many human lives and found ways to justify it. Others would argue that our current failure to provide adequate comprehensive health care and shelter for all Americans shows that we do not adequately value human life.

Discuss this idea. Can you think of further examples of the devaluation of human life in American history or in the present? On the other hand, can you think of historical or current examples of ways that we value and protect human life? Given your answers, does Smith's assertion seem accurate and fair to you? What implications does your conclusion have for the debate on abortion?

For Analysis

1.   Smith appears to weigh impartially the pros and cons, rejecting some arguments and accepting others. Upon close examination, how impartial do you think she really is? Does she treat each side equally? To help you analyze the essay, make a chart outlining the pro-life and pro-choice arguments Smith cites and her judgments of them.

2.   Smith claims that both camps—pro-life as well as pro-choice—"present themselves in absolutes." Why does she apparently assume that thinking in absolutes is wrong? What do you think?

3.   Consider how this section begins, noticing the repetition of sentence structure in the first two paragraphs. What exactly is repeated and what effect does this repetition have? From this way of beginning, what can you infer about Smith's argumentative strategy? How effective would you say it is?

For a discussion of refuting counterarguments, see pp. 483–86.

4.   In paragraphs 12 and 13, Smith addresses the question of whether or not abortion constitutes murder. The pro-life argument centers on the judgment that abortion is the taking of a life. How does Smith refute this argument? Given her argumentative strategy, how effective is this refutation?

For Your Own Writing

Think of an issue about which you feel ambivalent. What exactly are your contradictory feelings on this issue? If you were to write a position paper on this issue, how would you construct your argument? What points would you have to consider further and learn more about?

Commentary   Whereas Goss and Harjo state their positions explicitly in the opening paragraphs, Smith doesn't announce her thesis until the end. She starts out by saying that she is neither in favor of abortion nor against choice, and goes on to criticize both the anti-abortion and pro-choice activists for the way they argue. A reader might think that Smith is undecided on the issue, but by paragraph 14 her position becomes clear: although she thinks that abortion is a "human tragedy," she argues that women should have the right to make the "anguished" decision for themselves.

You might ask why Smith withholds her thesis for so long. The answer lies in her argumentative strategy. Knowing that on this issue many people tend to be intolerant of others' views, she tries to establish some common ground on which most of her readers can stand. She does this by showing us her own process of deliberation, admitting in paragraph 7 to having "conflicting emotions." This ambivalence, she explains, comes when "theory collides with reality." By theory, Smith means an ideal world where abortion would be unnecessary, contraceptives would be foolproof, and people would always be responsible. People would have all the children they wanted and could afford. However, Smith knows, and assumes all reasonable people know, that reality inevitably falls short of theory. So, she concludes, if abortion is evil (and Smith seems to agree that it is), it may be a necessary evil.

Not only does Smith try to give readers the impression that she, like them, is honestly struggling to make a reasonable decision, but she also presents herself as an independent thinker by critizing both camps. She describes herself as "horrified" and "alienated" by their tactics. Ticking off the arguments proposed by each side, she agrees with some and disagrees with others. By seeing merit as well as weakness on both sides, she demonstrates that she is fair-minded. In this way, Smith attempts to establish a bond with readers who also want to think of themselves as caring and reasonable, independent and fair-minded.

In addition to noticing how Smith establishes her credibility, you might also consider how she uses definition to support her position. Definition is essential to all kinds of writing, but it is especially important in a position paper. Smith relies on defining as her primary argumentative strategy. By defining abortion as "the taking of human life," she appears to concede an important point to the pro-life advocates. In effect, she agrees with them that a fetus, though unborn, should still be regarded as a human life. This idea is crucial to the pro-life argument because it supports the argument that abortion is murder.

But Smith will not go this far. While she concedes that "abortion ends a life," she disagrees that it is murder. She draws a distinction—some would say too fine a distinction—between taking a human life and murder. Defi-

*For more on defining,
see pp. 440–51. For
more on classifying, see
pp. 452–60.*

nition always involves classification, and Smith classifies homicide (the taking
of a human life) into two categories: justifiable homicide (in which she
includes the death penalty, war, killing in self-defense, and abortion) and
unjustifiable homicide (which she also calls murder). Readers may or may
not be convinced, but nearly everyone can admire the ingenuity of her argument. Basing an argument on definition is not a sure bet; as this example
illustrates, it is just as risky as any other kind of reasoning.

One last feature of this essay—Smith's use of repetition—deserves special
comment. She uses a common kind of repetition called anaphora, the repeating of sentence openers. For example, the first sentence of each of the
first two paragraphs follows the identical pattern: "I cannot bring myself to
say I am. . . ." These sentences set up the opposition with which the author
struggles throughout the essay. Moreover, the following sentences in these
two paragraphs all begin the same way, with one important variation; "I
don't want . . . I want . . . I want. . . ."

Skimming the essay, you will find many other examples of Smith's deliberate repetition of this "*I* + verb" sentence pattern. She also repeats other
sentence patterns such as "*They* + verb" (paragraph 10), "*No woman* + verb"
(paragraphs 14, 15, and 16), and "*Why* + verb" (paragraph 17).

Sometimes repeating words and sentence patterns is simply redundant,
making the rhythm monotonous and unemphatic. But done well, as in
Smith's essay, repetition can make prose more memorable and moving. When
you find yourself using repetition in an essay taking a position, consider
carefully whether this strategy adds to the impact of your argument or detracts from it.

■　　■　　■

Jessica Statsky wrote the following essay about children's competitive sports
for her freshman composition course. Before reading, recall your own experiences as an elementary school child playing competitive sports, either in
or out of school. If you weren't actively involved yourself, did you know
anyone who was? Looking back, do you think that winning was unduly
emphasized? What value was placed on having a good time? On learning to
get along with others? On developing athletic skills and confidence?

**CHILDREN NEED
TO PLAY, NOT
COMPETE**
JESSICA STATSKY

Over the past three decades organized sports for children have increased dra- 1
matically in the United States. And though many adults regard Little League Baseball
and Peewee Football as a basic part of childhood, the games are not always joyous
ones. When overzealous parents and coaches impose adult standards on children's
sports, the result can be activities that are neither satisfying nor beneficial to children.

I'm concerned about all organized sports activities for children between the ages 2
of six and twelve. The damage I see results from noncontact as well as contact sports,
from sports organized locally as well as those organized nationally. Highly organized

competitive sports such as Peewee Football and Little League Baseball are too often played to adult standards, which are developmentally inappropriate for children and can be both physically and psychologically harmful. Furthermore, because they eliminate many children from organized sports before they are ready to compete, they are actually counterproductive for developing either future players or fans. Finally, because they emphasize competition and winning, they unfortunately provide occasions for some parents and coaches to place their own fantasies and needs ahead of children's welfare.

One readily understandable danger of overly competitive sports is that they entice children into physical actions that are bad for growing bodies. For example, a twelve-year-old trying to throw a curve ball may put abnormal strain on developing arm and shoulder muscles, sometimes resulting in lifelong injuries (Koppett 294). Contact sports like football can be even more hazardous. Thomas Tutko, a psychology professor at San Jose State University, and coauthor of the book *Winning is Everything and Other American Myths,* said: "I am strongly opposed to young kids playing tackle football. It is not the right stage of development for them to be taught to crash into other kids. Kids under the age of fourteen are not by nature physical. Their main concern is self-preservation. They don't want to meet head on and slam into each other. But tackle football absolutely requires that they try to hit each other as hard as they can. And it is too traumatic for kids" (qtd. in Tosches A1). 3

As Tutko indicates, even when children are not injured, fear of being hurt detracts from their enjoyment of the sport. One mother of an eight-year-old Peewee Football player explained, "The kids get so scared. They get hit once and they don't want anything to do with football anymore. They'll sit on the bench and pretend their leg hurts . . ." (qtd. in Tosches A32). Some children are driven to even more desperate measures. For example, in one Peewee Football game a reporter watched the following scene as a player took himself out of the game: 4

"Coach, my tummy hurts. I can't play," he said. The coach told the player to get back onto the field. "There's nothing wrong with your stomach," he said. When the coach turned his head the seven-year-old stuck a finger down his throat and made himself vomit. When the coach turned back, the boy pointed to the ground and told him, "Yes there is, coach. See?" (Tosches A1).

Besides physical hazards and anxieties, competitive sports pose psychological dangers for children. Martin Rablovsky, a former sports editor for the *New York Times,* said that in all his years of watching young children play organized sports, he noticed very few of them smiling. "I've seen children enjoying a spontaneous pre-practice scrimmage become somber and serious when the coach's whistle blows," Rablovsky said. "The spirit of play suddenly disappears, and sport becomes joblike" (qtd. in Coakley 94). The primary goal of a professional athlete—winning—is not appropriate for children. Their goals should be having fun, learning, and being with friends. Although winning does add to the fun, too many adults lose sight of what matters and make winning the most important goal. Several studies have shown that when children are asked whether they would rather be warming the bench on a winning team or playing regularly on a losing team, about 90 percent choose the latter (Smith, Smith, and Smoll 11). 5

Winning and losing may be an inevitable part of adult life, but they should not be part of childhood. Too much competition too early in life can affect a child's 6 development. Children are easily influenced, and when they sense that their competence and worth are based on their ability to live up to their parents' and coaches' high expectations—and on their ability to win—they can become discouraged and depressed. According to Dr. Glyn C. Roberts, a professor of kinesiology at the Institute of Child Behavior and Development at the University of Illinois, 80 to 90 percent of children who play competitive sports at a young age drop out by sixteen (Kutner C8).

This statistic illustrates another reason I oppose competitive sports for children: because they are so highly selective, very few children get to participate. Far too soon a few children are singled out for their athletic promise, while many others, who may be on the verge of developing the necessary strength and ability, are screened out and discouraged from trying out again. Like adults, children fear failure, and so even those with good physical skills may stay away because they lack self-confidence. Consequently, teams lose many promising players who with some encouragement and experience might have become stars. The problem is that many parent-sponsored, out-of-school programs give more importance to having a winning team than to developing children's physical skills and self-esteem. 7

Indeed, it is no secret that too often scorekeeping, league standings, and the drive to win bring out the worst in adults who are more absorbed in living out their own fantasies than in enhancing the quality of the experience for children (Smith, Smith, and Smoll 9). Recent newspaper articles on children's sports contain plenty of horror stories. A *Los Angeles Times* reporter, for example, tells the story of a brawl among seventy-five parents following a Peewee Football game. As a result of the brawl, which began when a parent from one team confronted a player from the other team, the teams are now thinking of hiring security guards for future games. Another example is provided by a *Times* editorial about a Little League manager who intimidated the opposing team by setting fire to one of their team's jerseys on the pitching mound before the game began. As the editorial writer commented, the manager showed his young team that "intimidation could substitute for playing well." 8

Although not all parents or coaches behave so inappropriately, the seriousness of the problem is illustrated by the fact that Adelphi University in Garden City, New York, offers a sports psychology workshop for Little League coaches, designed to balance their "animal instincts" with educational theory in hopes of reducing the "screaming and hollering," in the words of Harold Weisman, manager of sixteen Little Leagues in New York City. In a three-and-one-half hour Sunday morning workshop, coaches learn how to make practices more fun, treat injuries, deal with irate parents, and be "more sensitive to their young players' fears, emotional frailties, and need for recognition" (Schmitt B2). Little League is to be credited with recognizing the need for such workshops. 9

Some parents would no doubt argue that children can't start too soon preparing to live in a competitive free-market economy. After all, secondary schools and colleges require students to compete for grades, and college admission is extremely competitive. And it is perfectly obvious how important competitive skills are in finding a job or a mate. Yet the ability to cooperate is also important for success in life. Before children are psychologically ready for competition, maybe we should emphasize cooperation and individual performance in team sports rather than winning. 10

Many people are ready for such an emphasis. In 1988 one New York Little League official who had attended the Adelphi workshop tried to ban scoring from six-to-eight-year-olds' games—but parents wouldn't support him (Schmitt B2). An innovative children's sports program in New York City, City-Sports-For-Kids, emphasizes fitness, self-esteem, and sportsmanship. In this program's basketball games, every member on a team plays at least two of six eight-minute periods. The basket is seven feet from the floor, rather than ten feet, and a player can score a point just by hitting the rim (Bloch C12). I believe this kind of local program should replace overly competitive programs like Peewee Football and Little League Baseball.

Authorities have clearly documented the excesses and dangers of many competitive sports programs for children. It would seem that few children benefit from these programs and that those who do would benefit even more from programs emphasizing fitness, cooperation, sportsmanship, and individual performance. Thirteen- and fourteen-year-olds may be eager for competition, but few younger children are. These younger children deserve sports programs designed specifically for *their* needs and abilities.

11

Works Cited

Bloch, Gordon B. "Thrill of Victory Is Secondary to Fun." *New York Times* 2 Apr. 1990, late ed.:C12.

"The Bad News Pyromaniacs?" Editorial. *Los Angeles Times* 16 June 1990:B6.

Coakley, Jay J. *Sport in Society: Issues and Controversies.* St. Louis: Mosby, 1982.

Koppett, Leonard. *Sports Illusion, Sports Reality.* New York: Houghton, 1981.

Kutner, Lawrence. "Athletics, Through a Child's Eyes. *New York Times* 23 Mar. 1989, late ed.:C8.

Schmitt, Eric. "Psychologists Take Seat on Little League Bench." *New York Times* 14 Mar. 1989, late ed.:B2.

Smith, Nathan, Ronald Smith, and Frank Smoll. *Kidsports: A Survival Guide for Parents.* New York: Addison-Wesley, 1983.

Tosches, Rich. "Peewee Football: Is It Time to Blow the Whistle?" *Los Angeles Times* 3 Dec. 1988:A1.

For Discussion

Statsky makes the point that whereas competition is highly valued in our culture, cooperation tends to be downplayed. In what ways does our society encourage competition? How is cooperation encouraged? Does the educational system, in your experience, encourage one more than the other? Which of the two seems to be valued most highly in advertising, television, and movies? What advantages or disadvantages do you see in emphasizing competition over cooperation?

For Analysis

For discussion and illustration of these cueing devices, see Chapter 12.

1.   Make a scratch outline of Statsky's argument. Then evaluate her organization. Put brackets around the cueing devices—statements forecasting what is to come, summaries of what has just been said, topic sentences, and transitions—she uses to help readers stay on track. Point to any places where you lose track or get confused.

2.   Statsky's argumentative strategy includes showing that she and her readers share the same values. Point to a passage where you feel she is trying to build a bridge of shared values between herself and her readers. How does this appeal affect your responsiveness to this particular passage?

3.   Skim the essay, noting each time Statsky quotes authorities. What do you think is the cumulative effect of quoting so many different people? Choose the quotation that you find most effective, and explain why.

4.   Reread the conclusion. What is Statsky trying to accomplish by ending the essay this way? How well do you think her conclusion works?

5.   Read the Writer at Work discussion on pp. 211–13. Notice in her analysis of purpose and audience how Statsky describes the readers she intends to address and her proposed argumentative strategy. Review the revised essay to see whether she kept to this plan or modified it in some way.

**For Your
Own Writing**

Make a list of issues related to childhood and adolescence. (Should elementary and secondary schools be on a year-round schedule? Should children be required to learn a foreign language? Should parents be legally responsible for the cost of vandalism committed by their adolescent children?) Then choose an issue that you think you could write about. What position do you think you would take? Why?

Commentary

Writers of position papers must be especially careful not to define the issue too broadly or to overstate their position. Statsky defines her issue by identifying several parameters such as age, geography, school affiliation, and type of sport. She restricts the subject by both age and school affiliation, limiting it to children between the ages of six and twelve (paragraph 2), and to "parent-sponsored out-of-school" sports (paragraph 7). On the other hand, she allows for sports organized nationally as well as locally and for all kinds of sports, noncontact as well as contact. Finally, to ensure that her readers know the kind of organized, competitive team sports she's talking about, Statsky gives two familiar examples: Peewee Football and Little League Baseball.

Statsky also qualifies her thesis by avoiding absolute or unconditional language. In the opening paragraph, for example, she uses the word *always* to soften her assertion: "These games are not always joyous ones." Similarly, in the next sentence, instead of saying "the result is" she allows for other possibilities by saying "the result can be." These minor adjustments in word choice have an enormous effect because they make Statsky's position seem reasonable. They also make her appear temperate, not given to extreme opinions, and therefore reliable and trustworthy as an advocate.

PURPOSE AND AUDIENCE

In a position paper, every decision you make—from the words you choose to the way you organize your evidence—depends on your purpose and audience. To develop an appropriate argumentative strategy, one that will have a good chance of achieving your purpose with your intended readers, you need to understand your audience. You need to know where your readers stand on the issue—whether they oppose your position, are undecided, or basically agree with you—and also to know how they think about the issue—for example, whether they see it as a moral issue, an issue of civil liberties, an issue that affects them personally. An effective argumentative strategy seeks to build a bridge of shared values and beliefs between writer and reader.

If you are writing primarily to readers with whom you disagree fundamentally, it is highly unlikely that you will be able to change their minds with a single essay, no matter how well written it is. Most writers addressing this kind of audience would be satisfied if they could simply win their readers' respect for their point of view. An even greater achievement would be to convince such readers to reconsider their own position. Kristin Goss, for example, knows that some of her audience will disagree with her position, and she is careful to appeal to shared values. On the one hand, she seeks to convince her readers that, like them, she opposes censorship—but that denying *Playboy* advertising space is not an act of censorship. On the other hand, she argues that running the ad would perpetuate the "institutionalized exploitation of women," something that she assumes her readers do not want to encourage.

Of course, it is easier to persuade readers who have not made up their minds. This is probably the kind of audience to which Rachel Richardson Smith addresses her essay on abortion. She identifies herself as being in neither the pro-life nor the pro-choice camp, assuming that her readers, like her, are undecided and also unhappy with the way both sides have argued their positions. Her argumentative strategy depends on readers' identifying with her. She shows them how, after weighing the pros and cons, she has arrived at a conclusion. An important part of her strategy is to offer readers a new way of looking at the issue—not as a moral or pragmatic question but as a tragic situation.

When you address readers who are inclined to agree with your position, your purpose is primarily to strengthen their understanding and commitment. You can do this by offering an especially compelling argument, as Suzan Shown Harjo does in her essay on American Indian remains. Her argumentative strategy is to remind readers of the issue's continuing relevance and to provide new evidence to refute counterarguments. She also tries to inspire them to action by appealing to their emotions. If handled judiciously, emotional appeals can strengthen an argument. But if they seem manipulative or if they are used as a substitute for reasoned argument, they will more likely backfire, undermining even the most sympathetic readers' confidence in your argument.

BASIC FEATURES OF POSITION PAPERS

Position papers generally share the following basic features: a well-defined issue, a clear position, a convincing argument, and a reasonable tone.

A Well-defined Issue

Position papers concern controversial issues, matters on which reasonable people disagree. The issue may arise from a particular occasion (as in the Goss essay) or be part of an ongoing debate (as in the Smith selection). In either case, the writer must clearly explain the issue.

Kristin Goss, because she is writing about a campus controversy, can safely assume that her immediate readers, Harvard students, will be familiar with the issue. Nevertheless, she reminds them that it centers on *The Crimson*'s decision not to print a *Playboy* ad recruiting Harvard women.

In contrast, Suzan Shown Harjo cannot assume that her readers will know about the injustice that she contends has been done to American Indians. Not only must she inform readers about history, but she also has to explain that the laws protecting "ordinary Americans" do not protect American Indians.

In addition to establishing that the issue exists, a writer needs to define it for the writing purpose. Defining an issue means saying what kind of issue it is. Goss, for example, defines the *Playboy* ad issue in terms of sexism, whereas some of her readers see it as a matter of censorship. Smith argues that abortion is not a moral or even a legal question, but an agonizing personal crisis. She uses a series of rhetorical questions to try to change her readers' way of looking at the issue. Similarly, by calling the American Indian remains "bodies" instead of "collector's items," Harjo defines the issue in human terms rather than in terms of property rights. Sometimes, defining the issue also involves marking its boundaries. Jessica Statsky, for example, limits the organized team sports she is talking about to those sponsored by parents outside schools for children of certain ages.

A Clear Position

In addition to defining the issue, the essay should also clearly indicate the writer's position. Writers may qualify their claims to accommodate strong counterarguments, but they should avoid vagueness or indecision.

Very often writers declare their position in a thesis statement early in the essay. The advantage of this strategy is that it lets the audience know right away where the writer stands. Goss, for instance, opens with a sentence that both defines the issue and announces her position: "*The Crimson*'s decision not to run *Playboy*'s advertisement recruiting Harvard women . . . was both the very most and the very least the newspaper could do to fight the institutionalized exploitation of women." Similarly, Statsky states her thesis explicitly in the opening paragraph and sets forth her reasons at the end of the second paragraph.

For more about making claims, see pp. 468–69. For more about the thesis statement, see pp. 400–01.

The thesis may also appear later in the essay. Postponing the thesis is particularly appropriate when the writer wants to weigh the pros and cons before announcing his or her position. We see this strategy in Smith's essay on abortion. She never explicitly states a thesis, but her position is clearly implied in the last four paragraphs: even though she supports the right to abortion, Smith doesn't want to align herself with pro-choice activists because she disapproves of what she considers their matter-of-fact attitude toward a tragic situation.

A Convincing Argument

A position paper cannot merely assert a writer's views. To convince readers, writers must provide sound reasoning and solid evidence in support of their claims. They must also anticipate possible counterarguments and either accommodate or refute them.

Sound Reasoning and Solid Evidence.   To be sure that readers will be able to follow an argument, the main points supporting a claim should be not only stated clearly but also explained and fully developed. Goss, for example, explains that protesting *Playboy*'s brand of sexism is particularly important because it is so subtle. She develops this point by describing *Playboy* as an example of "socially acceptable" sexism. Then, arguing by analogy, she compares *Playboy*'s sexism to the kind of racism that was once socially accepted but is now widely condemned. Readers may or may not be convinced by this argument, but by explaining and developing it fully, Goss makes sure that they understand her reasoning.

For guidance on finding published sources, see pp. 505–22.

A writer can cite various kinds of evidence in support of a position, including examples, authorities, and statistics.

Examples are used to bolster and to illustrate an argument. Harjo cites the outrageous example of grave desecration in Kentucky as a graphic illustration of her argument.

Testimony from authorities—people especially knowledgeable about the issue—also enhances the credibility of an argument. Statsky cites many authorities, including professors, reporters, physicians, coaches, and parents. As most writers do, she identifies these authorities by giving their credentials. Similarly, Harjo, for example, quotes Dr. Emery A. Johnson, whom she identifies as a former assistant surgeon general. Not only is Johnson a noted authority, but he also has no apparent motive for agreeing with Harjo other than to see that justice is done; consequently, he comes across to most readers as an unbiased expert.

For more on these and other kinds of evidence, see pp. 471–80.

Statistics are another common kind of evidence. Statsky cites statistics to demonstrate that a very high proportion of children—between 80 and 90 percent—drop out of organized sports by the time they enter their teens. She wisely indicates the source of these statistics, a professor at the University of Illinois, because knowledgeable readers tend to be skeptical of statistics that are not attributed to a source.

Counterarguments.   In addition to presenting reasons and evidence, a writer may also need to acknowledge opposing points of view and to accommodate reasonable counterarguments. Accommodating a counterargument basically involves admitting that it has validity and qualifying one's own view to account for it. Counterarguments that strike the writer as wrong, on the other hand, can be refuted. Refuting a counterargument means trying to show how it is wrong.

Harjo offers a good example of a writer accommodating possible counterarguments when she acknowledges the "honorable" intentions of scientists studying American Indian remains today. Yet she also reminds readers that for ethical reasons scientists should request permission from these American Indians' descendants before continuing to use the bodies for research.

Goss's essay, on the other hand, demonstrates how a writer can refute counterarguments. To identify the counterargument and represent it fairly, Goss uses the opposition's own language: they "claim the staff endeavored to 'censor' *Playboy*." To refute this counterargument, Goss argues that *The Crimson*'s action does not fit the definition of censorship.

For a discussion of anticipating counterarguments, see pp. 480–86.

Some writers appear to accommodate counterarguments but actually refute them. In debating the issue of abortion, for example, Smith accepts as fact the argument that a fetus is a human life (paragraph 12). Since this point is the crux of the anti-abortion argument, it would seem that by accommodating it Smith is conceding the whole argument. However, she turns around and refutes the anti-abortion argument by arguing that homicide is sometimes justifiable. These examples from Goss and Smith also indicate how important definition is in constructing a convincing argument.

A Reasonable Tone

Because writers of position papers want readers to take them seriously, they must adopt a tone that will be likely to gain readers' confidence and respect. They need to demonstrate their sincerity both by the way they reason and by the language they use. In other words, writers should seek to create a favorable impression through their tone.

Goss, for example, adopts an impassioned tone when writing about sexism. When she calls attention to the plight of women, her tone carries the conviction of personal experience. When she defends political protest as the only means of fighting sexism, she seems genuinely frustrated and angry. Even readers who oppose her view on the issue are likely to respect her feelings. Some readers, however, may react negatively to her use of such feminist buzzwords as *exploitation, sexism,* and *sex object.* As terms associated with particular ideology, buzzwords can establish common ground with sympathetic readers. But an argument cannot be based on buzzwords alone. Though they may resonate for those who already agree, such words cannot be counted on to convince those who do not.

The language at the beginning of Smith's essay on abortion strikes a heartfelt, confessional tone. She gives the impression of someone who sees both sides of a complicated issue, but when she characterizes the sides as camps vying for her support, her tone changes. She criticizes both sides—the pro-choice advocates for treating abortion "coldly and factually," and the pro-lifers for their "meanness" and "unforgiving spirit." Some readers may respond negatively to this harsh language. Because she seems so sincere, however, many readers are apt to forgive this harshness.

Guide to Writing

THE WRITING ASSIGNMENT

Write a position paper on a controversial issue. Examine the issue critically, take a position, and develop a reasoned argument in support of your position.

INVENTION AND RESEARCH

At this point you need to choose and explore an issue, consider your purpose and audience, formulate your thesis, test your choice, develop your reasoning, and anticipate counterarguments.

Choosing an Issue   Writing a position paper offers an opportunity to think deeply about an important issue. Following are some activities that can help you choose a promising issue and that may suggest ways to begin thinking about it.

Listing Issues.   Begin by making a list of issues you might write about. Put them in the form of questions, like the following examples. Make the list as long as you can. Include both issues on which you already have ideas and ones you do not know much about but would like to explore further.

Your choice may be influenced by whether you have time for research or whether your instructor requires it. You would have to research issues like affirmative action programs fairly extensively before you could adequately define a position and argue it well. Such issues, which have been debated for years and written about repeatedly, make excellent topics for extended research projects. Other issues, like rock music, may be approached more confidently from personal experience or from limited research. Even this kind of topic may be surprisingly complex; nevertheless, you might argue it convincingly without research if you have firsthand knowledge and can discuss it with others. Still other topics may be more suitable if your time is limited or your instructor wants you to argue a position without doing research, topics like separate college organizations for African-American and Hispanic students or special academic assistance for athletes. One possibility is to write on an issue currently affecting your community or college. You could define and explore fully issues like these with classmates or friends; and, with care, you could identify a wide range of counterarguments.

- Should drug testing be required in sports and industry?
- Should school boards be able to keep certain books out of school libraries?
- Should the primary purpose of a college education be job preparation?

- Should parents limit the amount of television their children watch?
- Should schools attempt to teach spiritual and moral values?
- Should undercover police officers be permitted to pose as high school students in order to identify sellers and users of drugs?
- Should a standard American history and literature course be taught in high schools so that all graduates have a common cultural experience?
- Should extended training in music performance or art making (drawing, painting, sculpting) be required of all high school students?
- Should college admission be based solely on academic achievement?
- Should college students work part time?
- Since fraternity hazing practices have caused injuries and even deaths, should fraternities be banned from college campuses?
- Should lesbians and gay men be allowed to adopt children?
- Should women serve in combat positions in the military?
- Should teenagers accused of serious crimes be tried as adults?

Choosing an Intriguing Issue.   Select an issue from your list that seems especially interesting, one that you would like to know more about. It should be an issue about which people disagree.

Exploring the Issue

To understand the issue and the rhetorical situation, you will need to define the issue, examine the pros and cons, and decide on your position.

Defining the Issue.   To begin thinking about the issue, write for about five minutes trying to define it. Do not take sides or present an argument; just state what you think the issue is. Who is involved in this issue? Identify individuals or groups. What kind of issue is it? Describe its features, scope, and history. Name and detail its aspects or parts. Try to find just the right words for naming aspects of the issue.

Doing Research.   If you do not know very much about the issue or the various views on it, do some research before continuing. You can gather information by talking to others or by reading what others have written. Refer to Chapter 19 for advice on interviewing an expert or surveying opinion and to Chapter 20 for guidelines on doing library research.

   If you do not have time for research but do not feel confident that you know enough about your topic to write a thoughtful essay, you should consider another subject, one about which you are better informed. Return to your list of possible issues and start over again.

On pp. 520–21 is a list of sources representing particular viewpoints.

Jessica Statsky's Pro/Con chart appears on pp. 211–12.

Determining the Pros and Cons.   Begin by dividing a page into two columns. Write the word *Pro* at the top of the left-hand column and *Con* at the top of the right-hand column. Then, in the appropriate column, list the reasons on each side of the issue. Try to be as thorough as you can now, even if you find later that you need to do research.

Deciding on a Tentative Position.   Once you have examined the pros and cons of an issue, decide on the tentative position you take on the issue.

Considering Your Purpose and Audience

After you've studied the issue and the various views people hold, you are ready to consider your purpose and audience. Write a couple of paragraphs analyzing your purpose and readers and trying to determine an argumentative strategy. Consider the following questions as you write.

- How do these particular readers define the issue?
- What basic values or assumptions about the issue do we share?
- What kinds of evidence are they likely to find convincing?
- Given the answers to the previous questions, what argumentative strategy should I adopt?

Consider several different ways of appealing to your readers. By considering various strategies now, you prepare yourself to make thoughtful decisions later.

Stating Your Thesis

Write a sentence or two stating your thesis. Choose your words carefully. Try to make your position clear and arguable, and be sure to qualify it appropriately.

You will have ample opportunity to revise your thesis as you learn more about the issue and develop your argument. Stating it now, even tentatively, will help you to focus the rest of your invention and planning.

Testing Your Choice

This is a good time to evaluate whether or not you should proceed with this particular issue. To make this decision, ask yourself the following questions:

- Does this topic really interest me?
- Do I know enough about it now to plan and write my essay, or can I learn what I need to know in the time I have remaining?
- Is the topic manageable within my time and space limits?
- Do I have a good sense of how others view this issue and what readers I might address in my essay?
- Have I begun to understand the issue and to formulate my own view?

As you explore the issue further and develop your argument, you will want to reconsider these questions. If at any point you decide that you cannot answer them affirmatively, you may want to choose a different issue.

For Group Inquiry

You might find it useful at this point to get together with two or three other students and run your chosen topics by one another. Assess the group's interest in the issue you've chosen to write about, and invite their advice about whether it sounds promising. Does it seem likely to lead to a paper they would care to read? Your purpose is to decide whether you have chosen a good issue to write about and thus to be able to proceed confidently to develop your position paper.

Developing Your Reasoning

To construct a convincing argument, you should list reasons for your position, choose the strongest ones, and develop them fully.

Listing Reasons.   Write down every plausible reason you could give to convince readers that your position on this issue should be taken seriously. To get started, it might help to think of your reasons as *because* clauses attached to your thesis statement. For example, "My position is X because . . ." or "A reason I think X is that. . . ."

Choosing the Strongest Reasons.   Review your list with your readers in mind. Mark the reasons that you think would carry most weight with them. If none of your reasons seems very strong, you might need to reconsider your position, do some more research, or even pick another topic.

Developing Your Best Reasons.   Take your strongest reasons and write for five minutes on each one, explaining it to your readers and providing evidence to support it. You may discover that you need some specific information: Do not stop to locate it now; just make a note about what you need and continue writing. If you decide not to include some of these reasons, you may not need the information after all. Later, before drafting or even when revising your draft, you will be able to follow up and locate any information you still need.

Anticipating Counterarguments

This section will help you to anticipate counterarguments and to decide which ones you will accommodate and which you will refute.

Listing Counterarguments.   Begin by listing all the counterarguments you can think of. You will almost certainly have discovered some in the process of exploring and researching the issue. If you cannot think of any counterarguments at all, write out an imaginary conversation with someone who disagrees with you on the issue.

Accommodating Counterarguments.   Review your list of counterarguments, and decide which of them you think you should accommodate. Write a few sentences for each one indicating how you will have to modify or qualify your thesis. Also, briefly explain why you are conceding this point.

Refuting Counterarguments.   Review the list to find counterarguments that you can refute. For each one, write for five minutes developing your refutation. Be careful not to criticize unfairly those who make these counterarguments. Instead, try to explain to them why you do not find the arguments convincing: they may be irrelevant, only partially true, or not true at all. If you need to check facts or find some other information, do so later. It will be most efficient at this point simply to list the points you need to check and to save the research until you take a break.

Restating Your Thesis   Now that you have developed your argument, you may want to reformulate your thesis. Consider whether you should change your language to qualify or limit your claim.

PLANNING AND DRAFTING

Before you begin drafting your essay, take some time to review your notes and see what you have, to set goals for your essay, to prepare an outline, and to draft your position paper.

Seeing What You Have   If you have completed all the invention work, you will have accumulated several pages of notes. Review these carefully to see what you might use in your draft. Mark passages that seem especially promising, that show conviction, have vivid writing, contain pointed examples, demonstrate strong reasoning. Note places where you reach out to readers, share their concerns and values, acknowledge their feelings, and modify your own views to accommodate theirs.

For more on general invention activities, see pp. 382–87.   If your invention notes are skimpy, you may not have given enough thought to the issue or know enough at this time to write a convincing essay about it. You have several alternatives. You can do more invention and research. You can go on to write a draft, hoping that you will get more ideas as you write. Or you can go back and choose a new topic.

Setting Goals   Experienced writers set overall goals for themselves before drafting their essays. They decide what they will try to achieve and how they will go about it. To help you set realistic goals, consider the following questions now. You may also find it helpful to return to some of these questions as you outline and draft your essay.

Your Purpose and Audience

- What can I realistically hope to accomplish by addressing these particular readers? Are they deeply committed to their opinions? Should I try, as

Goss does, to make readers see that their view is mistaken? Should I appeal, as Smith does, to their ambivalence?

- Can I address readers' special concerns, acknowledge the legitimacy of their feelings, or define the issue in terms that appeal to common values and beliefs? Shall I appeal, as Harjo does, to readers' sense of fairness and equality? Can I demonstrate, as Goss does, that I am aware of the need to protect the freedom of the press?
- Can I draw on any common experiences that relate to this issue? Could I share my own experience, as Smith and Goss do?

The Beginning

- How can I engage readers' attention immediately? Should I begin by identifying the controversy and stating my thesis, as Goss does? Should I use a rhetorical question, as Harjo does, or a surprising example, a personal anecdote, or startling statistics to draw readers into the argument?
- How much do I need to explain about the controversy and define the terms before proceeding with my argument? Should I summarize both sides, as Goss does? Should I limit the issue, as Statsky does?

Your Argument

- If I have more than one reason, how should I order the reasons? From strongest to weakest? From the most to the least predictable? From simplest to most complex? Can I sequence them logically, so that one leads inevitably to the next?
- Which counterarguments should I mention, if any? Shall I acknowledge and refute them all, as Goss does? Shall I focus, as Statsky does, on one? What would I gain from conceding something? What would I lose?

The Ending

- How can I conclude my argument effectively? Should I repeat my thesis, as Goss and Statsky do? Shall I look to the future, possibly to redefine the issue, as Smith does or to urge readers to take action, as Harjo does?
- Can I end on a note of agreement by reminding readers of the common concerns and values we share? Shall I look forward, as Smith does, to a new way of understanding the issue that transcends our differences?

Outlining

Some position papers include everything—an extended definition of the issue, an elaborate argument with multiple reasons and evidence, and several counterarguments, some of which are accommodated while others are refuted. Your essay may not be so complicated, but you will still have to decide how to arrange the different parts. Once you have considered strategies for beginning and ending your essay and determined how you might order your reasons, consider the organization more carefully and prepare a tentative outline.

Here is how Statsky organized her position paper on children's competitive sports:

identifies issue, states thesis, and gives reasons

explains and suggests reason 1—competing at too early an age is developmentally inappropriate and may be harmful physically

explains and supports reason 2—competing at too early an age also may be harmful psychologically

refutes counterargument—that children need to learn to live in a competitive world—by arguing that childhood is just the training period, not the real thing

explains and supports reason 3—because competitive sports are so selective, very few children can participate and reap the potential benefits

explains and supports reason 4—parents and coaches sometimes use children's sports to act out their own fantasies in ways harmful to the children

refutes counterargument—that children need to learn to live in a competitive world—by arguing that cooperation ought to be emphasized because it is as important to society as is competition

concludes by reasserting the position and framing the essay

Smith organized her essay differently, weighing the pros and cons before arguing for her own position. Her outline looks like this:

introduces both sides without advocating either

considers the strengths and weaknesses of one side's argument

considers the strengths and weaknesses of the other side's argument

implies thesis advocating a new way to view the issue

These are by no means the only ways to arrange an essay. Whatever way you choose, though, making an outline before drafting your essay will help you to get started. An outline presents a route, neither the only one nor necessarily the best, but one that will get you going in the right direction.

Drafting

You might want to review the general advice on drafting on pp. 9–11.

With an outline and goals as your guide, begin drafting your essay. As you draft, remember the importance of audience in a position paper. Keep your audience in mind by writing to a particular (real or imaginary) reader, thinking of your writing as a transcript of what you would say to this person. Also keep in mind your purpose in addressing this particular reader. Remember that establishing common ground depends on acknowledging the intelligence, experience, values, and concerns of your readers.

Use your outline to guide your drafting, but do not worry if you diverge from your original plan. Writing sometimes has a logic of its own that carries the writer along. As you pick up momentum, you may leave the outline behind. If you get stuck, refer to it again.

GETTING CRITICAL COMMENTS

Now is the time for your draft to get a good critical reading. Your instructor may arrange such a reading as part of your course work; otherwise, you can ask a classmate, friend, or family member to read it over. If your school has a writing center, you might ask a tutor there to read and comment on your draft. The guidelines in this section are designed to be used by *anyone* reviewing a position paper. (If you are unable to have someone else review your draft, turn ahead to the Revision section on pp. 208–11 for help reading your own draft with a critical eye.)

In order to provide focused, helpful comments, your reader must know your intended purpose and audience. Briefly write out this information at the top of your draft.

> *Audience.* To whom are you directing your argument? What do you assume they already know and think about this issue?
>
> *Purpose.* What effect can you reasonably expect your argument to have on these particular readers? If they are unlikely to adopt your position, what influence could you have on them?

Reading with a Critical Eye

Reading a draft critically means reading it more than once, first to get a general impression and then to analyze its basic features.

Reading for a First Impression.   Read the essay through quickly to get a sense of its argument. Then, write a few sentences describing your initial reaction. Does the issue interest you? What is your personal view of it? What did you find most convincing in the essay? Least convincing?

Now read the draft again, this time noticing any words or passages that contribute to your first impression, weak ones as well as strong ones. A good way of highlighting noteworthy language is to use the *pointings* system.

Pointings

- Draw a straight line under words or images that you find especially effective: strong verbs, precise descriptive details, memorable phrases, striking images.
- Draw a wavy line under words or images that seem flat, stale, or vague. Also put a wavy line under words or phrases that seem unnecessary or repetitious.
- Look for pairs or groups of sentences that you think should be combined. Put brackets [ ] around these sentences.

- Look for sentences that are garbled, overloaded, or awkward. Put parentheses ( ) around these sentences. Parenthesize any sentence that seems even slightly questionable; don't worry about whether anything is actually wrong with it. The writer needs to know that you, as one reader, had even the slightest difficulty understanding a sentence.

See pp. 195–98 to review the basic features.

Reading to Analyze.   Read now to evaluate the argument, focusing on basic features of writing a position paper.

Is the Issue Well-defined?

Check to see how the issue is defined. Is there enough information to understand the issue and why it is important? What questions still need to be answered? Determine whether the issue, as it is stated, is even arguable. For example, does it seem to be a question of fact or is it basically a matter of faith—and therefore not worth arguing about?

Is the Thesis Clear?

Find the clearest statement of the thesis. Given the readers and purpose, is the thesis stated in appropriate terms? Is it qualified? (Should it be?) If the thesis is implied rather than stated, summarize it. Should it be stated directly?

Is the Argument Supported by Convincing Reasons and Evidence?

Find the reasons given to support the claim, and number them in the margin: Reason 1, Reason 2, and so on. Then consider each reason in turn, looking at how it is explained and supported. Point to any reasons that need to be explained more clearly or supported more convincingly. Have any important reasons been left out or any weak ones overemphasized? Note any supporting evidence that seems weak as well as places where more evidence is needed.

Look for faulty reasoning. Note any sweeping generalizations (broad statements asserted without support). Indicate if the issue has been oversimplified or if either/or reasoning (unfairly limiting the argument to only two alternatives) is being used.

How Are Counterarguments Handled?

Look for places where other positions on this issue are mentioned, and specifically places where objections are acknowledged and counterarguments entertained. Note any areas of potential agreement that could be emphasized and any concessions that need to be made. Check for any attempts to refute counterarguments, and see whether the refutation could be strengthened.

Again, look for faulty reasoning. Point out any personal attacks on opponents rather than on their reasoning. Have only the weakest counterarguments been acknowledged, thus misrepresenting the opposition? What other counterarguments could be made?

Is the Tone Reasonable?

Note places where the tone comes across as thoughtful, reasonable, moderate, believable, and trustworthy. Also indicate where the writing seems too emotional or out of proportion to what is being discussed. For example, does the writing ever seem bitter, sarcastic, or too lighthearted?

Is the Organization Effective?

Look at the beginning and ending to evaluate their effectiveness and, if necessary, suggest how they might be made stronger. In particular, note whether the beginning gives a preview of the argument or whether one is needed. Review the sequence in which the reasons and counterarguments are presented to see if they should be reordered. Check to see if any evidence is misplaced. Point to effective uses of transitions, summaries, and topic sentences and places where they could be added.

What Final Thoughts Do You Have?

What is the strongest part of the argument? What is the weakest part, most in need of further work?

REVISING AND EDITING

This section will help you identify problems in your draft and then to revise and edit to solve the problems.

Identifying Problems

To discover problems in your draft, you need to read it objectively, analyze its basic features, and study any comments you've received from others.

Getting an Overview.   Consider the draft as a whole, trying to see it objectively. It may help to do so in two steps:

Reread. If at all possible, put the draft aside for a day or two before rereading it. When you do, start by reconsidering your purpose. Then read the draft straight through, trying to see it as your intended readers will.

Outline. Quickly outline the draft to see where the issue is defined, where the position is stated, how each reason is explained and supported, and how any counterarguments are handled.

Charting a Plan for Revision.   You may want to use a chart like the one that follows to keep track of the work you need to do as you revise. The left-hand column lists the basic features of position papers; as you analyze your draft and study any comments from other readers, use the right-hand column for noting any problems to solve.

Basic Features   *Problems to Solve*

Definition of the Issue

Thesis Statement

Reasons and Evidence

Counterarguments

Tone

Organization

Analyzing the Basic Features of Your Draft.   Turn now to the questions for analyzing a draft on pp. 207–08. Following these guidelines, note any specific problems you need to solve on the chart above.

Studying Critical Comments.   Review any comments you've gotten from other readers, and add to the chart any that you intend to act on. Try not to react defensively to these comments; by letting you see how other readers respond to your draft, they provide invaluable information about how you might improve it.

Solving the Problems

Having identified problems in your draft, you now need to figure out solutions and—most important of all—to carry them out. Following are some suggestions on how you might respond to some of the problems common to writing position papers.

Definition of the Issue

- If the essay does not provide enough information about the issue for a reader to understand it, add more. Consider adding examples, quoting authorities, or simply explaining the issue further.
- If the issue might strike readers as unimportant, state explicitly why you think it is important and why, in your view, they should think so too. Try to think of an anecdote that would demonstrate its importance.

Thesis Statement

- If readers might not find or recognize your thesis, you may need to rewrite your thesis statement to make it clearer. If your thesis is implied but not directly expressed, consider stating it explicitly so as to avoid misunderstanding.
- If your thesis is not appropriately qualified to account for exceptions or strong counterarguments, modify it by limiting its scope.

Reasons and Evidence

- If readers might have difficulty separating your reasons, announce them more directly.

- If any of your reasons seem vague or weak, explain them more fully. Consider telling an anecdote or making a comparison or contrast to show how this reason relates to the others.
- If your evidence seems weak or scanty, review your invention notes or do some more research to gather additional facts, statistics, or quotations from authorities.
- If you use any sweeping generalizations, try to be more specific and to support your assertions with evidence and examples.
- If you have oversimplified the argument, for example by using either/or reasoning, add some qualifying language that shows you are aware of the issue's true complexity.

Counterarguments

- If you can make any concessions to opposing views, consider doing so. Try to find common ground with readers by acknowledging the legitimacy of their concerns. Show readers where you share their values and beliefs.
- If your refutation of a counterargument seems unconvincing, try to strengthen it. Avoid attacking your opponents. Instead, provide solid evidence—known authorities, facts and statistics from reputable sources—to convince readers that you can argue objectively.
- If you have ignored strong counterarguments, take account of them. If you cannot refute them, you might have to acknowledge their legitimacy.

Tone

- If the tone seems inappropriately negative, consider altering your language. You may need to think some more about your feelings and determine whether you have enough emotional distance from this issue to write convincingly about it. You don't have to be disinterested or dispassionate, of course, but you have to be able to adjust your tone appropriately to your purpose and audience.

Organization

- If the beginning seems weak or dull, consider opening with a striking anecdote or surprising quotation.
- If readers might have trouble following your argument, consider adding at the beginning a brief forecast of your main points.
- If the reasons and counterarguments are not logically arranged, reorder them. Consider announcing each reason and counterargument more explicitly.
- If any evidence does not closely follow the point it is intended to support, move it.

■ If the ending seems weak or vague, search your invention notes for a strong quotation or add language that will reach out to readers.

Editing and Proofreading

As you've been working on your draft so far, you've probably corrected some obvious errors, but grammar and style have not been a priority. Now is the time to edit it carefully to correct any errors of mechanics, usage, punctuation, or style. You may find that studying your draft in separate passes—first for paragraphs, then for sentences, and finally for words—will help you to recognize any problems. After you have produced the final copy, be sure to proofread it carefully and make corrections before handing it in.

LEARNING FROM YOUR OWN WRITING PROCESS

Spend a few moments reflecting on the process you followed in writing this essay. Review your invention writing, drafts, critical reading notes, and final revision. What problems did you encounter in constructing your essay? Could you have avoided any of them by gathering more information, by understanding your purpose and readers better, by having more time to plan your draft, or by some other means?

What have you learned about writing an argumentative essay from this experience? Is it very different from the other kinds of writing you have done in this course? What would you do differently next time?

A Writer at Work

EXPLORING THE ISSUE

Jessica Statsky, whose revised essay appears on pp. 190–93, began exploring her chosen issue by making a Pro/Con chart. Since she opposes competitive sports programs for young children, the items on the Con side of the chart identify the reasons supporting her position, while the items on the Pro side anticipate the reasons of those who support such programs. At the bottom of each column she briefly identifies the groups of people who would likely hold opposing views on the issue.

PRO	CON
--competition teaches the child how to succeed in later life	--teaches the child to be vengeful, burns the child out
--when a child is allowed to feel the thrill of	--causes the child depression when he or she

PRO	CON
winning, he or she experiences a boost in self-esteem --allows children to prove to themselves and others their capabilities --gives the child an incentive to excel	loses and does not please the parents and/or coach --takes away the spontaneous fun of sports and free playing --causes children unnecessary physical strain (not good for growing kids to be overworking their bodies in stressful and unusual ways) --instills characteristics and values that are based on negative attitudes --when major stress is placed on winning, the development of each child's potential is made less important --parents and coaches indulge their own crazy ideas about winning and ignore best interests of children
People supporting this position would include coaches and parents who favor discipline and value competition.	People supporting this position might include sports psychologists, some doctors who treat injured children, and parents who want to protect their children from too much stress and competition. Many sports reporters who have covered Little League or Peewee Football also seem to support this position.

Library research was essential for Statsky's project. She was surprised to find a number of books devoted to children's sports and pleased to locate several articles readily in indexes to the *New York Times* and the *Los Angeles Times*.

Surveying and selecting research furthered her understanding of the purpose and audience for her essay. Here is what she wrote in her notes on considering purpose and audience:

I think I will write mainly to parents who are considering letting their children get involved in competitive sports and to those whose children are already on teams and who don't know about the possible dangers. Parents who are really into competition and winning probably couldn't be swayed by my arguments anyway. I don't know how to reach coaches (but aren't they parents?) or league organizers. I'll tell parents some horror stories and also present solid evidence from psychologists that competitive sports can really harm children under the age of twelve. I think they'll be impressed with this scientific evidence.

I share with parents one important value: the best interests of children. Competition really works against children's best interests. Maybe parents' magazines (don't know of any specific ones) publish essays like mine.

■ The business manager of a large hospital writes a proposal to the board of directors requesting the purchase of a new word-processing and billing system that she recently saw demonstrated at a convention. She argues that the new system would both improve efficiency and save money. In support of her proposal she reminds the board of the limitations of the present system and points out the advantages of the new one.

■ Researchers at an oceanographic institute write a proposal to the National Science Foundation for funding to study the effects of ocean temperatures on weather patterns. To convince the foundation that their research should have priority over other proposed projects, they argue that the world economy is being adversely affected by erratic weather conditions. They discuss in detail the El Niño phenomenon of 1983, with its extreme temperatures and severe storms, as evidence of the catastrophic effects changes in ocean temperature can have.

■ For a political science class, a student analyzes the question of presidential terms of office. Citing examples from recent history, she argues that presidents spend the first year of each term getting organized and the fourth year either running for reelection or weakened by their status as a lame duck. Consequently, they are fully productive for only half of their four-year terms.

She proposes limiting presidents to one six-year term, claiming that this change would remedy the problem by giving presidents four or five years to put their programs into effect. She acknowledges that it could make presidents less responsive to the public will, but insists that the system of legislative checks and balances would make that problem unlikely.

■ A newspaper columnist writes about the problem of controlling the spread of AIDS. Since symptoms may take years to appear, she notes, people infected with the AIDS virus unwittingly pass it on to their sexual partners. She discusses three solutions that have been proposed: having only one sexual partner, engaging in safer sexual practices, or notifying and testing the sexual partners of those found to have the disease. She argues that the first solution would solve the problem but may not be feasible, and that the second would not work because safer sexual practices are not absolutely reliable. In support of the third solution—tracing of sexual partners—she argues that tracing has worked to control other diseases and that it should help overcome a major obstacle in controlling AIDS—the widespread but false assumption that heterosexuals are not really at risk.

■ Several students in the predentistry program at a large state university realize how uncertain they are about requirements, procedures, and strategies for applying to dental school. One of them writes a proposal to the head of the program suggesting the need for a handbook for predentistry students. To dramatize that a problem exists and is considered serious by students, he points out their declining rate of admission to dental schools of students in the program and includes an informal survey of students currently enrolled in it. He mentions other programs that provide this kind of pamphlet. Realizing that few faculty members would take time for such a project, he proposes that students do the actual writing as well as handle the printing and distribution; two faculty members would serve simply as advisers. He asks that the publication costs be borne by the predentistry program, however, pointing out that students would donate their time.

■ A college student who works part-time at a pizzeria notices certain problems caused by rapid turnover of employees. Newcomers often misplace things, forget procedures for cleaning up, and interrupt other employees to ask for help operating the espresso machine. Since the company offers cash awards for ideas for improving procedures or service, the student writes a letter to the owners suggesting ways to reduce these problems. Knowing that rapid turnover is inevitable in such a job, she concentrates on procedures for orienting and training new staff.

P roposals serve an important role in a democracy, informing citizens about problems affecting their well-being and that of the society and also suggesting actions that could be taken to remedy these problems. As the examples to the left demonstrate, people write proposals every day in business, government, education, and the professions. Proposals are a basic ingredient of the world's work.

As a special form of argument, proposals have much in common with position papers, described in Chapter 6. Both analyze a subject and take a definite stand on it. Both seek to convince readers to share this position by giving reasons and evidence and by acknowledging readers' likely objections or questions. Proposals, however, go beyond inviting readers to share the writer's views; they urge them to support a particular policy or take specific action. They argue for a proposed solution to a problem, succeeding or failing by how well they argue for the solution.

To most disciplines and professions, problem solving is a basic way of thinking. For example, scientists use the scientific method, a systematic form of problem solving; political scientists and sociologists propose solutions to troubling political and social problems; engineers regularly employ problem-solving techniques to build bridges, automobiles, or computers; attorneys find legal precedents to solve their clients' problems; teachers continually make decisions about how to help students with specific learning problems; counselors devote themselves to helping clients solve personal problems; business owners or managers define themselves as problem-solvers. Problem solving depends on a questioning attitude, what is called critical thinking. In addition, it demands imagination and creativity. To solve a problem, you need to see it anew, to look at it from new angles and in new contexts.

As the writing scenarios to the left illustrate, college students find occasions both in class and at work to propose solutions to problems. Below are some further examples of college assignments calling for problem-solving skills:

■ *For an economics class:* The *maquiladora* industry along the U.S.-Mexican border provides foreign exchange for Mexico and low-paying jobs for half a million Mexicans, as well as profits for American manufacturers. Yet this innovative binational arrangement has created serious problems on the Mexican side of the border: inadequate housing, health care, and public services; on-the-job injuries; and environmental damage. Study one of these problems, research it, and propose a solution. Address your proposal to the mayor of Nogales, Tijuana, or Juarez.

■ *For a business class:* Take the case of a corporation wishing to install a workstation network but unwilling as yet to give up its mainframe computers. Propose a solution to this problem. Research the possibilities of mainframe-workstation integration, explain the problem carefully, and argue convincingly for your solution. Address your proposal to the CEO of the corporation:

■ *For a biology class:* Apply the principle of circadian rhythm to the problem of jet lag. Explain circadian rhythm, define jet lag in light of it, and speculate about how knowledge of it might help reduce the effects of jet lag. It might help to think of yourself as writing an article for the travel section of a newspaper.

Since a proposal tries to convince readers that its way of defining and solving the problem makes sense, proposal writers must be sensitive to readers' needs and expectations. As you plan and draft a proposal, you will want to determine whether your readers are aware of the problem and whether they recognize its seriousness. In addition, you will want to consider what they might think of any other solutions. Knowing what your readers know, what their assumptions and biases are, what kinds of arguments will be appealing to them is a central part of proposal writing, indeed of all good argumentative writing.

The reading selections that follow illustrate many of the strategies proposal writers use to analyze a problem and persuade readers to accept their solution. As you read them, you will see strategies you find effective and wish to use in your own writing.

For Group Inquiry

You can readily experience the complexities and possibilities involved in proposing solutions by thinking through a specific problem and trying to come up with a feasible proposal. With two or three other students, form a group and select someone to take notes during your discussion. List several problems within your college or community, and select one that you all know something about. Then consider possible solutions to this problem, and identify one that you can all support. Decide on an individual or group who could take action on your proposed solution, and figure out how you would go about convincing this audience that the problem is serious and must be solved and that your proposed solution is feasible and should have their support. Consider carefully what questions readers might ask about your solution and how they might object to it. Before the group separates, reflect on your efforts at proposing a solution to a problem. What surprised or pleased you? What difficulties did you encounter?

Readings

Samuel D. Proctor is minister emeritus of the Abyssinian Baptist Church in New York City. In this essay, published as a 1989 guest column in the *New York Times,* he proposes what he calls a national youth academy as a solution to the problems caused, for themselves and for others, by teenagers who are "unsocialized" and "unparented." What proposals have you heard recently for helping such teenagers? Can you imagine a special kind of school that would help them? As you read, notice what Proctor does to convince you of the seriousness of the problem. Notice also how he presents the idea of a youth academy, defining it as he develops his proposal.

**TO THE RESCUE:
A NATIONAL
YOUTH ACADEMY**
SAMUEL D. PROCTOR

Recently a junior high school teacher announced to me that she was leaving 1
teaching. She loved to teach, but in each of her classes there were six to eight out of 30 who had no respect for order or authority, were unmoved by punishment, rejected gestures of good will and concern and bullied other students. They made teaching and learning impossible.

This population of unsocialized pupils extends beyond the schools. It is the core 2
of a growing number of young people for whom the new jails and prison cells are being built. They create the staggering statistics on teen-age pregnancies and the high abortion rate. They are involved in drug trafficking, crimes that are committed to finance drug habits, and they keep us all from looking forward to traveling the city streets or the public transportation system.

Moreover, our responses to them are doing something to us. They have us 3
committing ourselves to capital punishment; indulging in levels of hatred that are unhealthy; abandoning public education and opting for vouchers to finance private schools; allowing our cities to remain gutted slums; permitting police brutality; and allowing an uneducated, illiterate, impoverished, violent underclass to grow like a cancer.

The costs also are getting out of hand. Prisons are expensive, both in dollar costs 4
and in net social losses. The price is $20,000 to $30,000 per year per head. The welfare costs for their offspring are something else.

There is no way to estimate what a society loses when, for example, 10,000 of 5
its young adults have to be incarcerated and supported at public expense, as compared to the same 10,000 supporting families inventing, producing and consuming, participating in churches and civic groups and reproducing their kind.

Research must be conducted to ferret out the hidden or subtle causes of this 6 disaster. But a few hypotheses are glaring and point us to a basis for doing something feasible and constructive in the national interest.

These children are victims of a breakdown in our most basic institution: the 7 family. In fact, these young people do not come from broken families, but from nonfamilies.

There never were breakfasts with others at a table. There were hamburgers and 8 fries all day long, eaten while walking. There were never stories read to them, only television with its fantasies and murders. There was no Sunday school. Sunday was like every other day: beer, noise, foul language, violence and no plans at all.

We must devise a response that is consonant with our freedom and those moral 9 principles that we wish to inculcate into the lives of the losers that are destroying our schools.

Something can be done. The costs may seem prohibitive in the light of our deficits 10 and budget reductions; but we are spending the money now, in a far less constructive way.

Our money is spent on "crime schools"—jails and prisons. Our money is spent 11 on unproductive police work that demoralizes the entire law enforcement system; our money is spent caring for the children of fathers who have learned to be irresponsible and cynical about work.

All of this can be turned around by creating a new institution: a national youth 12 academy with 50 campuses on our inactive military bases. This academy would service 250,000 students annually, 5,000 on each location.

We would enlist in these academies those young boys and girls, ages 12 to 18, 13 who are unparented and whose communities are morally bankrupt. There are legal ways of finding out who they are and enrolling them. These academies should also be open to others, whose parents may feel the need, provided they accept the program and pay the necessary fees.

The program is the key. This is the real investment. It is not a penal institution, 14 not a prep school, not a Job Corps Center, not a Civilian Conservation Camp, but it borrows from them.

It is an effort to provide for the academic, moral and social development of 15 young people, to cause them to be responsible and productive citizens. It is a "parenting" situation and an educational endeavor that takes seriously the needs of young people who never had what most of us could not avoid: strong parenting.

First, the facilities would be our deactivated military bases, where we already 16 own the real estate with power, water and sewer lines, and with roads and buildings standing. The students would provide all of the services required.

They would be trained to do the repairs, the cooking, the bookkeeping, the 17 gardening, the cleaning, truck and tractor service and repair, health services, farming and the security. And they would be paid nominally, along with some savings for separation pay at graduation. This kind of training and work would be one-third of the program.

Another third would be basic academics from grade levels 7 through 12. The 18 most successful people in education would recruit the most committed teachers, who would undergo special training. An emphasis would be placed on securing husband and wife teams to accentuate the family image and experience.

The final third would be human development activities: music, drama, oratory, 19 sports, horticulture, photography, gymnastics, painting, swimming. Every opportunity

to teach health care, a drug-free life, respect for oneself and others and civic participation would be sought.

These three components—the learning of lifelong skills, discipline, self-respect 20
and accomplishment; the mastery of subject matter at the junior and senior high
school levels; and the development of the body and the cultivation of esthetic taste—
would all be correlated.

We need to find out really how many candidates there are. During the 60's we 21
learned that there were 500,000 young people out of school, out of work and not
in jail. There could be as many as 250,000 today in need of a national youth academy.

Costs? If it costs $9,000 per student to provide a modest college education, 22
these students could cost $14,000 a head. But it costs nearly $30,000 today to keep
one drug addict in the penal system for one year. And the addict will never be likely
to return any of that to the society.

I am proposing an investment that has both moral and economic thrusts. Such 23
a program would have to be embarked upon in stages, but not with bureaucratic
sluggishness. There should be only a skeletal staff in Washington to establish guidelines and to recruit a national staff. But, beyond that, grants should be made to the
states to conduct the academies, within established guidelines.

It is also possible to include a junior military training program so that students 24
who choose military careers could begin with advanced preparation. This program
could be coordinated with some form of national service, Peace Corps-style, by which
students of commitment and character could become teachers of other young people. All other students would leave the academy ready for college, work or self-
employment.

Has this been tried before? No. But the crisis that we face now compels us to 25
create an intervention that will reverse an awful development—one that contradicts
the best that we desire for our country and the rising generation.

For Discussion

Proctor proposes a solution that is national rather than local, institutional
rather than voluntary, and standardized rather than free-form. Try to imagine
a local, voluntary, and unstandardized solution to the social problem created
by "unsocialized" teenagers. For solving this particular problem, what advantages and disadvantages do you see in a local approach?

Do you think it is possible that certain social problems are best solved
on a local level? Which current problems seem to require this approach?
How do you think we can decide when a social problem requires a national
rather than a local response?

For Analysis

*For an illustration of
scratch outlining, see
pp. 384–87.*

1.   To analyze Proctor's plan, construct a scratch outline of the essay. Then
divide the outline into two parts—presentation of the problem and proposal
of the solution—and note what proportion of the essay is devoted to each
part. Given Proctor's purpose and readers, what advantages or disadvantages
do you see in his plan?

2.   Perhaps because of space limitations, Proctor considers few objections
and no alternatives to his proposal. What questions and objections do you
have? Think of ones others might have. What other solutions do you think
might reasonably be proposed? Choose two or three of these questions,

objections, or alternative solutions, and explain how Proctor's argument would have been strengthened by acknowledging them.

3.   In proposing a solution, writers may appeal to readers' logic, feelings, and trust in them as an authoritative and well-meaning writer. Identify one instance of each kind of appeal in Proctor's proposal. How well does he succeed overall in appealing to readers' logic? to their feelings? to their trust?

4.   In paragraphs 17–20, underline each word or phrase that connects a sentence or paragraph to previous ones or that anticipates following ones. These connecting or cueing strategies are relatively obvious. What advantages do you see in using such explicit cues in Proctor's proposal and in proposals in general?

For further illustrations of cueing strategies, see pp. 410–15.

For Your Own Writing

What social problems—of national importance or of interest in your own community—concern you? List some, and choose one you might write about. How would you define and present the problem? What solution would you propose, and how might you convince readers of its feasibility?

Commentary

Writing for the *New York Times,* Proctor assumes an audience of college-educated readers and policy makers, people who are in a position to support his proposal or even write the legislation to implement it. In the political climate of 1989, however, when federal spending for existing social programs was being reduced and Congress was reluctant to establish new ones, many of Proctor's readers would have been skeptical of his proposal. This conservative political climate favored programs sponsored by state and local governments or by voluntary groups, President Bush's "thousand points of light," rather than standardized national programs of the kind associated with liberal politics.

As a politically astute religious leader, Proctor would have understood the social and political context at the time his proposal was published, and he knew he had to devise an argumentative strategy to achieve his purpose with his readers. Every decision a writer makes in proposing a solution must be guided by an argumentative strategy—what words to choose, how to begin, how fully to present the problem, how to argue for the feasibility of the solution, what details to provide about implementing it, how to acknowledge readers' questions and objections, and how to establish shared values with them.

Proctor begins with an anecdote about a teacher who had given up in frustration. Though it is brief and general, it creates an image of classrooms made intolerable by a few disruptive students. As the first stage in presenting the problem, it dramatizes the problem and is part of Proctor's strategy to convince readers—or perhaps merely remind them—that the problem is ominous. He focuses on its effects (paragraphs 2–5), noting among other things the increase in crime, the public's fears, the decline of public schooling, and prison and welfare costs. He concludes this section with an inventive contrast between 10,000 people in jail and the same 10,000 as productive citizens. Proctor then speculates about the causes of the problem (paragraphs 6–8) — broken families and "nonfamilies," bad eating habits, never having been read to, too much television, and no Sunday school. As he intends, it is an ominous list. Readers must be thinking "This really is terrible."

Since proposal writers must convince readers of the seriousness of the problem, they often emphasize its harmful effects. They may also give its history and, for readers unfamiliar with it, describe it in some detail. Since Proctor assumes that his readers are all too familiar with the problem he is discussing, he does not give much detail, simply pointing briefly to chaotic classrooms and dangerous streets and characterizing problematic teenagers as "unsocialized," "unparented," and "losers."

Despite space constraints, Proctor provides a surprising number of specifics about his proposed academy (paragraphs 12–24). He seems to assume that readers are not so concerned about how such an academy would be administered as they are about its curriculum, activities, and costs.

Though Proctor considers no alternative solutions, he does anticipate and acknowledge readers' counterarguments, their questions about his proposed solution and their objections to it. For example, in paragraphs 10, 11, 13, and 14 we can easily imagine him anticipating these questions: How much will a solution cost? How can we afford it with our national debt and other budget constraints? Can students be legally required to attend an academy? Can students who are not "losers" attend? How is an academy different from a jail, prep school, Job Corps Center, or Civilian Conservation Camp?

Proctor attempts to answer these questions even before he has detailed his solution. Placement of counterarguments is crucial because a shrewd writer does not want to keep readers waiting too long for answers to urgent questions. In fact, a careful writer brings up likely questions before the reader has thought of it. If a writer fails to answer predictable questions, readers may think the proposal has not really been thought through.

Notice finally what Proctor does to establish shared values with diverse readers. He knows that readers of all social classes and political persuasions share with him a fervent desire for orderly schools and safe streets, that they regret as much as he that any teacher who "loved to teach" is driven from the classroom. By finding values that many readers share with him, he wins a much wider audience for his solution.

■   ■   ■

Edward L. Palmer is one of the founders of Children's Television Workshop, which began in 1968 and is perhaps best known for creating and producing *Sesame Street*. Palmer has organized international conferences on children's television programming and has traveled to study such programming around the world. This work and travel produced a book, *Television and America's Children: A Crisis of Neglect* (1988), from which this selection is taken. In the book, Palmer seeks to convince policy makers and concerned adults that there is a serious problem with children's television programming in the United States—its virtual disappearance from commercial television and a decline in support for it on public television. He believes the solution lies in support for the creation of new programs to be shown on public television.

Before you read his proposal, reflect on the educational television programs you watched as a child. Did you watch *Captain Kangaroo* on commercial television? Did you watch *Sesame Street, Electric Company, WonderWorks,* or *Mister Rogers' Neighborhood* on public television? What made these programs entertaining or informative?

IMPROVING TV FOR AMERICA'S CHILDREN
EDWARD L. PALMER

All the ingredients to create and air a full schedule of high-quality educational shows for children are in place. America has the expertise, the production capability, the pedagogical and research skills, the audience, and the need. Public television [PTV] has abundant air space, and might be prevailed upon by parents and outside underwriters to become a willing host. Parents, children, and educators have shown great enthusiasm for all the fine quality programs so far made available. 1

Thanks to the many outstanding successes of the past twenty years, we have fashioned our own unique national vision of quality. Why, then, have we lacked the will to carry it through? Why is our government so short-sighted in failing to create the national policy and provide the funding to make full and effective use of the most cost-efficient teaching medium ever invented—broadcast television? . . . 2

The lapses we countenance in our own television institutions are seen in cross-cultural comparisons to be woefully shortsighted, or even bizarre. For instance, the Japanese Broadcasting Corporation, NHK, reports that in 85 percent of all Japanese schools, every classroom has a color television. The NHK reports further that each year 97 percent of all classrooms in Japan make some use of NHK's school television service. Yet, by contrast, the U.S. Department of Education places almost no priority whatsoever on television's development and use to advance learning for America's children. The bizarre part is that where another country's provision for the use of television in education is so vital and so far advanced, we are utterly without any well-informed, long-term, or dependable policy to guide our own educational uses of television, and this is true in spite of the unarguable fact that U.S. schools are drastically and chronically burdened by performance demands that exceed their capacity to deliver, and that television languishes as a proven but neglected cost-efficient ally. 3

It is fitting that we begin exploring a minimally adequate PTV children's schedule that places children's needs first. . . . The schedule most likely to attract funding support must be modest—minimally adequate to serve all children aged two through thirteen—and, I believe, must consist of programs geared to our most urgent national education problems. Moreover, for each educational outcome sought, television must be seen to be more effective, and substantially more cost-efficient, than any other means available. This high standard is well within broadcast television's capability. 4

The schedule which will be proposed here in detailed outline calls for a multi- 5
year program build-up, in phases, eventually yielding a one-hour weekday schedule,
year round, for each of three child age-groups: 2- to 5-year-olds, 6- to 9-year-olds,
and 10- to 13-year-olds. The scale of yearly funding support is $62.4 million. Al-
though modest, this amount is about double the current expenditure from all sources
for children's PTV programming. Anything more ambitious to begin is unrealistic;
anything less ambitious short-changes children by drastically under-utilizing this powerful educational resource.

This yearly budget, as shown below, will buy enough programming at today's 6
rates to continue the preschool service and provide a quarter of a full year's schedule
each for 6- to 9- and 10- to 13-year-olds. By simple arithmetic, this yearly program
build-up rate will fill a year's schedule for each age group in four years. "Simple
arithmetic" is misleading in this case, however, because not all programming will
bear up well in repeats—some will be topical, for instance—so that perhaps five or
more build-up years will be required to fill a year-long program schedule.

Whether one's concern may be with funding or with managing a children's 7
schedule, the following summary suggests some desirable schedule conditions:

- *Fill the children's TV schedule through the entire calendar year.* Children of all
  ages watch TV and can learn from it all year round. There are no "school va-
  cations" with at-home television. A constantly fresh program offering maintains
  a loyal audience, allowing the children's schedule to be its own best promotion.
  Television can help counteract the well-known drop-off in achievement which
  occurs in the summer between school years. During school years, those programs
  not actually used in the classroom can be assigned as homework.

- *Make optimum use of previously broadcast materials each year.* This practice is
  the key to schedule building. It is an important factor not only in creating an
  adequate quantity and diversity of programs but also in achieving the best possible cost-efficiency.

- *Aim to provide each four-year child age band with a full, four-year cycle of
  programs.*

- *Provide a sensible ratio of new to repeat programming.* Preschool children, as
  compared with their school-age counterparts, both enjoy repeat exposure to the
  same programs and derive greater educational benefit from it. Older children,
  like adults, have little tolerance for program repetition. The minimum renewal
  rate which will allow new educational needs to be met, and fresh new approaches taken, is a quarter of a year's new programming annually.

- *Slot children's programs at convenient and appropriate viewing times.*

Table I outlines the budget figures for a proposed national children's TV schedule. 8
This proposal assumes that we will incorporate, and build upon, the backlog of
excellent and durable programs which already exist, eventually to provide an hour
each weekday for each of the three age groups. The total amount of programming
required to fill this schedule is 780 hours a year.

Children grow up with this amount of programming in Japan and Great Britain 9
and thereby enjoy an opportunity to encounter new and useful information and
ideas each weekday. Over the important twelve-year learning period between two
and thirteen, they grow up "through" programs geared to successive levels of in-

Table 1. Initial Yearly Costs for Proposed National Children's TV Schedule[a,b]

Age Group	Scheduled Hours Each Year	New Hours Each Year	Cost per New Hour[c] (thousands)	Yearly Total (millions)	Annual Cost per Child
2–5	260	60	$200	$12.0	$ 0.86
6–9	260	65	$375	$24.4	$ 1.74
10–13	260	65	$400	$26.0	$ 1.86
Total	780	190		$62.4	$14.9 (avg)

[a]The calculations in the table are based on 14 million children per four-year age group, for a total of 42 million, as a convenient approximation. (Population source: U.S. Bureau of the Census, Current Population Reports Series, P-25, No. 952.)
[b]A factor of 50 percent has been added to production, to cover the activities of series development, curriculum planning, pre-production research and child testing, pilot production and review, and audience building.
[c]The cost per hour is based on prevailing mid-1980s production costs in U.S. public TV in general and in children's PTV programming in particular.

terest and understanding, "graduating" every three to five years from one level of difficulty and interest to the next.

Sesame Street is an excellent case study to show how a sustained investment 10 over several years can create a backlog of reusable programming. This reuse only improves the series' already highly favorable cost-efficiency, as programs and program elements are played again and again for successive "generations" of preschool children. Sesame Street in 1987 costs more than $11 million annually to produce. The actual expenditure for its first season was $7.2 million in 1979 dollars. Each year since, a substantially renewed series of 130 hour-long programs has been produced and broadcast. Today, however, expensively produced films, animation, and Muppet segments, reused from previous years, make up about two-thirds of each hour-long program. In times of inflated costs the savings are significant.

Only a fraction of the many hundreds of pieces of carefully crafted film and 11 videotape contained in this treasure store are called into use each year to assemble what is, for the children, a largely fresh 130-hour series. Most of the new program elements created consist of less costly studio-produced scenes.

Without doing a detailed cost analysis, one could estimate that the cost today 12 to inaugurate a wholly new, 130-hour Sesame Street series from scratch would easily exceed $25 million. This means that the replacement value of the program segments that are now carried forward into each new Sesame Street season from previous years is more than $15 million.

This system of building a backlog of reusable programs and program elements 13 is the key to creating an efficient and affordable children's schedule.

Sesame Street and its successors among CTW [Children's Television Workshop] 14 productions represent a massive number of program hours, outstanding in technical and artistic quality. By renewing Sesame Street each year as a 130-hour series, the Workshop is able to provide for an uninterrupted year-round presence in the weekday PTV schedule—and make learning an everyday pastime in preschool children's lives. This continuity is accomplished to some degree with mirrors, as it were, because

each year's 130 programs exactly fill a six-month broadcast schedule, then are repeated one time in their entirety to fill out the year. This rate of repeat will not hold
up in audience appeal with older children or with programs designed other than
with *Sesame Street*'s largely unthemed, variety format.

Sesame Street is seen by many as a model of collaborative production and re-   15
search activities, but as the above illustration makes clear, it also offers some important lessons on how to develop and manage a TV schedule. This realm of concern
will become especially important if and when we enter a new and expanded phase
in quality children's television.

The CTW experience is instructive and may be looked upon as the model for an   16
even larger national program package for all children. The *Sesame Street* case has
shown that judicious reuse of programs and program elements can introduce major
cost savings without any compromise of educational benefits.

For Discussion

Palmer accuses the federal government of negligence in funding educational
television programming for children. Recall the television programs you
watched as children, and name any that you now identify as educational.
Were you aware at the time of whether these programs were intended as
education or as entertainment? Do you recall learning specific things from
them? Does your own experience support the argument that educational
television is so important that it deserves federal funding?

For Analysis

1.   How does Palmer define the problem? How does he demonstrate that
it exists and is serious?

2.   Palmer concludes his proposal with what he calls a "case study." Review
this case study, and decide what role it contributes to his argument.

3.   To analyze the organization of Palmer's proposal, begin by making a
scratch outline of it. Given his purpose and readers, what advantages or
disadvantages do you see in this organization?

4.   Palmer lists in paragraph 7 the criteria he thinks should apply to any
proposal for a schedule of children's educational television programming.
How reasonable do these criteria seem to you as a general reader? Is anything
important left out? How well does Palmer's own proposal stand up when
you apply these criteria to it?

**For Your
Own Writing**

Consider some of the problems concerning schools or school children today.
Select one problem, and think about a solution you might propose. How
you would demonstrate the seriousness of the problem? How would you
convince readers of the feasibility of your solution?

Commentary

Palmer's proposal is typical of many that appear in books aimed at solving
social problems. Some such books are visionary: their proposals are not taken
seriously for years, if ever. Others influence public policy immediately: their
proposals are drafted directly into legislation. Legislators, lobbyists, policy

makers, and academics rely on writers like Palmer to define problems, establish their seriousness, outline solutions, and devise arguments for them. From these definitions and arguments come the ideas and the language of public policy debates.

Both Palmer and Proctor propose solutions to problems of national interest and write for readers nationwide, yet their writing situations and particular readers differ. While Proctor writes for a general educated readership, Palmer writes for specialists interested in children's education and welfare or in public policy and the media. While Proctor must accept the length constraints of a newspaper column, Palmer enjoys the expansive possibilities of a book. While Proctor proposes an untried solution to general readers who may need some time just to get used to the idea, Palmer proposes a proven one to readers who may be prepared to consider the actual details of implementing it. Consequently, Palmer focuses on elaborating the solution.

Palmer knows that readers will be skeptical that a complex solution can be realized within proposed cost and time limits. Consequently, he is careful to show how his solution can be staged, with its challenging creative work completed gradually over four or five years. He outlines yearly development costs and argues that his estimates are reasonable. He attempts to reassure readers that though the overall project is costly, it is achievable and a bargain in terms of cost per child.

Palmer's proposal shows how graphics can clarify or highlight important information. For example, he highlights desirable scheduling conditions with "bullets" in paragraph 7 and presents the proposed yearly costs of his solution in Table 1. He might also have used a chart to clarify the stages of programming development for each age group. Many writers of proposals rely on charts, tables, or drawings to help answer readers' predictable questions about costs or other details of a solution.

■   ■   ■

Adam Paul Weisman wrote the next selection for the *New Republic,* a national news and opinion magazine. It proposes a solution to the problem of teenage pregnancy. As you read, ask yourself how Weisman's admission that his solution is not original—that it has already been tried—affects your reaction to it.

BIRTH CONTROL IN THE SCHOOLS
ADAM PAUL WEISMAN

Should contraceptives be distributed to teenagers in public schools? A research panel of the National Academy of Sciences spent two years studying adolescent pregnancy in America, and decided they should. Its 1986 report, *Risking the Future,* prompted a new wave of angry debate about how to reduce the high rate of teenage pregnancy in the United States. 1

No one disputes the severity of the problem. Teen pregnancy ruins young lives and perpetuates a tragic cycle of poverty. According to the Alan Guttmacher Institute, the rate of pregnancy among American women aged 15 to 19 was almost ten 2 percent in 1981. That far outstrips the next closest industrialized nation, England, where the rate is less than five percent. Guttmacher estimates that more than 80 percent of teenage pregnancies in the United States are unintended and unwanted. Every year about four in 100 women aged 15 to 19 have an abortion. But those looking for ways to reduce these statistics have divided into two distinct camps: one favoring contraception, the other, sexual abstinence.

The contraception advocates point out that a majority of teenagers have already 3 rejected abstinence. In 1986, 57 percent of 17-year-olds say they have had sex. This camp believes that schools, as a central location in young peoples' lives, are a good place to make contraceptives available. Three recent studies (by the National Academy of Sciences, the Guttmacher Institute, and the Children's Defense Fund) have taken this view, while also calling for programs geared toward postponing adolescent sexual involvement and including parents in school sex education classes.

The abstinence advocates believe the answer lies in inculcating values based on 4 a clear understanding that sex is simply wrong for teenagers. They say that moral lessons are best taught by parents in the home, but that schools should continue the job by teaching a chaste morality. Secretary of Education William Bennett has been the most outspoken proponent of this view. Exposing students to "mechanical" means of pregnancy prevention, he says, encourages "children who do not have sexual intimacy on their minds to . . . be mindful of it."

Bennett concedes that "birth control clinics in schools may prevent some births." 5 And indeed, whatever the drawbacks, the contraception advocates have one strong advantage in this debate: their approach works. The only rigorous study of a pregnancy prevention program for urban teenagers was conducted in Baltimore from 1982 to 1983 by researchers from Johns Hopkins Medical School. The Hopkins-run birth-control clinic, located across the street from one school and nearby another, reduced the pregnancy rate in the schools it served by 30 percent while pregnancy rates in control schools soared 58 percent.

"Why did this program work?" asks Dr. Laurie Zabin, the program's director, in 6 her report on the experiment. "Access to high-quality, free services was probably crucial to its success. Professional counseling, education, and open communications were, no doubt, also important. All these factors appear to have created an atmosphere that allowed teenagers to translate their attitude into constructive preventive behavior." And what of those students who were virgins? According to Zabin, that group of girls (not very large) delayed initiation of sexual activity an average of seven months longer than those in the control groups, strong evidence that awareness of contraception is not directly linked to promiscuity.

But the existing school-based clinics that distribute or arrange for birth control 7 are not just rooms plastered with Planned Parenthood posters where contraceptives are handed out. They are full-service health clinics that came into existence to provide young people with comprehensive health care. Public health officials, including many who have doubts about distributing contraceptives in schools, agree that in many places, particularly the inner city, health care for adolescents is inadequate. The school-based clinic, like the school lunch program, seeks to make all students healthy enough to get the most out of education.

This is not to say that school-based clinics don't do a lot in the way of contra- 8 ception. According to Douglas Kirby, director of research for the Center for Population Options, a group that advocates and monitors school-based clinics, 15 percent to 20 percent of visits to clinics are for family planning. The majority are for general health care. Twenty-eight percent of the clinics actually dispense contraceptives or other prescription drugs. About half of the clinics write prescriptions that are filled off-campus; the rest diagnose and counsel teens before making referrals to outside health agencies.

These clinics also seem to help reduce unintended pregnancies. In St. Paul 33 9 percent of girls made use of the clinic's contraceptive services, and birth rates dropped by 50 percent. Thanks to the clinic's counseling, four out of five of the girls who did have children stayed in school, and only 1.4 percent of them had another pregnancy before graduation. Nationally, about 17 percent of teenage mothers become pregnant again within a year.

Bennett argues that distributing birth control is "not what school is for," and 10 that doing so represents "an abdication of moral authority." Many educators have similar concerns. They fear that communities and government are trying to dump another social problem—like drug counseling and AIDS education—on the schools when they could better be handled in the home. Diane Ravitch, an adjunct professor of history and education at Teachers College in New York, says, "Schools are increasingly being pushed to be social service centers, and they don't do that well."

Yet clearly schools do more than teach students the three R's. Schools are where 11 many teenagers learn to drive, weld, and cook. And numerous surveys reveal that over 80 percent of parents think it is a proper place for their children to learn about sex. Dr. Stephen Joseph, health commissioner for New York City, explains that if it weren't for the involvement of schools, the United States never could have achieved 100 percent immunization rates, a worthy goal that "wasn't perceived as the role of the school either at that time."

If the pressing health crisis were non-sexual in nature—tuberculosis, for example—it's hard to believe that educators such as Bennett wouldn't be the first to volunteer schools as a locus for a solution. And of course, if the problem of teen pregnancy is one that the schools shouldn't be expected to deal with, that would exclude any program of anti-sex indoctrination as well as the distribution of contraceptives. Putting such indoctrination into the curriculum is, arguably, more intrusive on the schools' basic function than the existence of a birth control or general health clinic. Bennett's speeches rule out the very real possibility that schools could prosecute a moral agenda and *also* support a clinic.

Despite the success of Zabin's off-campus model, there is a good reason school- 13 based clinics receive such wide support in the health services community: teenagers are notoriously lazy. As Cheryl Hayes, director of the NAS study explains, "If teenagers have to wait in the rain for a bus to take them to a clinic, there is a good chance they will never make it to the clinic." If the goal is providing health care and family planning services to teenagers, it is unlikely that anything will work as well as locating those services where most teenagers are: at school.

Of course the real question that excites people isn't whether teenagers should 14 get birth control at school, but whether they should get it at all. There is no hard evidence linking exposure to contraception with promiscuity, and it is unlikely any teenager who watches prime-time television is less than "mindful" (as Bennett puts it) of sexual intimacy. Although Bennett has dismissed the recommendations of *Risking the Future* as "stupid," the opponents of making contraception available to teenagers have yet to offer an effective alternative. As for the "parental authority" that birth control availability is said to undermine, a 1986 Planned Parenthood survey of 1,000 teenagers revealed that 31 percent of parents discuss neither sex nor birth control with their children. The failure of parental authority is manifest in the almost 900,000 unintended teenage pregnancies in 1983. *Risking the Future* only makes that failure painfully clear.

For Discussion

How do you react to Weisman's proposal that school-based health clinics be permitted to distribute birth-control information and contraceptives? Do you think it is appropriate for schools to play such a role? What advantages or dangers do you see?

For Analysis

1. How does Weisman set the stage for his argument in the title and opening paragraph? How effectively does his proposal begin? What criteria are appropriate for judging the effectiveness of a proposal's beginning?

2. Weisman at first appears to be a neutral reporter rather than an advocate for a particular solution. How does the first paragraph convey an objective tone? Is this tone maintained consistently throughout the essay? Point to passages where the same tone is evident or where a different tone emerges. How does the neutral reporter's tone serve Weisman's overall argumentative strategy?

3. In paragraph 5, Weisman cites the example of the Johns Hopkins University birth-control clinic. How does he use this example to support his argument? How effective is the example?

4. What are the advantages of Weisman's proposed solution? How does he present these advantages so that they will appeal to supporters of the abstinence solution? What common values and concerns does he call upon?

For Your Own Writing

Teenagers are part of the problem in this proposal, but they can also play a positive role in solving social problems. For example, high school students can teach illiterate adults to read or refurbish playgrounds and parks. Think of a problem that teenagers might be able to help solve. If you were to propose a solution to this problem, how would you explain the problem? How would you go about convincing other students that they should participate?

Commentary

Instead of developing an original proposal, like Proctor and Palmer, Weisman advocates a solution others have proposed, researched, and argued for. His essay illustrates a strategy that is often important in proposals: acknowledging an alternative solution, evaluating that alternative, and refuting it.

After establishing the problem, Weisman introduces the two solutions that have been proposed: encouraging teenagers to abstain from sexual activity and providing birth-control information to them. To demonstrate his fairness, Weisman presents the abstinence solution objectively, even sympathetically. He accepts the legitimacy of this proposed solution and objects only on the grounds that it does not work.

The fact that Weisman's proposed solution does appear to work is the cornerstone of his argument. He uses Secretary Bennett's own words to argue that the contraception solution works in at least some cases, then cites the Johns Hopkins study as the centerpiece of his argument. Furthermore, by noting that birth-control counseling "delayed initiation of sexual activity" for some of the teenagers, he makes a forceful appeal to those in favor of abstinence.

Not only does Weisman support his solution with reasons and evidence, but he also anticipates and refutes a major objection to it. This counterargument, that schools should not be used to solve social and moral problems, he refutes in two ways. First, he reasons that the problem of teenage pregnancy is a health crisis and that there is ample precedent for dealing with such problems through the schools. This argument appeals to humanitarian concerns, but is unlikely to convince those who consider teenage pregnancy a moral issue. To those readers, he offers a second argument: if birth-control information is excluded from the schools, then "any program of anti-sex indoctrination" must also be excluded. In other words, the argument against school-based birth-control clinics could also be made against teaching sexual abstinence. Both are forms of sex education.

For more on anticipating counterarguments, see pp. 480–86.

Weisman's argumentative strategy in this proposal is to show that he understands and respects the values of those who advocate an alternative solution and that he shares their desire to remedy the problem. He appeals to them on practical grounds, arguing that his solution will get the job done.

■   ■   ■

Patrick O'Malley wrote the following essay when he was a college freshman. In it, he proposes that college professors give students frequent brief examinations in addition to the usual midterm and final exams. After discussing with his instructor his unusual rhetorical situation—a freshman advising professors—he decided to revise the essay into the form of an open letter to professors on his campus, a letter that might appear in the campus newspaper.

O'Malley's essay may strike you as unusually authoritative. This air of authority is due in large part to what O'Malley learned about the possibilities and problems of frequent exams as he interviewed two professors (his writing instructor and the writing program director) and talked with several students. As you read, notice particularly how he is able to anticipate professors' likely objections to his proposals and their preferred solutions to the problem he identifies.

MORE TESTING, MORE LEARNING
PATRICK O'MALLEY

It's late at night. The final's tomorrow. You got a C on the midterm, so this one   1
will make or break you. Will it be like the midterm? Did you study enough? Did you study the right things? It's too late to drop the course. So what happens if you fail? No time to worry about that now—you've got a ton of notes to go over.

Although this last-minute anxiety about midterm and final exams is only too 2
familiar to most college students, many professors may not realize how such major,
infrequent, high-stakes exams work against the best interests of students both psychologically and intellectually. They cause unnecessary amounts of stress, placing too
much importance on one or two days in the students' entire term, judging ability
on a single or dual performance. They don't encourage frequent study, and they fail
to inspire students' best performance. If professors gave additional brief exams at
frequent intervals, students would be spurred to study more regularly, learn more,
worry less, and perform better on midterms, finals, and other papers and projects.

Ideally, a professor would give an in-class test or quiz after each unit, chapter, 3
or focus of study, depending on the type of class and course material. A physics
class might require a test on concepts after every chapter covered, while a history
class could necessitate quizzes covering certain time periods or major events. These
exams should be given weekly, or at least twice monthly. Whenever possible, they
should consist of two or three essay questions rather than many multiple-choice or
short-answer questions. To preserve class time for lecture and discussion, exams
should take no more than 15 or 20 minutes.

The main reason why professors should give frequent exams is that when they 4
do, and when they provide feedback to students on how well they are doing, students learn more in the course and perform better on major exams, projects, and
papers. It makes sense that in a challenging course containing a great deal of material, students will learn more of it and put it to better use if they have to apply or
"practice" it frequently on exams, which also help them find out how much they
are learning and what they need to go over again. A recent Harvard study notes
students' "strong preference for frequent evaluation in a course." Harvard students
feel they learn least in courses that have "only a midterm and a final exam, with no
other personal evaluation." They believe they learn most in courses with "many
opportunities to see how they are doing" (Light, 1990, p. 32). In a review of a
number of studies of student learning, Frederiksen (1984) reports that students who
take weekly quizzes achieve higher scores on final exams than students who take
only a midterm exam and that testing increases retention of material tested.

Another, closely related argument in favor of multiple exams is that they en- 5
courage students to improve their study habits. Greater frequency in test taking
means greater frequency in studying for tests. Students prone to cramming will be
required—or at least strongly motivated—to open their textbooks and notebooks
more often, making them less likely to resort to long, kamikaze nights of studying
for major exams. Since there is so much to be learned in the typical course, it makes
sense that frequent, careful study and review are highly beneficial. But students need
motivation to study regularly, and nothing works like an exam. If students had
frequent exams in all their courses, they would have to schedule study time each
week and gradually would develop a habit of frequent study. It might be argued
that students are adults who have to learn how to manage their own lives, but
learning history or physics is more complicated than learning to drive a car or balance
a checkbook. Students need coaching and practice in learning. The right way to
learn new material needs to become a habit, and I believe that frequent exams are
key to developing good habits of study and learning. The Harvard study concludes
that "tying regular evaluation to good course organization enables students to plan
their work more than a few days in advance. If quizzes and homework are scheduled
on specific days, students plan their work to capitalize on them" (Light, 1990, p. 33).

By encouraging regular study habits, frequent exams would also decrease anxiety 6
by reducing the procrastination that produces anxiety. Students would benefit psychologically if they were not subjected to the emotional ups and down caused by
major exams, when after being virtually worry-free for weeks they are suddenly ready
to check into the psychiatric ward. Researchers at the University of Vermont found
a strong relationship between procrastination, anxiety, and achievement. Students
who regularly put off studying for exams had continuing high anxiety and lower
grades than students who procrastinated less. The researchers found that even "low"
procrastinators did not study regularly and recommended that professors give frequent assignments and exams to reduce procrastination and increase achievement
(Rothblum, Solomon, & Murakami, 1986, pp. 393, 394).

Research supports my proposed solution to the problems I have described. Com- 7
mon sense as well as my experience and that of many of my friends support it. Why,
then, do so few professors give frequent brief exams? Some believe that such exams
take up too much of the limited class time available to cover the material in the
course. Most courses meet 150 minutes a week—three times a week for 50 minutes
each time. A 20-minute weekly exam might take 30 minutes to administer, and that
is one-fifth of each week's class time. From the student's perspective, however, this
time is well spent. Better learning and greater confidence about the course seem a
good tradeoff for another 30 minutes of lecture. Moreover, time lost to lecturing or
discussion could easily be made up in students' learning on their own through careful
regular study for the weekly exams. If weekly exams still seem too time-consuming
to some professors, their frequency could be reduced to every other week or their
length to 5 or 10 minutes. In courses where multiple-choice exams are appropriate,
several questions take only a few minutes to answer.

Another objection professors have to frequent exams is that they take too much 8
time to read and grade. In a 20-minute essay exam a well-prepared student can
easily write two pages. A relatively small class of 30 students might then produce
60 pages, no small amount of material to read each week. A large class of 100 or
more students would produce an insurmountable pile of material. There are a number of responses to this objection. Again, professors could give exams every other
week or make them very short. Instead of reading them closely they could skim them
quickly to see whether students understand an idea or can apply it to an unfamiliar
problem; and instead of numerical or letter grades they could give a plus, check, or
minus. Exams could be collected and responded to only every third or fourth week.
Professors who have readers or teaching assistants could rely on them to grade or
check exams. And the scantron machine is always available for instant grading of
multiple-choice exams. Finally, frequent exams could be given *in place of* a midterm
exam or out-of-class essay assignment.

Since frequent exams seem to some professors to create too many problems, 9
however, it is reasonable to consider alternative ways to achieve the same goals.
One alternative solution is to implement a program that would improve study skills.
While such a program might teach students how to study for exams, it cannot
prevent procrastination or reduce "large test anxiety" by a substantial amount. One
research team studying anxiety and test performance found that study skills training
was "not effective in reducing anxiety or improving performance" (Dendato &
Diener, 1986, p. 134). This team, which also reviewed other research that reached
the same conclusion, did find that a combination of "cognitive/relaxation therapy"

and study skills training was effective. This possible solution seems complicated, however, not to mention time-consuming and expensive. It seems much easier and more effective to change the cause of the bad habit rather than treat the habit itself. That is, it would make more sense to solve the problem at its root: the method of learning and evaluation.

Still another solution might be to provide frequent study questions for students 10 to answer. These would no doubt be helpful in focusing students' time studying, but students would probably not actually write out the answers unless they were required to. To get students to complete the questions in a timely way, professors would have to collect and check the answers. In that case, however, they might as well devote the time to grading an exam. Even if it asks the same questions, a scheduled exam is preferable to a set of study questions because it takes far less time to write in class, compared to the time students would devote to responding to questions at home. In-class exams also ensure that each student produces his or her own work.

Another possible solution would be to help students prepare for midterm and 11 final exams by providing sets of questions from which the exam questions will be selected or announcing possible exam topics at the beginning of the course. This solution would have the advantage of reducing students' anxiety about learning every fact in the textbook, and it would clarify the course goals, but it would not motivate students to study carefully each new unit, concept, or text chapter in the course. I see this as a way of complementing frequent exams, not as substituting for them.

From the evidence and from my talks with professors and students, I see frequent, 12 brief in-class exams as the only way to improve students' study habits and learning, reducing their anxiety and procrastination, and increase their satisfaction with college. These exams are not a panacea, but only more parking spaces and a winning football team would do as much to improve college life. Professors can't do much about parking or football, but they can give more frequent exams. Campus administrators should get behind this effort, and professors should get together to consider giving exams more frequently. It would make a difference.

References

Light, R. J. (1990). *Explorations with students and faculty about teaching, learning, and student life*. Cambridge, MA: Harvard University Graduate School of Education and Kennedy School of Government.

Frederiksen, N. (1984). The real test bias: Influences of testing on teaching and learning. *American Psychologist, 39,* 193–202.

Rothblum, E. D., Solomon, L., & Murakami, J. (1986). Affective, cognitive, and behavioral differences between high and low procrastinators. *Journal of Counseling Psychology, 33,* 387–394.

Dendato, K. M., & Diener, D. (1986). Effectiveness of cognitive/relaxation therapy and study-skills training in reducing self-reported anxiety and improving the academic performance of test-anxious students. *Journal of Counseling Psychology, 33,* 131–135.

For Discussion | O'Malley advocates frequent brief exams as a solution to the problems of midterm-and-final anxiety, poor study habits, and disappointing exam performance. What do you think of his proposal in light of your own experience? Which of your high school or college courses have included frequent exams? Did they offer the benefits O'Malley claims? Did you learn more because of them? Did courses without frequent exams produce the problems he identifies?

For Analysis

1. Reread paragraph 3 carefully to discover how O'Malley defines and qualifies the solution. Underline key words and phrases that indicate what kind of exams he advocates. For his purpose and readers, does he adequately qualify the solution? Does anything seem unnecessary? Should anything be added? Does each key term hold up usefully throughout the essay?

For a discussion of forecasting statements, see p. 402.

2. In paragraph 2, how does O'Malley forecast the plan of his essay? Does the forecast predict the order of main parts? What else, if anything, might he have included in the forecast?

3. Reread paragraphs 4–6 and underline the most direct statements of the reasons O'Malley gives in support of his proposal. Why do you think he makes these reasons so easy to notice? What role do they play in the proposal?

4. Compare how O'Malley and Weisman, the author of the previous selection, acknowledge alternative solutions and establish shared values with their readers. What role do these two strategies play in the overall argumentative strategy of each essay? How successfully does each writer manage the two strategies?

5. Turn to the Writer at Work discussion on pp. 252–254. Compare the last paragraph in the section of O'Malley's draft with paragraph 4 in his revision, and list specific changes he made from draft to revision. Knowing his purpose and readers, what advantages do you see in his changes?

For Your Own Writing | Consider writing about a problem you have encountered in learning something new, either in or out of school. What problem would you select, and to whom would you propose a solution to it? What solution would you propose, and how might you convince these readers to take action on it?

Commentary | O'Malley's essay demonstrates the importance of taking readers seriously. Not only did he interview both those who would carry out his proposal (professors) and those who would benefit from it (students), but he featured in his essay what he had learned in these interviews. Paragraphs 7–11 directly acknowledge professors' objections, their questions, and the alternative solutions they would probably prefer. If at all possible, it is good to interview possible readers and thus to find out their likely objections, questions, and preferred solutions.

O'Malley's plan is also worth noting:

opening: a scenario to introduce the problem
presentation of the problem and introduction of the solution
details of the solution
reason 1 to support the solution: improved learning and performance
reason 2: improved study habits
reason 3: decreased procrastination and anxiety
accommodate objection 1: class time is limited
accommodate objection 2: too much work
refute alternative solution 1: offer study skills training
refute alternative solution 2: provide study questions
accommodate alternative solution 3: provide sample exam questions
closing: reiterate the proposed solution and advise briefly about first steps in implementing it

The essay seems to follow an appropriate order for O'Malley's purpose and readers. It is especially easy to follow because of explicit cues to readers: forecasts (previews of what is coming next), paragraph breaks, transitions, and summaries. Most important, the plan is logical and convincing. It is not the only possible plan—the alternative solutions might have been acknowledged before O'Malley argues for his solution, for example—but it is a very effective plan. This orderly plan developed over several days of invention, drafting, and revising.

PURPOSE AND AUDIENCE

More than any other kind of writing, proposals depend on the writer to anticipate readers' needs and concerns—because most proposals are calls to action. They attempt not only to convince readers but also to inspire them, to persuade them to support or to put into effect the proposed solution. What your particular readers know about the problem and what they are capable of doing to solve it determine how you address them.

Readers of proposals are often unaware of the problem. In this case, your task is clear: present them with facts that will convince them of its existence. These facts may include statistics, testimony from witnesses or experts, and examples. You can also speculate about the cause of the problem and describe its ill effects.

Sometimes readers recognize the existence of a problem but fail to take it seriously. When this is so, you may need to connect the problem closely to readers' own concerns. For instance, you might show how much they have in common with those directly affected by it, or how it affects them indirectly. However you appeal to readers, you must do more than alert them to the problem; you must also make them care about it. You want to touch readers emotionally as well as intellectually.

There will be occasions when readers are concerned about the problem but assume that someone else is taking care of it and that they need not become personally involved. Faced with this situation, you might want to demonstrate that those they thought were taking care of the problem have failed. Another assumption readers might make is that a solution they supported in the past has already solved the problem. You might point out that the original solution has proved unworkable or that new solutions have become available through changed circumstances or improved technology. Your aim is to rekindle these readers' interest in the problem.

Perhaps the most satisfying proposals are addressed to those who can take immediate action to remedy the problem. Your chances of writing such a proposal are good if you choose a problem faced by a group to which you belong. You not only have a first-hand understanding of the problem but also have a good idea what solution other members of the group will support. (You might informally survey some of them before you submit your proposal in order to test your definition of the problem and your proposed solution.) When you address readers who are in a position to take action, you obviously want to assure them that it is wise to do so. You must demonstrate that the solution is feasible, that it can be implemented, and that it will work.

BASIC FEATURES OF PROPOSALS

Effective proposals include the following features: a well-defined problem, a clear proposed solution, a convincing argument, and a reasonable tone.

A Well-defined
Problem

A proposal is written to offer a solution to a problem. Before presenting the solution, a proposal writer must be sure that readers know what the problem is. Samuel D. Proctor spends the first eleven paragraphs of his essay defining the problem, Patrick O'Malley the first three. All the writers in this chapter state the problem explicitly. Adam Paul Weisman identifies it as teenage pregnancy. Edward L. Palmer asserts that America has too little educational television for children, and Proctor describes a complex social problem of youth without families. O'Malley points to several specific problems caused by "major, infrequent, high-stakes exams."

Stating the problem is not enough, however: the writer may have to establish that it indeed exists and is serious enough to need solving. Sometimes a writer can assume that readers will recognize the problem. For example, Proctor describes unsocialized youth but offers few precise statistics about them. He does remind readers of the problem's seriousness, though, pointing out its negative consequences for schools and society. At other times readers may not be aware of the problem. O'Malley, for example, explicitly says that many professors do not realize the harmful effects of infrequent exams.

In addition to stating the problem and establishing its existence and seriousness, a proposal writer must analyze the problem: its causes and its consequences, its history and past efforts of dealing with it. This information not only helps readers understand the problem, but it may also provide grounds for the proposed solution. When Weisman points out that most teenagers have had sex, for instance, he is preparing readers for his argument that offering contraceptives is a better way to reduce unwanted teenage pregnancies than preaching abstinence.

A Proposed Solution

Once the problem is established, the writer must present and argue for a particular solution, which constitutes the thesis of the proposal. Weisman states his thesis thus: "Whatever the drawbacks, the contraception advocates have one strong advantage in this debate: their approach works." In the same way, O'Malley asserts, "If professors gave additional brief exams at frequent intervals, students would be spurred . . ." and Palmer advises that "It is fitting that we begin exploring a minimally adequate PTV children's schedule that places children's needs first."

A Convincing Argument

The main purpose of a proposal is to convince readers that the writer's solution is the best way of solving the problem. Proposal writers argue for their solutions by trying to demonstrate all of the following:

> that the proposed solution will solve the problem
> that it is a feasible way of solving the problem
> that it stands up against anticipated counterarguments
> that it is better than other ways of solving the problem

Arguing That the Proposed Solution Will Solve the Problem. A writer must give reasons and evidence to show that the proposed solution will indeed solve the problem. To this purpose, Weisman cites the Johns Hopkins study as evidence that the program he proposes will work, and Palmer argues for alleviating the shortage of educational television for children by creating new programs.

Arguing That the Proposed Solution Is Feasible. In arguing that the proposal is feasible, the writer must demonstrate how it can be implemented. The easier it seems to implement, the more likely it is to win readers' support. Therefore, writers generally set out the steps required to put the proposal into practice, an especially important strategy when the solution might seem difficult, time-consuming, or expensive to enact.

All the writers in this chapter offer specific suggestions for implementing their proposals. Weisman points to an actual instance in which his proposal has been effectively implemented. And Palmer devotes many paragraphs to discussing how his solution can be financed and realized.

Anticipating Counterarguments.   An important part of arguing for a proposal is to anticipate counterarguments, objections or reservations readers may have about the proposed solution. Weisman anticipates the counterargument that schools should not be used as "social service centers." He attempts to refute it by arguing that schools have provided health-related services in the past and that if birth-control information is banned from the schools, then teaching sexual abstinence must also be banned. O'Malley understands that professors will object to the time required to give and grade frequent exams but outlines several ways to reduce the time.

For illustrations of other ways to anticipate counterarguments, see pp. 480–86.

Considering and Rejecting Alternative Solutions.   Finally, the writer has to convince readers that his or her solution is preferable to other possible solutions. This is done by examining the other possibilities and demonstrating what is wrong with them. Weisman considers the proposal that teenagers be encouraged to abstain from sexual activity. O'Malley considers study skills training, study questions, and sample exam questions as alternatives to frequent exams.

The best way to reject an alternative solution is simply to demonstrate that it does not work, as Weisman tries to do. Another way is to show that the alternative solves only part of the problem. This is O'Malley's strategy in rejecting the idea of sample exam questions.

A Reasonable Tone

Regardless of the proposal or the argument made on its behalf, proposal writers must adopt a reasonable tone. The objective is to advance an argument without "having" an argument. That is, writers must never take an adversarial or quarrelsome stance with their readers. The aim is to bridge any gap that may exist between writer and readers, not widen it.

Writers can build such a bridge of shared concerns by showing respect for their readers and treating their concerns seriously. They discuss counterarguments as an attempt to lay to rest any doubts readers may have. They consider alternative solutions as a way of showing they have explored every possibility in order to find the best possible solution.

Most important, they do not attack those raising counterarguments or offering other solutions by questioning their intelligence or goodwill. Attacking people personally is called *argumentum ad hominem* (Latin for "argument to the man") and is considered a fallacy, or error in reasoning.

For information on fallacies, see pp. 486–87.

Guide to Writing

THE WRITING ASSIGNMENT

Write an essay proposing a solution to a problem. Choose a problem faced by a community or group to which you belong, and address your proposal either to one or more members of the group or to an outsider who might help solve the problem.

INVENTION AND RESEARCH

As you prepare to write a proposal, you will need to choose a problem you can write about, identify your prospective readers, find a tentative solution to it, and develop reasons for adopting your proposal rather than an alternative.

Choosing a Problem

One possible problem you could write about may come to mind immediately. Even so, you will want to think about various problems before settling on a topic. The following exercise is a good way to get started.

Considering Problems in Various Communities. Divide a piece of paper into two columns. In the left-hand column list all communities, groups, or organizations to which you belong. Include as many communities as possible: college, neighborhood, hometown, cultural or ethnic groups. Also include groups you participate in: sports, musical, work, religious, political, support, hobby, and so on. In the right-hand column list any problems that exist within each group. Here's how a chart might begin:

Community	*Problem*
Your College	poor advising or orientation
	too many required courses
	no financial aid for part-time students
Your Neighborhood	inadequate trash collection
	need for traffic light at dangerous intersection

Choose one problem from your list that you consider especially important. It should be one that seems solvable, though you need not know the exact solution now; and it should concern others in the group. It should of course be a problem you can explore in detail—and one you are willing to discuss in writing.

Analyzing
and Defining
the Problem

You need now to analyze the problem carefully and then to try to define it. Keep in mind that you will have to be able to demonstrate to readers that the problem exists and is serious and that you have a more than casual understanding of its causes and consequences. If you find that you cannot do so, you will want to select some other problem to write about.

Analyzing.   Start by writing a few sentences in response to each of the following questions:

- Does the problem really exist? How can I tell?
- What caused this problem? Can I identify any immediate causes? any deeper causes? Is the problem caused by a flaw in the system, a lack of resources, individual misconduct or incompetence? How can I tell?
- What is the history of the problem?
- What are the bad effects of the problem? How is it hurting members of the community or group? What goals of the group are endangered by the existence of this problem? Does it raise any moral or ethical questions?
- Who in the community or group is affected by the problem? Be as specific as possible: Who is seriously affected? minimally affected? unaffected? Does anyone benefit from its existence?
- What similar problems exist in this the same community or group? How can I distinguish my problem from these?

Defining.   Write a definition of the problem, being as specific as possible. Identify who or what seems responsible for it, and give one recent example.

Identifying
Your Readers

Whom do you wish to address—everyone in the community or group, a committee, an individual, an outsider? In a few sentences, describe your readers, stating your reason for directing your proposal to them. Then take ten minutes to write about these readers. Use these questions to stimulate your writing:

- How informed are they likely to be about the problem? Have they shown any awareness of it?
- Why would this problem be important to them? Why would they care about solving it?
- Have they supported any other proposals to solve the problem? If so, what do their proposals have in common with mine?
- Do they ally themselves with any group that might cause them to favor or reject my proposal? Do we share any values or attitudes that could bring us together to solve the problem?
- How have they responded to other problems? Do their past reactions suggest anything about how they may respond to my proposal?

Finding a Tentative Solution

Solving problems takes time. Apparent solutions often turn out to be impossible because so many factors must be considered. After all, a solution has to be both workable and acceptable to the community or group involved. Consequently, you should strive to come up with several possible solutions whose advantages and disadvantages can be weighed. Keep in mind that the most imaginative solutions sometimes occur only after you've struggled with a number of other possibilities.

Look back at the way you defined the problem and described your readers. Then, with your readers and the particular community or group in mind, list as many possible solutions as you can think of. For ideas, reflect on the following problem-solving questions:

- What solutions to this problem have already been tried?
- What solutions have been proposed for related problems? Might they solve this problem as well?
- Is a solution required that would disband or change the community or group in some way?
- What solution might eliminate some of the causes of the problem?
- What solution would eliminate any of the bad effects of the problem?
- Maybe the problem is too big to be solved all at once. Try dividing it into several parts. What solutions might solve these parts?
- If the problem requires a series of solution, which one should come first? Second?
- What solution would ultimately solve the problem?
- What might be a daring solution?
- What would be the most conservative solution, acceptable to nearly everyone in the community or group?

Give yourself enough time to let your ideas percolate, continuing to add to your list of possible solutions and to consider the advantages and disadvantages of each one in light of your prospective readers. If possible, discuss your solutions with members of the community or group. Those actually involved with the problem can best help you consider the advantages and disadvantages of the possible solutions.

Choosing the Most Promising Solution.   In a sentence or two, state what you would consider the best possible way of solving the problem.

Determining Specific Steps.   Write down the steps necessary to carry out your solution. This list will provide an early test of whether your solution can, in fact, be implemented.

Defending
Your Solution

Proposals have to be feasible—that is, they must be both reasonable and practical. Imagine that one of your readers opposes your proposed solution and confronts you with the following statements. Write several sentences refuting each one.

- It won't really solve the problem.
- We can't afford it.
- It will take too long.
- People won't do it.
- Too few people will benefit.
- I don't even see how to get started on your solution.
- It's already been tried, with unsatisfactory results.
- You're making this proposal because it will benefit you personally.

Answering these questions now should help you to prepare responses to possible objections to your proposal. You may find that you need a better idea of how others are likely to feel about your proposal. If so, try to talk to a few people involved with the problem. The more you know about your readers and their concerns, the better you will be able to anticipate any counterarguments they may offer or alternative solutions they might prefer.

Testing
Your Choice

Now you should examine the problem and your chosen solution to see whether they will result in a strong proposal. Start by asking the following questions:

- Is this a significant problem? Do other people in the community or group really care about it, or can they be persuaded to care?
- Will my solution really solve the problem? Can it be implemented?
- Can I answer objections from enough people in the community or group to win support for my solution?

As you plan and draft your proposal, you will probably want to consider these questions again. If at any point you decide that you cannot answer them affirmatively and confidently, you may want to find another solution or even to write about some other problem.

For Group Inquiry

Now might be a good time to get together in a group with two or three other students and run your chosen topics by one another. Assess their awareness of the problem you wish to write about, and "try out" your solution on them. Are they convinced that it is a possible solution? a good solution? What counterarguments can they offer? What alternative solutions do they suggest? Your purpose is to decide whether the problem you have chosen to write about is one that matters and whether your solution seems feasible.

Offering Reasons
for Your Proposal

To make a convincing case for your proposed solution, you will need to offer your readers good reasons for adopting your proposal.

Listing Reasons.   Write down every plausible reason you could give that might persuade readers to accept your proposal. These reasons should answer readers' key question: "Why is this the best solution?"

Choosing the Strongest Reasons.   Keeping your readers in mind, look over your list and put an asterisk next to the strongest reasons. If you do not consider two or three of your reasons strong, you may anticipate difficulty developing a strong proposal and should reconsider your topic.

Developing Your Strongest Reasons.   Now look at these strongest reasons and explain briefly why you think each one will be effective with your particular readers. Then take around five minutes to write about each reason, developing your argument on its behalf.

Considering
Alternative
Solutions

Even if your readers are likely to consider your proposal reasonable, they will probably want to compare your proposed solution with other possible solutions. List alternative solutions that might be offered, and consider the advantages and disadvantages of each one next to your solution. You might find it helpful to chart the information as follows:

Possible Solutions	Advantages	Disadvantages
My solution		
Alternative solution 1		
Alternative solution 2		

Doing Research

For guidelines on library research, see Chapter 20.

Thus far you have relied largely upon your own knowledge and instincts for solving the problem. You may now feel that you need to know more. It has already been suggested that you talk to members of the group or community in order to anticipate their counterarguments or alternative proposals. You may also need to do some further research: to learn more about the causes of the problem, perhaps, or to find more technical information about implementing the solution. If you are proposing a solution to a problem about which others have written, you will probably want to find out how they have defined it and what solutions they have proposed. You may need to acknowledge these solutions in your essay, either accommodating or refuting them. Now is a good time—before beginning to draft—to get any additional information you need.

PLANNING AND DRAFTING

To help you plan your essay and begin drafting, review what you have done so far, set some specific goals for yourself, and prepare an outline.

Seeing What You Have

Reread your invention notes, asking yourself whether you have a good topic—an interesting problem with a feasible solution. If at this point you are doubtful about the significance of the problem or the success of your proposed solution, you might want to look for a new topic. If you are unsure about these basic points, you cannot really expect to produce a persuasive draft.

If your invention material seems thin but promising, however, you may be able to strengthen it with additional invention writing. Consider the following questions:

- Could I make a stronger case for the seriousness of the problem?
- Could I find more reasons for readers to support my solution?
- Are there any other ways of refuting attractive alternative solutions or troubling counterarguments?

Setting Goals

Before beginning to draft, think seriously about the overall goals of your proposal. Not only will the draft be easier to write once you have clear goals, but it will almost surely be more convincing.

Following are some goal-setting questions to consider now. You may find it useful to return to them while drafting, for they are designed to help you focus on exactly what you want to accomplish with this proposal.

Your Readers

- What do my readers already know about this problem?
- Are they likely to welcome my solution or resist it?
- Can I anticipate any specific reservations or objections they may have?
- How can I gain readers' enthusiastic support? How can I get them to help implement the solution?
- What kind of tone would be most appropriate? How can I present myself so that I seem both reasonable and authoritative?

The Beginning

- How can I immediately engage my readers' interest? Should I open with an anecdote, like Proctor? With a dramatic scenario, like O'Malley? With a statement that the time and conditions are right to solve the problem, like Palmer? With a question, like Weisman?
- What information should I give first?

Defining the Problem

■ How much do I need to say about the problem's causes or history?

■ How can I establish the seriousness of the problem? Should I quote statistics, like Weisman? Stress unfortunate consequences, like O'Malley?

■ Is it an urgent problem? How can I emphasize this? Should I outline dangers, like Proctor? Set up an unfavorable comparison, like Palmer?

■ How much space should I devote to defining the problem? Will I need to devote only a little space, like O'Malley, or much space, like Proctor?

Proposing a Solution

■ How can I present my solution so that it looks like the best way to proceed? Should I describe its basic features, like Proctor? Outline its implementation, like Palmer? Focus on reasons to support it, like O'Malley?

■ How can I make the solution seem easy to implement? Can I present the first step so that it looks easy to take?

Anticipating Counterarguments

■ Should I mention every possible counterargument to my proposed solution? How might I choose among them?

■ Has anyone already raised these counterarguments? If so, should I name the person?

■ Should I accommodate certain counterarguments?

■ What specific reasons can I give for refuting each counterargument? How can I support these reasons?

■ How can I refute the counterarguments without criticizing anyone?

Rejecting Alternative Solutions

■ How many alternative solutions do I need to mention? Which ones should I discuss?

■ Should I indicate where these alternatives come from? Like Weisman, should I name those who proposed them?

■ What reasons should I give for rejecting the alternative solutions? Like O'Malley, can I offer any evidence in support of my reasons?

■ How can I reject these other solutions without seeming to criticize their proponents? Both Weisman and O'Malley succeed at this.

The Ending

■ How should I conclude? Should I end by restating the seriousness of the problem, as Proctor does? With a case proving that the solution is workable, as Palmer does? By arguing that some readers' preferred solution is sure to fail, as Weisman does? Or should I simply end by summarizing my solution and restating its advantages, as does O'Malley?

- Is there something special about the problem itself I should remind readers of at the end?
- Should I end with an inspiring call to action or a scenario suggesting the dreaded consequences of a failure to solve the problem?
- Would a shift to humor or satire be an effective way to end?

Outlining

After setting goals for your proposal, you will be ready to make a working outline. The basic outline for a proposal is quite simple:

> the problem
> the solution
> the reasons for accepting the solution

This simple plan is nearly always complicated by other factors, however. In outlining your material you must take into consideration many other details, such as whether readers already recognize the problem, how much agreement exists on the need to solve the problem, how many alternative solutions are available, how much attention must be given to the other solutions, and how many counterarguments should be expected.

A possible outline for a proposal where readers may be unlikely to understand the problem fully and where other solutions have been proposed might look like this:

> presentation of the problem
> > its existence
> > its seriousness
> > its causes
>
> consequences of failing to solve the problem
>
> description of the proposed solution
>
> list of steps for implementing the solution
>
> discussion of reasons to support the solution
> > acknowledgment of counterarguments
> > accommodation or refutation of counterarguments
>
> consideration of alternative solutions and their disadvantages
>
> restatement of the proposed solution and its advantages

See p. 235 for another sample outline.

Your outline will of course reflect your own writing situation. As you develop it, think about what your readers know and feel, and about your own writing goals. Once you have a working outline, you should not hesitate to change it as necessary while writing. For instance, you might find it more effective to hold back on presenting your own solution until you have dismissed other possible solutions. Or you might find a better way to order the reasons for adopting your proposal. The purpose of an outline is to identify the basic features of your proposal and help you organize them effectively, not to lock you into a particular structure.

Most of the information you will need to develop each feature can be found in your invention writing and research notes. How much space you devote to each feature is determined by the topic, not the outline. Do not assume that each entry on your outline must be given one paragraph—in the preceding example, each of the reasons for supporting the solution may require a paragraph, but you might also discuss the reasons, counterarguments, and refutations all in one paragraph.

Drafting

After reviewing your outline, start drafting the proposal. Let the outline help you write, but don't hesitate to change it if you find that drafting takes you in an unexpected direction. If you get stuck in drafting, return to the invention activities earlier in this chapter. As you draft, keep in mind the two main goals of proposal writing: (1) to establish that a problem exists that is serious enough to require a solution; and (2) to demonstrate that your proposed solution is feasible and is the best possible alternative.

You might want to review the general advice on drafting on pp. 9–11.

GETTING CRITICAL COMMENTS

At this point your draft would benefit from a good critical reading. All writers find it helpful to have someone else read and comment on their drafts, and your instructor may schedule such a reading as part of your coursework. Otherwise, you can ask a classmate, friend, or family member to read it over. If your campus has a writing center, you might ask a tutor there to read and comment on your draft. In this section are guidelines designed to be used by *anyone* reviewing an essay proposing a solution to a problem. (If you are unable to get someone else to review your draft, turn to the Revision section on pp. 249–52, where you will find guidelines for approaching your own draft with a critical eye.)

To provide focused, helpful comments, your reader must know your intended audience and purpose. At the top of your draft, write out the following information:

Audience. Who are your readers?

Purpose. What do you hope will happen as a result of your proposal?

Reading with a Critical Eye

Reading a draft critically means reading it more than once, first to get a general impression and then to analyze its basic features.

Reading for a First Impression. Read first to get a basic understanding of the problem and the proposed solution to it. As you read, try to notice any words or passages that contribute either favorably or unfavorably to your impression. A good way to highlight noteworthy language is to use the pointings system.

Pointings

- Draw a straight line under any words or images that impress you as especially effective: strong verbs, specific details, memorable phrases, striking images.
- Draw a wavy line under any words or images that seem flat, stale, or vague. Also put a wavy line under any words or phrases that you consider unnecessary or repetitious.
- Look for pairs or groups of sentences that you think should be combined. Put brackets [ ] around these sentences.
- Look for sentences that are garbled, overloaded, or awkward. Put parentheses ( ) around these sentences. Put them around any sentence that seems even slightly questionable; don't worry about whether or not you're certain about your judgment. The writer needs to know that you, as one reader, had even the slightest problem understanding a sentence.

After reading the draft, briefly write out your impressions. How convincing do you think the essay will be for its particular readers? What do you notice about the way the problem is presented and the solution argued for?

See pp. 236–38 to review the basic features.

Reading to Analyze.   Now read to focus on the basic features of proposal writing. Consider the following questions:

How Well Is the Problem Defined?

Decide whether the problem is stated clearly. Is enough information given about its causes and consequences? What more might be done to establish its seriousness? Is there more readers might need or wish to know about it?

How Clearly Is the Solution Presented?

Restate the solution. Is it clear? Could its presentation be strengthened? How? Are steps for implementing the solution not laid out? If not, might readers expect or require them? Does the solution seem practical? If not, why not?

How Convincing Is the Argument for the Solution?

Look at the reasons and evidence offered in support of this solution. Are they sufficient? Which are the most convincing? Which are the least convincing? Why?

Consider the treatment of counterarguments to the proposed solution. What reasons and evidence refuting counterarguments seem most convincing? Which seem least convincing? Why? Are there other counterarguments that need to be acknowledged?

Are alternative solutions discussed and either accommodated or refuted? What are the most convincing reasons given against any other solutions? Which are least convincing, and why?

Are there any errors in reasoning, such as false analogies or personal attacks?

How Appropriate Is the Tone?

Is the proposal advanced in a reasonable tone, one that argues forcefully yet finds some common ground with readers who may advocate alternative solutions? Are such solutions accommodated or rejected without a personal attack on those who propose them?

How Effective Is the Organization?

Evaluate the *overall plan* of the proposal, perhaps by outlining it briefly. Would any parts be more effective earlier or later? Look closely at the ordering of the argument for the solution—the presentation of the reasons and the accommodation or refutation of counterarguments and alternative solutions. How might the sequence be revised to strengthen the argument? Point to any gaps in the argument.

Is the *beginning* engaging? If not, how might it be revised to capture the readers' attention? Does it adequately forecast the main ideas and the plan of the proposal? Can you think of other ways to begin.

Evaluate the *ending*. Does it frame the proposal by echoing or referring to something at the beginning? If not, how might it do so? Does the ending convey a sense of urgency? Can you think of a stronger way to conclude?

What Final Thoughts Do You Have?

What is the strongest part of this proposal? What part of the draft most needs additional work?

REVISING AND EDITING

This section will help you to identify problems in your draft and to revise and edit to solve them.

Identifying Problems

To identify problems in your draft, you need to read it objectively, analyze its basic features, and study any comments you've received from others.

Getting an Overview.   Consider the draft as a whole, trying to see it objectively. It may help to do so in two steps:

Reread. If at all possible, put the draft aside for a day or two before rereading it. When you reread, start by reconsidering your audience and purpose. Then read the draft straight through, trying to see it as your intended readers will.

Outline. Make a scratch outline to get an overview of the essay's development. This outline can be sketchy—words and phrases instead of complete sentences—but it should identify the basic features as they appear.

Charting a Plan for Revision.   Use the following chart to keep track of any problems you need to solve. The left-hand column lists the basic features of writing proposals. As you analyze your draft and study any comments you've gotten from others, note in the right-hand column the problems you want to solve.

Basic Features	*Problems to Solve*
Definition of the problem	
Presentation of the solution	
Argument for the solution	
Acknowledgement of alternative solutions	
Tone	
Organization	

Analyzing the Basic Features of Your Draft.   Turn now to the questions for analyzing a draft on pp. 248–49. Using these questions as guidelines, identify problems in your draft. Note anything you need to solve on the chart above.

Studying Critical Comments.   Review any comments you've received from other readers, and add to the chart any points that need attention. Try not to react too defensively to these comments; by letting you see how others respond to your draft, they provide invaluable information about how you might improve it.

Solving the Problems

Having identified problems, you now need to figure out solutions and to carry them out. Basically, you have three ways of finding solutions: (1) review your invention and planning notes for additional information and ideas; (2) do further invention to answer questions your readers raised; and (3) look back at the readings in this chapter to see how other writers have solved similar problems.

Following are suggestions to get you started on solving some of the problems common to writing proposals. For now, focus on solving those problems identified on your chart. Avoid tinkering with sentence-level problems; that will come later, when you edit.

Definition of the Problem

- If the problem is not clearly defined, you may need to sketch out its history, including past attempts to deal with it. Consider discussing its causes and consequences more fully or dramatizing its seriousness more vividly. It may help to compare it to other problems readers may be familiar with.

Presentation of the Solution

- If the solution is not adequately described, add details of how it will work when implemented. Try outlining the steps or phases in implementation. Help readers see how easy the first step will be.

Argument for the Solution

- If the argument seems weak, try to think of more reasons why readers should support your proposal.
- If your refutation of any counterargument seems unconvincing, consider accommodating it by modifying your proposal.
- If you have left out any likely objections readers will have to the solution, add acknowledgments of them, either accommodating or refuting them.
- If you have made errors in reasoning, such as false analogies or personal attacks, correct or eliminate them.
- If you neglected to mention alternative solutions some readers are likely to prefer, do so now. Consider whether you want to accommodate or reject these alternatives. For each one, try to acknowledge its good points but argue that it is not so good a solution as your own. You may, in fact, want to strengthen your own solution by incorporating into it some of the good points from alternatives. If you have made errors in reasoning, correct or eliminate them.

Tone

- If your tone seems too adversarial, revise to acknowledge your readers' fears, biases, and expectations.

Organization

- If the argument or the essay is hard to follow, find a better sequence for major parts. Try to put reasons supporting your solution in a more convincing order—leading up to the strongest one rather than putting it first, perhaps. Shift refutation of objections or alternative solutions so that they do not interrupt the main argument. Add explicit cues to keep the reader on track: previews of what is coming, transitional phrases and sentences, brief summaries of points just made.
- If the beginning is weak, see if there is a better place to start. Would an anecdote or an example of the problem's effects engage readers more quickly?

- If the ending doesn't work, consider framing your proposal by mentioning something from the beginning of your essay. Consider ending with a call for action that expresses the urgency behind implementing your solution.

Editing and Proofreading

Thus far you've probably corrected some obvious errors, but grammar and style have not been a priority. Now is the time to check carefully for errors in usage, punctuation, and mechanics, and also to consider matters of style. You may find that studying your draft in separate passes—first for paragraphs, then for sentences, and finally for words—will help you to recognize any problems.

Once you have edited your draft and produced a final copy, proofread it carefully to be sure there are no typos, misspellings, or other mistakes.

LEARNING FROM YOUR OWN WRITING PROCESS

Take time now to look over all the work you have done on your proposal. Start with your invention materials—what was easiest? what was hardest? Did the readings influence your invention and drafting in any way? What difficulties did you encounter in drafting? How did you solve them?

Consider your final revision. What changes did you make from draft to revision? Did other readers' comments affect the final version? Look at specific changes you made, and explain why you made them.

What do you consider best about your proposal? What would you still like to improve if you had more time?

A Writer at Work

STRENGTHENING THE ARGUMENT

This section focuses on Patrick O'Malley's successful efforts to strengthen the argument for his proposed solution in his essay "More Testing, More Learning." Read first the three paragraphs below from his draft. Then compare these with paragraphs 4–6 in his revision on pp. 231–232. As you read, take notes on differences you observe between draft and revision.

> The predominant reason why students perform better with
> multiple exams is that they improve their study hab-
> its. Greater regularity in test taking means greater
> regularity in studying for tests. Students prone to
> cramming will be forced to open their textbooks more

often, keeping them away from long, "kamikaze" nights of
studying. Regularity prepares them for the "real world"
where you rarely take on large tasks at long intervals.
Several tests also improve study habits by reducing procrastination. An article about procrastination from the
Journal of Counseling Psychology reports that "students
view exams as difficult, important, and anxiety provok-
ing." These symptoms of anxiety leading to procrastination could be solved if individual test importance was
lessened, reducing the stress associated with the perceived burden.

   With multiple exams, this anxiety decrease will
free students to perform better. Several, less important
tests may appear as less of an obstacle, allowing the
students to worry less, leaving them free to concentrate
on their work without any emotional hindrances. It is
proven that "the performance of test-anxious subjects
varies inversely with evaluation stress." It would also
be to the psychological benefit of students if they were
not subjected to the emotional ups and downs of large
exams where they are virtually worry-free one moment and
ready to check into the psychiatric ward the next.

   Lastly, with multiple exams, students can learn how
to perform better on future tests in the class. Regular
testing allows them to "practice" the information they
learned, thereby improving future test scores. In just
two exams, they are not able to learn the instructor's
personal examination style, and are not given the chance
to adapt their study habits to it. The *American Psychologist* concludes: "It is possible to influence teaching
and learning by changing the type of tests."

One difference you may have noted between draft and revision paragraphs is the sequencing of specific reasons why readers should accept the
solution and take action on it. Whereas the draft moves in three paragraphs
from improving study habits to decreasing anxiety to performing better on
future tests, the revision moves from learning more and performing better
on major exams to improving study habits to decreasing anxiety. The reason
for the change was that a response from a classmate and a conference with
his instructor helped O'Malley to see that the most convincing reason to his
readers—professors—would probably be the improved quality of students'
learning, not their habits and feelings. As he continued thinking about his
argument and discovering further relevant research, he shifted his emphasis
from the psychological to the intellectual benefits of frequent exams.

You may also have noticed that each paragraph of the revision is better focused. The psychological benefits (reduced anxiety as a result of less procrastination) are now discussed mainly in a single paragraph (the third), whereas in the draft they were mixed in with the intellectual benefits in the first two paragraphs. O'Malley also tried to use more precise language: for example, he changed "future tests" to "major exams, projects, and papers."

Another change you may have noticed is that all of the quoted research material in the draft has been replaced in the revision. Extending his library research for evidence to support his reasons, O'Malley discovered the very useful Harvard report. As his argument found a more logical sequence, more precise terms, and fuller elaboration, he saw different ways to use the research studies he had turned up initially and quoted in the draft.

A final difference is that in the revision O'Malley argues his reasons more effectively. Consider the paragraphs on improved study habits. In the draft paragraph O'Malley shifts abruptly from study habits to procrastination to anxiety. Except for study habits, none of these topics is developed; and the quotation adds nothing to what he has already said. By contrast, the revision paragraph focuses strictly on study habits. O'Malley keeps the best sentences from the draft for the beginning of the revised paragraph, but he adds several new sentences attempting to convince readers of the soundness of his argument that frequent exams change students' study habits. These sentences anticipate a possible objection ("It might be argued . . ."), note a contrast between complex academic learning and familiar survival skills, and assert claims about the special requirements of regular academic study. The quotation from the Harvard report supports rather than merely repeats O'Malley's claims, and it effectively concludes the paragraph.

■ In an article about the upcoming Rose Bowl game, a reporter for the *Los Angeles Times* evaluates the two competing teams, who represent the Pacific Ten and Big Ten conferences. She predicts victory for the Pacific Ten team, contending that it has a better-balanced offense as well as more depth and experience at each position. As support for her prediction, the reporter names several specific players and mentions some key plays from earlier games. To refute the likely counterargument that the Pacific Ten team won fewer games during the regular season, she argues that it played a much tougher schedule than the Big Ten team.

■ The president of a large computer corporation writes a letter recommending one of his employees for an upper-level management position at another company. He praises her judgment, energy, and interpersonal skills, mentioning several incidents as support for his claims. He describes in detail her contributions to several specific projects.

■ A *Skiing* reporter writes an article evaluating two popular makes of slalom skis. He assumes his audience to be made up of experienced downhill skiers who may not have actually done any slalom racing. Using one technical criterion, design, he argues that one make is superior to the other. He cites specific differences in waist width, sidecut radius, camber, and shovel stiffness as support for his judgment.

■ In a column syndicated to college newspapers, a writer reviews two newly revised paperback thesauri. Both are selling well in college bookstores. The reporter compares the two on the criteria of size, price, and usefulness. The criterion of usefulness leads to further comparisons of format and specific sample entries. She concludes by recommending one thesaurus over the other.

■ For her senior thesis, a political science major evaluates a state senator whom she dislikes and distrusts. After researching the senator's legislative activities and voting record, she decides that the best criteria for evaluating the senator are three: responsibility in carrying out legislative duties, voting record in support of public programs, and willingness to educate the voters on important issues. These criteria provide adequate support for her negative judgment: the senator is often absent for important votes, he votes consistently against antipoverty bills, and he makes little effort to provide his constituents with news about important issues. She documents each of these reasons—and all the others in her paper—with specific evidence gathered in her research. At several points in the paper she contrasts the senator's activities and voting record with those of other state senators.

■ **A midterm exam for a literature course includes two poems by John Updike that the students are unlikely to have seen before. They are to decide which is the better poem and write an essay explaining why. Evaluating the poems according to criteria he learned in the class, a student argues that one is better because its rhythms are less predictable and more conversationlike and also because its imagery is more visual and hence more memorable. He provides several examples from the poems in support of each reason.**

We all make judgments. Many times each day we make evaluations, usually spontaneously, in response to events, people, things. In everyday conversation we often state our evaluations without thorough justification or development. Rarely do we think out a reasoned, detailed argument for our evaluations based on specific criteria, although we constantly give reasons for our opinions in a casual way. By contrast, we expect judgments stated in writing to be authoritative and persuasive, with a planned, coherent, reasoned argument. We expect that the writer will use appropriate standards of evaluation, and that the argument will be supported with reasons, evidence, and examples.

Evaluation is basic to thinking and learning—and thus to writing. It underlies all types of argument, forming with cause-and-effect analysis the basic building blocks of argument. As a college student, you may be asked to evaluate books, artworks, scientific discoveries, or current events. Following are some typical evaluation assignments:

■ *For an astronomy course:* Which of two theories—the big bang theory or the pulsating universe theory—better explains the origin of the universe?

■ *For a political science course:* Evaluate the two major presidential candidates' performances during one of their scheduled televised debates. If possible, record the debate so that you can analyze it closely and quote the candidates directly. Make a file of newspaper and magazine clippings on the debate, along with reports of polls taken before and after it. Take notes on the post-debate television commentary. Use this material to support your judgment of who won the debate.

■ *For a twentieth-century American history course:* Review one of several published studies of the Vietnam War. Your review should describe the approach taken in the book and evaluate both the accuracy of its facts and the quality of its interpretation.

If your college has a system of student course evaluations, you will regularly evaluate your instructors. On the job, you will be evaluated and may eventually evaluate others for promotions, awards, or new jobs. You may also be asked to evaluate various plans and proposals, and your success at these important writing tasks may in large part determine how quickly you yourself are promoted. In a more fundamental way, studying and writing evaluations contributes to your intellectual development, teaching you to define the criteria that provide the standards for any judgments you are called upon to make and then to develop a reasoned argument with evidence to support your evaluation.

Your purpose in writing evaluations is to convince readers that you have made an informed and correct judgment. You may want to convince them that a particular movie is worth seeing, a research report seriously flawed, a competitor's product brilliantly innovative, an applicant for a position not the person to hire. In these and innumerable other writing situations in college and on the job, you must establish your authority and credibility in order to win the trust of your readers. You do that essentially by basing your judgment on sound reasoning, appropriate criteria, and solid evidence. This evidence comes from a thorough analysis of your subject, an analysis that ensures a detailed and comprehensive understanding.

For Group Inquiry

Assume that you have been asked to review some form of popular entertainment. Get together with two or three other students and choose a type of entertainment you all know fairly well: country-western music, horror movies, music videos, magic acts, or any other kind of entertainment. Then discuss what criteria, or standards for judgment, should be used in reviewing this type of entertainment. For example, the criteria for a movie review might include the movie's entertainment value (if it's a comedy, is it funny?), the quality of its ideas (if it's about relationships, is it insightful?), and its technical qualities (such as acting, direction, cinematography). Try to agree on the two or three most important criteria. Then reflect on what you have learned about the role of criteria in making evaluations:

- Which criteria did you agree about readily, and which created disagreement in the group?
- How can you account for these differences?
- Where do you suppose your criteria came from?
- How do you think experts decide on theirs?

Readings

David **Ansen** wrote the following review of a controversial 1989 movie, *Do the Right Thing*, for *Newsweek* magazine. *Newsweek*, along with other magazines and television talk shows, ran special features on the movie and its producer-director-writer, Spike Lee.

If you have not seen *Do the Right Thing*, you might want to rent the video, but seeing the movie is not essential, since reviews are written primarily for readers who are trying to decide whether or not to see a particular film. As you read this review, consider whether you would decide to see *Do the Right Thing* on the basis of what Ansen says about it.

SEARING, NERVY AND VERY HONEST
DAVID ANSEN

Somewhere near the midpoint in Spike Lee's "Do the Right Thing"—as the summer heat in Bedford-Stuyvesant reaches the boiling point—there occurs an astonishing outpouring of racial invective, five short soliloquies of ethnic slurs directed straight at the camera. A black man insults Italians. An Italian defames blacks. A Puerto Rican castigates Koreans. A white cop rips into Puerto Ricans. A Korean slanders Jews. At which point Lee cuts to the neighborhood radio deejay, Mister Señor Love Daddy, screaming into his mike "Time out! . . . 1

Nigger, dago, kike, spic. There they are, America's dirtiest words, hurled across the screen in Lee's nervy, complex, unsettling movie. The sequence makes you catch your breath, but you also laugh as you laughed when Lenny Bruce or Richard Pryor touched a raw nerve of publicly unspoken experience. And Lee's rude comic impulse is the same as theirs: unless we air these noxious fumes, and acknowledge just how dire the racial situation has become, this great unmelted pot might well explode. 2

When white filmmakers deal with race (from Stanley Kramer's "The Defiant Ones" to Alan Parker's "Mississippi Burning"), no matter how fine their intentions, they tend to speak in inflated, self-righteous tones, and they always come down to Hollywood's favorite dialectic, bad guys versus good guys. They allow the audience to sit comfortably on the side of the angels. In "Do the Right Thing," Lee blows away the pieties and the easy answers. He prefers abrasion and ambiguity to comfort and tidiness. As a black filmmaker, he's too close to the subject—and too much the artist—to oversimplify the issues. The beauty of "Do the Right Thing" is that all the characters, from the broadest cartoons to the most developed, are given their humanity and their due. 3

At the end of the story there is violence, police brutality, a riot. Sal's pizzeria, a white-run business that has existed peacefully in the black community for 25 years, suddenly becomes the target of pent-up rage. The owner, Sal (Danny Aiello, who's never been better), is no ogre—he's a sympathetic figure, a peacemaker who's arguably an unconscious racist. His son Pino (John Turturro), on the other hand, is blatantly antiblack, the closest to a villain the movie gets. Lee isn't saying the violence is inevitable, or even just. But we see how it comes to pass, a combination of heat, irritation, insensitivity, stubbornness and centuries of systematic oppression. 4

Lee trusts his audience: he doesn't need to stack the deck. You can feel he's working out his own ambivalence on screen. His rich portrait of the Bed-Stuy community is both affectionate and critical. Take the character of Buggin' Out (Giancarlo Esposito). He's the most militant black in the movie, but Lee shows his rage as misplaced and foolish. His attempt to boycott Sal's because there are no pictures of blacks on the walls—only Italian-Americans—is greeted by most with derision. When Mother Sister (Ruby Dee), the block's wise old watchdog, sees Sal's go up in flames we're startled by her exhilaration at the violence. But moments later she's wailing in despair at the destruction. It's one of the movie's points that we are all nursing wildly 5 contradictory impulses: our heads and hearts aren't always in sync. This is no cop-out, it's unusually honest reporting.

"Do the Right Thing" is a kind of compacted epic played out in jazzy, dissonant   6
scenes that dance in and out of realism. Lee's deliberately discordant style didn't jell in "School Daze," an ambitious but turgid look at the divisions in a black college. Here the clashing styles add up and pay off. You leave this movie stunned, challenged and drained. To accuse Lee of irresponsibility—of inciting violence—is to be blind to the movie he has made. The two quotes that end the film—Martin Luther King's eloquent antiviolent testament and Malcolm X's acknowledgment that violence in self-defense may be necessary—are the logical culmination of Lee's method. There can be no simple, tidy closure. Not now. Not yet. Lee's conscience-pricking movie is bracing and necessary: it's the funkiest and most informed view of racism an American filmmaker has given us.

For Discussion

Ansen refers to the two quotations that appear at the end of *Do the Right Thing*: The first, by Martin Luther King, Jr., asserts that violence is always to be avoided, whereas the second, by Malcolm X, counters that violence may sometimes be necessary. Is violence ever justifiable? Can you recall an occasion when you used violence or were tempted to? What did you think the use or the show of force would accomplish in this particular situation? What alternatives did you have? In general, why do you think people resort to violence? In what ways does American culture encourage or discourage the use of force? (You may want to read and discuss "The Use of Force," a short story on pp. 373–75.)

For Analysis

1.   If you have not seen *Do the Right Thing*, what did you learn about it from reading this essay? What information does it give about the movie? What kinds of information do you ordinarily expect from a movie review? How well does this review meet your expectations?

For a discussion of comparison and contrast, see Chapter 17.

2.   Ansen uses the writing strategy of comparing and contrasting at two different points in the essay. Find these passages. Which of the two strategies—comparison or contrast—is being used in each case? What does each accomplish in this essay?

3.   In paragraph 6 Ansen refers to an objection by others that *Do the Right Thing* incites people to violence. On what grounds does he refute this criticism? In your view, how effective is his refutation? What advantages or disadvantages do you see in placing this refutation in the last paragraph?

4.   To influence readers' decision whether or not to see a movie, a reviewer needs to gain readers' confidence. Has Ansen won your confidence? If so, how? If not, why not?

For Your Own Writing

If you were to review a movie, which one would you choose? What would be your basic judgment of this movie? What reasons would you give to convince your readers to support your judgment? Are there any criticisms of the movie that you would need to respond to in your review? If so, how would you handle them?

Commentary

This essay is typical of most movie reviews in that it primarily addresses readers who have heard about the movie and are trying to decide whether or not to see it. What these readers want to know is whether the film is worth their time and money. Ansen answers this question for *Do the Right Thing* with a thumbs up, but he knows that a good review must do more than simply assert a judgment. It must also give reasons for that judgment and cite evidence from the movie to support these reasons.

Ansen's title—"Searing, Nervy and Very Honest"—lets us know immediately what he thinks about the film. This judgment is echoed in paragraph 2 in slightly different terms: "nervy, complex, unsettling." Although Ansen doesn't state explicitly, "I like this film," readers can readily see that he is praising *Do the Right Thing* and on what grounds.

His reasons for admiring the film center on the way it represents the current racial situation in America. Ansen argues that Spike Lee departs from the safe route most other filmmakers have taken when dealing with racial tensions. Instead of oversimplifying the situation, he says, Lee portrays relations between blacks and whites in all their disturbing complexity. Instead of leaving viewers feeling complacent and self-satisfied, Lee challenges them to reflect on their own values and actions.

Because Ansen knows that most moviegoers won't like being challenged, he must convince his readers that *Do the Right Thing* unsettles viewers for a good reason, and that we should admire Lee for being "nervy" and "honest." This is the essence of his argumentative strategy. (An argumentative strategy is the plan a writer develops to accomplish a particular purpose with particular readers.) Ansen carries through this strategy by trying to convince his readers that "honest reporting" is especially important in this case, airing the "noxious fumes" of racial hatred and thus helping us to realize "how dire the racial situation has become." He even goes so far as to suggest that this film might possibly help to prevent an explosion of violence.

This idea that a movie attempting to portray reality should do so honestly, without oversimplifying or giving easy answers to the difficult questions it poses, is Ansen's primary criterion, the basis for his judgment of the film. Writers do not always have to justify their criteria, as Ansen does here. If they think that their criteria will not be readily understood or accepted by their readers, however, they must develop an argumentative strategy like Ansen's that establishes their criteria as a reasonable basis for judgment.

Finally, Ansen offers evidence from the movie to support his argument. In arguing that *Do the Right Thing* doesn't oversimplify, for example, he shows that Sal is portrayed sympathetically, even though he's "arguably an unconscious racist," while the militant Buggin' Out is shown to be "foolish."

And to illustrate his point about the tension being explosive he summarizes a sequence of scenes in which members of different ethnic groups verbally attack one another.

Concrete details and examples drawn from the movie give a review credibility, helping readers both to understand and to accept the writer's argument. They also give readers a taste of the movie so that they can make their own judgments about whether it seems interesting and worth seeing. To achieve this degree of specificity, the reviewer probably has to see the film more than once and almost certainly has to take notes during or immediately after it. When you plan your own evaluation essay, make sure that you will have the opportunity to do this kind of intensive note taking, whether you review a film or some other subject.

■   ■   ■

Terrence Rafferty, in this *New Yorker* review of *Do the Right Thing*, makes a judgment that opposes David Ansen's. Whereas Ansen argues that the film is a success, Rafferty claims that it ultimately fails. Reading these two reviews side by side shows how reviewers base their evaluation on different criteria. As you read this essay, try to identify Rafferty's criteria.

OPEN AND SHUT
TERRENCE RAFFERTY

In his first scene in ''Do the Right Thing,'' Spike Lee wears a Chicago Bulls jersey 1 with a big ''23'' on it—Michael Jordan's number. Mookie, the character Lee plays, is no superstar: he's an ordinary young man who lives with his sister in a Bedford-Stuyvesant apartment, works—just hard enough to hang on to his job—at the pizzeria at the end of his block, and gets along pretty well with everybody. Amiable Mookie as the divinely inspired Jordan—who plays basketball so brilliantly that it sometimes looks as if he didn't need his teammates at all—is a bit of a joke. It's Spike Lee who's the one-man team here: he's also the writer, the producer, and the director of ''Do the Right Thing,'' and, as the most prominent black director in the American movie industry, he probably feels as if he were sprinting downcourt with no one to pass to and about five hundred towering white guys between him and the basket. Lee has all the moves. Since graduating from N.Y.U.'s film school, in 1983, he has managed to get off three improbable shots, all lofted over the outstretched arms of the movie establishment—three movies, made and distributed, about black experience in America. The first, the buoyant and imaginative sex comedy ''She's Gotta Have It,'' seemed to come out of nowhere: made independently, speedily, and on the cheap, it just streaked past all the obstacles, scored big commercially, and earned Lee the chance, almost unprecedented for a black filmmaker, to make entirely personal movies with major-studio backing. On the evidence of ''Do the Right Thing,'' Lee is all too conscious of both the responsibility and the power of his position. (Later in the movie, Mookie changes into a Dodgers shirt with Jackie Robinson's number on it.) He seems willing to do anything—to take on huge themes and assume the burden of carrying them both in front of and behind the camera.

He just won't accept being ignored. He turns himself into the whole show, acting like Superman because he refuses, absolutely, to be an Invisible Man.

In "Do the Right Thing" this apparently fearless young moviemaker has, in Hol- 2 lywood terms, cut to the chase. His two previous films (or three if we count—and we should—his splendid hour-long N.Y.U. thesis film, "Joe's Bed-Stuy Barbershop: We Cut Heads") tried to dramatize what American movies weren't showing us about the real lives of black people in this gruelling, reactionary decade; to find, if possible, a visual style specific to that experience, not borrowed from Hollywood or Europe; and to make it all so funny and vivid that everyone would have to pay attention. That's more than enough ambition to sustain a filmmaker through an entire career, but Spike Lee's no ordinary artist. Eager to keep things moving, to force the tempo of the game, he has decided to go for it right now, to catch us off guard—again— by rushing head on at the biggest, most dauntingly complex subject imaginable: racism itself. Who's to stop him? He's got the talent, the passion, the crew, the cast, and the money. But he stops himself: the gigantic theme ultimately exposes his weaknesses, overshadows his strengths. In the end, he takes what looks like a big risk, goes for the killer shot, and blows it. . . .

It's a very unusual movie experience—two hours of bombardment with New 3 York-style stimuli. You feel your senses alternately sharpened and dulled, as on a sweltering midsummer day, when the sights and sounds of the city are dazzlingly clear individually yet somehow unassimilable as a whole, overwhelming, brain-fogging, oppressive. Lee is nimble-witted, and he's always on the offensive; he stays in your face until you're too exhausted to resist. You have to watch your reactions closely or he'll speed right past you, get you to nod assent to an argument you haven't fully realized he was making. Most American movies just want to knock you senseless immediately and get it over with; "Do the Right Thing" tries to wear you down, and its strategies are fascinating.

In form, "Do the Right Thing" is a multi-character, portrait-of-a-community 4 movie. When this sort of picture is done skillfully, it can be exhilarating: Renoir's "The Crime of Monsieur Lange," Altman's "McCabe & Mrs. Miller," and Scorsese's "Mean Streets" come to mind. The pleasure of community movies is their open-endedness, the (relative) freedom they allow us to observe the particulars of relationships in small, self-contained social units; they seem unusually responsive to the ambiguity and variety of experience. For long stretches, Lee's movie is enjoyable in this way. Characters are introduced, and while we wait to find out what they'll have to do with each other we can take in an abundance of atmospheric details—the lack of air-conditioning in the apartments, the way the sunlight looks sort of hopeful at the beginning of the day and then turns mean, the street wardrobe of T-shirts, bicycle shorts, and pristine Nikes—and listen to the casual speech of the neighborhood's residents, learn to hear in its varied rhythms how people who have lived too close for too long express their irritation and their affection. As we get our bearings, the movie has an easy, colloquial vivacity, and a sensational look. The superb cinematographer Ernest Dickerson (who has worked on all Lee's movies) gives the images a daring, Hawaiian-shirt glare: if the light were just a touch brighter, the colors a shade bolder, we'd have to turn away, but Dickerson somehow makes these clashing sensations seem harmonious. Lee's script seems to be trying to do something similar, but, despite its ingenuity, it doesn't succeed. As the long, sticky day goes on and the exchanges between the characters get edgier, nastier, more elaborately insulting, we begin to feel something ominous creeping in, which at the time we may take to be our realization that racial violence is inevitable, but which later on we may identify as our intuition of a different kind of disharmony—the jarring incongruity of Lee's "open" manner and his open-and-shut argument. . . .

At its most basic, Lee's intention in "Do the Right Thing" is to demonstrate how 5 in the context of a racially polarized society the slow accumulation of small irritations—the heat, some casual slights, bits of anger left over from old injuries, the constant mild abrasions of different cultural perspectives rubbing against each other—can swell to something huge and ugly and lethal. It's a solid idea for a movie—to show us the everyday texture of racial misunderstanding. But Lee wants to go further, to prove the inevitability of race conflict in America, and he can't do it, because no filmmaker could: movies aren't very good at proving things. The obvious inspiration for the story is the appalling incident in Howard Beach, Queens, in 1986: three young black men, stranded by car trouble in that very white neighborhood, were attacked outside a pizzeria by a bunch of youths armed with baseball bats; one of the victims, Michael Griffith, ran in front of a car while trying to escape and was killed. From this tragic event Lee has retained the charged iconography—the pizza parlor and the baseball bat—and changed everything else, with a view to making its significance larger, more general. He wants to create an event that can't be explained away as an isolated incident. And he's not about to let us believe that racism comes only in the form of teen-age thugs.

So in "Do the Right Thing" it isn't Sal's vicious son who precipitates the violence 6 but Sal himself—a man who, despite a fairly limited imagination, isn't an obvious racist. For most of the movie, Sal is a sympathetic figure: he's proud of the place he owns and proud of having fed the people of the neighborhood for twenty-five years, and he won't listen to Pino's suggestion that he sell the pizzeria and get out of Bed-Stuy. ("I've never had no trouble with these people," Sal says.) But in the end he becomes the enemy, and Mookie—the most easygoing and most rounded of the young black characters—becomes his adversary. By pitching his battle between the two most likable characters in the piece, Lee makes room in his story for the big statement: that in this society blacks and whites, even the best of us, are ultimately going to find ourselves on opposite sides. . . .

Does Lee really believe that, as he says in his published production diary, "sooner 7 or later it comes out"—that, any white person, pushed hard enough, will betray his contempt for blacks? Does he believe, for that matter, the tired notion that anger brings out people's *true* feelings? And does he also think that lashing out at Sal because he's white and owns a business and is therefore a representative of the racist power structure of the American economy is a legitimate image of "fighting the power"? If you can buy all these axioms smuggled in from outside the lively and particular world this movie creates, then "Do the Right Thing" is the great movie that so many reviewers have claimed it is. But if you think—as I do—that not every individual is a racist, that angry words are no more revealing than any other kind, and that trashing a small business is a woefully imprecise image of fighting the power, then you have to conclude that Spike Lee has taken a wild shot and missed the target. He ends his movie with a pair of apparently contradictory quotations—one from Dr. King, advocating peaceful change, and one from Malcolm [X], advocating violence (in self-defense). The juxtaposition suggests an admission that he doesn't know all the answers, but the movie, perhaps inadvertently, gives the lie to this confession of ambivalence. The imagery of the riot overwhelms the more incidental truths about human relations in the rest of the film, and Lee pays the price of all the little feints and evasions necessary to give his movie a socko ending: the half-truths add up, too. By the end, when Sal and Mookie are standing toe to toe in front of the burned-out shell of the pizzeria, and Mookie accepts his back wages, and more, from his employer, Lee actually seems to be saying that although Sal may not be the worst oppressor around, *someone's* got to pay; the implicit message to the small businessman is "Too bad it had to be you, but what did you expect?" I think audiences, black and white, have the right to expect something more thoughtful than this from one of our best young filmmakers.

The "power" isn't guys like Sal, even though they benefit, modestly, from the   8
biases of the economic system; they're just guilty by association, responsible for the deaths of young blacks like Raheem only in the most theoretical, distanced way. Although Lee must know this, he's clearly willing to sacrifice some political clarity for the sake of movie-style power. In order to make himself heard, he has chosen to adopt the belligerent, in-your-face mode of discourse that has been the characteristic voice of New York City in the Koch years. Spike Lee's movie isn't likely to cause riots (as some freaked-out commentators have suggested), but it winds up bullying the audience—shouting at us rather than speaking to us. It is, both at its best and at its worst, very much a movie of these times.

For Discussion

In this review Rafferty calls into question the idea that "in this society blacks and whites, even the best of us, are ultimately going to find ourselves on opposite sides." There are many differences among people in American society in addition to racial ones. Make a list of these differences, and discuss whether they can—or should—be eliminated. Some would even say that difference should be celebrated. Should America be a melting pot or a garden salad? How do you think language, and the media in general, might help to encourage, eliminate, or bridge the differences in our society?

For Analysis

1. In the opening paragraphs Rafferty focuses on Spike Lee rather than on the film itself. Given his purpose and audience, why do you think he begins this way? What advantages or disadvantages do you see in this way of beginning a movie review?

2. In paragraph 4 Rafferty indicates several ways in which the movie is "enjoyable." What aspects of the movie does he single out for praise? Underline specific evidence he uses to support this judgment. How convincing do you find this part of his argument?

3. Rafferty asserts in paragraph 6 that Lee wants to go beyond representing the "everyday texture of racial misunderstanding . . . to prove the inevitability of race conflict in America, and he can't do it, because no filmmaker could." How convincing do you find Rafferty's reasoning and evidence in paragraphs

For a discussion of the use of reasons and evidence, see pp. 471–80.

6 and 7? Look, for instance, at what he says about Sal, the pizzeria owner. How does Rafferty's evaluation of Sal's character compare with Ansen's?

4.   Rafferty uses dashes extensively. Skim the essay, putting brackets around the sentences with dashes. Read each one aloud in order to see how sentences like these are patterned. Select one sentence that you think is especially effective. What kind of material is enclosed or set off with dashes in this sentence?

For Your Own Writing

Some of the most interesting movie reviews evaluate a group of related movies. Consider writing a review of two or more films of the same type (such as horror, detective, or screwball comedy), by the same director, with the same actor, or from a series (such as the *Back to the Future* or *Godfather* films). Which kind of movies would you choose? Then choose one particular movie to evaluate, either as being better or worse than the others.

Commentary

Good reviewers don't apply criteria randomly but choose them according to whether they are appropriate and universal. Clearly, judging an action film like *Die Hard* in the same way as a social commentary film like *Do the Right Thing* would be inappropriate. Different types of movies should be judged by different criteria. In order to determine the criteria for evaluating a particular movie, you first need to consider what kind it is. Rafferty classifies *Do the Right Thing* as a "multi-character, portrait-of-a-community movie" (paragraph 4). On this basis, he finds the movie "enjoyable." It is only when he considers it as a film trying to make a political statement that he judges it a failure.

In addition to being appropriate, criteria must also be somewhat universal—they must be shared by others, and not be merely a matter of the writer's own personal taste. Most readers of Rafferty's review would readily agree that the film's rich atmospheric detail and excellent cinematography are qualities that make it "enjoyable."

Rafferty's second criterion—that the film portray the racial situation realistically—is also one that most readers would accept. In fact, it is the criterion that Ansen uses in his review of the film. Even though they base their overall judgments on the same criterion, however, the two writers reach different conclusions: for Ansen the film is a success, while for Rafferty it fails.

The disparity arises because Ansen and Rafferty interpret the ending differently. Rafferty claims Spike Lee "wants to prove the inevitability of race conflict in America." Ansen, on the other hand, claims that "Lee isn't saying the violence is inevitable," only showing how it could come to pass if nothing is done to remedy the situation. Whereas Ansen sees the ending as intentionally ambiguous, forcing readers to face the complexity and seriousness of the situation, Rafferty sees it simply as confused. For example, he argues that the two quotations ending the film serve only as Lee's "confession of ambivalence," not as "the logical culmination of Lee's method," as Ansen would have it.

As readers, we need to study evaluations critically, deciding for ourselves whether the writer's interpretation makes sense and whether the evaluation is sound. As writers, on the other hand, we need to be as clear and specific as possible when making an evaluation, and to present the best possible argument we can to support our judgment.

■   ■   ■

Barbara Ehrenreich is the author of seven books, including a critique of the 1980s, *The Worst Years of Our Lives: Irreverent Notes from a Decade of Greed* (1989), and a study of the middle class, *Fear of Falling* (1989). Her essays appear regularly in the *American Scholar*, the *Atlantic*, and the *New Republic*, where this selection originally appeared in April 1990. In it she reviews the situation comedy *Roseanne*, starring Roseanne Barr. As you read, notice how she includes numerous specific details and examples from different episodes of the show.

**THE WRETCHED
OF THE HEARTH**
BARBARA
EHRENREICH

"Roseanne" the sitcom, which was inspired by Barr the standup comic, is a radical 1 departure simply for featuring blue-collar Americans—and for depicting them as something other than half-witted greasers and low-life louts. The working class does not usually get much of a role in the American entertainment spectacle. In the seventies mumbling, muscular blue-collar males (*Rocky, The Deer Hunter, Saturday Night Fever*) enjoyed a brief modishness on the screen, while Archie Bunker, the consummate blue-collar bigot, raved away on the tube. But even these grossly stereotyped images vanished in the eighties, as the spectacle narrowed in on the brie-and-chardonnay class. Other than "Roseanne," I can find only one sitcom that deals consistently with the sub-yuppie condition: "Married . . . with children," a relentlessly nasty portrayal of a shoe salesman and his cognitively disabled family members. There may even be others, but sociological zeal has not sufficed to get me past the opening sequences of "Major Dad," "Full House" or "Doogie Howser."

Not that "Roseanne" is free of class stereotyping. The Connors must bear part 2 of the psychic burden imposed on all working-class people by their economic and occupational betters. . . . They indulge in a manic physicality that would be unthinkable among the more controlled and genteel Huxtables. They maintain a traditional, low-fiber diet of white bread and macaroni. They are not above a fart joke.

Still, in "Roseanne" I am willing to forgive the stereotypes as markers designed 3 to remind us of where we are: in the home of a construction worker and his minimum-wage wife. Without the reminders, we might not be aware of how thoroughly the deeper prejudices of the professional class are being challenged. Roseanne's fictional husband Dan (played by the irresistably cuddly John Goodman) drinks domestic beer and dedicates Sundays to football; but far from being a Bunkeresque boor, he looks to this feminist like the fabled "sensitive man" we have all been pining for. He treats his rotund wife like a sex goddess. He picks up on small cues signaling emotional distress. He helps with homework. And when Roseanne works overtime, he cooks, cleans, and rides herd on the kids without any of the piteous whining we have come to expect from upscale males in their rare, and lavishly documented, encounters with soiled Pampers.

Roseanne Connor has her own way of defying the stereotypes. Variously em- 4 ployed as a fast-food operative, a factory worker, a bartender, and a telephone salesperson, her real dream is to be a writer. When her twelve-year-old daughter Darlene (brilliantly played by Sara Gilbert) balks at a poetry-writing assignment, Rose-anne gives her a little talking-to involving Sylvia Plath:[1] "She inspired quite a few women, including *moi*." In another episode, a middle-aged friend thanks Roseanne for inspiring her to dump her chauvinist husband and go to college. We have come a long way from the dithering, cowering Edith Bunker.

Most of the time the Connors do the usual sitcom things. They have the little 5 domestic misunderstandings that can be patched up in twenty-four minutes with wisecracks and a round of hugs. But "Roseanne" carries working-class verisimilitude into a new and previously taboo dimension—the workplace. In the world of employment, Roseanne knows exactly where she stands: "All the good power jobs are taken. Vanna turns the letters. Leona's got hotels. Margaret's running England . . . 'Course she's not doing a very good job. . . .''

The class conflict continues on other fronts. In one episode, Roseanne arrives 6 late for an appointment with Darlene's history teacher, because she has been forced to work overtime at Wellman. The teacher, who is leaning against her desk stretching her quadriceps when Roseanne arrives, wants to postpone the appointment because she has a date to play squash. When Roseanne insists, the teacher tells her that Darlene has been barking in class, "like a dog." This she follows with some psychobabble—on emotional problems and dysfunctional families—that would leave most mothers, whatever their social class, clutched with guilt. Not Roseanne, who calmly informs the yuppie snit that, in the Connor household, everybody barks like dogs.

It is Barr's narrow-eyed cynicism about the family, even more than her class 7 consciousness, that gives "Roseanne" its special frisson. Archie Bunker got our attention by telling us that we (blacks, Jews, "ethnics," WASPs, etc.) don't really like each other. Barr's message is that even within the family we don't much like each other. We love each other (who else do we have?); but The Family, with its impacted emotions, its lopsided division of labor, and its ancient system of age-graded humiliations, just doesn't work. Or rather, it doesn't work unless the contradictions are smoothed out with irony and the hostilities are periodically blown off as humor. Coming from mom, rather than from a jaded teenager or a bystander dad, this is scary news indeed. . . .

On the one hand, she presents the family as a zone of intimacy and support, 8 well worth defending against the forces of capitalism, which drive both mothers and fathers out of the home, scratching around for paychecks. On the other hand, the family is hardly a haven, especially for its grown-up females. It is marred from within by—among other things—the patriarchal division of leisure, which makes dad and the kids the "consumers" of mom's cooking, cleaning, nurturing, and (increasingly) her earnings. Mom's job is to keep the whole thing together—to see that the mort-

---

[1]American poet and novelist (1932–63).

gage payments are made, to fend off the viperish teenagers, to find the missing green sock—but mom is no longer interested in being a human sacrifice on the altar of "pro-family values." She's been down to the feminist bookstore; she's been reading Sylvia Plath.

This is a bleak and radical vision. Not given to didacticism, Barr offers no pro- 9 grammatic ways out. Surely, we are led to conclude, pay equity would help, along with child care, and so on. But Barr leaves us hankering for a quality of change that goes beyond mere reform: for a world in which even the lowliest among us—the hash-slinger, the sock-finder, the factory hand—will be recognized as the poet she truly is.

For Discussion

Some people consider America a classless country, but Ehrenreich apparently thinks there are definite class divisions within our society. How aware are you of these divisions? How difficult do you think it is for people to pull themselves out of the lower class and into the middle class or even higher? In other words, to what extent is the "American dream" really possible? What determines who will achieve it? If you think moving up is largely a myth, why do so many people continue to believe in it? Do you ever feel you want to move up? Do you have a plan for doing so?

For Analysis

For more on thesis statements, see pp. 400–02.

1. What is Ehrenreich's judgment of *Roseanne*? Find the passage that you think is the most explicit statement of her thesis. On what basis does she make this judgment? In other words, what criteria does she rely on?

2. Skim the essay, noting where Ehrenreich refers to other television programs and films. In each case, note how she uses the strategy of comparison and contrast. What part does comparison and contrast play in her overall argumentative strategy?

3. In providing evidence from the *Roseanne* series, Ehrenreich refers both to specific episodes and to elements that occur throughout the series. Skim her essay, marking references to specific episodes with a line in the margin and general references to the series with a double line. If she is evaluating the series as a whole, why do you think she refers to specific episodes? What does each kind of reference contribute to her review?

4. Ehrenreich has some fun with this essay. Reread it, noting any passages where her writing seems especially witty. How does her use of humor influence your willingness to accept her judgment?

For Your Own Writing

Ehrenreich evaluates a television series, not just a single program. If you were assigned to evaluate a series of something—such as the *Star Wars* or *Jaws* movies, Rembrandt's or Van Gogh's self-portraits, the *Lord of the Rings* books, or a television series—what would you choose? On what criteria might you base your evaluation? Why?

Commentary

A great temptation for writers evaluating a subject they feel strongly about is to give it unqualified praise or blame. Few things, however, are all good or all bad, and readers are likely to see such a characterization as either/or thinking—a logical fallacy, or error in reasoning, that weakens an argument partly by undermining the writer's credibility. Ehrenreich is enthusiastic about *Roseanne* but tempers her praise in paragraph 2, where she points out that the program is not "free of class stereotyping."

Also notable is the way Ehrenreich makes her writing readable by careful use of topic sentences. Not only do they announce the topic of the paragraph they introduce, but topic sentences may also connect this paragraph to preceding ones. Paragraph 2, for example, begins with a sentence that refers explicitly to class stereotyping, the central idea of the first paragraph. The opening sentence of paragraph 7 makes similarly helpful connection, summarizing the central point of the first six paragraphs and identifying the main topic of the next few paragraphs.

For more on strategies for coherence, see pp. 411–13.

Two stylistic features also deserve mention: the use of the colon and repetition of sentence openings. Ehrenreich uses the colon for a variety of purposes. Sometimes it introduces an example: "Other than 'Roseanne,' I can find only one sitcom that deals consistently with the sub-yuppie condition: 'Married . . . with children,'. . ." (paragraph 1). At other times it specifies or defines: "Still, in 'Roseanne,' I am willing to forgive the stereotypes as markers designed to remind us of where we are: in the home of a construction worker and his minimum-wage wife" (paragraph 3). And at still other times it introduces a quotation: "Roseanne gives her a little talking-to involving Sylvia Plath: 'She inspired quite a few women, including *moi*.' "

Ehrenreich repeats sentence openings—a device called *anaphora*—to strengthen the bonds between sentences, to create a pleasing rhythm, and to emphasize the material that is repeated. The last three sentences in paragraph 2, for example, open with a "*they* + verb" construction. In paragraph 3, Ehrenreich uses a "*he* + verb" pattern in three consecutive sentences but then varies it by beginning the next sentence with a prepositional phrase followed by the expected pattern.

■   ■   ■

Jason Thornton wrote this essay as a college freshman. With his classmates in mind as readers, Thornton evaluates a newly released album, *Document*, by the rock group REM. As you read, notice the many references he makes to other albums and groups.

DOCUMENTING
DOCUMENT
JASON THORNTON

Joshua Tree may well become the best-remembered rock album of 1987. Certainly it is one of the best-selling and one of the most talked-about LPs of the year. But the biggest isn't always the best, and the one album released this year that truly surpasses U2's epic is REM's masterpiece, *Document*. Although REM—"America's most successful fringe band," according to rock critic David Fricke—is often overshadowed by bigger, more pop-oriented groups, this four-man band from Athens,

Georgia, has a large cult following. Its first release, 1981's *Murmur*, was recently voted one of the top 100 albums of the past 20 years by *Rolling Stone* rock critics. REM makes music like no one else, incorporating a large range of sounds from punk to country-Western, from Aerosmith-like hard rock to folkish melodies to a style not unlike Andy Warhol's art rock band, the Velvet Underground. Many bands try to incorporate as many sound styles as REM, but no one does it as well.

Like *Joshua Tree*, *Document* is an 11-song collection of straightforward rock 'n' 2 roll with lyrics that are easy to relate to. The music on *Document*, like that on REM's *Life's Rich Pageant*, is more catchy and more pop-oriented than the group's older albums like *Reckoning* or this year's strange B-side compilation, *Dead Letter Office*. REM's songs have become more vivid, forceful, and straightforward. The group had a hand (along with Scott Litt) in producing *Document*, and they show they can handle this task as well as they handle their instruments. They also show they can bring more life and energy to their vinyl sound than their past producers could. Singer Michael Stipe's stinging, haunting lyrics are more prominent than on past REM LPs, creating a wonderful verbal richness and bringing forth powerfully suggestive images. Stipe's words on *Document*, much like those of Bono Vax on *The Joshua Tree*, are loaded with symbolism of America and its people. But while U2 sees America as a distant land and relates to it in an almost spiritual sense, REM *is* American and its lyrics show a vivid sense of this land that the Irish U2 could never fully grasp.

REM has always been a band of contrasts and paradoxes. *Murmur* sounded like 3 folk music, a style that generally uses acoustic instruments, except that REM used electric guitars. By all rights, the music of its past five albums would be ideal for keyboards or synthesizers, but REM rarely uses a single keyboard track. Instead, it relies on the simple trio of Peter Buck's wide range of guitar playing; Mike Mills's rough bass lines; and Bill Berry's droning, occasionally militant drums. Despite the simple methods, REM forges complex songs through a mixture of melodies, simple chords, numerous rhythms, and staggering vocal harmonies. Once together, this mixture forms a swirly, moody track that manages not to sound muddy, bogged down, or inconsistent. Sometimes with REM the finest points seem to be the roughest edges: each feedback whine from the guitar amp and rough vocal from Stipe seems well planned and strategically placed.

Often REM shows its originality in the sharp contrast between bitter lyrics and 4 upbeat music. In *Document*'s "Disturbance at the Heron House," for example, the band plays a catchy, cheerful sixties-influenced tune as Stipe describes a democracy gone mad by way of mob rule:

> They gathered up the cages
> The cages and courageous
> The followers of chaos
> Out of control.

Throughout the song Berry pounds out a foot-stomping drum beat that keeps the rhythm while Stipe sings about a "stampede at the monument"—a symbol of a large mass of people assaulting their government.

One of the best traits of *Document* is the constant theme of social and political 5 protest. The album opens with "Finest Worksong," a riveting rock anthem in which Stipe sings, "The time to rise/ Has been engaged/ We're better/ Best to rearrange," a call for an uprising by the lower classes of society. As the song progresses, Stipe continues to discuss the faults of society until he finally comes to a conclusion on what he feels is the basis of America's social and economic difficulties: "What we want/What we need,/Has been confused." Greed is expressed as a single three-line concept, as Buck's guitars, sounding almost like heavy metal, carry the song along with Mills's and Berry's rhythms.

In "Exhuming McCarthy," with its sleazy bass line and trumpeting horn playing   6 by guest musician Steve Berlin, REM recalls an embarrassing event in American political history, Senator Joseph McCarthy's Communist "witchhunts" of the 1950s. Stipe sings about McCarthy's belief that he was able to spot and slay the Communist dragon in society: "Enemy sighted, enemy met/I'm addressing the real politic." "Exhuming McCarthy" starts off with a strange typewriter sound, contains an actual taped voice from a McCarthy hearing mixed into the guitar solo, and ends with an superbly harmonized double vocal, where two tracks of Stipe's voice sing drastically different things yet blend together wonderfully.

There have been few criticisms of the album. Although most of REM's lyrics tend   7 to be abstract, the ones in "Fireplace" go too far. The song is made up of confusing extracts from a speech by Mother Ann Lee, an eighteenth-century leader of the Shaker religious sect, and its mixture of slow rock and waltz rhythms struggle to carry these lyrics along. "Strange," originally performed by the British band Wire, seems out of place on a REM album, with its lyrical style different from Stipe's norm; but Buck, Mills, and Berry still manage to create a reasonably decent version of the song. Another *Document* song, "It's the End of the World As We Know It (And I Feel Fine)," has been considered by many to be only an imitation of Bob Dylan's "Subterranean Homesick Blues."

REM makes up for these shortcomings, however, on other songs such as the   8 album's ballads. No REM album would be complete without a few ballads like *Document*'s strange but appealing "Oddfellows Local 151." In this song Stipe creates a character more typical of John Steinbeck than of a modern rock star: a small-town storyteller who has taken to drinking but still manages to impress his fellow townspeople with his tales and "wisdom."

The most important song on this album, however, is "The One I Love," REM's   9 finest song to date. "The One I Love" starts off as a melancholy, regretful love song relying on lyrics such as

> This one goes out to the one I love,
> This one goes out to the one I left behind,
> A simple prop to occupy my time.

Slowly, the song goes beyond the simple boy/girl relationships of most love songs and introduces the complex problem of the effect on a relationship of distance and time away from a loved one. In the end, "The One I Love" becomes an expression of the pain and guilt one feels because of unfaithfulness to a loved one.

> This one goes out to the one I love,
> This one goes out to the one I left behind,
> Another prop has occupied my time.

"The One I Love" and the other songs on *Document* constitute the best REM   10 album yet and one of the best LPs of the year. With its upbeat tunes mixed with contrasting lyrics, its themes of social and political protest, and its touching ballads,

REM shows that it deserves to be classified in the same league with some of the top bands around today, such as U2. *Document* may not end up getting as much air play as *The Joshua Tree*, and it may not sell as many copies; but artistically it equals or betters the other album, breaking through the boundaries of conventional song-writing and record making, taking rock music to a plateau never before achieved.

For Discussion

Thornton says that One of *Document's* best traits is the "constant theme of social and political protests." Although he doesn't claim that every song should have a political message, he does seem to be saying that social protest is an important criterion for judging rock music in general. What other rock songs from the late 1980s and early 1990s deal with America's social and economic difficulties? Make a list of recent songs of this kind and discuss Thornton's association of rock with social protest. Why do you think he associates the two? Do you?

For Analysis

1.   Reread the opening and closing paragraphs to see how Thornton frames the essay by referring at the end to something from the beginning. What advantages or disadvantages do you see in this strategy?

2.   In paragraph 1, Thornton quotes a rock critic and refers to a *Rolling Stone* list of top albums. How do these two pieces of evidence contribute to his argument?

3.   Throughout the essay Thornton quotes song lyrics. Reread the essay, stopping to consider how well each quotation works. Note particularly what he says about the lyrics. How does he introduce them? Does he seem to assume his readers will already know the songs he's quoting? How much does he explain? Are there any places where you have difficulty figuring out the point he's trying to make?

4.   In paragraph 7 Thornton discusses the album's shortcomings. What advantages or disadvantages do you see in his including this negative criticism in an otherwise positive review? Also, why do you think he places this passage where he does? Where else might he have put it?

For Your Own Writing

What recording, music video, or live performance would you wish to evaluate? On what basis would you judge it, and how would you justify your criteria?

Commentary

The process of evaluating is essentially comparative because criteria for judging things are based on comparison with other things of the same kind. Consequently, evaluators nearly always make judgments about one thing in relation to another. So to assert the importance of *Document,* Thornton compares it with the best-selling and most talked-about album of the year, U2's *Joshua Tree*. After pointing out that they have attributes in common—such as "whimsical lyrics that are easy to relate to" and "symbolism of America and its people"—he goes on to argue that *Document* "equals or betters" *The Joshua Tree* because of its special insight into America. He also compares

Document with earlier REM albums to show how the group has matured, pointing out that its recent music is "more catchy and pop-oriented" and the lyrics are "more vivid, forceful, and straightforward."

Comparison is not used only to praise *Document*. Thornton also identifies two songs that are weak in comparison with the other songs on the album: "Strange," originally performed by another group, and "It's the End of the World As We Know It (And I Feel Fine)," widely considered an imitation of a Bob Dylan song.

These comparisons show that Thornton knows a lot about the kind of music he's evaluating, and they also help to support his judgment of the album.

PURPOSE AND AUDIENCE

When you evaluate something, you seek to influence readers' judgments and possibly also their actions. Your primary aim is to convince readers that your judgment is well informed and reasonable, and therefore that they can feel confident in making decisions based on it. Good readers don't simply accept reviewers' judgments, however, especially on subjects of importance. More likely, they read reviews to learn more about a subject so that they can make an informed choice themselves. Consequently, most readers care less about the forcefulness with which you assert your judgment than about the reasons and evidence you cite to support it.

The most effective writers develop an argumentative strategy designed for their particular readers. Your argumentative strategy determines every writing decision you make, from what you reveal about the subject to the way you construct your argument—which reasons you use, whether you try to justify your choice of criteria, how much and what kinds of evidence you cite.

You may want to acknowledge directly your readers' knowledge of the subject, perhaps revealing that you understand how they might judge it according to different criteria. You might even let readers know that you have anticipated their counterarguments, or objections to your argument. In responding to counterarguments, you should try to build a bridge of shared values, perhaps agreeing to disagree on certain points but finding common ground on others.

BASIC FEATURES OF EVALUATIONS

Evaluations generally include the following basic features: a well-defined subject, a clear and well-balanced judgment of the subject, and a convincing argument for this judgment. They often also include pointed comparisons between the subject and other things of the same kind.

A Clearly
Defined Subject

The subject being evaluated should be clearly identified, usually with some description. Both David Ansen and Terrence Rafferty name the movie they're reviewing in the opening sentence. Barbara Ehrenreich names her subject and also provides some descriptive details, identifying it as a "sitcom" inspired by Roseanne Barr "the stand-up comic" and "featuring blue-collar Americans." Similarly, Jason Thornton describes *Document* as REM's "11-song collection of straightforward rock 'n' roll with lyrics that are easy to relate to."

In general, evaluations provide only enough information to give readers a context for the judgment. Movie and book reviews may include more information than other kinds of evaluations because reviewers assume readers will be unfamiliar with the subject and are reading, in part, to learn more about it. Readers of movie reviews, for example, want to know who the actors and director are, where the movie takes place, and generally what happens in it. Ansen therefore explains that *Do the Right Thing* takes place "as the summer heat in Bedford-Stuyvesant reaches the boiling point" and identifies some of the actors and the characters they play, telling us, for instance, that Ruby Dee is Mother Sister, "the block's wise old watchdog."

For a recently released movie, the writer must decide how much of the plot to reveal. Here reviewers must walk a fine line—trying not to spoil the suspense while explaining how well or how poorly the suspense is managed. When reviewing a movie everyone is talking about, like *Do the Right Thing*, reviewers are released from this constraint, for they can assume that most readers are already familiar with the general plot outline and mostly want to know the reviewer's opinion of the film. Neither Ansen nor Rafferty bothers keeping from readers the outcome of the plot. Ansen talks about police brutality and the destruction of Sal's pizzeria. Rafferty describes the final confrontation between Sal and Mookie "standing toe to toe in front of the burned-out shell of the pizzeria."

A Clear,
Balanced
Judgment

Evaluation essays are focused around a judgment—an assertion that something is good or bad or that it is better or worse than something of the same kind. This judgment is the thesis, or main point, of the essay. Usually the judgment is clearly stated in various ways throughout the essay and reasserted at the end. For example, Thornton claims in his opening paragraph that *Document* is a "masterpiece" and concludes by saying that it "equals or betters [*The Joshua Tree*], breaking through the boundaries of conventional songwriting and record making, taking rock music to a plateau never before achieved."

Although readers expect a definitive judgment, they also appreciate a balanced one that acknowledges both good and bad points of the subject. Ehrenreich, for instance, praises *Roseanne* for representing blue-collar Americans more realistically than other programs have, but also acknowledges that the show is not free of class stereotyping.

A Convincing
Argument

An evaluation cannot merely state its judgment but must argue for it. To be convincing, an evaluative argument must give reasons that are based on criteria shared with readers and are supported by reliable evidence.

Writers of evaluations usually establish their criteria when discussing the reasons for their judgment. Thornton, for example, praises the music on *Document* for being catchy and pop-oriented. Later he adds the point that REM shows its originality by combining catchy, upbeat music with bitter, disturbing lyrics. He does not bother to justify his criteria, probably because he assumes their importance will be self-evident to his particular readers.

Ansen and Rafferty both, on the other hand, make the effort to justify their criteria. To make his point, Ansen uses comparison and contrast to argue that Spike Lee succeeds where other filmmakers have failed.

In addition to giving reasons based on shared criteria, writers of evaluations must support their judgments with evidence. The kinds of evidence used vary according to the subjects. All of the essays in this chapter rely primarily on textual evidence—describing, quoting, paraphrasing, and summarizing aspects of the movie, television program, or album. Ansen, for example, paraphrases an exchange of insults, and Ehrenreich summarizes some typical actions of Roseanne's television husband. Thornton quotes song lyrics. In addition, some of the essays use other kinds of evidence. Thornton refers to authorities: a rock critic and *Rolling Stone*. Rafferty mentions an actual racial incident similar to the one in the film and also quotes from Lee's film diary.

Sometimes reviewers anticipate and respond to counterarguments. They may accommodate these objections by making concessions, as Thornton does when he acknowledges that some of REM's lyrics are too abstract. Or they may refute them, as Ansen does when he claims that "to accuse Lee of irresponsibility—of inciting violence—is to be blind to the movie he has made."

Pointed
Comparisons

Comparisons are not a requirement of evaluative writing, but they are often useful. One good way to assess something, after all, is to set it next to another of its kind. If you are evaluating a movie, for instance, you naturally judge it relative to other movies of the same kind. You can compare it with other movies, looking at similarities; or you can contrast it, looking at differences.

All of the pieces in this chapter include comparisons or contrasts. Thornton's evaluation of *Document* centers on a comparison and contrast with the more successful, better-known *Joshua Tree*. Ansen contrasts *Do the Right Thing* with other movies dealing with race relations, and Rafferty compares it to other movies portraying the life of a community. Ehrenreich contrasts *Roseanne* with other television sitcoms featuring working-class characters and with *The Cosby Show*'s portrait of genteel family life.

Guide to Writing

THE WRITING ASSIGNMENT

Choose a subject to evaluate. Write an essay assessing your subject addressed to a particular group of readers, giving them all of the background information, reasons, and evidence they will need to accept your evaluation. Your principal aim is to convince these readers that your judgment of this subject is informed and reasonable, based on criteria that are generally accepted as appropriate for judging this kind of subject.

INVENTION AND RESEARCH

At this point you need to choose a subject, evaluate it closely, analyze your readers, and develop an argument to support your evaluation.

Choosing a Subject

You may already have something in mind to evaluate. Even so, consider some other possibilities to be sure you're making the best choice.

Listing Possible Subjects.   List anything you would be interested in evaluating, trying to think of at least one subject in each of the following categories.

- *Media:* a television program, magazine, or newspaper
- *Arts:* a movie or play; a musical recording, video, or performance; a work of art or art exhibit; a building
- *Literature:* a poem, short story, novel, or essay
- *Education:* a school, program, teacher, or textbook
- *Government:* a government department or official; a proposed or existing law; a candidate for public office
- *Campus:* a class, department, library, or sports team
- *Leisure:* an amusement park, museum, restaurant, or resort

Making a Choice.   Review your list, and choose the subject that seems most promising. Look for a subject that you could evaluate with authority—something you already know well or could reexamine. Consider whether you know the criteria people ordinarily use to evaluate something of this kind.

Exploring Your Subject

Before going much further, you need to ascertain what you already know about the subject and what additional information you may need. Write down whatever you now know about the subject and the questions you have about it. Don't worry about leaving things out; just get started thinking. Later you will have the opportunity to reexamine the subject and gather more specifics.

Considering Your Present Opinion.   You may already have an opinion about your subject, but it probably will change somewhat as you think more and you reexamine the subject. For now, your aim is to set down your current opinion on paper as clearly as you can and to begin exploring what you now think about the subject. In a sentence or two, simply state your judgment. At this time, don't explain why you're making this judgment; just say what it is.

Considering What You Think and Know about Your Subject.   Write for around ten minutes about your feelings and knowledge about your topic, considering these questions for guidance:

■ How certain am I of my judgment? Do I have any doubts? Why do I feel the way I do?

■ Do I like (or dislike) everything about my subject, or only certain parts?

■ Are there any similar things I should consider (other products or movies, for example)?

■ Is there anything I will need to do right away in order to evaluate this subject authoritatively? If I need to do any research, can I get the information I need?

Analyzing Your Readers

You will be trying to convince particular readers to consider your evaluation seriously, perhaps even to take some action as a result—to see a certain movie, for instance, or take a specific class. Consequently, you must analyze these readers carefully, considering what they are likely to know and think about your subject. Take ten minutes to analyze your readers in writing. Use these questions to stimulate your analysis:

■ Who are my readers? What values and attitudes do we share that might enable me to gain their trust?

■ What are they likely to know and think about my subject?

■ What other subjects of the same type might they be familiar with? How have they judged these other subjects?

■ What about my judgment might surprise them? On what grounds might they disagree with me?

Developing an Argumentative Strategy

Once you have some sense of who your readers will be, you can begin to think about your argumentative strategy. Basically, an argumentative strategy is a plan for how to accomplish a particular purpose with specific readers.

For an evaluation, your purpose will be to convince your readers to accept your judgment about the subject; your argumentative strategy would be to present reasons for your judgment and to show evidence to support those reasons. The reasons you give should be based on criteria appropriate to the subject and must be selected with your readers' sensibilities in mind.

It might help you in working out your argumentative strategy to keep track of your reasons, criteria, and evidence on a chart. Simply divide a piece of paper into three vertical columns, labeling the first *Reasons,* the second *Criteria,* and the third *Evidence.* Putting all your material on such a chart will help you to see at a glance where your argument is strong and where you need to give it more thought or collect more evidence.

A completed chart of this sort is shown on pp. 288–89.

Listing the Reasons for Your Judgment.   Consider the reasons for your judgment: why do you like or dislike the film or city or restaurant or whatever you are evaluating? To identify your reasons, try completing the following statement:

_____ is a good/bad _____ because _____.

Jason Thornton, for example, might have begun to state his reasons for liking the REM album *Document* as follows:

Document is a good rock album because its lyrics are easy to relate to.

Put down all the reasons you can think of for your judgment about your subject, and then look over your list to decide which ones would be the most convincing for your particular readers. Imagine you were evaluating the new Walt Disney hotel designed by Michael Graves, for instance. If your readers were professional architects, you would probably look for architectural reasons; that it is the most architecturally distinctive hotel at Walt Disney World, for instance. If, however, your readers were school children, you'd surely focus on some other reasons: that it is the only hotel filled with familiar Disney characters, perhaps.

Finding Evidence.   When you have listed as many reasons as you can, look to find evidence to illustrate each reason. Evidence comes in many forms: descriptive details, quotations, statistics, authoritative testimony, anything that demonstrates the existence of a reason. Thornton, for example, quotes specific lyrics as evidence of easy-to-relate-to lyrics. Evidence for the architectural distinctiveness of the Disney hotel might be that it's designed by the celebrated architect Michael Graves; for the hotel's featuring Disney characters everywhere, that it has Mickey Mouse doorknobs and Dumbo lampposts. You will probably find that the amount of evidence you can show for each reason will vary. Some reasons will have only one piece of evidence, while others may have many.

Identifying Criteria.   Criteria are standards for judging something. To evaluate a restaurant for a family with young children, you might ask: does it have high chairs? The availability of high chairs would be one criterion for judging a restaurant for such families. High chairs would not matter, however, to many college students. Criteria more appropriate to them might be a good jukebox and an interesting menu. In deciding on the criteria for an evaluation, therefore, you need to keep your readers in mind.

You need, as well, to match the criteria to the subject that's being evaluated. If you're shopping for a jeep, the criteria you'd use to evaluate those you see would be different from those for evaluating a sports car. In the same way, the standards you apply to a documentary film would be different from those you'd use to judge a Saturday morning cartoon. For your evaluation to seem informed, thoughtful, and convincing, it must be based on appropriate criteria.

Consider each of your reasons, one by one, and decide what criterion it is based on. Then look at the criteria all together, to make sure you haven't overlooked any that your readers might consider important. Finally, consider each criterion with your particular readers in mind: would they accept it as a reasonable basis for judging the subject at hand?

Justifying Your Criteria. If your readers are likely to be unfamiliar with some of your criteria, object to any of them, or expect you to apply criteria other than the ones you've chosen, you will need to justify your criteria. Consider them individually and as a set. Begin by writing about each one, explaining why it is appropriate for judging this kind of subject. Then write about the set, explaining why you've chosen to use these criteria and not others that readers might expect you to use. Try comparing your subject with other examples of the same type of thing to show that your criteria are the ones on which subjects like these are typically judged.

Drawing Comparisons. It is a good idea to apply the criteria to other subjects like yours, to get some sense of how your subject compares. Doing this will help you to recognize strengths and weaknesses in your subject, and may lead you to material you can use in your essay. In comparing the REM album with one by U2, for instance, Jason Thornton compares his subject, which he thinks readers may not be completely familiar with, to another similar subject, one they are more likely to know.

Testing Your Choice

Pause now to ask yourself whether you have the makings of a good convincing argument. Ask yourself the following questions:

- Do I know enough about my subject to evaluate it fully?
- Do I care enough about this subject really to want to convince readers to accept my opinion about it?
- Are my reasons for thinking what I do about my subject strong ones? Are they reasons that will appeal to my readers?

■ Are the criteria I've applied to my subject appropriate to it, and will my readers accept them as the right ones for evaluating something of this kind?

■ Do I have adequate evidence to convince readers that my reasons have a basis? Will I be able to check out my subject closely again if I need additional evidence?

For Group Inquiry

At this point it might be helpful to get together in a group with two or three other students. Announce your subject and intended readers, and name the criteria you're using for your evaluation. Then ask the group whether these seem to be reasonable criteria for your topic. Can they suggest any other criteria they'd like to see considered? This kind of feedback can help you to know whether you have to explain in your essay why your chosen criteria are appropriate.

PLANNING AND DRAFTING

The following will help you to review your invention writings to see what you have so far, to establish goals for your evaluation, and to make a tentative outline to guide you as you draft.

Seeing What You Have

By now you have done considerable thinking and writing about your evaluation. You have explored many aspects of your subject, analyzed your readers, and developed an argumentative strategy. Take some time now to reread your invention notes thoughtfully, highlighting anything you think you will be able to use in the draft and noting connections between ideas. Also keep an eye out for problems you may have overlooked earlier, and consider how you might deal with them. For example, look for places where your evidence is thin or contradictory or your reasoning weak.

Setting Goals

Before you actually begin drafting, think seriously about the overall goals of your evaluation. Establishing clear goals will make the draft not only easier to write but almost surely more focused as well, and therefore more convincing.

Following are some questions designed to help you focus on what exactly you want to accomplish with this evaluation. You may find it useful to return to them while you are drafting.

Your Readers

■ What do I want my readers to think about the subject as a result of reading my essay? Do I want to show them how it succeeds, as Ansen does, or how it fails, as Rafferty does?

- Should I assume, as Ansen and Rafferty do, that my readers are likely to have read other evaluations of the subject? Or should I assume, as Thornton does, that I am introducing them to it?

- How can I gain my readers' trust? Should I show them, as all the writers in this chapter do, how familiar I am with comparable subjects? Should I indicate my special knowledge, as Rafferty does when he refers to Spike Lee's thesis film?

- What tone should I take? Should I be witty like Ehrenreich, serious like Ansen and Rafferty, enthusiastic like Thornton?

Presentation of the Subject

- Should I place the subject historically, as Thornton, Rafferty, and Ehrenreich try to do?

- If the subject has a plot, how much of it should I tell?

- How can I capture the flavor of my subject? Can I cite notable details, as Ansen does, or refer to some typical incidents, as Ehrenreich does?

Your Argument

- How should I state my judgment? Should I make it a comparative judgment, as Thornton and Ansen do? Should I put it up front, as Thornton does, or wait a bit, like Rafferty, until I've provided a context?

- How can I show that my judgment is fair and well balanced? Shall I balance my criticism with praise, as Rafferty does? Can I refer to specific weaknesses without taking away from the larger strengths, as Thorton does?

- Should I simply assert my reasons, or do I need to explain or justify the criteria underlying them?

- How can I support my reasons? Can I find textual evidence to quote or paraphrase? Are there any authorities I can call upon, as Thornton does? What facts, statistics, or other evidence could I use?

The Beginning and the Ending

- Should I open by stating my judgment, as Ehrenreich does? By comparing my subject with one more familiar to readers, as Thornton does? By describing the subject, as Rafferty and Ansen do?

- How should I conclude? Should I try to frame the essay by echoing something from the opening, or from another part of the essay? Should I conclude by restating my judgment, as Ansen and Thornton do?

Outlining

Evaluations may be organized in various ways. The important thing is to include all essential parts: a presentation of the subject, a judgment of some kind, and reasons and evidence to support the judgment. In addition, you will want to arrange your reasons in some logical order: from most obvious to least obvious, most general to most technical, least convincing to most convincing, least important to most important.

If your readers are already familiar with the topic, your outline might look like this:

> presentation of the subject
>
> any discussion of criteria to be considered
>
> judgment
>
> reason 1
> > evidence
>
> reason 2
> > evidence
>
> reason 3
> > evidence, with a comparison
>
> consideration of an opposing judgment
>
> conclusion

If your readers are unfamiliar with the topic, you will need to begin with some description of your subject, including perhaps some background discussion and definition of terms.

There are many other possible organizations. Whichever you choose, remember that an outline should serve only as a guide. It can help you to organize your invention materials and provide a sense of direction as you start drafting, but you should feel free to depart from it if you see a better way of developing your argumentative strategy.

Drafting

Before you begin to draft your evaluation, reread all your notes and, if possible, take a last look at your subject. If you are evaluating a published work (such as a poem, story, novel), reread it. If you are writing about a movie, see it again. Your subject must be completely fresh in your mind.

Start drafting, focusing on your readers and how you can convince them to share your judgment of the subject. If you run into trouble, reconsider each element in your evaluation. Perhaps you should think of better reasons or add more evidence to support the reasons you give. You may need to take another look at your criteria. If you really get stuck, turn back to the invention activities in this chapter to see if you can fill out your material.

You might want to review the general advice about drafting on pp. 9–11.

GETTING CRITICAL COMMENTS

All writers find it helpful to have someone else read their drafts and give them critical comments. Your instructor may arrange such a reading as part of your coursework; if not, you can ask a classmate, friend, or family member to read it over. If your college has a writing center, you might ask a tutor there to read and comment on your draft. Following are guidelines designed to be used by *anyone* reviewing an evaluation essay. (If you are unable to get someone else to read over your draft, turn ahead now to the Revision section on pp. 285–88, which includes guidelines for reading your own draft with a critical eye.)

In order to provide helpful comments, your reader must know your intended audience and purpose. Briefly write out this information at the top of your draft:

Audience. Who are your readers?

Purpose. What do you want your readers to think about your subject from reading this essay?

Reading with a Critical Eye

Reading a draft critically means reading it more than once, first to get a general impression and then to analyze its basic features.

Reading for a First Impression.   Read first to understand the essay's judgment. As you read, try to notice any words or passages that contribute, either favorably or unfavorably, to your first impression. A good way of highlighting noteworthy language is to use the pointings system:

Pointings

- Draw a straight line under any words or images that impress you as especially effective: strong verbs, specific details, memorable phrases, striking images.

- Draw a wavy line under any words or images that seem flat, stale, or vague. Also put a wavy line under any words or phrases that you consider unnecessary or repetitious.

- Look for pairs or groups of sentences that you think should be combined. Put brackets [ ] around these sentences.

- Look for sentences that are garbled, overloaded, or awkward. Put parentheses ( ) around these sentences. Put them around any sentence that seems even slightly questionable; don't worry about whether or not you're certain about your judgment. The writer needs to know that you, as one reader, had even the slightest problem understanding a sentence.

After you've finished reading the draft, briefly write down your impressions. What is the essay's judgment? How convincing do you think the argument will be for the intended readers?

See pp. 274–76 to review the basic features.

Reading to Analyze.   Read the draft again, this time focusing on the basic features of an evaluation.

Is the Subject Clearly Presented?

Check to see how the subject is described. Is there anything else the intended readers might be curious about or might need to know? Point to any details that seem unnecessary or redundant.

Is the Judgment Clear and Balanced?

Is the judgment about the subject stated explicitly enough? Is it clear? Check to see that there is a balanced appraisal, acknowledging how the subject succeeds as well as fails.

Is the Argument Convincing?

Do the reasons given for the judgment seem relevant? If they seem inappropriate or vague, try to determine the criteria on which they are based. Are the criteria appropriate? Is sufficient evidence given for each reason? Is the argument convincing?

Are Any Comparisons Pointed and Appropriate?

Look at any comparisons or contrasts between the subject and other things of the same kind. What do they contribute to the evaluation? Do there seem to be too many comparisons? Are there places where comparisons might be added?

Is the Organization Effective?

Note any places where the essay seems disorganized or confusing. Are there topic sentences at the beginning of paragraphs? Would adding some make the essay easier to read? Consider whether any reasons ought to be reordered.

Look at the *beginning*. Is it engaging? If not, can you see any other passages in the draft that might be more interesting? Does it provide sufficient background information?

Look at the *ending*. Does the ending leave you thinking about the subject? Point to any passages elsewhere in the draft that might work nicely as a conclusion.

What Final Thoughts Do You Have?

What is the strongest part of the argument? What is the weakest part, most in need of further work?

REVISING AND EDITING

This section will help you to identify problems in your draft and to revise and edit to solve them.

Identifying
Problems

To identify problems in your draft, you need to read it objectively, analyze its basic features, and study any comments you've gotten from others.

Getting an Overview.   Consider the draft as a whole, trying to judge it objectively. It may help to do so in two steps:

Reread. If possible, put the draft aside for a day or two before rereading it. When you do, start by reconsidering your audience and purpose. Then read the draft straight through, trying to see it as your intended readers will.

Outline. Make a scratch outline to get an overview of the essay's development. This outline can be sketchy—words and phrases instead of complete sentences—but it should identify the basic features as they appear.

Charting a Plan for Revision.   You may want to use the following chart to keep track of any problems you need to solve. The left-hand column lists the basic features of evaluative writing. As you analyze your draft yourself and study any comments you've gotten from others, use the right-hand column to notice the problems you want to solve.

Basic Features	*Problems to Solve*
The subject	
The judgment	
The argument	
Comparisons	
Organization	

Analyzing the Basic Features of Your Draft.   Turn now to the questions for analyzing a draft on pp. 284–85. Using these questions as guidelines, identify problems in your draft. Note anything you need to solve on the chart above.

Studying Critical Comments.   Review any comments you've received from other readers, and add to the chart any points that need attention. Try not to react too defensively to these comments: by letting you see how others respond to your draft, they provide invaluable information about how you might improve it.

Solving
the Problems

Having identified problems, you now need to figure out solutions and to carry them out. Basically, you have three ways of finding solutions: (1) review your invention and planning notes for information and ideas to add to the draft; (2) do further invention and research to answer questions your readers raised; and (3) look back at the readings in this chapter to see how other writers have solved similar problems.

Following are suggestions to get you started on solving some of the problems common to evaluative writing. For now, focus on solving those issues identified on your chart. Try not to worry about sentence-level problems at this time; that will come later when you edit.

The Subject

- If the subject is not clear, name it explicitly and describe it in specific detail. Try to anticipate and answer your intended readers' questions.
- If the subject is presented in too much detail, cut extraneous and repetitive details. If your subject has a plot, try to sketch it without telling the whole story.

The Judgment

- If the judgment is vague or ambiguous, restate it so that there can be no confusion about your evaluation.
- If the judgment seems too one-sided, consider balancing your praise or criticism. Think of something praiseworthy to applaud or a weakness to note.

The Argument

- If any reasons seem inappropriate or vague, try to clarify them. The problem might be that the underlying criteria need to be explained or defended. Review your invention writing, looking for material to strengthen your reasons. Or you may need to explore your reasons and criteria further. Consider whether any of the reasons should be combined or separated.
- If the evidence is thin, review your invention writing and reexamine the subject for additional evidence.

Comparisons

- If any comparisons or contrasts seem pointless or inappropriate, eliminate them.
- If there are too many comparisons, consider dropping some.
- If you don't compare or contrast your subject with anything else, try to do so and see whether it strengthens your judgment.

Organization

- If the essay seems disorganized or confusing, you may need to add transitions, summaries, or topic sentences. You may also need to do some major restructuring, such as moving your presentation of the subject or reordering your reasons.

- If the beginning is weak, see if there's a better place to start. Review your notes for an interesting quotation, image, or scene that might arouse readers' interest in your subject.

- If the ending doesn't work, see if you can frame the essay by echoing a point made earlier.

Editing and Proofreading

As you've been working on your draft so far, you've probably corrected some obvious errors, but grammar and style have not been a priority. Now is the time to check carefully for errors in usage, punctuation, and mechanics; and also to consider matters of style. You may find that studying your draft in separate passes—first for paragraphs, then for sentences, and finally for words—will help you to recognize any problems.

Once you have edited your draft and produced a final copy, proofread it carefully to be sure there are no typos, misspellings, or other mistakes.

LEARNING FROM YOUR OWN WRITING PROCESS

Reflect now on the process you followed in writing this essay. Look over all your work—invention writing, draft, and revision. Think about the various problems you encountered choosing a subject or defining criteria or articulating reasons or finding evidence. Study any changes you made between draft and revision, and think about why you made them. What are the strong points in your essay? What would you still like to improve?

A Writer at Work

PLANNING AN ARGUMENTATIVE STRATEGY

In developing an evaluative essay, a writer must decide what reasons will be most convincing to readers and whether their underlying criteria need to be justified. In this section, we will see how Jason Thornton, the writer of "Documenting *Document*," charted his reasons, criteria, and evidence and then explored ways of justifying his criteria. Following is a chart he made when he was working on the reasons, criteria, and evidence for his essay.

REASONS	CRITERIA	EVIDENCE
lyrics are easy to relate to	lyrics	"Finest Worksong"
lyrics are literary, intellectual		"Oddfellows Local 151"
haunting lyrics		"Exhuming McCarthy"
		"The One I Love"

REASONS	CRITERIA	EVIDENCE
catchy, poplike music	music	"Disturbance at the Heron House"
Document shows REM's great versatility freshness, originality	style	mixes hard rock, folk, punk, country-western like folk music, but with electric guitars
lyrics work well with music	songs	"Disturbance at the Heron House" combines bitter lyrics and upbeat music
Document well produced	production quality	REM had a hand in album's production

After charting out his plans, Thornton considered which reasons he should use in the essay. He then explored the criteria underlying his reasons to gauge the strength of his argumentative strategy. Following is his written analysis of the criteria and reasons, first individually and then as a set.

Justifying Criteria. Much of the song's strength comes from the quality of its lyrics. Thus, this must be an important basis for evaluating an album. How easily you can relate to a song's lyrics can greatly affect how much you like the song. Why do alienated teenagers listen to heavy metal? Because the music reflects aspects of their lives. People enjoy music that reveals something of themselves.

I should be able to demonstrate how easy REM's lyrics are for most listeners to relate to because they are so abstract and "open." Their abstractness allows different interpretations, though it can be confusing. Mentioning this potential weakness might make me seem like a fair judge. My review would seem more objective, less one-sided. It might also be good to say something about the Americanism of the lyrics--one more reason we can relate to them! Also, by showing how literary and intellectual REM's lyrics can be, I might be able to convince readers that these songs are well thought-out and fairly artistic.

The music is, without a doubt, the most important reason why a person would buy an album. Therefore, I

have to convince readers that REM's music is both original and accessible. People like variety and newness, but
many folks shy away from the radically different. Thus,
it will be important that I focus on the familiar appeal
of the music on *Document*. So I should comment on the
pop-oriented, catchy aspects of these songs, mentioning
also their diversity of style. Even though it's an artistic record, *Document* can be enjoyed in mainstream
pop/rock terms.

Production, although often ignored, is also important. If an album isn't recorded or mixed well, it won't
sound good and this could distract from the music's
other merits. I need to make readers aware that *Document*
is well produced. I might want to compare its production
to that of U2's *Joshua Tree*.

And style is important. Listeners judge an album or
group on what kind of music it has. Convincing readers
of REM's diversity and style will be important. Plus,
REM's way of combining many styles--like working folk
with a typical rock assortment of guitars, bass, and
drums would show a freshness and originality in the
band's approach.

Finally, how well the songs are written must be included. I need to show how certain lyrics work with the
music. Also, I might want to mention songs that have
been criticized as imitative.

I've read numerous record reviews, and I think that
these criteria are the ones generally used. It seems
that they all come down to listener enjoyment. Other
points could be used to evaluate the band's performance,
such as musicianship or the conventionality of chord
progressions, but these are criteria used more often to
evaluate jazz, classical, or even art-rock. They would
be out of place here. Many of the reasons I'm citing
overlap, but that's because they're all related. It
might be best to evaluate *Document* on a song-by-song
basis, using specific songs as examples of specific
points.

I think I'll try to combine all the negative criticism in one paragraph and maybe put it somewhere in the
middle, to break up all the praise.

As he drafted the essay and again as he revised it, Thornton returned to the
chart and this exploratory writing for ideas.

■ In a popular magazine, a psychologist speculates about the causes of a phenomenon known to many parents: kids love Nintendo. She considers several possible causes for this phenomenon—the influence of television, the power of advertising—but concludes that the primary reason children like to play Nintendo is that it fills certain psychological needs. One such need is to escape from everyday reality, where the demands are many and often contradictory. Playing Nintendo, children know what is expected of them. This need for an ordered universe suggests a related and even more important need that Nintendo may satisfy: the need for mastery. Nintendo offers the child the opportunity for mastery. Unlike many other challenging games, Nintendo can be mastered in the privacy of one's own room, away from the judging eyes of peers, parents, and teachers. In addition, the child doesn't have to begin with much mastery to get satisfaction from playing. Games like the very popular *Super Mario* allow children to develop their skills incrementally, building their confidence and skill at the same time.

■ For a popular magazine, two anthropologists write an article in which they offer an explanation for the universal phenomenon of the "afternoon lull," the period of reduced energy after the midday meal. Referring to research studies, they reject the possibility that the lull is caused either by the biochemical effects of eating or by a change in body temperature. They also reject the possibility that the lull is due to laziness or a desire for diversion. They argue instead that it is caused by a biological rhythm established during early human evolution in the tropics, where heat peaks in the early afternoon.

■ For a university social policy institute, a survey researcher reports a steady 22-year decline in the percentage of college freshmen who say they plan to major in physical sciences or mathematics. He demonstrates the trend in a single table reporting survey results for the years 1966–1988. The researcher speculates that deteriorating math instruction in schools and the lure of computer science are sustaining the trend but that a significant underlying cause is materialism—students' interest in making money quickly rather than in developing their minds for careers that have a slower payoff.

Speculating about Causes 9

W e all quite naturally attempt to explain causes. Because we assume everything has a cause, we predictably ask "Why?" when we notice something new or unusual or puzzling.

Many things can be fully and satisfactorily explained. When children ask "Why is the sky blue in the day and black at night?" parents can provide an answer. But there are other questions we can answer only tentatively: Why did the United States become involved in Vietnam? Why do minority groups in American society continue to suffer discrimination? Questions such as these often have only plausible, not definitive, explanations because we cannot design a scientific experiment to identify the actual cause conclusively. The decline in SAT scores, for example, has been attributed to the rise in television viewing among children. Though this cause is plausible, we cannot know for certain that it is actually responsible for the drop in scores.

Much of what we want to know about can never be known definitively and unarguably, but can only be speculated about on the basis of the best available evidence and experience. Writing that speculates about causes plays an important role in academic and professional life, as the scenarios that open this chapter suggest. Government specialists analyze the causes of unemployment or homelessness to design policies intended to solve social problems. Business executives study the reasons for increases in sales or declines in worker productivity. Educators look at why some teaching techniques work and others do not or how family problems affect students' performance in school.

As a student, you too face assignments that call for you to speculate about causes. Here are some typical assignments:

■ *For an American history course:* When Japanese-Americans on the West Coast were forcibly moved to "relocation camps" during World War II, the government officially cited the danger that they would prove disloyal to the United States in its war with Japan. Some historians, however, have argued that racial prejudice and economic jealousy played a large part in the government's decision. On the basis of the assigned readings on this topic, how important do you think these unofficial reasons were?

■ *For a political science course:* During 1989 Communist governments crumbled almost without resistance in the Soviet Union and much of eastern Europe, while in China the government succeeded in crushing a movement toward a more open political system. From what you have learned about the characteristics of Communist rule in the Soviet bloc and in China, why do you think the movements against the party succeeded in one case and not the other?

■ *For a literature course:* Why does Huck Finn "light out for the Territory" at the end of the novel? Defend your answer with evidence from the book.

■ *For a biology course:* Why is AIDS concentrated among homosexuals in this country but among heterosexuals in Africa? In your answer, consider differences in such factors as sexual practices and attitudes and general standards of health and medical care.

This chapter presents several essays arguing for the causes of some phenomenon or trend. A phenomenon is something notable about the human condition or social order—fear of failure, for example, or racial discrimination. A trend is a significant change extending over some period of time, generally months or years. It can be identified by an increase or decrease— for example, a rise in the rate of births of babies with AIDS or a decline in the number of applicants to law school.

When you speculate about causes, you first need to describe your subject and then to propose some causes and argue for one or more as the best available explanation. You do not have to prove that your explanation is right, but you must convince readers that it is plausible.

This chapter is designed to introduce you to one of the more common and important writing situations you will meet in college. Speculating about why things are the way they are or why things change will help you to develop your powers of creativity as you speculate about possible causes, your powers of judgment as you weigh these possibilities and choose the most plausible ones, and your powers of reasoning as you devise an argumentative strategy to present your conclusions to your readers.

For Group Inquiry

Get together with two or three other students and make a list of a dozen or so trends—such as the decline in voting in the United States or the increasing popularity of Mexican food—whose causes you are interested in speculating about. Choose one trend that interests all of you, and spend ten or fifteen minutes discussing its likely causes and how important each one is. When you've finished, take a few more minutes to reflect on the process you've been engaged in.

■ Where did your ideas about causes come from—reading, television, your own imagination?

- How did you decide which causes were more important than others?
- Do you recall other occasions when you tried to analyze the causes of something? How did you go about it?

Readings

Stephen King is America's best-known writer of horror fiction. In the following essay, written for *Playboy*, King speculates about the popular appeal of horror movies. Before you begin reading, think about your own attitude toward horror films. Do you enjoy them? "Crave" them? Dislike them? Or are you indifferent?

As you read, notice how assertively King presents his assumptions about people, such as the one in the opening sentence. How does he try to get you to accept these assumptions? Is he successful?

**WHY WE CRAVE
HORROR MOVIES**
STEPHEN KING

I think that we're all mentally ill; those of us outside the asylums only hide it a little better—and maybe not all that much better, after all. We've all known people who talk to themselves, people who sometimes squinch their faces into horrible grimaces when they believe no one is watching, people who have some hysterical fear—of snakes, the dark, the tight place, the long drop . . . and, of course, those final worms and grubs that are waiting so patiently underground. 1

When we pay our four or five bucks and seat ourselves at tenth-row center in a theater showing a horror movie, we are daring the nightmare. 2

Why? Some of the reasons are simple and obvious. To show that we can, that we are not afraid, that we can ride this roller coaster. Which is not to say that a really good horror movie may not surprise a scream out of us at some point, the way we may scream when the roller coaster twists through a complete 360 or plows through a lake at the bottom of the drop. And horror movies, like roller coasters, have always been the special province of the young; by the time one turns 40 or 50, one's appetite for double twists or 360-degree loops may be considerably depleted. 3

We also go to re-establish our feelings of essential normality; the horror movie is innately conservative, even reactionary. Freda Jackson as the horrible melting woman in *Die, Monster, Die!* confirms for us that no matter how far we may be removed from the beauty of a Robert Redford or a Diana Ross, we are still light-years from true ugliness. 4

And we go to have fun. 5

Ah, but this is where the ground starts to slope away, isn't it? Because this is a very peculiar sort of fun, indeed. The fun comes from seeing others menaced—sometimes killed. One critic has suggested that if pro football has become the voyeur's version of combat, then the horror film has become the modern version of the public lynching. 6

It is true that the mythic, "fairy-tale" horror film intends to take away the shades   7
of gray. . . . It urges us to put away our more civilized and adult penchant for analysis
and to become children again, seeing things in pure blacks and whites. It may be
that horror movies provide psychic relief on this level because this invitation to lapse
into simplicity, irrationality and even outright madness is extended so rarely. We are
told we may allow our emotions a free rein . . . or no rein at all.

If we are all insane, then sanity becomes a matter of degree. If your insanity   8
leads you to carve up women like Jack the Ripper or the Cleveland Torso Murderer,
we clap you away in the funny farm (but neither of those two amateur-night surgeons was ever caught, heh-heh-heh); if, on the other hand, your insanity leads you
only to talk to yourself when you're under stress or to pick your nose on your morning
bus, then you are left alone to go about your business . . . though it is doubtful that
you will ever be invited to the best parties.

The potential lyncher is in almost all of us (excluding saints, past and present;   9
but then, most saints have been crazy in their own ways), and every now and then,
he has to be let loose to scream and roll around in the grass. Our emotions and our
fears form their own body, and we recognize that it demands its own exercise to
maintain proper muscle tone. Certain of these emotional muscles are accepted—
even exalted—in civilized society; they are, of course, the emotions that tend to
maintain the status quo of civilization itself. Love, friendship, loyalty, kindness—these
are all the emotions that we applaud, emotions that have been immortalized in the
couplets of Hallmark cards and in the verses (I don't dare call it poetry) of Leonard
Nimoy.

When we exhibit these emotions, society showers us with positive reinforcement;   10
we learn this even before we get out of diapers. When, as children, we hug our
rotten little puke of a sister and give her a kiss, all the aunts and uncles smile and
twit and cry, "Isn't he the sweetest little thing?" Such coveted treats as chocolate-
covered graham crackers often follow. But if we deliberately slam the rotten little
puke of a sister's fingers in the door, sanctions follow—angry remonstrance from
parents, aunts and uncles; instead of a chocolate-covered graham cracker, a
spanking.

But anticivilization emotions don't go away, and they demand periodic exercise.   11
We have such "sick" jokes as, "What's the difference between a truckload of bowling balls and a truckload of dead babies?" (You can't unload a truckload of bowling
balls with a pitchfork . . . a joke, by the way, that I heard originally from a ten-year-
old). Such a joke may surprise a laugh or a grin out of us even as we recoil, a
possibility that confirms the thesis: If we share a brotherhood of man, then we also
share an insanity of man. None of which is intended as a defense of either the sick
joke or insanity but merely as an explanation of why the best horror films, like the
best fairy tales, manage to be reactionary, anarchistic, and revolutionary all at the
same time.

The mythic horror movie, like the sick joke, has a dirty job to do. It deliberately   12
appeals to all that is worst in us. It is morbidity unchained, our most base instincts
let free, our nastiest fantasies realized . . . and it all happens, fittingly enough, in
the dark. For those reasons, good liberals often shy away from horror films. For
myself, I like to see the most aggressive of them—*Dawn of the Dead*, for instance—
as lifting a trap door in the civilized forebrain and throwing a basket of raw meat
to the hungry alligators swimming around in that subterranean river beneath.

Why bother? Because it keeps them from getting out, man. It keeps them down 13 there and me up here. It was Lennon and McCartney who said that all you need is love, and I would agree with that.

As long as you keep the gators fed. 14

For Discussion

"The potential lyncher is in almost all of us," says Stephen King, "and every now and then, he has to be let loose to scream and roll around in the grass." King seems to say that horror films perform a social function by allowing us to exercise (or possibly exorcise) our least civilized emotions. How do you react to this idea? What value do horror movies have for you personally? What do you think about the social value of horror films—or of some other kind of film? It might help to think in terms of a specific film you've seen recently.

For Analysis

1. A successful argument often depends on a careful definition of a key term. Which term does King define? What significance does the definition have for King's argument? How convincing do you find his definition?

2. Why do you think King begins as he does? Given his argument and his particular readers, what advantage do you see in this beginning?

Scratch outlines are discussed on pp. 397–98; transitions, on pp. 408–09.

3. Causal arguments must be carefully organized and developed. To discover King's plan, make a scratch outline of the selection. Then, to follow one way he keeps readers on track, analyze the transitions at the beginning of each paragraph. Begin by underlining the word or phrase that makes the exact connection with the previous paragraph.

Turn to pp. 465–67 for a discussion of analogy.

4. How effective do you find the analogy in paragraph 3? To analyze its effectiveness, consider carefully the ways in which horror movies and roller coaster rides are similar and dissimilar. Can you think of another analogy that would work?

For Your Own Writing

Think of some phenomenon of popular culture that interests you. Speculate about its causes. For instance, have you ever wondered why romance novels are so popular? Police shows and soap operas? Survivalist war games? Singles bars? Computer hacking? How would you present the phenomenon to your readers and develop an argument for its causes?

Commentary

To understand King's argument, it may help to distinguish between obvious and hidden causes. King begins with a cause that seems obvious but is still worth mentioning: we go to horror films because we want to prove that we can sit through them, just as we ride roller coasters to show ourselves and others that we have the courage to do it (paragraph 3). This cause seems plausible, though not at all surprising. We can assume that King mentions it right away because he assumes readers will be thinking of it. It enables him both to connect to a very common experience of his readers and to set an obvious cause aside in order to move on to the not-so-obvious causes, which are the heart of his argument.

King next entertains a very different cause: we go to horror movies "to re-establish our feelings of essential normality." This cause is much less predictable than the first. It may even be somewhat puzzling, and King might have argued it further. He asserts that horror movies are conservative and gives one illustration about the ugliness of their actors. However plausible this cause, it does move us from obvious causes toward the one hidden (unexpected, unlikely, risky) cause that King is to argue at length—we "crave" horror movies (not just attend them casually) in order to manage our uncivilized emotions of fear, violence, and aggression.

We may not accept King's psychology or find this hidden cause convincingly argued, but we are almost certainly interested in the argument itself, perhaps intrigued, maybe even shocked by either the idea or the examples. Whatever our reaction, King has not bored us with causes so obvious that we could have predicted all of them before reading the selection. In your own causal analysis essay, your first goal will be to speculate creatively about your subject so that you can come up with at least one not-so-obvious cause. Like King, you may want to place this cause last, after discussing other more obvious causes, and to argue for it at length and with ingenuity.

Experienced writers let their readers know that they are taking into account their values and beliefs as well as anticipating their counterarguments. We see this strategy in the way King attempts to get us to accept his striking assertions about our basic nature: "we're all mentally ill" (paragraph 1), "the potential lyncher is in almost all of us" (paragraph 9), and "anticivilization emotions . . . demand periodic exercise" (paragraph 11). Knowing these are debatable assertions, King defines his terms and qualifies them in a way that will enable most readers to consider his argument seriously, instead of rejecting it irritably. For example, he defines the disguised insanity in all of us in terms of all too familiar private habits and personal fears. Later he reminds us that sick jokes, which nearly all readers have told or laughed at from time to time, reveal our "anticivilization emotions." At the end of paragraph 11, he says, to paraphrase: "Look, I know you may be resisting my argument; but if I acknowledge that we share a brotherhood of man, then I think you should be able to acknowledge that we share an insanity of man, as I have been arguing. I'm not trying to encourage sick jokes or excuse aggression and violence but only to explain why we crave horror movies." This kind of direct acknowledgment of readers' points of view increases a writer's credibility and results in a more convincing argument.

Befitting his subject, King's tone is tough but engaging. We know what his thesis is and where he is going with the argument. Whether or not we are convinced, we can admire this thoughtfulness and craft.

For more about anticipating counterarguments, see pp. 480–86.

■   ■   ■

K. C. Cole began her writing career as a reporter and editor and has written several books on education, science, and women's issues: *Facets of Light* (1980), *Between the Lines* (1982), and *Sympathetic Vibrations: Physics as a Way of Life* (1984). In the following essay, written for the *New York Times* in 1981, she seeks to explain why so few women go into science. Like Stephen King, she speculates about the causes of a familiar phenomenon.

Before you begin reading, give some thought to her topic. Why don't more women become scientists, mathematicians, or engineers? Reflect on your own experience: Did you like or dislike science in high school? How would you explain your feelings?

WHY THERE ARE SO FEW WOMEN IN SCIENCE
K. C. COLE

I know few other women who do what I do. What I do is write about science, mainly physics. And to do that, I spend a lot of time reading about science, talking to scientists and struggling to understand physics. In fact, most of the women (and men) I know think me quite queer for actually liking physics. "How can you write about that stuff?" they ask, always somewhat askance. "I could never understand that in a million years." Or more simply, "I hate science." 1

I didn't realize what an odd creature a woman interested in physics was until a few years ago when a science magazine sent me to Johns Hopkins University in Baltimore for a conference on an electrical phenomenon known as the Hall effect. We sat in a huge lecture hall and listened as physicists talked about things engineers didn't understand, and engineers talked about things physicists didn't understand. What *I* didn't understand was why, out of several hundred young students of physics and engineering in the room, less than a handful were women. 2

Sometime later, I found myself at the California Institute of Technology reporting on the search for the origins of the universe. I interviewed physicist after physicist, man after man. I asked one young administrator why none of the physicists were women. And he answered: "I don't know, but I suppose it must be something innate. My seven-year-old daughter doesn't seem to be much interested in science." 3

It was with that experience fresh in my mind that I attended a conference in Cambridge, Mass., on science literacy, or rather the worrisome lack of it in this country today. We three women—a science teacher, a young chemist and myself—sat surrounded by a company of august men. The chemist, I think, first tentatively raised the issue of science illiteracy in women. It seemed like an obvious point. After all, everyone had agreed over and over again that scientific knowledge these days was a key factor in economic power. But as soon as she made the point, it became clear that we women had committed a grievous social error. Our genders were suddenly showing; we had interrupted the serious talk with a subject unforgivably silly. 4

For the first time, I stopped being puzzled about why there weren't any women in science and began to be angry. Because if science is a search for answers to fundamental questions then it hardly seems frivolous to find out why women are excluded. Never mind the economic consequences. 5

A lot of the reasons women are excluded are spelled out by the Massachusetts Institute of Technology experimental physicist Vera Kistiakowsky in a recent article in *Physics Today* called "Women in Physics: Unnecessary, Injurious and Out of Place?" 6

The title was taken from a nineteenth-century essay written in opposition to the appointment of a female mathematician to a professorship at the University of Stockholm. "As decidedly as two and two make four," a woman in mathematics is a "monstrosity," concluded the writer of the essay.

Dr. Kistiakowsky went on to discuss the factors that make women in science 7 today, if not monstrosities, at least oddities. Contrary to much popular opinion, one of those is *not* an innate difference in the scientific ability of boys and girls. But early conditioning does play a stubborn and subtle role. A recent *Nova* program, "The Pinks and the Blues," documented how girls and boys are treated differently from birth—the boys always encouraged in more physical kinds of play, more active explorations of their environments. Sheila Tobias, in her book, *Math Anxiety,* showed how the games boys play help them to develop an intuitive understanding of speed, motion and mass.

The main sorting out of the girls from the boys in science seems to happen in 8 junior high school. As a friend who teaches in a science museum said, "By the time we get to electricity, the boys already have had some experience with it. But it's unfamiliar to the girls." Science books draw on boys' experiences. "The examples are all about throwing a baseball at such and such a speed," said my stepdaughter, who barely escaped being a science drop-out.

The most obvious reason there are not many more women in science is that 9 women are discriminated against as a class, in promotions, salaries and hirings, a conclusion reached by a recent analysis by the National Academy of Sciences.

Finally, said Dr. Kistiakowsky, women are simply made to feel out of place in 10 science. Her conclusion was supported by a Ford Foundation study by Lynn H. Fox on the problems of women in mathematics. When students were asked to choose among six reasons accounting for girls' lack of interest in math, the girls rated this statement second: "Men do not want girls in the mathematical occupations."

A friend of mine remembers winning a Bronxwide mathematics competition in 11 the second grade. Her friends—both boys and girls—warned her that she shouldn't be good at math: "You'll never find a boy who likes you." My friend continued nevertheless to excel in math and science, won many awards during her years at Bronx High School of Science, and then earned a full scholarship to Harvard. After one year of Harvard science, she decided to major in English.

When I asked her why, she mentioned what she called the "macho mores" of 12 science. "It would have been O.K. if I'd had someone to talk to," she said. "But the rules of comportment were such that you never admitted you didn't understand. I later realized that even the boys didn't get everything clearly right away. You had to stick with it until it had time to sink in. But for the boys, there was a payoff in suffering through the hard times, and a kind of punishment—a shame—if they didn't. For the girls it was O.K. not to get it, and the only payoff for sticking it out was that you'd be considered a freak."

■   ■   ■

Science is undeniably hard. Often, it can seem quite boring. It is unfortunately 13 too often presented as laws to be memorized instead of mysteries to be explored. It is too often kept a secret that science, like art, takes a well-developed esthetic sense. Women aren't the only ones who say, "I hate science."

That's why everyone who goes into science needs a little help from friends. For 14 the past ten years, I have been getting more than a little help from a friend who is a physicist. But my stepdaughter—who earned the highest grades ever recorded in her California high school on the math Scholastic Aptitude Test—flunked calculus in her first year at Harvard. When my friend the physicist heard about it, he said, "Harvard should be ashamed of itself."

What he meant was that she needed that little extra encouragement that makes 15 all the difference. Instead, she got that little extra discouragement that makes all the difference.

"In the first place, all the math teachers are men," she explained. "In the second 16 place, when I met a boy I liked and told him I was taking chemistry, he immediately said 'Oh, you're one of those science types.' In the third place, it's just a kind of a social thing. The math clubs are full of boys and you don't feel comfortable joining."

In other words, she was made to feel unnecessary, injurious and out of place. 17

A few months ago, I accompanied a male colleague from the science museum 18 where I sometimes work to a lunch of the history of science faculty at the University of California. I was the only woman there, and my presence for the most part was obviously and rudely ignored. I was so surprised and hurt by this that I made an extra effort to speak knowledgeably and well. At the end of the lunch, one of the professors turned to me in all seriousness and said: "Well, K.C., what do the women think of Carl Sagan?" I replied that I had no idea what "the women" thought about anything. But now I know what I should have said: I should have told him that his comment was unnecessary, injurious and out of place.

For Discussion

Does your own experience in math and science support or contradict Cole's argument? How much math and science did you take in high school? Are girls in the 1990s still made to feel out of place in these courses? If you believe they are, can you think of any causes in addition to the ones Cole presents? Were there certain math and science courses that girls were more likely to take or enjoy? If so, what do you think are the reasons?

For Analysis

1. Cole writes for educated newspaper readers. Does she seem to be writing primarily to men or to women or to both equally? What do you think is her purpose? Point to specific evidence in the essay to support your answer.

2. In paragraphs 1–5, how does Cole present the phenomenon she speculates about? Given her readers and purpose, what advantages or disadvantages do you see in her beginning?

3. Unlike King, Cole relies on published sources as support for her argument. Review the essay to identify all these sources, and then decide what each contributes to the essay.

4. Cole also makes effective use of her own personal experiences. List each example that she mentions from this source and note briefly what it contributes to her argument. What can you conclude about the role of personal experience in arguments speculating about causes?

**For Your
Own Writing**

Consider some well-recognized social or educational problem you might write about for a specific group of readers—discriminatory university hiring practices, cheating on exams, diminishing aid for the poor. Choose a topic, and consider its causes. What plausible causes can you think of now, without doing any research? Which of these causes would be obvious to these readers? Which might surprise them?

Commentary

Whereas Stephen King relies solely on his own inventive speculations to explain why we crave horror movies, K. C. Cole relies on others' speculations, primarily those of physicist Vera Kistiakowsky, to explain why there are so few women in science. Cole goes well beyond reporting Kistiakowsky's proposed causes, however. Primarily, she evaluates them against her own experience. For example, after she reports Kistiakowsky's claim that girls are "sorted out" of science in junior high, Cole mentions two specific examples, one of a friend, the other of her stepdaughter. And after she notes Kistiakowsky's argument that girls are made to feel out of place in science, Cole recalls a friend who excelled in science through high school but majored in English in college because of the "macho mores" in her college science courses.

From her wide experience of discrimination against women in science, Cole could have relied entirely on her own speculations for the causes that make up her argument. Instead, she relies on Kistiakowski, whose book may even have inspired Cole to write the essay. Cole's strategy is not at all unusual for a writer of such an essay. In any writing that you do speculating about causes, you too may want to research causes others have proposed to explain your subject. When you do so, you must explicitly evaluate each cause, not only acknowledging its source but also then refuting it or, like Cole, accommodating it—acknowledging its validity and incorporating it into your own argument.

For more about refuting and accommodating counterarguments, see pp. 481–86.

Though Cole mentions several sources, she does not give formal citations for any of them because newspaper writing rarely cites sources formally. She does, however, identify her sources—Kistiakowsky's "recent article" in *Physics Today,* a "recent" *Nova* program—so that readers could easily track them down. Your instructor may expect you to cite your sources formally, as does the writer of the final selection in this chapter. If so, Chapter 21 provides guidance.

The commentary following King's essay distinguishes between obvious and hidden causes. Cole's essay demonstrates other classifications of causes that are important in causal analysis. In her argument, differences in early conditioning of boys and girls are a *remote or background* cause: since she discounts innate or genetic differences, conditioning through experience seems the earliest possible cause for women's absence from science. Such conditioning seems a *sufficient* cause, since it is so difficult to overcome. It is not, however, a *necessary* cause, since other causes Cole mentions would be sufficient to reduce the number of women in science. With early conditioning as a plausible remote cause, the remaining causes in Cole's list—sorting in junior high, discrimination, the peripheral status of women science majors in college, and lack of encouragement—seem plausible *immediate* causes—things that cause individual women to abandon science at a particular point. They are also *perpetuating* causes, helping to maintain or strengthen an aversion to science that has already begun.

Your own essay will be much more thoughtful and convincing if you can analyze the causes you are considering to determine whether they could be considered remote, immediate, sufficient, necessary, or perpetuating causes of the subject. You probably will not want to use these labels in the essay, but such an analysis can help you understand how convincing your causes are and how they are related to one another. For instance, if a cause is immediate or perpetuating, you will want to ask yourself what other causes might lie behind it, because these might be more important and influential.

■　　■　　■

Victor Fuchs, a professor of economics at Stanford, has for many years been a research associate at the National Bureau of Economic Research. This selection is from his book *How We Live: An Economic Perspective on Americans from Birth to Death* (1983). Here he speculates about the causes of a trend. As you begin reading, notice the care with which Fuchs documents the existence of the trend.

The tone of Fuchs's essay is more serious than that of King's. Fuchs does not let his personality show. His essay is not only impersonal, it is dryly factual; it seems to move slowly, but such slowness is actually a tribute to the rigor of Fuchs's careful reasoning and attention to detail.

As you read, pay attention to both the causes Fuchs rejects and the ones he proposes to explain the increase in suicides among young people.

SUICIDE AMONG YOUNG PEOPLE
VICTOR FUCHS

Although the vigor and vitality of most young people are the envy of their elders, a significant range of serious health problems are present at ages 15–24, including venereal disease, alcoholism, and drug abuse. Moreover, a large number of adolescents and youth are making themselves vulnerable to future health problems through cigarette smoking, poor diet, and inadequate exercise (Institute of Medicine 1978). One of the most disturbing trends is rising mortality among youth at a time when death rates at all other ages are declining rapidly. Male death rates at ages 15–19 and 20–24 were 12 percent *higher* in 1977 than in 1960, while mortality at other ages *declined* an average of 12 percent. A large differential in mortality trends by age is also evident for women. The deaths of young people take a tremendous emotional toll and are also particularly costly because these men and women are at the threshold of productive lives during which they and society could realize a return on the investment that has been made in them.

The principal reason for the divergent trends in mortality by age is the increase 2 in self-destructive behavior by young men and women (see the tabulation below). Among young men, suicide and motor vehicle accidents now account for half of all deaths, and among women for well over 40 percent. More youth die from suicide alone than from cancer, cardiovascular disease, diabetes, pneumonia, and influenza combined. The rising death rate from homicide also contributes to the rising death rate among the young. Homicide rates have approximately doubled at most ages, but because it is a relatively more important cause of death among the young, this doubling has had more of an impact on their overall rate. The high homicide rate among nonwhite men is particularly shocking, averaging about 50 per year per hundred thousand at ages 15–19 and over 100 per hundred thousand at ages 20–24. These rates imply that almost one out of every 100 black youths who turn 15 becomes a homicide victim before the age of 25! Apart from violent deaths, the trends in mortality of young men and women have been as favorable as at older ages.

	Percent change in age-sex-specific death rates, 1960 to 1977	
	Ages 15–24	Ages 25 and over
Suicide	145	6
Motor vehicle accidents	25	−15
Homicide	113	83
All other causes	−22	−21

Why did suicide rates among young people increase so rapidly in the 1960s and 3 1970s? It is much easier to rule out answers to this question than to find ones that will withstand critical examination. For instance, it is highly unlikely that the trend is a result of differences in the reporting of suicides, although reporting practices do vary considerably over time and in different areas. Changes in reporting, however, would affect the suicide rate at all ages, and there was no comparable increase at other stages of life. The emotional trauma of the Vietnam War was felt more keenly by young people and this may have contributed to the increase in suicides, but there are two problems with this explanation. First, after the war ended the suicide rate among young people kept on rising, rather than falling back to prewar levels (see Figure 9.1). Second, suicide rates at ages 15–24 in Canada and Sweden have been rising as rapidly and are as high as in the United States. Neither country was much affected by the Vietnam War.

Suicides have been blamed on deteriorating economic conditions, but Figure 9.1 4 shows that the rate has been rising in good times as well as bad; the long-term trend is much stronger than any response to business cycle fluctuations. Furthermore, the suicide level is slightly higher among white than nonwhite youth and the rate of increase has been as rapid for whites as for nonwhites, despite the large race differentials in youth employment. One of the more mischievous arguments currently in vogue is that the problems of children and youth are the result of high unemployment and that their solution lies in better macroeconomic policies. Of course

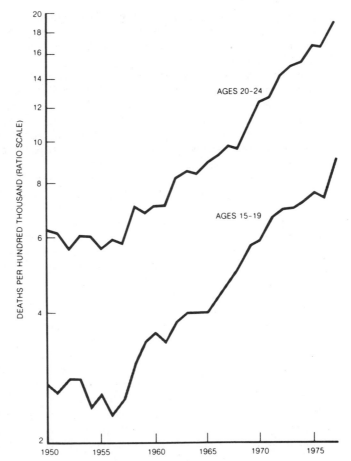

FIGURE 9.1.
Suicide rates among
youth, 1950–1977
Sources: U.S. Bureau of the
Census, *Vital Statistics of the
United States,* 1950–1977;
idem, *Current Population Reports,* series P-25, nos. 310,
519, 721, and 870.

low unemployment is better than high, and price stability is preferable to inflation, but anyone who believes that the increases in suicides among youth, births to unwed mothers, juvenile crime, and one-parent homes are primarily the result of macro-economic conditions is ignoring readily available evidence. All these problems were increasing particularly rapidly during the second half of the 1960s, when the un-employment rate averaged 3.8 percent and economic growth was extremely rapid.

Some mental health experts attribute the increases in suicides among the young   5
to the rapid changes in the American family. A study at Bellevue Hospital in New York City of 102 teenagers who attempted suicide showed that only one-third of them lived with both parents (*Newsweek,* August 28, 1978, p. 74). Parents may be failing to provide enough structure and security for children either because they are not present or because they are preoccupied with their own lives and careers, or simply because they are too permissive. In a review of psychosocial literature on adolescence, Elder (1975) concludes: "Adolescents who fail to receive guidance, affection, and concern from parents — whether by parental inattention or absence — are likely to rely heavily on peers for emotional gratification, advice, and compan-

ionship, *to anticipate a relatively unrewarding future,* and to engage in antisocial activities'' (italics added). On the other hand, some experts contend that too many demands and the setting of unrealistic standards by parents also predispose young people toward suicide.

Some evidence of a relation between family background and suicide appears in 6 a long-term longitudinal study of fifty thousand male students of Harvard University and the University of Pennsylvania that compared the characteristics of 381 men who eventually committed suicide with a set of living control subjects randomly chosen from the same school and year as the suicides (Paffenbarger, King, and Wing 1969). One of the strongest results was a positive relation between suicide and loss of father. At the time of the original interview (average age 18) the future suicides were more likely than the controls to have a deceased father (12.4 percent versus 8.1 percent) or to have parents who had separated (12.6 percent versus 8.9 percent). The difference in paternal loss through death or separation was statistically significant at a high level of confidence. The future suicides also differed from the control by having a larger percentage of fathers who were college-educated (69.1 percent versus 56.6 percent) and who were professionals (48.8 percent versus 38.4 percent). Loss of mother did not differ between the suicides and the controls.

It must be emphasized that the rapid increase in suicide rates among youth is 7 unique to that age group—there is nothing comparable at other ages. By contrast, the doubling of death rates from homicide at young ages reflects a general increase in violent crime that has affected all age groups, although not in exactly equal degree.

For some problems, such as the sharp increase in suicides, no simple or even 8 moderately complex public policy solution is in the offing. Young people may be succumbing to what Abraham Maslow (1959) forecast as the ultimate disease of our time—''valuelessness.'' The rise in suicides and other self-destructive behavior such as motor vehicle accidents and drug abuse may be the result of weakening family structures and the absence of fathers, as suggested by the study of Harvard University and University of Pennsylvania students. We can't be sure of the cause, but if it's along the lines suggested above, the challenge to public policy is staggering.

References

Elder, Glen H., Jr. 1975. Adolescence in the life cycle: An introduction. In *Adolescence in the life cycle: Psychological change and social context,* ed. Sigmund E. Dragastin and Glen H. Elder, Jr. New York: Halsted-Wiley.

Institute of Medicine. 1978. *Adolescent behavior and health.* Washington, D.C.: National Academy of Sciences.

Maslow, Abraham H. 1959. *New knowledge in human values.* New York: Harper and Brothers.

Paffenberger, Ralph S. Jr.; Stanley H. King; and Alvin L. Wing. 1969. Characteristics in youth that predispose to suicide and accidental death in later life. *American Journal of Public Health* 59 (June): 900–908.

For Discussion

"The rise in suicides and other self-destructive behavior" among young people, Fuchs suggests, "may be the result of weakening family structures and the absence of fathers." How convincing do you find this explanation?

Among young people you know, to what extent does behavior like reckless driving and alcohol or drug abuse seem related to parental neglect or absence? If you've ever done something you consider self-destructive, do you know now why you did it?

For Analysis

1. How does Fuchs demonstrate that there is a trend of increased suicide among young people? What role do the table and figure play? Has he convinced you that the trend actually exists?

2. What causes does Fuchs propose to explain the increasing number of suicides among young people? Analyze his proposed causes in terms of the categories introduced earlier in this chapter: obvious, hidden, precipitating, perpetuating, necessary, and sufficient. (You may want to review the discussion of these categories in the Commentary following the King and Cole essays.)

3. What kind of evidence does Fuchs offer for his proposed causes? How convincing do you find his argument?

4. In "ruling out answers" to his question at the beginning of paragraph 3, Fuchs rejects alternatives to his own proposed causes. List the alternative causes he rejects in paragraphs 3 and 4. In paragraph 7, Fuchs reiterates his objections to an alternative cause he had discussed earlier. Why do you think he does this? Why do you think he devotes so much space to considering alternatives that he then rejects?

5. How does Fuchs conclude his essay? Does he frame it by repeating some element from the beginning? How successful do you find his ending? Can you suggest a more effective one?

For Your
Own Writing

Imagine that you've been asked to write about some recent trend as an example of "how we live" (to borrow the title of the book from which this essay was taken). What trends have caught your attention? Choose one. How would you demonstrate the increase or decrease that constitutes the trend? What causes come immediately to mind?

Commentary

Fuch's essay is easy to read because it follows a simple plan:

> beginning
>> context for suicide trend
>> demonstration of suicide trend
> consideration and rejection of alternative causes
> argument for proposed causes
>> parental failure
>> loss of father
> reiteration of why the most likely alternative cause should be rejected
> ending

Essays speculating about the causes of trends nearly always begin by demonstrating the existence of the trend and then move on to the causes. The challenge in planning such an essay is in ordering the causes to make the most convincing argument. Another decision that must be made is where to take up alternative causes.

Writing about trends involving people and groups usually demands the kind of careful arguments Fuchs presents. It is the sort of argumentative writing we rely on for help in making personal and social-policy decisions when there is no unarguable scientific evidence to tell us what to do. Such analysis helps us to consider plausible arguments, decide which is the best one, and then decide what to do.

Fuchs's essay provides causal analysis typical of the social sciences. You will encounter such analysis often in the texts you will be required to read as a college student as well as in the social or political analysis found on the editorial pages of newspapers and magazines. You may very well be asked to write a causal analysis yourself, either as an essay exam or as a term paper.

Chapter 21 provides detailed information on using each style.

The source citation style in Fuchs's essay is the style favored in the social sciences, that of the American Psychological Association. The following essay by Kim Dartnell also uses the APA style. The style favored in the humanities, that of the Modern Language Association, is used in the Mintz and Kellogg essay in Chapter 5.

■   ■   ■

Kim Dartnell looks at the plight of homeless women in the following essay, written when she was a college freshman. Like Fuchs's essay, it illustrates how a writer can use library research to document a trend and try to determine its causes.

Before reading the essay, recall what you know about the homeless in America and homeless women in particular. What reasons can you think of for Americans to find themselves without homes?

WHERE WILL THEY SLEEP TONIGHT?
KIM DARTNELL

On January 21, 1982, in New York City, Rebecca Smith froze to death, after   1
living for five months in a cardboard box. Rebecca was one of a family of thirteen children from a rural town in Virginia. After graduating from high school as the valedictorian of her class and giving birth to a daughter, she spent ten years in mental institutions, where she underwent involuntary shock treatment for schizophrenia. It was when she was released to her sister's custody that Rebecca began wandering the streets of New York, living from day to day. Many social workers tried unsuccessfully to persuade her to go into a city shelter, and she died only a few hours before she was scheduled to be placed in protective custody. (Hombs and Snyder, 1982, p. 56).

Rebecca Smith's story is all too typical of those of the increasing number of   2
homeless women in America. Vagrant men have always been a noticeable problem
in American cities, and their numbers have increased in the 1980s. Vagrancy among
women is a relatively new problem of any size, however. In 1979, New York City
had one public shelter for homeless women. By 1983 it had four. Los Angeles has
recently increased the number of beds available to women in its skid-row shelters
(Stoner, 1983, p. 571). Even smaller communities have noticed an increase in homeless women. It is impossible to know their number or the extent of their increase in
the 1980s, but everyone who has studied the problem agrees that it is serious and
that it is getting worse (Hombs and Snyder, 1982, p. 10; Stoner, 1984, p. 3).

Who are these women? Over half of all homeless women are under the age of   3
forty. Forty-four percent are black, forty percent white. The statistics for homeless
men are about the same (Stoner, 1983, p. 570). These women are almost always
unemployed and poorly educated, unlike Rebecca Smith, and few are homeless by
choice. An expert in the field has written, "Homeless women do not choose their
circumstances. They are victims of forces over which they have lost control." The
women try in various ways to cope with their dangerous lifestyle. To avoid notice,
especially by the police, some have one set of nice clothes that they wash often.
They shower in shelters or YWCA's and try to keep their hairstyle close to the latest
fashions. An extreme is the small number of women who actually sleep sitting up
on park benches to avoid wrinkling their clothes. On the other end of the spectrum
are the more noticeable "bag ladies," who purposely maintain an offensive appearance and body odor to protect themselves from rape or robbery (Stoner, 1983, pp.
568, 569).

Why has there been such an increase in the number of vagrant American   4
women? There are several causes of this trend. For one thing, more and more women
are leaving their families because of rape, incest, and other forms of abuse. To take
one example, the Christian Housing Facility, a private organization in Orange County,
California, that provides food, shelter, and counseling to victims of abuse, sheltered
1,536 people in 1981, a 300-percent increase from the year before (Stoner, 1983,
p. 573). It is unclear whether such increases are due to an actual increase of abuse
in American families, or whether they result from the fact that it is more socially
acceptable for a woman to be on her own today. Another factor is that government
social programs for battered women have been severely cut back, leaving victims of
abuse no choice but to leave home.

Evictions and illegal lockouts force some women onto the streets. Social welfare   5
cutbacks, unemployment, and desertion all result in a loss of income. Once a woman
cannot pay her rent, she is likely to be evicted, often without notice.

Another problem is a lack of inexpensive housing. Of today's homeless women,   6
over fifty percent lived in single rooms before they became vagrants. Many of the
buildings containing single-room or other cheap apartments have been torn down
to make way for more profitable use of the land or renovated into more expensive
housing. Hotels are being offered new tax incentives that make it economically
unfeasible to maintain inexpensive single rooms. This is obviously a serious problem,
one that sends many women out onto the streets every year.

Alcoholism has been cited as a major reason for the increase in the number of   7
homeless women. I don't feel this is a major contributing factor, however. First, there

hasn't been a significant general increase in alcoholism to parallel the rise in homeless women; second, alcoholism occurs at all levels of financial status, from the executive to the homeless. Rather, I would suggest that alcoholism is usually a result of homelessness rather than the cause.

Probably the biggest single factor in the rising number of homeless women is 8 the deinstitutionalization of the mentally ill. One study estimated that ninety percent of all vagrant women may be mentally ill (Stoner, 1983, p. 567), as was the case with Rebecca Smith. The last few years have seen an avalanche of mental patients released from institutions. Between 1955 and 1980 the number of patients in mental institutions dropped by 75 percent, from about 560,000 to about 140,000. There are several reasons for this decline. New psychotonic drugs can now "cure" patients with mild disturbances. Expanded legal rights for patients lead to early release from asylums. Government-funded services such as Medicare allow some patients to be released into nursing or boarding homes. The problem is that many of these women have not really known any life outside the hospital and suddenly find themselves thrust out into an unreceptive world, simply because they present no threat to society or are "unresponsive to treatment." Very few of them are ever referred to community mental health centers, as deinstitutionalization policies assumed. Instead, many go straight out on the streets. Others may live with family or in some other inexpensive housing at first, but sooner or later they are likely to end up in the streets as well.

Although deinstitutionalization seems to have been the biggest factor in the 9 increase in vagrant women, there is some evidence that the main cause is economic. Unemployment hit 10.1 percent in 1982, the highest it has been since 1940. Yet that same year saw $2.35 billion cut from food-stamp programs. Reductions in another federal welfare program, Aid to Families with Dependent Children (AFDC), hit women particularly hard because four out of five AFDC families are headed by women, two thirds of whom have not graduated from high school (Hombs and Snyder, 1982). Together with inflation, unemployment, and loss of other welfare benefits, these cuts have effectively forced many women into homelessness and can be expected to continue to do so at a greater rate in the years to come.

The United States may be one of the world's most prosperous nations, but for 10 Rebecca Smith and others like her, the American Dream is far from being fulfilled.

References

Hombs, M. E., & Snyder, M. (1982). *Homelessness in America*. Washington, DC: Community for Creative Non-Violence.

Stoner, M. R. (1983). The plight of homeless women. *Social Service Review, 57,* 565–581.

Stoner, M. R. (1984). An analysis of public and private sector provisions for homeless people. *The Urban and Social Change Review, 17,* 2–10.

For Discussion

What is your first response to Dartnell's essay? How frequently do you encounter homeless people, and how do you respond to them? How do you react to the fact that so many Americans are without homes? Why do you think our society allows people to remain in this condition?

For Analysis

1.   What is Dartnell's purpose in this essay? What does she seem to assume about her readers?

2.   In paragraphs 3 and 7, Dartnell rejects two alternative causes that are frequently used to explain why women are homeless. How does she construct her refutations? How convincing do you find them? Why do you think Dartnell makes a point of refuting these particular arguments?

3.   Write out a brief outline of this essay. How does Dartnell order her proposed causes? What advantages or disadvantages do you see in this order?

4.   How does Dartnell begin and end her essay? How effective is this way of beginning and ending a causal argument?

5.   Now that you have completed a comprehensive analysis of Dartnell's essay, how convincing do you find her explanation for the increasing number of homeless women? If you find it convincing, how would you explain its effectiveness? If it is not convincing, how could it be improved?

For Your
Own Writing

Think of a troubling social trend you might write about. How would you demonstrate its existence, and what causes would you propose to explain it?

Commentary

Dartnell's essay illustrates how important a small amount of research can be for an essay explaining the causes of a social trend. She uses only three sources, all located on one visit to the library, which provide adequate documentation for both the trend and her proposed causes. Her sources include two essays she found in social science journals and a book on the general topic of homelessness in America. Dartnell depends on these sources for her evidence—statistics and the particular case of Rebecca Smith. She also uses the authority of her sources to bolster her argument, quoting from Stoner in paragraph 3, for example, to persuade readers that they should not blame homeless women for their plight but rather see them as victims.

For more about these and other kinds of evidence, see pp. 471–80.

PURPOSE AND AUDIENCE

When you write an essay speculating about causes, your chief purpose is to convince readers that your proposed causes are plausible. Whatever your subject or available evidence, you must construct a coherent, logical, authoritative argument, one that readers will take seriously. Sometimes, like King and Cole, you may want readers to look at a phenomenon or trend in a new way. You can challenge them to think more deeply by taking them beyond obvious or familiar explanations. At other times, you may, like Dartnell, hope to influence policy decisions. You may hope that if policymakers hear sound arguments for possible causes of social problems, they will be influenced to take action.

Your purpose for writing about causes will inevitably be affected by your audience and what you expect them to think about the subject. If you think your readers are only mildly curious about the subject, you might write partly to stimulate their interest. If you feel they are judging your competency, you might try to impress them.

BASIC FEATURES OF ESSAYS SPECULATING ABOUT CAUSES

Essays that explain causes typically include two basic features: a presentation of the subject and a convincing causal argument.

A Presentation of the Subject

First of all, it is necessary to identify the subject. That involves naming it and could include a good deal more, depending on what the writer thinks the readers know or need to know. Writers sometimes devote a large portion of the essay to the subject—describing it with specific details and examples, establishing that it actually exists (or existed) with factual evidence, statistics, and statements by authorities.

In writing about a phenomenon he knows will be familiar to his readers, Stephen King simply asserts in his title the popular fascination with horror movies. If he had been concerned that his readers might not accept this assertion, he could have cited statistics to demonstrate the popularity of horror movies. In the original essay from which this selection was excerpted, King also describes a number of particular examples of the genre in all of their gory detail. Because we all know what horror movies are—whether we've seen or studiously avoided them—we do not need such detailed description to understand his analysis of why some people, at least, "crave" this type of film. But such details can still be useful for engaging readers' interest in the subject or impressing them with its importance.

In contrast, K. C. Cole goes to some lengths at the beginning of her essay to describe the phenomenon whose causes she speculates about—the paucity of women in science. Knowing that few readers have firsthand experience of professional science, Cole takes us to three different scientific conferences to show us how few women are present.

In an essay about a trend, a writer must always demonstrate that the trend exists. Notice how Victor Fuchs very carefully documents the increase in youth suicides, presenting figures to show the sharp increase in suicides since 1960 as well as other statistics. In the same way, Kim Dartnell uses well-documented statistics to demonstrate that the number of homeless women is increasing. Because her subject is likely to be personally unfamiliar to some readers, she also describes some typical homeless women and presents an example, the case of an individual woman.

In some cases the writer may have to show that the subject is in fact a trend—an established, significant change—as opposed to a fad, which is only a short-term, superficial change. For example, a new form of exercise might become a fad if many people try it out for a few months. But this brief popularity would not make it a trend. It might, however, be considered part of a trend—a general increase in health-consciousness, for example.

It may also be necessary to provide some other details about a trend. When did it start? Is it completed or continuing? Is the increase or decrease decelerating or accelerating? Where does the evidence for these details come from? Is it authoritative? A thorough presentation of the trend may have to answer all these questions.

A Convincing Causal Argument

At the heart of an essay that analyzes the causes of something is the causal argument itself—presentation of the causes, presentation of evidence in support of each cause, and anticipation of counterarguments and alternative causes. Causal arguments are tricky. Effects have a way of being mistaken for causes. Causes proposed as sufficient to explain a phenomenon may not be necessary to explain it. A proposed cause may turn out to have originated only after a trend started. Since skeptical readers are quick to spot these reasoning errors, writers must take care in constructing their argument.

In proposing causes, writers need to be very sensitive to their readers. First, they must present their causes in a logical order that readers will be able to follow. Thus Dartnell, writing for a somewhat uninformed readership, begins with an immediate and concrete cause (abuse) and concludes with a background and perpetuating cause (economics). To hold readers' interest, writers must also not emphasize causes readers would consider obvious or predictable.

Writers must marshal evidence for each cause they propose. They may use statistics, factual cases and examples, and anecdotes. Fuchs gives statistics (paragraphs 5 and 6) to support his argument about the most likely cause of the increase in suicide among young people. Similarly, Dartnell offers statistical evidence of the economic forces behind female homelessness. The best example of a case is also found in her essay, which opens with a short narrative about a particular homeless woman. Cole includes several examples and anecdotes, concrete, one-time incidents, as evidence of the causes she proposes for the scarcity of women in science.

For more about argumentative evidence, see pp. 471–80.

Most important, writers must anticipate readers' possible objections to and questions about the proposed causes, as well as showing they have considered (and rejected) any other possible causes. Cole twice acknowledges that many or even most men find science unpleasant or mystifying for the same reasons women do. Fuchs emphatically rejects several alternative causes before proposing his own explanation of the increase in youth suicides. Dartnell refutes the counterargument that many homeless women choose their condition, and she not only shows evidence that alcoholism is not a cause of increased homelessness among women but goes on to suggest that it is usually an effect instead.

Guide to Writing

THE WRITING ASSIGNMENT

Think of some important or intriguing phenomenon or trend, and explain why it has occurred. Describe your subject, demonstrate its existence if necessary, and propose possible causes for it. Your purpose is to convince your readers that the proposed causes are plausible.

INVENTION AND RESEARCH

Following are some activities to help you find a subject, explore what you know about it, and do any necessary research.

Finding a Subject   Consider both phenomena and trends as possible subjects. A *phenomenon* is something notable about the human condition or the social order—some people's fear of speaking to a group, for example, or opposition to gun-control legislation. A *trend* is a significant change extending over many months or years. It can be identified by some sort of increase or decrease—a rise in the birthrate, a decline in test scores.

Some subjects can be approached as either phenomena or trends. For example, you could, like Fuchs, speculate about the causes of the increasing rate of suicide among young people, or you could simply speculate about the causes of suicide in this age group, ignoring whether it is increasing or decreasing.

Listing Phenomena.   First list any current phenomena you might want to write about. Following are some possibilities to consider. Start with some of them, and see if they bring to mind other topics of interest to you.

- The workplace—satisfaction or dissatisfaction with a job, white-collar crime, discrimination against women, reliance on part-time help, loyalty to a company, respect or lack of respect for a supervisor
- College—a noisy library, a shortage of parking, an instructor's skill or popularity, cheating, a successful or unsuccessful class or course, a feeling or lack of community
- Personal life—competitiveness, idealism, creativity, popularity, jealousy, laziness, workaholics
- Politics and government—hostility to politicians, low voter turnout, political action committee (PAC) influence, high cost of running for public office, negative campaigning
- Environment—failure to reduce pollution, the garbage crisis, difficulty of

starting and maintaining recycling programs, public concern about food safety

- Life stages—the "terrible twos," teenage alienation or rebellion, midlife crises, abrupt career changes
- Popularity of current musical styles or other art forms
- Continuing influence or popularity of a book, movie, actor, novelist, movie director, athlete, politician, religious leader, television personality or program

Listing Trends.   List all the trends you can think of, from the past as well as the present. Consider trends you have studied and can research as well as those you know firsthand. Try to think of trends you would like to understand better and be sure that the possibilities you list are trends, not fads. To start, consider the following possibilities:

- Shifting patterns in education—increasing interest in computer science, increasing interest in teaching as a career, increase in home schooling, increase in time required to complete college, declining numbers of math and science majors, decline in civility on college campuses, increase in number of black students attending historically black colleges
- Changes in patterns of leisure or entertainment—increasing consumption of fast food, declining interest in a particular style of music, increase in competitive cycling, increase or decrease in a magazine's circulation
- Shifts in religious practices—decreasing support for television evangelists increasing incidence of women ministers or rabbis, increasing interest in Asian religions, increased membership in fundamentalist churches
- New patterns of political behavior—increase in conservatism or liberalism, a growing desire for isolationism from world affairs, developing power of minorities and women
- Societal changes—increases in the number of women working, unmarried teenagers having babies, single-parent households
- Changes in politics or world affairs—decline of Communism, increasing influence of political action committees (PACs), increasing terrorist activity, increasing numbers of women elected to political office
- Changes in economic conditions—the long-term rise or fall of interest rates, increase in low-paying service jobs, increasing cost of medical care
- Changing attitudes—diminishing concern about world hunger, growing concern for personal success
- Completed artistic movements or historical trends—impressionism, pop art, the struggle for female suffrage, industrialization

Choosing a Subject.   Now look over your list and pick one subject to write about. You may or may not already have some ideas about why this phenomenon or trend occurred. As you analyze it in some detail, you will have the opportunity to consider possible causes and to decide which ones are the most important.

Of the two types of subjects, a trend may be more challenging because you nearly always must do research to demonstrate that it actually exists, that something has been increasing or decreasing over an extended period of time. (Usually one or two references will be adequate.) Since a trend begins at a specific point, you must take care that the causes you propose as the sources of the trend actually precede its onset. You may also need to differentiate between causes that launched the trend and those that perpetuate it. Though trend analysis is challenging, it may be a challenge you are ready to take on.

Stop now to focus your thoughts. In one or two sentences, describe the subject you have decided to analyze.

Exploring What You Know about Your Subject

Do some thinking now about the subject you have chosen to analyze. Consider what you know about it, figure out why you are interested in it, decide where you might find more information about it. Write for around ten minutes, noting everything you know about the subject.

Considering Causes

Think now about what caused your subject, listing all the possible causes you can think of and then analzying the most promising of them.

Listing Possible Causes.   Write down all the things you can think of that might have caused your subject. There are several kinds of causes you should try to find, specifically:

- immediate causes: those responsible for making the phenomenon or trend begin when it did
- remote, background causes: those from the more distant past
- perpetuating causes: those that may have contributed to the phenomenon or trend
- obvious causes
- hidden causes

Selecting the Most Promising Causes.   Review your list and select five or six "promising" causes, ones that seem to you to provide a plausible explanation of your subject. Since you will next need to analyze these causes, it might be helpful to list them in table form. On a piece of paper, list the causes in a column on the left, leaving five or six lines between each cause.

See pp. 328–29 for an example of such a table.

Analyzing Promising Causes.   Next to each potential cause on the table, explain why you think it is real and important. Consider each of the following questions as you analyze the causes:

- Is it a necessary cause? Without it, could the subject have occurred?
- Is it a sufficient cause? Could it alone have caused this subject?
- Would this cause affect everybody the same way?
- Would this cause always lead to phenomena or trends like this?
- If the subject is a trend, do you know of any statistical evidence that this cause increases or decreases in correlation with the trend?
- Can you think of any particular anecdotes or examples that demonstrate the cause's importance?
- Can you recall that any authorities have suggested it is an important cause?
- Is it actually a result of the subject rather than a cause?
- Is it a remote cause or an immediate cause?
- Is it a perpetuating cause?
- Is it an obvious cause or a hidden cause?

Researching Your Subject

As you were exploring your subject, you may have found that you already know enough to describe or define it adequately for your readers. Should you want or need to know more, consult library sources.

As you do research, take careful notes and remember to record information necessary for acknowledging your sources in your essay.

If you are speculating about the causes of a *trend,* you will also need to do some research to confirm that it actually is a trend and not just a phenomenon or fad. To do so you will need to find factual, and probably statistical, evidence of an increase or decrease over time—and also of the date when this change began. (Recall that Fuchs uses a graph to show the increase in youth suicides and that Dartnell provides statistical evidence that the number of homeless women is increasing.) If you are unable to confirm the trend, you will need to select another that you can confirm.

On pp. 521–22 is a list of sources especially useful for researching trends.

Testing Your Choice

Once you have explored your subject, considered its possible causes, confirmed its existence, and described it in some detail, take some time to review your material and decide whether your subject is workable. Does the subject still interest you? Do you have some ideas about its causes? Would you like to research it further? If your subject does not seem promising, return to your list of possible subjects to select another.

For Group Inquiry

One good way of testing your subject is with a group of two or three other students. In turn, present your subjects and then name the causes you have in mind. See whether the other members of the group accept these as likely causes, and ask whether they can think of any others. Find out what, if anything, they already know about your subject. Feedback of this kind can help you to know what objections to expect from readers as well as to learn some other causes.

Researching
Causes

Some subjects can be explained fully and convincingly on the basis of your own knowledge and intuition. In fact, you may be on your own to explain very recent phenomena or new, emerging trends. Most subjects that catch your attention will already have been noticed by others, however, and you will want to find out what they have had to say about the causes. Doing research can be helpful in several ways: (1) to confirm or refute your own ideas, (2) to suggest other causes, (3) to provide evidence of causes, and (4) to identify evidence against possible counterarguments.

As you discover causes others have proposed, add the most interesting or plausible ones to your table of causes. Analyze these just as you did your own proposed causes. When you draft your essay, you may want to accommodate them—integrate them fully or partially into your own argument—or refute them.

For guidelines on acknowledging sources, see pp. 533–43.

As you gather evidence about causes, remember to record information for acknowledging your sources.

Considering Your
Readers

Because you will be trying to make a convincing case for some particular cases, you should know as much as possible about your prospective readers. Only after you have analyzed your readers can you confidently decide how to present these causes in your essay—which to emphasize, which will require the most convincing evidence, which will be obvious. Take a few minutes to answer the following questions:

- Who are my readers? (Describe them briefly.)
- What do they know about my subject, and how much proof of its existence or defining or describing of it might they require?
- What attitudes might they have about my subject? Do they care about it? Are they indifferent to it? Should I appeal to their feelings? If so, how?
- What causes would they be most likely to think of?
- Which of my possible causes might they be skeptical of, and why?
- What else do I know about my readers?

Developing Your
Argument

Once you have figured out your expectations of your readers, review the table of causes and analyses and make a list of all the causes that you believe contribute significantly to your subject. Make a separate list of any other causes for which you have evidence. When you write your essay, you may wish to mention these minor causes to show that you have considered a wide range of possibilities. To try out your arguments, write about each of the significant causes for around five minutes, summing up all the evidence you have found. Develop your argument with your readers in mind; remember that you must convince them that your causes are reasonble ones. With this brief rehearsal in mind, continue thinking of ways to convince your readers.

Anticipating
and Refuting
Objections

You should expect readers to evaluate your essay critically, considering your reasons and evidence carefully before accepting your explanation. It would be wise, therefore, to account for any possible objections they could raise. Consider the two most likely objections and figure out ways to refute them. Write out a few sentences to prepare your refutation.

Refuting
Alternative Causes

As they read your essay, your readers may think of other causes that seem more plausible to them than your cause. Try to think of two or three such causes now—perhaps ones you analyzed earlier—and write a few sentences about each one explaining why you did not consider it or want specifically to reject it. Why are these causes less plausible than your own? Why might readers prefer the causes they think of?

PLANNING AND DRAFTING

You should now review what you have learned about your topic and start to plan your first draft by setting goals and making an outline.

Seeing What
You Have

Pause now to reflect on your notes. Reread everything carefully in order to decide whether you can really prove that your subject exists (or existed) and can offer a convincing explanation of its causes.

Setting Goals

Before you begin your draft, you should consider some specific goals for your essay. Not only will the draft be easier to write once you have established goals, but it is likely to be more convincing.

Following are questions to help you set goals. You may find it useful to return to them while you are drafting, for they are designed to help you to focus on specific elements of an essay speculating about causes.

Your Readers

- What are my readers likely to know about the subject?
- How can I interest them in understanding its causes?
- How can I refute their potential objections or other causes they might propose without unduly irritating them?
- How can I present myself so that my readers will consider me reasonable, fair, and authoritative?

The Beginning

- What kind of beginning would make readers take this subject seriously and really want to think about what caused it? Should I personalize it? Should I begin with a case, as Dartnell does? Should I begin by citing statistics, as Fuchs does?

Presentation of the Subject

- Do I need to demonstrate that my subject really exists? If I am analyzing a trend, do I need to demonstrate that it is not just a fad? How much and what kind of evidence do I need for these points?

The Causal Argument

- How many causes should I propose? Should I mention or give evidence for minor causes?

- How can I present my proposed causes in the most effective order? Should I arrange them from most important to least important or vice versa? From most obvious to least obvious or vice versa? From immediate to remote or vice versa?

- Do I need to make other distinctions among causes, such as between a cause that starts a trend and one that keeps it going or between sufficient and necessary causes?

- How much and what kind of evidence do I need to offer to make each cause plausible to readers? Are any causes so obvious that evidence is unnecessary? Does any cause require evidence that it existed before the phenomenon or trend began?

- How can I refute readers' objections to my proposed causes?

- How can I refute alternative causes readers might propose?

The Ending

- How should I end my essay? Should I frame it by referring back to the beginning? Do I need to summarize my causes? Should I conclude with a conjecture about larger implications, as Fuchs does?

Outlining

A causal analysis may contain as many as four basic parts: (1) a presentation of the subject, (2) a presentation of proposed causes and evidence for them, (3) a consideration of counterarguments, and (4) a consideration and refutation of alternative causes. These parts can be organized in various ways. If your readers are not likely to think of any causes other than the ones you are proposing, you could begin with a statement describing the subject and indicating its importance or interest. Then state your first proposed cause and elaborate on the evidence that it has contributed to the subject and the reasons that likely objections are unconvincing. Follow the same pattern for any other causes you propose. Your conclusion could then refer to—and explain—the lack of other explanations for your subject.

> presentation of the subject
> first proposed cause with evidence and refutation of objections, if any
> second proposed cause with evidence and refutation of objections, if any
> (etc.)
> conclusion

If you need to account for alternative causes likely to occur to readers, you could discuss them first and give your reasons for rejecting them before offering your own proposed causes. Many writers save their own causes for last, hoping to leave their readers with a clear picture of it.

> presentation of the subject
> alternative causes and reasons for rejecting them
> proposed causes with evidence and refutation of objections, if any
> conclusion

Another option is to put your own causes first followed by alternatives. This is a good way to show the relative advantage of your causes over the others. You might then end with a restatement of your causes.

> presentation of the subject
> proposed causes with evidence and refutation of objections, if any
> alternative causes compared with your causes
> concluding restatement of proposed cause

There are of course many other possible ways to organize a causal analysis, but these outlines should help you to start planning your own essay.

Drafting

Begin drafting your essay, keeping in mind the following tips on writing an essay of causal analysis:

- Remember that in writing about causes you are dealing with probabilities rather than certainties; therefore, you should not try to claim you have the final, conclusive answer but only that your explanation is plausible. Qualify your statements and acknowledge the worth of opposing views.
- Try to enliven your writing and to appeal to your readers' interests and concerns. Causal analysis is potentially rather dry.
- Remember that your outline is just a plan. Writers often make major discoveries and reorganize as they draft. Be flexible. If you find your writing taking an interesting, unexpected turn, follow it to see where it leads. You will have an opportunity to look at it critically later.
- If you run into a problem as you draft, see whether any of the invention activities earlier in this chapter will help. If, for instance, you are having difficulty making the subject seem important or interesting, you could analyze your readers further, find a way to personalize the subject with a quotation or an anecdote, or look for some attention-getting statistical evidence.
- If you are having difficulty refuting counterarguments, try composing a dialogue between yourself and an imaginary reader who does not agree with you.
- If you find you need more information, you might want to interview an expert, survey a group, or do further library research.

You may now want to review the general advice on drafting given on pp. 9–11.

GETTING CRITICAL COMMENTS

At this point your draft should get a good critical reading. All writers find it helpful to have someone else read their draft and give them critical comments. Your instructor may arrange such a reading as part of your coursework; otherwise, you can ask a classmate, friend, or family member to read it over. If your campus has a writing center, you might ask a tutor there to read and comment on your draft. (If you are unable to have someone else read over your draft, turn ahead to the Revision section on pp. 324–27, which gives guidelines for reading your own draft with a critical eye.)

In order to provide focused, helpful comments, your reader must know your intended audience and purpose. Briefly write out this information at the top of your draft:

Audience. Who are your readers? What do you assume they already know and think about your subject and its causes?

Purpose. What conclusions do you want readers to reach about your subject and its causes from reading this essay?

Reading with a
Critical Eye

Reading a draft critically means reading it more than once, first to get a general impression and then to analyze its basic features. Following are guidelines designed to be used by anyone reviewing an essay speculating about causes.

Reading for a First Impression.   Read the essay straight through. As you read, try to notice any words or passages that contribute to your first impression, weak ones as well as strong ones. A good way to highlight noteworthy language is to use the pointings system.

Pointings

- Draw a straight line under any words or images that seem especially effective: strong verbs, specific details, memorable phrases.
- Draw a wavy line under any words or images that sound flat, stale, or vague. Also put a wavy line under any words or phrases that you consider unnecessary or repetitious.
- Look for pairs or groups of sentences that you think should be combined. Put brackets [ ] around these sentences.
- Look for sentences that are garbled, overloaded, or awkward. Put parentheses ( ) around these sentences. Parenthesize any sentence that seems even slightly questionable; don't worry now about whether or not it is actually incorrect. The writer needs to know that you, as one reader, had even the slightest problem in following a sentence.

After you've finished reading the draft, write a few sentences giving your impressions. Did the essay hold your interest? What most surprised you? What did you like best? Did you find the causal argument convincing?

See pp. 312–13 to review the basic features.

Reading to Analyze. Now read to focus on the basic features of writing an essay speculating about causes.

Is the Subject Presented Well?

How well does the draft present the phenomenon or trend? Does it give enough information to make readers understand and care about the subject? Does it establish that the subject actually exists? If the subject is a trend, does it demonstrate a significant increase or decrease over time? Where might additional details, examples, facts, or statistics help?

Are the Causes and Evidence Convincing?

Look first at the proposed causes and list them. Do there seem to be too many? Too few? Do any seem either too obvious (not worth mentioning) or too obscure (remote in time or overly complicated)? Note any causes that seem merely to have been the immediate trigger of the subject or to have kept it going rather than starting it, or that are not sufficient in themselves to result in the subject. Are the limitations of these causes mentioned? If not, do they need to be?

Next, examine the evidence for each cause—anecdotes, facts, statistics, reference to authorities, and so on. Which evidence is most convincing? Which seems unconvincing? Where would more evidence or a different kind strengthen the argument? Might readers expect additional evidence that a cause existed before the phenomenon or trend began?

Check for errors in reasoning. Does the argument mistakenly assume that something that occurred before the beginning of the phenomenon or trend was therefore a cause? Are any of the proposed causes of the subject actually effects of it instead?

Are Possible Objections and Questions Acknowledged Adequately?

Look for places where readers' possible objections to or questions about the proposed causes are acknowledged. How well are they handled? Should any of them be taken more seriously? Can you see other ways of either accommodating or refuting any objections? Do any of the refutations attack or ridicule the persons raising the objections? Can you think of other questions or objections that might be raised?

Are Alternative Causes Acknowledged Adequately?

If causes proposed by others are acknowledged, are they presented fairly and adequately? Is it clear why they have been rejected? Do the refutations of them seem convincing? Do any of the refutations attack or ridicule the persons proposing the causes? Can you think of other plausible causes readers might propose?

Is the Organization Effective?

Given the expected readers, are the causes presented in an effective order? Can you think of a better order?

Reread the *beginning*. Will it engage the readers? Imagine at least one other way to open. Look for sections of the essay that could be moved to the beginning—an intriguing anecdote, for instance, or a surprising statistic.

Study the *ending*. Does the essay conclude decisively and memorably? Think of an alternative ending, possibly a passage that could be moved to the end.

What Final Thoughts Do You Have?

What is this draft's strongest part? What about it is most memorable? What is weak, most in need of further work?

REVISING AND EDITING

This section will help you to identify problems in your draft and to revise and edit to solve them.

Identifying Problems

To identify problems in your draft, you need to get an objective overview of it, analyze its basic features in detail, and assess any critical comments on it by other readers.

Getting an Overview.   Begin by considering your draft as a whole, trying to see it as objectively as you can. The following steps will help you do this:

Reread. If at all possible, put the draft aside for a day or two before rereading it. When you go back to it, start by reconsidering your audience and purpose. Then read the draft straight through, trying to see it as your intended readers will.

Outline. Make a scratch outline of the draft to chart its development. Words and phrases will do as long as they identify the subject and any important details, the proposed causes, and the supporting evidence, and any treatment of counterarguments and alternative causes.

Charting a Plan for Revision.   Once you have an overview of your draft, use the following chart to keep track of specific problems you need to solve. The left column lists the basic features of essays speculating about causes. As you analyze your draft and study any comments you've gotten from others, use the right column to note any problems with each feature.

Basic Features	*Problems to Solve*

Basic Features

Presentation of the subject

Presentation of causes and evidence

Acknowledgment of possible objections
and questions .

Acknowledgment of alternative causes

Organization

Analyzing the Basic Features of Your Draft.   Turn now to the questions for analyzing a draft on pp. 323–24. Using these questions as guidelines, identify problems in your draft, noting specific points on the chart above.

Studying Critical Comments.   Now review any comments you've received from other readers. Try not to react defensively to these comments. Rather, look at them as information that can help you to improve your draft. Add to the chart any problems readers have identified.

**Solving
the Problems**

You now need to figure out solutions to the problems in your draft and to carry them out. Basically, you have three ways of finding solutions: (1) review your invention and planning notes for other information and ideas; (2) do additional invention or research; and (3) look back at the readings in this chapter to see how other writers have solved similar problems. Following are suggestions to get you started on addressing some of the problems common to writing that speculates about causes.

Presentation of the Subject

- If your subject is less than clear or its existence is not clearly established, you may need to discuss it in greater detail. Consider adding anecdotes, statistics, citations from authorities, or other details. If your subject is a trend, be sure you show evidence of a significant increase or decrease over an extended period.

Presentation of Causes and Evidence

- If you've proposed what seem like too many causes, clarify the role each one plays: is it obvious? hidden? sufficient? necessary? immediate, remote, or perpetuating? (You need not use these labels.) In addition, you may need to emphasize one or two causes or delete some that seem too obvious, too obscure, or relatively minor.
- If you've proposed what seem like too few causes for a complex subject, try to think of other possible causes, especially hidden or remote ones. Do further research if necessary.
- If your evidence is skimpy or weak, look for more or stronger evidence to offer.

■ If you've made errors in reasoning, correct them. For example, if you cannot argue convincingly that a proposed cause not only occurred before the phenomenon or trend began but also contributed to it, you will have to delete that cause or at least present it more tentatively. If you have confused a cause with an effect, clarify their relationship.

Acknowledgment of Possible Objections and Questions

■ If any refutations of objections to your proposed causes don't seem convincing, try to provide stronger evidence. If you cannot do so, you may have to accommodate the objections.

■ If any refutations attack or ridicule people, revise to focus on the issue instead.

■ If readers have raised questions about your argument, you may need to provide more information about your subject or more evidence for proposed causes.

■ If readers have made any additional objections to your argument, consider whether you need to accommodate or refute them. That is, you can acknowledge their validity and incorporate them into your own argument, or you can give reasons and evidence why they are wrong.

Acknowledgment of Alternative Causes

■ If any refutations of alternative causes don't seem convincing, try to provide stronger evidence, or consider accommodating the alternative causes.

■ If any refutations attack or ridicule people, revise to focus on the issue.

■ If readers have suggested any causes you had not considered, analyze them to see whether they are plausible and should be integrated into your argument. If they seem implausible, decide if you want to mention and refute them.

Organization

■ If your readers found the argument disorganized, hard to follow, or uninteresting, consider reordering it—for example, arranging the causes in order of increasing rather than decreasing importance, grouping related causes together, or moving the refutations of alternative causes ahead of your own causes. Your plan may be more understandable if you forecast it at the beginning. Provide summaries, transitions, and other cues to keep readers on track.

■ If the beginning is dull, try opening with a surprising fact about your subject, emphasizing its puzzling nature, or telling an engaging anecdote about it.

■ If the ending is weak, try to make it more emphatic or interesting, perhaps by restating your main cause or causes, framing (referring to something mentioned at the beginning of the essay), or inviting readers to speculate further.

Editing and Proofreading

Although you have probably already corrected some obvious errors in your draft, now you should check it thoroughly for errors in grammar, mechanics, usage, punctuation, and spelling. You should also consider matters of style at this point. Studying a draft in separate passes—first for paragraphs, then for sentences, and finally for words—may help you recognize problems. After editing your draft to correct errors you find, proofread your final copy carefully for typos and other mistakes.

LEARNING FROM YOUR OWN WRITING PROCESS

Your instructor may ask you to analyze your own composing process. If so, begin by rereading your draft and revision. Focus on the way you analyzed causes, mentioning uncertainties you may still have about your analysis. Point to some specific changes you made in your revision, and explain why you made them. Indicate what you like best about your revision, as well as what still seems to need work.

A Writer at Work

ANALYZING CAUSES

For a writer planning an essay explaining causes, the most important part of invention and research is analyzing the causes. Because the causes are the heart of the argument, it takes rigorous analysis of each cause during the invention stage to compose a convincing argument.

Here we will look at the table of causes and analyses that Kim Dartnell developed for her essay on homeless women. (The revised version of her essay appears on pp. 308–10 in this chapter.)

Dartnell began this invention activity intending to write about the trend of homelessness in general, without considering men and women separately. Only after she had started to do some research did she realize that not only were there an increasing number of homeless women but that there had been several recent reports on the subject.

She began her analysis before going to the library, entering the first four causes on her table and completing a partial analysis. After she decided to focus on women, she added the other causes and completed the analysis. Examine her table of causes and analyses now. As you study her analysis, remember the questions she was asking herself about each cause.

TABLE OF CAUSES AND ANALYSES

Causes	Analyses
1. unemployment	Necessary cause for this trend. Could be sufficient, would affect everybody the same way, causes loss of income. Immediate cause that has grown in importance recently.
2. inflation	Relates to unemployment--as such, may be necessary but not sufficient by itself, especially affects unemployed and poor. Perpetuating, immediate, hidden cause.
3. alcoholism	Not necessary, not sufficient. Common conception is all homeless are drunks. Refute this cause since alcohol use hasn't risen in proportion to homelessness. Alcoholism is found at all levels of society, and so can't say that it causes homelessness. May be a result of unemployment or homelessness. No one really knows what causes alcoholism--or what it causes.
4. cutbacks in welfare	Necessary cause, could be sufficient. Affects women especially, causes loss of income, homelessness. Immediate cause--with no money, people forced to beg or move in with others.
5. abuse	There's always been abuse. Neither necessary nor sufficient. Affects women and children more. Research shows it's risen in proportion to homelessness (Stoner).
6. release from institutions	Many women being released from mental institutions. Necessary, may be sufficient. Immediate cause for the mentally ill. May be coupled with economic prob-

```
                              lems. Rebecca Smith is a good ex-
                              ample. Evidence shows this is in-
                              creasing as homelessness
                              increases. Couldn't be a result.
                              Perpetuates the trend. (Use
                              Stoner, Hombs and Snyder data.)
7. evictions                  Necessary and sufficient cause,
                              due to economic reasons. Immedi-
                              ate cause. Affects females more,
                              but also affects men. As evic-
                              tions increase, more homeless.
                              Perpetuating cause.
8. lack of housing            Necessary and sufficient, but re-
                              lated to economic reasons. Cheap
                              housing is harder to find due to
                              redevelopment and gentrification.
                              Renovation affects those already
                              without housing more. Could men-
                              tion Rebecca Smith. Perpetuating
                              cause.
```

Once she had analyzed all these possible causes, Dartnell could decide how to use them to make the most convincing explanation. She had to decide which causes to emphasize, which ones to combine, which ones to omit, and how to order the causes to produce the most effective argument. Also, she had to consider whether or not any of her causes should be refuted. Last, she had to try to find any potential objections to her arguments, which she would then have to answer. As it happened, she decided to use all of these causes except for alcoholism, which she would mention and refute.

She begins her essay with a discussion of abuse, thinking it was the one cause of homelessness that most affects women. She then discusses evictions and housing, treating each of these causes in a separate paragraph. Next she mentions—and refutes—alcoholism as a cause. Only then does she develop the cause for which she had the most evidence—deinstitutionalization. Finally, she combines several causes—unemployment, inflation, welfare cutbacks—into one paragraph on economic causes.

Certainly these causes might be presented in a different order—deinstitutionalization might be effectively placed either first or last, for example—but Dartnell's plan serves her topic well. By covering her topic so comprehensively and discussing it in a clear, logically organized manner, she presents a convincing argument.

■ For a history of science class, a student writes about the myth of the mad scientist in literature, focusing on two classic works: *Frankenstein* and *Dr. Jekyll and Mr. Hyde*. From her reading, she concludes that as a fictional figure, the mad scientist is socially isolated, obsessed with the desire for knowledge and power, and reckless of his own and others' safety. To demonstrate the accuracy of her analysis, the student quotes descriptions of the scientists in the two works and discusses their behavior.

■ A journalist writing about the American newspaper publisher William Randolph Hearst (1863–1951) decides to model his article on the classic film about a Hearstlike character, *Citizen Kane*. He organizes his piece around a series of imagined interviews with people who knew and worked for Hearst. Throughout the article, he draws parallels between Hearst and his film counterpart to support the point that Hearst is finally as unknowable as Kane.

■ In an introductory literature class, a student analyzes the structure and meaning of Edgar Allan Poe's poem "The Raven." As the thesis of her essay, she claims the poem's theme of inescapable despair is conveyed by its repetition of words and sounds as well as by its monotonous rhythm. As evidence for her conclusion, the student points to specific examples of repetition, alliteration, and rhythmic uniformity in the poem.

■ A freshman in a composition course explores the relationship between setting and action in William Faulkner's story "Dry September." He argues that the setting can be viewed metaphorically, as a projection of the characters' emotions. To support his point, he draws parallels between descriptions of the setting and descriptions of the characters.

■ For a political science course, a student writes a research paper arguing that the films Alfred Hitchcock made before, during, and after World War II are more complex politically than most people think. He claims that while Hitchcock's films appear to be pro-American, they actually call into question the assumption of American moral superiority. As evidence of the filmmaker's sense of the moral ambiguity in world politics, he points to the way that Hitchcock makes viewers regard the enemy with sympathy and understanding in films like *Foreign Correspondent* and *Notorious,* and how he shows that the American government has as little regard for human life as the other side in films like *North by Northwest* and *Torn Curtain.*

Interpreting Stories 10

■ After seeing Henrik Ibsen's *A Doll's House*, a student decides to write in her diary about the play's feminist themes. She is disturbed by the decision of the play's protagonist, Nora, to leave her home and children. If Nora felt she had never grown up or accepted responsibility, the student asks, why was she leaving her children? To answer this question, she attempts to examine Nora's character in light of the expectations Nora's husband and society in general have of women.

Interpreting what we read is an intuitive as well as an intellectual process. We engage a story with our feelings and values, our imaginations and minds. Not only do we examine its parts to see how they influence our understanding, but we also immerse ourselves in its language.

As we read works of literature and try to understand their meanings, we often see reflections of our own experience. We may recognize characters in a story and sympathize with them because we share their problems and motives, even if their situations differ radically from our own. From seeing our own lives mirrored in the stories of others, we can begin to appreciate how much we have in common. Thus, studying literature reinforces the bonds that hold people together.

Sharing our interpretations with others also forges shared understanding and connection. When we read and write about literature, we join an ongoing conversation, becoming members of what the literary critic Stanley Fish calls the "interpretive community." As members of this community, we exchange our views and share our insights. This process of inquiry and exchange enables us to clarify and deepen our understanding.

Writing an essay interpreting a story means that we must probe our initial response to the work, examining the story closely to find the basis for our thinking. This analysis of the story and of our reactions to it helps us to discover and create new meaning. But we do not write for ourselves alone, we also write for others. We present our interpretations as arguments, making a claim about the story's meaning and providing evidence to convince readers that our interpretation is plausible. Since stories can be interpreted in different ways, we do not seek to prove that we have discovered the one correct or final meaning. Instead, we try to convince our readers—instructors, classmates, or other students of literature—that we have analyzed the story carefully and thoughtfully and have found a reasonable way of understanding it.

In college, you will probably take literature courses in which you will be asked to write interpretive essays. Other courses also may require you to analyze works of literature, film, or other media, as the following assignments suggest:

■ *For a health course:* The media play a major role in educating people about difference. Analyze the portrayal of physical disability in a particular film or television program of your choice. (Some possibilities include the films *Rainman* and *Born on the Fourth of July* and the television programs *L.A. Law* and *Life Goes On.*)

■ *For a philosophy course:* If war is hell, why is it so often glorified? Analyze the attitude toward war represented in one of the following novels: *War and Peace, Gravity's Rainbow, The Red Badge of Courage, All Quiet on the Western Front.*

■ *For an American history course:* The study of history gives us many facts about the immigrant experience—when the great waves of immigration occurred, how many people came to America, where they came from, and where they settled. To fully understand the experience, however, you need the immigrant's perspective. Read one of the books on the reserve list in the library, and write an essay analyzing the writer's perspective.

■ *For a sociology course:* How are minorities represented in the media? Are they stereotyped or invisible, as some critics claim? To examine this situation, analyze one evening's worth of television programs. Pay attention not only to the programs themselves but to the commercials as well.

For Group Inquiry

Read "Araby" and then discuss it for fifteen minutes with two or three other students. Focus on this question: Why does the boy at the end of the story feel "anguish and anger"?

Then take some time to reflect on the nature of your discussion by considering the following questions:

■ Did the members of your group express different views? What led to the greatest disagreement?

■ Did you finally reach a consensus? How?

■ Roughly what proportion of your discussion was spent making general observations and sharing ideas and what proportion was spent rereading or analyzing particular passages?

■ On which aspects of the story did you focus most: what it means, what happens, what is said, what is thought or felt, the narrator?

■   ■   ■

James **J**oyce (1882–1941) was a native of Dublin, Ireland. "Araby," the short story that follows, appears in *Dubliners,* a collection of stories published in 1914. Along with Joyce's other stories and novels, "Araby" is considered a major work of modern literature.

In every detail, "Araby" reflects Dublin around the turn of the century. As a boy, Joyce lived on the North Richmond street of the opening sentence of the story and attended the Christian Brothers' School for a short while. In 1894, the year that his family moved to North Richmond Street, the *Grand Oriental Fete, Araby in Dublin* attracted many visitors, the young Joyce almost certainly among them. Araby was a bazaar with stalls selling cheap merchandise with an exotic Middle Eastern flavor. A special train, like the one mentioned in the story, carried visitors to the bazaar.

Ireland is a predominantly and devoutly Catholic country, and the story is filled with religious references. The girl in the story ("Mangan's sister") cannot go to Araby because she must attend a special week of communal living and prayer arranged by her convent school. (The girl is not a nun.) The narrator's family lives in a house formerly occupied by a priest, whose possessions the narrator mentions. The story ends in an epiphany, a sudden insight. In Christianity, the Feast of the Epiphany celebrates the revelation of Christ's divinity to the Magi, the three wise men who traveled to the scene of Christ's birth.

In the second paragraph, the narrator mentions three of the priest's books: *The Abbot* by Sir Walter Scott (1771–1832), a story about a poor boy in the court of Mary, Queen of Scots, who becomes important because he knows a valuable state secret; the *Devout Communicant*, a book of religious meditations; and *The Memoirs of Vidocq*, a sexually suggestive story about a criminal who becomes a detective.

Joyce chose the Dublin details with great care to create a story with significance far beyond its particular setting. It is this significance you will be inquiring into as you analyze the story and read what others have written about it.

ARABY
JAMES JOYCE

North Richmond Street, being blind, was a quiet street except at the hour when the Christian Brothers' School set the boys free. An uninhabited house of two storeys stood at the blind end, detached from its neighbours in a square ground. The other houses of the street, conscious of decent lives within them, gazed at one another with brown imperturbable faces. 1

The former tenant of our house, a priest, had died in the back drawing-room. Air, musty from having been long enclosed, hung in all the rooms, and the waste room behind the kitchen was littered with old useless papers. Among these I found a few paper-covered books, the pages of which were curled and damp: *The Abbot,* by Walter Scott, *The Devout Communicant* and *The Memoirs of Vidocq.* I liked the last best because its leaves were yellow. The wild garden behind the house contained a central apple-tree and a few straggling bushes under one of which I found the late tenant's rusty bicycle-pump. He had been a very charitable priest; in his will he had left all his money to institutions and the furniture of his house to his sister. 2

When the short days of winter came dusk fell before we had well eaten our   3
dinners. When we met in the street the houses had grown sombre. The space of
sky above us was the colour of ever-changing violet and towards it the lamps of the
street lifted their feeble lanterns. The cold air stung us and we played till our bodies
glowed. Our shouts echoed in the silent street. The career of our play brought us
through the dark muddy lanes behind the houses where we ran the gauntlet of the
rough tribes from the cottages, to the back doors of the dark dripping gardens
where odours arose from the ashpits, to the dark odorous stables where a coachman
smoothed and combed the horse or shook music from the buckled harness. When
we returned to the street light from the kitchen windows had filled the areas. If my
uncle was seen turning the corner we hid in the shadow until we had seen him
safely housed. Or if Mangan's sister came out on the doorstep to call her brother in
to his tea we watched her from our shadow peer up and down the street. We waited
to see whether she would remain or go in and, if she remained, we left our shadow
and walked up to Mangan's steps resignedly. She was waiting for us, her figure
defined by the light from the half-opened door. Her brother always teased her before
he obeyed and I stood by the railings looking at her. Her dress swung as she moved
her body and the soft rope of her hair tossed from side to side.

Every morning I lay on the floor in the front parlour watching her door. The blind   4
was pulled down to within an inch of the sash so that I could not be seen. When
she came out on the doorstep my heart leaped. I ran to the hall, seized my books
and followed her. I kept her brown figure always in my eye and, when we came
near the point at which our ways diverged, I quickened my pace and passed her.
This happened morning after morning. I had never spoken to her, except for a few
casual words, and yet her name was like a summons to all my foolish blood.

Her image accompanied me even in places the most hostile to romance. On   5
Saturday evenings when my aunt went marketing I had to go to carry some of the
parcels. We walked through the flaring streets, jostled by drunken men and bar-
gaining women, amid the curses of labourers, the shrill litanies of shop-boys who
stood on guard by the barrels of pigs' cheeks, the nasal chanting of street-singers,
who sang a *come-all-you* about O'Donovan Rossa, or a ballad about the troubles in
our native land. These noises converged in a single sensation of life for me: I imagined
that I bore my chalice safely through a throng of foes. Her name sprang to my lips
at moments in strange prayers and praises which I myself did not understand. My
eyes were often full of tears (I could not tell why) and at times a flood from my heart
seemed to pour itself out into my bosom. I thought little of the future. I did not
know whether I would ever speak to her or not or, if I spoke to her, how I could
tell her of my confused adoration. But my body was like a harp and her words and
gestures were like fingers running upon the wires.

One evening I went into the back drawing-room in which the priest had died. It   6
was a dark rainy evening and there was no sound in the house. Through one of the
broken panes I heard the rain impinge upon the earth, the fine incessant needles of
water playing in the sodden beds. Some distant lamp or lighted window gleamed
below me. I was thankful that I could see so little. All my senses seemed to desire
to veil themselves and, feeling that I was about to slip from them, I pressed the
palms of my hands together until they trembled, murmuring: ''O love! O love!''
many times.

At last she spoke to me. When she addressed the first words to me I was so   7
confused that I did not know what to answer. She asked me was I going to *Araby*.

I forgot whether I answered yes or no. It would be a splendid bazaar, she said she would love to go.

"And why can't you?" I asked.   8

While she spoke she turned a silver bracelet round and round her wrist. She 9 could not go, she said, because there would be a retreat that week in her convent. Her brother and two other boys were fighting for their caps and I was alone at the railings. She held one of the spikes, bowing her head towards me. The light from the lamp opposite our door caught the white curve of her neck, lit up her hair that rested there and, falling, lit up the hand upon the railing. It fell over one side of her dress and caught the white border of a petticoat, just visible as she stood at ease.

"It's well for you," she said.   10

"If I go," I said, "I will bring you something."   11

What innumerable follies laid waste my waking and sleeping thoughts after that 12 evening! I wished to annihilate the tedious intervening days. I chafed against the work of school. At night in my bedroom and by day in the classroom her image came between me and the page I strove to read. The syllables of the word *Araby* were called to me through the silence in which my soul luxuriated and cast an Eastern enchantment over me. I asked for leave to go to the bazaar on Saturday night. My aunt was surprised and hoped it was not some Freemason affair. I answered few questions in class. I watched my master's face pass from amiability to sternness; he hoped I was not beginning to idle. I could not call my wandering thoughts together. I had hardly any patience with the serious work of life which, now that it stood between me and my desire, seemed to me child's play, ugly monotonous child's play.

On Saturday morning I reminded my uncle that I wished to go to the bazaar in 13 the evening. He was fussing at the hallstand, looking for the hatbrush, and answered me curtly:

"Yes, boy, I know."   14

As he was in the hall I could not go into the front parlour and lie at the window. 15 I left the house in bad humour and walked slowly towards the school. The air was pitilessly raw and already my heart misgave me.

When I came home to dinner my uncle had not yet been home. Still it was early. 16 I sat staring at the clock for some time and, when its ticking began to irritate me, I left the room. I mounted the staircase and gained the upper part of the house. The high cold empty gloomy rooms liberated me and I went from room to room singing. From the front window I saw my companions playing below in the street. Their cries reached me weakened and indistinct and, leaning my forehead against the cool glass, I looked over at the dark house where she lived. I may have stood there for an hour, seeing nothing but the brown-clad figure cast by my imagination, touched discreetly by the lamplight at the curved neck, at the hand upon the railings and at the border below the dress.

When I came downstairs again I found Mrs. Mercer sitting at the fire. She was 17 an old garrulous woman, a pawnbroker's widow, who collected used stamps for some pious purpose. I had to endure the gossip of the tea-table. The meal was prolonged beyond an hour and still my uncle did not come. Mrs. Mercer stood up to go: she was sorry she couldn't wait any longer, but it was after eight o'clock and she did not like to be out late, as the night air was bad for her. When she had gone I began to walk up and down the room, clenching my fists. My aunt said:

"I'm afraid you may put off your bazaar for this night of Our Lord."   18

At nine o'clock I heard my uncle's latchkey in the halldoor. I heard him talking   19
to himself and heard the hallstand rocking when it had received the weight of his
overcoat. I could interpret these signs. When he was midway through his dinner I
asked him to give me the money to go to the bazaar. He had forgotten.

"The people are in bed and after their first sleep now," he said.   20

I did not smile. My aunt said to him energetically: 21

"Can't you give him the money and let him go? You've kept him late enough   22
as it is."

My uncle said he was very sorry he had forgotten. He said he believed in the old   23
saying: "All work and no play makes Jack a dull boy." He asked me where I was
going and, when I had told him a second time he asked me did I know *The Arab's
Farewell to his Steed.* When I left the kitchen he was about to recite the opening
lines of the piece to my aunt.

I held a florin tightly in my hand as I strode down Buckingham Street towards   24
the station. The sight of the streets thronged with buyers and glaring with gas
recalled to me the purpose of my journey. I took my seat in a third-class carriage of
a deserted train. After an intolerable delay the train moved out of the station slowly.
It crept onward among ruinous houses and over the twinkling river. At Westland
Row Station a crowd of people pressed to the carriage doors; but the porters moved
them back, saying that it was a special train for the bazaar. I remained alone in the
bare carriage. In a few minutes the train drew up beside an improvised wooden
platform. I passed out on to the road and saw by the lighted dial of a clock that it
was ten minutes to ten. In front of me was a large building which displayed the
magical name.

I could not find any sixpenny entrance and, fearing that the bazaar would be   25
closed, I passed in quickly through a turnstile, handing a shilling to a weary-looking
man. I found myself in a big hall girdled at half its height by a gallery. Nearly all the
stalls were closed and the greater part of the hall was in darkness. I recognised a
silence like that which pervades a church after a service. I walked into the centre of
the bazaar timidly. A few people were gathered about the stalls which were still
open. Before a curtain, over which the words *Café Chantant* were written in coloured
lamps, two men were counting money on a salver. I listened to the fall of the coins.

Remembering with difficulty why I had come I went over to one of the stalls and   26
examined porcelain vases and flowered tea-sets. At the door of the stall a young
lady was talking and laughing with two young gentlemen. I remarked their English
accents and listened vaguely to their conversation.

"O, I never said such a thing!"   27

"O, but you did!"

"O, but I didn't!"

"Didn't she say that?"

"Yes. I heard her."

"O, there's a . . . fib!"

Observing me the young lady came over and asked me did I wish to buy anything.   28
The tone of her voice was not encouraging; she seemed to have spoken to me out
of a sense of duty. I looked humbly at the great jars that stood like eastern guards
at either side of the dark entrance to the stall and murmured:

"No, thank you."   29

The young lady changed the position of one of the vases and went back to the 30
two young men. They began to talk of the same subject. Once or twice the young
lady glanced at me over her shoulder.

I lingered before her stall, though I knew my stay was useless, to make my interest 31
in her wares seem the more real. Then I turned away slowly and walked down the
middle of the bazaar. I allowed the two pennies to fall against the sixpence in my
pocket. I heard a voice call from one end of the gallery that the light was out. The
upper part of the hall was now completely dark.

Gazing up into the darkness I saw myself as a creature driven and derided by 32
vanity; and my eyes burned with anguish and anger.

APPROACHES TO INTERPRETING "ARABY"

Every reader of "Araby" finds it puzzling. Events seem strange and exaggerated. We wonder about the importance to the narrator of the Araby bazaar and of his relationship to Mangan's sister. Most of all, we wonder what to make of the narrator's final insight. For over seventy-five years, readers have been interpreting this story. To work out your own interpretation, you will need to find a way into the story. The following approaches present some of the ways experienced readers have discovered meanings in puzzling stories. Each approach invites you to reread the story, looking at it from a new perspective, annotating what you notice, and then making an inventory of your annotations in order to discover patterns, relations, and insights. These approaches will help you interpret "Araby" and can also be used with other stories, as shown in the Guide to Writing in this chapter.

Puzzling Statements

Readers often approach a story by starting from one statement in the story that surprises or puzzles them. Following are three statements that readers of "Araby" have found surprising or puzzling and that eventually led them to understand the story better:

> Her image accompanied me even in places the most hostile to romance.
>
> I bore my chalice safely through a throng of foes.
>
> Gazing up into the darkness I saw myself as a creature driven and derided by vanity; and my eyes burned with anguish and anger.

To investigate an intriguing statement, begin by looking closely at its content. Then look closely at the context of the statement: what is happening at that point in the story, what do the key words mean, and what attitudes and values are associated with them? Then reread the entire story, annotating words, images, events, and ideas that help you understand the importance of the statement. Inventory your annotations in order to probe further.

Patterns of Words and Images	Another way to interpret stories is through specific patterns of words and images. Such a pattern may lead a patient reader to a larger understanding of the story. Here are three of the many patterns of words and images you may discover in "Araby": religion, water, blindness and vision. Reread the story, annotating evidence of such a pattern. Inventory your annotations to try to discover what this particular pattern discloses about the meaning of the story.
Character	Another useful approach is to analyze one or more characters closely in terms of their attributes and development in the course of the story. Reread the story, annotating information about each character you have chosen (physical characteristics, attitudes, values), key events in which the character is directly or indirectly involved, and important relationships or interactions with other characters. Your goal is to understand the characters you are studying as fully as possible, piecing together all the clues Joyce offers and making inferences from this evidence. It is important not only to notice what characters say about themselves and one another, but also to make your own judgments about their behavior and ways of thinking.
Point of View	Point of view refers to how the story is told, who tells it, and how much trust the reader can have in the narrator. Examining a story's point of view can be a productive first step in deciding what the story might mean. "Araby" is written in the first person, with the narrator telling his own story. Reread the story, annotating it with the following questions in mind. Your purpose is to probe the implications of the story being told by this narrator (rather than by some other possible narrator).

Who exactly is the narrator in "Araby"?

How does the narrator reveal his values and beliefs?

Are the events being narrated as they happen, soon after, or years later? How can you tell?

How well does the narrator seem to understand his experience? What are his perceptive insights? His blind spots?

In light of the revelation the narrator has at the end, can you find evidence of hindsight or of irony in the way he tells the story?

Can you trust the narrator? Why or why not?

Ironies or Contradictions	Frequently, readers begin their analysis by noticing ironies or contradictions in the story. Something is ironic when it appears to say one thing but actually says something else. Here are three ironies readers have found in "Araby":

1. Mrs. Mercer appears to be religious and to serve the church, but everything about her suggests money rather than spirit: her name, Mercer, means dealer in merchandise; her husband was a pawnbroker; even her

church work involves acquisitiveness, collecting cancelled stamps, presumably to sell. She embodies the contradiction between the spiritual and the material that is evident throughout the story.

2. The boy appears to worship Mangan's sister as a religious object, yet he describes her in sensual, not spiritual, images. These images point to a contradiction between the way the boy feels and the way he allows himself to think, a contradiction between illusion and reality.

3. The boy likes the dead priest's book *The Memoirs of Vidocq* not because of its content but because of its appearance. Ironically, the book is about the criminal and sexual adventures of a notorious impostor. This irony points up the idea of disguise and suggests that below surface respectability lurks something criminal or antisocial.

Some other irony or contradiction might strike you as you read. Reread the story with one of these ironies or contradictions in mind. Annotate any evidence you find of it elsewhere in the story—in events; in what the main character thinks, says, or does; in how characters relate to one another and to their environment.

Literary Motifs

"Araby" is remarkable in that many of the most familiar literary motifs, or themes, are reflected in it. Select one of the following motifs, or any other you happen to notice, and then reread the story carefully, annotating it as a story of that type.

- a journey or quest for something of value, like self-knowledge
- a conflict or disparity between appearance and reality
- an individual in relation to society
- a coming of age or initiation into new experience
- a conflict between spiritual and material values
- relations between generations, genders, groups—children and parents, men and women, blacks and whites, employees and owners
- the double, in which two or more characters represent alternative realities, perhaps one good and one evil or one desired and one denied (consider Mangan's sister and the "young lady" at the bazaar or the narrator and the "young gentlemen" as doubles)

Setting

The physical setting of particular scenes can often be a productive starting point for interpreting a story. In "Araby" the narrator mentions many details of setting, which create an unmistakable mood. Annotating and inventorying these details may lead you to a full understanding of the influence of setting on the characters' lives and the narrator's motives, feelings, and final insight.

You might examine one of these scenes closely—the Saturday evening streets, the drawing room of the narrator's house, the train the narrator rides to the bazaar, the bazaar. Look for connections between this scene and any other parts of the story, noticing especially how this scene and its events compare or contrast with others in the story. Annotate what you notice. Your purpose is to understand the significance of the scene in the story and to let this understanding lead you to a fuller understanding of the story as a whole.

Structure

Exploring structure or plot can lead to unexpected insights about the story. "Araby" is a straightforward narrative encompassing a few weeks in the narrator's life, moving through winter days of growing adoration for Mangan's sister to the time of the Araby bazaar. You could outline the story's narrative to identify conventional features of narrative structure such as foreshadowing, points of suspense, climax, and ending or denouement.

You could also look for structural relationships beyond the conventional narrative pattern. For example, you could see the story as organized into stages and annotate to discover what is revealed by the events in each stage and how they relate to one another. Or you might look for structural patterns—repeated or contrasting events such as the narrator's conversation with Mangan's sister and the conversation between the shop attendants at the bazaar.

Historical and Social Context

Every story reflects a historical, social, and economic context specific to its time and place. You can deepen your understanding of the story by learning about these conditions from outside sources and by looking at the story's events and details for references to them.

"Araby," for example, subtly refers to the long-term political, religious, and economic tensions between the Irish and the British, who ruled all of Ireland until 1921. It also reflects a religious and patriarchal tradition of viewing a woman as either angel or whore. Read the story with one of these contexts in mind, annotating and inventorying what you find. Your aim is to discover how the story's particular context informs its meaning.

Readings

Cleanth Brooks and Robert Penn Warren wrote this essay on "Araby" for *Understanding Fiction,* a classic introduction to literary interpretation. As Brooks and Warren demonstrate, interpretations consist of two essential elements: general ideas about the story and particular details from the story. The key to constructing an interpretation is establishing clear and compelling relationships between the general ideas and the particular details. As you read this essay, notice Brooks and Warren's general ideas about the story. Also ask yourself how they tie these ideas together. What conclusion do these ideas lead to? How convincing do you find this interpretation?

THE CHALICE BEARER
CLEANTH BROOKS
AND ROBERT PENN
WARREN

On what may be called the simplest level "Araby" is a story of a boy's disap-   1
pointment. The description of the street in which he lives, the information about the dead priest and the priest's abandoned belongings, the relations with the aunt and uncle—all of these items, which occupy so much space, seem to come very naturally into the story. That is, they may be justified individually in the story on realistic grounds. But when one considers the fact that such material constitutes the bulk of the story, one is led to observe that, if such items *merely* serve as "setting" and atmosphere . . . , the story is obviously overloaded with nonfunctional material. Obviously, for any reader except the most casual, these items do have a function. If we find in what way these apparently irrelevant items in "Araby" are related to each other and to the disappointment of the boy, we shall have defined the theme of the story.

What, then, is the relation of the boy's disappointment to such matters as the   2
belongings of the dead priest, the fact that he stands apart talking to the girl while his friends are quarreling over the cap, the gossip over the tea table, the uncle's lateness, and so on? One thing that is immediately suggested by the mention of these things is the boy's growing sense of isolation, the lack of sympathy between him and his friends, teachers, and family. He says, "I imagined that I bore my chalice safely through a throng of foes." For instance, when the uncle is standing in the hall, the boy could not go into the front parlor and lie at the window; or at school his ordinary occupations began to seem "ugly monotonous child's play." But this sense of isolation has, also, moments which are almost triumphant, as for example is implied when the porters at the station wave the crowds back, "saying that it was a special train for the bazaar" and was not for them. The boy is left alone in the bare carriage, but he is going to "Araby," which name involves, as it were, the notion of romantic and exotic fulfillment. The metaphor of the chalice implies the same kind of precious secret triumph. It is not only the ordinary surrounding world, however, from which he is cruelly or triumphantly isolated. He is also isolated from the girl herself. He talks to her only once, and then is so confused that he does not know how to answer her. But the present which he hopes to bring her from Araby would somehow serve as a means of communicating his feelings to her, a symbol for their relationship in the midst of the inimical world.

In the last scene at the bazaar, there is a systematic, though subtle, preparation   3
for the final realization on the part of the boy. There is the "improvised wooden platform" in contrast with the "magical name" displayed above the building. Inside, most of the stalls are closed. The young lady and young men who talk together are important in the preparation. They pay the boy no mind, except in so far as the young lady is compelled by her position as clerk to ask him what he wants. But her tone is not "encouraging." She, too, belongs to the inimical world. But she, also, belongs to a world into which he is trying to penetrate: she and her admirers are on terms of easy intimacy—an intimacy in contrast to his relation to Mangan's sister. It is an exotic, rich world into which he cannot penetrate; he can only look "humbly at the great jars that stood like eastern guards at either side of the dark entrance to

the stall. . . ." But, ironically, the young lady and her admirers, far from realizing that they are on holy, guarded ground, indulge in a trivial, easy banter, which seems to defile and cheapen the secret world from which the boy is barred. How do we know this? It is not stated, but the contrast between the conversation of the young lady and her admirers, and the tone of the sentence quoted just above indicates such an interpretation.

This scene, then, helps to point up and particularize the general sense of isolation 4 suggested by the earlier descriptive materials, and thereby to prepare for the last sentence of the story, in which, under the sudden darkness of the cheap and barnlike bazaar, the boy sees himself as "a creature driven and derided by vanity," while his eyes burn with anguish and anger.

We have seen how the apparently casual incidents and items of description do 5 function in the story to build up the boy's sense of intolerable isolation. But this is only part of the function of this material. The careful reader will have noticed how many references, direct or indirect, there are to religion and the ritual of the church. The atmosphere of the story is saturated with such references. We have the dead priest, the Christian Brothers' School, the aunt's hope that the bazaar is not "some Freemason affair," her reference, when the uncle has been delayed, to "this night of Our Lord." These references are all obvious enough. At one level, these references merely indicate the type of community in which the impressionable boy is growing up. But there are other, less obvious, references, which relate more intimately to the boy's experience. Even the cries of the shop boys for him are "shrill litanies." He imagines that he bears a "chalice safely through a throng of foes." When he is alone the name of Mangan's sister springs to his lips "in strange prayers and praises." For this reason, when he speaks of his "confused adoration," we see that the love of the girl takes on, for him, something of the nature of a mystic, religious experience. The use of the very word *confused* hints of the fact that romantic love and religious love are mixed up in his mind.

It has been said that the boy is isolated from a world which seems ignorant of, 6 and even hostile to, the experience of his love. In a sense he knows that his aunt and uncle are good and kind, but they do not understand him. He had once found satisfaction in the society of his companions and in his school work, but he has become impatient with both. But there is also a sense in which he accepts his isolation and is even proud of it. The world not only does not understand his secret but would cheapen and contaminate it. The metaphor of the chalice borne through a throng of foes, supported as it is by the body of the story, suggests a sort of consecration like that of the religious devotee. The implications of the references to religion, then, help define the boy's attitude and indicate why, for him, so much is staked upon the journey to the bazaar. It is interesting to note, therefore, that the first overt indication of his disillusionment and disappointment is expressed in a metaphor involving a church: "Nearly all the stalls were closed and the greater part of the hall was in darkness. I recognized a silence like that which pervades a church after a service. . . . Two men were counting money on a salver. I listened to the fall of the coins." So, it would seem, here we have the idea that the contamination of the world has invaded the very temple of love. (The question may arise as to whether this is not reading too much into the passage. Perhaps it is. But whatever interpretation is to be made of the particular incident, it is by just such suggestion and implication that closely wrought stories, such as this one, are controlled by the author and embody their fundamental meaning.)

Is this a sentimental story? It is an adolescent love affair, about "calf love," a 7
subject which usually is not to be taken seriously and is often the cause of amusement. The boy of the story is obviously investing casual incidents with a meaning
which they do not deserve; and himself admits, in the end, that he has fallen into
self-deception. How does the author avoid the charge that he has taken the matter
over-seriously?

The answer to this question would involve a consideration of the point of view 8
from which the story is told. It is told by the hero himself, but after a long lapse of
time, after he has reached maturity. This fact, it is true, is not stated in the story,
but the style itself is not that of an adolescent boy. It is a formal and complicated
style, rich, as has already been observed, in subtle implications. In other words, the
man is looking back upon the boy, detachedly and judicially. For instance, the boy,
in the throes of the experience, would never have said of himself: "I had never
spoken to her, except for a few casual words, and yet her name was like a summons
to all my foolish blood." The man knows, as it were, that the behavior of the boy
was, in a sense, foolish. The emotions of the boy are confused, but the person telling
the story, the boy grown up, is not confused. He has unraveled the confusion long
after, knows that it existed and why it existed.

If the man has unraveled the confusions of the boy, why is the event still signifi- 9
cant to him? Is he merely dwelling on the pathos of adolescent experience? It seems,
rather, that he sees in the event, as he looks back on it, a kind of parable of a
problem which has run through later experience. The discrepancy between the real
and the ideal scarcely exists for the child, but it is a constant problem, in all sorts of
terms, for the adult. This story is about a boy's first confrontation of that problem—
that is, about his growing up. The man may have made adjustments to this problem,
and may have worked out certain provisional solutions, but looking back, he still
recognizes it as a problem, and an important one. The sense of isolation and disillusion which, in the boy's experience, may seem to spring from a trivial situation,
becomes not less, but more aggravated and fundamental in the adult's experience.
So, the story is not merely an account of a stage in the process of growing up—it
does not merely represent a clinical interest in the psychology of growing up—but
is a symbolic rendering of a central conflict in mature experience.

For Discussion

In the final paragraph of their essay, Brooks and Warren write: "The discrepancy between the real and the ideal scarcely exists for the child, but it is
a constant problem, in all sorts of terms, for the adult." Discuss this idea. In
what contexts have you noticed that reality falls short of the ideal? To what
extent is this awareness a problem for you? Do you think you've become
increasingly aware of this problem as you've gotten older? Why do you think
Brooks and Warren connect becoming an adult to seeing this discrepancy as
a problem and recognizing that it can never be adequately solved?

For Analysis

*For more about
classifying, see pp.
452–59.*

1. In paragraph 2, Brooks and Warren introduce the idea that the boy feels
isolated. To develop this idea, they use the writing strategy of division and
classification. How do they categorize his feeling of isolation? How do these
distinctions contribute to your understanding of this idea?

2. Brooks and Warren argue that the boy's sense of isolation is particularized in the details used to set the scene at the bazaar. They use the writing

*For more about
comparison and contrast,
as writing strategies see
Chapter 17.*

strategy of comparison and contrast to reveal a pattern in the scene's details. What pattern do they find? How does this pattern illustrate their idea about the boy's feelings of isolation?

3. In paragraphs 5 and 6, Brooks and Warren turn their attention to another pattern of details—language referring to religion and church ritual. What ideas do they connect to these details? How do they relate these ideas about the story's religious imagery to their idea about the boy's sense of isolation? How important do you think it is, in general, to relate different ideas in an essay of interpretation?

4. In the last two paragraphs, Brooks and Warren discuss the point of view from which "Araby" is told in order to argue that it is not just a "sentimental story" about a boy's growing up. Why do you think they challenge this interpretation? What does *sentimental* mean? In what ways does the story seem sentimental to you? How does it avoid sentimentality?

**For Your
Own Writing**

In discussing the point of view of "Araby," Brooks and Warren note that the story "is told by the hero himself, but after a long lapse of time . . . looking back upon the boy, detachedly and judicially" (paragraph 8). Reread "Araby," paying close attention to the narrator's voice and tone. How do you think the narrator regards his younger self?

If you were to write an essay on this subject, what might you want to say? How do you think the particular way the story is told influences your interpretation of it? Imagine the story being told from another point of view—for example, by the boy as he's going through the experience, by Mangan's sister, or by Mangan. How do you think the story would be different if it were told from one of these perspectives?

Commentary

Brooks and Warren seem to have relied on four approaches: character and character change, setting, patterns of words and images, and point of view. These approaches allow them to draw a conclusion about the meaning of "Araby" that serves as the thesis of their essay. The thesis, stated explicitly in the last sentence, claims that the story is "a symbolic rendering of a central conflict in mature experience," the conflict between reality and illusion.

Though Brooks and Warren present their thesis at the end of the essay, other writers about literature, as you will see, put their thesis near the beginning. Whether it appears in the first paragraph or in the last, the thesis represents the writer's conclusion. The thesis is not your initial idea about the story but the result of a process of inquiry that leads to the discovery of new meanings, even in familiar works of literature. As Brooks and Warren show us, it is not possible to know in advance what discoveries you will make or what connections you will find from using different approaches.

Brooks and Warren begin their analysis with two approaches: character and setting. Looking at the boy leads them to the idea that the story is about the boy's state of mind—specifically, his disappointment. Another approach—the setting—reveals many interesting details, but as Brooks and Warren explain, these seem to be unrelated to each other and to the idea of the boy's disappointment. For them, the key to interpreting "Araby," to defining the story's theme, is forging connections between these apparently unrelated ideas and details.

By considering the boy's disappointment in the context of the other characters and the setting, Brooks and Warren come up with the idea that the boy experiences a "growing sense of isolation." This sense of isolation, they note, has a positive as well as a negative side. His estrangement from others is painful; he feels "cruelly" isolated. But he also feels "triumphant" in being separate from and somehow raised above his ordinary surroundings. This contrast between the ordinary and extraordinary, or actual and ideal, provides the basis for Brooks and Warren's thesis about reality and illusion.

To this analysis of character and setting, Brooks and Warren add two more approaches: patterns of words and images, and point of view. In the story's religious references they find a pattern that suggests a distinction between romantic love and religious love. The boy, they argue, confuses these two kinds of love. By making his love for Mangan's sister a religious experience, the boy attempts to protect it, like a chalice, from everything that would "cheapen and contaminate it"—from the real, material world.

By thinking about the story's point of view, Brooks and Warren are able to put their various discoveries into perspective. They observe that the story is told by the boy after he has grown up. This hindsight allows the narrator to understand the significance of the boy's experience: "The emotions of the boy are confused, but the person telling the story, the boy grown up, is not confused. He has unraveled the confusion long after, knows that it existed and why it existed." This insight enables Brooks and Warren to recognize that "Araby" is not simply about a particular experience but presents a universal theme, the continuing conflict between the real and the ideal.

From this essay on "Araby," you can see how different approaches to interpreting a story might be productive. Brooks and Warren make use of several approaches. The writer of the next essay only one. As you plan and write an essay interpreting a story, you'll need to decide which approach or approaches to use in developing your own interpretation.

■

David Ratinov wrote this essay for his freshman composition class. Like most readers of "Araby," Ratinov wanted to understand what the narrator's final statement meant and what motivated it. Rereading and annotating the story, he focused on the narrator's relationships with the other characters and on how he uses evidence from these relationships to argue that isolation and hypocrisy are the central ideas of the story.

**FROM INNOCENCE
TO INSIGHT:
"ARABY" AS AN
INITIATION STORY**
DAVID RATINOV

"Araby" tells the story of an adolescent boy's initiation into adulthood. The story 1
is narrated by a mature man reflecting upon his adolescence and the events that
forced him to cross over the threshold from childhood innocence to a more mature
understanding of the realities of the human condition. The minor characters play a
pivotal role in this initiation process. The boy's infatuation with the girl ultimately
ends in disillusionment, and Joyce uses the specific example of the boy's disillusionment with love to act as a metaphor for disillusionment with life itself. From the
beginning the boy deludes himself about his relationship with Mangan's sister.
Through this self-delusion, he increasingly resembles the adult characters, and later,
at Araby, he realizes the parallel between his own self-delusion and the hypocrisy
and vanity of the adult world.

From the beginning, the boy's infatuation with Mangan's sister draws him away 2
from childhood toward adulthood. He breaks his ties with his childhood friends and
luxuriates in his isolation. He can think of nothing but his love for her: "From the
front window I saw my companions playing below in the street. Their cries reached
me weakened and indistinct and, leaning my forehead against the cool glass, I looked
over at the dark house where she lived." The friends' cries are weak and indistinct
because they are distant emotionally as well as spatially. He imagines he carries his
love as if it were a sacred object, a chalice: "Her image accompanied me even in
places the most hostile to romance. . . . I imagined that I bore my chalice safely
through a throng of foes." Even in the active, distracting marketplace, he is able to
retain this image of his pure love. But his love is not pure.

Although he worships Mangan's sister as a religious object, his lust for her is 3
undeniable. He idolizes her as if she were the Virgin Mary: "her figure defined by
the half-opened door. . . . The light from the lamp opposite our door caught the
white curve of her neck, lit up her hair that rested there, and falling, lit up the hand
upon the railing." Yet even this image is sensual with the halo of light accentuating
"the white curve of her neck." The language makes obvious that his attraction is
physical rather than spiritual: "Her dress swung as she moved her body and the soft
rope of her hair tossed from side to side." His desire for her is strong and undeniable:
"her name was like a summons to all my foolish blood"; "my body was like a harp
and her words and gestures were like fingers running upon the wires." But in order
to justify his love, to make it socially acceptable, he deludes himself into thinking
his love *is* pure. He is being hypocritical, although at this point he does not

obvio...isy is characteristic of the adults in this story. The priest is by far the most 4
romanti...der. What is a man of the cloth doing with books like *The Abbott* (a
imply that ...nd *The Memoirs of Vidocq* (a sexually suggestive tale)? These books
when he die... ...double life. Moreover, the fact that he had money to give away
Mercer appear... ...Her... that he was far from saintly. Similarly, at first glance Mrs.
materialistic. ...
(presumably to sell ...ligious, but upon closer inquiry it seems that she too is
name, Mercer, identifi...k — collecting used stamps for some "pious purpose"
a pawnbroker, a profess...h) — associates her with money and profit. Even her
money, she pretends to b... ...ealer in merchandise. In addition, her husband is
Mercer is hypocritical. ...church frowns upon. Despite being linked to
...spectable. Therefore, like the priest, Mrs.

The uncle may not be hypocritical, but as the boy's only living male relative he 5
is a failure as a role model and the epitome of vanity. He is a self-centered old man
who cannot handle responsibility. When the boy reminds him on Saturday morning
about the bazaar, the uncle brushes him off, devoting all his attention to his own
appearance. After being out all afternoon the uncle returns home at 9:00, talking
to himself. He rocks the hallstand when hanging up his overcoat. These details
suggest that he is drunk. "I could interpret these signs" indicates that this behavior
is typical of his uncle. The uncle is the only character in the story the boy relies upon,
but the uncle fails him. Only after the aunt persuades him does the uncle give the
boy the money he promised. From the priest, Mrs. Mercer, and his uncle, the boy
learns some fundamental truths about the world, but it is only after his visit to Araby
that he is able to recognize what he has learned.

Araby to the adolescent represents excitement, a chance to prove the purity of 6
his love and, more abstractly, his hope; however, Araby fulfills none of these expectations. Instead, the boy finds himself in utter disillusionment and despair. Araby
is anything but exciting. The trip there is dreary, and uneventful, lonely and intolerably
slow—not the magical journey he had expected. When he arrives, Araby itself is
nearly completely dark and in the process of closing. With his excitement stunted,
he can barely remember why he came (to prove the purity of his love by buying a
gift for Mangan's sister). The trip is a failure. He does nothing to prove himself or
his faithfulness, and as a result his illusion that his love for her is pure begins to
break down.

The young lady selling porcelain and her gentlemen friends act as catalysts, 7
causing the boy to recognize the truth of his love for Mangan's sister. Their conversation is flirtatious—a silly lovers' game that the boy recognizes as resembling his
own conversation with Mangan's sister. He concludes that his love for her is no
different than the two gentlemen's "love" for this "lady." Neither love is pure. He
too had only been playing a game, flirting with a girl and pretending that it was
something else and that he was someone else.

His disillusionment with love is then extended to life in general. Seeing the last 8
rays of hope fading from the top floors of Araby, the boy cries: "I saw myself as a
creature driven and derided by vanity; and my eyes burned with anguish and anger."
At last he makes the connection—by deluding himself, he has been hypocritical and
vain like the adults in his life. Before these realizations he believed that he was driven
by something of value (such as purity of love), but now he realizes that his quest
has been in vain because honesty, truth, and purity are only childish illusions and he
can never return to the innocence of childhood.

For Discussion   Ratinov appears to agree with Brooks and Warren that the boy confuses
several different kinds of love: sexual, romantic, and religious. Both essays
also seem to assume that this confusion about love is somehow symptomatic
of adolescence. What distinguishes these different kinds of love from one
another? In what ways does the boy's experience in "Araby" seem to you to
be typical of adolescent experience with which you're familiar? To what
extent does the boy's confusion seem specific to his cultural situation (growing up Catholic in Ireland early in the century) and not necessarily representative of adolescence in general?

For Analysis

For a discussion of ways to integrate quotations into your writing, see pages 528–29.

1.   In paragraphs 2 and 3, Ratinov quotes repeatedly from the story in order to supply the textual evidence essential to his argument. Examine each quotation to see how it contributes to his argument and how he integrates it into his own text. Then compare Ratinov's use of quotation with Brooks and Warren's. What conclusions can you make about how literary critics use quotations from the texts they are interpreting?

2.   In paragraph 7, Ratinov focuses on what happens at the bazaar, particularly the conversation the boy overhears between the shop girl and the two men. Look back at this conversation in paragraph 27 of "Araby." How convincing is Ratinov's interpretation of this conversation? What does it lead you to understand about the significance of the conversation for the boy?

3.   In the last paragraph, Ratinov ties together his two main ideas: that the boy's love for Mangan's sister is an illusion, and that the boy's adult role models are either hypocritical or vain. How effectively does he connect these ideas? How could the connection be made even clearer?

4.   Minor characters sometimes play a major role in conveying meaning. Analyzing Mrs. Mercer, for example, enables Ratinov to gain insight into the theme of hypocrisy. Turn to the Writer at Work section on pages 363–66, and focus particularly on his efforts to understand what Mrs. Mercer stands for in the context of the story. Read his annotations of paragraph 17 (where Mrs. Mercer appears) as well as the inventory of his annotations and his written analysis. Would you add anything to his annotations or analysis? What else might Ratinov have wanted readers to think of Mrs. Mercer?

For Your Own Writing

On page 366, you will find an anthology of three short stories: "Everyday Use," by Alice Walker, "The Use of Force" by William Carlos Williams, and "The Smallest Woman in the World," by Clarice Lispector. Skim these stories in order to choose the one that seems most intriguing to you, and read it more closely. Then select one approach to interpreting stories—surprising statement, words and images, character, point of view, irony or contradiction, literary motif, setting, structure, or context—that you think would be most productive for analyzing this particular story. Why do you think it would be productive?

Commentary

Like Brooks and Warren, David Ratinov presents an interpretation of "Araby." His audience, purpose, and argumentative strategy, however, differ markedly from theirs. Brooks and Warren wrote their piece for a book introducing literary interpretation to college students. They therefore sought to demonstrate how students might go about analyzing a story like "Araby." Ratinov, on the other hand, wrote his essay for his English teacher and classmates. His aim was to show that his interpretation of the story is plausible, carefully reasoned, and well-supported.

Their respective argumentative strategies reflect the special constraints of writing for a particular audience and purpose. Brooks and Warren arrange their argument inductively, ending with their thesis. This arrangement allows them to show how an interpretation develops from discoveries made by taking various approaches to the work. Ratinov arranges his argument deductively, beginning with the thesis. Such a strategy allows him to lay out his argument so that readers can judge his reasoning and evidence.

Ratinov sets forth his thesis in the opening sentence and elaborates it extensively in the first paragraph, which introduces the key terms and main ideas in his argument. The key terms in Ratinov's thesis are *initiation, self-delusion, hypocrisy,* and *vanity.* The clarity and coherence of an argument depends largely on its key terms, and terms that are vague or ambiguous lead to confusing writing. Good writers, therefore, carefully define and explain their terms in the context of the story they are analyzing.

The last two sentences of Ratinov's introductory paragraph forecast the main points of the essay and the order in which they are presented: that the boy deludes himself about his infatuation with Mangan's sister (paragraphs 2 and 3); that the adult characters are hypocritical (paragraphs 4 and 5); and finally that the boy's self-delusion parallels the adults' hypocrisy (paragraphs 6 to 8). In addition, each succeeding paragraph begins with a topic sentence that announces the point developed in that paragraph. This careful, systematic presentation of the thesis, forecast, and topic sentences ensures that the argument will be easy for readers to follow.

For a discussion of strategies for cueing your readers, see Chapter 12.

PURPOSE AND AUDIENCE

When you write an essay interpreting a literary work, your purpose is to present an idea about what the work means. This idea is your interpretation. Since your readers may favor other interpretations, your task is to convince them that yours is reasonable or plausible and that it reflects thoughtful analysis. Even if it were possible for all serious readers to agree about a general theme for a work, such readers might focus on quite diverse aspects of the work, just as the writers in this chapter do. A story, such as this one, can be interpreted in many different ways. A community of readers—your composition class or all English majors on your campus or all literary scholars who have written about "Araby"—accepts this diversity and enjoys it.

There is, then, no single or best interpretation. There are only interesting or plausible ideas, intriguing ideas presented convincingly. Consequently, in writing an essay interpreting a story you are not trying to win a contest or prove that only your idea should be taken seriously. Instead, you are trying to share your idea and to develop a reasonable and well-supported argument for it. Your readers will not immediately assume that they disagree with what you are about to say. Quite the contrary, as members of your community of readers, they will be anticipating a new intriguing idea about the story, one that may lead them to a new understanding and appreciation for it.

Your readers do not expect you to come up with a startling insight into the story, though they will be pleased if you do. What readers do expect is a logical argument supported by an interesting "reading" of the story. If you have been discussing the same story (like "Araby") or a group of stories by the same author (like Joyce's *Dubliners,* in which "Araby" appears), they may even find your thesis predictable or similar to their own. But a predictable thesis can be argued in an interesting way, showing readers new ways to look at the story. Your readers will be disappointed only if you propose an unclear or unfocused thesis with unworkable terms, propose a thesis that can be challenged by evidence in the text, argue illogically, neglect to include numerous examples and quotations from the text, or fail to provide the necessary cues to keep readers on track. Readers will be especially disappointed if they think you are summarizing the story rather than developing a particular idea about it.

BASIC FEATURES OF LITERARY INTERPRETATION

Writing about literature generally has only two key ingredients: an interpretation of the work and a convincing argument based on textual evidence for that interpretation.

The Writer's Interpretation

At the center of a literary interpretation lies the writer's analysis of the story's meaning. This interpretation provides the main focus for the essay. Without such a central idea, the essay would be just an accumulation of ideas about the story rather than a coherent analysis of it.

In literary interpretation, this main idea is usually given directly in a thesis statement. A focal point, the thesis brings the parts of the essay into perspective, helping readers to understand how the subordinate ideas relate to one another as well as how they combine to illuminate the story.

For example, Ratinov states his thesis in his opening paragraph: " 'Araby' tells the story of an adolescent boy's initiation into adulthood. . . . Through this self-delusion, he increasingly resembles the adult characters, and later, at Araby, he realizes the parallel between his own self-delusion and the hypocrisy and vanity of the adult world." The key terms in Ratinov's interpretation—*initiation, self-delusion, hypocrisy,* and *vanity*—are clear, appropriate, and workable. Brooks and Warren begin with a general statement about the story ("On what may be called the simplest level 'Araby' is a story of a boy's disappointment") that they explore in the essay. Their thesis, however, is not explicitly stated until the final sentence: "So, the story is not merely an account of a stage in the process of growing up . . . but is a symbolic rendering of a central conflict in mature experience."

Although skilled literary critics may want their analysis to account for subtleties in the work, they do not want their readers to have difficulty understanding their interpretation. No matter how complex their ideas, they strive to make their writing direct and clear. Therefore, they usually alert readers early to the points they will be making, giving readers a context in which to understand their analysis of the story. Ratinov, for example, forecasts in the last two sentences of the opening paragraph the points he develops in the essay: "From the beginning, the boy deludes himself about his relationship with Mangan's sister. Through this self-delusion, he increasingly resembles the adult characters, and later, at Araby, he realizes the parallel between his own self-delusion and the hypocrisy and vanity of the 'adult world.' "

A Convincing Argument

In addition to stating their interpretation, writers must try to present a convincing argument for it. They may sometimes assume that readers are familiar with the story, but never can they expect readers to see it as they do or automatically to understand—let alone accept—their interpretation.

Writers argue for their interpretation not so much to convince readers to adopt it but rather to convince them that it makes sense. They must demonstrate to readers how they "read" the story, pointing out specific details and explaining what they think these details mean.

The primary source of evidence for literary interpretation, then, is the work itself. Writers quote the story, describe it, summarize it, and paraphrase it. They do more than just refer to a specific passage, however: they explain the meaning of the passage in light of their thesis. Brooks and Warren, for example, paraphrase, summarize, and quote from the story throughout their essay. This textual evidence alternates with their serious and energetic explanation of its significance to their thesis. In paragraph 2 alone, in which they explore the idea of the boy's sense of isolation, they quote from the story three times and also summarize several events.

It is also possible to find ideas and evidence in support of an interpretation from outside sources—other critics, biographical information about the author, historical facts. Not only can such evidence provide insight into the work, but it may also increase the writer's authority and lend the argument credibility. Occasionally, writers may refer to other critics to build their own case not on, but in opposition to, alternative interpretations. Disagreements over interpretations are productive and healthy, leading to clearer insights and deeper understanding of the work.

Guide to Writing

THE WRITING ASSIGNMENT

Write an essay interpreting a work of short fiction. Your aim is not primarily to convince readers to adopt your view, but to convince them that it is a reasonable one based on a thoughtful and imaginative reading of the story.

INVENTION AND RESEARCH

At this point you should choose a short story, analyze it carefully, develop a thesis, and find evidence in the story for that thesis.

Choosing a Story

Your instructor may have asked you to write about a particular story. If this is the case, turn now to the next section, Analyzing the Story.

If you must choose a story on your own, consider—and read—several stories before deciding on one to write about. Choose a story that impresses, surprises, or puzzles you, one that excites your interest and imagination. You should not expect to understand the story completely on the first reading; just be sure to select a story that you want to study closely.

Analyzing the Story

To discover meaning in a story, you need a way of analyzing the story that will lead to ideas about it. There are various different approaches you can try, including several that are listed below. Most of them will lead you to read looking for some specific element in the story. Reading with an eye for a certain element can help you to discover patterns in the story and lead you to insights about the story's meaning. Following are nine approaches for interpreting a story. You won't need to use all of them, but most writers try several different approaches.

A Catalog of Approaches

Puzzling Statements. Select a surprising or puzzling statement that especially interests you, and begin by looking closely at the context in which it appears. Then reread, annotating to explore the significance of the statement throughout the story.

Patterns of Words and Images. To find patterns of related words or images, reread the story, watching for unusual words; words that suggest a particular feeling or mood; words identifying visual details (shape, color, texture), sounds, smells; words that form patterns of repetition, contradiction, or tension; images (simile, metaphor) and patterns of images. When you have identified a pattern, annotate the text carefully in order to discover what the pattern discloses about the story.

Character. Examine the personality and state of mind of one or more characters. Annotate the story, noticing the character's name; way of talking; actions; reported thoughts; values, beliefs, motives, and goals; relations with other characters; differences from and similarities to other characters. Also notice any contradictions among the character's thoughts, words, and actions and any changes in or development of the character from beginning to end of the story. Ask yourself what brought about the change and in what way it is significant.

Point of View. Analyze how the story is told, who tells it, and how much this narrator knows. Consider how you learn about the narrator (whether through description, action, dialogue, statements that reveal attitudes and opinions, or other characters' statements); whether the narrator is a character or just a disembodied voice; whether the narrator knows everything, including characters' thought and feelings, or has only limited knowledge; whether the narrator can be trusted; how the work would be changed with a different narrator. Your goal is to decide just who the narrator is and how the story is shaped by this narrator.

Ironies or Contradictions. Identify ironies or contradictions in events; in what characters think, say, or do; and in ways characters relate to one another and to their environment.

Literary Motifs. Analyze the story as an example of a conventional literary motif, such as coming of age or initiation, a journey or quest, the disparity between appearance and reality, or the double. Or you may identify motifs associated with traditional literary genres such as the fairy tale, fable, detective story, or gothic romance.

Setting. Consider the physical setting of the story: where and when the events take place; whether the setting or scene changes; how different scenes are related; how the writer presents the setting (features and objects singled out for attention or naming; particular colors, shapes, sizes, textures, sounds, smells); what mood the setting creates; whether the setting causes, reflects, or contradicts the characters' actions, values, or moods; how a different setting might alter the story's meaning.

Structure. Analyze the story in terms of its arrangement: the opening, foreshadowing, points of suspense or tension, the climax, the ending. Look for repetition, framing, unresolved conflicts, as well as stages in the story's development (repeated or opposite events).

Historical and Social Context. Analyze the story for specific historical, political, economic, social, or religious references. Stories are written and set in a particular time and place. If you know anything about the conditions in which a story was written or the period in which it takes place or the cultural and historical background of it, you can gain a valuable perspective on the story. You can also ask questions like the following: Who has the money, power, privilege, or status? Do the political, economic, and social conditions trivialize or ennoble human activities and relationships? Do people seem to be trapped in gender or economic roles? Do institutions appear to support or to thwart human needs and dreams?

Using These Approaches to Analyze a Story. Whichever approaches you follow in analyzing the story, you may find it helpful to read (and reread) in the following way:

1. *Read.* First read the story for pleasure, diversion, and insight—for the same reasons you always read stories and novels or watch movies.

2. *Approach.* Look over the list of approaches that follows to find one that interests you. Since you will want to try at least two or three approaches, this first choice is not crucial. Review the approach carefully so that you fully understand its possibilities. To ensure that your annotating and inventorying (Steps 3 and 4) are focused and productive, you should refer continually to the suggestions listed in the approach.

3. *Annotate.* Reread the story with a pencil in hand, annotating anything you notice that is at all relevant to the approach you are taking. To annotate, mark on the text itself and write in the margins. Look up any unfamiliar words and phrases, making a note of their meanings and connotations.

You will find an example of annotating in the Writer at Work section at the end of this chapter.

Annotating is most productive when it is "layered up" over several readings. Reread the story more than once, using a different approach and adding a new layer of annotations each time. Annotate freely. Annotating leads to the discovery of unexpected connections and patterns that you cannot predict while you are doing it, so you should not limit yourself in this early stage of inquiry.

4. *Inventory.* Look over your annotations and inventory them by listing related items in groups on a sheet of paper and then naming the groupings. Try out several different ways of grouping your annotations. By organizing and reorganizing your annotations in this manner, you will begin to discover different patterns of meanings in the story.

You will find examples of inventorying in the Writer at Work Section at the end of this chapter and in Chapter 11.

5. *Write.* Analyze your inventory by writing at least a page about the connections and patterns you have discovered. This writing will record what you have learned and may also lead you to further discoveries. Answer this question as you write: What does this inventory reveal about the story?

6. *Reflect.* Think about what you have learned about the story by using this approach. You may have clarified an idea you had earlier or arrived at a new understanding. Sometimes, approaching a story raises more questions than answers. Write down your conclusions—ideas you can assert confidently as well as questions you cannot yet answer. These reflections may help lead you to a thesis about the story.

Finding a Thesis

In approaching the story from several different perspectives, you have begun the process of finding a focus for further exploration. Your aim now is to consider the possible focuses you have discovered and to formulate a tentative thesis, a hypothesis that will guide your further analysis of the story.

Listing Possible Focuses.   Begin by reviewing the reflections you wrote as you completed each approach. Some will be in the form of ideas, while others will be questions. List the ones that most interest you, those that you would like to explore further. Add to this list any ideas that you now have. Consider how your ideas relate to one another. What generalizations do they lead you to make about the story?

Exploring Your Ideas.   Choose what seems to you now to be the most intriguing idea from your list and write about it for five minutes. Focus your exploratory writing on these points:

- What will this idea enable me to say about the story's meaning and significance?
- What in the story will I be able to point to as evidence to support and develop my idea?

If at the end of five minutes, you are not satisfied with your choice—satisfied that it allows you to say something new and worthwhile about the story—try exploring another of your ideas. It may take a few tries before you settle on a focus worth taking.

Writing a Tentative Thesis Statement.   When you decide on a focus, put it in the form of a thesis statement. Formulating a thesis, even one that you know will undergo change, will help you to clarify your idea. Pay special attention to the key terms you use. These stand for important concepts you will need to explain and illustrate.

It may help to recall David Ratinov's thesis (the key terms are italicized): " 'Araby' tells the story of an adolescent boy's *initiation* into adulthood [by which] he realizes the parallel between his own *self-delusion* and the *hypocrisy* and *vanity* of the adult world."

For Group Inquiry

At this point you may find it helpful to get together with two or three other students and get some response to one another's thesis statements. One by one, read your thesis aloud, and ask the other members to say what the thesis leads them to expect will be argued in the essay. For example, if you were a member of a group with David Ratinov, you might have said it led you to expect his essay to demonstrate the following ideas: (1) that the boy is self-deluded, (2) that the adults are hypocritical or vain, and (3) that the boy ultimately realizes he is like the adults.

Finding Evidence

Having settled on a tentative thesis, you now need to marshal evidence to support it. You will find this evidence in the story and in your annotations, inventories, and exploratory writings about the inventories. After identifying evidence, you can begin to organize and evaluate it.

With your thesis in mind, search for evidence that will support it. Note and annotate everything you can find that seems relevant to your thesis—

dialogue, events, descriptive details, key words, images. If you find evidence that seems to contradict your thesis, do not ignore it. Instead, let it lead you to clarify and revise your thesis.

Organizing Your Evidence.   The evidence you've discovered already may be organized in a certain way. You may now, however, see different ways to organize it. Or you may have identified new evidence that you overlooked in your earlier work. Your goal is only to begin grouping evidence, rather than to organize it precisely, since you cannot predict the exact sequence of your argument at this point.

Evaluating Your Evidence.   Determine whether you have sufficient evidence to support your thesis and develop a convincing argument for your particular readers. Also test the fit between your ideas and the available evidence. If you have trouble supporting your thesis or fitting evidence to it logically, you will need to revise your thesis or try out a different one.

Researching Other Interpretations

Interpretations of the story you have chosen may have been published by others in articles and books that you can find in the library. Of course, you need not read theirs for assurance that yours is appropriate, nor can their interpretations substitute for your own. After you have examined the story closely and have devised a thesis, however, your instructor may encourage you to search out other interpretations to help you clarify and develop your ideas. Reading what others have written is like entering a conversation about the story. You may agree or disagree, find your own ideas supported or challenged, discover new insights, or learn nothing at all.

If you do research, be sure to cite any ideas from other critics that you use in your essay. You might acknowledge interpretations supporting your own or refute those that contradict yours. You could mention different but complementary interpretations. Be careful, however, to keep the focus on your own interpretive argument. Do not write a report surveying what others think about the story; write an essay arguing for your own interpretation. Keep careful notes of your research, including direct quotations you may want to use. Keep a record of your sources, including page numbers.

See Chapter 21 for discussion of using sources.

PLANNING AND DRAFTING

You now need to review your notes, set goals, and make an outline before writing a first draft.

Seeing What You Have

Review your notes. If you wish or need to, reread the story. As you review what you have discovered about it, ask yourself these questions:

■   Can I express my thesis more clearly?

- What are my reasons for holding this thesis?
- Can my evidence be interpreted in some other way?
- Have I overlooked any important evidence?
- Have I glossed over or ignored any contradictions or problems?

Decide now whether or not you need to do further research. Postpone starting to draft if you find problems that still need to be worked out.

Setting Goals

Before you start to draft, consider the special demands of literary interpretation and of the story you are interpreting. Let the following questions guide you in setting goals for what you want to achieve in your essay and how you can meet these demands:

Your Readers

- Are my readers likely to know this story? If not, how much of the plot should I relate? If so, how can I lead them to see the story as I do?
- How can I organize the essay so that my readers will find it easy to follow? What cues can I provide about my organization and sequence? How can I integrate quotations?
- What questions or objections might my readers raise about my interpretation?

The Beginning

- Must I begin by describing the work for readers who have not read it?
- Should I pose an interpretive problem about the work and ask a question about it, as Brooks and Warren do?
- Should I state my thesis and forecast my plan, as Ratinov does?

The Argument

- Is my thesis clear enough to act as the focus for all parts of my argument? Have I used key terms that forecast ideas I will develop in my argument?
- How can my argument be considered authoritative and at the same time thoughtful and reasonable?
- Is the organization of the main parts of my argument logical? Have I arranged the evidence so that each new bit of evidence builds on earlier ones, making the argument convincing as a whole?
- How much textual evidence must I include in order for my argument to seem informed and convincing?
- How much evidence from outside sources should I include to support my interpretation?
- Should I acknowledge readers' possible objections to my argument or differing interpretations? If so, how can I accommodate or refute these arguments?

The Ending

- Should I repeat my key terms, as the writers in this chapter do?
- Should I restate my thesis, as Ratinov does?
- Should I end with a provocative question suggested by my analysis of the story?

Outlining

Each of these kinds of outlines is discussed in Chapter 11.

At this point you should try to develop a plan for your draft. You may compose a formal outline, a simple list of key points, or a clustering diagram. Whichever method you choose, remember that an outline is only a tentative plan; if you have other thoughts while drafting, try them out.

Drafting

You might want to review the general advice on drafting on pp. 9–11.

If some time has gone by since you last read the story, reread it quickly. Then begin to draft, keeping in mind the two goals of all literary analysis: presenting your interpretation and supporting that interpretation with textual evidence. Try to be as direct as you can. Explain your ideas fully. Make the relations between the thesis, the points you use to develop it, and the supporting evidence explicit for readers. Remember that they will have different ways of understanding the passages you refer to. Show them how you are using specific evidence from the work to make your own point about it.

GETTING CRITICAL COMMENTS

Now is the time to try to get a good critical reading. All writers find it helpful to have someone else read and comment on their drafts, and your instructor may schedule such a reading as part of your coursework. Otherwise, you can ask a classmate, friend, or family member to read it over. If your campus has a writing center, you might ask a tutor there to read and comment on your draft. The guidelines that follow are designed to be used by *anyone* reviewing an essay interpreting a story. (If you are unable to have someone else read over your draft, turn ahead to the Revision section on pp. 360–62, which gives guidelines for reading your own draft with a critical eye.)

In order to provide focused, helpful comments, your reader must know your intended audience and purpose. The reader must also have read the story you were writing about. Attach a copy of the story to your draft if you think your reader may not already have one, and briefly write out answers to the following questions at the top of your draft:

Audience. What do you expect your readers will think about the story?

Purpose. What do you want your readers to learn about the story from reading your essay?

Reading with a Critical Eye

Reading an essay critically means reading it more than once, first to get a general impression and then to analyze its basic features.

Reading for a First Impression.   Read first to grasp the interpretation. As you read, notice any passages that are particularly well-written and convincing as well as any that seem especially weak. A good way of highlighting note-worthy language is to use the pointings system.

Pointings

- Draw a straight line under words or images that impress you as especially effective: strong verbs, specific details, memorable phrases, striking images.

- Draw a wavy line under any words or images that seem flat, stale, or vague. Also put the wavy line under any words or phrases that you consider unnecessary or repetitious.

- Look for pairs or groups of sentences that you think should be combined. Put brackets [ ] around these sentences.

- Look for sentences that are garbled, overloaded, or awkward. Put paren-theses ( ) around these sentences. Put them around any sentence that seems even slightly questionable; don't worry about whether or not you're certain about your judgment. The writer needs to know that you, as one reader, had even the slightest problem understanding a sentence.

After you've finished reading the draft, briefly write out your impressions. Summarize what you think the essay says about the story, and indicate whether you think this interpretation makes sense. If your view of the story differs, you might indicate briefly how you interpret it.

See pp. 350–51 for an explanation of the basic features.

Reading to Analyze.   Now reread to focus on the basic features of interpretive writing.

Is the Thesis Clear and Effective?

Identify the thesis statement. Do any of the key terms seem unclear or un-workable? Number the ideas expressed in the thesis and then skim the rest of the essay, identifying by number where each idea is developed. Note any ideas that do not reappear or are only identified vaguely. Also note any important ideas that should be added to the thesis.

Is the Argument Developed and Supported Adequately?

Take each point in turn. Note where a particular idea could be developed further. Also note where evidence from the story is lacking or where the evidence could be more explicitly connected to the idea it is supposed to illustrate.

Is the Argument Logical?

Does any idea seem to contradict the thesis or other ideas? Note where logical connections between ideas could be strengthened. Also note any places where there are gaps in the logic, where connecting ideas appear to be left out.

Is the Organization Effective?

Note any places where the argument is confusing or hard to follow. Point out places where the order of the evidence weakens the argument because new ideas do not build on previously stated ones. Look again at the *beginning* and note whether it adequately anticipates the rest of the essay. Look at the *ending* and note whether it is too abrupt or raises too many new ideas.

What Final Thoughts Do You Have?

What do you find most satisfying about this draft? Which part needs the most work?

REVISING AND EDITING

This section will help you to identify problems in your draft and to revise and edit to solve them.

Identifying Problems

To identify problems in your draft, you need to get an overview of it, analyze its basic features, and study any critical comments you've received from other readers.

Getting an Overview.   First consider the draft as a whole, trying to see it objectively. Two simple steps will help you begin to look somewhat objectively at your own writing:

Reread. If at all possible, put the draft aside for a day or two before rereading it. When you do, start by reconsidering your purpose. Then read the draft straight through, trying to see it as your intended readers will.

Outline. Make a scratch outline to get an overview of the essay's development. This outline can be sketchy—words and phrases instead of complete sentences—but it should identify the basic features as they appear.

Charting a Plan for Revision.   You may wish to make a chart like the one below to keep track of any problems you need to solve. The left-hand column lists the basic features of writing interpretations of stories. As you analyze your draft and study any comments you've gotten, note the problems you want to solve in the right-hand column next to the appropriate feature.

Basic Features   *Problems to Solve*

Thesis

Argument

Organization

Analyzing the Basic Features of Your Draft.   Turn now to the questions for analyzing a draft on pp. 359–60. Using these questions as guidelines, identify problems in your draft. Note anything you need to solve on the preceding chart.

Studying Critical Comments.   Review any comments you've received from other readers, and add to the chart any points that need attention. Try not to react too defensively to these comments; by letting you see how others respond to your draft, they provide invaluable information about how you might improve it.

Solving the Problems

Having identified problems, you now need to figure out solutions and carry them out. Basically, you have three ways of finding solutions: (1) review your invention and planning notes for additional information and ideas; (2) do further invention to answer questions your readers raised; and (3) look back at the readings in this chapter to see how other writers have solved similar problems.

Following are suggestions to get you started solving some of the problems common to writing interpretations of stories. For now, focus on solving those problems identified on your chart. Avoid tinkering with sentence-level issues now; that will come later when you edit.

The Thesis

- If the thesis statement is hard to identify, make it more explicit. Be sure that you have announced your main idea somewhere in the essay. Even writers who place the thesis at the end, like Brooks and Warren, announce it in general terms at the beginning ("On what may be called the simplest level 'Araby' is a story of a boy's disappointment").

- If the ideas in the thesis don't match the points developed in the argument, revise the thesis or consider adding, deleting, or revising something in the argument.

The Argument

- If an idea seems undeveloped, try discussing it more—break it into subordinate ideas and discuss them, say what it tells about the story as a whole, compare or contrast it with related ideas. Also consider providing a theoretical framework to help explain the idea—for example, discussing character development by using psychoanalytical terms or discussing the power relationships among characters by using Marxist terms.

- If evidence seems lacking, add more detail by quoting, paraphrasing, or summarizing specific parts of the story. Also consider using other kinds of evidence, such as information about the story's historical or cultural context.

- If the connection between an idea and evidence seems vague, clarify it by explaining why you think the evidence illustrates or supports the idea. Remember that what seems obvious to you may be obscure to your readers. Don't just quote from the story. Explain how you interpret the quotation, which words seem significant, and what they suggest about the point you're making.

- If there are contradictions in the argument or the evidence, you may need to rethink, reorganize, or rewrite whole sections of your essay. Consider whether you can eliminate apparent contradictions by explaining more clearly.how your ideas relate to one another.

- If there are gaps in the logic or missing connections, fill them in. Remember that your readers cannot follow your train of thought unless you lay it out for them.

The Organization

- If the essay is hard to follow, you may need to provide more explicit cues, such as topic sentences for paragraphs, transitions between paragraphs and sentences, or brief forecasts and summaries to let readers know where they're going and where they've been.

- If the beginning doesn't adequately prepare readers, you may need to revise it to better forecast your ideas.

- If the ending seems abrupt, you may need to tie all the strands of the essay together, reiterate your thesis, or discuss its implications.

Editing and Proofreading

As you've been working on your draft so far, you've probably corrected some obvious errors, but grammar and style have not been a priority. Now is the time to check carefully for errors in usage, punctuation, and mechanics, and also to consider matters of style. You may find that studying your draft in separate passes—first for paragraphs, then for sentences, and finally for words—will help you to recognize any problems.

Once you have edited your draft and produced a final copy, proofread it carefully to be sure there are no typos, misspellings, or other mistakes.

LEARNING FROM YOUR OWN WRITING PROCESS

Your instructor may ask you to write about what you learned from writing this essay. If so, consider the following questions:

- How did my thesis evolve as I planned and drafted the essay?
- How did I go about analyzing the story?
- What problems, if any, did I have finding evidence to support the thesis?

- Why did I decide to organize the essay as I did?
- What specific revisions, if any, did I make in the draft, and what were my reasons for making these changes?

A Writer at Work

ANNOTATING AND INVENTORYING A LITERARY WORK

Annotating and taking inventory of annotations are basic tools for understanding and interpreting short stories. Used with various traditional approaches to analyzing stories, they provide an instructive strategy of critical reading, inquiry, and interpretation. Here you can see a portion of the results of one student's annotation and inventory of "Araby." The student is David Ratinov, whose essay appears earlier in this chapter on pages 341–43.

Ratinov chose two approaches to analyzing "Araby": (1) character and character change, and (2) literary motifs. Following the instructions in the Guide to Writing, he reread the story and annotated it from these two perspectives, took inventory to discover connections and ideas among his annotations, wrote briefly about his discoveries, and then wrote several generalizations asserting his ideas about the story. One of these generalizations led to the thesis you see in his essay.

Here are Ratinov's annotations on paragraphs 13 through 23. Notice the diversity of his annotations. On the text itself, he underlines key words, circles words to be defined, and connects related words and ideas. In the margin, he defines words, makes comments, poses questions, and expresses tentative insights, personal reactions, and judgments.

2nd mention of uncle fussing—vain? irritable? rude	On Saturday morning I reminded my <u>uncle</u> that I wished to go to the bazaar in the evening. He was fussing at the hallstand, looking for the hatbrush, and answered me ⟨curtly⟩.
always unkind to the boy? uncle's effect on the boy	"Yes, boy, I know."
	As he was in the hall I could not go into the front parlour and lie at the window. I left the house in <u>bad humour</u> and walked slowly towards the school. The air was <u>pitilessly raw</u> and already my <u>heart misgave me</u>.
uncle will be late sudden change in mood: *big* contrast	When I came home to dinner my uncle had not yet been home. Still it was early. I <u>sat staring</u> at the clock for some time and, when its ticking began to <u>irritate</u> me, I
liberated from uncle?	left the room. I mounted the staircase and gained the upper part of the house. The high cold empty gloomy rooms liberated me and I went from room to room singing.
isolated from friends	From the front window I saw my companions playing below in the street. Their cries reached me weakened and indistinct and, leaning my forehead against the cool glass, I looked over at the dark house where she lived. I may have stood there for

romantic, even sensual

merchandise
talkative
hypocritically religious
boy doesn't seem to like
or trust the adults

uncle and Mercer both try
to give a false impression
aunt seems pious too

boy knows uncle is drunk
boy's fears are justified
excuses

aunt to the rescue

hypocritical
what a bore!
boy determined to go to
bazaar to buy girl a gift

an hour, seeing nothing but the brown-clad figure cast by my imagination, touched discreetly by the lamplight at the curved neck, at the hand upon the railings and at the border below the dress.

When I came downstairs again I found Mrs. Mercer sitting at the fire. She was an old garrulous woman, a pawnbroker's widow, who collected used stamps for some pious purpose. I had to endure the gossip of the tea-table. The meal was prolonged beyond an hour and still my uncle did not come. Mrs. Mercer stood up to go: she was sorry she couldn't wait any longer, but it was after eight o'clock and she did not like to be out late, as the night air was bad for her. When she had gone I began to walk up and down the room, clenching my fists. My aunt said:

"I'm afraid you may put off your bazaar for this night of Our Lord."

At nine o'clock I heard my uncle's latchkey in the halldoor. I heard him talking to himself and heard the hallstand rocking when it had received the weight of his overcoat. I could interpret these signs. When he was midway through his dinner I asked him to give me the money to go to the bazaar. He had forgotten.

"The people are in bed and after their first sleep now," he said.

I did not smile. My aunt said to him energetically:

"Can't you give him the money and let him go? You've kept him late enough as it is."

My uncle said he was very sorry he had forgotten. He said he believed in the old saying: "All work and no play makes Jack a dull boy." He asked me where I was going and, when I had told him a second time he asked me did I know *The Arab's Farewell to his Steed*. When I left the kitchen he was about to recite the opening lines of the piece to my aunt.

Annotating the story to analyze the boy's character, Ravinov finds himself paying a lot of attention to the boy's relations with other characters. Taking inventory of these annotations for the entire story, he notices how negatively the narrator portrays the priest, Mrs. Mercer, and the uncle. He decides that what these characters have in common is hypocrisy. This notion would become a key term in his thesis and a major idea in his essay. In his essay, of course, he would have to prove with textual evidence that all these minor characters are hypocrites. In addition, he would have to be sure that no textual evidence challenged this idea.

Here Ratinov tries to organize his textual and marginal annotations in paragraphs 13 through 23 under the idea of hypocrisy:

```
adult hypocrisy
Mrs. Mercer
   name means "merchandise"
   pious--a religious hypocrite
   widow of pawnbroker--makes money by lending money to
      poor people for their possessions
   collected stamps--to sell for a church charity?
   gossip--talk about others behind their backs
Uncle
   a banker or manager
```

```
brushes hat--obsessive about appearance
fussy, vain, irritable, curt
boy distrusts him, hides from him, seems to have no
    real relationship with him*
lives in a big house only partly furnished and heated
drinks, often drunk--Irish habit or stress of social
    pretense?
"all work and no play"--uncle is the player--plays at
    social status, vain about appearance; also "plays"
    in bar (pub?) every night (most nights?)
lets boy down--can't be trusted, irresponsible,
    insensitive to the boy's feelings, forgets, doesn't
    keep promises*

*irresponsibility, not hypocrisy
```

You can see that Ratinov labels this portion of his inventory with the connection he makes among the adult characters. He then lists relevant annotations under the characters' names. (Ratinov also inventoried information about the priest, but it is not included here because the priest is not mentioned in paragraphs 13 through 23.) Many inventories of text annotations use labels and lists in this way. The labels indicate connections, patterns, or ideas about the story. The lists bring together annotations relevant to the labels.

To analyze his inventory, Ratinov writes these sentences about the section on hypocrisy:

```
Mrs. Mercer may be a good neighbor to the boy's aunt,
but the boy dislikes her. Joyce plants many clues that
she is a hypocrite. She thinks of herself as a good re-
ligious Christian, but she is pious (an exaggerated
Christian, not a believable one), collects stamps to
sell for charity instead of doing good works firsthand
(my guess), and she is a gossip. Her husband got his
money in an unchristian way. Does the boy know all this
or only the narrator much later? I'm sure the boy senses
it. He says he has to endure Mrs. Mercer and her gossip
with his aunt. Now that I look over the evidence for the
uncle's hypocrisy, it seems that his unguardianlike ac-
tions toward the boy, his irresponsibility toward him,
is just as big a flaw as his hypocrisy. He seems to be
trying to hide something by drinking and being obsessive
about his appearance—a failure to advance at work? He
tries to impress people with a bigger house than he can
afford. Says he believes in things that don't apply to
```

```
his own actions. I think I can show that he's a hypo-
crite like Mrs. Mercer. Because the boy distrusts him,
he must sense this hypocrisy.
```

Writing about this portion of his inventory enables Ratinov to try out his ideas about hypocrisy. He confirms that the term itself is workable for discussing the story and that the evidence in the text supports the idea of hypocrisy. He also makes the important discovery that some annotations listed under the uncle concern his irresponsibility, so he goes back to the inventory to asterisk these items. This discovery leads in his essay to a more complex presentation of the uncle as a flawed adult inadvertently teaching lessons the boy will discover at the Araby bazaar.

After completing his written analysis of his annotations involving the boy's relations with other characters, Ratinov writes several generalizations about what he discovered.

```
All the adult characters are hypocrites.

If this is just a story about romance, then all the
adult characters wouldn't have to be so weak and flawed.

Mangan's sister is different from the adults, but
through her he has to face up to what the adult world is
all about.

The adults are initiating the boy into adulthood, but he
doesn't see it until the end of the story.

Growing up means being able to see the world for what it
actually is, not what you want it to be.
```

From these generalizations about initiation, epiphany, romance, and hypocrisy, Ratinov devised the thesis for his essay.

An Anthology of Stories

Following are three additional stories for you to read. You'll find all of them intriguing, subject to many, varied interpretations.

■   ■   ■

Alice **Walker** (b. 1944) is probably best known for her Pulitzer Prize–winning novel, *The Color Purple* (1982). Her other novels include *Meridian* (1976) and *The Temple of My Familiar* (1989). She has also written essays and short stories. "Everyday Use" originally appeared in her first collection of stories, *In Love and Trouble: Stories of Black Women* (1973).

EVERYDAY USE
ALICE WALKER

for your grandmama

I will wait for her in the yard that Maggie and I made so clean and wavy yesterday 1
afternoon. A yard like this is more comfortable than most people know. It is not just
a yard. It is like an extended living room. When the hard clay is swept clean as a
floor and the fine sand around the edges lined with tiny, irregular grooves, anyone
can come and sit and look up into the elm tree and wait for the breezes that never
come inside the house.

Maggie will be nervous until after her sister goes: she will stand hopelessly in 2
corners, homely and ashamed of the burn scars down her arms and legs, eying her
sister with a mixture of envy and awe. She thinks her sister has held life always in
the palm of one hand, that "no" is a word the world never learned to say to her.

You've no doubt seen those TV shows where the child who has "made it" is 3
confronted, as a surprise, by her own mother and father, tottering in weakly from
backstage. (A pleasant surprise, of course: What would they do if parent and child
came on the show only to curse out and insult each other?) On TV mother and child
embrace and smile into each other's faces. Sometimes the mother and father weep,
the child wraps them in her arms and leans across the table to tell how she would
not have made it without their help. I have seen these programs.

Sometimes I dream a dream in which Dee and I are suddenly brought together 4
on a TV program of this sort. Out of a dark and soft-seated limousine I am ushered
into a bright room filled with many people. There I meet a smiling, gray, sporty man
like Johnny Carson who shakes my hand and tells me what a fine girl I have. Then
we are on the stage and Dee is embracing me with tears in her eyes. She pins on
my dress a large orchid, even though she has told me once that she thinks orchids
are tacky flowers.

In real life I am a large, big-boned woman with rough, man-working hands. In 5
the winter I wear flannel nightgowns to bed and overalls during the day. I can kill
and clean a hog as mercilessly as a man. My fat keeps me hot in zero weather. I can
work outside all day, breaking ice to get water for washing; I can eat pork liver
cooked over the open fire minutes after it comes steaming from the hog. One winter
I knocked a bull calf straight in the brain between the eyes with a sledge hammer
and had the meat hung up to chill before nightfall. But of course all this does not
show on television. I am the way my daughter would want me to be: a hundred
pounds lighter, my skin like an uncooked barley pancake. My hair glistens in the hot
bright lights. Johnny Carson has much to do to keep up with my quick and witty
tongue.

But that is a mistake. I know even before I wake up. Who ever knew a Johnson 6
with a quick tongue? Who can even imagine me looking a strange white man in
the eye? It seems to me I have talked to them always with one foot raised in flight,
with my head turned in whichever way is farthest from them. Dee, though. She
would always look anyone in the eye. Hesitation was no part of her nature.

．　　　．　　　．

"How do I look, Mama?" Maggie says, showing just enough of her thin body 7
enveloped in pink skirt and red blouse for me to know she's there, almost hidden
by the door.

''Come out into the yard,'' I say.   8

Have you ever seen a lame animal, perhaps a dog run over by some careless   9
person rich enough to own a car, sidle up to someone who is ignorant enough to
be kind to him? That is the way my Maggie walks. She has been like this, chin on
chest, eyes on ground, feet in shuffle, ever since the fire that burned the other house
to the ground.

Dee is lighter than Maggie, with nicer hair and a fuller figure. She's a woman   10
now, though sometimes I forget. How long ago was it that the other house burned?
Ten, twelve years? Sometimes I can still hear the flames and feel Maggie's arms
sticking to me, her hair smoking and her dress falling off her in little black papery
flakes. Her eyes seemed stretched open, blazed open by the flames reflected in them.
And Dee. I see her standing off under the sweet gum tree she used to dig gum out
of; a look of concentration on her face as she watched the last dingy gray board of
the house fall in toward the red-hot brick chimney. Why don't you do a dance around
the ashes? I'd wanted to ask her. She had hated the house that much.

I used to think she hated Maggie, too. But that was before we raised the money,   11
the church and me, to send her to Augusta to school. She used to read to us without
pity; forcing words, lies, other folks' habits, whole lives upon us two, sitting trapped
and ignorant underneath her voice. She washed us in a river of make-believe, burned
us with a lot of knowledge we didn't necessarily need to know. Pressed us to her
with the serious way she read, to shove us away at just the moment, like dimwits,
we seemed about to understand.

Dee wanted nice things. A yellow organdy dress to wear to her graduation from   12
high school; black pumps to match a green suit she'd made from an old suit somebody gave me. She was determined to stare down any disaster in her efforts. Her
eyelids would not flicker for minutes at a time. Often I fought off the temptation to
shake her. At sixteen she had a style of her own: and knew what style was.

■   ■   ■

I never had an education myself. After second grade the school was closed down.   13
Don't ask me why: in 1927 colored asked fewer questions than they do now. Sometimes Maggie reads to me. She stumbles along good-naturedly, but can't see well.
She knows she is not bright. Like good looks and money, quickness passed her by.
She will marry John Thomas (who has mossy teeth in an earnest face) and then I'll
be free to sit here and I guess just sing church songs to myself. Although I never
was a good singer. Never could carry a tune. I was always better at a man's job. I
used to love to milk till I was hooked in the side[1] in '49. Cows are soothing and
slow and don't bother you, unless you try to milk them the wrong way.

I have deliberately turned my back on the house. It is three rooms, just like the   14
one that burned, except the roof is tin; they don't make shingle roofs any more.
There are no real windows, just some holes cut in the sides, like the portholes on a
ship, but not round and not square, with rawhide holding the shutters up on the
outside. This house is in a pasture, too, like the other one. No doubt when Dee sees
it she will want to tear it down. She wrote me once that no matter where we
''choose'' to live, she will manage to come see us. But she will never bring her

[1]kicked by a cow

friends. Maggie and I thought about this and Maggie asked me, ''Mama, when did Dee ever *have* any friends?''

She had a few. Furtive boys in pink shirts hanging about on washday after school. Nervous girls who never laughed. Impressed with her they worshiped the well-turned phrase, the cute shape, the scalding humor that erupted like bubbles in lye. She read to them.   15

When she was courting Jimmy T she didn't have much time to pay to us, but turned all her faultfinding power on him. He *flew* to marry a cheap city girl from a family of ignorant flashy people. She hardly had time to recompose herself.   16

·   ·   ·

When she comes I will meet—but there they are!   17

Maggie attempts to make a dash for the house, in her shuffling way, but I stay her with my hand. ''Come back here,'' I say. And she stops and tries to dig a well in the sand with her toe.   18

It is hard to see them clearly through the strong sun. But even the first glimpse of leg out of the car tells me it is Dee. Her feet were always neat-looking, as if God himself had shaped them with a certain style. From the other side of the car comes a short, stocky man. Hair is all over his head a foot long and hanging from his chin like a kinky mule tail. I hear Maggie suck in her breath. ''Uhnnnh,'' is what it sounds like. Like when you see the wriggling end of a snake just in front of your foot on the road. 'Uhnnnh.'   19

Dee next. A dress down to the ground, in this hot weather. A dress so loud it hurts my eyes. There are yellows and oranges enough to throw back the light of the sun. I feel my whole face warming from the heat waves it throws out. Earrings gold, too, and hanging down to her shoulders. Bracelets dangling and making noises when she moves her arm up to shake the folds of the dress out of her armpits. The dress is loose and flows, and as she walks closer, I like it. I hear Maggie go ''Uhnnnh'' again. It is her sister's hair. It stands straight up like the wool on a sheep. It is black as night and around the edges are two long pigtails that rope about like small lizards disappearing behind her ears.   20

''Wa-su-zo-Tean-o!''[2] she says, coming on in that gliding way the dress makes her move. The short stocky fellow with the hair to his navel is all grinning and he follows up with ''Asalamalakim,[3] my mother and my sister!'' He moves to hug Maggie but she falls back, right up against the back of my chair. I feel her trembling there and when I look up I see the perspiration falling off her chin.   21

''Don't get up,'' says Dee. Since I am stout it takes something of a push. You can see me trying to move a second or two before I make it. She turns, showing white heels through her sandals, and goes back to the car. Out she peeks next with a Polaroid. She stoops down quickly and lines up picture after picture of me sitting there in front of the house with Maggie cowering behind me. She never takes a shot without making sure the house is included. When a cow comes nibbling around the edge of the yard she snaps it and me and Maggie *and* the house. Then she puts the Polaroid in the back seat of the car, and comes up and kisses me on the forehead.   22

[2]a Black Muslim greeting

[3]peace with you

Meanwhile Asalamalakim is going through motions with Maggie's hand. Mag- 23
gie's hand is as limp as a fish, and probably as cold, despite the sweat, and she
keeps trying to pull it back. It looks like Asalamalakim wants to shake hands but
wants to do it fancy. Or maybe he don't know how people shake hands. Anyhow,
he soon gives up on Maggie.

"Well," I say. "Dee."   24

"No, Mama," she says. "Not 'Dee,' Wangero Leewanika Kemanjo!"   25

"What happened to 'Dee'?" I wanted to know.   26

"She's dead," Wangero said. "I couldn't bear it any longer, being named after 27
the people who oppress me."

"You know as well as me you was named after your aunt Dicie," I said. Dicie is 28
my sister. She named Dee. We called her "Big Dee" after Dee was born.

"But who was *she* named after?" asked Wangero.   29

"I guess after Grandma Dee," I said.   30

"And who was she named after?" asked Wangero.   31

"Her mother," I said, and saw Wangero was getting tired. "That's about as far 32
back as I can trace it," I said. Though, in fact, I probably could have carried it back
beyond the Civil War through the branches.

"Well," said Asalamalakim, "there you are."   33

"Uhnnnh," I heard Maggie say.   34

"There I was not," I said, "before 'Dicie' cropped up in our family, so why should 35
I try to trace it that far back?"

He just stood there grinning, looking down on me like somebody inspecting a 36
Model A car. Every once in a while he and Wangero sent eye signals over my head.

"How do you pronounce this name?" I said.   37

"You don't have to call me by it if you don't want to," said Wangero.   38

"Why shouldn't I?" I asked. "If that's what you want us to call you, we'll call 39
you."

"I know it might sound awkward at first," said Wangero.   40

"I'll get used to it," I said. "Ream it out again."   41

Well, soon we got the name out of the way. Asalamalakim had a name twice 42
as long and three times as hard. After I tripped over it two or three times he told
me to just call him Hakim-a-barber. I wanted to ask him was he a barber, but I didn't
really think he was, so I didn't ask.

"You must belong to those beef-cattle peoples down the road," I said. They said 43
"Asalamalakim" when they met you, too, but they didn't shake hands. Always too
busy: feeding the cattle, fixing the fences, putting up salt-lick shelters, throwing
down hay. When the white folks poisoned some of the herd the men stayed up all
night with rifles in their hands. I walked a mile and a half just to see the sign.

Hakim-a-barber said, "I accept some of their doctrines, but farming and raising 44
cattle is not my style." (They didn't tell me, and I didn't ask, whether Wangero (Dee)
had really gone and married him.)

We sat down to eat and right away he said he didn't eat collards and pork was 45
unclean. Wangero, though, went on through the chitlins and corn bread, the greens
and everything else. She talked a blue streak over the sweet potatoes. Everything
delighted her. Even the fact that we still used the benches her daddy made for the
table when we couldn't afford to buy chairs.

"Oh, Mama!" she cried. Then turned to Hakim-a-barber. "I never knew how 46 lovely these benches are. You can feel the rump prints," she said, running her hands underneath her and along the bench. Then she gave a sign and her hand closed over Grandma Dee's butter dish. "That's it!" she said. "I knew there was something I wanted to ask you if I could have." She jumped up from the table and went over in the corner where the churn stood, the milk in it clabber[4] by now. She looked at the churn and looked at it.

"This churn top is what I need," she said. "Didn't Uncle Buddy whittle it out of 47 a tree you all used to have?"

"Yes," I said.   48

"Uh huh," she said happily. "And I want the dasher, too."   49

"Uncle Buddy whittle that, too?" asked the barber.   50

Dee (Wangero) looked up at me.   51

"Aunt Dee's first husband whittled the dash," said Maggie so low you almost 52 couldn't hear her. "His name was Henry, but they called him Stash."

"Maggie's brain is like an elephant's," Wangero said, laughing. "I can use the 53 churn top as a centerpiece for the alcove table," she said, sliding a plate over the churn, "and I'll think of something artistic to do with the dasher."

When she finished wrapping the dasher the handle stuck out. I took it for a 54 moment in my hands. You didn't even have to look close to see where hands pushing the dasher up and down to make butter had left a kind of sink in the wood. In fact, there were a lot of small sinks; you could see where thumbs and fingers had sunk into the wood. It was beautiful light yellow wood, from a tree that grew in the yard where Big Dee and Stash had lived.

After dinner Dee (Wangero) went to the trunk at the foot of my bed and started 55 rifling through it. Maggie hung back in the kitchen over the dishpan. Out came Wangero with two quilts. They had been pieced by Grandma Dee and then Big Dee and me had hung them on the quilt frames on the front porch and quilted them. One was in the Lone Star pattern. The other was Walk Around the Mountain. In both of them were scraps of dresses Grandma Dee had worn fifty and more years ago. Bits and pieces of Grandpa Jarrell's Paisley shirts. And one teeny faded blue piece, about the size of a penny matchbox, that was from Great Grandpa Ezra's uniform that he wore in the Civil War.

"Mama," Wangero said sweet as a bird. "Can I have these old quilts?"   56

I heard something fall in the kitchen, and a minute later the kitchen door 57 slammed.

"Why don't you take one or two of the others?" I asked. "These old things was 58 just done by me and Big Dee from some tops your grandma pieced before she died."

"No," said Wangero. "I don't want those. They are stitched around the borders 59 by machine."

"That'll make them last better," I said.   60

"That's not the point," said Wangero. "These are all pieces of dresses Grandma 61 used to wear. She did all this stitching by hand. Imagine!" She held the quilts securely in her arms, stroking them.

[4]curdled

"Some of the pieces, like those lavender ones, come from old clothes her mother 62
handed down to her," I said, moving up to touch the quilts. Dee (Wangero) moved
back just enough so that I couldn't reach the quilts. They already belonged to her.

"Imagine!" she breathed again, clutching them closely to her bosom. 63

"The truth is," I said, "I promised to give them quilts to Maggie, for when she 64
marries John Thomas."

She gasped like a bee had stung her. 65

"Maggie can't appreciate these quilts!" she said. "She'd probably be backward 66
enough to put them to everyday use."

"I reckon she would," I said. "God knows I been saving 'em for long enough 67
with nobody using 'em. I hope she will!" I didn't want to bring up how I had offered
Dee (Wangero) a quilt when she went away to college. Then she had told me they
were old-fashioned, out of style.

"But they're *priceless*!" she was saying now, furiously; for she has a temper. 68
"Maggie would put them on the bed and in five years they'd be in rags. Less than
that!"

"She can always make some more," I said. "Maggie knows how to quilt." 69

Dee (Wangero) looked at me with hatred. "You just will not understand. The 70
point is these quilts, *these* quilts!"

"Well," I said, stumped. "What would *you* do with them?" 71

"Hang them," she said. As if that was the only thing you *could* do with quilts. 72

Maggie by now was standing in the door. I could almost hear the sound her 73
feet made as they scraped over each other.

"She can have them, Mama," she said, like somebody used to never winning 74
anything, or having anything reserved for her. "I can 'member Grandma Dee without
the quilts."

I looked at her hard. She had filled her bottom lip with checkerberry snuff and 75
it gave her face a kind of dopey, hangdog look. It was Grandma Dee and Big Dee
who taught her how to quilt herself. She stood there with her scarred hands hidden
in the folds of her skirt. She looked at her sister with something like fear but she
wasn't mad at her. This was Maggie's portion. This was the way she knew God to
work.

When I looked at her like that something hit me in the top of my head and ran 76
down to the soles of my feet. Just like when I'm in church and the spirit of God
touches me and I get happy and shout. I did something I never had done before:
hugged Maggie to me, then dragged her on into the room, snatched the quilts out
of Miss Wangero's hands and dumped them into Maggie's lap. Maggie just sat there
on my bed with her mouth open.

"Take one or two of the others," I said to Dee. 77

But she turned without a word and went out to Hakim-a-barber. 78

"You just don't understand," she said, as Maggie and I came out to the car. 79

"What don't I understand?" I wanted to know. 80

"Your heritage," she said. And then she turned to Maggie, kissed her, and said, 81
"You ought to try to make something of yourself, too, Maggie. It's really a new day
for us. But from the way you and Mama still live you'd never know it."

She put on some sunglasses that hid everything above the top of her nose and 82
her chin.

Maggie smiled; maybe at the sunglasses. But a real smile, not scared. After we 83
watched the car dust settle I asked Maggie to bring me a dip of snuff. And then the
two of us sat there just enjoying, until it was time to go in the house and go to bed.

■ ■ ■

William Carlos Williams (1883–1963) is one of the most important poets of this century, best known for his long poem *Paterson* (1946–58). He has also written essays, plays, novels, and short stories. "The Use of Force" was published initially in *The Doctor Stories* (1933), a collection loosely based on Williams' experiences as a pediatrician.

THE USE OF FORCE
WILLIAM CARLOS
WILLIAMS

They were new patients to me, all I had was the name, Olson. Please come down 1
as soon as you can, my daughter is very sick.

When I arrived I was met by the mother, a big startled looking woman, very 2
clean and apologetic who merely said, Is this the doctor? and let me in. In the back, she added. You must excuse us, doctor, we have her in the kitchen where it is warm. It is very damp here sometimes.

The child was fully dressed and sitting on her father's lap near the kitchen table. 3
He tried to get up, but I motioned for him not to bother, took off my overcoat and started to look things over. I could see that they were all very nervous, eyeing me up and down distrustfully. As often, in such cases, they weren't telling me more than they had to, it was up to me to tell them; that's why they were spending three dollars on me.

The child was fairly eating me up with her cold, steady eyes, and no expression 4
to her face whatever. She did not move and seemed, inwardly, quiet; an unusually attractive little thing, and as strong as a heifer in appearance. But her face was flushed, she was breathing rapidly, and I realized that she had a high fever. She had magnificent blonde hair, in profusion. One of those picture children often reproduced in advertising leaflets and the photogravure sections of the Sunday papers.

She's had a fever for three days, began the father and we don't know what it 5
comes from. My wife has given her things, you know, like people do, but it don't do no good. And there's been a lot of sickness around. So we tho't you better look her over and tell us what is the matter.

As doctors often do I took a trial shot at it as a point of departure. Has she had 6
a sore throat?

Both parents answered me together, No . . . No, she says her throat don't hurt 7
her.

Does your throat hurt you? added the mother to the child. but the little girl's 8
expression didn't change nor did she move her eyes from my face.

Have you looked?   9

I tried, said the mother, but I couldn't see.   10

As it happens we had been having a number of cases of diphtheria in the school 11
to which this child went during that month and we were all, quite apparently, thinking of that, though no one had as yet spoken of the thing.

Well, I said, suppose we take a look at the throat first. I smiled in my best 12
professional manner and asking for the child's first name I said, come on, Mathilda, open your mouth and let's take a look at your throat.

Nothing doing.   13

Aw, come on, I coaxed, just open your mouth wide and let me take a look. Look, 14
I said opening both hands wide, I haven't anything in my hands. Just open up and let me see.

Such a nice man, put in the mother. Look how kind he is to you. Come on, do 15
what he tells you to. He won't hurt you.

At that I ground my teeth in disgust. If only they wouldn't use the word "hurt" 16
I might be able to get somewhere. But I did not allow myself to be hurried or
disturbed but speaking quietly and slowly I approached the child again.

As I moved my chair a little nearer suddenly with one catlike movement both 17
her hands clawed instinctively for my eyes and she almost reached them too. In fact
she knocked my glasses flying and they fell, though unbroken, several feet away
from me on the kitchen floor.

Both the mother and father almost turned themselves inside out in embarrass- 18
ment and apology. You bad girl, said the mother, taking her and shaking her by one
arm. Look what you've done. The nice man . . .

For heaven's sake, I broke in. Don't call me a nice man to her. I'm here to look 19
at her throat on the chance that she might have diphtheria and possibly die of it.
But that's nothing to her. Look here, I said to the child, we're going to look at your
throat. You're old enough to understand what I'm saying. Will you open it now by
yourself or shall we have to open it for you?

Not a move. Even her expression hadn't changed. Her breaths however were 20
coming faster and faster. Then the battle began. I had to do it. I had to have a throat
culture for her own protection. But first I told the parents that it was entirely up to
them. I explained the danger but said that I would not insist on a throat examination
so long as they would take the responsibility.

If you don't do what the doctor says you'll have to go to the hospital, the mother 21
admonished her severely.

Oh yeah? I had to smile to myself. After all, I had already fallen in love with the 22
savage brat, the parents were contemptible to me. In the ensuing struggle they grew
more and more abject, crushed, exhausted while she surely rose to magnificent
heights of insane fury of effort bred of her terror of me.

The father tried his best, and he was big man but the fact that she was his 23
daughter, his shame at her behavior and his dread of hurting her made him release
her just at the critical times when I had almost achieved success, till I wanted to kill
him. But his dread also that she might have diphtheria made him tell me to go on,
go on though he himself was almost fainting, while the mother moved back and
forth behind us raising and lowering her hands in an agony of apprehension.

Put her in front of you on your lap, I ordered, and hold both her wrists. 24

But as soon as he did the child let out a scream. Don't, your hurting me. Let go 25
of my hands. Let them go I tell you. Then she shrieked terrifyingly, hysterically. Stop
it! Stop it! You're killing me!

Do you think she can stand it, doctor! said the mother. 26

You get out, said the husband to his wife. Do you want her to die of diphtheria? 27
Come on now, hold her, I said. 28

Then I grasped the child's head with my left hand and tried to get the wooden 29
tongue depressor between her teeth. She fought, with clenched teeth, desperately!
But now I also had grown furious—at a child. I tried to hold myself down but I
couldn't. I know how to expose a throat for inspection. And I did my best. When
finally I got the wooden spatula behind the last teeth and just the point of it into
the mouth cavity, she opened up for an instant but before I could see anything she
came down again and gripping the wooden blade between her molars she reduced
it to splinters before I could get it out again.

Aren't you ashamed, the mother yelled at her. Aren't you ashamed to act like 30
that in front of the doctor?

Get me a smooth-handled spoon of some sort, I told the mother. We're going 31
through with this. The child's mouth was already bleeding. Her tongue was cut and
she was screaming in wild hysterical shrieks. Perhaps I should have desisted and
come back in an hour or more. No doubt it would have been better. But I have seen
at least two children lying dead in bed of neglect in such cases, and feeling that I
must get a diagnosis now or never I went at it again. But the worst of it was that I
too had got beyond reason. I could have torn the child apart in my own fury and
enjoyed it. It was a pleasure to attack her. My face was burning with it.

The damned little brat must be protected against her own idiocy, one says to 32
one's self at such times. Others must be protected against her. It is a social necessity.
And all these things are true. But a blind fury, a feeling of adult shame, bred of a
longing for muscular release are the operatives. One goes on the the end.

In a final unreasoning assault I overpowered the child's neck and jaws. I forced 33
the heavy silver spoon back of her teeth and down her throat till she gagged. And
there it was—both tonsils covered with membrane. She had fought valiantly to keep
me from knowing her secret. She had been hiding that sore throat for three days
at least and lying to her parents in order to escape just such an outcome as this.

Now truly she was furious. She had been on the defensive before but now she 34
attacked. Tried to get off her father's lap and fly at me while tears of defeat blinded
her eyes.

■   ■   ■

Clarice Lispector (1925–1977), a Brazilian writer, is known for her short
stories and novels. "The Smallest Woman in the World" was originally translated by the American poet Elizabeth Bishop for an English-language collection of Latin American stories, *The Eye of the Heart* (1973).

THE SMALLEST WOMAN IN THE WORLD
CLARICE LISPECTOR

In the depths of Equatorial Africa the French explorer, Marcel Pretre, hunter and 1
man of the world, came across a tribe of surprisingly small pygmies. Therefore he
was even more surprised when he was informed that a still smaller people existed,
beyond forests and distances. So he plunged farther on.

In the Eastern Congo, near Lake Kivu, he really did discover the smallest pygmies 2
in the world. And—like a box within a box within a box—obedient, perhaps, to the
necessity nature sometimes feels of outdoing herself—among the smallest pygmies
in the world there was the smallest of the smallest pygmies in the world.

Among mosquitoes and lukewarm trees, among leaves of the most rich and lazy 3
green, Marcel Pretre found himself facing a woman seventeen and three-quarter
inches high, full-grown, black, silent—"Black as a monkey," he informed the press—
who lived in a treetop with her little spouse. In the tepid miasma of the jungle, that
swells the fruits so early and gives them an almost intolerable sweetness, she was
pregnant.

So there she stood, the smallest woman in the world. For an instant, in the 4
buzzing heat, it seemed as if the Frenchman had unexpectedly reached his final
destination. Probably only because he was not insane, his soul neither wavered nor

broke its bounds. Feeling an immediate necessity for order and for giving names to what exists, he called her Little Flower. And in order to be able to classify her among the recognizable realities, he immediately began to collect facts about her.

Her race will soon be exterminated. Few examples are left of this species, which, 5 if it were not for the sly dangers of Africa, might have multiplied. Besides disease, the deadly effluvium of the water, insufficient food, and raging beasts, the great threat to the Likoualas are the savage Bahundes, a threat that surrounds them in the silent air, like the dawn of battle. The Bahundes hunt them with nets, like monkeys. And eat them. Like that: they catch them in nets and eat them. The tiny race, retreating, always retreating, has finished hiding away in the heart of Africa, where the lucky explorer discovered it. For strategic defense, they live in the highest trees. The women descend to grind and cook corn and to gather greens; the men, to hunt. When a child is born, it is left free almost immediately. It is true that, what with the beasts, the child frequently cannot enjoy his freedom for very long. But then it is true that it cannot be lamented that for such a short life there had been any long, hard work. And even the language that the child learns is short and simple, merely the essentials. The Likoualas use few names; they name things by gestures and animal noises. As for things of the spirit, they have a drum. While they dance to the sound of the drum, a little male stands guard against the Bahundes, who come from no one knows where.

That was the way, then, that the explorer discovered, standing at his very feet, 6 the smallest exciting human thing. His heart beat, because no emerald in the world is so rare. The teachings of the wise men of India are not so rare. The richest man in the world has never set eyes on such strange grace. Right there was a woman that the greed of the most exquisite dream could never have imagined. It was then that the explorer said timidly, and with a delicacy of feeling of which his wife would never have thought him capable: "You are Little Flower."

At that moment, Little Flower scratched herself where no one scratches. The 7 explorer—as if he were receiving the highest prize for chastity to which an idealistic man dares aspire—the explorer, experienced as he was, looked the other way.

A photograph of Little Flower was published in the colored supplement of the 8 Sunday Papers, life-size. She was wrapped in a cloth, her belly already very big. The flat nose, the black face, the splay feet. She looked like a dog.

On that Sunday, in an apartment, a woman seeing the picture of Little Flower 9 in the paper didn't want to look a second time because "It gives me the creeps."

In another apartment, a lady felt such perverse tenderness for the smallest of 10 the African women that—an ounce of prevention being worth a pound of cure— Little Flower could never be left alone to the tenderness of that lady. Who knows to what murkiness of love tenderness can lead? The woman was upset all day, almost as if she were missing something. Besides, it was spring and there was a dangerous leniency in the air.

In another house, a little girl of five, seeing the picture and hearing the com- 11 ments, was extremely surprised. In a houseful of adults, this little girl had been the smallest human being up until now. And, if this was the source of all caresses, it was also the source of the first fear of the tyranny of love. The existence of Little Flower made the little girl feel—with a deep uneasiness that only years and years later, and for very different reasons, would turn into thought—made her feel, in her first wisdom, that "sorrow is endless."

In another house, in the consecration of spring, a girl about to be married felt 12 an ecstasy of pity: "Mama, look at her little picture, poor little thing! Just look how sad she is!"

"But," said the mother, hard and defeated and proud, "it's the sadness of an animal. It isn't human sadness." 13

"Oh, Mama!" said the girl, discouraged. 14

In another house, a clever little boy had a clever idea: "Mummy, if I could put this little woman from Africa in little Paul's bed when he's asleep? When he woke up wouldn't he be frightened? Wouldn't he howl! When he saw her sitting on his bed? And then we'd play with her! She would be our toy!" 15

His mother was setting her hair in front of the bathroom mirror at the moment, and she remembered what a cook had told her about life in an orphanage. The orphans had no dolls, and, with terrible maternity already throbbing in their hearts, the little girls had hidden the death of one of the children from the nun. They kept the body in a cupboard and when the nun went out they played with the dead child, giving her baths and things to eat, punishing her only to be able to kiss and console her. In the bathroom, the mother remembered this, and let fall her thoughtful hands, full of curlers. She considered the cruel necessity of loving. And she considered the malignity of our desire for happiness. She considered how ferociously we need to play. How many times we will kill for love. Then she looked at her clever child as if she were looking at a dangerous stranger. And she had a horror of her own soul that, more than her body, had engendered that being, adept at life and happiness. She looked at him attentively and with uncomfortable pride, that child who had already lost two front teeth, evolution evening itself, teeth falling out to give place to those who could bite better. "I'm going to buy him a new suit," she decided, looking at him, absorbed. Obstinately, she adorned her gap-toothed son with fine clothes; obstinately, she wanted him very clean, as if his cleanliness could emphasize a soothing superficiality, obstinately perfecting the polite side of beauty. Obstinately drawing away from, and drawing him away from, something that ought to be "black as a monkey." Then, looking in the bathroom mirror, the mother gave a deliberately refined and social smile, placing a distance of insuperable millenniums between the abstract lines of her features and the crude face of Little Flower. But, with years of practice, she knew that this was going to be a Sunday on which she would have to hide from herself anxiety, dreams, and lost millenniums. 16

In another house, they gave themselves up to the enthralling task of measuring the seventeen and three-quarter inches of Little Flower against the wall. And, really, it was a delightful surprise: she was even smaller than the sharpest imagination could have pictured. In the heart of each member of the family was born, nostalgic, the desire to have that tiny and indomitable thing for itself, that thing spared having been eaten, that permanent source of charity. The avid family soul wanted to devote itself. To tell the truth, who hasn't wanted to own a human being just for himself? Which, it is true, wouldn't always be convenient; there are times when one doesn't want to have feelings. 17

"I bet if she lived here it would end in a fight," said the father, sitting in the armchair and definitely turning the page of the newspaper. "In this house everything ends in a fight." 18

"Oh, you, José—always a pessimist," said the mother. 19

"But, Mama, have you thought of the size her baby's going to be?" said the oldest little girl, aged thirteen, eagerly. 20

The father stirred uneasily behind his paper. 21

"It should be the smallest black baby in the world," the mother answered, 22 melting with pleasure. "Imagine her serving our table, with her big little belly!"

"That's enough!" growled father. 23

"But you have to admit," said the mother, unexpectedly offended, "that it is 24 something very rare. You're the insensitive one."

And the rare thing itself? 25

In the meanwhile, in Africa, the rare thing herself, in her heart—and who knows 26 if the heart wasn't black, too, since once nature has erred she can no longer be trusted—the rare thing herself had something even rarer in her heart, like the secret of her own secret: a minimal child. Methodically, the explorer studied that little belly of the smallest mature human being. It was at this moment that the explorer, for the first time since he had known her, instead of feeling curiosity, or exhaltation, or victory, or the scientific spirit, felt sick.

The smallest woman in the world was laughing. 27

She was laughing, warm, warm—Little Flower was enjoying life. The rare thing 28 herself was experiencing the ineffable sensation of not having been eaten yet. Not having been eaten yet was something that at any other time would have given her the agile impulse to jump from branch to branch. But, in this moment of tranquility, amid the thick leaves of the eastern Congo, she was not putting this impulse into action—it was entirely concentrated in the smallness of the rare thing itself. So she was laughing. It was a laugh such as only one who does not speak laughs. It was a laugh that the explorer, constrained, couldn't classify. And she kept on enjoying her own soft laugh, she who wasn't being devoured. Not to be devoured is the most perfect feeling. Not to be devoured is the secret goal of a whole life. While she was not being eaten, her bestial laughter was as delicate as joy is delicate. The explorer was baffled.

In the second place, if the rare thing herself was laughing, it was because, within 29 her smallness, a great darkness had begun to move.

The rare thing herself felt in her breast a warmth that might be called love. She 30 loved that sallow explorer. If she could have talked and had told him that she loved him, he would have been puffed up with vanity. Vanity that would have collapsed when she added that she also loved the explorer's ring very much, and the explorer's boots. And when that collapse had taken place, Little Flower would not have understood why. Because her love for the explorer—one might even say "profound love," since, having no other resources, she was reduced to profundity—her profound love for the explorer would not have been at all diminished by the fact that she also loved his boots. There is an old misunderstanding about the word love, and, if many children are born from this misunderstanding, many others have lost the unique chance of being born, only because of the susceptibility that demands that it be me! me! that is loved, and not my money. But in the humidity of the forest these cruel refinements do not exist, and love is not to be eaten, love is to find a boot pretty, love is to like the strange color of a man who isn't black, is to laugh for love of a shiny ring. Litte Flower blinked with love, and laughed warmly, small, gravid, warm.

The explorer tried to smile back, without knowing exactly to what abyss his smile 31 responded, and then he was embarrassed as only a very big man can be embarrassed. He pretended to adjust his explorer's hat better; he colored, prudishly. He turned a lovely color, a greenish-pink, like a lime at sunrise. He was undoubtedly sour.

Perhaps adjusting the symbolic helmet helped the explorer to get control of 32 himself, severely recapture the discipline of his work, and go on with his note-taking. He had learned how to understand some of the tribe's few articulate words, and to interpret their signs. By now, he could ask questions.

Little Flower answered "Yes." That it was very nice to have a tree of her own 33 to live in. Because—she didn't say this but her eyes became so dark that they said it—because it is good to own, good to own, good to own. The explorer winked several times.

Marcel Pretre had some difficult moments with himself. But at least he kept busy 34 taking notes. Those who didn't take notes had to manage as best they could:

"Well," suddenly declared one old lady, folding up the newspaper decisively, 35 "well, as I always say: God knows what He's doing."

PART TWO

Writing Strategies

Writers are like scientists: they ask questions, systematically inquiring about how things work, what they are, where they occur, and how more information can be learned about them. Writers are also like artists using what they know and learn to create something new and imaginative.

The invention and inquiry strategies described in this chapter are not mysterious or magical. They are tricks of the trade available to everyone and should appeal to your common sense and experience in solving problems. Developed by writers, psychologists, and linguists, they represent the ways writers, engineers, scientists, composers—in fact, all of us—creatively solve problems.

Once you've mastered these strategies, you can use them to tackle any writing situation you encounter in college or on the job. The best way to learn them is to use them as you write an actual essay. Part I, Chapters 2–10, shows you when these strategies can be most helpful and how to make the most efficient use of them. The guides to invention and research in these chapters offer easy-to-use adaptations of these general strategies, adaptations designed to satisfy the special requirements of each kind of writing.

The strategies for invention and inquiry in this chapter are grouped into three categories:

Mapping: a brief visual representation of your thinking or planning

Writing: the composition of phrases or sentences to discover information and ideas and to make connections among them

Reading: a systematic use of reading to understand and to explore information and ideas for your own writing

These invention and inquiry strategies can give you powerful help in the thinking and planning you need to do as a writer. They will help you to explore and research a topic fully before you begin drafting and then to solve problems as you are drafting and revising. In this chapter strategies are arranged alphabetically within each of the three categories.

MAPPING

Mapping involves making a visual record of invention and inquiry. Many writers find that mapping helps them think about a topic. In making maps, they usually use key words and phrases to record material they want to remember, questions they need to answer, and even new sources of information they want to check. The maps show the ideas, details, and facts they are examining. They also show possible ways materials can be connected and focused. Maps might be informal graphic displays with words and phrases circled and connected by lines to show relationships, or they might be formal sentence outlines. Mapping can be especially useful because it provides visual representation of your thinking and planning. Mapping strategies include clustering, listing, and outlining.

Clustering

Clustering is a strategy for revealing possible relations among facts and ideas. Unlike listing (the next mapping strategy), clustering requires a brief period of initial planning. You must first come up with a tentative division of the topic into subparts or main ideas. Clustering works as follows:

1. In a word or phrase, write your topic in the center of a piece of paper. Circle it.

2. Also in a word or phrase, write down the main parts or central ideas of your topic. Circle these, and connect them to the topic in the center.

3. The next step is to generate facts, details, examples, or ideas related in any way to these main parts. Cluster these around the main parts.

Clustering can be useful for any kind of writing. You can use it in the early stages of planning an essay in order to find subtopics and to organize information. You may try and discard several clusters before finding one that is promising. Many writers use clustering to plan brief sections of an essay as they are drafting or revising. (A model of clustering is on p. 384.)

Listing

Listing is a familiar activity. We make shopping lists and lists of errands to do or people to call. Listing can also be a great help in planning an essay. It enables you to recall what you already know about a topic and suggests what more you may need to find out. It is an easy way to get started doing something productive, instead of just worrying about what you will write. A list rides along on its own momentum, the first item leading naturally to the next.

Listing is a basic activity for writers, especially useful for those who have little time for planning—for example, reporters facing deadlines or college

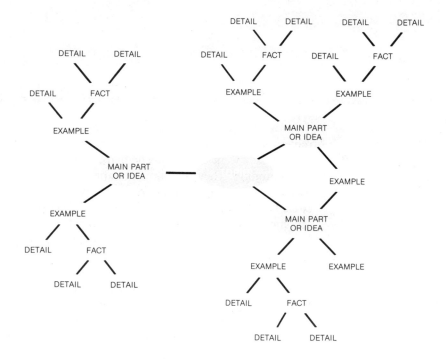

students taking essay exams. Listing lets you order your ideas quickly. It can also help as a first step in discovering possible writing topics.

Listing is a solitary form of brainstorming, a popular technique of problem solving in groups. If you were working with a group to generate ideas for a collaborative writing project, then you would be engaged in true brainstorming. Here is how listing works best for invention work: (1) Give your list a title that indicates your main idea or topic. (2) Write as fast as you can, relying on short phrases. (3) Include anything that seems at all useful. Do not try to be judgmental at this point. (4) After you have finished, or even as you write, reflect on the list and organize it in the following way. This is a very important step, for it may lead you to further discoveries about your topic.

Put an asterisk by the most promising items.
Number key items in order of importance.
Put items in related groups.
Cross out items that do not seem promising.
Add new items.

Outlining

Outlining is both a way of planning and a means of inventing. An outline may, of course, be used to organize an essay. Yet, as soon as you start making an outline, you begin to see new possibilities in your subject, discovering new ways of dividing or grouping information and seeing where you need additional information to develop your ideas. Outlining also lets you see at a glance whether your plan is appropriate.

There are three main forms of outlining: scratch, topic, and sentence. (Keep in mind that clustering is also a way of outlining.)

A scratch outline is an informal outline, really only a rough list of the main points (and sometimes subpoints as well) of an essay. You have no doubt made scratch outlines many times—both to clarify difficult reading and to plan essays or essay exams. As an example, here is a *scratch outline* for Victor Fuchs's essay in Chapter 9.

SUICIDE AMONG YOUNG PEOPLE

death rate rising for 15–24 year olds

mainly more murders and suicides

why more suicides?—not a result of new ways of reporting suicides or of Vietnam War or of bad economy

causes probably in family—divorce, no discipline, loss of father

increase in suicide really is unique to this age group

no simple solution possible

Fuchs may have made such a scratch outline before he began drafting his essay. Notice that the items in a scratch outline do not necessarily coincide with paragraphs. Sometimes two or more items may be developed in the same paragraph or one item may represent two or more paragraphs. (A different scratch outline emphasizing strategies of causal analysis rather than content follows Fuchs's essay on p. 307.)

Scratch outlines are especially helpful for organizing information while you are still gathering it and for deciding how to revise an essay after it has been drafted. The writing guide for each chapter in Part I reminds you when you might use scratch outlining most profitably.

Topic and sentence outlines are more formal than scratch outlines. They follow a conventional format of numbered and lettered headings and subheadings. Some instructors require such an outline with term or research papers. Following is a *topic outline* of Fuchs's essay:

SUICIDE AMONG YOUNG PEOPLE

I. Increasing death rate in the 15–24 age group
II. Increase explained by self-destructive behavior
  A. Homicide
  B. Suicide
III. Unacceptable causes of the increase
  A. Change in reporting of suicides
  B. Attitudes toward Vietnam War
  C. Unemployment and weak economy

IV. Probable causes of the increase
   A. Divorce or lack of discipline
   B. Loss of father
 V. Increase in suicides unique to 15–24 age group
VI. Challenge of this problem for public policy

Notice that a period follows the Roman numerals and capital letters. The items in a topic outline are words or brief phrases, not sentences. Items are not followed by a period, but the first word is capitalized. It is customary in a topic outline for items at the same level of indentation to be grammatically parallel. Under Item IV, for instance, the A and B items both begin with nouns:

A. *Divorce* or lack of discipline
B. *Loss* of father

The items would not be grammatically parallel if B began with an infinitive phrase (*to* plus a verb), like this:

A. *Divorce* or lack of discipline
B. *To lose* a father

Following is a *sentence outline* of Fuchs's essay. Each item is a complete sentence, with the first word capitalized and the last word followed by a period.

SUICIDE AMONG YOUNG PEOPLE

  I. The death rate is rising only for Americans in the age group 15–24.
 II. This increase is a result of self-destructive behavior.
   A. The homicide rate is rising in the 15–24 age group, especially among blacks.
   B. The suicide rate is also increasing.
III. Many explanations have been offered for the increasing suicide rate.
   A. The trend is not the result of a change in ways of reporting suicides.
   B. The trend cannot be explained by attitudes toward the Vietnam War.
   C. The trend cannot be explained by unemployment or a bad economy.
IV. The causes of the trend can most probably be located in family situations.
   A. Children in families where little guidance is provided or where parents are divorced are more likely to commit suicide.
   B. Children who have lost a father are more likely to commit suicide.
 V. The increase in suicide rates is unique to the 15–24 age group.
VI. Whatever the cause of the increasing suicide rate among young people, since there is no apparent solution, it creates a serious challenge to public policy.

Sentence outlines can be considerably more detailed, to the point of containing most of the information in the essay; but for an essay the length of Fuchs's they are usually about as detailed as this one. Should you want to make a more detailed outline, you would probably need more levels of information than the preceding two outlines contain. A rule of thumb for subdividing topics is that there must be at least two items in every level. You would follow this convention for identifying levels:

```
I. (Main topic)
  A. (Subtopic of I)
  B.
    1. (Subtopic of I.B)
    2.
      a. (Subtopic of I.B.2)
      b.
        (1) (Subtopic of I.B.2.b.)
        (2)
          (a) (Subtopic of I.B.2.b.(2) )
          (b)
          (c)
```

WRITING

Writing itself is a powerful tool for thinking. By writing, you can recall details of scenes or people, remember facts and ideas, find connections in new information you have collected.

Unlike most mapping strategies, writing strategies of invention invite you to produce complete sentences. The sentence provides considerable generative power. Because sentences are complete statements, they take you further than listing or clustering. They enable you to explore ideas and define relationships, to bring ideas together or show how they differ, to identify causes and effects. Sentences can follow one another naturally and develop a chain of thought.

This section presents several invention and inquiry strategies which invite you to formulate complete sentences and thus produce brief exploratory pieces of writing. Some are guided, systematic strategies, while others are more flexible. Even though they call for complete sentences that are related to one another, they do not require planning or polishing.

These writing strategies include cubing, dialogues, diaries, dramatizing, quick drafting, journals, looping, and questioning.

Cubing

Cubing is useful for quickly exploring a writing topic. It lets you probe the topic from six different perspectives. (It is known as cubing because a cube has six sides.) Following are the six perspectives in cubing:

Describing. What does your subject look like? What size is it? Color? Shape? Texture? Name its parts.

Comparing. What is your subject similar to? Different from?

Associating. What does it make you think of? What connections does it have to anything else in your experience? Be creative here. Include any connection you can think of.

Analyzing. How is it made? Where did it come from? Where is it going? How are its parts related?

Applying. What can you do with it? What uses does it have?

Arguing. What arguments can you make for it? Against it?

Following are some guidelines to help you use cubing productively:

1. Select a topic, subject, or part of a subject. This can be a person, scene, event, object, problem, idea, or issue. Hold it in focus.

2. Limit yourself to three to five minutes for each perspective. The whole activity will then take no more than a half hour.

3. Keep going until you have written about your subject from *all six* perspectives. Remember that the special advantage of cubing is the quick *multiple* perspectives it provides.

4. As you write from each perspective, begin with what you know about your subject. However, do not limit yourself to your present knowledge. Indicate what else you need to know about your subject, and suggest where you might find that information.

5. Reread what you have written. Look for bright spots, surprises. Recall the part that was easiest for you to write. Recall the part where you felt a special momentum and pleasure in the writing. Look for an angle or an unexpected insight. These special parts may suggest a focus or a topic within a larger subject, or they may provide specific details to include in a draft.

Dialogues

A dialogue is a conversation between two or more people. You can use dialogue to search for topics, find a focus, explore ideas, or consider opposing viewpoints. As an invention strategy, writing a dialogue requires you to make up all parts of the conversation. Imagine two particular people talking, or hold a conversation yourself with some imagined person, or simply talk out loud to yourself. Follow these steps:

An example of dialogue used for invention and inquiry is on pp. 49–50.

1. Write a conversation between two speakers. Label the speakers "1" and "2," or make up names for them.

2. If you get stuck, you might have one of the speakers ask the other a question.

3. Write brief responses in order to keep the conversation moving fast. Do not spend much time planning or rehearsing responses. Write what first occurs to you—just as in a real conversation, where people take quick turns to prevent any awkward silences.

Dialogues can be especially useful with personal experience and persuasive essays because they help you remember conversations and anticipate counterarguments.

Dramatizing

Dramatizing is an invention activity developed by the philosopher Kenneth Burke as a way of thinking about how people interact and as a way of analyzing literature and the arts.

Thinking about human behavior in dramatic terms can be very productive for writers. Drama has action, actors, setting, motives, and methods. Since stars and acting go together, you can use a five-pointed star to remember these five points of dramatizing:

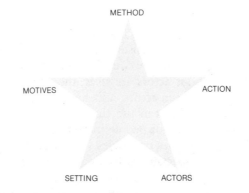

METHOD

MOTIVES   ACTION

SETTING   ACTORS

Each point provides a different perspective on human behavior. We can think of each point independently and in combination. Let us begin by looking at each point to see how it helps us analyze people and their interactions.

Action.   An action is anything that happens, has happened, will happen, or could happen. Action includes events that are physical (running a marathon), mental (thinking about a book you read), and emotional (falling in love). This category also refers to the results of activity (a term paper).

Actor.   The actor is involved in the action. He or she may be responsible for it or simply be affected by it. The actor does not have to be a person. It can be a force, something that causes an action. For example, if the action is a rise in the price of gasoline, the actor could be increased demand or short supply. Dramatizing may also include a number of co-actors working together or at odds.

Setting.   This is the situation, the background of the action. We usually think of setting as the place and time of an event, but it can be the historical background of an event or the childhood of a person.

Motive.   The motive is the purpose or reason for an action. It refers to the intention actors may have or the end an action serves.

Method.   Method is the way an action occurs, the techniques an actor uses. It refers to whatever makes things happen.

Each of these points suggests a simple invention question:

> Action = What?
> Actor = Who?
> Setting = When and where?
> Motive = Why?
> Method = How?

This list looks like the questions reporters typically ask. But dramatizing goes further because it enables us to ask a much fuller set of invention questions generated by considering relations between these five elements. We can think about actors' motives, the effect of the setting on the actors, the relations between actors, and so on.

You can use this activity to learn more about yourself or about other significant people in your life. You can use it, as well, to explore characters in stories or movies you are analyzing or evaluating. Moreover, dramatizing is especially useful in analyzing readers you are trying to inform or convince.

To use dramatizing, imagine the person you want to understand better in a particular situation. Holding this image in mind, write answers to any questions in the following list that apply. You may draw a blank on some questions, have little to say to some, and a lot to say to others. Be exploratory and playful. Write quickly, relying on words and phrases, even drawings.

- What is the actor doing?
- How did the actor come to be involved in this situation?
- Why does the actor do what he or she does?
- What else might the actor do?
- What is the actor trying to accomplish?
- How do other actors influence—help or hinder—the main actor?
- What do the actor's actions reveal about him or her?
- What does the actor's language reveal about him or her?
- How does the event's setting influence the actor's actions?
- How does the time of the event influence what the actor does?
- Where did this actor come from?
- How is this actor different from what he or she used to be?
- What might this actor become?
- How is this actor like or unlike the other actors?

Quick Drafting

Sometimes writers know basically what they want to say or don't have time for much invention. In these situations, quick drafting may be a good invention strategy.

There are no special rules for quick drafting, but you should not rely on it unless you know your subject well, have had experience with the kind of writing you are doing, and will have a chance to revise your draft. Quick drafting can help you discover what you already know about the subject and what you need to find out. It can also help you develop and organize your thoughts.

Journals

Professional writers often use journals to keep notes, and so might you. It is quite easy to start a writer's journal. Buy a special notebook, and start writing. Here are some possibilities:

- Keep a list of new words and concepts you learn in your courses. You could also write about the progress and direction of your learning in particular courses—the experience of being in the course, your feelings about what is happening and what you are learning.

- Respond to your reading, assigned and personal. Write about your personal associations as you read, your reflections, reactions, evaluations. Summarize important passages. Copy memorable passages and comment on them. (Copying and commenting has been practiced by students and writers for centuries, keeping a special kind of journal called a *commonplace book*.)

- Write to prepare for particular class meetings. Write about the main ideas you have learned from assigned readings and about the relation of these new ideas to other ideas in the course. After class, write to summarize what you have learned. List questions you have about the ideas or information discussed in class. Journal writing of this kind involves reflecting, evaluating, interpreting, synthesizing, summarizing, and questioning.

- Record observations and overheard conversations.

- Write for ten or fifteen minutes every day about whatever is on your mind. Focus these meditations on your new experiences and your understandings, interpretations, and reflections on them.

- Write sketches of people who catch your attention.

- Organize a day or a week. You could write about your goals and priorities. You could list specific things to accomplish and what you plan to do.

- Keep a log over several days or weeks about a particular event unfolding in the news—a sensational trial, an environmental disaster, a political campaign, a campus controversy, the fortunes of a sports team.

If you begin a journal, you may think of still other ways to use it. There are many possibilities. All of the writing in your journal has value for learning, observing experience closely, and organizing your life. It may also end up in other writing.

Looping

Looping—the strategy of writing quickly but *returning* to your topic—is especially useful for the first stages of exploring a topic. From almost any starting point, no matter how general or unfocused, looping enables you to find a center of interest and eventually a thesis. The steps are simple:

1. Write down your area of interest. You may know only that you have to write about another person or a movie or a cultural trend that has caught your attention. Or, you may be searching for a topic in a broad historical period or one related to a major political event. Although you may wander from this topic as you write, you will want to keep coming back to it. Your purpose is to find a focus for writing, or even a thesis.

2. Write nonstop for ten minutes. Start with the first thing that comes to mind. Write rapidly, without looking back to reread or to correct anything. *Do not stop writing. Keep your pencil moving.* That is the key to looping. If you get stuck for a moment, rewrite the last sentence. Trust the act of writing to lead you to new insights. Follow diversions and digressions, but keep returning to your topic.

3. At the end of ten minutes, pause to reread what you have written. Decide what is most important—a single insight, a pattern of ideas, an emerging theme, a visual detail, anything at all that stands out. Some writers call this a "center of gravity" or a "hot spot." To complete the first loop, express this center in a single sentence.

4. Beginning with this sentence, write nonstop for ten minutes.

5. Summarize in one sentence again to complete the second loop.

6. Keep looping until one of your summary sentences produces a focus or thesis. You may need only two or three loops; you may need more.

Questioning

Asking questions about a subject is a way to learn about it and decide what to write. However, when we first encounter a subject, our questions may be scattered. Also, we are not likely to think right away of all the important questions we ought to ask. The advantage of a basic list of questions for invention, like the ones for cubing and for dramatizing discussed earlier in this chapter, is that it provides a systematic approach to exploring a subject.

The questions here come from classical rhetoric (what the Greek philosopher Aristotle called "topics") and a modern approach to invention called *tagmemics*. Tagmemics, based on the work of American linguist Kenneth Pike, provides questions about all the ways we make sense of the world, all the ways we sort and classify experience and come to understand it.

Here are the steps in using questions for invention: (1) Think about your subject. (Subjects could be any event, person, problem, project, idea, or issue—in other words, anything you might write about.) (2) Start with the first question, and move right through the list. Try to answer each question at least briefly with a word or phrase. Some questions may invite several sentences, or even a page or more of writing. You may draw a blank on a few questions. Skip them. Later, with more experience with questions for invention, you can start anywhere in the list. (3) Write your responses quickly, without much planning. Follow digressions or associations. Do not screen anything out. Be playful.

What is your subject?

- What is your subject's name and what other names does it have, now or in the past?
- What aspects of the subject do these different names emphasize?
- Imagine a still photograph or moving picture of your subject. What would it look like?
- What would you put into a time capsule to stand for your subject?
- What are its causes and results?
- How would it look from different vantage points or perspectives?
- What particular experiences have you had with the subject? What have you learned?

What parts or characteristics does your subject have and how are they related?

- Name the parts or characteristics.
- Describe each one, using the questions in the preceding subject list.
- How is each part or characterisic related to the others?

How is your subject similar to and different from other subjects?

- What is your subject similar to? In what ways are they alike?
- What is your subject different from? In what ways are they different?
- Of all the things in the world, what seems to you most unlike your subject? In what ways are they unlike each other? Now, just for fun, note how they are alike.

How much can your subject change and still remain the same?

- How has your subject changed from what it once was?
- How is it changing now—from moment to moment, day to day, year to year?
- How much can it change and still remain the same?
- What are some different forms your subject takes?
- What does it become when it is no longer itself?

Where does your subject fit in the world?

- When and where did your subject originate?
- Imagine a time in the future when your subject will not exist.
- When and where do you usually experience the subject?
- What is this subject part of and what are its parts?
- What is the relationship between the subject and that of which it is a part?
- What do other people think of your subject?

READING

In many situations, writers must rely on information and ideas in books, articles, letters, and other archival documents. Their invention and inquiry in these situations involves gathering, analyzing, selecting, and organizing what they learn from such sources.

Most of the writing you do in college or on the job will be based at least in part on printed texts. This section presents several strategies that will help you to write about ideas and information you acquire in your reading. The strategies include annotating, inventorying, outlining, paraphrasing, and summarizing. They will help you in the following ways:

to gather and organize new information from your reading

to understand the new information

to connect information from different sources

to relate information to what you already know, believe, and feel

to condense and record information so that you can use it when writing exams, research papers, and essays about issues and policies

Annotating

Annotations are the notes we make in margins of books we own. Annotations can be exclamations of outrage or of approval, insights, questions, brief summaries, sequential labeling of main points, even doodles—anything at all that records succinctly what the reader is learning and feeling. Some readers annotate consistently, even obsessively, filling margins with notes. Others rarely do it. Most also underline important sentences or passages, or they may highlight them with colored markers.

Annotation serves two purposes: (1) to record reactions, questions, and understandings, and (2) to organize the text for reviewing, studying, or writing about. As a preliminary step to writing, annotation can be a very important invention activity, marking crucial details, examples, quotations, and main points that might be needed for a summary, essay, or research report. Annotating takes various forms:

- Writing words, phrases, or sentences: these writings can comment, question, evaluate, define, relate, challenge

- Underlining or highlighting words or phrases
- Circling or boxing words or phrases
- Connecting related items with lines
- Numbering a sequence of related items: points, examples, names
- Bracketing a part of the text, either within the text itself or with a line in the margin

Annotating can be light or heavy, depending on the difficulty of the material and your plans for writing about it. For a literary text you plan to analyze and interpret, your annotations may be heavy and quite varied. You will make some annotations the first time you read it and more when you reread it. Here is the way one reader annotated a paragraph James Joyce's "Araby." The complete story appears in Chapter 10.

When the short days of winter came dusk fell before we had well eaten our dinners. When we met in the street the house had grown sombre. The space of sky above us was the colour of ever-changing violet and towards it the lamps of the street lifted their feeble lanterns. The cold air stung us and we played till our bodies glowed. Our shouts echoed in the silent street. The career of our play brought us through the dark muddy lanes behind the houses where we ran the gauntlet of the rough tribes from the cottages, to the back doors of the dark dripping gardens where odours arose from the ashpits, to the dark odorous stables where a coachman smoothed and combed the horse or shook music from the buckled harness. When we returned to the street light from the kitchen windows had filled the areas. If my uncle was seen turning the corner we hid in the shadow until we had seen him safely housed. Or if Mangan's sister came out on the doorstep to call her brother in to his tea we watched her from our shadow peer up and down the street. We waited to see whether she would remain or go in and, if she remained, we left our shadow and walked up Mangan's steps resignedly. She was waiting for us, her figure defined by the light from the half-opened door. Her brother always teased her before he obeyed and I stood by the railings looking at her. Her dress swung as she moved her body and the soft rope of her hair tossed from side to side.

Margin annotations:

light, faint

circular movement— from light, to dark, back to light

why hide from uncle?

Mangan's sister introduced

time of year: winter

time of day: dusk

"career" = play, not job

repetition of "where" clauses

again—light to shadow to light

enticing, almost sexual image of friend's sister (light)—older than boys?

At a glance you can see how many different annotating activities this writer found useful: writing comments and questions, connecting related items, circling unusual or unknown words, underlining certain words, and bracketing part of the text in the margin. The written comments indicate that the reader actively sought to understand the story.

Annotating an expository text is different from annotating a story or a poem. You are not so much probing for meaning as you are organizing and

You might compare this annotation of "Araby" to the one on pp. 363–64.

clarifying information. Consequently, in annotating an expository text, you might want to concentrate on underlining main ideas, deciding how the information and ideas are organized, and marking the most important points. Here is the way one student annotated a paragraph in an essay on Native American writing systems.

The Native American groups which, despite all obstacles, have developed traditions of literacy in their own languages seem to share certain characteristics. All of them, of course, have preserved some sort of social organization, at least at the local community level. It would seem that such groups have also found one or more functions for their own literacy. Thus the spread of Fox, Winnebago, Cherokee, and Mahican literacy occurred at the same time that these several tribes were divided by migrations. In all four cases it seems reasonable to suppose that the first individuals to become literate were motivated by a desire to communicate with relatives who had departed for the west or, as the case may be, had lingered behind in the east. The Aleuts and Yupiks were never forcibly "removed" or broken into separate reservation communities; but their dispersed settlements and frequent hunting and fishing expeditions made the ability to read and write letters a useful skill. Motivation for literacy is not always based on the need to correspond with absent friends and relatives, however. The Cherokee syllabary, for example, has long been used in the context of religious services and religious instruction where those to whom messages are read are all present in the same room with those who are reading. Likewise, the Cherokee medical practitioners who record curing formulas in the syllabary do so primarily for their own reference, not for unspecified readers at some remote place and time. The factors that tend to perpetuate native literacy, then, need not include a felt need to communicate with distant members of a tightly knit society; but they do seem to include the perception of literacy as a useful skill which enables the literate to achieve some worthwhile objective.

Left margin annotations:

certain characteristics—social organization, literacy functions (letters, religious services, records)

6 different tribes mentioned—strong evidence

Right margin annotations:

what kinds of obstacles?

1. for communication

2. for religious services

3. for reference

main point

Inventorying

Inventorying is a useful activity for understanding, analyzing, and interpreting a reading. It is a natural follow-up to annotating. When you annotate you try to identify significant ideas and information. Inventorying helps you find relationships and patterns in this material, which in turn helps you to decide how you might interpret or evaluate it. Once you have a thesis, inventorying enables you to review the reading for evidence to support your thesis.

An inventory to find patterns in a text involves making several lists of related items. Consider the following possibilities:

- Recurring images (similes, metaphors)
- Noticeable stylistic features

- Repeated descriptions
- Consistent ways of characterizing people or events and of defining terms
- Repeated words and phrases
- Repeated subjects or topics
- Repeated examples or illustrations
- Reliance on particular writing strategies

What patterns you discover depend on the kind of reading you are analyzing and what you are looking for. Here is an inventory one student made from the annotations of the excerpt from James Joyce's "Araby."

```
Movement between light and darkness
space of sky
lanterns
bodies glowed
dark muddy lanes
dark dripping gardens
ashpits
dark odorous stables
light from kitchen windows
shadow . . . shadow . . . shadow
light from half-opened door

Mangan's sister enticing to narrator
figure defined by the light
dress swung as she moved her body
soft rope of her hair tossed from side to side
I stood by the railings looking at her

Childishness of narrator
played till our bodies glowed
our shouts echoed in the quiet streets
walked up to Mangan's steps resignedly
```

You may find it useful to inventory your annotations of a literary work before writing about it. You may also want to inventory the reading you do to find information for a report, evidence demonstrating that a trend exists, or background on an activity you are profiling. In inventorying a long work, you might want to include page numbers of items in your lists and put quotation marks around quoted words and phrases. For much of the writing you do as a college student, you will find inventorying (and annotating) not just helpful but essential.

Outlining

Outlining is not only a good way of organizing your own ideas, but it can help you understand and remember the material you are reading. An outline displays the framework of main features or ideas of a written work. An outline may be an informal list of phrases, a formal numbered and indented set of sentences, or a visual cluster. Each of these types of outlines is illustrated in the earlier discussion of mapping strategies.

Paraphrasing

In many of the writing assignments in this book and in much of the writing you do in college, you will use information from sources. The three basic ways of integrating this information into your own writing are by means of quotation, paraphrase, and summary. One of the most important writing decisions you will have to make again and again is which one of these to use. A *quotation* is an exact reproduction of the language in the source. A *paraphrase* is a presentation in your own words of *all* the information in a brief passage. Paraphrase may alternate with quotations and with your own analysis or commentary. When you *summarize*, you present in your own words just the main ideas in a passage.

Strategies for integrating quoted material smoothly into your writing are demonstrated in Chapter 21.

Here is how one student paraphrased the first five sentences of a paragraph from the article on Native American writing systems printed earlier in this chapter.

Original

The Native American groups which, despite all obstacles, have developed traditions of literacy in their own languages seem to share certain characteristics. All of them, of course, have preserved some sort of social organization, at least at the local community level. It would seem that such groups have also found one or more functions for their own literacy. Thus the spread of Fox, Winnebago, Cherokee, and Mahican literacy occurred at the same time that these several tribes were divided by migrations. In all four cases it seems reasonable to suppose that the first individuals to become literate were motivated by a desire to communicate with relatives who had departed for the west or, as the case may be, had lingered behind in the east.

Paraphrase

```
Native American groups had to overcome many obstacles in
order to develop writing systems in their own languages.
The groups that did develop writing are alike in several
ways: they maintained their social structure, and they
were able to put writing to good use. For example, writ-
ing became more common in the Fox, Winnebago, Cherokee,
and Mahican tribes after they were separated through mi-
gration. Tribal members probably wanted to write to
relatives they could no longer see regularly.
```

The first thing to note about the paraphrase is that it contains *all* the information in the original. It is not just a summary. It is a complete reproduction in the student's own words. Although it has the same number of sentences as the original, the information is grouped into sentences in somewhat different ways. In using this information in an essay, the writer might quote the original; but, unless it contains crucial evidence or memorable language, it probably should be paraphrased.

Without changing the information significantly, paraphrase aims to clarify and simplify the original. It may explain difficult material, or it may restate a complicated argument. As a way of understanding difficult material by restating it in your own words, paraphrase is useful as a strategy of inquiry. It is very time-consuming, though, and should be used only with short passages.

Summarizing

A summary is a selection of main ideas. All talking and writing involves some degree of summary. If we tell someone what our day was like, we summarize. When we write, we summarize our experience or knowledge.

As you write, you occasionally summarize your own writing, especially in longer pieces, when you pause to remind the reader what you have said so far and forecast what is to come next. Some essays conclude with a summary.

As a writer, you also summarize information from other writers. In informative and argumentative essays, essay exams and research reports, you interweave your own analysis and commentary with quotations, paraphrases, and summaries from other writers. Just as you must indicate the source of quotations, you must also indicate the source of paraphrased or summarized material.

Chapter 21 illustrates ways to document your sources.

Here is one student's summary of the paragraph from the essay on Native American writing systems that appeared earlier in this chapter. Read the complete paragraph, and then examine the student's summary.

Summary

```
Native Americans developed their own writing systems in
order to write letters, perform religious services, and
keep records.
```

The preceding sentence is one possible summary of the main idea of the paragraph. It does not leave out any important part of the main idea, nor does it include any of the examples or illustrations. It is stated in the student's own language, not the language of the original, though, of course, certain key terms must be repeated.

To summarize a longer selection, you would read and reread it carefully, annotating as you go. You could then outline the selection in order to be certain you have identified all the main ideas. You would then be able to write a coherent summary based on your outline.

n order to guide readers through a piece of writing, a writer can provide four basic kinds of cues or signals: (1) thesis and forecasting statements, to orient readers to ideas and organization; (2) paragraphing, to group related ideas and details; (3) cohesive devices, to connect ideas to one another and bring about coherence and clarity; and (4) transitions, to signal relationships or shifts in meaning. This chapter will examine how each of these cueing strategies works.

ORIENTING STATEMENTS

To help readers find their way, especially in difficult and lengthy works, you can provide two kinds of orienting information: thesis statements that declare the main point and forecasting statements that, in addition to stating the thesis, preview the way the thesis will be developed.

Thesis Statements

Although they may have a variety of forms and purposes, all essays are essentially assertive. That is, they assert or put forward the writer's point of view on a particular subject. We call this point of view the essay's *thesis,* or main idea.

To help readers understand what is being said about a subject, writers often provide a thesis statement early in the essay. The *thesis statement* is usually a single sentence that declares the essay's main idea. It operates as a cue by letting readers know which is the most important, general idea among the writer's many ideas and observations. Like the focal point of a picture, the thesis statement directs the reader's attention to the one idea that brings all the other ideas and details into perspective. Here are two thesis statements from essays in Part I:

> Two great partnerships are celebrated in this Oklahoma arena: the indispensable one between man and animal that any rancher or cowboy takes on, enduring the joys and punishments of the alliance; and the one between man and man, cowboy and cowboy. —Gretel Ehrlich, Chapter 4

> *The Crimson*'s decision not to run *Playboy*'s advertisement recruiting Harvard women for its October ''Women of the Ivy League'' issue was both the very most and the very least the newspaper could do to fight the institutionalized exploitation of women. —Kristin A. Goss, Chapter 6

Cueing the Reader   12

Read an essay by Gretel Ehrlich (Chapter 4), Kristin A. Goss (Chapter 6), or Stephen King (Chapter 9); then briefly explain how its thesis statement brings the ideas and details of the essay into perspective.

Each of the two preceding thesis statements is expressed directly in a single sentence. But sometimes writers need several sentences to state their thesis, and sometimes they imply the thesis rather than state it directly. For example, Rachel Richardson Smith in "Abortion, Right and Wrong" (Chapter 6) states her thesis this way:

> I find myself in the awkward position of being both anti-abortion and pro-choice. Neither group seems to be completely right—or wrong. It is not that I think abortion is wrong for me but acceptable for someone else. The question is far more complex than that.   –Rachel Richardson Smith, Chapter 6

Smith presents her thesis in terms of a dichotomy between two extremes, neither of which she finds acceptable. Rather than imposing a single viewpoint directly, Smith suggests the complexity of the matter of abortion and, in the course of her argument, encourages her readers to regard abortion less in ideologically single-minded terms than in terms of the variety of difficult human, ethical, and political questions involved.

Readers by necessity look for something that will tell them the point of an essay, a focus for the many diverse details and ideas they encounter as they read. The lack of an explicit thesis statement can make this task more difficult. Therefore, careful writers keep in mind the needs and expectations of readers in deciding whether or not to state the thesis explicitly.

A further important decision is where to place the thesis statment. Most readers expect to find some information early in the text that will give them a context for the essay. They expect essays to open with thesis statements, and they need such statements to orient them, particularly if they are reading about a new and difficult subject. A thesis statement placed at the beginning of an essay helps give readers a sense of control over the subject, enabling them to anticipate the content of the essay and more easily understand the relationship between its various ideas and details.

Occasionally, however, particularly in fairly short, informal essays and in some argumentative essays, a writer will save a direct statement of the thesis

See Victor Fuchs's essay on pp. 303–06 for an example of a concluding thesis.

until the conclusion. Such a thesis is designed to bring together the various strands of information or evidence introduced over the course of the essay and to suggest the essay's overall point; in many cases, a concluding thesis is also used to point the way toward future developments or goals.

Forecasting Statements

Actually a special kind of thesis statement, a *forecasting statement* not only identifies the thesis but also gives an overview of the way that thesis will be developed. The opening paragraph of an essay by William Langer on the bubonic plague illustrates the role of the forecasting statement:

> In the three years from 1348 through 1350 the pandemic of plague known as the Black Death, or, as the Germans called it, the Great Dying, killed at least a fourth of the population of Europe. It was undoubtedly the worst disaster that has ever befallen mankind. Today we can have no real conception of the terror under which people lived in the shadow of the plague. For more than two centuries plague has not been a serious threat to mankind in the large, although it is still a grisly presence in parts of the Far East and Africa. Scholars continue to study the Great Dying, however, as a historical example of human behavior under the stress of universal catastrophe. In these days when the threat of plague has been replaced by the threat of mass human extermination by even more rapid means, there has been a sharp renewal of interest in the history of the 14th-century calamity. With new perspective, students are investigating its manifold effects: demographic, economic, psychological, moral and religious.
>
> —William Langer, "The Black Death"

This paragraph informs us that Langer's article is about the effects of the Black Death. His thesis, however, is not stated explicitly. It is implied by the forecasting statement that concludes the paragraph. With this sentence, Langer states that the study of the plague currently is focused on five particular categories. As a reader would expect, Langer then goes on to divide his essay into analyses of these five effects, taking them up in the order in which they appear in the forecasting statement.

EXERCISE 12.2

Choose an essay from Chapter 5 and read it, underlining the thesis and forecasting statements. If you do not find any sentences that perform these functions, try drafting them yourself. Then reflect on the usefulness of those cueing devices.

PARAGRAPHING

Paragraph Cues

The indentation that signals the beginning of a new paragraph is a relatively modern printing convention. Old manuscripts show that paragraph divisions were not always marked. In order to make reading easier, scribes and printers began to use the symbol ¶ to mark paragraph breaks. Later indenting became common practice, but even that relatively modern custom has changed in some forms of writing today. Instead of indenting, most writers in business now set paragraphs apart from the rest of the text by leaving an extra line of space above and below each paragraph.

The lack of paragraph cues makes reading extremely difficult. To illustrate this fact, the paragraph indentions have been removed from the following introductory section of a chapter in Stephen Jay Gould's book *Ever Since Darwin*. Even with proper paragraphing, this selection might be difficult because it includes unfamiliar information and technical language. Without paragraphing, however, Gould's logic becomes hard to follow, and the mind and the eye long for a momentary rest. (Each of the thirty sentences in the selection is numbered at the beginning.)

(1) Since man created God in his own image, the doctrine of special creation has never failed to explain those adaptations that we understand intuitively. (2) How can we doubt that animals are exquisitely designed for their appointed roles when we watch a lioness hunt, a horse run, or a hippo wallow? (3) The theory of natural selection would never have replaced the doctrine of divine creation if evident, admirable design pervaded all organisms. (4) Charles Darwin understood this, and he focused on features that would be out of place in a world constructed by perfect wisdom. (5) Why, for example, should a sensible designer create only on Australia a suite of marsupials to fill the same roles that placental mammals occupy on all other continents? (6) Darwin even wrote an entire book on orchids to argue that the structures evolved to insure fertilization by insects are jerry-built of available parts used by ancestors for other purposes. (7) Orchids are Rube Goldberg machines; a perfect engineer would certainly have come up with something better. (8) This principle remains true today. (9) The best illustrations of adaptation by evolution are the ones that strike our intuition as peculiar or bizarre. (10) Science is not "organized common sense"; at its most exciting, it reformulates our view of the world by imposing powerful theories against the ancient, anthropocentric prejudices that we call intuition. (11) Consider, for example, the cecidomyian gall midges. (12) These tiny flies conduct their lives in a way that tends to evoke feelings of pain or disgust when we empathize with them by applying the inappropriate standards of our own social codes. (13) Cecidomyian gall midges can grow and develop along one of two pathways. (14) In some situations, they hatch from eggs, go through a normal sequence of larval and pupal molts, and emerge as ordinary, sexually reproducing flies. (15) But in other circumstances, females reproduce by parthenogenesis, bringing forth their young without any fertilization by males. (16) Parthenogenesis is common enough among animals, but the cecidomyians give it an interesting twist. (17) First of all, the parthenogenetic females stop at an early age of development. (18) They never become normal, adult flies, but reproduce while they are still larvae or pupae. (19) Secondly, these females do not lay eggs. (20) The offspring develop live within their mother's body—not supplied with nutrient and packaged away in a protected uterus but right inside the mother's tissues, eventually filling her entire body. (21) In order to grow, the

offspring devour the mother from the inside. (22) A few days later, they emerge, leaving a chitinous shell as the only remains of their only parent. (23) And within two days, their own developing children are beginning, literally, to eat them up. (24) *Micromalthus debilis,* an unrelated beetle, has evolved an almost identical system with a macabre variation. (25) Some parthenogenetic females give birth to a single male offspring. (26) This larva attaches itself to his mother's cuticle for about four or five days, then inserts his head into her genital aperture and devours her. (27) Greater love hath no woman. (28) Why has such a peculiar mode of reproduction evolved? (29) For it is unusual even among insects, and not only by the irrelevant standards of our own perceptions. (30) What is the adaptive significance of a mode of life that so strongly violates our intuitions about good design?   —Stephen Jay Gould, *Ever Since Darwin*

A major difficulty in reading this selection is the need to hold the meaning of each sentence "in suspension" as you read ahead, because the meaning of an earlier sentence may be affected by the meaning of succeeding sentences. For instance, the second sentence clarifies the meaning of the first sentence by giving specific examples; the third sentence restates the idea, while sentences 4 through 7 clarify and illustrate it. Without paragraphing, you are forced to remember each sentence separately and even to anticipate such close connections among sentences in order to make sense of the text.

EXERCISE 12.3

Here is the way the Gould selection divides into its six original paragraphs: sentences 1–7, 8–10, 11–12, 13–23, 24–27, 28–30. Put a paragraphing symbol ¶ in your own book before the opening sentence of each paragraph. Later exercises will ask you to analyze aspects of Gould's paragraphing.

Paragraphing helps readers by signaling when a sequence of related sentences begins and ends. The use of such paragraph signals tells you when you can stop holding meaning in suspension. The need for this kind of closure is a major consideration of writers. Gould, for example, begins a new paragraph with sentence 8 in order to draw a sharp distinction between the examples and the general principle. Similarly, he begins a new paragraph with sentence 24 to signal a shift from a description of the reproductive mode of the cecidomyian gall midge to that of *Micromalthus debilis.* In this way, paragraphing keeps readers from being overloaded with information and at the same time helps them follow the development of ideas.

Paragraphing also helps readers judge what is most important in what they are reading. Writers typically emphasize important information by placing it at the two points where readers are most attentive—the beginning and ending of a paragraph. Many writers put information to orient readers at the beginning of a paragraph and save the most important information for last, as Gould does when he ends a paragraph with sentence 27.

See pp. 406–10 for discussion of topic sentences.

You can give special emphasis to information by placing it in a paragraph of its own. Gould, for example, puts sentences 11 and 12 together in a separate paragraph. These two sentences could have been attached to either the preceding or following paragraphs. But Gould gives them a separate paragraph in order to emphasize the general point he is making. In addition, this paragraph serves as an important transition between the general discussion of how science explains things that go against intuition and the specific example of the bizarre adaptation of the cecidomyian gall midge.

Paragraph Conventions

Some writing situations call for fairly strict conventions for paragraphing. Readers may not be conscious of these conventions, but they would certainly notice if the custom were not observed. For example, readers would be surprised if a newspaper did not have narrow columns and short paragraphs. This paragraphing convention is not accidental; it is designed to make newspaper reading easy and fast and to allow the reader to take in an entire paragraph at a glance. Business writing also tends to have short paragraphs. Memo readers frequently do not want an excess of details or qualifications. Instead, they prefer a concise overview, a capsule that is easy to swallow.

College instructors, on the other hand, expect students to qualify their ideas and support them with specifics. They care less about how long it takes to read a paragraph than about how well developed the writing is. Therefore, paragraphs in college essays usually have several sentences. In fact, it is not unusual to find quite long paragraphs, as this example from an undergraduate history essay on the status of women in Victorian England illustrates:

> A genteel woman was absolutely dependent upon the two men in her life: first her father, and then her husband. From them came her economic and social status; they were the center of her thoughts and the objects of any ambitions she might have. The ideal woman did not live for herself; she barely had a self, because her entire existence was vicarious. Legally, a woman had almost no existence at all. Until her marriage, a daughter was completely in the power of her father; upon her marriage, she was legally absorbed by her husband. Any money she had became his, as did all of her property, including her clothes and even those things that had been given her as personal gifts before her marriage. Any earnings she might make by working belonged to her husband. A woman could not be sued for debt separately from her husband because legally they were the same person. She could not sign a lease or sue someone in court without having her husband be the complainant, even in cases of long separation. In cases of a husband's enmity, she had almost no legal protection from him. Under English law, divorces could be obtained, in practice, only by men. A man could divorce his wife on the grounds of adultery, but the reverse was not the case.

If any rule for paragraphing is truly universal, it is this: paragraphs should be focused, unified, and coherent. That is, the sentences in a paragraph should be meaningfully related to one another, and the relationships among the sentences should be clear. The following sentences—although they may look like a paragraph—do not constitute a meaningful paragraph because they lack focus, unity, and coherence.

> Maturity and attitude go together because both determine why you want to become a model. I went to the university for two years, not because I wanted to but because I was pushed into it. I used to think models were thought of as dumb blondes, but after being here at the university I realized that people still have respect for modeling and know all the hard work put in it.

Even though each of these sentences mentions either modeling or the university or both, the two topics are not connected. With each sentence, the focus shifts—from the general desire to become a model, to the writer's attending university, to the attitude of people toward models. There is no unity because there is no single idea controlling the sentences. The various elements of the writing do not "stick together" to form a coherent meaning, and the reader may well become disoriented. The topic-sentence strategies discussed in the following section are useful for ensuring coherence.

EXERCISE 12.4

Look at the Gould passage earlier in this chapter. Analyze how Gould's paragraphing helps you follow his meaning. Would you have paragraphed this passage differently? Explain how and why.

Topic-sentence Strategies

A *topic sentence* lets readers know the focus of a paragraph in simple and direct terms. It is a cueing strategy for the paragraph much as a thesis or forecasting statement is for the whole essay. Because paragraphing usually signals a shift in focus, readers expect some kind of reorientation in the opening sentence. They need to know whether the new paragraph is going to introduce another aspect of the topic or develop one already introduced.

Announcing the Topic.　Some topic sentences simply announce the topic. Here are a few examples taken from Barry Lopez's book *Arctic Dreams:*

> A polar bear walks in a way all its own.

> What is so consistently striking about the way Eskimos used parts of an animal is the breadth of their understanding about what would work.

> Distinctive landmarks that aid the traveler and control the vastness, as well as prominent marks on the land made inadvertently in the process of completing other tasks, are very much apparent in the Arctic.

> The Mediterranean view of the Arctic, down to the time of the Elizabethan mariners, was shaped by two somewhat contradictory thoughts.

These topic sentences do more than merely identify the topic; they also indicate how the topic will be developed in subsequent sentences—by citing examples, describing physical features, presenting reasons and evidence, relating anecdotes, classifying, defining, comparing, or contrasting.

Other strategies that can be used for paragraph development are discussed in Chapters 13 through 18.

Following is one of Lopez's paragraphs that shows how the topic in the first sentence is developed:

What is so consistently striking about the way Eskimos used parts of an animal is the breadth of their understanding about what would work. Knowing that muskox horn is more flexible than caribou antler, they preferred it for making the side prongs of a fish spear. For a waterproof bag in which to carry sinews for clothing repair, they chose salmon skin. They selected the strong, translucent intestine of a bearded seal to make a window for a snowhouse—it would fold up for easy traveling and it would not frost over in cold weather. To make small snares for sea ducks, they needed a springy material that would not rot in salt water—baleen fibers. The down feather of a common eider, tethered at the end of a stick in the snow at an aglu, would reveal the exhalation of a quietly surfacing seal. Polar bear bone was used anywhere a stout, sharp point was required, because it is the hardest bone.   —Barry Lopez, *Arctic Dreams*

EXERCISE 12.5

Read the Weisman essay in Chapter 7. Indicate which paragraphs begin with topic sentences, and explain how these sentences help you anticipate the paragraph's topic and its method of development.

Forecasting Subtopics.   Other topic sentences actually give readers a detailed overview of subtopics that follow. In the following paragraph the subtopics mentioned in the opening sentence appear later in the paragraph. The subtopics are underscored in the first sentence and then connected by lines to the point in the paragraph where they subsequently appear.

Notice that the subtopics are taken up in the same order as in the opening sentence: education first, followed by economic independence, power of office, and so on. This correlation makes the paragraph easy to follow. Even so, one subtopic may be developed in a sentence while another requires two or more sentences. The last two subtopics—equality of status and recognition as human beings—are not directly brought up but are implied in the last sentence.

Oppressed groups are denied education, economic independence, the power of office, representation, an image of dignity and self-respect, equality of status, and recognition as human beings. Throughout history women have been consistently denied all of these, and their denial today, while attenuated and partial, is nevertheless consistent. The education allowed them is deliberately designed to be inferior, and they are systematically programmed out of and excluded from the knowledge where power lies today—e.g., in science and technology. They are confined to conditions of economic dependence based on the sale of their sexuality in marriage, or a variety of prostitutions. Work on a basis of economic independence allows them only a subsistence level of life—often not even that. They do not hold office, are represented in no positions of power, and authority is forbidden them. The image of woman fostered by cultural media, high and low, then and now, is a marginal and demeaning existence, and one outside the human condition—which is defined as the prerogative of man, the male.

—Kate Millett, *Sexual Politics*

Asking a Rhetorical Question.   Writers occasionally put their topic sentences in a question-answer format, posing a rhetorical question in one sentence which is then answered in the next sentence. Question-answer topic sentences do not always appear at the beginning of a paragraph. On occasion, a question at the end of one paragraph may combine with the first sentence of the following paragraph. Here is a paragraph illustrating the rhetorical question strategy.

> What about motion that is too slow to be seen by the human eye? That problem has been solved by the use of the time-lapse camera. In this one, the shutter is geared to take only one shot per second, or one per minute, or even one per hour—depending upon the kind of movement that is being photographed. When the time-lapse film is projected at the normal speed of twenty-four pictures per second, it is possible to see a bean sprout growing up out of the ground. Time-lapse films are useful in the study of many types of motion too slow to be observed by the unaided human eye.   —James C. Rettie, "But a Watch in the Night"

EXERCISE 12.6

Look at the selection by Rachel Richardson Smith in Chapter 6. Where does the writer use the rhetorical question as a topic-sentence strategy? Analyze how the rhetorical question is answered.

Making a Transition.   Not all topic sentences simply point forward to what will follow. Some also refer back to earlier sentences. Such sentences work both as topic sentences, stating the main point of the paragraph, and as transitions, linking that paragraph to the previous one. Here are a few topic sentences from *Aristotle for Everybody* by Mortimer J. Adler that use specific transitional terms (underscored) to tie the sentence to a previous statement:

> Nevertheless there is something permanent in this special kind of change.
>
> Like sensations, ideas are neither true nor false.
>
> On the other hand, a piece of music—a song that is sung over and over again—does not exist just at one place and at one time.
>
> So, too, are teachers.
>
> There is one further difference between a song or a story and a painting or a statue.
>
> Not only must these basic biological needs be satisfied beyond the level of the barest minimum required to sustain life but, in addition, many other human needs must be satisfied in order to approach the fulfillment of all our capacities and tendencies.

Sometimes the first sentence of a paragraph serves as a transition, while a subsequent sentence—in this case the last—states the topic. The underscored sentences illustrate this strategy in the following example:

> . . . What a convenience, what a relief it will be, they say, never to worry about how to dress for a job interview, a romantic tryst, or a funeral!
>
> Convenient perhaps, but not exactly a relief. Such a utopia would give most of us the same kind of chill we feel when a stadium full of Communist-bloc athletes in identical sports outfits, shouting slogans in unison, appears on TV. Most people do not want to be told what to wear any more than they want to be told what to say. In Belfast recently four hundred Irish Republican prisoners "refused to wear any clothes at all, draping themselves day and night in blankets," rather than put on prison uniforms. Even the offer of civilian-style dress did not satisfy them; they insisted on wearing their own clothes brought from home, or nothing. Fashion is free speech, and one of the privileges, if not always one of the pleasures, of a free world.   —Alison Lurie, *The Language of Clothes*

Occasionally, particularly in long essays, whole paragraphs serve as transitions, linking one sequence of paragraphs with those that follow. Even though we have taken the next transition paragraph out of its context, you can see that it summarizes what went before (evidence of contrast) and sets up what will follow (evidence of similarity):

> Yet it was not all contrast, after all. Different as they were—in background, in personality, in underlying aspiration—these two great soldiers had much in common. Under everything else, they were marvelous fighters. Furthermore, their fighting qualities were really very much alike.
>
> —Bruce Catton, "Grant and Lee: A Study in Contrasts"

Positioning the Topic Sentence.   Although topic sentences may occur anywhere in a paragraph, stating the topic in the first sentence has the advantage of giving readers a sense of how the paragraph is likely to be developed. The beginning of the paragraph is therefore the most commonly favored position for a topic sentence.

A topic sentence that does not open a paragraph is most likely to appear at the end. When placed in the concluding position, topic sentences usually summarize or generalize preceding information. In the following example, the topic is not stated explicitly until the last sentence.

> Every moment of the day the world bombards the human speaker with information and experiences. It clamors for his attention, claws his senses, intrudes into his thoughts. Only a very small portion of this total experience is language—yet the speaker must use this small portion to report on all the experiences that exist or ever existed in the totality of the world since time began. Try to think about the stars, a grasshopper, love or hate, pain, anything at all—and it must be done in terms of language. There is no other way; thinking is language spoken to oneself. Until language has made sense of experience, that experience is meaningless.   —Peter Farb, *Word Play*

When a topic sentence is used in a narrative, it will often appear as the last sentence. This concluding topic sentence often evaluates or reflects on events, as illustrated in the following paragraph:

I hadn't known she could play the piano. She wasn't playing very well, I guess, because she stopped occasionally and had to start over again. She concentrated intensely on the music, and the others in the room sat absolutely silently. My mother was facing me but didn't seem to see me. She seemed to be staring beyond me toward something that wasn't there. All the happy excitement died in me at that moment. <u>Looking at my mother, so isolated from us all, I saw her for the first time as a person utterly alone.</u>   —Russell Baker, *Growing Up*

In rare cases, the topic sentence for one paragraph will appear at the end of the preceding paragraph, as in this example:

<u>. . . And apart from being new, psychoanalysis was particularly threatening.</u>
French psychiatrists tended to look at the sufferings of their patients either as the result of organic lesions or moral degeneration. In either case, the boundary between the "healthy" doctor and the "sick" patient was clear. Freud's theory makes it hard to draw such lines by insisting that if the psychiatrist knew himself better, he would find more points in common with the patient than he might have thought. . . .   —Sherry Turkle, *Psychoanalytic Politics*

In addition, it is possible for a single topic sentence to introduce two (or occasionally more) paragraphs. Subsequent paragraphs in such a series consequently have no separate topic sentence of their own. Following is an example of a two-paragraph sequence in which the topic sentence opens the first paragraph:

<u>Almost without exception all human languages have built into them a polarity, a veer to the right.</u> "Right" is associated with legality, correct behavior, high moral principles, firmness, and masculinity; "left," with weakness, cowardice, diffuseness of purpose, evil, and femininity. In English, for example, we have "rectitude," "rectify," "righteous," "right-hand man," "dexterity," "adroit" (from the French "*à droite*"), "rights," as in "the rights of man," and the phrase "in his right mind." Even "ambidextrous" means, ultimately, two right hands.
On the other side (literally), we have "sinister" (almost exactly the Latin word for "left"), "gauche" (precisely the French word for "left"), "gawky," "gawk," and "left-handed compliment." The Russian "*nalevo*" for "left" also means "surreptitious." The Italian "*mancino*" for "left" signifies "deceitful." There is no "Bill of Lefts."   —Carl Sagan, *Dragons of Eden*

EXERCISE 12.7

Now that you have seen several topic-sentence strategies, look again at the Gould passage earlier in this chapter and identify the strategies he uses. Then evaluate how well his topic sentences work to orient you as a reader.

COHESIVE DEVICES

Writers can also use certain cohesive devices to guide the reader. Cohesive devices help readers follow a writer's train of thought by connecting key words and phrases throughout a passage. Among such devices are pronoun reference, word repetition, synonyms, repetition of sentence structure, and collocation.

Pronoun Reference

One common cohesive device is pronoun reference. As noun substitutes, pronouns refer to nouns that either precede or follow them, and thus serve to connect phrases or sentences. The nouns that come before the pronouns are called antecedents. In the following paragraph, the pronouns (all *it*) form a chain of connection with their antecedent, *George Washington Bridge*.

> In New York from dawn to dusk to dawn, day after day, you can hear the steady rumble of tires against the concrete span of the George Washington Bridge. The bridge is never completely still. It trembles with traffic. It moves in the wind. Its great veins of steel swell when hot and contract when cold; its span often is ten feet closer to the Hudson River in summer than in winter. —Gay Talese, "New York"

In the preceding example, there is only one pronoun-antecedent chain, and the antecedent comes first so all the pronouns refer back to it. When there are multiple pronoun-antecedent chains with references forward as well as back, writers have to make certain that readers will not mistake one pronoun's antecedent for another's.

Word Repetition

To avoid confusion, a writer will often use a second cohesive device: the repetition of words and phrases. This device is used especially if a pronoun might confuse readers:

> The first step is to realize that in our society we have permitted the kinds of vulnerability that characterize the victims of violent crime and have ignored, where we could, the hostility and alienation that enter into the making of violent criminals. No rational person condones violent crime, and I have no patience with sentimental attitudes toward violent criminals. But it is time that we open our eyes to the conditions that foster violence and that ensure the existence of easily recognizable victims. —Margaret Mead, "A Life for a Life: What That Means Today"

In the next example several overlapping chains of word repetition prevent confusion and help the reader follow the ideas:

> Natural selection is the central concept of Darwinian theory—the fittest survive and spread their favored traits through populations. Natural selection is defined by Spencer's phrase "survival of the fittest," but what does this famous bit of jargon really mean? Who are the fittest? And how is "fitness" defined? We often read that fitness involves no more than "differential reproductive success"—the production of more surviving offspring than other competing members of the population. Whoa! cries Bethell, as many others have before him. This formulation defines fitness in terms of survival only. The crucial phrase of natural selection means no more than "the survival of those who survive"—a vacuous tautology. (A tautology is a phrase—like "my father is a man"—containing no information in the predicate ["a man"] not inherent in the subject ["my father"]. Tautologies are fine as definitions, but not as testable scientific statements—there can be nothing to test in a statement true by definition.)
>
> —Stephen Jay Gould, *Ever Since Darwin*

Notice that Gould uses repetition to keep readers focused on the key concepts of "natural selection," "survival of the fittest," and "tautology." These key terms may vary in form—*fittest* becomes *fitness* and *survival* changes to *surviving* and *survive*—but they serve as links in the chain of meaning.

Synonyms

In addition to repeating the same word, you can also use synonyms, words with identical or very similar meanings, to connect important ideas. In the following example, the author develops a careful chain of synonyms and word repetitions:

> Over time, small bits of knowledge about a region accumulate among local residents in the form of stories. These are remembered in the community; even what is unusual does not become lost and therefore irrelevant. These narratives comprise for a native an intricate, long-term view of a particular landscape. . . . Outside the region this complex but easily shared "reality" is hard to get across without reducing it to generalities, to misleading or imprecise abstraction.
>
> —Barry Lopez, *Arctic Dreams*

Note the variety of synonym sequences: "region," "particular landscape"; "local residents," "community," "native"; "stories," "narratives"; "accumulate," "remembered," "does not become lost," "comprise"; "intricate long-term view," "complex . . . reality," "without reducing it to generalities." The result is a coherence of paragraph development that constantly reinforces the point the author is making.

Sentence-structure Repetition

Writers occasionally repeat the same sentence structure in order to emphasize the connections among their ideas. For example:

> But the life forms are as much part of the structure of the Earth as any inanimate portion is. It is all an inseparable part of a whole. If any animal is isolated totally from other forms of life, then death by starvation will surely follow. If isolated from water, death by dehydration will follow even faster. If isolated from air, whether free or dissolved in water, death by asphyxiation will follow still faster. If isolated from the Sun, animals will survive for a time, but plants would die, and if all plants died, all animals would starve.   —Isaac Asimov, "The Case against Man"

From the third sentence to the last, Asimov repeats the "If this . . . then that" sentence structure to emphasize the various points he is making.

Collocation

Words collocate when they occur together in expected ways around a particular topic. For example, in a paragraph on a high school graduation, a reader might expect to encounter words such as *valedictorian, diploma, commencement, honors, cap and gown,* or *senior class.* Collocations occur quite naturally to a writer, and they usually form a recognizable network of meaning for readers. The paragraph that follows uses five collocation chains:

1. housewife—cooking—neighbor—home
2. clocks—calculated cooking times—progression—precise

3. obstinacy—vagaries—problem

4. sun—clear days—cloudy ones—sundial—cast its light—angle—seasons—sun—weather

5. cooking—fire—matches—hot coals—smoldering—ashes—go out—bed-warming

> The seventeenth-century housewife not only had to make do without thermometers, she also had to make do without clocks, which were scarce and dear throughout the sixteen hundreds. She calculated cooking times by the progression of the sun; her cooking must have been more precise on clear days than on cloudy ones. Marks were sometimes painted on the floor, providing her with a rough sundial, but she still had to make allowance for the obstinacy of the sun in refusing to cast its light at the same angle as the seasons changed; but she was used to allowing for the vagaries of sun and weather. She also had a problem starting her fire in the morning; there were no matches. If she had allowed the hot coals smoldering under the ashes to go out, she had to borrow some from a neighbor, carrying them home with care, perhaps in a bed-warming pan.
> —Waverly Root and Richard de Rouchement, *Eating in America*

EXERCISE 12.8

The preceding section illustrates the following cohesive devices: pronoun reference, word repetition, synonyms, sentence-structure repetition, and collocation. Look again at the Gould passage on adaptation earlier in the chapter, and identify the cohesive devices you find in it. How do these cohesive devices help you to read the essay and make sense of it?

TRANSITIONS

The final type of cueing discussed in this chapter is the transition. A *transition,* sometimes called a connective, serves as a bridge, connecting one paragraph, sentence, clause, or word with another. Not only does a transition signal a connection, it also identifies the kind of connection by indicating to readers how the item preceding the transition relates to that which follows it. Transitions help readers anticipate how the next paragraph or sentence will affect the meaning of what they have just read. Following is a discussion of three basic groups of transitions, based on the relationships they indicate: logical, temporal, and spatial.

Logical
Relationships

Transitions help readers follow the logic of an argument. How such transitions work is illustrated in this tightly—and passionately—reasoned paragraph by James Baldwin:

> The black man insists, by whatever means he finds at his disposal, that the white man cease to regard him as an exotic rarity <u>and</u> recognize him as a human being.

This is a very charged and difficult moment, <u>for</u> there is a great deal of will power involved in the white man's naivete. Most people are not naturally malicious, <u>and</u> the white man prefers to keep the black man at a certain human remove <u>because</u> it is easier for him <u>thus</u> to preserve his simplicity <u>and</u> to avoid being called to account for crimes committed by his forefathers, <u>or</u> his neighbors. He is inescapably aware, <u>nevertheless</u>, that he is in a better position in the world <u>than</u> black men are, <u>nor</u> can he quite put to death the suspicion that he is hated by black men <u>therefore</u>. He does not wish to be hated, <u>neither</u> does he wish to change places, <u>and</u> at this point in his uneasiness he can scarcely avoid having recourse to those legends which white men have created about black men, the most unusual effect of which is that the white man finds himself enmeshed, so to speak, in his own language which describes hell, <u>as well as</u> the attributes which lead one to hell, <u>as being</u> black as night.

—James Baldwin, "Stranger in the Village"

Following is a partial list of transitions showing logical relations:

To introduce another item in a series: first, second; in the second place; for one thing . . . for another; next; then; furthermore; moreover; in addition; finally; last; also; similarly; besides; and; as well as.

To introduce an illustration or other specification: in particular; specifically; for instance; for example; that is; namely.

To introduce a result or a cause: consequently; as a result, hence; accordingly; thus; so; therefore; then; because; since; for.

To introduce a restatement: that is; in other words; in simpler terms; to put it differently.

To introduce a conclusion or summary: in conclusion; finally; all in all; evidently; clearly; actually; to sum up; altogether; of course.

To introduce an opposing point: but; however; yet; nevertheless; on the contrary; on the other hand; in contrast; still; neither . . . nor.

To introduce a concession to an opposing view: certainly; naturally; of course; it is true; to be sure; granted.

To resume the original line of reasoning after a concession: nonetheless; all the same; even though; still; nevertheless.

Temporal Relationships

In addition to showing logical connections, transitions indicate sequence or progression in time (temporal relationships), as this example illustrates:

<u>That night</u>, we drank tea and <u>then</u> vodka with lemon peel steeped in it. The four of us talked in Russian and English about mutual friends and American railroads and the Rolling Stones. Seryozha loves the Stones, and his face grew wistful <u>as we spoke</u> about their recent album, "Some Girls." He played a tape of "Let It Bleed" over and over, <u>until</u> we could translate some difficult phrases for him; <u>after that,</u> he came out with the phrases <u>at intervals during the evening,</u> in a pretty decent imitation of Jagger's Cockney snarl. He was an adroit and oddly formal host, inconspicuously filling our teacups and politely urging us to eat bread and cheese and chocolate. <u>While he talked to us,</u> he teased Anya, calling

her "Piglet," and she shook back her bangs and glowered at him. It was clear that theirs was a fiery relationship. After a while, we talked about ourselves. Anya told us about painting and printmaking and about how hard it was to buy supplies in Moscow. There had been something angry in her dark face since the beginning of the evening; I thought at first that it meant she didn't like Americans; but now I realized that it was a constant, barely suppressed rage at her own situation.   —Andrea Lee, *Russian Journal*

Following is a partial list of temporal transitions:

To indicate frequency: frequently; hourly; often; occasionally; now and then; day after day; again and again.

To indicate duration: during; briefly; for a long time; minute by minute.

To indicate a particular time: now; then; at that time; in those days; last Sunday; next Christmas; in 1995; at the beginning of August; at six o'clock; first thing in the morning; two months ago.

To indicate the beginning: at first; in the beginning; since; before then.

To indicate the middle: in the meantime; meanwhile; as it was happening; at that moment; at the same time; simultaneously; next; then.

To indicate the end and beyond: eventually; finally; at last; in the end; subsequently; later; afterwards.

Spatial Relationships

Spatial transitions orient readers to the objects in a scene, as illustrated in this paragraph:

On Georgia 155, I crossed Troublesome Creek, then went through groves of pecan trees aligned one with the next like fenceposts. The pastures grew a green almost blue, and syrupy water the color of a dusty sunset filled the ponds. Around the farmhouses, from wires strung high above the ground, swayed gourds hollowed out for purple martins.

The land rose again on the other side of the Chattahoochee River, and Highway 34 went to the ridgetops where long views over the hills opened in all directions. Here was the tail of the Appalachian backbone, its gradual descent to the Gulf. Near the Alabama stateline stood a couple of LAST CHANCE! bars. . . .

—William Least Heat Moon, *Blue Highways*

Following is a partial list of transitions showing spatial relationships:

To indicate closeness: close to; near; next to; alongside; adjacent to; facing.

To indicate distance: in the distance; far; beyond; away; there.

To indicate direction: up or down; sideways; along; across; to the right or left; in front of or behind; above or below; inside or outside.

EXERCISE 12.9

Return to the Gould passage on page 403, and underline the logical, temporal, and spatial transitions. How do they help to relate the many details and ideas?

Narration is a basic writing strategy for presenting action. You can use narration for a variety of purposes: to illustrate and support ideas with anecdotes, entertain readers with suspenseful or revealing stories, analyze causes and possible effects with scenarios, and explain procedures with process narrative. This chapter focuses on narrative techniques—how to sequence narrative action, shape narrative structure, and present the narrative from various points of view. Finally, it looks at one special narrative form, how to present a process.

SEQUENCING NARRATIVE ACTION

Narration presents a sequence of actions taking place over a period of time. The most common way of ordering a narrative is to present the actions chronologically, beginning with the first action and going straight through to the last.

On occasion, however, writers complicate the narrative sequence by referring to something that occurred earlier, with a *flashback,* or to one that will occur later, with a *flashforward.*

The following excerpt from "Death of a Pig," an essay by E. B. White, shows how writers typically organize narratives chronologically. The essay from which the passage is taken tells us what happened when the pig White was raising became ill and died. This passage is referred to often in the pages that follow to illustrate the ways writers control readers' sense of passing time in a narrative and shape actions into meaningful stories.

It was about four o'clock in the afternoon when I first noticed that there was something wrong with the pig. He failed to appear at the trough for his supper, and when a pig (or a child) refuses supper a chill wave of fear runs through any household, or ice-household. After examining my pig, who was stretched out in the sawdust inside the building, I went to the phone and cranked it four times. Mr. Dameron answered. "What's good for a sick pig?" I asked. (There is never any identification needed on a country phone; the person on the other end knows who is talking by the sound of the voice and by the character of the question.)

"I don't know, I never had a sick pig," said Mr. Dameron, "but I can find out quick enough. You hang up and I'll call Henry."

Mr. Dameron was back on the line again in five minutes. "Henry says roll him over on his back and give him two ounces of castor oil or sweet oil, and if that doesn't do the trick give him an injection of soapy water. He says he's almost sure the pig's plugged up, and even if he's wrong, it can't do any harm.''

I thanked Mr. Dameron. I didn't go right down to the pig, though. I sank into a chair and sat still for a few minutes to think about my troubles, and then I got up and went to the bar, catching up on some odds and ends that needed tending to. Unconsciously I held off, for an hour, the deed by which I would officially recognize the collapse of the performance of raising a pig; I wanted no interruption in the regularity of feeding, the steadiness of growth, the even succession of days. I wanted no interruption, wanted no oil, no deviation. I just wanted to keep on raising a pig, full meal after full meal, spring into summer into fall. I didn't even know whether there were two ounces of castor oil on the place.

Shortly after five o'clock I remembered that we had been invited out to dinner that night and realized that if I were to dose a pig there was no time to lose. The dinner date seemed a familiar conflict: I move in a desultory society and often a week or two will roll by without my going to anybody's house to dinner or anyone's coming to mine, but when an occasion does arise, and I am summoned, something usually turns up (an hour or two in advance) to make all human intercourse seem vastly inappropriate. I have come to believe that there is in hostesses a special power of divination, and that they deliberately arrange dinners to coincide with pig failure or some other sort of failure. At any rate, it was after five o'clock and I knew I could put off no longer the evil hour.

When my son and I arrived at the pigyard, armed with a small bottle of castor oil and a length of clothesline, the pig had emerged from his house and was standing in the middle of his yard, listlessly. He gave us a slim greeting. I could see that he felt uncomfortable and uncertain. I had brought the clothesline thinking I'd have to tie him (the pig weighed more than a hundred pounds) but we never used it. My son reached down, grabbed both front legs, upset him quickly, and when he opened his mouth to scream I turned the oil into his throat—a pink, corrugated area I had never seen before. I had just time to read the label while the neck of the bottle was in his mouth. It said Puretest. The screams, slightly muffled by oil, were pitched in the hysterically high range of pig-sound, as though torture were being carried out, but they didn't last long; it was all over rather suddenly, and, his legs released, the pig righted himself.

—E. B. White, ''Death of a Pig''

EXERCISE 13.1

Think of something memorable you did that lasted a few hours. You might recall a race you ran in, a school play you performed in, an unusual activity you participated in, or an adventure in a strange place. Reflect on what you did, making a list of the events in the order in which they occurred. Then, write a brief, one-page narrative following the chronological sequence set out in your list.

**Narrative
Time Signals**

Writers basically rely on three methods of sequencing actions for their readers: time markers, verb tense markers, and references to clock time.

Time Markers.   A common way of showing the passage of time is with temporal transitions, words and phrases that locate an action at a particular point in time or that relate one point to another. Some familiar time markers include *then, when, at that time, before, after, while, next, later, first,* and *second.* Look back at the passage from "Death of a Pig" to see how White uses time markers. Notice, for example, that *when* in the first sentence labels the initial point at which he recognized something was seriously wrong. *After* in the third sentence signals the relationship between two actions—examining the pig and calling for advice.

EXERCISE 13.2

Skim the White passage, underlining all the time markers. In each case, consider whether your understanding of the narrative would be hampered if the time marker had been left out.

Time markers are particularly crucial when explaining procedures to be followed or analyzing the steps in a complicated process, as you can see in this passage from an explanatory essay about the predatory relationship between wasps and tarantulas.

> When the grave is finished, the wasp returns to the tarantula to complete her ghastly enterprise. First, she feels it all over once more with her antennae. Then her behavior becomes more aggressive. She bends her abdomen, protruding her sting, and searches for the soft membrane at the point where the spider's legs join its body—the only spot where she can penetrate the horny skeleton. From time to time, as the exasperated spider slowly shifts ground, the wasp turns on her back and slides with the aid of her wings, trying to get under the tarantula for a shot at the vital spot. During all this maneuvering, which can last for several minutes, the tarantula makes no move to save itself. Finally the wasp corners it against some obstruction and grasps one of its legs in her powerful jaws. Now at last the harassed spider tries a desperate but vain defense. The two contestants roll over and over on the ground. It is a terrifying sight and the outcome is always the same.   —Alexander Petrunkevitch, "The Spider and the Wasp"

Verb Tense Markers.   Verb tense also plays an important role in presenting time in narrative. It indicates when the actions occur and whether they are complete or in progress. White, for example, sets most of his narrative in the simple past tense, complicating his narrative only when he reports actions occurring simultaneously: "When my son and I arrived at the pigyard, . . . the pig had emerged from his house and was standing in the middle of his yard. . . ." To convey the time relations among these actions, he uses three past tenses in one sentence:

simple past to indicate a completed action: "my son and I arrived"

past perfect to indicate the action occurred before another action: "the pig had emerged"

past progressive to indicate an ongoing action that had been in progress for some time: the pig "was standing"

Note that, in addition to these past tense forms, White also uses the present tense, to distinguish habitual, continually occurring, actions: "When a pig (or a child) refuses supper a chill wave of fear runs through any household." In fact, whole narratives may be written primarily in the present tense. This is generally the case for process narratives, as illustrated by the excerpt from "The Spider and the Wasp" in the preceding discussion. In addition, contemporary writers of profiles often use the present tense to give their writing a sense of "you-are-there" immediacy.

Verb tense and temporal transitions can be used in various ways to distinguish actions that occurred repeatedly from those that occurred only once. In the following passage, for example, Willie Morris uses the tense marker *would* along with the time markers *many times* and *often* to indicate recurring actions. When he moves from action which occurred repeatedly to action which occurred only once, he shifts to the simple past tense, signaling this shift with the phrase *on one occasion*.

The pieces by Gretel Ehrlich and David Noonan in Chapter 4 are good examples of this use of the present tense.

> Many times, walking home from work, I would see some unknowing soul venture across that intersection against the light and then freeze in horror when he saw the cars ripping out of the tunnel toward him. . . . Suddenly, the human reflex would take over, and the pedestrian would jackknife first one way, then another, arms flaying the empty air, and often the car would literally *skim* the man, brushing by him so close it would touch his coat or his tie. . . . On one occasion, feeling sorry for the person who had brushed against the speeding car, I hurried across the intersection after him to cheer him up a little. Catching up with him down by 32nd I said, "That was good legwork, sir. Excellent moves for a big man!" but the man looked at me with an empty expression in his eyes, and then moved away mechanically and trancelike, heading for the nearest bar.
>
> —Willie Morris, *North toward Home*

Clock Time.   Most writers use clock time sparingly to signal the passage of time in a narrative, but it is a valuable device. White uses clock time to orient readers and to give a sense of duration. He tells us that the action lasted a little over an hour, beginning at about four o'clock and ending a little after five. He indicates that he called Mr. Dameron as soon as he had assessed the situation and then had to wait five minutes for him to call back. More important, he makes clear that once he learned what to do, he spent most of the hour avoiding the task.

In the following brief example, clock time serves the writer's purpose by making readers aware of the speed with which actions were taken:

> 9:05 P.M. An ambulance backs into the receiving bay, its red and yellow lights flashing in and out of the lobby. A split second later, the glass doors burst open as a nurse and an attendant roll a mobile stretcher into the lobby. When the nurse screams, "Emergent!" the lobby explodes with activity as the way is cleared to the trauma room. Doctors appear from nowhere and transfer the bloodied body of a black man to the treatment table. Within seconds his clothes are stripped away.   —George Simpson, "The War Room at Bellevue"

EXERCISE 13.3

Look back at any of the essays in Chapter 2. Read the essay to see how the writer signals the passage of time in the narration. How many time markers, verb tense markers, and references to clock time do you find? Identify any places where a signal should be added and any place where it seems unnecessary. What can you conclude from analyzing this particular essay about the importance of signaling in narrative?

EXERCISE 13.4

Look back at the narrative you wrote for Exercise 13.1. Did you use time markers, verb tense markers, or clock time in your own writing? If you did, try to explain what they add. If you did not, how would your writing be improved if you added some of them? Which ones would you add, and where? Explain why you would add these particular transitions at these places.

SHAPING NARRATIVE STRUCTURE

In addition to clear sequencing of action, writers of effective narrative create a structure to give their stories interest and to focus the action. They shape the narrative around a central conflict, building tension by manipulating the narrative pace.

Conflict and Tension

The basic device writers use to turn a sequence of actions into a story is *conflict*. Conflict adds the question "So what?" to "What happened next?" It provides motivation and purpose for the actions of characters. In this way, conflict gives narrative its dramatic structure.

The conflict in most narrative takes the form of a struggle between the main character and an opposing force. This force may take many forms—another person or creature, nature, society's rules and values, internal characteristics such as conflicting values or desires.

Conflict focuses the action toward some purpose. That is, instead of the simple "and then-and then-and then" structure which a time line gives, conflict provides a one-thing-leads-to-another structure. Along with conflict in a narrative comes *tension,* and this tension or suspense is what makes readers want to read on to find out what will happen. Tension in narrative does not refer to hostility or anxiety, but to tautness. This sense of tension comes from its Latin root, *tendere,* meaning "to stretch." By setting up an unresolved conflict, a writer can stretch the narrative line, creating a sense of tautness or suspense. Readers thus are involved in the action because they care about the ultimate resolution of the conflict. They look forward to the climax, the highest point of tension where the conflict is most focused and explicit.

We can see these concepts illustrated in the excerpt from "Death of a Pig." The opposing forces seem to be the man and the pig, but the conflict is really more elemental—between health and illness or life and death. We see the conflict as an internal drama within the narrator himself who initially resists acknowledging that the routine of his life—not to mention the pig's—has been disrupted. Tension grows as he begins to face reality and consider what he can do to save the pig. In the pages that follow, we see how his efforts to forestall the inevitable are hopeless. The climax of the excerpt occurs when the narrator finally takes action, but the climax of the story does not occur until the pig dies.

EXERCISE 13.5

Look back at the essay you read for Exercise 13.3 and try to identify its conflict and climax. At what points do you feel the tension grow? When do you have a sense of anticipation or suspense? How do these feelings affect your enjoyment of the story?

Narrative Pace

Although you may place actions in the context of clock time, few writers really try to reproduce time as it is measured by clocks. Clock time moves at a uniform rate. If everything were emphasized equally, readers would be unable to distinguish the importance of particular actions. Such a narrative would be monotonous and unnatural.

Pacing techniques allow writers to represent the passage of narrative time. You can pace narratives by emphasizing more important actions and deemphasizing less important ones. To emphasize a sequence of action, you can heighten tension, thus making the action last longer or seem more intense.

Common techniques for doing this are to concentrate on specific narrative action, to present action through dialogue, and to vary sentence rhythm.

Specific Narrative Action.   The writer George Plimpton participated in the Detroit Lions football training camp in order to write a book about professional football. In this passage from his book, Plimpton tells what happened when he had his big chance in a practice scrimmage.

> Since in the two preceding plays the concentration of the play had been elsewhere, I had felt alone with the flanker. Now, the whole heave of the play was toward me, flooding the zone not only with confused motion but noise—the quick stomp of feet, the creak of football gear, the strained grunts of effort, the faint *ah-ah-ah,* of piston-stroke regularity, and the stiff calls of instruction, like exhalations. "Inside, inside! Take him inside!" someone shouted, tearing by me, his cleats thumping in the grass. A call—a parrot squawk—may have erupted from me. My feet splayed in hopeless confusion as Barr came directly toward me, feinting in one direction, and then stopping suddenly, drawing me toward him for the possibility of a buttonhook pass, and as I leaned almost off balance toward him, he turned and came on again, downfield, moving past me at high speed, leaving me poised on one leg, reaching for him, trying to grab at him despite the illegality, anything to keep him from getting by. But he was gone, and by the time I had turned to set out after him, he had ten yards on me, drawing away fast with his sprinter's run, his legs pinwheeling, the row of cleats flicking up a faint wake of dust behind.   —George Plimpton, *Paper Lion*

Although the action lasted only a few moments, Plimpton gives a close-up of it. He focuses on what we are calling *specific narrative action*—specific and concrete movements, gestures, and activities. Instead of writing "Someone ran by me shouting," he writes:

> "Inside, inside! Take him inside!" someone <u>shouted</u>, (verb) <u>tearing</u> by me, (participial phrase) <u>his cleats thumping</u> in the grass. (absolute phrase)

The underlined verbs and verb phrases identify a player's specific actions: shouting, tearing by, thumping cleats. In the long fifth sentence Plimpton gives us another series of specific narrative actions: "feet splayed," "came directly toward me," "feinting in one direction," "stopping suddenly," "drawing me toward him," "leaned almost off balance," "turned and came on again," and then "moving/leaving/reaching/trying" in quick succession. The specific actions slow the narrative pace and heighten the tension. In addition, because they are concrete, they enable us to imagine what is happening.

EXERCISE 13.6

Look at the selection by Maya Angelou in Chapter 3. Note particularly what happens in paragraph 18. How does Angelou's use of specific narrative action here contribute to the overall effectiveness of the selection?

EXERCISE 13.7

Look back at the narrative you wrote for Exercise 13.1. How effectively have you used specific narrative action to pace your narrative and make it concrete? Choose a sentence or a series of sentences to revise, emphasizing a particular part of your narrative by adding specific narrative action. Then, compare the two versions, analyzing the different effects of pacing.

Dialogue.   Another way of dramatizing narrative action is dialogue. Writers use it to reveal conflict directly, without the narrator's intruding commentary. Dialogues are not mere recordings of conversation, but pointed representations of conversation. Through dialogue, readers gain insight into the personality and motives of the characters.

Richard Wright uses dialogue to show what happened when a white man confronted a black delivery boy. Notice that the dialogue does not have the free give-and-take of conversation. Instead, it is a series of questions which get evasive answers: "he said" . . . "I lied" . . . "he asked me" . . . "I lied." The dialogue is tense, revealing the extent of the boy's fear and defensiveness.

> I was hungry and he knew it; but he was a white man and I felt that if I told him I was hungry I would have been revealing something shameful.
>
> "Boy, I can see hunger in your face and eyes," he said.
>
> "I get enough to eat," I lied.
>
> "Then why do you keep so thin?" he asked me.
>
> "Well, I suppose I'm just that way, naturally," I lied.
>
> "You're just scared, boy," he said.
>
> "Oh, no, sir," I lied agan.
>
> I could not look at him. I wanted to leave the counter, yet he was a white man and I had learned not to walk abruptly away from a white man when he was talking to me. I stood, my eyes looking away. He ran his hand into his pocket and pulled out a dollar bill.
>
> "Here, take this dollar and buy yourself some food," he said.
>
> "No, sir," I said.
>
> "Don't be a fool," he said. "You're ashamed to take it. God, boy, don't let a thing like that stop you from taking a dollar and eating."
>
> The more he talked the more it became impossible for me to take the dollar. I wanted it, but I could not look at it. I wanted to speak, but I could not move my tongue. I wanted him to leave me alone. He frightened me.
>
> "Say something," he said.   —Richard Wright, *Black Boy*

Wright does not try to communicate everything through dialogue. He intersperses information which supports the dialogue—description, reports of the boy's thoughts and feelings, as well as some movement—in order to help readers understand the unfolding drama.

You can also use dialogue to reveal a person's character and show the dynamics of interpersonal relationships. Notice the way Lillian Hellman uses dialogue to write about a long-time friend, Arthur W. A. Cowan:

> . . . Cowan said, "What's the matter with you? You haven't said a word for an hour." I said nothing was the matter, not wishing to hear his lecture about what was. After an hour of nagging, by the repetition of "Spit it out," "Spit it out," I told him about a German who had fought in the International Brigade in the Spanish Civil War, been badly wounded, and was now very ill in Paris without any money and that I had sent some, but not enough.
>
> Arthur screamed, "Since when do you have enough money to send anybody a can to piss in? Hereafter, I handle all your money and you send nobody anything. And a man who fought in Spain has to be an ass Commie and should take his punishment."
>
> I said, "Oh shut up, Arthur."
>
> And he did, but that night as he paid the dinner check, he wrote out another check and handed it to me. It was for a thousand dollars.
>
> I said, "What's this for?"
>
> "Anybody you want."
>
> I handed it back.
>
> He said, "Oh, for Christ sake take it and tell yourself it's for putting up with me."
>
> "Then it's not enough money."
>
> He laughed. "I like you sometimes. Give it to the stinking German and don't say where it comes from because no man wants money from a stranger."
>
> –Lillian Hellman, *Pentimento*

This dialogue is quite realistic. It shows the way people talk to one another, the rhythms of interactive speech and its silences. But the dialogue does something more: it gives readers real insight into the way Hellman and Cowan were with each other, their conflicts and their shared understanding. Such dialogue allows readers to listen in on private conversations.

The Hellman passage also exemplifies two methods of presenting dialogue: quoting and summarizing. In summarizing, writers choose their own words instead of quoting actual words used; this allows them to condense dialogue as well as to emphasize what they wish. When Hellman writes "I told him about a German . . . ," she is summarizing her actual spoken words.

EXERCISE 13.8

Turn to Chapter 3 and read Gerald Haslam's essay about his grandmother, paying attention to his use of dialogue. What does the dialogue reveal about the grandmother's character, and about the boy's relationship with her?

EXERCISE 13.9

Write several paragraphs of narrative, including some dialogue. Write about an incident that occurred between you and someone you consider a close friend or associate—a friend, a relative, an enemy, a boss. Try to compose a dialogue that conveys the closeness of your relationship.

Read over your dialogue, and reflect on the impression it gives. In a sentence or two, state what you think the dialogue reveals about your relationship with this person.

Sentence Rhythm. Sequences of short sentences and phrases also contribute to narrative pace. You can see how this works in the following paragraph by Russell Baker about taking a flight test. See how the pace quickens until it reaches an apex in the dramatic series of quick phrases that make up the last sentence:

> The wheels were hardly off the mat before I experienced another eerie sensation. It was a feeling of power. For the first time since first stepping into an airplane I felt in complete mastery of the thing. I'd noticed it on takeoff. It had been an excellent takeoff. Without thinking about it, I'd automatically corrected a slight swerve just before becoming airborne. Now as we climbed I was flooded with a sense of confidence. The hangover's residue of relaxation had freed me of the tensions that had always defeated me before. Before, the plane had had a will of its own; now the plane seemed to be part of me, an extension of my hands and feet, obedient to my slightest whim. I leveled it at exactly 5,000 feet and started a slow roll. First, a shallow dive to gain velocity, then push the stick slowly, firmly, all the way over against the thigh, simultaneously putting in hard rudder, and there we are, hanging upside down over the earth and now—keeping it rolling, don't let the nose drop—reverse the controls and feel it roll all the way through until—coming back to straight-and-level now—catch it, wings level with the horizon, and touch the throttle to maintain altitude precisely at 5,000 feet. —Russell Baker, *Growing Up*

TAKING A POINT OF VIEW

In narrative writing, point of view refers to the narrator's relation to the action at hand. Basically, writers use two points of view: first person and third person.

First person is used to narrate action in which the writer participated. For instance, when Piri Thomas writes, "Big-mouth came at me and we grabbed each other and pushed and pulled and shoved," he is using a first-person point of view. Third person, on the other hand, is used to narrate action performed by people other than the narrator. When Paul Theroux writes, "The Suns fought for it. One man gained possession, but he was pounced upon and the ball shot up and ten Suns went tumbling after it," he is using a third-person point of view. Because they are telling about their own experiences, autobiographers typically write first-person narrative, using the first-person pronouns *I* and *we,* as Piri Thomas does. When writers tell another person's story, as in biography, they use the third-person pronouns *he, she,* and *they* instead of the first-person *I* or *we.*

Of course, first-person narrators often observe and report on the actions of others. In such cases they may shift, perhaps for long stretches, into what seems to be primarily a third-person point of view. This is especially true when the writer is neither participating in the action nor introducing personal thoughts or feelings. However, the presence of the narrative "I" at any point in a piece of writing suggests a first-person point of view throughout.

EXERCISE 13.10

In Chapter 4, compare the profiles written by David Noonan and by Brian Cable, noting particularly each writer's point of view, first-person or third-person. Take a paragraph from each profile and rewrite it, using another point of view. What is the effect of the change of point of view in each case?

EXERCISE 13.11

Think of a brief incident involving you and one other person. Write about the incident from your own, first-person, point of view. Then write about the incident from the third-person point of view, as though another person is telling it. What impact does a change in point of view have on your story?

PRESENTING A PROCESS

Process narrative typically explains how something is done or how to do it. For example, in *Oranges,* a book about the Florida citrus industry, John McPhee tells how the technical operation of bud grafting is done. He is not writing directions for readers to follow. If he were, his narrative would be much more detailed and precise. Instead, he tells us as much as he thinks nonspecialists need or want to know.

> One of Adams' men was putting Hamlin buds on Rough Lemon stock the day I was there. He began by slicing a bud from a twig that had come from a registered budwood tree—of which there are forty-five thousand in groves around Florida, each certified under a state program to be free from serious virus disease and to be a true strain of whatever type of orange, grapefruit, or tangerine it happens to be. Each bud he removed was about an inch long and looked like a little submarine, the conning tower being the eye of the bud, out of which would come the shoot that would develop into the upper trunk and branches of the ultimate tree. A few inches above the ground, he cut a short vertical slit in the bark of a Rough Lemon liner; then he cut a transverse slit at the base of the vertical one, and, lifting the flaps of the wound, set the bud inside. The area was bandaged with plastic tape. In a couple of weeks, Adams said, the new shoot would be starting out of the bud and the tape would be taken off. To force the growth of the new shoot, a large area of the bark of the Rough Lemon would be shaved off above the bud union. Two months after that, the upper

trunk, branches, and leaves of the young Rough Lemon tree would be cut off altogether, leaving only a three-inch stub coming out of the earth, thick as a cigar, with a small shoot and a leaf or two of the Hamlin flippantly protruding near the top. —John McPhee, *Oranges*

EXERCISE 13.12

Look at the selection by Brian Cable in Chapter 4. Read it carefully, noting the way the author tells about the funeral home's process of dealing with a "client." Why do you think Cable includes this process narrative in his essay? Write a few sentences explaining Cable's purpose.

In contrast to the McPhee example, here is a process narrative that provides both information and directions. This selection comes from an article written for the *American Journal of Physiology*. Notice all the precise detail, technical terminology, and careful, step-by-step narrating. Because objectivity is important to such writing, the writers use the passive voice.

Ten 20- to 25-kg male baboons *(Papio anubis)* were tranquilized with ketamine, 10 mg/kg, intubated, mechanically ventilated, and anesthetized with halothane, 1.5 vol%. Instrumentation was implanted through a thoracotomy in the fifth left intercostal space. A miniature pressure transducer (Konigsberg P22, Konigsberg Instruments, Pasadena, CA) was implanted in the left ventricle through a stab wound in the apex, and a pair of ultrasonic transducers was implanted on opposing endocardial surfaces of the left ventricle. Tygon catheters were implanted in the left atrium and aorta. The transducer wires and catheters were run subcutaneously and buried in the interscapular area. —Steven F. Vatner and Michael Zimpfer, "Brainbridge Reflex in Conscious, Unrestrained, and Tranquilized Baboons"

EXERCISE 13.13

Read through the essay by David Quammen in Chapter 5, noting the places where he presents a process. How does this process narrative help you to understand the concept of parthenogenesis?

EXERCISE 13.14

Write a simple process narrative, explaining how to do something—make a sandwich, build a doghouse, write a poem, perform a scientific experiment, fly a kite. Address your narrative to someone who knows nothing about performing the task you are telling about.

CREATING A DOMINANT IMPRESSION

The most effective description creates some dominant impression, a mood or atmosphere that reinforces the writer's purpose. In fact, writers will often attempt to create a dominant impression—for example, when they describe a place in order to set a scene and make readers aware of its atmosphere. Naming, detailing, and comparing—all the choices about what to include and what to call things—come together to create this effect, as the following passage by Mary McCarthy illustrates. Notice that McCarthy directly states the idea she is trying to convey in the last sentence, the paragraph's topic sentence.

> Whenever we children came to stay at my grandmother's house, we were put to sleep in the sewing room, a bleak, shabby, utilitarian rectangle, more office than bedroom, more attic than office, that played to the hierarchy of chambers the role of a poor relation. It was a room seldom entered by the other members of the family, seldom swept by the maid, a room without pride; the old sewing machine, some cast-off chairs, a shadeless lamp, rolls of wrapping paper, piles of pins, and remnants of material united with the iron folding cots put out for our use and the bare floor boards to give an impression of intense and ruthless temporality. Thin, white spreads, of the kind used in hospitals and charity institutions, and naked blinds at the windows reminded us of our orphaned condition and of the ephemeral character of our visit; there was nothing here to encourage us to consider this our home. —Mary McCarthy, *Memories of a Catholic Girlhood*

Everything in the room made McCarthy and her brothers feel unwanted, discarded, orphaned. The room itself is described in terms applicable to the children. (Like them it "played to the hierarchy of chambers the role of a poor relation.") The objects she names, together with their distinguishing details—"cast-off chairs," "shadeless lamp," "iron folding cots," "bare floor boards," "naked blinds"—contribute to this overall impression, thus enabling McCarthy to convey her purpose to her readers.

Sometimes writers comment directly in a description. McCarthy, for instance, states that the sewing room gave "an impression of intense and ruthless temporality," everything serving to remind the children that they were orphans and did not live there. Often, however, writers want description to speak for itself. They *show* rather than tell, letting the descriptive language evoke the impression by itself. Such is the case in the following description by George Orwell of a room for hire:

> Hanging from the ceiling there was a heavy glass chandelier on which the dust was so thick that it was like fur. And covering most of one wall there was a huge hideous piece of junk, something between a sideboard and a hall-stand, with lots of carving and little drawers and strips of looking-glass, and there was a once-gaudy carpet ringed by the slop-pails of years, and two gilt chairs with burst seats, and one of those old-fashioned armchairs which you slide off when you try to sit on them. The room had been turned into a bedroom by thrusting four squalid beds in among the wreckage. —George Orwell, *The Road to Wigan Pier*

EXERCISE 14.1

Write a paragraph or two describing some room where you have spent a lot of time. Describe the room in a way that conveys its mood or atmosphere. Then write a few sentences describing the dominant impression you want your description to make, explaining your purpose in describing the room this way.

NAMING

All writers point to and name things they wish to describe. In the following passage, for example, Annie Dillard identifies the face, chin, fur, underside, and eyes of a weasel she once encountered in the woods:

> He was ten inches long, thin as a curve, a muscled ribbon, brown as fruitwood, soft-furred, alert. His <u>face</u> was fierce, small and pointed as a lizard's; he would have made a good arrowhead. There was just a dot of <u>chin</u>, maybe two browns hairs' worth, and then the pure white <u>fur</u> began that spread down his <u>underside</u>. He had two black <u>eyes</u> I didn't see, any more than you see a window.
> —Annie Dillard, *Teaching a Stone to Talk*

The underscored nouns name the parts of the weasel on which Dillard focuses her attention. The nouns she uses are concrete: they refer to actual, tangible parts of the animal. They are also fairly specific: they identify parts of one particular animal, the weasel she saw.

In looking for the right word to name something, you can usually choose from a variety of words. Some words may be concrete (referring to tangible objects or actual instances), while others are abstract (referring to ideas or qualities). *Nose, tooth,* and *foot* are concrete words, whereas *love, faith,* and *justice* are abstract.

Some words may be specific (referring to a particular instance or individual), while others are general (referring to a class which includes many particular instances). *Specific* and *general* are relative terms. That is, the specificity of a word cannot be measured absolutely but only by contrasting it with other words that could be substituted for it. For example, *vegetable* is more specific than *food* but more general than *carrot.*

If you compare the following description to Dillard's, you will see how each writer has made particular word choices:

> The expression of this snake's <u>face</u> was hideous and fierce; the <u>pupils</u> consisted of a vertical slit in a mottled and coppery <u>iris</u>; the <u>jaws</u> were broad at the base, and the <u>nose</u> terminated in a triangular projection.
>
> —Charles Darwin, *The Voyage of the Beagle*

Like Dillard, Darwin uses the word *face,* though he specifies the *expression* on the snake's face. He could have used *eyes,* as Dillard does, but he uses the more specific *pupils* and *iris* instead. *Chin,* however, would not substitute for *jaws* because *jaws* refers to the bone structure of the lower face, while *chin* refers to something different—the prominence of the lower jaw. Darwin could have used the technical terms *maxilla* and *mandible,* the names of the upper and lower jaw bones. He chose not to use these words, even though they are more specific than *jaws,* possibly because they might be unfamiliar to readers or more specific than necessary. As a rule of thumb, most writers prefer more specific nouns for naming, but they adjust the degree of specificity to the particular needs of their readers.

EXERCISE 14.2

This is an exercise in close observation and naming. Go to a place where you can sit for a while and observe the scene. It might be a landscape or a cityscape, indoors or outdoors, crowded or solitary. Write for five minutes, listing everything in the scene that you can name.

Then, for each noun on your list, try to think of two or three other nouns you could use in its place. Write these other names down.

Finally, write a paragraph describing the scene. Use the nouns you think go together best, assuming your readers are unfamiliar with the scene.

In addition to naming perceivable objects and features, writers name sensations (*stink* and *plunk*) and qualities (the *sweetness* of the lumber):

> When the sun fell across the great white pile of the new Telephone Company building, you could smell the stucco burning as you passed; then some liquid

<u>sweetness</u> that came to me from deep in the rings of the freshly cut lumber stacked in the yards, and the fresh plaster and paint on the brand-new storefronts. <u>Rawness,</u> sunshiny <u>rawness</u> down the end streets of the city, as I thought of them then—the hot ash-laden <u>stink</u> of the refuse dumps in my nostrils and the only sound at noon the resonant metal <u>plunk</u> of a tin can I kicked ahead of me as I went my way.   —Alfred Kazin, *A Walker in the City*

EXERCISE 14.3

Read "Father," the personal essay by student Jan Gray printed in Chapter 3, and notice how much naming she does in her description. Then, write a few sentences explaining why you think Gray uses so much naming in this passage. What impression does all this naming make on you? How specific is her naming? How subjective or objective is it?

DETAILING

Although nouns can be quite specific, adding details is a way of making them more specific, and thus describing something more precisely. Naming answers the questions "What is it?" and "What are its parts or features?" Detailing answers questions like these:

- What size is it?
- How many are there?
- What is it made of?
- Where is it located?
- What is its condition?
- What is its use?
- Where does it come from?
- What is its effect?
- What is its value?

To add details to names, add modifiers—adjectives and adverbs, phrases and clauses. Modifiers make nouns more specific by supplying additional information about them. Notice, in this passage about a weasel, how many modifying details Annie Dillard provides. She indicates size, shape, color, texture, value, and amount.

He was <u>ten inches long</u>, <u>thin</u> as a curve, a <u>muscled</u> ribbon, <u>brown</u> as fruitwood, soft-furred, <u>alert</u>. His face was fierce, <u>small</u> and <u>pointed</u> as a lizard's; he would have made a <u>good</u> arrowhead. There was just a <u>dot</u> of chin, maybe <u>two brown hairs'</u> worth, and then the <u>pure white</u> fur began that spread down his underside. He had <u>two black</u> eyes I didn't see, any more than you see a window.

—Annie Dillard, *Teaching a Stone to Talk*

Like names, details can be more or less specific. For example, because "ten inches long" is a measurable quantity, it is more precise than the relative term *small*. Other detailing words like *good* and *pure* are also relative. Even *brown,* although it is more precise than the general word *color,* could be specified further, as Dillard does, by comparing it to the color of fruitwood.

EXERCISE 14.4

Choose a common household item such as a clock, vacuum cleaner, television set, or toaster which you can examine closely. Study this object for at least ten minutes. Then describe it for someone who has never seen it, using as many specific naming and detailing words as you can.

Modifiers are also used to identify a person's character traits, as the following passage illustrates:

> By no amount of agile exercising of a wishful imagination could my mother have been called lenient. Generous she was; indulgent, never. Kind, yes; permissive, never.   –Maya Angelou, *Gather Together in My Name*

EXERCISE 14.5

Look at Forrest Carter's description of Willow John in the excerpt from his autobiography printed in Chapter 3. What modifiers does he use? How does this detailing contribute to the overall impression the selection gives you of Willow John?

COMPARING

Whereas naming and detailing call on the power of observation, comparing brings the imagination into play. Comparison makes language even more precise and description more evocative. Look again at Annie Dillard's description of a weasel to see how she uses comparison:

> He was ten inches long, thin as a curve, a muscled ribbon, brown as fruitwood, soft-furred, alert. His face was fierce, small and pointed as a lizard's; he would have made a good arrowhead. There was just a dot of chin, maybe two brown hairs' worth, and then the pure white fur began that spread down his underside. He had two black eyes I didn't see, any more than you see a window.
>
> –Annie Dillard, *Teaching a Stone to Talk*

This passage illustrates two kinds of comparison: simile and metaphor. Both figures of speech compare things that are essentially dissimilar. A *simile* directly expresses a similarity by using the word *like* or *as* to announce the comparison. Dillard uses a simile when she writes that the weasel was "thin as a curve." A *metaphor,* on the other hand, is an implicit comparison by which one thing is described as though it were the other. Dillard uses a metaphor when she describes the weasel as "a muscled ribbon."

Here are more examples of comparison used descriptively:

Sometimes I rambled to pine groves, <u>standing like temples</u>, or <u>like fleets at sea</u>, full-rigged, with wavy boughs, and rippling with light. . . .

–Henry David Thoreau, *Walden*

Just below the path, <u>raising their heads</u> above the endless white crosses of a soldier's cemetery, were strange red flowers.   –Alfred Kazin, *A Walker in the City*

Comparing enhances a description by showing readers that which is being described in a surprising new way that can be suggestive and revealing. Although this strategy is called comparing, it includes both comparing and contrasting because differences can be as illuminating as likenesses. Once two things are compared, they are put into a context that causes them to play off each other in unexpected ways.

EXERCISE 14.6

Most writers use comparison only occasionally to achieve particular effects. Look at Gretel Ehrlich's profile of a rodeo event in Chapter 4. Mark each metaphor and simile. Then reflect on how these comparisons contribute to the dominant impression you get of the event.

Useful as comparison is, there are a few pitfalls to avoid with this strategy. Be sure that the connection between the two things being compared is clear and appropriate to your description. Avoid using clichéd expressions, comparisons that are so overused that they have become predictable and consequently do not reveal anything new. Following are some examples of comparisons that have been worn out and thus do not enrich a description:

The kiss was as sweet as honey.

I am as busy as a bee.

That picture stands out like a sore thumb.

EXERCISE 14.7

Take five minutes to list as many clichés as you can think of. Then, pair up with another student, and discuss your lists to decide whether the entries are all clichés. When you are done, figure out what turns a comparison into a cliché for you, and together write a sentence defining a cliché.

EXERCISE 14.8

Turn to Jan Gray's essay about her father in Chapter 3. Reread the essay, noting the use of naming, describing, and comparing. What impression do you get of Gray's father from this description? How do these three strategies contribute to this impression?

USING SENSORY DESCRIPTION

If there are three basic descriptive strategies—naming, detailing, and comparing—there are many language resources, and some limitations, for reporting sense impressions. These resources help convey sights, sounds, smells, touches, and tastes.

In describing, the sense of sight seems to have primacy over the other senses. *Describere,* the Latin root for describe, even means "to sketch or copy." In general, people rely more on the sense of sight than on the other senses. Certainly our vocabulary for reporting what we see is larger and more varied than our vocabulary for reporting any other sense impression.

For the other senses, quite a few nouns and verbs designate sounds; a smaller number of nouns, but few verbs, describe smells; and very few nouns or verbs convey touch and taste. Furthermore, these nonvisual sensations do not invite as much naming as sights do because they are not readily divided into constituent features. For example, we have many names to describe the visible features of a car, but few to describe the sounds a car makes. Nevertheless, writers detail the qualities and attributes of nonvisual sensations—the loudness or tinniness or rumble of an engine, for instance.

The Sense of Sight   When people describe what they see, they identify the objects in their field of vision. As the following passages illustrate, these objects may include animate as well as inanimate things and their features. Details may range from words delineating appearance to those evaluating it.

The first selection, by Henry David Thoreau, depicts a nature scene with a lot of activity; the second passage, by Ernest Hemingway, describes F. Scott Fitzgerald's face.

> As I sit at my window this summer afternoon, hawks are circling about my clearing; the tantivy of wild pigeons, flying by twos and threes athwart my view, or perching restless on the white pine boughs behind my house, gives a voice to the air; a fish hawk dimples the glassy surface of the pond and brings up a fish; a mink steals out of the marsh before my door and seizes a frog by the shore; the sedge is bending under the weight of the reed-birds flitting hither and thither. . . .   —Henry David Thoreau, *Walden*

> Scott was a man then who looked like a boy with a face between handsome and pretty. He had very fair wavy hair, a high forehead, excited and friendly eyes and a delicate long-lipped Irish mouth that, on a girl, would have been the mouth of a beauty. His chin was well built and he had good ears and a handsome, almost beautiful, unmarked nose.   —Ernest Hemingway, *A Moveable Feast*

EXERCISE 14.9

Using Hemingway's description of Fitzgerald's face as a model, write a few sentences describing someone's face. Do not rely on memory for this exercise: describe someone who is before you as you write. You can even look in the mirror and describe your own face.

When you are done, read what you have written and identify the dominant impression of this description. Which words contribute most to creating the impression? Which words, if any, seem to you now to contradict or weaken it?

The Sense of Hearing

In reporting auditory impressions, writers seldom name the objects from which the sounds come without also naming the sounds themselves: the murmur of a voice, the rustle of the wind, the squeak of a hinge, the sputter of an engine. *Onomatopoeia* is the term for names of sounds that echo the sounds themselves: *squeak, murmur, hiss, boom, tinkle, twang, jangle, rasp.* Sometimes writers make up words like *plink, chirr, sweesh-crack-boom,* and *cara-wong* to imitate sounds they wish to describe. Qualitative words like *powerful* and *rich* as well as relative terms like *loud* and *low* often specify sounds further. Detailing sounds sometimes involves the technique called *synesthesia,* applying words commonly used to describe one sense to another, such as describing sounds as *sharp* and *soft.*

To write about the sound of Yosemite Falls, John Muir uses all these naming and describing techniques. He also uses comparison when he refers metaphorically to the water's powerful "voice":

> This noble fall has far the richest, as well as the most powerful, voice of all the falls of the Valley, its tones varying from the sharp hiss and rustle of the wind in the glossy leaves of the live oaks and the soft, sifting, hushing tones of the pines, to the loudest rush and roar of storm winds and thunder among the crags of the summit peaks. The low bass, booming, reverberating tones, heard under favorable circumstances five or six miles away, are formed by the dashing and exploding of heavy masses mixed with air upon two projecting ledges on the face of the cliff, the one on which we are standing and another about 200 feet above it. The torrent of massive comets is continuous at time of high water, while the explosive, booming notes are wildly intermittent, because, unless influenced by the wind, most of the heavier masses shoot out from the face of the precipice, and pass the ledges upon which at other times they are exploded.
>
> —John Muir, *The Story of My Boyhood and Youth*

EXERCISE 14.10

Find a noisy spot—a restaurant, a football game, a nursery school, a laundry room—where you can perch for a half hour or so. Listen attentively to the sounds of the place and make notes about what you hear. Then, write a paragraph describing the place through its sounds.

When you are done, read your description and identify the dominant impression. Which words contribute most to creating this impression and which detract from it?

The Sense of Smell

The English language has a meager stock of words to express the sense of smell. In addition to the word *smell,* only about ten commonly used nouns name this sensation: *odor, scent, vapor, aroma, fragrance, perfume, bouquet, stench, stink.* Although there are other, rarer words like *fetor* and *effluvium,* few writers use them, probably for fear their readers will not know them. Few verbs describe receiving or sending odors—*smell, sniff, waft*—but a fair number of detailing adjectives are available: *redolent, pungent, aromatic, perfumed, stinking, musty, rancid, putrid, rank, foul, acrid, sweet,* and *cloying.*

In the next passage, Conroy uses comparing in addition to naming and detailing. Notice how he describes the effect the odor has on him:

> The perfume of the flowers rushed into my brain. A lush aroma, thick with sweetness, thick as blood, and spiced with the clear acid of tropical greenery. My heart pounded like a drowning swimmer's as the perfume took me over, pouring into my lungs like ambrosial soup.   —Frank Conroy, *Stop-time*

In reporting smells, naming the objects from which they come can also be very suggestive:

> It is the smells of the school that I remember best; the sour smell of the oil they rubbed the desks with; the classroom smell of chalk dust and old pulled-down maps; the smell of fuller's earth scattered in wide arcs along the corridors, ahead of the pushbrooms that formed fat kittens out of the dirt tracked daily in by some 300 pairs of feet; the smell of a master's unlighted pipe; the smell that would periodically drift through the school late in the morning to tell us that we were going to have corned beef and cabbage for lunch; the steamy, chlorinated smell of the indoor pool; the smell of the gym, which was a mixture of wintergreen oil and sneakers.   —Stephen Birmingham, "New England Prep School"

EXERCISE 14.11

Go someplace with noticeable, distinctive smells where you can stay for ten or fifteen minutes. You may choose an eating place (a cafeteria, a donut shop, a cafe), a place where something is being manufactured (a saw mill, a bakery, a pizza parlor), or some other place that has distinctive odors (a fishing dock, a garden, a locker room). Take notes while you are there on what you smell, and then write a paragraph describing the place through its smells. What is the dominant impression you were trying to create with this description?

The Sense of Touch

Writers describing the sense of touch tend not to name the sensation directly or even to report the act of feeling. Probably this omission occurs because only a few nouns and verbs name tactile sensations besides words like *touch, feel, tickle, brush, scratch, sting, itch, tingle.* Nevertheless, a large stock of words describe temperature *(hot, warm, mild, tepid, cold, arctic)*, moisture content *(wet, dry, sticky, oily, greasy, moist, crisp)*, texture *(gritty, silky, smooth, crinkled, coarse, soft, leathery)*, and weight *(heavy, light, ponderous, buoyant, feathery)*. Read the following passages with an eye for descriptions of touch.

> The midmorning sun was deceitfully mild and the wind had no weight on my skin. Arkansas summer mornings have a feathering effect on stone reality.
> –Maya Angelou, *Gather Together in My Name*

> It was an ordeal for me to walk the hills in the dead of summer for then they were parched and dry and offered no shade from the hot sun and no springs or creeks where thirst could be quenched. –William O. Douglas, *Go East, Young Man*

EXERCISE 14.12

Briefly describe the feel of a cold shower, a wool sweater, an autumn breeze, bare feet on hot sand, or any other tactile sensation you might think of. What is the dominant impression you were trying to create with this description?

The Sense of Taste   Other than *taste, savor,* and *flavor,* few words name the gustatory sensations directly. Certain words do distinguish among the four types of taste—*sweet (saccharine, sugary, cloying); sour (acidic, tart); bitter (acrid, biting); salty (briny, brackish),* while several other words describe specific tastes (*piquant, spicy, pungent, peppery, savory,* and *toothsome*).

   In addition to these words, the names of objects tasted and other details may indicate the intensity and quality of a taste. Notice Hemingway's descriptive technique in the following selection.

> As I ate the oysters with their strong taste of the sea and their faint metallic taste that the cold wine washed away, leaving only the sea taste and the succulent texture, and as I drank their cold liquid from each shell and washed it down with the crispy taste of the wine, I lost the empty feeling and began to be happy and to make plans. –Ernest Hemingway, *A Moveable Feast*

EXERCISE 14.13

Describe the taste of a particular food or meal as Hemingway does in the preceding passage. What is the dominant impression you were trying to create with this description?

EXERCISE 14.14

Turn to "Unripened Light" in Chapter 2. Reread the essay and put brackets around any instances where Young uses sensory language to describe the scene and people. What is the dominant impression you get from this description? How do you think sensory description helps to create this impression?

ASSUMING A VANTAGE POINT

Writing effectively about a scene requires taking a vantage point—that is, selecting the point or position from which to describe the scene. By presenting objects and features from a particular vantage point, the writer creates a perspective by which readers can enter the scene.

A Stationary
Vantage Point

A writer of description who stays still assumes a fixed or stationary vantage point. In the following passage, the author takes a position in a subway station and describes what he sees without moving around the station:

> Standing in a subway station, I began to appreciate the place—almost to enjoy it. First of all, I looked at the lighting: a row of meager electric bulbs, unscreened, yellow, and coated with filth, stretched toward the black mouth of the tunnel, as though it were a bolt hole in an abandoned coal mine. Then I lingered, with zest, on the walls and ceiling: lavatory tiles which had been white about fifty years ago, and were now encrusted with soot, coated with the remains of a dirty liquid which might be either atmospheric humidity mingled with smog or the result of a perfunctory attempt to clean them with cold water; and, above them, gloomy vaulting from which dingy paint was peeling off like scabs from an old wound, sick black paint leaving a leprous white subsurface. Beneath my feet, the floor was a nauseating dark brown with black stains upon it which might be stale oil or dry chewing gum or some worse defilement; it looked like the hallway of a condemned slum building. Then my eye traveled to the tracks, where two lines of glittering steel—the only positively clean objects in the whole place—ran out of darkness into darkness above an unspeakable mass of congealed oil, puddles of dubious liquid, and a mishmash of old cigarette packets, mutilated and filthy newspapers, and the debris that filtered down from the street above through a barred grating in the roof. As I looked up toward the sunlight, I could see more debris sifting slowly downward, and making an abominable pattern in the slanting beam of dirt-laden sunlight. I was going on to relish more features of this unique scene: such as the advertisement posters on the walls—here a text from the Bible, there a half-naked girl, here a woman wearing a hat consisting of a hen sitting on a nest full of eggs, and there a pair of girl's legs walking up the keys of a cash register—all scribbled over with unknown names and well-known obscenities in black crayon and red lipstick; but then my train came in at last. . . .   –Gilbert Highet, "The Subway Station"

Although Highet stays still, he shifts his field of vision, using these shifts to order the description of what he sees, looking first at the lights, then at the walls and ceilings, at the floor, at the tracks, toward the sunlight, and finally at the posters on the wall. He seems to describe things as they catch his attention. Sometimes writers give details in a more orderly pattern—for example, from left to right, top to bottom, big to small.

A Moving
Point of View

Instead of remaining fixed in one spot, a writer may move through a scene. Such is the case with the next author, who describes what he sees as he drives along a highway:

The highway, without warning, rolled off the plateau of green pastures and entered a wooded and rocky gorge; down, down, precipitously down to the Kentucky River. Along the north slope, man-high columns of ice clung to the limestone. The road dropped deeper until it crossed the river at Brooklyn Bridge. The gorge, hidden in the table and and wholly unexpected, was the Palisades. At the bottom lay only enough ground for the river and a narrow strip of willow-rimmed.

Houses on stilts and a few doublewides rose from the damp flats like toad-stools. Next to one mobile home was a partly built steel boat longer than the trailer.   –William Least Heat Moon, *Blue Highways*

See pp. 413–15 for a discussion of transitions and a list of those commonly used to indicate spatial relations.

Notice how the author uses spatial transitions like *down, along, from,* and *next* to orient his readers to his movements.

Combined Vantage Points

Sometimes writers use more than one stationary vantage point or combine stationary and moving vantage points. In these cases, the important thing is to orient the readers to any change in position.

In the next selection, Willie Morris begins with a moving vantage point and then uses several stationary points.

One walked up the three flights through several padlocked doors, often past the garbage which the landlords had neglected to remove for two or three days. Once inside our place, things were not bad at all. There was a big front room with an old floor, a little alcove for a study, and to the back a short corridor opening up into a tiny bedroom for my son and a larger bedroom in the back. The kitchen was in the back bedroom. I had not been able to find a view of an extensive body of water at popular prices, but from the back window, about forty-yards out, there *was* a vista of a big tank, part of some manufacturing installation in the building under it, and the tank constantly bubbled with some unidentified greenish substance. From this window one could see the tarred rooftops of the surrounding buildings, and off to the right a quiet stretch of God's earth, this being the parking lot next door.   –Willie Morris, *North toward Home*

EXERCISE 14.15

Look back at the paragraph you wrote for Exercise 14.1. What vantage point did you take in that description? How do you think your choice of vantage point contributes to the dominant impression the description creates? Try rewriting a few sentences taking another vantage point. How does this vantage point change the dominant impression?

EXERCISE 14.16

Look at Brian Cable's profile, "The Last Stop," in Chapter 4. Mark places in the text where you notice that a particular vantage point is used or that a vantage point shifts. What effect does the use of a vantage point have on Cable's descriptions of the mortuary?

Defining is an essential strategy for all kinds of writing. Autobiographers, for example, must occasionally define objects, conditions, events, and activities for readers likely to be unfamiliar with particular terms. The following example (with definitions underlined) is from Chapter 3.

> My father's hands are grotesque. He suffers from psoriasis, <u>a chronic skin disease that covers his massive, thick hands with scaly, reddish patches that periodically flake off, sending tiny pieces of dead skin sailing to the ground.</u>   —Jan Gray, "Father"

Writers sharing information or explaining how to do something must very often define important terms for readers who are unfamiliar with the subject. This example comes from Chapter 5.

> <u>What we are talking about here is celibate motherhood, procreation without copulation,</u> a phenomenon that goes by the technical name parthenogenesis.
> —David Quammen, "Is Sex Necessary?"

To convince readers of a position or an evaluation or to move readers to take action on a proposal, a writer must often define concepts important to an argument. This example comes from Chapter 6.

> Social acceptability is <u>a function of which group controls society and to what extent minority voices can influence the spectrum of opinion.</u>
> —Kristin A. Goss, "Taking a Stand against Sexism"

As these examples illustrate, there are many kinds of definitions and many forms that they can take. This chapter illustrates the major kinds and forms of definitions, beginning with those that we find in dictionaries and other reference sources. After dictionary definitions come various forms of sentence definition. This type of definition, the most common form in writing, relies on various sentence patterns to provide concise definitions. Following this are illustrations of multi-sentence extended definitions, including definition by etymology, or word history, and by stipulation.

DICTIONARY DEFINITIONS

The most familiar source of definitions is the dictionary, where words are defined briefly with other words. In a short space, dictionaries tell us a lot about words: what they mean, how they are pronounced, how they look in context in a sample phrase or clause, where they originated, what forms they take as they function differently in sentences. Here is an example from *The American Heritage Dictionary:*

definition ⸺⸺⸺⸺⸺⸺⸺⸺⸺⸺⸺⸺
part of speech ⸺⸺⸺⸺⸺⸺⸺⸺⸺
syllabification ⸺⸺⸺⸺⸺⸺⸺

> in-trep-id (ĭn-trĕp′ĭd) *adj.* Marked by reso-

pronunciation ⸺⸺⸺⸺⸺⸺⸺

> lute courage; fearless and bold: *an intrepid*

illustrative use ⸺⸺⸺⸺⸺⸺

> *mountaineer.* [Fr. *intrépule* < Lat. *intrepidus*

etymology ⸺⸺⸺⸺⸺⸺⸺

> : *in-*, not + *trepidus,* alarmed.] —in′tre-pid′i-
> ty (-trə-pĭd′ĭ-tē), in-trep′id-ness *n.* —in-
> trep′id-ly *adv.*

other forms ⸺⸺⸺⸺⸺⸺

Other dictionary entries may include still more information. For example, if a word has more than one meaning, all of its meanings will be presented. From the context in which you read or hear the word, you can nearly always tell which meaning applies.

A good dictionary is an essential part of your equipment as a college student. It should always be within reach when you are reading so that you can look up unfamiliar words in order to understand what you read and to expand your vocabulary. When you are writing, you can use a dictionary to check spellings and the correct forms of words as well as to make sure of the meanings of words you might not have used before.

You may want to ask your instructor for advice about which dictionary to buy in your college bookstore. A good current dictionary like *The American Heritage Dictionary* or *Webster's New Collegiate Dictionary* is most useful. Though a hardback dictionary version will cost two or three times more than a paperback, it will be a sound and relatively inexpensive investment (about fifteen dollars). Hardback dictionaries usually have the advantages of more entries, fuller entries, larger type, and a thumb index.

To present a great deal of information in a small space, dictionaries have to rely on many abbreviations, codes, and symbols. These differ somewhat from one dictionary to the next, but you can learn the system of abbreviations in your dictionary by reading the front matter carefully. You will also find a range of interesting topics and lists in the front and end matter of some dictionaries: articles on usage and language history, reviews of punctuation rules, biographical entries, geographical entries, and lists of colleges and universities.

Any dictionary you are likely to buy for desk use would be an *abridged* dictionary, which does not include many technical or obsolete words. Much larger *unabridged* dictionaries contain every known current and obsolete word in the language. Two unabridged dictionaries are preeminent: *Oxford English Dictionary* and *Webster's Third New International Dictionary*, the latter the standard reference for American English. Libraries have these impressive dictionaries available for specialized use.

A special dictionary called a *thesaurus* can be useful for a writer, but only if it is used judiciously. It is a dictionary of synonyms, words with identical or very similar meanings. The motive for searching out synonyms should be to use just the right word, not to impress readers. Straining to impress readers with unusual words will more often than not lead to the embarrassing use of a word in the wrong context.

Here is an example from *Roget's II, The New Thesaurus*. It offers alternatives to *brave*, used as an adjective. Among the synonyms for *brave* is *intrepid*, noted in the dictionary definition on the preceding page.

> **brave** *adjective*
> Having or showing courage: *a brave effort to rescue the drowning child.* **Syns:** audacious, bold, courageous, dauntless, doughty, fearless, fortitudinous, gallant, game, gutsy (*Informal*), gutty, heroic, intrepid, mettlesome, plucky, stout, stouthearted, unafraid, undaunted, valiant, valorous.

Some thesauri also offer antonyms, words opposite in meaning to the word of interest. (An antonym of *brave*, for example, would be *cowardly*.)

The great limitation of a thesaurus is that it does not tell you which synonym is most appropriate for a particular writing situation. *Brave* and *intrepid* are not simply interchangeable. Which word you might use would depend on your readers, your purpose, your subject, and the exact meaning you hoped to convey with the sentence in which the word appears. In the preceding list, the only clue to appropriateness is the information that *gutsy* is informal. Checking each word in a good dictionary would be necessary to select the most appropriate word from a set such as the preceding one. Because of this troublesome limitation, a thesaurus is most useful in reminding you of a synonym whose shades of meaning you are already closely familiar with.

A solution to the limitations of a thesaurus is a dictionary of synonyms with words in a set like the preceding one but with each synonym defined, contrasted, and illustrated with quotations. An excellent source is *Webster's New Dictionary of Synonyms,* which provides enough information to let you make an appropriate choice among words with similar meanings. Your college bookstore will have this book for about the cost of a hardback dictionary. This volume's entry for *brave,* for example, notes eleven common synonyms for *brave* as an adjective, ranging from *courageous* to *audacious.* Each synonym is defined and then quoted in context from a respected source, as this portion of the entry shows:

brave *adj* **Brave, courageous, unafraid, fearless, intrepid, valiant, valorous, dauntless, undaunted, doughty, bold, audacious** are comparable when they mean having or showing no fear when faced with something dangerous, difficult, or unknown. **Brave** usually indicates lack of fear in alarming or difficult circumstances rather than a temperamental liking for danger ⟨the *brave* soldier goes to meet Death, and meets him without a shudder—*Trollope*⟩ ⟨he would send an explosion ship into the harbor . . . a *brave* crew would take her in at night, right up against the city, would light the fuses, and try to escape—*Forester*⟩ **Courageous** implies stouthearted resolution in contemplating or facing danger and may suggest a temperamental readiness to meet dangers or difficulties ⟨I am afraid . . . because I do not wish to die. But my spirit masters the trembling flesh and the qualms of the mind. I am more than brave, I am *courageous*—*London*⟩ ⟨a man is *courageous* when he does things which others might fail to do owing to fear—

Russell⟩ **Unafraid** simply indicates lack of fright or fear whether because of a courageous nature or because no cause for fear is present ⟨enjoy their homes *unafraid* of violent intrusion—*MacArthur*⟩ ⟨a young, daring, and creative people—a people *unafraid* of change—*MacLeish*⟩ **Fearless** may indicate lack of fear, or it may be more positive and suggest undismayed resolution ⟨joyous we too launch out on trackless seas, *fearless* for unknown shores—*Whitman*⟩ ⟨he gives always the impression of *fearless* sincerity . . . one always feels that he is ready to say bluntly what every one else is afraid to say—*T. S. Eliot*⟩ **Intrepid** suggests either daring in meeting danger or fortitude in enduring it ⟨with the *intrepid* woman who was his wife, and a few natives, he landed there, and set about building a house and clearing the scrub—*Maugham*⟩ ⟨the *intrepid* guardians of the place, hourly exposed to death, with famine worn, and suffering under many a perilous wound—*Wordsworth*⟩

This entry shows that *brave* and *intrepid* are very close in meaning, but that *intrepid* would be the better choice if you wanted to suggest "daring in meeting danger" rather than "lack of fear" in facing danger when it comes. You might call a person setting off on a solo sea voyage in a small craft an *intrepid* sailor, but a flight attendant who faced down a potential hijacker is better described as *brave.*

To summarize our advice about dictionaries: buy a respected hardback dictionary for looking up the meanings of new words you encounter and for checking spellings and correct usage. Buy an inexpensive paperback thesaurus for a quick look at sets of synonyms. Buy a respected hardback dictionary of synonyms in order to discriminate among synonyms and pick the most appropriate word. These resources will enable you to write essays with correct spellings and verb forms and with just the right words.

SENTENCE DEFINITIONS

Every field of study and every institution and activity has its own unique concepts and terms. Coming to a new area for the first time, a participant or a reader is often baffled by the many unfamiliar names for objects and activities. In college, a basic course in a field often seems like an entire course in definitions of new terms. In the same way, a sport like sailing requires newcomers to learn much specialized terminology. In such cases, writers of textbooks and sailing manuals rely on brief sentence definitions, involving a variety of sentence strategies.

Following are some sentence strategies from one widely used introductory college biology text, Sylvia Mader's *Inquiry into Life*. These examples illustrate some of the sentence strategies an author may use to name and define terms for readers.

The most obvious sentence strategies simply announce a definition. (In each of the following examples the word being defined is in italics, while the definition is underlined.)

Homo habilis means handyman.

Somatic mutations are mutations that affect the individual's body cells.

At the time of ejaculation, sperm leaves the penis in a fluid called *seminal fluid*.

Thus an ecosystem contains both a *biotic* (living) and *abiotic* (nonliving) environment.

The human blastula, termed the blastocyst, consists of a hollow ball with a mass of cells — *the inner cell mass* — at one end.

The sentence strategies illustrated so far all declare in a straightforward way that the writer is defining a term. Other strategies, signaled by certain sentence relationships, are less direct but still quite apparent.

Fraternal twins, which originate when two different eggs are fertilized by two different sperm, do not have identical chromosomes.

Hemophilia is called the bleeders disease because the afflicted person's blood is unable to clot.

When a mutagen leads to an increase in the incidence of cancer it is called a *carcinogen*.

If the thyroid fails to develop properly, a condition called *cretinism* results.

These sentence definitions — all of them relying on subordinate clauses — play an important role in sentences by adding details, expressing time and cause, and indicating conditions or tentativeness. In all these examples from *Inquiry into Life,* however, the clauses have a specific defining role to play in the sections of the text where they appear. In this specialized way, they are part of a writer's repertoire for sentence definitions.

There are, in addition, several other defining strategies. One of the most common is the appositive phrase. Here one noun defines another noun in a brief inserted phrase called an appositive. Sometimes the appositive contains the definition; other times it contains the word to be defined.

> Sperm are produced in the testes, but they mature in the *epididymus,* a tightly coiled tubule about twenty feet in length that lies just outside each testis.

> Breathing consists of taking air in, *inspiration,* and forcing air out, *expiration.*

Finally, in a comparative definition, two or more terms are defined in part by comparison or contrast with each other. For these multiple definitions, writers rely on a great variety of syntactic and stylistic strategies including the two illustrated below: (1) a series of phrases following either the main verb or a colon and (2) contrasting clauses beginning with words or phrases like *even though, in spite of,* or *whereas.* The various parts of the comparison are always grammatically parallel, that is, similar in form.

> The special senses include the *chemoreceptors* for taste and smell, the *light receptors* for sight, and the *mechanoreceptors* for hearing and balance.

> Whereas a *miscarriage* is the unexpected loss of an embryo or fetus, an *abortion* is the purposeful removal of an embryo or fetus from the womb.

EXERCISE 15.1

Look up any three of the following words in a dictionary. Define each one in a sentence. Try to use a different sentence pattern, like those illustrated above, for each of your definitions.

clinometer	mnemonic
ecumenism	testosterone
harangue	buyer's market
ectomorph	Shakespearean sonnet
senile dementia	edema
carcicature	samba

EXERCISE 15.2

Turn to the essay by David Noonan in Chapter 4, and analyze the sentence definitions in paragraphs 2, 6, 9, 13, and 18. (Some of these paragraphs contain more than one sentence definition.) Classify each definition as one of the preceding sentence types. What is the purpose of all these definitions in the selection as a whole?

EXTENDED DEFINITIONS

Rather than a brief sentence definition, a writer may need to go further and provide readers with a fuller definition extending over several sentences.

Here, for example, is how Mark Twain defines a word he learned on a trip to New Orleans.

We picked up one excellent word—a word worth traveling to New Orleans to get; a nice limber, expressive, handy word—"lagniappe." They pronounce it lanny-*yap*. It is Spanish—so they said. We discovered it at the head of a column of odds and ends in the Picayune, the first day; heard twenty people use it the second; inquired what it meant the third; adopted it and got facility in swinging it the fourth. It has a restricted meaning, but I think the people spread it out a little when they choose. It is the equivalent of the thirteenth roll in a "baker's dozen." It is something thrown in, gratis, for good measure. The custom originated in the Spanish quarter of the city. When a child or a servant buys something in a shop—or even the mayor or the governor, for aught I know—he finishes the operation by saying—

"Give me something for lagniappe."

The shopman always responds; gives the child a bit of licorice root, gives the servant a cheap cigar or a spool of thread; gives the governor—I don't know what he gives the governor; support, likely.

When you are invited to drink—and this does occur now and then in New Orleans—and you say, "What, again?—no, I've had enough"; the other party says, "But just this one more time—this is for lagniappe." When the beau perceives that he is stacking his compliments a trifle too high, and sees by the young lady's countenance that the edifice would have been better with the top compliment left off, he puts his "I beg pardon—no harm intended," into the briefer form of "Oh, that's for lagniappe." If the waiter in the restaurant stumbles and spills a gill of coffee down the back of your neck, he says, "For lagniappe, sah," and gets you another cup without extra charge.   —Mark Twain, *Life on the Mississippi*

This extended definition relies on a variety of strategies—word history, personal experience, many examples, and even dialogue.

An ecology text provides another example of the way certain important concepts require extended definition.

Demes   A deme is a small local population, such as all the deer mice or all the red oaks in a certain woodland or all the perch in a given pond. Although no two individuals in a deme are exactly alike, the members of a deme do usually resemble one another more closely than they resemble the members of other demes, for at least two reasons: (1) They are more closely related genetically, because pairings occur more frequently between members of the same deme than between members of different demes; and (2) they are exposed to more similar environmental influences and hence to more nearly the same selection pressures.

It must be emphasized that demes are not clear-cut permanent units of population. Although the deer mice in one woodlot are more likely to mate among themselves than with deer mice in the next woodlot down the road, there will almost certainly be occasional matings between mice from different woodlots. Similarly, although the female parts of a particular red oak tree are more likely to receive pollen from another red oak tree in the same woodlot, there is an appreciable chance that they will sometimes receive pollen from a tree in another nearby woodlot. And the woodlots themselves are not permanent ecological features. They have only a transient existence as separate and distinct ecological units; neighboring woodlots may fuse after a few years, or a single large woodlot may become divided into two or more separate smaller ones. Such changes in ecological features will produce corresponding changes in the demes of deer mice and red oak trees. Demes, then, are usually temporary units of population that intergrade with other similar units.

–William T. Keeton, *Biological Science*

As a writer drafting an essay, your choice of appropriate definition strategies will be guided by your awareness of what you want to accomplish and by your knowledge of who your readers will be. You need not even be consciously aware of particular choices while you are writing a first draft. Later, though, when you are revising this first draft, you will have a special advantage if you can look critically at the way you have defined key terms. If your repertoire of defining strategies includes all the variations illustrated in this chapter, you will be able to revise with much more confidence and power.

Though it happens fairly rarely, some published essays and reports are concerned primarily with the definition of a little understood or problematic concept or thing—for example, the essay about parthenogenesis by David Quammen in Chapter 5. Usually, however, definition is only a part of an essay. A long piece of writing, like a term paper or a textbook or a research report, may include many kinds of brief and extended definitions, all of them integrated with other writing strategies.

EXERCISE 15.3

Choose one term that names some concept or feature of central importance in an activity or subject you know well. Choose a word with a well-established definition, one agreed on by everyone knowledgeable about the topic.

Write an extended definition of several sentences for this important term. Write for readers your own age who will be encountering the term for the first time when they read your definition.

EXERCISE 15.4

Read "Inside the Brain," David Noonan's essay in Chapter 4, and analyze the extended definition of *sterile field* in paragraph 6. How does he define this term? What purpose does the definition have within the whole selection?

HISTORICAL DEFINITIONS

Occasionally a writer will trace the history of a word—from its first use, to its adoption into other languages, to its shifting meanings over the centuries.

Such a strategy can be a rich addition to an essay, bringing to the definition of an important concept a surprising depth and resonance. A historical definition usually begins with the roots of a word, but it extends well beyond that to trace the word's history over a long period of time. Such a history should always serve a writer's larger purpose, as the example here shows.

In this example, from a book discussing the recent rise of witchcraft and paganism in America, the writer uses a historical definition of the word *pagan* as background to her own definition and also as a way of instructing us in how we should feel about the new pagans.

> *Pagan* comes from the Latin *paganus*, which means a country dweller, and is itself derived from *pagus*, the Latin word for village or rural district. Similarly, *heathen* originally meant a person who lived on the heaths. Negative associations with these words are the end result of centuries of political struggles during which the major prophetic religions, notably Christianity, won a victory over the older polytheistic religions. In the West, often the last people to be converted to Christianity lived on the outskirts of populated areas and kept to the old ways. These were the Pagans and heathens—the word *Pagan* was a term of insult, meaning "hick."
>
> *Pagan* had become a derogatory term in Rome by the third century. Later, after the death of Julian, the last Pagan emperor, in 362 A.D. the word *Pagan* came to refer to intellectual Pagans like Julian. Gore Vidal, in his extraordinary novel *Julian*, wrote a fictional description of this event in which the Pagan orator Libanius, after attending the funeral of a Christian notable, writes in his journal: "There was a certain amount of good-humored comment about 'pagans' (a new word of contempt for us Hellenists) attending Christian services. . . . " Julian, by the way, has long been one of Neo-Paganism's heroes, and an early Neo-Pagan journal was called *The Julian Review*. Centuries later the word *Pagan* still suffers the consequences of political and religious struggles, and dictionaries still define it to mean a godless person or an unbeliever, instead of, simply, a member of a different kind of religion.
>
> *Pagan* is also often associated with hedonism. This makes some sense, since many ancient Pagan religions incorporated sexuality into ecstatic religious practice. One scholar, writing on the use of mystical experience by young people in the 1960s, observed that a characteristic of many groups was "the idea of paganism—the body is a temple in which there is nothing unclean, a shrine to be adorned for the ritual of love." New attitudes toward sexuality play a part in some, but not all, Neo-Pagan groups, and the old Pagan religions had their share of ascetics, but generally, Neo-Pagans seem to have healthy attitudes toward sex.
>
> I use *Pagan* to mean a member of a polytheistic nature religion, such as the ancient Greek, Roman, or Egyptian religions, or, in anthropological terms, a member of one of the indigenous folk and tribal-religions all over the world. People who have studied the classics or have been deeply involved with natural or aboriginal peoples are comparatively free of the negative and generally racist attitudes that surround the word *Pagan*.   –Margot Adler, *Drawing Down the Moon*

EXERCISE 15.5

Any good dictionary tells the origins of words. Historical, or etymological, dictionaries, however, give much more information, enough to trace changes in use of a word over long periods of time. The preeminent historical dictionary of our language is 'the *Oxford English Dictionary*. Less imposing is *A Dictionary of American English*, and even less imposing is *A Dictionary of Americanisms*.

Look up the historical definition of any one of the following words in *A Dictionary of Americanisms*, and write several sentences on its roots and development. As an alternative, you may choose any word with a complex history from one of these dictionaries.

basketball	eye-opener
bazooka	filibuster
bedrock	gerrymander
blizzard	jazz
bogus	pep
bonanza	picayune
bushwhack	podunk
canyon	rubberneck
carpetbag	sashay
dugout	two bits

STIPULATIVE DEFINITIONS

The historical definition of pagans in the preceding section concludes with a stipulative definition: "I use *Pagan* to mean a member of a polytheistic nature religion. . . . " *To stipulate* means to seek or assert agreement on something. A stipulative definition is one in which the writer declares a certain meaning, generally not one found in the dictionary.

Stipulative definitions have a variety of important functions, several of which are illustrated here. In the next example, a prominent historian of science proposes a stipulative definition of the word *ecology*.

Ernst Haeckel, the great popularizer of evolutionary theory in Germany, loved to coin words. The vast majority of his creations died with him a half-century ago, but among the survivors are "ontogeny," "phylogeny," and "ecology." The last is now facing an opposite fate—loss of meaning by extension and vastly inflated currency. Common usage now threatens to make "ecology" a label for anything good that happens far from cities or anything that does not have synthetic chemicals in it. In its more restricted and technical sense, ecology is the study of

organic diversity. It focuses on the interactions of organisms and their environments in order to address what may be the most fundamental question in evolutionary biology: "Why are there so many kinds of living things?"

—Stephen Jay Gould, *Ever Since Darwin*

Important concepts in technical fields like biology may gradually take on
fuzzy or overly broad popular definitions. The specialists may then have to
rescue a concept by redefining it, as Gould does here. He is asking his readers
to agree with him that *ecology* means "the study of organic diversity." He
stipulates a redefinition and asks us to use the word only as he defines it, at
least for the duration of his book.

Another use of stipulative definition is to sort through alternative definitions of a problematic concept—*pure breed of cats* in the next example—in
order to reject these definitions and argue for another definition the writer
favors.

What is a pure breed of cats, and what constitutes a pure-bred animal? These
terms can have a number of meanings. One of the simplest is merely to regard
as pure-bred a cat that has been properly registered with a responsible body
(such as the Governing Council of the Cat Fancy [GCCF] in Britain, or the Cat
Fanciers' Association [CFA] or one of the other similar associations in the United
States). Such a cat will have a pedigree of similarly registered parents, grandparents and so on for a given number of generations—normally at least four.
This ensures that the cat has "respectable" parentage and is likely to be a representative specimen of the breed—though it says nothing about its quality.

However, the process of registration and the writing of pedigrees is, in a
sense (and without meaning to be derogatory), merely window dressing. They
simply set a seal upon a more fundamental definition of pure breeds of cats.
This relates to the characteristics of the individuals constituting a recognized
breed and how these may differ from those of other cats: from alley cats and
from other recognized breeds. In one sense, a breed is a group of animals that
sufficient people are mutually agreed to recognize as such. This is not enough
in itself, however; the group must have coherent distinguishing features that set
them apart from all other cats, and hence distinctive underlying genetic characteristics.   —Michael Wright and Sally Walters, *The Book of the Cat*

EXERCISE 15.6

In his Chapter 7 proposal about birth control in the schools, Adam Paul
Weisman offers a stipulative definition of the role schools play in students'
lives (paragraph 11). Read the essay, paying particular attention to this definition. What function does it serve in the essay as a whole?

EXERCISE 15.7

Write several sentences of a stipulative definition for one of the following
alternatives.

1.   Define in your own way game shows, soap operas, police dramas, or horror movies. Try for a stipulative definition of what these (or some other form of entertainment) are generally like. In effect, you will be saying to your readers, other students in your class who are familiar with these shows, "Let's for now define X this way."

2.   Do the same for some hard-to-define concept—such as *loyalty, love, bravery, shyness, sportsmanship, male chauvinism,* or *worthwhile college courses.*

3.   Think of a new development or phenomenon in contemporary romance, music, television, leisure, fashion, or eating habits. Invent a name for it, and write a stipulative definition for it.

In a variety of writing situations, you will be faced with the task of sorting various scattered materials into an orderly presentation. A common strategy for doing so is *classifying*—combining items into a number of discrete groupings and then labeling each new group. In many instances classifying is a matter of *dividing* something into its constituent parts in order to consider the elements of each part separately.

In using classification and division, you will be particularly concerned with organization, principles of division, and coherence.

ORGANIZATION

As a strategy, classification and division serve primarily as a means of organization, of creating a framework for the presentation of information, whether in a few paragraphs of an essay or an entire book. Other strategies—definition, illustration, contrast—are often used to develop a topic in detail.

Authors of technical documents and textbooks often rely on classification and division as an organizing principle. In the following example from a book on the computer revolution, a three-part division of the topic is announced in the first sentence, and each part is labeled. Based on the order forecast by this sentence, each part is then defined and discussed in a separate paragraph.

> There are essentially three categories of machine: simple machines, programmable machines and robots.
>
> Simple machines, to all intents and purposes, are nothing more than powerful mechanical muscles; they are either controlled by a human being, or have been designed and constructed to perform an endless series of repetitive acts. Hydraulic excavators, steam engines and motor cars all fall into this category.
>
> Programmable machines are more sophisticated. They are devices which can be programmed to do any of a number of different tasks or, in the more ambitious cases, a sequence of tasks. The program is set into the device by the human who controls it. They have only become widely used in recent years, though some of the very earliest versions were invented at around the same time as the first simple machines. Jacquard's loom was a programmable machine—and it was also one of the first true machines.
>
> The robot is different, and in an important way. It, too, is capable of performing a variety of tasks, or a sequence of tasks, but the choice of tasks at any

particular moment is determined not only by a pre-set program, but also by some information *fed into it from the outside world which is relevant to the task it is performing.* The information it absorbs is fed into it through sensing devices attached to its own structure, and not by command signals from a human. A simple machine, or even a programmed one, is capable of performing quite a complex task, but it will go on doing it indefinitely in really blockheaded fashion until something intervenes to stop it; a robot, on the other hand, will take account of change in its environment and adjust its behavior accordingly.

–Christopher Evans, *The Micro Millennium*

The division of a topic into parts can be used for a variety of purposes. See how Ernest Hemingway uses the strategy to open a chapter in *Death in the Afternoon,* his classic book on bullfighting in Spain. To help us understand how a bullfight develops, Hemingway describes it as divided into three acts, each of which is named for the major action (the trial of the lances, the banderillas, and the death). Hemingway subdivides the third act further, into three parts (or scenes, to continue his analogy between a bullfight and a play). Finally, he summarizes his discussion in terms of a three-act "tragedy."

There are three acts to the fighting of each bull and they are called in Spanish los tres tercios de la lidia, or the three thirds of the combat. The first act, where the bull charges the picadors, is the suerte de varas, or the trial of the lances. Suerte is an important word in Spanish. It means, according to the dictionary: Suerte, f., chance, hazard, lots, fortune, luck, good luck, haphazard; state, condition, fate, doom, destiny, kind, sort; species, manner, mode, way, skillful manœuvre; trick, feat, juggle, and piece of ground separated by landmark. So the translation of trial or manœuvre is quite arbitrary, as any translation must be from the Spanish.

The action of the picadors in the ring and the work of the matadors who are charged with protecting them with their capes when they are dismounted make up the first act of the bullfight. When the president signals for the end of this act and the bugle blows the picadors leave the ring and the second act begins. There are no horses in the ring after the first act except the dead horses which are covered with canvas. Act one is the act of the capes, the pics and the horses. In it the bull has the greatest opportunity to display his bravery or cowardice.

Act two is that of the banderillas. These are pairs of sticks about a yard long, seventy centimetres to be exact, with a harpoon-shaped steel point four centimetres long at one end. They are supposed to be placed, two at a time, in the humped muscle at the top of the bull's neck as he charges the man who holds them. They are designed to complete the work of slowing up the bull and regulating the carriage of his head which has been begun by the picadors: so that his attack will be slower, but surer and better directed. Four pair of banderillas are usually put in. If they are placed by the banderilleros or peones they must be placed, above all other considerations, quickly and in the proper position. If the matador himself places them he may indulge in a preparation which is usually accompanied by music. This is the most picturesque part of the bullfight and the part most spectators care for the most when first seeing fights. The mission of the banderilleros is not only to force the bull by hooking to tire his neck muscles and carry his head lower but also, by placing them at one side or another, to correct a tendency to hook to that side. The entire act of the banderillas should not take more than five minutes. If it is prolonged the bull becomes discomposed and the fight loses the tempo it must keep, and if the bull is an uncertain and dangerous one he has too many opportunities to see and charge men unarmed with any lure, and so develops a tendency to search for the man, the bundle, as the Spanish call him, behind the cloth when the matador comes out for the last act with the sword and muleta.

The president changes the act after three or at most four pairs of banderillas have been placed and <u>the third and final division is the death.</u> It is made up of three parts. First the brindis or salutation of the president and dedication or toasting of the death of the bull, either to him or to some other person by the matador, followed by the work of the matador with the muleta. This is a scarlet serge cloth which is folded over a stick which has a sharp spike at one end and a handle at the other. The spike goes through the cloth which is fastened to the other end of the handle with a thumb screw so that it hangs in folds along the length of the stick. Muleta means literally crutch, but in bullfighting it refers to the scarlet-serge-draped stick with which the matador is supposed to master the bull, prepare him for killing and finally hold in his left hand to lower the bull's head and keep it lowered while he kills the animal by a sword thrust high up between his shoulder blades.

These are the three acts in the tragedy of the bullfight, and it is the first one, the horse part, which indicates what the others will be and, in fact, makes the rest possible. It is in the first act that the bull comes out in full possession of all of his faculties, confident, fast, vicious and conquering. All his victories are in the first act. At the end of the first act he has apparently won. He has cleared the ring of mounted men and is alone. In the second act he is baffled completely by an unarmed man and very cruelly punished by the banderillas so that his confidence and his blind general rage goes and he concentrates his hatred on an individual object. In the third act he is faced by only one man who must, alone, dominate him by a piece of cloth placed over a stick, and kill him from in front, going in over the bull's right horn to kill him with a sword thrust between the arch of his shoulder blades.   —Ernest Hemingway, *Death in the Afternoon*

The way a topic is divided can be illustrated with a diagram showing its parts and subparts. Here is such a diagram of the organization of Hemingway's excerpt:

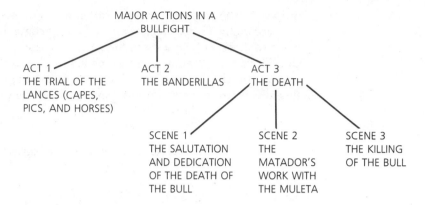

Using this division, the various actions of the bullfight can be classified according to the "act" in which they occur.

PRINCIPLES OF DIVISION

When you divide materials up, you must be sure the division meets several basic requirements. First of all, it must be appropriate to your writing purpose. You shouldn't divide material simply to have smaller bits of information; rather, it should help you to make some point about your topic. In addition, your divisions should be consistent, exclusive, and complete. These may be defined as follows:

Consistency.   The resulting parts must all be based on the same principle of division.

Exclusiveness.   Parts resulting from the division should not overlap.

Completeness.   No important parts should be omitted in the division.

The Hemingway excerpt illustrates each of these requirements. The *point* of Hemingway's division is to suggest the formalized, tragic drama of a bullfight and to highlight the contribution of the key action in each act to the noble defeat of the bull. This division is *consistent* in that the parts, or acts—the trial of the lances, the banderillas, and the death—are all formed on the same principle. Each one is a primary segment of the drama and revolves around a particular major action. The division is *exclusive* because there is no overlap: actions in one act do not usually occur again in other acts. It is *complete* because Hemingway's acts include all the actions responsible for the defeat of the bull. (Note that the subdivision of the third act into the major activities of the matador fulfills these same requirements.)

The principle of division one uses depends primarily on one's purpose. Most topics can be divided in a number of ways. For example, based on the purpose of the study, a team of sociologists might divide a survey's respondents according to age, education, income, geographic location, or answer given to a particular question. Similarly, a landscape gardener choosing deciduous trees for a midwestern park might be concerned, among other matters, with variations in leaf coloration or in shade-giving characteristics and thus divide the subject into groupings such as one of the following:

DECIDUOUS TREES OF THE MIDWEST

Writers likewise divide topics according to principles based on their purposes for writing. The division itself results from the writer's analysis of the topic and of all information gathered regarding the topic plus any ideas or insights he or she may have. Only full and thoughtful analysis of the topic and a carefully defined principle of division can assure that the division or system of classification will be consistent, exclusive, and complete.

EXERCISE 16.1

Diagram the division in the first example in this chapter, the selection from *The Micro Millennium* by Christopher Evans. Then decide whether the division is consistent, exclusive, and complete. What would you say is the point of the division?

EXERCISE 16.2

Pick at least two of the following topics, and divide them according to two or three different principles of division. Diagram each division, and then state its point. Be sure that each division is consistent, exclusive, and complete.

teachers   crimes
dreams   poets

lies	popular music groups
restaurants	tools for writing
bars	ways of avoiding writing
movies	football offenses
students	field hockey defenses

MAINTAINING COHERENCE

Anytime you divide information into parts, you have to take care to present the material in a way that readers can follow easily. Biologist Sylvia Mader's *Inquiry into Life*, featured in Chapter 15, includes many good examples of cues a writer can provide to bring coherence to a discussion and to guide readers sufficiently. In the following example from that book, Mader offers a straightforward three-part division to identify the parts of the human ear. In the larger context of the chapter in which it appears, its purpose is to name and classify the parts so that readers will be able to follow a discussion of how the ear functions.

The ear has three divisions: outer, middle, and inner. The **outer ear** consists of the **pinna** (external flap) and **auditory canal**. The opening of the auditory canal is lined with fine hairs and sweat glands. In the upper wall are modified sweat glands that secrete earwax to help guard the ear against the entrance of foreign materials such as air pollutants.

The **middle ear** begins at the **tympanic membrane** (eardrum) and ends at a bony wall in which are found two small openings covered by membranes. These openings are called the **oval** and **round windows**. The posterior wall of the middle ear leads to many air spaces within the **mastoid process**.

Three small bones are found between the tympanic membrane and the oval window. Collectively called the **ossicles,** individually they are the **hammer** (malleus), **anvil** (incus), and **stirrup** (stapes) because their shapes resemble these objects. The hammer adheres to the tympanic membrane, while the stirrup touches the oval window.

The eustachian tube extends from the middle ear to the nasopharynx and permits equalization of air pressure. Chewing gum, yawning, and swallowing in elevators and airplanes helps move air through the eustachian tubes upon ascent and descent.

Whereas the outer ear and middle ear contain air, the inner ear is filled with fluid. The **inner ear,** anatomically speaking, has three areas: the first two, called the vestibule and semicircular canals, are concerned with balance; and the third, the cochlea, is concerned with hearing.

The **semicircular canals** are arranged so that there is one in each dimension of space. The base of each canal, called the **ampulla,** is slightly enlarged. Within the ampullae are little hair cells.

The **vestibule** is a chamber that lies between the semicircular canals and the cochlea. It contains two small sacs called the **utricle** and **saccule**. Within both of these are little hair cells surrounded by a gelatinous material containing calcium carbonate granules, or **otoliths.**

The **cochlea** resembles the shell of a snail because it spirals. Within the tubular cochlea are three canals: the vestibular canal, the **cochlear canal,** and the tympanic canal. Along the length of the basilar membrane, which forms the lower wall of the cochlear canal, are little hair cells, and just above them is another membrane, called the **tectorial membrane.** The hair cells plus the tectorial membrane are called the **organ of Corti.** When this organ sends nerve impulses to the cerebral cortex, it is interpreted as sound.

—Sylvia Mader, *Inquiry into Life*

The Ear

	Outer Ear	Middle Ear	Inner Ear *Cochlea*	*Sacs plus semicircular canals*
Function	Directs sound waves to tympanic membrane	Picks up and amplifies sound waves	Hearing	Maintains equilibrium
Anatomy	Pinna Auditory canal	Tympanic membrane Hammer (malleus) Anvil (incus) Stirrup (stapes)	Vestibular canal Tympanic canal Cochlear canal Contains organ of Corti Auditory nerve starts here	Saccule and utricle (contain otoliths and hair cells) Semicircular canals (contain hair cells in ampullae)
Media	Air	Air (eustachian tube)	Fluid	Fluid

Path of vibration: Sound waves—vibration of tympanic membrane—vibration of hammer, anvil, and stirrup—vibration of oval window—fluid pressure waves of fluids in canals of inner ear lead to stimulation of hair cells—bulging of round window.

Mader's plan for her division is a *spatial* one, moving from inside to outside. (Note, in contrast, that Hemingway's division of the bullfight into three acts follows a *temporal* plan, moving across time.) In the initial statement of the division, Mader forecasts the plan of the presentation and names the three divisions in the order in which she will take them up: outer, middle, and inner ear. Each division is then introduced in a new paragraph and always with the same syntax at the beginning of a sentence: "The outer ear . . . The middle ear . . . The inner ear . . ." Furthermore, Mader includes a chart to diagram the division and to classify all the main anatomical terms within each part. (She also provides several drawings of the ear, not included here.)

General strategies for coherence are discussed on pp. 410–13.

With each of these strategies, Mader helps readers to understand and to follow her explanation easily and without confusion.

EXERCISE 16.3

Look again at the first selection in this chapter (from *The Micro Millennium* by Christopher Evans) to examine the strategies the writer uses to present a coherent division of information. Does the initial statement of the division name all the groups and forecast the order in which they will be discussed? What other writing strategies does the writer use to steer the reader through the presentation?

USING CLASSIFICATION WITH OTHER WRITING STRATEGIES

The last example comes from a book that explains the new physics to non-physicists.

There are two kinds of mass, which means that there are two ways of talking about it. The first is gravitational mass. The gravitational mass of an object, roughly speaking, is the weight of the object as measured on a balance scale. Something that weighs three times more than another object has three times more mass. Gravitational mass is the measure of how much force the gravity of the earth exerts on an object. Newton's laws describe the effects of this force, which vary with the distance of the mass from the earth. Although Newton's laws describe the effects of this force, they do not define it. This is the mystery of action-at-a-distance. . . .

The second type of mass is inertial mass. Inertial mass is the measure of the resistance of an object to acceleration (or deceleration, which is negative acceleration). For example, it takes three times more force to move three railroad cars from a standstill to twenty miles per hour (positive acceleration) than it takes to move one railroad car from a standstill to twenty miles per hour. . . . Similarly, once they are moving, it takes three times more force to stop three cars than it takes to stop the single car. This is because the inertial mass of the three railroad cars is three times more than the inertial mass of the single railroad car.

Inertial mass and gravitational mass are equal. This explains why a feather and a cannonball fall with equal velocity in a vacuum. The cannonball has hundreds of times more gravitational mass than the feather (it weighs more) but it also has hundreds of times more resistance to motion than the feather (its inertial mass). Its attraction to the earth is hundreds of times stronger than that of the feather, but then so is its inclination not to move. The result is that it accelerates downward at the same rate as the feather, although it seems that it should fall much faster.

The fact that inertial mass and gravitational mass are equal was known three hundred years ago, but physicists considered it a coincidence. No significance was attached to it until Einstein published his general theory of relativity.

—Gary Zukav, *The Dancing Wu Li Masters: An Overview of the New Physics*

This example illustrates the relation of classification and division to other essential writing strategies. Zukav divides his topic into two kinds of mass: gravitational and inertial. Then he defines each one. In the first paragraph, to define gravitational mass, he relies in part on the illustration of an ordinary balance scale. In the second paragraph, to define inertial mass, he contrasts the action of three railroad cars with that of one railroad car. These two paragraphs show how naturally dividing and classifying work together with definition, illustration, and contrast.

Dividing his material into two parts serves to emphasize his point: that inertial mass and gravitational mass (the two parts) are equal. This point is then illustrated by contrasting a feather with a cannonball.

As this example and the others in this chapter indicate, classification and division are basically an organizational strategy rather than one for development. Only when used together with other writing strategies can they be used to *explain* a topic.

EXERCISE 16.4

Analyze the following classifications, each from a selection in Part I of this book. First, within the context of the whole selection, decide the point of the division and the principle used. Then decide whether the division is consistent, exclusive, and complete. To focus your analysis, you might want to diagram the division.

> *Chapter 7*. "Birth Control in the Schools," Adam Paul Weisman, paragraphs 2–5
>
> *Chapter 7*. "To the Rescue: A National Youth Academy," Samuel D. Proctor, paragraphs 14–20
>
> *Chapter 9*. "Suicide among Young People," Victor Fuchs, paragraph 2 and table

EXERCISE 16.5

Choose one of the following writing activities. Each one asks for some division; state briefly what point your division might make. Be sure, in addition, that your groupings have consistency, exclusiveness, and completeness. Include in your writing appropriate strategies of coherence: forecasting, paragraphing (optional in a brief piece), repeated sentence patterns, and so on.

1.   Write several sentences in which you identify the major periods in your life. Label and briefly define each period.

2.   Describe a familiar activity (running, sleeping, eating Chinese food) in a new way by dividing it into stages. Label and define each stage.

3.   Develop in writing one of the classification systems you created in Exercise 16.2.

When you analyze and evaluate two or more things, you compare those things. You might compare two people you know well, three motorcycles you are considering buying for a cross-country tour, four Stephen King novels, three tomato plants being grown under different laboratory conditions, or two theories about the causes of inflation and unemployment. But as soon as comparison begins, contrast edges its way in, for rarely are two things totally alike. The contrasts, or differences, between the three motorcycles are likely to be more enlightening than the similarities, many of which may be so obvious as to need no analysis. *Comparison,* then, brings similar things together for examination, to see how they are alike. *Contrast* is a form of comparison that emphasizes their differences.

Comparison and contrast is more than a writing strategy, of course. It is a basic way of thinking and learning. A basic principle of learning theory says that we acquire new concepts most readily if we can see how they are similar to or different from concepts we already know.

Professional writers say that comparison and contrast is a basic strategy they would not want to be without. For some writing situations (like the ones above) it has no substitute. Indeed, some writing is essentially extended comparison. But for all kinds of writing, comparison and contrast regularly alternates with other writing strategies in presenting information.

Chances are that you will confront many test questions and essay assignments asking you to compare and contrast—two poems, three presidents, four procedures. This is a popular format in all academic disciplines, for it is one of the best ways to challenge students intellectually.

TWO WAYS OF COMPARING AND CONTRASTING

There are two ways to organize comparison and contrast in writing: in chunks and in sequence. In *chunking,* each object of the comparison is presented separately; in *sequencing,* the items are compared point by point. For example, a chunked comparison of two motorcycles would first detail all pertinent features of the Pirsig 241X and then consider all features of the Kawazuki 500S, whereas a sequenced comparison would analyze the Pirsig and the Kawazuki feature by feature. In a chunked comparison discussion is organized around each separate item being compared. In a sequenced comparison it is organized around characteristics of the items being compared.

Comparing and Contrasting 17

Look now at an example of chunked comparison, one that contrasts the effects westward migration had on American men in the nineteenth century with its effects on women:

> The westward move for many men was the physical expression of a break with the past and a setting out for a new life. The journey occurred when the rhythms of maturity were primed for a change. The determination to go West was either the initial separation from a man's parental family or the second major move, the move "upward" in the search for economic mobility and success. The adventure took on the color of some "dramatic rite of passage to mastery and adulthood" in the life cycle of frontier men.
>
> But the journey could have no natural place in the life cycle of the women. The journey was a violation of life's natural rhythms for women of childbearing years. There was simply no way that the rigorous exertions of the overland journey could be considered "normal" for a pregnant woman. And yet a woman's pregnancy mattered very little to emigrant families; certainly it was not sufficient cause to defer the trip.
>
> Even with the best of care, childbirth was a precarious business in the nineteenth century. It was even more risky on the open road, followed by immediate travel in a wagon with no springs and with very little access to water for drinking or for bathing. Any complications of delivery proved critical. And frailty in the newborn was life-threatening. The prospect of childbirth on the Trail must have meant months of heightened anxiety to women.
>
> —Lillian Schlissel, *Women's Diaries of the Westward Journey*

The two parts of the comparison—men and women—are discussed separately, first one and then the other. The shift from the first discussion to the contrasting one is signaled by the word *but* and by a new paragraph. Each discussion begins with a general statement which is then developed by examples.

Schematically, a chunked comparison looks simple enough. As the preceding example shows, it is easy to block off such a discussion in a text and then provide a clean transition between the various parts. And yet it can in fact be more complicated for a writer to plan than a sequenced comparison. Sequenced comparison may be closer to the way people perceive and think about similarities or differences in things. For example, while your awareness that two navy blazers are different might come all at once, you would identify the specific differences—buttons, tailoring, fabric—one at a time. A sequenced comparison would point to the differences in just this way—one at a time—whereas a chunked comparison would present all the features of one blazer and then do the same for the second. Thus the chunked strategy requires that a writer organize all the points of comparison before starting to write. With sequencing, however, it is possible to take up each point of comparison as it comes to mind.

In the next example, from a natural history of the earth, sequencing is used to contrast bird wings and airplane wings:

> Bird wings have a much more complex job to do than the wings of an aeroplane, for in addition to supporting the bird they must act as its engine, rowing it through the air. Even so the wing outline of a bird conforms to the same aerodynamic principles as those eventually discovered by man when designing his aeroplanes, and if you know how different kinds of aircraft perform, you can predict the flight capabilities of similarly shaped birds.
>
> Short stubby wings enable a tanager and other forest-living birds to swerve and dodge at speed through the undergrowth just as they helped the fighter planes of the Second World War to make tight turns and aerobatic manoeuvres in a dog-fight. More modern fighters achieve greater speeds by sweeping back their wings while in flight, just as peregrines do when they go into a 130 kph dive, stooping to a kill. Championship gliders have long thin wings so that, having gained height in a thermal up-current they can soar gently down for hours and an albatross, the largest of flying birds, with a similar wing shape and a span of 3 metres, can patrol the ocean for hours in the same way without a single wing beat. Vultures and hawks circle at very slow speeds supported by a thermal and they have the broad rectangular wings that very slow flying aircraft have. Man has not been able to adapt wings to provide hovering flight. He has only achieved that with the whirling horizontal blades of a helicopter or the downward-pointing engines of a vertical landing jet. Hummingbirds have paralleled even this. They tilt their bodies so that they are almost upright and then beat their wings as fast as 80 times a second producing a similar down-draught of air. So the hummingbird can hover and even fly backwards.   –David Attenborough, *Life on Earth*

The important thing to note about this example is the limited, focused basis for the comparison: the shape of wings. Attenborough specifies this basis in the second sentence of the passage (underscored here). Though birds and planes both fly, there is almost nothing else they have in common. They are so obviously different that it would even seem silly to compare them in writing. But Attenborough finds a valid—and fascinating—basis for comparison and develops it in a way that is both informative and entertaining. A successful comparison always has these qualities: a valid basis for comparison, a limited focus, and information that will catch a reader's attention.

EXERCISE 17.1

Pick any one of the following subjects and write several sentences comparing and contrasting. Be careful to limit the basis for your comparison, and underline the sentence that states that basis.

two ways of achieving the same goal (travel by bus or subway, using flattery or persuasion to get what you want)

two seemingly unlikely subjects for comparison (a child and an old man, soccer and ballet)

two sports

two explanations or theories

EXERCISE 17.2

Analyze the specified comparisons in the following selections from Part I. How is each comparison organized? (It may or may not be neatly chunked or sequenced.) Why do you think the writer organizes the comparison in that way? What is the role of the comparison in the whole piece? How effective do you consider the comparison?

Chapter 2. "On Being a Real Westerner," Tobias Wolff, paragraphs 3, 4

Chapter 4. "Inside the Brain," David Noonan, paragraphs 21–23

Chapter 5. "Is Sex Necessary?," David Quammen, paragraph 14

Chapter 8. "Searing, Nervy and Very Honest," David Ansen, paragraph 3

Chapter 8. "Open and Shut," Terrence Rafferty, paragraphs 1–2, 4

Chapter 9. "Suicide among Young People," Victor Fuchs, paragraph 2

EXERCISE 17.3

Some of the selections in Part I are organized around comparisons. Identify and evaluate the comparisons in each of the following pieces. (Remember that the comparison may be stated or implied.)

Chapter 5. "American Individualism," Robert N. Bellah et al.

Chapter 6. "Abortion, Right and Wrong," Rachel Richardson Smith

ANALOGY

One special form of comparison is the *analogy,* in which one part of the comparison is used simply to explain the other. See how John McPhee uses two different analogies—the twelve-month calendar and the distance along two widespread arms—to explain the duration of geologic time.

In like manner, geologists will sometimes use the calendar year as a unit to represent the time scale, and in such terms the Precambrian runs from New Year's Day until well after Halloween. Dinosaurs appear in the middle of December and are gone the day after Christmas. The last ice sheet melts on December 31st at one minute before midnight, and the Roman Empire lasts five seconds. With your arms spread wide again to represent all time on earth, look at one hand with its line of life. The Cambrian begins in the wrist, and the Permian

Extinction is at the outer end of the palm. All of the Cenozoic is in a fingerprint, and in a single stroke with a medium-grained nail file you could eradicate human history. Geologists live with the geologic scale. Individually, they may or may not be alarmed by the rate of exploitation of the things they discover, but, like the environmentalists, they use these repetitive analogies to place the human record in perspective—to see the Age of Reflection, the last few thousand years, as a small bright sparkle at the end of time.   —John McPhee, *Basin and Range*

Scientists have always made good use of analogy—in both their thinking and their writing. Modern physics, in particular, is full of concepts that strain the comprehension and imagination of the nonscientist. One such concept is the uncertainty principle, a concept that is very difficult for anybody but a physicist to define. In the following excerpt, Gary Zukav does so with an analogy—likening the uncertainty principle to a movie projector that is always slightly out of focus.

The uncertainty principle reveals that as we penetrate deeper and deeper into the subatomic realm, we reach a certain point at which one part or another of our picture of nature becomes blurred, and there is no way to reclarify that part without blurring another part of the picture! It is as though we are adjusting a moving picture that is slightly out of focus. As we make the final adjustments, we are astonished to discover that when the right side of the picture clears, the left side of the picture becomes completely unfocused and nothing in it is recognizable. When we try to focus the left side of the picture, the right side starts to blur and soon the situation is reversed. If we try to strike a balance between these two extremes, both sides of the picture return to a recognizable condition, but in no way can we remove the original fuzziness from them.

The right side of the picture, in the original formulation of the uncertainty principle, corresponds to the position in space of a moving particle. The left side of the picture corresponds to its momentum. According to the uncertainty principle, we cannot measure accurately, at the same time, both the position *and* the momentum of a moving particle. The more precisely we determine one of these properties, the less we know about the other. If we precisely determine the position of the particle, then, strange as it sounds, there is *nothing* that we can know about its momentum. If we precisely determine the momentum of the particle, there is no way to determine its position.

—Gary Zukav, *The Dancing Wu Li Masters: An Overview of the New Physics*

Notice what a strong visual image Zukav's analogy produces—it is very easy to imagine alternating sides of the movie screen going in and out of focus. Explanatory analogies almost always use very familiar objects for comparison, probably because they are trying to explain something very unfamiliar.

Analogies can also be used for subjects other than abstract, scientific concepts. Indeed, writers often offer analogies to make nontechnical descriptions of explanations more vivid and entertaining. Here is a sports analogy from a sociological study of Hamilton, Ohio. It comes from a chapter describing a hearing held to examine a school board's decision to fire one teacher, Sam Shie. In it, the writer uses analogy to describe Shie's three lawyers, comparing them to an aggressive basketball team.

> The cross-examination of Dr. Helms was conducted by Randy Rogers, the young associate of Holbrock's. Rogers was tall and strongly built, lacking by only a couple of inches the height of a professional basketball player who weakens the opposition by fouling often and drawing fouls in return. This was close to the function Rogers performed for the defense. With Hugh Holbrock, Robert Dunlevey, and Randy Rogers all ranged against Carl Morgenstern, it was sometimes hard to tell just who the underdog was at the hearings. Sam Shie, to be sure, was a lone teacher up against a community's educational establishment which was trying to purge him. But at the hearings themselves, almost all the spectators were on Shie's side; he was being supported by the Ohio Education Association, and he had three articulate, variously styled lawyers who disputed virtually everything Carl Morgenstern or one of his witnesses said. Each came at Morgenstern from a different angle with a new tactic, trying to wear him down the way a basketball team will use a full-court press, a fast break, the setting of a pick or screen, the switching of defensive assignments to bewilder an opponent. Hugh Holbrock made long, arcing, oratorical shots from outside the key, Robert Dunlevey dribbled spectacularly around any position Morgenstern took, and Randy Rogers would try to provoke Morgenstern into exchanges of anger and procedural wrangles. Rogers was surly to Morgenstern, who would respond by being loftily sardonic. A few times Morgenstern slipped and got mad at Rogers, who was polite to witnesses but steeled himself to a single pitch of fury when he was addressing Morgenstern. The rest of the time Rogers sat moodily at the defense table—in effect on the bench—while Holbrock and Dunlevey performed their own specialties.   —Peter Davis, *Hometown*

Analogies are tricky. They may at first seem useful, but actually it is a rare analogy that is consistently useful at all the major points of comparison. Some analogies break down early; others are downright misleading. To be successful, a writer must be sure the analogy really holds.

Thus, most writers exercise caution with analogy. Nevertheless, you will run across analogies regularly; indeed, it would be hard to find a book without one. For certain very abstract information as well as some writing situations, analogy is the writing strategy of choice.

EXERCISE 17.4

Choose a principle or process that you know well. You might select a basic principle from the natural or social sciences; or you could consider a bodily movement, a physiological process, or a process of social change.

Write an analogy of several sentences that explains this principle or process to a reader who is unfamiliar with it. Look for something very familiar to compare it with that will help the reader understand the principle or process without a technical explanation.

The word *arguing* connotes a dispute—raised voices, doors slammed, names called. As a writing strategy, however, arguing means something quite different. It means presenting a carefully reasoned, well-supported argument that takes into account other points of view. Arguing here, then, connotes both inquiry and advocacy, presenting a position in a thoughtful and convincing way.

This chapter presents the basic argumentative strategies available to a writer, focusing first on the structure of an argument—making claims, offering supporting reasons and evidence, and handling counterarguments—and then on common abuses or errors in arguing.

MAKING A CLAIM

Central to any writer's argument is a claim. The claim is whatever view or thesis or conclusion the writer puts forth about the subject. Argumentative essays present the claim in a thesis statement.

Here are some claims that appear as thesis statements in argumentative essays in Part I of this book:

> *The Crimson*'s decision not to run *Playboy*'s advertisement recruiting Harvard women for its October "Women of the Ivy League" issue was both the very most and the very least the newspaper could do to fight the institutionalized exploitation of women. —Kristin A. Goss, "Taking a Stand against Sexism" (Chapter 6)

> All of this [social problems caused by unsocialized youth] can be turned around by creating a new institution: a national youth academy with 50 campuses on our inactive military bases. This academy would service 250,000 students annually, 5,000 on each location.
> —Samuel D. Proctor, "To the Rescue: A National Youth Academy" (Chapter 7)

> *Document* may not end up getting as much air play as *The Joshua Tree*, and it may not sell as many copies; but artistically it equals or betters the other album, breaking through the boundaries of conventional songwriting and record making, taking rock music to a plateau never before achieved.
> —Jason Thornton, "Documenting *Document*" (Chapter 8)

> The mythic horror movie, like the sick joke, has a dirty job to do. It deliberately appeals to all that is worst in us. It is morbidity unchained, our most base instincts let free, our nastiest fantasies realized . . . and it all happens fittingly enough, in the dark. —Stephen King, "Why We Crave Horror Movies" (Chapter 9)

"Araby" tells the story of an adolescent boy's initiation into adulthood. . . . From the beginning, the boy deludes himself about his relationship with Mangan's sister. Through this self-delusion, he increasingly resembles the adult characters, and later, at Araby, he realizes the parallel between his own self-delusion and the hypocrisy and vanity of the adult world.

—David Ratinov, "From Innocence to Insight: 'Araby' as an Initiation Story" (Chapter 10)

Claims can be classified according to the kinds of questions they seek to answer. Each of the preceding thesis statements, for example, illustrates a different kind of claim:

Claim of judgment: What is your position on the issue? (Goss)
Claim of policy: What should be done to solve the problem? (Proctor)
Claim of value: What is something worth? (Thornton)
Claim of cause: Why is something the way it is? (King)
Claim of interpretation: What does something mean? (Ratinov)

Chapters 6–10 contain essays that argue for each of these kinds of claims, along with guidelines for constructing an argument to support such a claim.

Successful claims must be arguable, clear, and appropriately qualified. Following is a discussion of each of these characteristics of successful claims.

Arguable Statements

To be arguable, a claim must have some probability of being true. It should not, however, be generally accepted as true. In addition, a claim must be arguable on grounds shared by writer and readers.

Facts are unarguable as claims because they are objectively verifiable. Facts are easy to verify—whether by checking an authoritative reference book, asking an authority, or observing it with your own eyes. For example, these statements assert facts:

Jem will be twenty-one years old on May 6, 1991.

I am less than five feet tall.

Eucalyptus trees were originally imported into California from Australia.

Each of these assertions can be easily verified. To find out Jem's age, you can do many things including asking him and looking up his school records. To determine a person's height, you can use a tape measure. To discover where California got its Eucalyptus trees, you can refer to a source in the library. There is no point in arguing over such statements (though you might question the authority of a particular source or the accuracy of someone's measurement). If a writer were to claim something as fact and attempt to support the claim with authorities or statistics, the essay would not be considered an argument but a report of information. Facts, as you will see in the next section, are used in arguments as evidence to support a claim and not as claims themselves.

Like facts, expressions of personal feeling are not arguable claims. While facts are unarguable because they can be definitively proven true or false, feelings are unarguable because they are purely subjective. Personal feelings can be explained, but it would be unreasonable to attempt to convince others to change their views or take action solely on the basis of your personal feelings.

You can declare, for example, that you love rocky road ice cream or that you detest eight o'clock classes, but you cannot offer an argument to support such claims. All you can do is explain why you feel as you do. You might explain that the combination of chocolate, marshmallow, and nuts in rocky road feels good in your mouth. Similarly, even though many people undoubtedly share your dislike of eight o'clock classes, it would be pointless to try to convince others to share your feelings. If, however, you were to restate the claim as "Eight o'clock classes are counterproductive," you could then construct an argument to support your claim that does not depend solely on your subjective feelings, memories, or preferences. Your argument could be based on reasons and evidence that apply to others as well as to yourself. For example, you might argue that students' ability to learn is at an especially low ebb after breakfast and provide scientific as well as statistical evidence as support, in addition, perhaps, to personal experience and informal interviews with your friends.

Clear and
Exact Wording

The way a claim is worded is as important as whether or not it is arguable. The wording of a claim, especially its key terms, must be clear and exact. Two common kinds of imprecision are vagueness and ambiguity.

Consider the following claim: "Democracy is a way of life." The meaning of this claim is vague and uncertain. The problem stems both from the abstractness of the word *democracy* and the inexactness of the phrase *way of life*. Abstract ideas like democracy, freedom, and patriotism are by their very nature hard to grasp, and they become even less clear with overuse. Too often, such words take on connotations that may obscure their original meaning. *Way of life* suffers from fuzziness: What does it mean? Moreover, can a form of government be a way of life? It depends on what is meant by *way of life*. Does it refer to daily life, to a general philosophy or attitude toward life, or to something else?

A related problem is ambiguity. While a claim is considered vague if its meaning is unclear, it is ambiguous if it has more than one possible meaning. For example, the statement "my English instructor is mad" can be understood in two ways: The teacher is either angry or insane. Obviously, these are two very different claims. You wouldn't want readers to think you mean one when you actually mean the other.

In any argumentative writing, you should pay special attention to the way you phrase your claims and take care to avoid vague and ambiguous language.

Appropriate Qualification

In addition to being arguable and clear, the forcefulness with which a writer asserts a claim should be appropriate to the writing situation. If you are confident that your case is so strong that readers will accept your argument without question, you will want to state your claim emphatically and unconditionally. If, however, you expect readers to challenge your assumptions or conclusions, then you will want to qualify your statement. Qualifying the extremity or forcefulness of a claim makes it more likely that readers will take it seriously. Expressions like *probably, very likely, apparently, it seems* all serve to qualify a claim.

EXERCISE 18.1

Write a claim of judgment that asserts your position on one of the following controversial issues: flag burning, working part time during college, censorship of music lyrics, drug testing for college athletes. These issues are complicated and have been debated for a long time. Constructing a persuasive argument would obviously require careful deliberation and probably some research as well. For the limited purpose of practicing writing claims, however, try simply to construct a claim that is arguable, clear, and appropriately qualified.

EXERCISE 18.2

Find the claim in any one of the selections in Chapter 6 and read the entire essay. Then decide whether the claim meets the three requirements of successful claims: that it be arguable, clear, and appropriately qualified.

SUPPORTING CLAIMS WITH REASONS AND EVIDENCE

Claims are supported with reasons and evidence. Whether you are taking a stand, proposing a solution, making an evaluation, speculating about causes, or interpreting a literary work, you need reasons and evidence to construct a convincing argument.

Reasons can be thought of as the main points supporting a claim. Often they are the answers to the question "Why do you make that claim?" For example, you might value a movie highly *because* of its challenging ideas, unusual camera work, and memorable acting. You might oppose mandatory drug testing for college athletes *because* it singles out one group for unusual treatment, cannot be conducted reliably with current technology, and in your view violates athletes' civil rights. These *because* phrases are the reasons you make your claim. You may have one or many reasons for a claim, depending on your subject and writing situation. These reasons need evidence in order for them to be convincing and in order for your whole argument to succeed with your readers.

The main kinds of evidence writers use to construct arguments include facts, statistics, authorities, anecdotes, scenarios, cases, and textual evidence. Following is a discussion of each one, along with criteria for judging the reliability of that particular kind of evidence and examples from published works. In each example, you will be able to see readily how the evidence supports a main point or reason in a larger argument.

Facts

Facts may be used as supporting evidence in all types of arguments. A fact is generally defined as a statement accepted as true. Facts refer to a reality that can be measured or verified by objective means. The reliability of facts depends on their accuracy (they should not distort or misrepresent reality), completeness (they should not omit important details), and the trustworthiness of their sources (sources should be qualified and unbiased). Facts come from such sources as almanacs, encyclopedias, and research studies as well as from our own observations and experience.

In this example, a scholar who studies Mexican migration to the United States uses facts to argue against three assumptions about illegal migrants, assumptions he asserts are false.

> The case for a more restrictive immigration policy is based on three principal assumptions: that illegal aliens compete effectively with, and replace, large numbers of American workers; that the benefits to American society resulting from the aliens' contribution of low-cost labor are exceeded by the "social costs" resulting from their presence here; and that most illegal aliens entering the United States eventually settle here permanently, thus imposing an increasingly heavy, long-term burden upon the society.
>
> There is as yet no direct evidence to support any of these assumptions, at least with respect to illegal aliens from Mexico, who still constitute at least 60 to 65 percent of the total flow and more than 90 percent of the illegal aliens apprehended each year.
>
> Where careful independent studies of the impact of illegal immigration on local labor markets have been made, they have found no evidence of large-scale displacement of legal resident workers by illegal aliens. Studies have also shown that Mexican illegals make amazingly little use of tax-supported social services while they are in the United States, and that the cost of the services they do use is far out-weighed by their contributions to Social Security and income tax revenues.

There is also abundant evidence indicating that the vast majority of illegal aliens from Mexico continue to maintain a pattern of "shuttle" migration, most of them returning to Mexico after six months or less of employment in the United States. In fact, studies have shown that only a small minority of Mexican illegals even aspire to settle permanently in the United States.

While illegal aliens from countries other than Mexico do seem to stay longer and make more use of social services, there is still no reliable evidence that they compete effectively with American workers for desirable jobs. The typical job held by the illegal alien, regardless of nationality, would not provide the average American family with more than a subsistence standard of living. In most states, it would provide less income than welfare payments.

Certainly in some geographic areas, type of enterprises, and job categories, illegal aliens may depress wage levels or "take jobs away" from American workers. But there is simply no hard evidence that these effects are as widespread or as serious as most policy-makers and the general public seem to believe.

–Wayne A. Cornelius, "When the Door Is Closed on Illegal Aliens, Who Pays?"

Notice that Cornelius refers to facts as "hard evidence." They are considered hard or solid evidence because once accepted, a fact carries a great deal of weight in an argument. To encourage readers to accept his statements as fact, Cornelius says they come from "careful independent studies." Although he does not cite the sources of these studies here, they are included in the list of works cited at the end of the book in which this selection appears. Citing sources is especially important when your facts are not commonly accepted. Skeptical readers can review the research cited, as well as other relevant research, and draw their own conclusions.

Any facts you include in an argument should be current because what is accepted as "the facts" does change as new observations and studies are completed. In addition, you should use only those facts relevant to your argument, even if it means leaving out interesting peripheral information. Cornelius, for example, does not include facts about the kind of transportation Mexican illegals rely on because he wants to keep the focus on their brief periods of employment in the United States.

EXERCISE 18.3

Select one essay from Chapters 6–9 and evaluate its use of fact. Identify the statements presented as fact and comment on their reliability.

Statistics

In many kinds of arguments about economic, educational, or social issues, statistics may be essential. When you use statistics in your own arguments, you will want to ensure that they come from reliable sources. Your readers will expect you to explain the statistics clearly and present them fairly.

The following example comes from a book by the economist Lester Thurow proposing a solution to the problem of America's economic decline.

To convince readers that the problem is serious, Thurow argues early in the book that American productivity is falling behind that of some of our chief competitors. The statistics in the table are key evidence in his argument.

The data in Table 2 show the level of manufacturing productivity for seven leading industrial countries in 1983. As the data show, the United States has already been surpassed by Germany and France. Since we know that most of the small northern European countries (Switzerland, Sweden, Norway, Holland, Austria) have productivity rates similar to those of Germany and France, all of northern Europe with the exception of Ireland and the United Kingdom may now have moved slightly ahead of the United States in manufacturing productivity.

TABLE 2
MANUFACTURING PRODUCTIVITY 1983

Country	Output Per Hour of Work (1983 prices)	Rate of Growth 1977–82	1983
United States	$18.21	0.6%	4.2%
Germany	20.22	2.1	4.6
France	19.80	3.0	6.1
Italy	17.72	3.6	0.6
Japan	17.61	3.4	6.2
Canada	17.03	−0.3	6.9
United Kingdom	11.34	2.7	6.1

To some it will come as a surprise that Japanese productivity is still slightly behind that of the United States. This is due to the fact that the Japanese manufacturing economy is a peculiar mixture of the superefficient and the real dogs. In America we see only the exporting superefficient industries whose productivity is second to none. Japan's inefficient industries do not export and as a result are simply invisible to American eyes. While average Japanese productivity may be slightly inferior to that of America, it is well to remember that it is possible to drown in a river which is "on average" two feet deep. Where it counts—in exporting industries such as steel, autos, and consumer electronics—the Japanese are second to none.   —Lester Thurow, *The Zero-Sum Solution*

Thurow comments on the table, explaining the information it contains and why it is important. He then immediately (and throughout the chapter in which the table appears) uses it to support his argument.

Chapter 20 provides help finding statistical data at the library. Whenever possible, use sources in which statistics first appeared rather than summaries or digests of others' statistics. For example, you would want to get medical statistics from a reputable and authoritative professional periodical like the *New England Journal of Medicine* rather than from a popular news weekly. If you are uncertain about the most authoritative sources, ask a reference librarian or a professor who is a specialist on your topic.

EXERCISE 18.4

Analyze the use of statistics in one of the following selections from Part I:

> *Chapter 7.* "Birth Control in the Schools," Adam Paul Weisman
> *Chapter 9.* "Suicide among Young People," Victor Fuchs
> *Chapter 9.* "Where Will They Sleep Tonight?," Kim Dartnell

1. Identify the sources of the statistics. Do they seem to be the original sources? How might you find out whether the sources are authoritative and reputable?
2. How does the writer integrate the statistics into the text of the selection? By direct quotation from the source? By paraphrase or summary? In tables or figures?
3. What part do the statistics play in the selection? Do you find the statistics convincing?

Authorities

To support their claims and reasons, writers do not hesitate to cite authorities. They establish their credentials and quote them. Quoting a respected authority on a topic generally adds weight to an argument.

From Loretta Schwartz-Nobel's book on starvation in America comes a typical example. The writer cites an authority, a researcher at a well-known oceanographic institute, to support her argument that we now have technical resources to eliminate hunger in America.

> Dr. John Ryther, a highly respected and well-known marine biologist at the Woods Hole (Massachusetts) Oceanographic Institution, points out that there are about one billion acres of coastal wetlands in the world. If only one-tenth of these wetlands were used to raise fish, the potential yield of fish using improved methods of production would be one hundred million tons a year. This is the equivalent of the yield from the entire world's commercial fisheries.
>
> Dr. Ryther has also devised a complex continuous culture system which produces oysters, seaweed, worms, flounder, and abalone. It ultimately becomes a biological sewage treatment plant returning clean water to the sea.
>
> If this kind of system were implemented on a large scale it could produce a million pounds of shellfish a year from each one-acre production facility. By using advanced culture techniques like those developed at Woods Hole, Dr. Ryther estimates that the yield could well be multiplied tenfold within the next three decades.   —Loretta Schwartz-Nobel, *Starving in the Shadow of Plenty*

The writer could simply have mentioned a system for wetland culture, but instead she emphasizes that it comes from a respected expert—thereby adding to her own authority and to the credibility of her material. (After all, she is not an expert on all the technical aspects of her topic.) Instead of quoting the expert directly, she paraphrases the information from him.

EXERCISE 18.5

Analyze the way authorities are used in one of the following selections from Part I of this book. Decide whether you find the use of authorities convincing. How might you find out whether the authorities are respected? How does the writer establish each authority's credentials?

How does the writer integrate the authority's words or opinions into the text of the selection? By direct quotation? By paraphrase or summary in the writer's own language? What role does the authority have in the piece as a whole?

Chapter 6. "Last Rites for Indian Dead," Suzan Shown Harjo

Chapter 7. "Birth Control in the Schools," Adam Paul Weisman

Chapter 9. "Suicide among Young People," Victor Fuchs

Anecdotes

Anecdotes are brief stories that can very effectively provide evidence in an argument. Their specificity may be quite convincing if they seem to readers to be true to life. A physician opens an essay arguing that funerals are good for people with this anecdote:

> While attending a medical meeting about a year ago, I ran into a fellow I'd known in residency. "What are you doing here, Bill?" he asked. "Giving a talk on the responses to death," I replied. "It will cover the psychological value of funerals as well as—"
>
> "Funerals!" he exclaimed. "What a waste *they* are! I've made it plain to my wife that *I* don't want a funeral. Why spend all that money on such a macabre ordeal? And why have the kids standing around wondering what it's all about?"
>
> "Look, Jim," I said patiently, "I've seen case after case of depression caused by the inability of patients—young and old—to work through their feelings after a death. I've found that people are often better off if they have a funeral to focus their feelings on. That lets them do the emotional work necessary in response to the loss." My friend still looked doubtful. And, as we parted company, I wondered how many other physicians are also overlooking the psychological value of funerals.　—William A. Lamers, Jr., "Funerals Are Good for People"

Notice that the anecdote characterizes one particular occurrence. Anecdotes are different from generalized narratives, which summarize recurring or typical events. They are also different from scenarios, which tell about something that might happen, and cases, which summarize observations made over a period of time. Anecdotes make a special contribution to argument through their concreteness.

See Chapter 2 and Chapter 13 for more on writing anecdotes.

In the next example, a historian repeats a secondhand anecdote to argue that we should take extrasensory perception more seriously than we do:

> At six o'clock one evening Swedenborg, while dining with friends in the town of Gothenburg, suddenly became excited and declared that a dangerous fire had broken out in his native city of Stockholm, some three hundred miles away. He

asserted a little later that the fire had already burned the home of one of his neighbors and was threatening to consume his own. At eight o'clock of that same evening, he exclaimed with some relief that the fire had been checked three doors from his home. Two days later, Swedenborg's every statement was confirmed by actual reports of the fire, which had begun to blaze at the precise hour that he first received the impression.

Swedenborg's case is only one among hundreds of similar instances recorded in history and biography of the great, the near-great, and the obscure. At some time in their lives Mark Twain, Abraham Lincoln, Saint-Saëns, to name but a few, had, according to their biographers and in some cases their own accounts, strange sudden visions of events taking place at a distance, or events that took place, down to the last minute detail, months or years later in their own lives. In the case of Swedenborg the ability to see at a distance developed later into a powerful and sustained faculty; in most other cases, the heightened perceptivity seemed to arise only in a moment of crisis.   —Gina Cerminora, *Many Mansions*

EXERCISE 18.6

Analyze the use of anecdote in one of the following selections from Part I of this book. How long is the anecdote in relation to the length of the whole essay? Does the writer comment on the significance of the anecdote or leave it to the reader to infer its importance? What role does the anecdote play in the selection as a whole? Do you find the anecdote convincing?

> *Chapter 6.* "Children Need to Play, Not Compete," Jessica Statsky, paragraphs 6, 8
> *Chapter 8.* "Searing, Nervy and Very Honest," David Ansen, paragraph 1

Scenarios

While an anecdote tells about something that actually happened, a scenario is a narrative that describes something that might happen. Writers create scenarios to make their arguments more vivid and convincing. Scenarios raise and answer the question "What if?"

The first example comes from a book on illiteracy in America. To help readers understand illiterates' plight, the author creates a scenario from a dream:

Since I first immersed myself within this work I have often had the following dream: I find that I am in a railroad station or a large department store within a city that is utterly unknown to me and where I cannot understand the printed words. None of the signs or symbols is familiar. Everything looks strange: like mirror writing of some kind. Gradually I understand that I am in the Soviet Union. All the letters on the walls around me are Cyrillic. I look for my pocket dictionary but I find that it has been mislaid. Where have I left it? Then I recall that I forgot to bring it with me when I packed my bags in Boston. I struggle to remember the name of my hotel. I try to ask somebody for directions. One person stops and looks at me in a peculiar way. I lose the nerve to ask. At last I reach into my wallet for an ID card. The card is missing. Have I lost it? Then I remember that my card was confiscated for some reason, many years before. Around this point, I wake up in a panic.

This panic is not so different from the misery that millions of adult illiterates experience each day within the course of their routine existence in the U.S.A.

–Jonathan Kozol, *Illiteracy in America*

EXERCISE 18.7

Analyze the use of scenario in Patrick O'Malley's proposal for more frequent testing (reprinted in Chapter 7). What role does the scenario play in the selection as a whole? Do you find the scenario convincing?

EXERCISE 18.8

Writers often use scenarios to discuss the possible effects of trends or phenomena. Choose one of the following subjects, and write a scenario illustrating the possible effects.

1. The effects of cable TV's popularity on commercial and public TV

2. The effects of the popularity of aerobic dancing and exercise on Americans

3. The effects of increasing tuition costs on college students

4. The effects on U.S. society if colleges were available only to the wealthy

5. The effects on U.S. culture if we actually ran out of gasoline

Cases

Like an anecdote, a case is an example that comes from a writer's firsthand knowledge. Cases summarize observations of people. They are meant to be typical or generalized. Case histories are an important part of the work of psychologists, doctors, and social workers. These cases may be quite lengthy, sometimes following the life of one individual over many months or years. In persuasive writing, however, cases are presented briefly as evidence for a claim or reason.

This example comes from a publication for school administrators. It was written by two sociologists studying the psychological problems of adolescents, particularly alienation. Notice how they use the John Kelly case both to define alienation and to argue that it is a serious problem.

Since the beginning of man's awareness of "self" and "other," alienation has frayed the fabric of social institutions. In recent decades the term has become a euphemism for every kind of aberrant behavior from drug use to rejection of the political system. Adolescents are especially affected by this malaise. Let us consider the case of John Kelly, for example.

When John Kelly was 10, he was curious and energetic, the mascot of his family. His inquisitiveness led him to railroad yards, museums, and bus adventures downtown alone. In school, he was charming, cooperative, and interested. At 13, John suddenly changed. His agreeable nature vanished as he quarreled endlessly with his older brothers. He became moody and sullen, constantly snapping at his parents. He began to skip school and disrupt class when he did attend. When he was finally expelled, his parents enrolled him in another junior high school, hoping the change would solve some of John's problems. Instead, his difficulties intensified as he dropped his boyhood friends, stopped communicating with his parents, and withdrew into himself. Now, 16-year-old John bears little resemblance to the loving, active child his family once knew. He has been suspended from yet another school, hangs out with an older crowd, and comes home only to sleep. His parents feel hurt, bewildered, frustrated, and frightened.

As John Kelly's case makes clear, adolescent alienation is a teenager's inability to connect meaningfully with other people. At its root is aloneness, a feeling that no one else is quite like you, that you are not what other people want you to be.

—James Mackey and Deborah Appleman, "Broken Connections: The Alienated Adolescent in the 80s"

As examples and evidence in persuasive writing, cases are usually brief, rarely longer than this one. Writers nearly always know much more about their cases than they tell us. They select just the details from the case that will support the claim they are making.

To be effective, a case must ring true. Readers need specific details: dress, manner, personal history. Though the person in this case is an abstraction, meant to represent many people like him or her, we still recognize a real person.

EXERCISE 18.9

Evaluate the use of a case in "Where Will They Sleep Tonight?" by Kim Dartnell (Chapter 9). Decide whether the case is relevant to the argument and whether it rings true. What does the case contribute to the essay?

Textual Evidence

When you argue claims of value (Chapter 8) and interpretation (Chapter 10), textual evidence may be very important. If you are criticizing a controversial book that your readers have not yet read, you may want to quote from it often so that readers can understand why you think the author's argument is not credible. If you are interpreting a novel for one of your classes, you may need to include numerous excerpts to show just how you arrived at your conclusion. In both situations, you are integrating bits of the text you are evaluating or interpreting into your own text and building your argument on these bits.

You can read "Araby" on pp. 333–37.

In the following example, a literary critic uses textual evidence to support the claim that the main character in James Joyce's story "Araby" is involved in a "vivid waiting." As you read, notice how the writer continually refers to events in the story and also regularly quotes phrases from the story.

"Araby," wrote Ezra Pound, "is much better than a 'story,' it is a vivid waiting." It is true; the boy, suspended in his first dream of love, is also held up by circumstance, and the subjective rendering of this total experience is indeed vivid. . . .

Every morning the boy kept watch from his window until Mangan's sister appeared, and then with a leaping heart he ran to follow her in the street until their ways diverged, hers toward her convent school. Of an evening, when she came out on the doorstep to call her brother to tea, the boys at play would linger in the shadows to see whether she "would remain or go in"; then while she waited they would approach "resignedly," but while Mangan still teased his sister before obeying, the boy of this story "stood by the railings looking at her," seeing "her figure defined by the light from the half-opened door" and waiting upon a summons of another kind. He must wait too for his uncle's late return and for the money to fetch the girl a present from the bazaar Araby; then the special train, almost empty, waited intolerably and he arrived late. Still he drove toward his goal, paying a shilling to avoid further delay in looking for a sixpenny entrance. Once inside, he found the place half-darkened and the stalls mostly closed. Though there was nothing for him to buy, he lingered still, baffled, stultified, prolonging only pretense of interest. What awaits him as the lights are being put out is a facing "with anguish and anger" of his obsessive mood and its frustration, of himself as "a creature driven and derided by vanity"—like Stephen in *A Portrait* "angry with himself for being young and the prey of restless foolish impulses."   —Warren Beck, *Joyce's Dubliners*

EXERCISE 18.10

Select one of the essays on "Araby" in Chapter 10 and analyze its use of evidence. Identify where "Araby" is quoted, paraphrased, summarized, or merely referred to. Indicate whether the evidence is simply cited or explained in some way.

ANTICIPATING READERS' COUNTERARGUMENTS

Claims, reasons, and evidence are essential to a successful argument. Thoughtful writers go further, however, by anticipating their readers' counterarguments. Counterarguments include any objections, alternatives, challenges, or questions. To anticipate counterarguments, try to imagine a reader's point of view on the subject, knowledge about the subject, and familiarity with the issues. Try also to imagine a reader's response to the argument as it unfolds step by step. What will readers be thinking and feeling? How will they react?

Anticipating readers' counterarguments, writers rely on three basic strategies: acknowledging, accommodating, and refuting counterarguments. They let readers know they are aware of their objections and questions (acknowledge), accept all or part of the objections into their argument (accommodate), or explicitly oppose (refute) the objections. Writers may use one or more of these strategies in the same essay. Research by communications specialists indicates that readers find arguments more convincing when writers have anticipated their readers in these ways.

At this point, you may have an objection: Isn't it manipulative to acknowledge and accommodate readers' counterarguments? In fact, cynical writers and speakers do try to manipulate their readers' responses. They may try to trick readers, sell something, ensure a donation, or win support for a policy based on lies and evasions. However, unless readers are especially ignorant or emotionally vulnerable and willing to grant uncritically the writer's credibility, readers recognize and scorn manipulation. Anticipating counterarguments is convincing when it builds a bridge of shared concerns between writer and reader. The writer bases the anticipation (and the argument) on shared values, assumptions, goals, or criteria. This approach to acknowledging, accommodating, and refuting counterarguments wins readers' respect and attention—and sometimes even their agreement.

Acknowledging Counterarguments

The primary purpose of argumentative writing is to influence readers. Therefore, careful writers seek to influence their readers with each choice of a word, each choice of a sentence. Sometimes writers may even address their readers openly, both to build a bridge of shared concerns and to acknowledge their questions or objections.

The first example comes from a book on hunger in America. The writer seeks to enlist readers' sympathies for neglected elderly people.

> This is South Philadelphia—a microcosm of America, a place where people have gone to work, raised children, and then retired. Their daughters are our secretaries, clerks, and teachers. Their sons are our policemen, longshoremen, bankers, doctors, and lawyers. Economically these retired people once represented America's middle class. Yet in this typical urban neighborhood with its tap dance school, businessmen's association, American Cancer Society chapter, and local fire station, a two-year survey conducted by the Albert Einstein Medical Center's Social Service Division concluded that "very few if any of the elderly were without need."
>
> These are men and women who have worked all their lives. These are our uncles, our aunts, our grandparents, our mothers, and our fathers. They live in a world of old newspaper clippings, pictures, and photographs of relatives who never visit.   —Loretta Schwartz-Nobel, *Starving in the Shadow of Plenty*

Here the writer seems to anticipate that readers—as citizens, voters, and taxpayers in any part of the country—might question whether they have any personal responsibility for elderly people in South Philadelphia. Her strategy is to argue that South Philadelphia is a representative American community, not a peculiar place with unique problems. She implies that we are one big American family, with familylike responsibilities for aging relatives. Since she eventually argues for a national solution to what she believes to be a widespread problem, her success depends on convincing readers of their personal responsibility for needy elderly people anywhere in America.

The next example acknowledges readers' possible counterarguments even more directly. These are the opening paragraphs in an article arguing that some of America's homeless have chosen that way of life. The writer knows that readers may immediately doubt this surprising claim. It seems inconceivable that people would choose to sleep on sidewalks and eat out of garbage cans. The writer acknowledges three different counterarguments.

> The homeless, it seems, can be roughly divided into two groups: those who have had marginality and homelessness forced upon them and want nothing more than to escape them, and a smaller number who have at least in part chosen marginality, and now accept, or, in a few cases, embrace it.
>
> I understand how dangerous it can be to introduce the idea of choice into a discussion of homelessness. It can all too easily be used for all the wrong reasons by all the wrong people to justify indifference or brutality toward the homeless, or to argue that they are getting only what they deserve.
>
> And I understand, too, how complicated the notion can become: Many of the veterans on the street, or battered women, or abused and runaway children, have chosen this life only as the lesser of evils, and because, in this society, there is often no place else to go.
>
> And finally, I understand how much that happens on the street can combine to create an apparent acceptance of homelessness that is nothing more than the absolute absence of hope.
>
> Nonetheless we must learn to accept that there may indeed be people on the street who have seen so much of our world, or have seen it so clearly, that to live in it becomes impossible.   –Peter Marin, "Go Ask Alice"

You might think that acknowledging readers' objections in this way—addressing readers directly, listing their possible objections, and discussing each one—would weaken an argument. It might even seem reckless to suggest objections that not all readers would think of. On the contrary, however, readers respond positively to this strategy. The writer appears to have explored the issue thoroughly. He seems thoughtful and reasonable, more interested in inquiry than advocacy, more concerned with seeking the truth about the homeless than in ignoring or overriding readers' objections in order to win their adherence to a self-serving claim. By researching your subject and analyzing your readers, you will be able to use this strategy confidently in your own argumentative essays.

EXERCISE 18.11

Evaluate the acknowledgment of readers in "Abortion, Right and Wrong" in Chapter 6. How does the author adapt this strategy to her purposes? What is the approach to readers and the tone? What does the acknowledgment seem to contribute to the essay?

Accommodating
Counterarguments

Careful argumentative writers often acknowledge their readers' objections, questions, and alternative causes or solutions. Occasionally, however, they may go even further. Instead of merely acknowledging their readers' objections, they accept them and incorporate them into their own arguments. You can imagine how disarming this strategy can be to readers.

This example comes from an essay speculating about the causes of people's interest in jogging. Before proposing his own cause (later in the essay), the writer acknowledges and then accommodates causes proposed by philosophers and theologists.

> Some scout-masterish philosophers argue that the appeal of jogging and other body-maintenance programs is the discipline they afford. We live in a world in which individuals have fewer and fewer obligations. The work week has shrunk. Weekend worship is less compulsory. Technology gives us more free time. Satisfactorily filling free time requires imagination and effort. Freedom is a wide and risky river; it can drown the person who does not know how to swim across it. The more obligations one takes on, the more time one occupies, the less threat freedom poses. Jogging can become an instant obligation. For a portion of his day, the jogger is not his own man; he is obedient to a regimen he has accepted.
>
> Theologists may take the argument one step further. It is our modern irreligion, our lack of confidence in any hereafter, that makes us anxious to stretch our mortal stay as long as possible. We run, as the saying goes, for our lives, hounded by the suspicion that these are the only lives we are likely to enjoy.
>
> All of these theorists seem to me more or less right. As the growth of cults and charismatic religions and the resurgence of enthusiasm for the military draft suggest, we do crave commitment. And who can doubt, watching so many middle-aged and older persons torturing themselves in the name of fitness, that we are unreconciled to death, more so perhaps than any generation in modern memory? —Carll Tucker, "Fear of Dearth"

Notice that this writer's accommodation is not grudging. He admits that the theorists (and any readers who favor them) are "more or less right," and he suggests reasons why they must be right. Considering alternative causes is very common in essays of causal analysis (see Chapter 9). Writers must include alternatives that their readers may be aware of and then either accommodate or refute these alternatives. To do anything less makes writers seem uninformed and weakens their credibility.

EXERCISE 18.12

Exactly how does Patrick O'Malley attempt to accommodate readers in his Chapter 7 essay on more frequent exams? What seems successful or unsuccessful in his argument? What do his efforts at accommodation contribute to the essay?

Refuting
Counterarguments

Readers' objections and questions cannot always be accommodated. Sometimes they must be refuted. When writers refute likely counterarguments, they assert that they are wrong and argue against them. Refutation does not have to be delivered arrogantly or dismissively, however. Writers can refute their readers' objections in a spirit of shared inquiry in solving problems, establishing probable causes, deciding the value of something, or understanding all the issues in a controversy. In argument, differences are inevitable. Argument remains centrally important in human discourse because informed, well-intentioned people disagree about issues and policies.

In this example, an economist refutes one explanation for the increasing numbers of women in the work force. First he describes a "frequently mentioned" counterargument. Then he concedes a point ("there is little doubt") before beginning his refutation.

> One frequently mentioned but inadequately evaluated explanation for the surge of women into paid employment is the spread of time-saving household innovations such as clothes washers and dryers, frozen foods, and dishwashers. There is little doubt that it is easier to combine paid employment with home responsibilities now than it was fifty years ago, but it is not clear whether these time-saving innovations were the *cause* of the rise in female labor force participation or whether they were largely a *response* to meet a demand created by working women. Confusion about this point is most evident in comments that suggest that the rapid growth of supermarkets and fast-food outlets is a cause of women going to work. Similar time-saving organizations were tried at least sixty years ago, but with less success because the value of time was much lower then. The absence of supermarkets and fast-food eating places in low-income countries today also shows that their rapid growth in the United States is primarily a *result* of the rising value of time and the growth of women in the work force, not the reverse.   —Victor Fuchs, "Why Married Mothers Work"

This selection illustrates very well that refutations must be supported. Writers cannot simply dismiss readers' counterarguments with a wave of the hand. Fuchs refutes one proposed cause by arguing that it is actually an effect or result of the trend. The last two sentences support his refutation.

The second example comes from a publication arguing for a revised English curriculum in the schools. In this section, the writers attempt to refute a predictable objection. Notice how they describe the objection and then assert their refutation.

> [An] argument against the teaching of literature, which enjoyed greater currency in the late 1960s and 1970s than it does now, goes something like this: Literature is an "elitist" discipline, a subterfuge for imposing ruling-class values on oppressed groups so that they will cooperate in their own exploitation. According to this argument, minority students will encounter a world view in literature classes that is either irrelevant to their own heritage or downright destructive of it. The rebuttal to this argument is straightforward: It is wrong. The treasure-house of literature is not oppressive; it is liberating—of the constraints of time, place, and personal experience into which each of us as an individual is born. The real injustice would be to deny any child access to the wealth of insights

that our best literature has to offer. To deny students the wisdom of our literary heritage may restrict their social mobility and limit the potential that schools have to create opportunities for students to develop their individual talents and to prepare for participation in our society.

Of course, in literature and the arts, local districts should adopt reading lists that recognize the natural desire of communities to maintain an ethnic identity. Quite rightly, black students are inspired by Alex Haley's *Roots* and Richard Wright's *Black Boy;* Hispanic students, by Rudolfo A. Anaya's *Bless Me, Ultima* and Peter Matthiessen's *Sal Si Puedes: Cesar Chavez and the New American Revolution;* Japanese-Americans, by Yoshiko Uchida's *Samurai of Gold Hill* and Monica Sone's *Nisei Daughter;* and so on. Like all great literature, these stories confer lasting benefits—intellectual, social, and spiritual—on those who read them. Furthermore, all students will profit from such literature to understand those whose experiences of America differ from theirs. The point is, far from being "elitist," the common culture belongs to all of us. And every child in the United States—rich or poor, male or female, black, Hispanic, Asian, or white—is entitled to experience it fully.

Our country was founded on the expectation that out of many traditions one nation could evolve that would be stronger and more durable than any single tradition. To argue that teaching a common core of literature in our pluralistic society is not feasible because there is no basis for consensus is to beg the question. It is, and always has been, precisely the task of the public schools to help form that consensus.

In a society that celebrates the prerogatives of the individual, the public schools are potentially one of the most meaningful forces for social cohesion. They are the modern equivalent of the village square—a forum for identifying the shared ethos of our diverse and cosmopolitan society; a place where all our children can come together and discover what it is that unites us as a people. Well-taught literature is an essential part of that consensus building.

—California State Education Department, *Handbook for Planning an Effective Literature Program*

This example and the previous one illustrate that effective refutation requires a restrained tone and careful argument. Although you may not accept the refutation, you can agree that it is thoughtfully argued. You do not feel attacked personally because the writers disagree with you.

The writers of the second article make an important concession in the second paragraph. They acknowledge the value of minority literature while still arguing for a common literature in school English programs. Here, accommodation blends with refutation.

EXERCISE 18.13

Analyze and evaluate the use of refutation in any one of the essays in Chapter 6. How does the writer manage the refutation? Does the objection seem to be clearly and accurately described? How is the refutation asserted and argued for? What seems most convincing and least convincing in the argument? What is the tone of the refutation?

EXERCISE 18.14

Briefly refute any of the refutations you analyzed in the preceding exercise. State the writers' refutation accurately, and argue your refutation of it convincingly. Try to use a restrained tone.

EXERCISE 18.15

Return to the claim you wrote in Exercise 18.1. Imagine how you might develop an essay arguing for this claim with reasons and evidence. Then identify one likely objection or question from your readers, and write a refutation of it. State the objection accurately, and argue your refutation in a way that will not alienate your readers.

LOGICAL FALLACIES

Fallacies are errors or flaws in reasoning. Although essentially unsound, fallacious arguments seem superficially plausible and often have great persuasive power. Fallacies are not necessarily deliberate efforts to deceive readers. They may be accidental, resulting from a failure to examine underlying assumptions critically, establish solid ground to support a claim, or choose words that are clear and unambiguous. Here, listed in alphabetical order, are the most common logical fallacies:

- *Begging the question.*   Arguing that a claim is true by repeating the claim in different words. Sometimes called circular reasoning.
- *Confusing chronology with causality.*   Assuming that because one thing preceded another, the former caused the latter. Also called *post hoc, ergo propter hoc* (Latin for "after this, therefore because of this").
- *Either/or reasoning.*   Assuming that there are only two sides to a question, and representing yours as the only correct one.
- *Equivocating.*   Misleading or hedging with ambiguous word choices.
- *Failing to accept the burden of proof.* Asserting a claim without presenting a reasoned argument to support it.
- *False analogy.*   Assuming that because one thing resembles another, conclusions drawn from one also apply to the other.
- *Overreliance on authority.*   Assuming that something is true simply because an expert says so and ignoring evidence to the contrary.
- *Hasty generalization.*   Offering only weak or limited evidence to support a conclusion.
- *Oversimplifying.*   Giving easy answers to complicated questions, often by appealing to emotions rather than logic.

- *Personal attack.*   Demeaning the proponents of a claim instead of their argument. Also called *ad hominen* (Latin for "against the man").
- *Red herring.*   Attempting to misdirect the discussion by raising an essentially unrelated point.
- *Slanting.*   Selecting or emphasizing the evidence that supports your claim and suppressing or playing down other evidence.
- *Slippery slope.*   Pretending that one thing inevitably leads to another.
- *Sob story.*   Manipulating readers' emotions in order to lead them to draw unjustified conclusions.
- *Straw man.*   Directing the argument against a claim that nobody actually holds or that everyone agrees is very weak.

PART THREE

Research Strategies

In universities, government agencies, and the business world, field research can be as important as library research or experimental research. In specialties such as sociology, political science, anthropology, polling, advertising, and news reporting, field research is the basic means of gathering information.

This chapter is a brief introduction to three of the major kinds of field research: observations, interviews, and questionnaires. The writing activities involved are central to several academic specialties. If you major in education, communication, or one of the social sciences, you probably will be asked to do writing based on observations, interviews, and questionnaire results. You will also read large amounts of information based on these ways of learning about people, groups, and institutions.

Observations and interviews are essential for writing profiles (Chapter 4). Interviewing could be helpful, as well, in documenting a trend or phenomenon and exploring its causes (Chapter 9)—for example, to consult an expert or conduct a survey to establish the presence of a trend. In proposing a solution to a problem (Chapter 7), you might want to interview people involved; or, if many people are affected, you might find it useful to do a questionnaire. In writing to explain an academic concept (Chapter 5), you might want to interview a faculty member who is a specialist on that subject.

OBSERVATIONS

This section offers guidelines for planning an observational visit, taking notes on your observations, and later writing them up. Some kinds of writing are based on observations from single visits—travel writing, social workers' case reports, insurance investigators' accident reports—but most observational writing is based on several visits. An anthropologist or sociologist studying an unfamiliar group or activity might observe it for months, filling several notebooks with notes. If you are profiling a place (Chapter 4), you almost certainly will want to make two or three (or more) observational visits, some of them perhaps combined with interviews.

Second and third visits to observe further are important because as you learn more about a place from observations, interviews, or reading, you will discover new ways to look at it. Gradually you will have more and more questions that can only be answered by follow-up visits.

Planning the Visit

To ensure that your observational visits are worthwhile, you must plan them carefully.

Getting Access.   If the place you propose to visit is public, you probably will have easy access to it. If everything you need to see is within view of anyone passing by or using the place, you can make your observations without any special arrangements. Indeed, you may not even be noticed.

However, most observational visits that are part of special inquiries require special access. Hence, you will need to arrange your visit, calling ahead or making a get-acquainted visit, in order to introduce yourself and state your purpose. Find out the times you may visit, and be certain you can gain access easily.

Announcing Your Intentions.   State your intentions directly and fully. Say who you are, where you are from, and what you hope to do. You may be surprised at how receptive people can be to a student on assignment from a college course. Not every place you wish to visit will welcome you, and a variety of constraints on outside visitors exist in private businesses as well as public institutions. But generally, if people know your intentions, they may be able to tell you about aspects of a place or activity you would not have thought to observe.

Taking Your Tools.   Take a notebook with a firm back so that you will have a steady writing surface. Remember also to take a writing instrument. Some observers dictate their observations into portable tape recorders. You might want to experiment with this method. We recommend, though, that for your first observations you record in writing. Your instructor or other students in your class may want to see your written notes.

Observing and Taking Notes

Following are some brief guidelines for observing and taking notes.

Observing.   Some activities invite multiple vantage points, whereas others seem to limit the observer to a single perspective. Take advantage of every perspective available to you. Come in close, take a middle position, and stand back. Study the scene from a stationary position and also try to move around it. The more varied your perspectives, the more you are likely to observe.

Your purpose in observing is both to describe the activity and to analyze it. You will want to look closely at the activity itself, but you will also want to think about what makes this activity special, what seems to be the point of it.

Try to be an innocent observer: pretend you have never seen anything like this activity before. Look for typical features of the activity as well as unusual features. Look at it from the perspective of your readers. Ask what details of the activity would surprise and inform and interest them.

Taking Notes.   You undoubtedly will find your own style of notetaking, but here are a few pointers.

- Write only on one side of the page. Later, when you organize your notes, you may want to cut up the pages and file notes under different headings.
- Take notes in words, phrases, or sentences. Draw diagrams or sketches, if they help you see and understand the place.
- Note any ideas or questions that occur to you.
- Use quotation marks around any overheard conversation you take down.

Since you can later reorganize your notes in any way you wish, you do not need to take notes in any planned or systematic way. You might, however, want to cover these aspects of a place:

The Setting. The easiest way to begin is to name objects you see. Just start by listing objects. Then record details of some of these objects—color, shape, size, texture, function, relation to similar or dissimilar objects. Although your notes probably will contain mainly visual details, you might also want to record sounds and smells. Be sure to include some notes about the shape, dimensions, and layout of the place as a whole. How big is it? How is it organized?

The People. Record the number of people, their activities, their movements and behavior. Describe their appearance or dress. Record parts of overheard conversations. Note whether you see more men than women, more members of one nationality or ethnic group than of another, more older than younger people. Most important, note anything surprising or unusual about people in the scene.

Your Personal Reactions. Include in your notes any feelings you have about what you observe. Also record, as they occur to you, any hunches or ideas or insights you have.

Reflecting on Your Observation   Immediately after your observational visit (within just a few minutes, if possible), find a quiet place to reflect on what you saw, review your notes, and add to your notes. Give yourself at least a half hour for quiet thought.

What you have in your notes and what you recall on reflection will suggest many more images and details from your observation. Add these to your notes.

Finally, review all of your notes, and write a few sentences about your main impressions of the place. What did you learn? How did this visit change your preconceptions about the place? What surprised you most? What is the dominant impression you get from your notes?

Writing Up Your Notes

Your instructor may ask you to write up your notes as a report on the observational visit. If so, review your notes, looking for patterns and vivid details. You might find inventorying or clustering (described in Chapter 11) useful for discovering patterns and relationships in your notes.

Decide on the main impression you want readers to have of the place. Use this as the focus for your report.

See Chapter 14 for a full discussion of descriptive strategies.

Now draft a brief description of the place. Your purpose is to present a general impression of the place through a selection of the details in your notes. Assume your readers have never been to the place, and try to present a vivid impression of it.

Follow-up Visits

Rather than repeat yourself in follow-up visits, try to build on what you have already discovered. You should probably do some interviewing and reading before another observational visit so that you will have a greater understanding of the subject when you observe it again. It is also important to develop a plan for your follow-up: questions to be answered, hypotheses to be tested, types of information you would like to discover.

INTERVIEWS

Like making observations, interviewing tends to involve four basic steps: (1) planning and setting up the interview, (2) notetaking, (3) reflecting on the interview, and (4) writing up your notes.

Planning and Setting Up the Interview

The initial step in interviewing involves choosing an interview subject and then arranging and planning the interview.

Choosing an Interview Subject.   First, decide whom to interview. If you are writing about some activity or enterprise in which several people are involved, choose subjects representing a variety of perspectives—a range of different roles, for example. If you are profiling a single person, most, if not all, of your interviews will be with that person.

You should be flexible because you may be unable to speak to the person you initially targeted and may wind up with someone else—the person's assistant, perhaps. Do not assume this interview subject will be of little use to you. With the right questions, you might even learn more from the assistant than you would from the person in charge.

Arranging an Interview.   You may be nervous about calling up a busy person and asking for some of his or her time. Indeed, you may get turned down. But if so, it is possible that you will be referred to someone who will see you, someone whose job it is to talk to the public.

Do not feel that just because you are a student you do not have the right to ask for people's time. You will be surprised how delighted people are to be asked about themselves, particularly if you reach them when they are not feeling harried. Most people love to talk—about anything! Usually, the problem is that no one will listen to them. And, since you are a student on assignment, some people may feel that they are doing a form of public service to talk with you.

Presenting Yourself. When introducing yourself to arrange the interview, give a short and simple description of your project. If you talk too much, you could prejudice or limit the interviewee's response. At the same time, it is a good idea to exhibit some enthusiasm for your project. If you lack enthusiasm, the person may see little reason to talk to you.

Keep in mind that the person you are interviewing is donating time to you. Be certain that you call ahead to arrange a specific time for the interview. Be on time. Bring all the materials you need, and express your thanks when the interview is over.

Planning for the Interview.   The best interview is generally the planned interview. It will help if you have made an observational visit and done some background reading before the interview. In preparation for the interview, you should do two things in particular: consider your objectives and prepare some questions.

Think about your main objectives. Do you want an orientation to the place (the "big picture") from this interview? Do you want this interview to lead you to interviews with other key people? Do you want mainly facts or information? Do you need clarification of something you have heard in another interview or observed or read? Do you want to learn more about the person, or learn about the place through the person, or both? Should you trust or distrust this person?

The key to good interviewing is flexibility. You may be looking for facts, but your interview subject may not have any to offer. In that case, you should be able to shift gears and go after whatever your subject has to discuss.

Composing Questions.   Take care in composing the questions you prepare in advance; they can be the key to a successful interview. Any question that places unfair limits on respondents is a bad question. Two specific types to avoid are forced-choice questions and leading questions.

Forced-choice questions are unsatisfactory because they impose your terms on your respondents. Consider this example: "Do you think rape is an expression of sexual passion or of aggression?" A person may think that neither sexual passion nor aggression satisfactorily explain rape. A better way to phrase the question would be to ask, "People often fall into two camps on the issue of rape. Some think it is an expression of sexual passion, while others argue it is really not sexual but aggressive. Do you think it is either of these? If not, what is your opinion?" This form of questioning allows you to get a reaction to what others have said at the same time that it gives the interviewee freedom to set the terms.

Leading questions are unsatisfactory because they assume too much. An example of this kind of question is this: "Do you think the increase in the occurrence of rape is due to the fact that women are perceived as competitors in a severely depressed economy?" This question assumes that there is an increase in the occurrence of rape, that women are perceived (apparently by rapists) as competitors, and that the economy is severely depressed. A better way of asking the question might be to make the assumptions more explicit by dividing the question into its parts: "Do you think there is an increase in the occurrence of rape? What could have caused it? I've heard some people argue that the economy has something to do with it. Do you think so? Do you think rapists perceive women as competitors for jobs? Could the current economic situation have made this competition more severe?"

Good questions come in many different forms. One way of considering them is to divide them into two types: open and closed. *Open questions* give the respondent range and flexibility. They also generate anecdotes, personal revelations, and expressions of attitudes. For example:

- I wonder if you would take a few minutes to tell me something about your early days in the business. I'd be interested to hear about how it got started, what your hopes and aspirations were, what problems you faced and how you dealt with them.
- Tell me about a time you were (name an emotion).
- What did you think of (name a person or event)?
- What did you do when (name an event) happened?

The best questions are those that allow the subject to talk freely but to the point. If the answer strays too far from the point, a follow-up question may be necessary to refocus the talk. Another tack you may want to try is to rephrase the subject's answer, to say something like "Let me see if I have this right," or "Am I correct in saying that you feel. . . ." Often, a person will take the opportunity to amplify the original response by adding just the anecdote or quotation you've been looking for.

Closed questions usually request specific information. For example:

- How do you do (name a process)?
- What does (name a word) mean?
- What does (a person, object, or place) look like?
- How was it made?

Taking Your Tools	As for an observational visit, you will need a notebook with a firm back so that you can write on it easily without the benefit of a table or desk. You might find it useful to divide several pages into two columns with a line drawn about one third of the width of the page from the left margin. Use the lefthand column to note details about the scene, the person, the mood of the interview, other impressions. Head this column DETAILS AND IMPRESSIONS. At the top of the righthand column, write several questions. You may not use them, but they will jog your memory. This column should be titled INFORMATION. In this column you will record what you learn from answers to your questions.

See pp. 130–32 for an example of notes of this sort.

Taking Notes during the Interview	Because you are not taking a verbatim transcript of the interview (if you wanted a literal account, you would use a tape recorder or shorthand), your goals are to gather information and to record a few good quotations and anecdotes. In addition, because the people you interview may be unused to giving interviews and so will need to know you are listening, it is probably a good idea to do more listening than notetaking. You may not have much confidence in your memory, but, if you pay close attention, you are likely to recall a good deal of the conversation afterward. Take some notes during the interview: a few quotations; key words and phrases; details of the scene, the person, and the mood of the interview. Remember that *how* something is said is as important as *what* is said. Look for material that will give texture to your writing—gesture, physical appearance, verbal inflection, facial expression, dress, hair, style, body language, anything that makes the person an individual.

Reflecting on the Interview	As soon as you finish the interview, find a quiet place to reflect on it, and review your notes. This reflection is essential because so much happens in an interview that you cannot record at the time. Spend at least a half hour, maybe longer, adding to your notes and thinking about what you learned.

At the end of this time, write a few sentences about your main impressions from the interview. What did you learn? What surprised you most? How did the interview change your attitude or understanding about the person or place? How would you summarize your impressions of the person? |

Writing Up Your Notes	Your instructor may ask you to write up your notes. If so, review them for useful details and information. Decide what main impression you want to give of this person. Choose details that will contribute to this impression. Select quotations and paraphrases of information you learned from the person.

To find a focus for your write-up, you might try looping or clustering. Invention questions can also help you consider the person from different perspectives. |

These strategies are discussed in Chapter 11.

QUESTIONNAIRES

Questionnaires let you survey the attitudes or knowledge of large numbers of people. You could carry out many face-to-face or phone interviews to get the same information, but questionnaires have the advantages of economy, efficiency, and anonymity. Some questionnaires, such as ones you filled out in applying to college, just collect demographic information: your name, age, sex, home town, religious preference, intended major. Others, such as the Gallup and Harris polls, collect opinions on a wide range of issues. Prior to elections we are bombarded with the results of these kinds of polls. Still other kinds of questionnaires, ones used in academic research, are designed to help answer important questions about personal and societal problems.

This section will briefly outline procedures you can follow to carry out an informal questionnaire survey of people's opinions or knowledge, and then to write up the results.

Focusing Your Study

A questionnaire study usually has a limited focus. You might need to interview a few people in order to find this focus.

Let us assume that you went to your campus Student Health Clinic (SHC) and had to wait over an hour to see a nurse. Sitting there with many other students, you decide this is a problem that needs to be studied. Furthermore, it seems an ideal topic for a proposal essay (Chapter 7) you have been assigned in your writing class.

To study this problem, you do not have to explore the entire operation of SHC. You are not interested in how nurses and doctors are hired or how efficient their system of ordering supplies is. You have a particular concern: how successful is SHC in scheduling appointments and organizing its resources to meet student needs? More specifically: do students often have to wait too long to see a nurse or doctor? You might also want to know *why* this is the case, if it is; but you can only seek an answer to that question by interviewing SHC staff. Your primary interest is in how long students usually wait for appointments, what times are most convenient for students to schedule appointments, whether SHC resources are concentrated at those times, and so on. Now you have a limited focus, and you can collect valuable information with a fairly brief questionnaire.

To be certain about your focus, however, you should talk informally to several students to find out whether they think there is a problem. You might also want to talk to people at SHC, explaining your plans and asking for their views on the problem.

Whatever your interest, be sure to limit the scope of your study. Try to focus on one or two important questions. With a limited focus, your questionnaire can be brief, and people will be more willing to fill it out. In addition, a study based on a limited amount of information will be easier to organize and report.

Writing Questions   Two basic forms of questions—closed and open—were introduced earlier in this chapter. In the following section are additional illustrations of how these types of questions may be used in the context of a questionnaire.

Closed Questions.   Following are examples of some forms of closed questions for a possible student questionnaire. You probably will use more than one form in a questionnaire, because you will have several kinds of information to collect.

Checklists

With your present work and class schedule, when are you able to visit the SHC? (Check as many boxes as necessary.)

☐ 8–10 A.M.
☐ 10–12 A.M.
☐ noon hour
☐ 1–3 P.M.
☐ 3–5 P.M.

Which services do you expect to use at the SHC this year?

☐ allergy desensitization
☐ immunization
☐ optometry
☐ dental care
☐ birth control
☐ illness or infection
☐ counseling
☐ health education

Two-way Questions

Have you made an appointment this year at SHC?
_____ yes
_____ no

Have you ever had to wait more than 30 minutes at SHC for a scheduled appointment?
_____ yes
_____ no

If you could, would you schedule appointments at the SHC after 7:00 P.M.?
_____ yes
_____ no
_____ uncertain

Multiple-choice Questions

How frequently have you had to wait more than 10 minutes at the SHC
for a scheduled appointment?

_____ always
_____ usually
_____ occasionally
_____ never

From your experience so far with SHC, how would you rate its services?
_____ inadequate
_____ barely adequate
_____ adequate
_____ better than adequate
_____ outstanding

Ranking Scales

With your present work and class schedule, which times during the day
(Monday through Friday) would be most convenient for you to schedule
appointments at SHC? Put a 1 by the most convenient time, a 2 by the
next most convenient time, until you have ranked all the choices.

_____ mornings
_____ afternoons before 5 P.M.
_____ 5–7 P.M.
_____ 7–10 P.M.

Open Questions.   Open questions ask for a brief answer.

What services do you expect to need at SHC this year?

_____
_____
_____

From your experiences with appointments at SHC, what advice would
you give students about making appointments?

_____
_____
_____

What do you believe would most improve services at SHC?

_____
_____
_____

You may want to use a combination of closed and open questions for your
questionnaire. Both offer advantages: closed questions will give you definite

answers, but open questions can give information you may not have expected as well as providing lively quotations for your report.

Trying Out the Questions.   As soon as you have a collection of possible questions, try them out on a few typical readers. You need to know which questions are unclear, which seem to duplicate others, which seem most interesting. These tryouts will enable you to assess which questions will give you the information you need. Readers also can help you come up with additional questions.

Designing the Questionnaire

Write a brief, clear introduction stating the purpose of the questionnaire and explaining how you intend to use the results. Give advice on answering the questions, and estimate the amount of time needed to complete the questionnaire. If you are going to give the questionnaire to groups of people in person, you can give this information orally.

Select your most promising questions, and decide on an order. Any logical order is appropriate. You might want to begin with the least complicated questions or the most general ones. You may find it necessary or helpful to group the questions by subject matter or form. Certain questions may lead to others. You might want to place open questions at the end.

Design the questionnaire so that it looks attractive and readable. Make it look easy to complete. Do not crowd questions together to save paper. Provide plenty of space for readers to answer open questions, and remind them to use the back of the page if they need more space.

Testing the Questionnaire

Make a few copies of your first design, and ask at least two or three readers to complete the questionnaire. Find out how much time they needed to complete it. Talk to them about any confusions or problems they experienced. Review their responses with them to be certain each question is doing what you want it to do. From what you learn, reconsider your design, and revise particular questions.

Administering the Questionnaire

Decide who will fill out your questionnaire and how you can arrange for them to do it. The more readers you have, the better; but constraints of time and expense almost certainly will limit the number. You can mail questionnaires or distribute them to dormitories or workplace mailboxes, but the return will be low. It is unusual for even half the people receiving mail questionnaires to return them. If you do mail the questionnaire, be sure to mention the deadline for returning it. Give directions for returning the questionnaire, and include a stamped, addressed envelope.

You might want to arrange to distribute the questionnaire yourself to some groups in class, at dormitory meetings, or at work.

Note that if you want to do a formal questionnaire, you will need a scientifically representative group of readers (a random or stratified random sample). Even for an informal study, you should try to get a reasonably representative group. For example, to study satisfaction with the appointments schedule at SHC, you would want to have readers who had been to SHC fairly often. You might even want to include a concentration of seniors rather than freshman readers because after four years seniors would have made more visits to SHC. If many students commute, you would want to be sure to have commuters among your readers.

Your report will be more convincing if you demonstrate that your readers represent the group whose opinions or knowledge you claim to be studying. As few as twenty-five readers could be adequate for an informal study.

Writing Up the Results

Now that you have the completed questionnaires, what do you do with them?

Summarizing the Results.   Begin by tallying the results from the closed questions. Take an unused questionnaire, and tally the responses next to each choice. Suppose you had twenty-five readers. Here is how the tally might look for the first checklist question.

> With your present work and class schedule, when are you able to visit the SHC? (Check as many boxes as necessary.)
>
> ☐ 8–10 A.M. ⳾⳾⳾ ||| (18)
> ☐ 10–12 A.M. ⳾ || (7)
> ☐ noon hour ⳾⳾ ||| (13)
> ☐ 1–3 P.M. ||| (3)
> ☐ 3–5 P.M. ⳾ |||| (9)

Each tally mark represents one response to that item. The totals add up to more than twenty-five because readers were asked to check *all* the times they could make appointments.

Next consider the open questions. Read all twenty-five answers to each question separately to see the kind and variety of response to each. Then decide whether you want to code any of the open questions so that you can summarize results from them quantitatively, as you would with closed questions. For example, you might want to classify the types of advice given as responses to an open question proposed earlier: "From your experiences with appointments at SHC, what advice would you give students about making appointments?" You could then report the numbers of readers (of your twenty-five) who gave each type of advice. For an opinion question ("How would you evaluate the most recent appointment you had at SHC?"), you might simply code the answers as positive, neutral, and negative and then tally the results accordingly for each kind of response. However, responses to open questions are perhaps most often used as a source of quotations for your report.

You can report results from the closed questions as percentages, either within the text of your report or in tables. (See the Fuchs essay in Chapter 9 for one possible format for a table. You can find other formats in texts you may be using or even in magazines or newspapers. Conventional formats for tables in social science reports are illustrated in *Publication Manual of the American Psychological Association,* 3rd edition, Washington, DC: American Psychological Association, 1983.)

See pp. 528–29 for strategies for integrating quoted material.

You can quote responses to the open questions within your text, perhaps weaving them into your discussion like quoted material. Or you can organize several responses into lists and then comment on them. Since readers' interests can be engaged more easily with quotations than with percentages, plan to use many open responses in your report.

There are computer programs that will provide quantitative results from closed questions and will even print out tables you can insert into your report. For a small informal study, however, such programs probably would not save you much time.

Organizing and Writing the Report.   In organizing the report of your results, you might want to consider a plan that usually is followed in the social sciences:

> Statement of the problem
>> context for your study
>> your question
>> need for your study
>> brief preview of your study and plan for your report
>
> Review of other related studies (if you know of any)
>
> Procedures
>> designing the questionnaire
>> selecting the readers
>> administering the questionnaire
>> summarizing the results
>
> Results: presentation of what you learned, with little commentary or interpretation
>
> Summary and discussion: brief summary of your results, and discussion of their significance (commenting, interpreting, exploring implications, and comparing to other related studies)

A college library presents a complex challenge. Unlike a course—with its limited number of texts, easy-to-find classroom, and familiar activities—the library contains thousands of texts organized in unfamiliar ways. Each new research project you undertake there presents surprises and unexpected problems. Each project leads you to new catalogs, indexes, floors, corners. You may find yourself keyboarding commands to access a computer database, threading a microfilm reader, viewing a videodisc, or squinting at the fine print in an index. You may read the latest weekly magazine or a rare book hundreds of years old. You may breeze through an encyclopedia entry introducing you to a new subject or struggle with a just-published report of a highly technical research study on the same subject.

A library's resources are so immense and so diverse that complete mastery of them is something only professional librarians have. With the help of these librarians and the guidelines in this chapter, however, you will be able to manage all the research assignments in this text and in your other college courses as well.

One way to make your college library seem more manageable is to think of its diverse materials as two different types of resources: the actual materials for your research, and the resources that enable you to find these materials. The search for research materials requires patience, careful planning, good advice, and even luck. The rewards are great, however. One of life's greatest intellectual pleasures is to learn about a subject and then be able to put diverse information together in a new way—creating new knowledge, for yourself and others.

This chapter is designed to help you learn how to use your college library's catalogs and indexes to locate the materials you need. It gives advice on how to learn about the library, develop a search strategy, keep track of your research, and locate and evaluate sources.

ORIENTING YOURSELF TO THE LIBRARY

Make a point of taking a tour of the library. Then, when you first research a subject, be sure you understand your research task well. Consult a reference librarian if you need help.

Taking a Tour

Your instructor may arrange a library orientation tour for your composition class. If not, you can join one of the regular orientation tours scheduled by the librarians. Unless you are already using the library frequently, a tour is essential because nearly all college libraries are more complex and offer more services than typical school or public libraries. On a library tour you will learn how the card catalog and reference room are organized, how to gain access to computer catalogs and databases, whom to ask for help if you are confused, and how to get your hands on books and periodicals.

Pick up copies of any available pamphlets and guidelines. Nearly every library offers handouts describing the resources and services it provides. Also look for a floor map of materials and facilities. See whether your library offers any research guidelines or strategies for locating resources. Some libraries offer special workshops or presentations on search strategies, recommending ways of setting out to do research.

Consulting a Librarian

Think of college librarians as advisors whose job is to help you understand the library and get your hands on sources you need to complete your research projects. Think of them also as instructors who can help you with the business of learning. Librarians on duty at the information or reference desk are there to provide reference services, and most have years of experience answering the very questions you are likely to ask. You should not hesitate to approach them with any questions you have about locating sources. Remember, however, that they can be most helpful if you can explain your research assignment clearly.

Knowing Your Research Task

Before you go to the library to start an assigned research project, learn as much as you can about the assignment. Should you need to ask a librarian for advice, it is best to have the assignment in writing. Ask your instructor to clarify any confusing terms and to define the purpose and scope of the project. Find out whether you can narrow or focus the project once you begin the research. Asking a question or two in advance can prevent hours— or even days—of misdirected work.

A RECOMMENDED SEARCH STRATEGY

In order for your library research to be manageable and productive, you will want to work carefully and systematically. The search strategy presented in this chapter was developed by college librarians with undergraduate needs firmly in mind. Although specific search strategies may vary to fit the needs

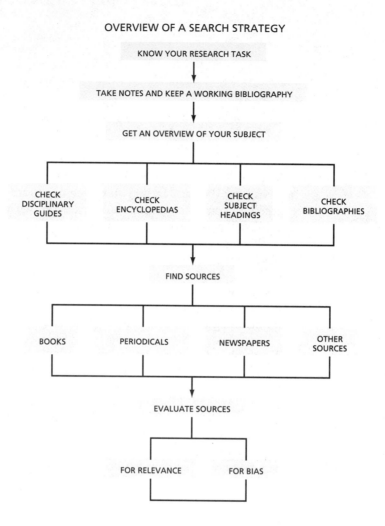

OVERVIEW OF A SEARCH STRATEGY

KNOW YOUR RESEARCH TASK

TAKE NOTES AND KEEP A WORKING BIBLIOGRAPHY

GET AN OVERVIEW OF YOUR SUBJECT

CHECK DISCIPLINARY GUIDES   CHECK ENCYCLOPEDIAS   CHECK SUBJECT HEADINGS   CHECK BIBLIOGRAPHIES

FIND SOURCES

BOOKS   PERIODICALS   NEWSPAPERS   OTHER SOURCES

EVALUATE SOURCES

FOR RELEVANCE   FOR BIAS

of individual research tasks, the general process presented here should help you to get started, to keep track of all your research, to use library materials to get an overview of your subject, to find the sources you need, and to evaluate those sources.

KEEPING TRACK OF YOUR RESEARCH

As you research your topic, you will want to keep careful records of all your sources by setting up a working bibliography.

Keeping
a Working
Bibliography

A working bibliography is a preliminary, ongoing record of books, articles, pamphlets—all the sources of information you discover as you research your subject. (A final bibliography, on the other hand, lists only sources actually used in your paper. Some of the sources in your working bibliography may turn out to be irrelevant, while others simply will be unavailable.) In addition, you can use your working bibliography as a means of keeping track of any encyclopedias, bibliographies, and indexes you consult, even though you may not list these resources in your final bibliography.

Because you probably will have to cite many different sources, you must decide on a documentation style before you write. Chapter 21 presents two different documentation styles, one adopted by the Modern Language Association (MLA) and widely used in the humanities, and the other adopted by the American Psychological Association (APA) and used in the social sciences. Individual disciplines often have their own preferred styles of documentation, which your instructor may wish you to use. Determine a style to use at the beginning, when you are constructing a working bibliography, as well as later, when you compile a final bibliography.

Practiced researchers keep their working bibliography in a notebook, in a computer file, or on index cards. They make a point of keeping bibliographical information separate from notes they take on the sources listed in their bibliography. Many researchers find index cards most convenient because they are so easily alphabetized. Others find them too easy to lose and prefer instead to keep everything—working bibliography, notes, and drafts—in one notebook. Researchers who use computers set up working bibliographies in word-processing or database programs, printing out hard copies to aid in library searches. Whether you use a computer, cards, or a notebook, the important thing is to make your entries accurate and complete. If the call number for a book is incomplete or inaccurate, you will not be able to find the book in the stacks. If the volume number for a periodical is incorrect, you may not be able to locate the article. If the author's name is misspelled, you may have trouble finding the book in the library catalog.

Taking Notes

Outlining, paraphrasing, and summarizing are discussed on pp. 397–99; quoting, on pp. 526–28.

Take notes as you read. If you own the work or can photocopy the relevant parts, you may want to annotate right on the page. Otherwise, you can paraphrase, summarize, and outline useful information as separate notes. In addition, you will want to write down quotations you might use in your essay.

You may already have a method of notetaking you prefer. Some researchers like to use index cards for notes as well as for their working bibliography. They use 3″ × 5″ cards for their bibliography and larger ones (4″ × 6″ or 5″ × 7″) for notes. Some even use a different color card for each of their sources. Other people prefer to keep their notes in a notebook, and still others enter their notes into a computer. It really does not matter what method you use as long as you keep accurate notes.

Care in notetaking is of paramount importance in order to minimize the risk of copying facts incorrectly or of misquoting. Another common error in notetaking is to copy the author's words without enclosing them in quotation marks. This error could lead easily to plagiarism, the unacknowledged use of another's words or ideas. Double-check all your notes and try to be as accurate as you can.

See pp. 526–28 for tips on avoiding plagiarism.

You might consider photocopying materials from sources that look especially promising. All libraries house a photocopy machine or offer a copying service. Photocopying can be costly, of course, so you'll want to be selective. It will facilitate your work, however, allowing you to reread and analyze important sources as well as to highlight material you may wish to quote, summarize, or paraphrase.

GETTING STARTED

"But where do I start?" is a question easily answered. You first need an overview of your topic. If you are researching a concept or issue in a course you are taking, then your textbook or other course materials provide the obvious starting point. Your instructor can advise you about other sources providing overviews of your topic. If your topic is just breaking in the news, then current newspapers and magazines might be sufficient. For all other topics—and for background information—disciplinary guides and encyclopedias are often the place to start. They let you test your interest in a topic before you start gathering sources on it, and they introduce you to diverse aspects of a subject, from which you might find a focus for your research. In a typical college essay or research project, you do not have the time or space to summarize everything that is known on a subject, but you can inquire productively into some unusual or controversial aspect of it.

Consulting Disciplinary Guides

If your research project falls within an academic discipline, you will want to start with one of the guides to research in that discipline. The following guides can help you to identify the major handbooks, encyclopedias, bibliographies, computer databases, journals, and periodical indexes in the various disciplines. You will probably not want to read one of these extensive works straight through before beginning your research, but you will find it to be a valuable reference.

GENERAL   *Guide to Reference Books,* 10th ed., 1986. Edited by Eugene P. Sheehy.

HUMANITIES   *The Humanities: A Selective Guide to Information Sources,* 3rd ed., 1988. By Ron Blazek.

SCIENCE AND TECHNOLOGY	Chen, Ching-chih. *Scientific and Technical Information Sources.* 2nd ed. Cambridge, Mass.: MIT Press, 1987.
SOCIAL SCIENCES	*Sources of Information in the Social Sciences: A Guide to the Literature,* 3rd ed., 1986. Edited by William Webb.
ANTHRO-POLOGY	*Introduction to Library Research in Anthropology,* 1989. By Mary M. Koenig and John M. Weeks.
ART	*Visual Arts Research: A Handbook,* 1986. By Elizabeth B. Pollard.
EDUCATION	*Education: A Guide to Reference and Information Sources,* 1989. By Lois Buttlar.
FILM	*On the Screen: A Film, Television, and Video Research Guide,* 1986. By Kim N. Fisher.
HISTORY	*A Student's Guide to History,* 4th ed., 1987. By Jules R. Benjamin.
LITERATURE	*Reference Works in British and American Literature,* 1990. By James K. Bracken. *Literary Research Guide,* 2nd ed., 1983. By Margaret Patterson.
MUSIC	*Music: A Guide to the Reference Literature,* 1987. By William S. Brockman.
PHILOSOPHY	*Philosophy: A Guide to the Reference Literature,* 1986. By Hans E. Bynagle.
POLITICAL SCIENCE	*Information Sources of Political Science,* 4th ed., 1986. By Frederick L. Holler.
PSYCHOLOGY	Douglas, Nancy E. *Library Research Guide to Psychology: Illustrated Search Strategy and Sources,* 1984. By Nancy E. Douglas.
SOCIOLOGY	*Sociology: A Guide to Reference and Information Sources,* 1987. By Stephen H. Aby.
WOMEN'S STUDIES	*Introduction to Library Research in Women's Studies,* 1985. By Susan E. Searing.

Consulting Encyclopedias

Specialized encyclopedias can be a good place to explore early in your research. While general encyclopedias such as *World Book* and *Encyclopedia Americana* cover many topics superficially, only specialized encyclopedias cover topics in the depth appropriate for college writing. In addition to providing an overview of a topic, a specialized encyclopedia will often include an explanation of issues related to the topic, definitions of specialized terminology, and selective bibliographies of additional sources.

As starting points, specialized encyclopedias have two further advantages: (1) they provide a comprehensive introduction to key terms related to your topic, terms that will be useful in identifying the "subject headings" that enable you to locate research materials in catalogs and indexes; and (2) by comprehensively presenting a subject, they enable you to see many possibilities for focusing your research on one aspect of it.

Following are some specialized encyclopedias in the major academic disciplines:

ART   *Encyclopedia of World Art*

MUSIC   *New Grove Dictionary of Music and Musicians*

CHEMISTRY   *Encyclopedia of Chemistry*

COMPUTERS,   *Encyclopedia of Computer Science and Engineering*
ENGINEERING

ECONOMICS   *Encyclopedia of American Economic History*

EDUCATION   *Encyclopedia of Education*

ENVIRONMENT   *McGraw-Hill Encyclopedia of Environmental Sciences*

FOREIGN   *Encyclopedia of American Foreign Policy*
RELATIONS   *Encyclopedia of the Third World*

HISTORY   *Dictionary of American History*
                           Dictionary of the History of Ideas

LAW   *Encyclopedia of Crime and Justice*

LITERATURE   *Encyclopedia of World Literature in the 20th Century*

MEDICINE   *Oxford Companion to Medicine*

MINORITIES   *Encyclopedia of American Ethnic Groups*

PHILOSOPHY   *Encyclopedia of Philosophy*

PSYCHOLOGY   *Encyclopedia of Psychology*

RELIGION   *New Catholic Encyclopedia*

SCIENCE   *McGraw-Hill Encyclopedia of Science and Technology*

SOCIAL   *International Encyclopedia of the Social Sciences*
SCIENCES

WOMEN'S   *Nature of Women: An Encyclopedia and Guide*
STUDIES

You can locate any of these encyclopedias in the library by looking up its call number in the computer or card catalog. Other specialized encyclopedias can be found by looking in the catalog under the subject heading for the subject or discipline, such as "psychology," and the subheading "dictionaries and encyclopedias."

Two reference sources can help you to identify specialized encyclopedias covering your topic:

ARBA Guide to Subject Encyclopedias and Dictionaries lists specialized encyclopedias by broad subject category, with descriptions of coverage, focus, and any special features.

First Stop: The Master Index to Subject Encyclopedias lists specialized encyclopedias by broad subject category and also provides access to individual articles within them. By looking under the key terms that describe your topic, you will find references to specific articles in any of over four hundred specialized encyclopedias.

Checking Subject Headings

To carry your research beyond encyclopedias, you need to find appropriate subject headings. Subject headings are specific words and phrases used in libraries to categorize the contents of books and periodicals. As you read about your subject in an encyclopedia or other reference book, you will discover possible subject headings.

To begin your search for subject headings, consult the *Library of Congress Subject Headings* (LCSH). This reference book lists the standard subject headings used in catalogs and in many encyclopedias and bibliographies. It usually can be found near the library catalog. For example, if you were researching "toxic wastes" and looked for that subject in the LCHS, you would find the following:

Toxic wastes
    USE Hazardous wastes

Looking under "hazardous wastes" you would find this:

Hazardous wastes
    UF Hazardous waste disposal
        Poisonous wastes
        Toxic wastes
        Waste disposal
        Wastes, Hazardous
    BT Factory and trade waste
        Hazardous substances
        Refuse and refuse disposal
    RT Pollution
    NT Hazardous waste management industry
        Hazardous waste treatment facilities

In this entry, UF means "used for," BT "broader term," RT "related term," and NT "narrower term." Assume you are interested not in hazardous wastes generally but in recent improvements in treatment of them. Looking at the last line above, you decide that this term seems most closely related to your subject. Now you are ready to begin your search for sources by locating this subject heading—your key word or phrase—in catalogs and indexes. There you will find listed the books and articles that will provide the materials of your research. Should you find that you need more materials than the first subject heading provides, you can go back and pursue related headings, such as "Hazardous waste management industry" or "Pollution."

Consulting Bibliographies

A bibliography is simply a list of publications on a given subject. Whereas an encyclopedia may give you only background information on your subject, a bibliography gives you an overview of what has been published on the subject. Its scope may be broad or narrow. Some bibliographers try to be exhaustive, including every title they can find, but most are selective. To discover how selections were made, check the bibliography's preface or introduction. Occasionally, bibliographies are annotated: that is, they provide brief summaries of the entries and, sometimes, also evaluate them. Bibliographies may be found in a variety of places: in encyclopedias, in the card catalog, and in research guides. All specialized encyclopedias and academic research guides include bibliographies.

The best way to locate a comprehensive, up-to-date bibliography on your subject is to look in the *Bibliographic Index*. A master list of bibliographies that contain fifty or more titles, the *Bibliographic Index* includes bibliographies from articles, books, and government publications. A new volume is published every year. (Note that because this index is not cumulative, you should check back over several years, beginning with the most current volume.)

Even if you attend a large research university, your library is unlikely to hold every book or journal article a bibliography might direct you to. Your library's catalog and serial record will tell you whether the book or journal is available.

Determining the Most Promising Sources

As you follow a subject heading into the library's catalog and bibliographic indexes, discovering many seemingly relevant books and articles, how do you decide which ones to track down and examine? With little to go on but author, title, date, and publisher or periodical name, you may feel at a loss; but these actually provide useful clues. Look, for example, at the card at the top of page 513 from a library card catalog. This particular card is called a subject card because it is found in a card file with other cards alphabetized by subject headings. (Libraries also use author and title card files, which are illustrated later in this chapter.) Notice that from the author's birthdate and the publication date of the book, you can tell that she writes toward the end of her career. She might, therefore, offer some historical perspective on the topic. From the subtitle phrase "the person within" and from the first subject heading at the bottom of the card, you can tell that the book focuses on psychological problems rather than physiological or medical details.

The book is a substantial 396 pages and includes a bibliography, which could lead you to other sources on anorexia nervosa. Since by the early 1990s this 1973 book could be dated in some respects, you might pass it over in

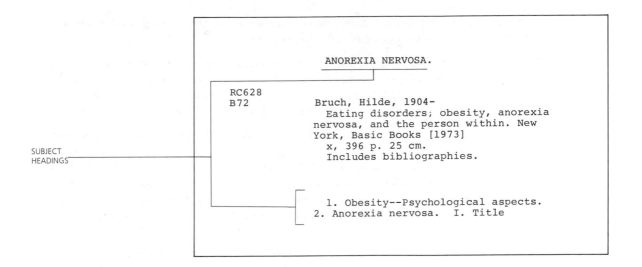

your first stage of research. You should not be surprised to discover later, however, that it is either still timely or valued because of its historical contribution. The call number in the upper left corner leads you to the book in the library's stacks.

Now look at the following entry from a periodical index.

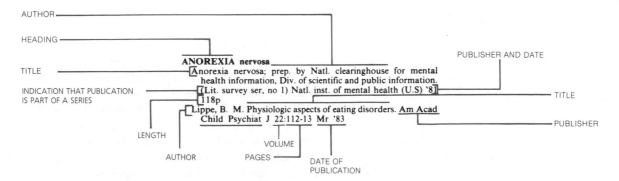

This entry identifies a research report, about ten years old by the early 1990s, which appeared in the journal of a prestigious national psychiatric association. From the volume number, you learn that this journal had been published for twenty-two years by 1973. The title indicates that the report concerns the physiology of eating disorders, not their psychology; and it is a concise two pages.

In the first stage of your research, you want to quickly extend your understanding of your topic beyond what an encyclopedia can offer. From the works listed in the indexes you consulted, you should look at three to five promising sources. Select these first sources on the basis of their recentness, range, and suggestion of further sources.

Recentness. Single out the most recent sources on your topic. For current controversies, emerging trends, and continuing technical or medical developments, you must see the very most recent material. Even for historical or biographical topics, you will want to begin with contemporary perspectives.

Range. Select at least one book, one research report in an academic journal, and one article in a popular magazine. Or select three or four publications that you can tell from their titles concern different aspects of your topic or approach it from different perspectives. In this first look beyond an encyclopedia, avoid selecting sources by the same author, from the same publisher, or in the same journal. Common sense will lead you to an appropriate decision about range.

Suggestion of Further Sources. Select sources that promise to lead you to other sources. For example, books and journal articles usually include citation lists or bibliographies.

LOCATING SOURCES

Following are guidelines to finding books; periodical articles; newspaper articles; and other, specialized sources.

Finding Books

The primary source for books is the library catalog. Until recently it was called the card catalog because it consisted entirely of cards filed in drawers; now nearly every college library also offers a computerized catalog, sometimes called an online catalog. The online catalog is accessed through computer terminals, which allow more people to find the information they need at various locations in the library. It provides more flexibility in searching subject headings and may even be able to tell you whether the book you are interested in has already been checked out. Another distinct advantage it provides is the ability to print out source information, making it unnecessary for you to copy it by hand. Since an online catalog typically contains material received and catalogued only after a certain date, however, you may need to check the card catalog as well.

Library catalogs organize sources by author, subject, and title. For each book there is a card or computer entry under the name of each author, under each subject heading to which the book is related, and under the title. Author, subject, and title cards or entries all give the same basic information.

1. The *call number*—always in the upper lefthand corner of cards in a card catalog, indicates the numerical code under which the book is filed in the library. Call numbers are assigned according to subject. Most college

research libraries use the Library of Congress subject headings and numbering system. Call numbers have at least two rows of numbers. The top row indicates the general subject classification, and the second row places the book within this classification. Subsequent rows identify the copyright and publication date for multiple editions. In an online catalog, the call number usually appears on a separate line.

2. The *author*—appears last name first, followed by birth and death dates. If there are multiple authors, there is an author card or entry under each author's name.

3. The *title*—appears exactly as it is printed on the title page of the book, except that only the first word and proper nouns and adjectives are capitalized.

4. The *imprint*—includes the place of publication (usually just the city), publisher, and year of publication. If the book was published simultaneously in the United States and abroad, both places of publication and both publishers are included.

5. The *collation*—offers descriptive information about the book's length and size. A roman numeral indicates the number of pages used for front matter (such as a preface, table of contents, and acknowledgments).

6. *Notes*—indicate any special features (for example, a bibliography or an index).

7. *Subject headings*—indicate how the book is listed in the subject catalog. These may be headings you can use to find other books related to your subject.

Following is the author card for the book for which a subject card was shown earlier in this chapter.

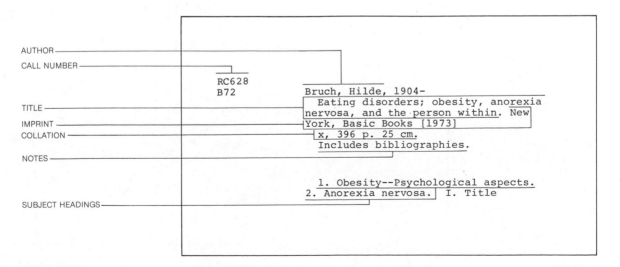

The title and subject cards for a book are just like the author card except that they have headings printed at the top above the author's name. On the title card the heading is the title (which also appears again below the author's name).

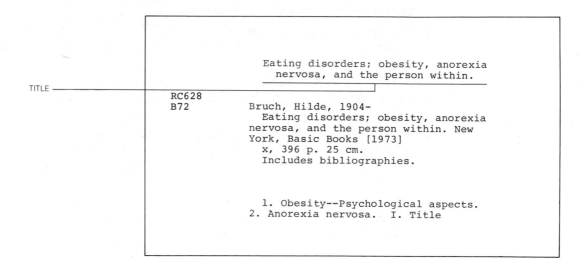

TITLE

```
                    Eating disorders; obesity, anorexia
                      nervosa, and the person within.

          RC628
          B72        Bruch, Hilde, 1904-
                       Eating disorders; obesity, anorexia
                     nervosa, and the person within. New
                     York, Basic Books [1973]
                       x, 396 p.  25 cm.
                       Includes bibliographies.


                       1. Obesity--Psychological aspects.
                     2. Anorexia nervosa.  I. Title
```

On a subject card the heading is one of the subject headings from the bottom of the card. Note that a separate catalog card or entry for a book will exist for each subject heading listed (see, for example, the subject card for this book shown on page 513).

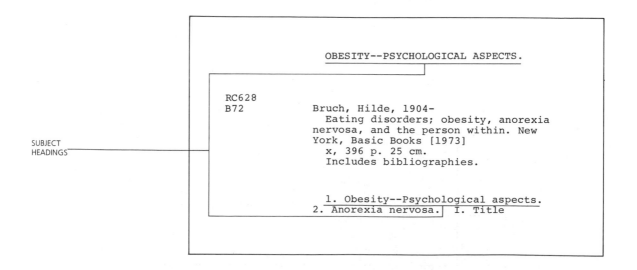

SUBJECT HEADINGS

```
                     OBESITY--PSYCHOLOGICAL ASPECTS.

          RC628
          B72        Bruch, Hilde, 1904-
                       Eating disorders; obesity, anorexia
                     nervosa, and the person within. New
                     York, Basic Books [1973]
                       x, 396 p.  25 cm.
                       Includes bibliographies.


                       1. Obesity--Psychological aspects.
                     2. Anorexia nervosa.  I. Title
```

Here is one college library's online catalog display of the author entry for a book in its collection. Notice the call number along the bottom line.

AUTHOR   Brown, Michael Harold, 1952-

TITLE   The toxic cloud/Michael H. Brown,
            1st ed.
            New York: Harper & Row, c1987.

DESCRIPTION 307 p.; 25 cm.

NOTES   Includes index.

SUBJECTS   Air pollution-Environmental
            aspects-United States.
            Pollutants-Environmental
            aspects-United States.
            Environmental chemistry-United States.
            Hazardous wastes-Environmental
            aspects-United States.

CALL NUMBER UCSD Undergrad TD883.2 .B66 1987

Finding Periodical Articles

The most up-to-date information on a subject usually is found not in books but in articles in magazines and journals, or periodicals. Articles in periodicals usually are not listed in the library catalog; to find them, you must instead use periodical indexes and abstracts. Indexes list articles, whereas abstracts summarize as well as list them.

Following is an example from an index you may be familiar with already—the *Readers' Guide to Periodical Literature:*

SUBJECT HEADING ——— Anorexia nervosa
                      Anorexia nervosa. D. K. Mano. *Natl Rev* 35:1626-8 D ——— PERIODICAL
TITLE ———   23 '83
                      Anorexia nervosa: a hormonal link [abnormal levels of
                        vasopressin] *Newsweek* 101:69 My 23 '83
VOLUME AND PAGE ——   A brother remembers [K. Carpenter] R. Carpenter. il ——— DATE
                        pors *People Wkly* 20:152-3+ N 21 '83
                      Can an athlete take fitness too far? [M. Wazeter's suicide
                        attempt linked to athletic competition] N. Amdur. il
                        pors *Seventeen* 42:24+ Jl '83

The *Readers' Guide* covers about two hundred popular periodicals and may help you start your search for sources on general and current topics. Even for general topics, however, you should not rely on it exclusively. Nearly all college libraries house far more than two hundred periodicals, and university research libraries house twenty thousand or more. *Readers' Guide* does not even attempt to cover the research journals that play such an important role in college writing.

The following example is from a specialized reference work, *Psychological Abstracts,* which both indexes and summarizes articles from a wide range of periodicals that publish psychological research:

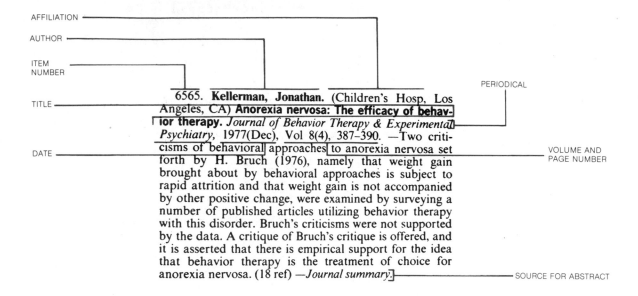

AFFILIATION

AUTHOR

ITEM NUMBER

PERIODICAL

TITLE

6565. **Kellerman, Jonathan.** (Children's Hosp, Los Angeles, CA) **Anorexia nervosa: The efficacy of behavior therapy.** *Journal of Behavior Therapy & Experimental Psychiatry,* 1977(Dec), Vol 8(4), 387–390. —Two criticisms of behavioral approaches to anorexia nervosa set forth by H. Bruch (1976), namely that weight gain brought about by behavioral approaches is subject to rapid attrition and that weight gain is not accompanied by other positive change, were examined by surveying a number of published articles utilizing behavior therapy with this disorder. Bruch's criticisms were not supported by the data. A critique of Bruch's critique is offered, and it is asserted that there is empirical support for the idea that behavior therapy is the treatment of choice for anorexia nervosa. (18 ref) —*Journal summary.*

DATE

VOLUME AND PAGE NUMBER

SOURCE FOR ABSTRACT

General indexes. These list articles in nontechnical, general interest publications. They cover a broad range of subjects. Most have separate author and subject listings as well as a list of book reviews. Following are some general indexes:

Humanities Index (1974–present) covers archaeology, history, classics, literature, performing arts, philosophy, and religion.

Social Sciences Index (1974–present) covers economics, geography, law, political science, psychology, public administration, and sociology.

Public Affairs Information Service Bulletin [PAIS] (1915–present) covers articles and other publications by public and private agencies on economic and social conditions, international relations, and public administration. Subject listing only.

Specialized Indexes and Abstracts. These list or abstract articles devoted to technical or scholarly research.

Accountant's Index (1944–present)
American Statistics Index (1973–present)
Applied Science and Technology Index (1958–present)
Biological and Agricultural Index (1964–present)

Education Index (1929–present)
Engineering Index (1920–present)
Historical Abstracts (1955–present)
Index Medicus (1961–present)
MLA International Bibliography of Books and Articles in the Modern Languages and Literature (1921–present)
Philosopher's Index (1967–present)
Psychological Abstracts (1927–present)
Science Abstracts (1898–present)

Many periodical indexes and abstracts use the Library of Congress subject headings, but some have their own systems. *Psychological Abstracts,* for example, has a separate volume for subject headings. Check the opening pages of the index or abstract you are using to see how it classifies its subjects. Then look for periodicals under your chosen Library of Congress subject heading or the heading that seems most similar to it.

Some libraries now have both printed and computerized versions of some periodical indexes. For example, microcomputer versions of *Social Sciences Index, Humanities Index,* and *General Science Index* are widely available. Since computerized indexes cover only the most recent years of an index, however, you might want to consult older printed issues as well. Like the online catalog, computerized indexes give you the ability to search quickly, to search for key words or fields not designated by subject headings, to limit your search in helpful ways, and to print out accurate source information rather than copy it by hand. A search for articles on the subject of schizophrenia, for example, might turn up hundreds or even thousands of entries; then you might narrow your search by using commands to limit the search to articles written in English and published within the last three years. Unlike print indexes, computerized periodical indexes allow you to search many years simultaneously, and to do so much more quickly.

When you identify a promising a magazine or journal article in a periodical index, you must go to the library's serial record to learn whether the library subscribes to the periodical and, if so, where you can find it. Recent issues of periodicals are usually arranged alphabetically by title on open shelves. Older issues are either bound like books and filed by call numbers or filmed and available on microfiche.

Finding Newspaper Articles

Newspapers provide useful information for many research topics in such areas as foreign affairs, economic issues, public opinion, and social trends. Libraries usually miniaturize newspapers and store them on microfilm (reels) or microfiche (cards), which must be placed in viewing machines to be read.

Newspaper indexes like the *Los Angeles Times Index, New York Times Index,* and *National Newspaper Index* will help you locate specific articles on your topic. The *National Newspaper Index* is on microfilm and covers the most recent three years of five leading newspapers: the *Christian Science Monitor, Los Angeles Times, Washington Post, Wall Street Journal,* and *New York Times.* College libraries usually have indexes to local newspapers as well.

Your library may also subscribe to newspaper article and digest services like the following:

NewsBank. Full-text articles from 450 U.S. newspapers. A good source of information on local and regional issues and on trends.

Newspaper Abstracts. An index and brief abstracts of articles from nineteen major regional, national, and international newspapers.

Facts on File. A weekly digest of U.S. and international news events arranged by subject, such as foreign affairs, arts, education, religion, and sports.

Editorials on File. Editorials from 150 U.S. and Canadian newspapers. Each entry includes a brief description of an editorial subject followed by fifteen to twenty editorials on the subject, reprinted from different newspapers. Published twice-monthly.

Editorial Research Reports. Reports on current and controversial topics, including brief histories, statistics, editorials, journal articles, endnotes, and supplementary reading lists.

African Recorder. Articles on African issues from African newspapers for 1970 to date.

Asian Recorder. Articles on Asian issues from Asian newspapers for 1971 to date.

Canadian News Facts. A digest of current articles from Canadian newspapers such as the *Montreal Star, Toronto Star,* and *Vancouver Sun* for 1972 to date.

Foreign Broadcast Information Service (FBIS). Foreign broadcast scripts, newspaper articles, and government statements from Asia, Europe, Latin America, Africa, the Soviet Union, and the Middle East for 1980 to date.

Current Digest of the Soviet Press. Articles on Soviet issues from Soviet and European newspapers for 1963 to date.

Keesing's Contemporary Archives. A weekly digest of events in all countries, compiled from British reporting services. Includes speeches and statistics. Index includes chronological, geographical, and topical sections.

Finding Other, Specialized Sources

Following is a description of some other materials that may help you to find sources for a particular purpose or a particular kind of subject.

Sources Representing Particular Viewpoints.

Some specialized periodical indexes tend to represent particular viewpoints and may help you identify different positions on an issue.

Alternative Press Index. A subject listing of articles from "alternative" publications; includes radical, environmental, feminist, revolutionary, ethnic, and non-American viewpoints. Some of the sources covered are not available in most libraries.

Index to Black Periodicals. An author and subject index to articles of both a general and a scholarly nature about African-Americans.

Left Index. An author and subject index to over eighty periodicals with a Marxist, radical, or left perspective. Listings cover primarily topics in the social sciences and humanities.

Chicano Index. An index to general and scholarly articles about Mexican-Americans. Articles are arranged by subject with author and title indexes. (Before 1989 the title was *Chicano Periodical Index.*)

Another useful source for identifying positions is *Editorials on File,* described on p. 520.

Sources for Political Subjects.   Two publications that report developments in the federal government can be rich sources of information on political issues. Types of material they cover include congressional hearings and debates, presidential proclamations and speeches, Supreme Court decisions and dissenting opinions, and compilations of statistics. These publications may not be included in catalogs and indexes but are accessible in a separate documents department within some college libraries. Ask a reference librarian for assistance.

Congressional Quarterly Almanac. An annual summary of legislation. Provides an overview of governmental policies and trends, including objective analysis as well as election results, records of roll-call votes, and the text of significant speeches and debates.

Congressional Quarterly Weekly Report. A news service that includes up-to-date summaries of committee actions, votes, and executive branch activities, as well as overviews of current policy discussions and activities within the federal government.

Chapter 9 provides guidance developing an argument speculating about the causes of a trend.

Sources for Researching Trends.   Research can help you identify trends to write about and, most important, provide the evidence you need to demonstrate the existence of a trend. The following resources can be especially helpful:

Statistical Abstract of the United States is issued annually by the Bureau of the Census. Provides a variety of social, economic, and political statistics, often covering several years. Includes tables, graphs, and charts and gives references to additional sources of information.

American Statistics Index (1974–present) is an annual with monthly supplements. Attempts to cover all federal government publications containing statistical information of research significance. Brief descriptions of references.

Statistical Reference Index (1980–present) is "a selective guide to American statistical publications from sources other than the U.S. government." Includes economic, social, and political statistical sources.

World Almanac and Book of Facts is published annually, presenting information on a variety of subjects drawn from many sources. Includes such things as a chronology of the year, climatological data, and lists of inventions and awards.

The Gallup Poll: Public Opinion (1935–present) is a chronological listing of the results of public opinion polls. Includes information on social, economic, and political trends.

NewsBank (1979–present) includes newspaper articles from across the country reproduced on microfiche. Topics include business and economics, politics, health, and others.

In addition to researching the trend itself, you may want to research others' speculations about its causes. If so, the reports of federal government activities described in the previous section may be helpful.

EVALUATING SOURCES

Suggestions for deciding which sources to consult at an early stage of your research are given on pp. 508–14.

From the beginning of your search you will be evaluating sources to determine which to use in your essay. Obviously, you must decide which sources provide information relevant to the topic. But you also must decide how credible or trustworthy your sources are. Just because a book or essay appears in print does not necessarily mean the information or opinions in it are reliable.

Selecting
Relevant Sources

Begin the evaluation of your sources by narrowing your working bibliography to the most relevant sources. Consider them in terms of scope, date, and viewpoint.

Scope and Approach.   To decide how relevant a particular source is, you need to examine it in depth. Do not depend on title alone, for it may be misleading. If the source is a book, check its table of contents and index to see how many pages are devoted to the precise subject you are exploring. You most likely will want an in-depth, not a superficial, treatment of the subject. Read the preface or introduction to a book or the opening paragraphs of an article to determine the author's basic approach to the subject or special way of looking at it. Abstracts, printed with many scholarly articles, give you a quick idea of the article's scope and approach.

Date of Publication.   Although you will always want to consult the most up-to-date sources available on your subject, older sources often establish the principles, theories, and data upon which later work rests and may provide a useful perspective for evaluating it. Since many older works are considered classics, you may want to become familiar with them. To determine which sources are classics, note the ones that are cited most often in encyclopedia articles, bibliographies, and recent works on the subject.

Viewpoint.   You will want your sources to represent a variety of viewpoints on the subject. Just as you would not depend on a single author for all of your information, so you do not want to use authors who all belong to the same school of thought. For suggestions on determining authors' viewpoints, see the next section, Identifying Bias.

Using sources that represent different viewpoints is especially important when you must develop an argument to support your own position about something, as in the essay assignments in Chapters 6–10. During the invention work in those chapters, you may want to research what others have said about your subject to see what positions have been staked out and what arguments have been made. You will then be able to define the issue more carefully, collect arguments supporting your position, and anticipate arguments opposing it. As a result, your essay will be more authoritative and convincing.

Inclusion in Bibliographies.   Selective bibliographies, particularly those with annotations, can also help you gauge the reliability of sources on your list. Check the bibliography's preface or introduction to discover the principle of selection. You may also want to check other bibliographies, particularly more recent ones and those included in respected books on the subject.

Bibliographies in specialized research guides are especially reliable because experts have already evaluated the available materials and are recommending only the best. Specialized encyclopedias also offer highly selective bibliographies.

Identifying Bias

A list of research guides is on pp. 508–09; one of specialized encyclopedias is on p. 510.

One of the most important aspects of evaluating a source is identifying any bias in its treatment of the subject. Although the word *bias* may sound like a criticism or drawback, it simply refers to the fact that most writing is not neutral or objective and does not try or claim to be. Authors come to their subjects with particular viewpoints, and in using sources you must consider carefully how these viewpoints are reflected in their writing.

Although the text of the source will give you the most precise indication of the author's viewpoint, you can often get a good idea by looking at the preface or introduction or at the sources the author cites. Even before you examine a reference, you can often determine the general point of view it represents by noting carefully its title, author, and (for a book) publisher and (for an article) by researching the editorial slant of the periodical in which it appears.

Title.   Often the most obvious indication of bias is the title or subtitle. Watch for "loaded" words or confrontational phrasing.

Author.   The citation may indicate an author's title and/or affiliation. Information on the author may also be available in the book or article itself or in biographical sources available in the library.

Publisher.   The publication information can also be useful in determining bias. Country or publication may be a clue, or the work may be published by an organization with a known bias.

Editorial Slant.   Many periodicals have definite editorial slants. In cases where the publication title does not indicate bias, there are reference sources that may help you to determine this information. Two of the most common are the following:

> *Gale Directory of Publications and Broadcast Media.* A useful source for descriptive information on newspapers and magazines. Entries often include an indication of intended audience and political or other bias. For example, the *San Diego Union* is described as a "newspaper with a Republican orientation."
>
> *Magazines for Libraries.* A listing of over 6,500 periodicals arranged by academic discipline. For each discipline there is a list of basic indexes, abstracts, and periodicals. Each individual listing for a periodical includes its publisher, the date it was founded, the places it is indexed, its intended audience, and an evaluation of its content and editorial focus. Here is one such listing:

>> **4917.*The Nation*.** 1865. w. $40. Victor Navasky. Nation Assocs., Inc., P.O. Box 1953, Marion, OH 43305. Illus., index, adv. Circ: 50,000. Vol. ends: June/Dec. Microform: UMI.
>> *Indexed:* BoRvI, PAIS, RG. *Bk rev:* 3–7, 1,400 words, signed, *Aud:* Hs, Ga, Ac.
>> Liberal to the left: first, foremost and always. That is the policy of the distinguished editor, who has given the journal new life with a series of investigative reports that often make headlines. The articles range from the Nicaraguan debate to abortion to Israel and the politics of Washington, D.C. It is partisan, yet witty and extremely intelligent. Some of the best stylists in journalism are regular columnists in the arts and entertainment sections, for example, Alexander Cockburn, I. F. Stone, Christopher Hitchens, Jefferson Morley, and Andrew Kopkind. The editorials are quite superior in both content and style. This is a required magazine for almost all types and sizes of libraries.

Much of the writing you will do in college requires you to use sources in combination with your own firsthand observation and reflection. Any time you get information and ideas from reading, lectures, and interviews, you are using sources.

In college, using sources is not only acceptable, it is expected. No matter how original their thinking, educated people nearly always base their original thought on the work of others. In fact, most of your college education is devoted to teaching you what Matthew Arnold called "the best that has been thought and said" along with ways of analyzing and interpreting this information so that your own understanding is informed but not limited by what others have said. In other words, your education prepares you to take part in an ongoing conversation. When you use and acknowledge sources in your writing, you let readers in on the conversation so that they can see whose ideas and information have influenced your thinking on the subject.

USING SOURCES

Writers commonly use sources by quoting directly as well as by paraphrasing and by summarizing. Be selective in using quotation. As a general rule, quote only when your source's language is particularly vivid, memorable, or well known, or when your source is so respected by your readers that quoting would lend authority to your writing. If the phrasing does not matter, it is preferable to paraphrase or summarize rather than quote.

Quoting   Quotations should duplicate the source exactly. If the source has an error, copy it and add the Latin word *sic* in brackets immediately after the error to indicate that it is not yours but your source's:

> According to a recent newspaper article, "Plagirism [*sic*] is a problem among journalists and scholars as well as students."

However, you can change quotations (1) to emphasize particular words by underlining or italicizing them, (2) to omit irrelevant information or to make

Using and
Acknowledging Sources *21*

the quotation conform grammatically to your sentence by using ellipses, and (3) to make the quotation conform grammatically or to insert information by using brackets.

Underlining or Italicizing for Emphasis.   Underline or italicize the words you want to emphasize, and add the phrase *(emphasis added)* at the end of the sentence. In his essay on youth suicide in Chapter 9, Victor Fuchs emphasizes that part of the quotation that refers specifically to suicide:

> In a review of psychosocial literature on adolescence, Elder (1975) concludes: "Adolescents who fail to receive guidance, affection, and concern from parents — whether by parental inattention or absence — are likely to rely heavily on peers for emotional gratification, advice, and companionship, *to anticipate a relatively unrewarding future,* and to engage in antisocial activities" (emphasis added).

Using Ellipsis for Omissions.   Ellipsis, a set of three spaced periods (. . .), signals that something has been left out of a quotation. If you quote single words or a portion of a sentence, it will be obvious that you have left out some of the original so you don't need to use an ellipsis:

> More specifically, Wharton's imagery of suffusing brightness transforms Undine before her glass into "some fabled creature whose home was in a beam of light" (21).

But when words are left out in the quotation, use an ellipsis to mark the missing words. When the omission occurs within the sentence, put a space *before, among, and after* the three periods:

> Hermione Roddice is described in Lawrence's *Women in Love* as a "woman of the new school, full of intellectuality and . . . nerve-worn with consciousness" (17).

When the omission falls at the end of the sentence, place a sentence *period directly after* the last word, followed by three spaced periods:

> But Grimaldi's recent commentary on Aristotle contends that for Aristotle rhetoric like dialectic had "no limited and unique subject matter upon which it must be

> exercised. . . . Instead, rhetoric as an art transcends all specific disciplines and may be brought into play in them" (6).

Four periods can indicate the omission of the rest of the sentence as well as whole sentences, paragraphs, even pages.

When a parenthetical reference follows the ellipsis at the end of your sentence, use three spaced periods and place the sentence period after the final parenthesis:

> But Grimaldi's recent commentary on Aristotle contends that for Aristotle rhetoric like dialectic had "no limited and unique subject matter upon which it must be exercised . . ." (6).

Using Brackets for Insertions or Changes. You may also use brackets to make a quotation conform grammatically to your sentence or to replace an unclear pronoun. In this example from an essay on James Joyce's "Araby," reprinted in Chapter 10, the writer adapts Joyce's phrases "we played till our bodies glowed" and "shook music from the buckled harness" to fit the tense of her sentences:

> In the dark, cold streets during the "short days of winter," the boys must generate their own heat by "[playing] till [their] bodies glowed." Music is "[shaken] from the buckled harness" as if it were unnatural, and the singers in the market chant nasally of "the troubles in our native land."

You may also use brackets to add or substitute explanatory material in a quotation:

> Any unfaithfulness is, as the candidate phrased it, "between me and Lee [his wife] and me and God."

Several kinds of changes necessary to make a quotation conform grammatically to another sentence may be made without any signal to readers: (1) the first letter of the first word in a quotation may be changed from capital to lowercase (or vice versa), (2) the punctuation mark at the end of a quotation may be changed, and (3) double quotation marks (enclosing the entire quotation) may be changed to single quotation marks (enclosing a quotation within the longer quotation).

Integrating Quotations

A quotation may either be integrated into the text by enclosing it in quotation marks or set off from the text in a block without quotation marks.

In-text Quotations. Incorporate brief quotations (no more than four typed lines of prose or three lines of poetry) into your text. You may place the quotation virtually any place in your sentence:

At the Beginning

"To live a life is not to cross a field," she quotes Pasternak at the beginning of her narrative (11), not acknowledging that she is in fact quoting Lowell's translation of Pasternak.

In the Middle

She begins and ends by speaking of the need of the woman writer to have "money and a room of her own" (4)—an idea that certainly spoke to Plath's condition, especially in her impoverished and harassed last six months.

At the End

In *The Second Sex,* Simone de Beauvoir has described such an experience as one in which the girl "becomes as object, and she sees herself as object" (378).

Or Divided by Your Own Words

"Science usually prefers the literal to the nonliteral term," Kinneavy writes, "—that is, figures of speech are often out of place in science" (177).

When you quote poetry, use a slash with spaces before and after (/) to signal the end of each line of verse:

Alluding to St. Augustine's distinction between City of God and Earthly City, Lowell writes that "much against my will / I left the City of God where it belongs" ("Beyond the Alps" ll. 4–5).

Block quotations.   Put in block form five or more typed lines of prose or four or more lines of poetry. Indent the quotation ten spaces from the left margin and double-space. *Do not* enclose the passage within quotation marks. Use a colon to introduce a block quotation, unless the context calls for another punctuation mark or none at all. When quoting a single paragraph or part of one, do not indent the first line of the quotation more than the rest. In quoting two or more paragraphs, indent the first line of each paragraph an additional three spaces.

In "A Literary Legacy from Dunbar to Baraka," Margaret Walker says of Paul Lawrence Dunbar's dialect poems:

> He realized that the white world in the United States tolerated his literary genius only because of his "jingles in a broken tongue," and they found the old "darky" tales and speech amusing and within the vein of folklore into which they wished to classify all Negro life. This troubled Dunbar because he realized that white America was denigrating him as a writer and as a man. (70)

Punctuating
Introductory
Statements

Statements that introduce quotations take a range of punctuation marks and
lead-in words. Here are some examples of ways writers typically introduce
quotations:

Introducing a Statement with a Colon

Protection of white privilege is critical to patterns of discrimination: "Whenever
a number of persons within a society have enjoyed for a considerable period of
time certain opportunities for getting wealth, for exercising power and authority,
and for successfully claiming prestige and social deference, there is a strong
tendency for these people to feel that these benefits are theirs 'by right'" (Williams 727).

Introducing a Statement with a Comma

Similarly, Duncan asserts, "As matters now stand, it is unwise to talk about
communication without some understanding of Burke" (259).

Introducing a Statement Using *That*

Noting this failure, Alice Miller asserts <u>that</u> "the reason for her despair was not
her suffering but the impossibility of communicating her suffering to another
person" (255)

Introducing a Statement Using *As . . . said*:

The token women writers authenticated the male canon without disrupting it,
for <u>as</u> Ruth Bleier has <u>said</u>, "the last thing society desires of its women has been
intellectuality and independence" (73).

Punctuating
within
Quotations

Although punctuation within a quotation should reproduce the original,
some adaptations may be necessary. Use single quotation marks for quotations within the quotation:

Original

The reviewers' comments pleased her because they supported her claim that her
novels "could never be designated as feminine writing" because "they were
written by a cerebral human being who had a knowledge of the technique of
writing" (APT 176).

Quoted Version

Winston claims that "the reviewers' comments pleased [Edna Ferber] because
they supported her claim that her novels 'could never be designated as feminine
writing' because 'they were written by a cerebral human being who had a knowledge of the technique of writing'" (106).

If the quotation ends with a question mark or an exclamation point,
retain the original punctuation:

"Did you think I loved you?" Edith later asks Dombey (566).

But if a quotation ending with a question mark or an exclamation point concludes your sentence, put the parenthetical reference and sentence period outside the quotation marks:

> Edith later asks Dombey, "Did you think I loved you?" (566).

Avoiding Grammatical Tangles

When you incorporate quotations into your writing and especially when you omit words, you run the risk of creating ungrammatical sentences. Here are three common errors you should make an effort to avoid: verb incompatibility, ungrammatical omissions, and sentence fragments.

Verb Incompatibility. When this error occurs, the verb form in the introductory statement is grammatically incompatible with the verb form in the quotation. When your quotation has a verb form that does not fit in with your text, it is usually possible to use just part of the quotation, thus avoiding verb incompatibility. In the following example, *suggests* and *saw* do not fit together as the sentence is written; see how the sentence is revised for verb compatibility.

NOT   The narrator suggests his bitter disappointment when "I saw myself as a creature driven and derided by vanity."

BUT   The narrator suggests his bitter disappointment when <u>he describes seeing himself</u> "as a creature driven and derided by vanity."

An Awkward Omission. Sometimes the omission of text from the quotation results in an ungrammatical sentence. In the following example, the quotation was awkwardly and ungrammatically excerpted. The revised sentences show two ways of correcting the grammar: first, by adapting the quotation (with brackets) so that its two parts fit together grammatically; second, by using only one part of the quotation.

NOT   From the moment of the boy's arrival in Araby, the bazaar is presented as a commercial enterprise: "I could not find any sixpenny entrance and . . . handing a shilling to a weary-looking man."

BUT   From the moment of the boy's arrival at Araby, the bazaar is presented as a commercial enterprise: "I could not find any sixpenny entrance and . . . hand[<u>ed</u>] a shilling to a weary-looking man."

OR   From the moment of the boy's arrival at Araby, the bazaar is presented as a commercial enterprise: he "could not find any sixpenny entrance" <u>and so paid</u> "a shilling" <u>to get in.</u>

An Incomplete Introductory Sentence. Sometimes when a quotation is a complete sentence, writers will carelessly neglect the introductory sentence—often, for example, forgetting to include a verb. Even though the quotation is a complete sentence, the total statement is then a sentence fragment.

NOT   The girl's interest in the bazaar leading the narrator to make what
               amounts to a sacred oath: "If I go . . . I will bring you something."

BUT   The girl's interest in the bazaar <u>leads</u> the narrator to make what amounts
               to a sacred oath: "If I go . . . I will bring you something."

Paraphrasing and Summarizing

Chapter 11 offers a fuller discussion of paraphrasing and summarizing techniques.

In addition to quoting their sources, writers have the option of paraphrasing or summarizing what others have written. This method allows writers to use the source's information, but to present it in their own words. The following examples show ways of summarizing statistics and facts as well as thoughts and ideas:

A study at Bellevue Hospital in New York City of 102 teenagers who attempted suicide showed that only one third of them lived with both parents (*Newsweek,* August 28, 1978, p. 74).

For an industry that says it already loses one and a half billion dollars annually to people who copy music from their friends, the record industry is fearful of that number growing astronomically (Buell 112).

William Faulkner, for example, had been working as a janitor and as a deckhand on a fishing boat in Mississippi while writing *The Sound and the Fury* and *As I Lay Dying.* When *Sanctuary* was published in 1931, he attended some New York literary parties, at one of which Tallulah Bankhead asked him to write a picture for her. The idea so appealed to him that he apparently began writing a screenplay immediately. Some months later, reporting to MGM for a six-week contract, he asked to write a picture script for Mickey Mouse but, no less absurdly, was assigned to a script for Wallace Beery. Despite the obvious need for trained screenwriters, no studio offered schooling. Faulkner was packed off to a small projection room to watch old movies. Bored after a few minutes, he wandered off for a week in Death Valley, then returned to write four treatments in five days, including one for Beery (Kawin 70–72).

In the first example the writer paraphrases a *Newsweek* article in order to highlight the survey statistics pertinent to his own thesis, while in the second the writer paraphrases the ideas he introduces from another writer's research. The third example is a good instance of summary: the writer has boiled down several pages of biographical data from her original source into a paragraph that focuses on the information of primary interest to her research.

Notice in the preceding examples that each writer acknowledges his or her source by name. Even when you use your own words to present someone else's information, you generally must acknowledge the fact that you borrowed the information. The only types of information that do not require acknowledgment are common knowledge (John F. Kennedy was assassinated in Dallas), familiar sayings ("haste makes waste"), and well-known quotations ("All's well that ends well").

ACKNOWLEDGING SOURCES

Although there is no universally agreed-upon system for acknowledging sources, there is agreement on both the need for documentation and the items that should be included. Writers should acknowledge sources for two reasons: to give credit to those sources, and to enable readers to consult the sources for further information. The following information should be included when documenting sources: (1) name of author, (2) title of publication, and (3) publication source, date, and page.

Most documentation styles combine some kind of citation in the text with a separate list of references keyed to the textual citations. There are basically two ways of acknowledging sources: (1) parenthetical citations keyed to a works cited list, and (2) footnotes (or endnotes) plus a bibliography. The Modern Language Association (MLA), a professional organization of English instructors, for many years endorsed the note style of documentation. But, with the 1984 revision of the *MLA Handbook,* the MLA went over to the simpler parenthetical citation method. The new MLA style is similar to the style endorsed by the American Psychological Association (APA)—the style used by many social and natural science instructors.

In Part I of this book, you can find examples of current MLA style (Jessica Statsky in Chapter 6) and APA style (Veronica Murayama in Chapter 5). This chapter presents the basic features of both these styles.

If you have any questions, consult the *MLA Handbook for Writers of Research Papers,* Third Edition (1988), or the *Publication Manual of the American Psychological Association,* Third Edition (1983). The *MLA Handbook* includes both the current MLA style using parenthetical citation and the old style using numbered notes.

Parenthetical Citation in Text

The MLA and APA styles both advocate parenthetical citations in the text keyed to a works cited list at the end of the paper. However, they differ on what should be included in the parenthetical citation. The MLA uses an author/page citation, while the APA uses an author/year (and page for a quotation) citation.

MLA   Dr. James is described as a "not-too-skeletal Ichabod Crane" (Simon 68).

APA   Dr. James is described as a "not-too-skeletal Ichabod Crane" (Simon, 1982, p. 68).

Notice that the APA style uses a comma between author, year, and page as well as "p." for page (Simon, 1982, p. 68), whereas the MLA puts nothing but space between author and page (Simon 68). Note also that the citations in both cases come before the final period. With block quotations, however, the citation comes after the final period preceded by two spaces.

If the author's name is used in the text, put the page reference in parentheses as close as possible to the quoted material, but without disrupting the flow of the sentence. For the APA style, cite the year in parentheses directly following the author's name, and place the page reference in parentheses before the final sentence period.

MLA   Simon describes Dr. James as a ''not-too-skeletal Ichabod Crane'' (68).

APA   Simon (1982) describes Dr. James as a ''not-too-skeletal Ichabod Crane'' (p. 68).

To cite a source by two or three authors, the MLA uses all the authors' last names; for works with more than three authors, it uses the first author's name followed by "et al." For more than three authors, the APA uses all the authors' last names the first time the reference occurs and the last name of the first author followed by "et al., " subsequently.

MLA   Dyal, Corning, and Willows identify several types of students, including the ''Authority-Rebel'' (4).

APA   Dyal, Corning, and Willows (1975) identify several types of students, including the ''Authority-Rebel'' (p. 4).

MLA   The Authority-Rebel ''tends to see himself as superior to other students in the class'' (Dyal, Corning, and Willows 4).

APA   The Authority-Rebel ''tends to see himself as superior to other students in the class'' (Dyal et al., 1975, p. 4).

To cite one of two or more works by the same author(s), the MLA uses the author's last name, a shortened version of the title, and the page. The APA uses the author's last name plus the year and page. When more than one work being cited was published by an author in the same year, APA style uses letters with the date (1973a, 1973b).

MLA   When old paint becomes transparent, it sometimes shows the artist's original plans: ''a tree will show through a woman's dress'' (Hellman, *Pentimento* 1).

APA   When old paint becomes transparent, it sometimes shows the artist's original plans: ''a tree will show through a woman's dress'' (Hellman, 1973, p. 1).

To cite a work listed only by its title, both the MLA and the APA use a shortened version of the title.

MLA   An international pollution treaty still to be ratified would prohibit all plastic garbage from being dumped at sea (''Awash'' 26).

APA   An international pollution treaty still to be ratified would prohibit all plastic garbage from being dumped at sea (''Awash,'' 1987, p. 26).

To quote material taken not from the original but from a secondary source that quotes the original, both the MLA and the APA give the secondary source in the works cited list, and acknowledge that the original was quoted in a secondary source in the text.

MLA   E. M. Forster says "the collapse of all civilization, so realistic for us, sounded in [Matthew Arnold's] ears like a distant and harmonious cataract" (qtd. in Trilling 11).

APA   E. M. Forster says "the collapse of all civilization, so realistic for us, sounded in [Matthew Arnold's] ears like a distant and harmonious cataract" (cited in Trilling, 1955, p. 11).

List of Works Cited

Providing full information for the parenthetical citations in the text, the list of works cited identifies all the sources the writer uses. Every source cited in the text must refer to an entry in the works cited list. And, conversely, every entry in the works cited list must correspond to at least one parenthetical citation in the text.

Whereas the MLA style uses the title "Works Cited," the APA prefers "References." Both alphabetize the entries according to the first author's last name. When several works by an author are listed, the APA recommends these rules for arranging the list:

- Same name single-author entries precede multiple-author entries:

  Aaron, P.   (1985).

  Aaron, P., & Zorn, C. R.   (1982).

- Entries with the same first author and different second author should be alphabetized according to the second author's last name:

  Aaron, P., & Charleston, W.   (1979).

  Aaron, P., & Zorn, C. R.   (1982).

- Entries by the same authors should be arranged by year of publication, in chronological order:

  Aaron, P., & Charleston, W.   (1979).

  Aaron, P., & Charleston, W.   (1984).

- Entries by the same author(s) with the same publication year should be arranged alphabetically by title (excluding *A, An, The*), and lowercase letters (*a, b, c,* and so on) should follow the year within the parentheses:

  Aaron, P. (1985a).   Basic . . .

  Aaron, P. (1985b).   Elements . . .

For multiple works by the same author (or group of authors), MLA style recommends alphabetizing by title. The author's name is given for the first entry only; subsequent entries are preceded by three hyphens and a period.

```
Vidal, Gore. Empire. New York: Random House, 1987.

---. Lincoln. New York: Random House, 1984.
```

The essential difference between the MLA and APA styles of listing sources is the order in which the information is presented. The MLA follows this order: author's name; title; publication source, year, and page. The APA puts the year after the author's name. Both systems call for two spaces after a period. The examples that follow indicate minor differences in capitalization and arrangement between the two documentation styles.

BOOKS

A Book by a Single Author

```
MLA        Simon, Kate. Bronx Primitive. New York: Harper,
              1982.

APA        Simon, K. (1982). Bronx primitive. New York:
              Harper & Row.
```

A Book by an Agency or Corporation

```
MLA        Association for Research in Nervous and Mental
              Disease. The Circulation of the Brain and
              Spinal Cord: A Symposium on Blood Sup-
              ply. New York: Hafner, 1966.

APA        Association for Research in Nervous and Mental
              Disease. (1966). The circulation of the brain
              and spinal cord: A symposium on blood sup-
              ply. New York: Hafner Publishing.
```

A Book by More Than One Author

```
MLA        Strunk, W., Jr., and E. B. White. The Elements of
              Style. 4th ed. New York: Macmillan, 1983.

APA        Strunk, W., Jr., & White, E. B. (1983). The ele-
              ments of style (4th ed.). New York: Macmillan.

MLA        Dyal, James A., William C. Corning, and Dale M.
              Willows. Readings in Psychology: The Search
              for Alternatives. 3rd ed. New York: McGraw,
              1975.
```

APA   Dyal, J. A., Corning, W. C., & Willows, D. M.
        (1975). Readings in psychology: The search for
        alternatives (3rd ed.). New York: McGraw-Hill.

For works by more than three authors, MLA style lists the name of the first
author followed by "et al."

MLA   Nielsen, Niels C., Jr., et al. Religions of the
        World. New York: St. Martin's, 1985.

A Book by an Unknown Author

Use title in place of author.

MLA   Webster's New Biographical Dictionary.
        Springfield, MA: Merriam-Webster, 1988.

APA   Webster's new biographical dictionary.
        (1988). Springfield, MA: Merriam-Webster.

An Edition

APA   Arnold, M. (1966). Culture and anarchy (J. Dover
        Wilson, Ed.). Cambridge: Cambridge University
        Press. (Original work published 1869)

If you refer to the text itself, begin with the author:

MLA   Arnold, Matthew. Culture and Anarchy. Ed. J.
        Dover Wilson. Cambridge: Cambridge UP, 1966.

If you cite the editor in your text, begin with the editor:

MLA   Wilson, J. Dover, ed. Culture and Anarchy. By
        Matthew Arnold. Cambridge: Cambridge UP,
        1966.

An Edited Collection

MLA   Dertouzos, Michael L., and Joel Moses, eds. The
        Computer Age: A Twenty-Year View. Cambridge,
        MA: MIT, 1979.

APA   Dertouzos, M. L., & Moses, J. (Eds.). (1979). The
        computer age: A twenty-year view. Cambridge,
        MA: MIT Press.

A Translation

APA   Tolstoy, L. (1972). War and peace. (C. Garnett,
        Trans.). London: Pan Books.
        (Original work published 1868–1869)

If you are referring to the work itself, begin with the author:

MLA   Tolstoy, Leo. War and Peace. Trans. Constance
          Garnett. London: Pan, 1972.

If you cite the translator in your text, begin the entry with the translator's
name:

MLA   Garnett, Constance, trans. War and Peace. By Leo
          Tolstoy. London: Pan, 1972.

A Work in an Anthology or Collection

MLA   Walker, Alice. "Beauty: When the Other Dancer Is
          the Self." Reading Critically, Writing Well.
          Ed. Rise B. Axelrod and Charles R. Cooper.
          2nd ed. New York: St. Martin's, 1990. 86–92.

APA   Bell, D. (1979). The social framework of the in-
          formation society. In M. L. Dertouzos & J.
          Moses (Eds.), The computer age: A twenty-year
          view (pp. 163–211). Cambridge, MA: MIT Press.

An Article in a Reference Book

MLA   Suber, Howard. "Motion Picture." Encyclopedia
          Americana. 1981 ed.

APA   Suber, H. (1981). Motion picture. Encyclopedia
          Americana.

An Introduction, Preface, Foreword, or Afterword

MLA   Holloway, John. Introduction. Little Dorrit. By
          Charles Dickens. Ed. John Holloway.
          Harmondsworth, England: Penguin, 1967. 13–29.

APA   Holloway, J. (1967). Introduction. In C. Dick-
          ens, Little Dorrit. (J. Holloway, Ed.). (pp.
          13–29). Harmondsworth, England: Penguin.

A Government Document

MLA   United States. Cong. Senate. Subcommittee
          on Constitutional Amendments of the Committee
          on the Judiciary. Hearings on the "Equal

Rights" Amendment. 91st Cong., 2nd sess.
S. Res. 61. Washington: GPO, 1970.

APA   U.S. Department of Health, Education and Welfare.
(1979). Healthy people: The surgeon general's
report on health promotion. (DHEW Publication
No. 79-55071). Washington, DC: U.S. Government
Printing Office.

An Unpublished Doctoral Dissertation

MLA   Bullock, Barbara. "Basic Needs Fulfillment among
Less Developed Countries: Social Progress
over Two Decades of Growth." Diss. Vanderbilt
U, 1986.

APA   Bullock, B. (1986). Basic needs fulfillment among
less developed countries: Social progress over
two decades of growth. Unpublished doctoral
dissertation, Vanderbilt University, Nashville,
TN.

ARTICLES

An Article from a Daily Newspaper

MLA   Burns, Jonathan F. "Afghans Seek Direct Talks
with U.S. on Elections." New York Times 6 May
1990: 4, 22.

APA   Burns, J.F. (1990, May 6). Afghans seek direct
talks with U.S. on elections. The New York
Times, pp. 4, 22.

An Article from a Weekly or Biweekly Magazine

MLA   Glastris, Paul. "The New Way to Get Rich." U.S.
News & World Report 7 May 1990: 26–36.

APA   Glastris, P. (1990, May 7). The new way to get
rich. U.S. News & World Report, pp. 26–36.

An Article from a Monthly or Bimonthly Magazine

MLA   Dolnick, Edward. "What Dreams Are (Really) Made
Of." Atlantic July 1990: 41–61.

APA   Dolnick, E. (1990, July). What dreams are
(really) made of. Atlantic, pp. 41–61.

An Article in a Scholarly Journal with Continuous Annual Pagination

MLA   Dworkin, Ronald. "Law as Interpretation."
           Critical Inquiry 9 (1982): 179–200.

APA   Dworkin, R. (1982). Law as interpretation.
           Critical Inquiry, 9, 179–200.

An Article in a Scholarly Journal That Paginates Each Issue Separately

MLA   Epstein, Alexandra. "Teen Parents: What They Need
           to Know." High/Scope Resource 1.2 (1982): 6.

APA   Epstein, A. (1982). Teen parents: What they need
           to know. High/Scope Resource, 1(2), 6–7.

An Anonymous Article

MLA   "Awash in Garbage." New York Times 15 Aug. 1987,
           sec. 1: 26.

APA   Awash in garbage. (1987, August 15). The New
           York Times, section 1, p. A26.

An Editorial

MLA   "Stepping Backward." Editorial. Los Angeles
           Times 4 July 1989, pt. 2: 6.

APA   Stepping backward. (1989, July 4). [Editorial].
           Los Angeles Times, part 2, p. 6.

A Letter to the Editor

MLA   Rissman, Edward M. Letter. Los Angeles Times
           29 June 1989, pt. 2: 5.

APA   Rissman, E. M. (1989, June 29). [Letter to the
           editor]. Los Angeles Times, part 2, p. 5.

A Review

MLA   Tyler, Anne. "Manic Monologue." Rev. of
           Tripmaster Monkey, by Maxine Hong Kingston.
           New Republic 17 Apr. 1989: 44–46.

If you don't know the author, start with the title. If the review is untitled, begin with the words "Rev. of" and alphabetize under the title of the work being reviewed.

APA   Tyler, A. (1989, April 17). Manic monologue. [Re-
           view of Tripmaster Monkey]. The New Republic,
           pp. 44–46.

OTHER SOURCES

Computer Software

MLA Nota Bene. Vers. 3.0. Computer software. 1988.
          MS-DOS 2.0, 512 KB, disk.

APA SuperCalc 3 Release 2.1. (1985). [Computer pro-
          gram]. San Jose, CA: Computer Associates, Micro
          Products Division.

Material from NewsBank

MLA Sharpe, Lora. "A Quilter's Tribute." Boston
          Globe 25 Mar. 1989. NewsBank [Microform], So-
          cial Relations, 1989, fiche 6, grids B4—6.

Material from an Information Service

MLA Belenky, Mary F. "The Role of Deafness in the
          Moral Development of Hearing Impaired Chil-
          dren." Teaching, Learning and Development.
          Ed. A. Areson and J. DeCaro. Rochester, NY:
          National Institute for the Deaf, 1984.
          115—184. ERIC ED 248 646.

APA Belenky, M. F. (1984). The role of deafness in
          the moral development of hearing impaired chil-
          dren. In A. Areson & J. DeCaro (Eds.), Teach-
          ing, learning and development (pp. 115—184).
          Rochester, NY: National Institute for the Deaf.
          (ERIC Document Reproduction Service No. ED 248
          646)

Material from a Computer Service

MLA Reece, Jerry S. "Measuring Investment Center Per-
          formance." Harvard Business Review 56.3
          (1978): 28—40. Dialog file 107, item
          673280 047658.

APA Reece, J. S. (1978). Measuring investment center
          performance. Harvard Business Review 56(3),
          28—40. (Dialog file 107, item 673280 047658)

Performances

MLA The Piano Lesson. By August Wilson. Dir. Lloyd
          Richards. Walter Kerr Theater, New York.
          23 Aug. 1989.

APA   Wilson, A. (Playwright), & Richards,
             L. (Director). (1989, Aug. 23). The piano
             lesson [play]. Walter Kerr Theater, New York.

Records and Tapes

MLA   Beethoven, Ludwig van. Violin Concerto in D Ma-
             jor, op. 61. Cond. Alexander Gauk. U.S.S.R.
             State Orchestra. David Oistrakh, violinist.
             Allegro, ACS 8044, 1980.

             Springsteen, Bruce. "Dancing in the Dark." Born
             in the U.S.A. Columbia, QC 38653, 1984.

APA   Beethoven, Ludwig van. (Composer). (1980).
             Violin concerto in D major, op. 61.
             (Cassette Recording No. ACS 8044). New York:
             Allegro.

             Springsteen, Bruce. (Singer and Composer).
             (1984). Dancing in the dark. Born in the
             U.S.A. (Record No. QC 38653). New York:
             Columbia.

Interviews

MLA   Lowell, Robert. "Robert Lowell." With Frederick
             Seidel. Paris Review 25 (1975): 56–95.

             Franklin, Anna. Personal interview. 3 Sept.
             1983.

APA   Lowell, R. (1975). [Interview with Frederick Sei-
             del]. Paris Review, 25, pp. 56–95.

When using APA style, you do not need to list personal interviews in your references list. Simply cite the person's name, "personal communication," and the date in parentheses in your text.

Writers—students and professionals alike—occasionally misuse sources by failing to acknowledge them properly. The word *plagiarism,* which derives from the Latin word for "kidnapping," refers to the unacknowledged use of another's words, ideas, or information. Students sometimes get into trouble because they mistakenly assume that plagiarizing occurs only when another writer's exact words are used without acknowledgment. Keep in mind, however, that depending on your topic and audience, you may need to indicate the source of any ideas or information you have taken note of in your research for a paper, even if you have paraphrased or summarized another's words rather than copied down direct quotations.

See pp. 507–08 for tips on keeping a working bibliography and taking notes.

Some people plagiarize simply because they do not know the conventions for using and acknowledging sources. This chapter makes clear how to incorporate sources into your writing and how to acknowledge your use of those sources. Others plagiarize because they keep sloppy notes and thus fail to distinguish between what is their own and what is their source's. Either they neglect to enclose their source's words in quotation marks or do not indicate when they are paraphrasing or summarizing a source's ideas and information. If you keep a working bibliography and careful notes, you will not make this serious mistake.

There is still another reason some people plagiarize: They fee unable to write the paper by themseslves. They feel overwhelmed by the writing task or by the deadline or by their own and others' expectations of them. This sense of inadequacy is not experienced by students alone. In a *Los Angeles Times* article on the subject, a journalist whose plagiarizing was discovered explained why he had done it. He said that when he read a column by another journalist on a subject he was preparing to write about, he felt that the other writer "said what I wanted to say and he said it better." If you experience this same anxiety about your work, speak to your instructor. Don't run the risk of failing a course or being expelled because of plagiarizing.

SOME SAMPLE RESEARCH PAPERS

As a writer you will have many occasions when you will want or need to use sources. You may be assigned to write a "research paper," complete with formal citation and documentation of outside sources. Several of the writing assignments in this book present logical opportunities to do library or field research—in other words, to turn to outside sources. Among the readings in Part I, those listed below cite and document sources. (The documentation style each follows is given in the parentheses.)

"Patriarchy in Puritan Family Life"
—by Steven Mintz and Susan Kellogg, pp. 144–47 (MLA)
"Schizophrenia: What It Looks Like, How It Feels"
—by Veronica Murayama, pp. 152–55 (APA)
"Children Need to Play, Not Compete"
—Jessica Statsky, pp. 190–93 (MLA)
"More Testing, More Learning"
—by Patrick O'Malley, pp. 230–33 (APA)
"Suicide among Young People"
—by Victor Fuchs, pp. 303–06 (APA)
"Where Will They Sleep Tonight?"
—by Kim Dartnell, pp. 308–10

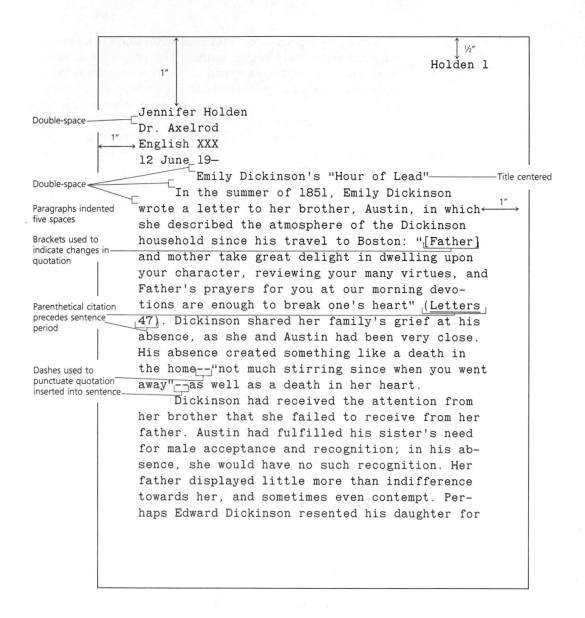

½"

Holden 1

Double-space

Jennifer Holden
Dr. Axelrod
English XXX
12 June 19—

1"

1"

Title centered

Double-space

Emily Dickinson's "Hour of Lead"

Paragraphs indented
five spaces

In the summer of 1851, Emily Dickinson
wrote a letter to her brother, Austin, in which
she described the atmosphere of the Dickinson

1"

Brackets used to
indicate changes in
quotation

household since his travel to Boston: "[Father]
and mother take great delight in dwelling upon
your character, reviewing your many virtues, and
Father's prayers for you at our morning devo-

Parenthetical citation
precedes sentence
period

tions are enough to break one's heart" (Letters
47). Dickinson shared her family's grief at his
absence, as she and Austin had been very close.
His absence created something like a death in
the home--"not much stirring since when you went

Dashes used to
punctuate quotation
inserted into sentence

away"--as well as a death in her heart.

Dickinson had received the attention from
her brother that she failed to receive from her
father. Austin had fulfilled his sister's need
for male acceptance and recognition; in his absence, she would have no such recognition. Her
father displayed little more than indifference
towards her, and sometimes even contempt. Perhaps Edward Dickinson resented his daughter for

AN ANNOTATED RESEARCH PAPER

Here is a student research paper on Emily Dickinson, in which the student
explores a recurrent theme she finds in Dickinson's poetry—a quest for recognition and understanding. The author cites primary and secondary
sources—Dickinson's letters and poems, a biography, and two works of literary criticism. She uses MLA documentation style.

Holden 2

being female. In a different letter to Austin,
Emily Dickinson wrote, "Father overheard some of
my intentions and said they were rather 'small'—
whether this remark was intended for the apples,
or for my noble self I did not think to ask
him . . ." (<u>Letters</u> 54). Never blind to her
father's insults or belittling comments about
her character or intelligence, she concluded by
saying "I rather think he intended to give us
both a cut."

Austin understood his sister's feelings
and, most important, her situation. He knew she
lived a sheltered life, stifled by the single-
mindedness of their mother and smothered by the
strictness of their father. While he lived at
home, Austin had shared with her secrets and
knowledge that she had been otherwise forbidden
to learn. Now that he was gone, all he could
give her was sympathy. When Emily wrote to Austin that "Father takes care of the doors and
mother of the windows, and Vinnie and I are se-
cure against all outward attacks" (<u>Letters</u> 47),
she knew that her brother would comprehend the
figurative meaning of her description. Her parents protected her and her sister to such an
extent that they became prisoners in their own
home. Although she made several attempts to
overcome this restrictive condition, it was a
situation that she ultimately found inescapable.
At the age of thirty-eight, she would insist
that the literary critic Thomas Wentworth Higginson travel to her because she was forbidden
to leave home alone, writing "I do not cross my

Marginal annotations:

Quotation reproduces original punctuation

Ellipsis used to indicate something left out of quotation

Completes quotation cited above; no need to repeat page reference

Quotation inserted in middle of sentence

Reference placed close to quotation, before punctuation

½″

Holden 3

Father's ground to any House or town" (<u>Letters</u>
197).

Poem 77 begins, "I never heard the word
'escape' / Without a quicker blood" (lines 1–2).
Although Dickinson's heart raced at the idea of
freedom, she was forced to add the words "But I
tug childish at my bars / Only to fail again"
(7–8). Freedom and autonomy represented unat-
tainable dreams, and she referred to her
"tug[ging]" as "childish" because her effort was
futile. The bars would never bend, and she would
never escape childhood. Dickinson found herself
perpetually treated as a child, patronized and
dominated by both the men and women in her life.
She felt powerless to change their attitudes or
change herself, having been conditioned since
birth to behave submissively and obediently.
Though she resented the subservient role, she
saw no other way to exist in Victorian society.

Writing allowed Dickinson to express her
pain, grief, and despair as well as her feelings
of injustice and resentment. In her day-to-day
life, she was forced to repress her emotions
just as she was forced to repress her physical
and intellectual capabilities, explaining to
Austin, "If we can get our hearts 'under' I
don't have much to fear--I've got all but three
feelings down, if I can only keep them!"
(<u>Letters</u> 47).

Dickinson's external being was completely
controlled, both by her father and by society.
Indeed, she looked and behaved according to Edward Dickinson's idea of what constituted a

Holden 4

woman. She was forbidden individuality and
creativity; as she remarked once, in a letter to
Higginson, "Father, too busy with his Briefs to
notice what we do—He buys me many Books—but begs
me not to read them—because he fears they boggle
the mind" (<u>Letters</u> 173).

Single space between title and page number. No *p.* used, and no punctuation separating title and number

In fact, her father paid her little attention, and when he did, it was either to scold or
instruct, never to compliment. It was treatment
that made her feel burdensome and insignificant,
and her poetry is filled with scenes of neglect
and endless longing for love.

Edward Dickinson could restrict his daughter's actions and suppress her emotions, but he
could not possess her mind. Emily Dickinson's
mind belonged solely to her. In poem 61, she
compares herself to a mouse, nibbling in "ser-
aphic Cupboards" while "unsuspecting Cycles /
Wheel solemnly away!" (6; 8—9). Here Dickinson
implies that her passive exterior did not hinder
her active interior. The wheels in her mind
turned incessantly no matter how "o-erpowered"
she felt. Poem 613 similarly demonstrates Dickinson's unconquerable inner life:

No need to repeat "lines" after first reference to poetry

Set off poetry of more than three lines

They shut me up in Prose—
As when a little Girl
They put me in the <u>Closet</u>—
Because they liked me <u>"still"</u>—

Double-space

Reproduce punctuation and capitalization of original source

Quadruple space between stanzas

Still! Could themself have peeped—
And seen my brain—go round—

Indent 10 spaces

Holden 5

Indent 10 spaces   They might as wise have lodged a Bird
                    For Treason—in the Pound—

                    Himself has but to will
                    And easy as a Star
                    Look down upon Captivity—
                    And laugh—No more have I— (1—12)

A bird "has but to will" away his captivity,
while Dickinson abolished hers through thinking
and writing. Unleashing her "Brain" and pen,
Dickinson rebelled against her father.
As Sandra Gilbert and Susan Gubar have written,
"In the context of a dramatic fiction, Dickinson
could metamorphose from a real person (to whom
aggressive speech is forbidden) into a series of
characters or supposed persons (for whom assertive speech must be supplied)" (584). Dickinson's mind and page served as the only places
where she could attain power and authority,
though the voice in many of her poems sounds
weak and inferior. Dickinson's voice varies from
poem to poem. In one poem, she may depict the
speaker as a martyr or heroine, while in another
the speaker may appear to be a docile wife or
servant.

        Marriage might have removed Dickinson from
her father's grasp; however, marriage would have
failed to give her even a glimpse of autonomy.
In her poetry, she portrays marriage as an escape from one kind of repression into another.
On the day of marriage, she writes in poem 1072,
a woman is "Born—Bridalled—Shrouded" (10). Mar-

Source cited parenthetically after block quotation

Explains language quoted in block; no need to repeat page reference

Names authors in sentence; parenthetical page reference placed at end of sentence

Holden 6

riage meant birth, an emancipation from one's
family; but it also meant death, a loss of
identity. In <u>Stealing the Language</u>, Alicia Ostriker asserts that "the perception that Romantic love tends to submerge rather than fulfill a
woman's identity begins to appear as far back as
. . . Emily Dickinson'' (61). "It's safer" to
be a "'wife,'" Dickinson remarks in poem 199
(4; 1). The "comfort," however, that accompanies
wifehood suggests numbness and inactivity. The
"wife" views life from "Behind this soft
Eclipse," no longer able to see imaginatively
(64). Once a woman becomes a "wife," she fails
to be perceived as anything else. Dickinson
longed for love, but she feared the containment
of wedded life.

Love itself appears as both the cure and
the cause of Dickinson's ailment. On one hand,
"Love is the Fellow of the Resurrection /
Scooping up the Dust and chanting 'Live'!"
(Poem 491: 9—10). Dickinson portrays herself as
being inanimate as dust, brought suddenly to
life by the power of affection. She continually
depicts herself as a valueless entity, unworthy
of romantic love. When love enters her life one
"Day at Summer's full," for example, she thinks
"that such were for the Saints, / Where Resur-
rections—be—(Poem 322: 1; 3—4). Love can provide
breath and meaning. But on the other hand,
Dickinson's speaker often welcomes love so
blindly that she neglects to realize its negative side-effects. Poem 303, for example, re-

---

Margin annotations:

Names title and author in sentence. Parenthetical page reference placed at end of sentence

Ellipsis used to indicate an omission

Sentence begins with quoted language

Quotation marks used within double quotation marks to indicate word appeared originally within quotation marks

Poem number given in parenthetical citation

Holden 7

veals the speaker's devotion to her selected
"Society" (1). After choosing "One" "from an
ample nation," she closes "the Valves of her
attention— / Like Stone—" (9—12). While the
speaker's dedication may be notable, her sacrifice seems too great. The consequence of her
loyalty is silence and stillness. Inadvertently,
she pinches off her own lifeforce, rolling a
stone over her senses. Ostriker writes:

> To love a man is to be dependent upon
> him. To be dependent is to be si-
> lenced. Prufrock believes he must
> speak, assuming a completeness and as-
> surance he does not have, to obtain
> feminine approval. Women, by contrast,
> feel that to gain male approval they
> must remain silent. (67)

Dickinson sees love as a way to revitalize her
life, when, in fact, it only succeeds in increasing her silence. In poem 430, she writes,
"Such bliss—had I" when love enters her life,
" 'Twas needless—any speak—" (7; 12). The "I" in
Dickinson's love poems rarely speaks to the man
she loves. Love has an effect on her similar to
grief. She becomes silent and immobile, falling
into a trancelike state. "Struck," "Maimed,"
"Robbed—was I," admits Dickinson in poem 925,
yet "I love the Cause that slew Me" (1; 5; 9;
17). She could not control her love for the unidentified man, though she allowed him to dev-
astate her. Eventually she may have realized
that love, instead of solving her problems,
would only intensify them.

Holden 8

In 1862, Dickinson wrote a series of poems on the tremendous pain of love-loss and love-lessness in which she continued to equate love with life, suggesting that without love her life was a living death. In poem 640, she writes, "I cannot live with You— / It would be Life— / And Life is over there" (1–3). In actuality, she could not "live" with the unnamed lover because he would not live with her. She did not turn away his love; she simply saw it as impossible to attain. Deprived of love, Dickinson sank into a world of darkness and solitude. "We grow accustomed to the Dark," she explains in poem 419 (1). Even the "larger [interior] Darknesses" become "almost" bearable. Poem 341 epitomizes Dickinson's hopeless condition, showing how a "formal feeling" sweeps over her, deadening her "Nerves" and stiffening her "Heart" (1–3). She walks through each day "mechanical[ly]," without thought or emotion, displaying a "contentment, like a stone" (5; 9). The "Hour of Lead" she describes occurred "after great pain" and seems to have lasted a lifetime (10; 2). She continued to perform "Life's little duties" as if they "were infinite" (Poem 443: 2; 4). Nevertheless, "Existence—some way back— / Stopped—struck—[her] ticking" (11–12), so that while she appeared to live and function normally, she really moved through life in an absentminded daydream. "We do life's labor—. . . With scrupulous exactness" (30–31), she wrote, simply "To hold our Senses—on" (32).

Movement served as a distraction from her suffering. Falling into routines allowed her to

Poetry of three lines is integrated into sentence, with slashes to indicate line breaks

Brackets used to indicate change in quotation to make it fit grammatically into the sentence

Quotes open and close sentence, interrupted by identifying phrase

endure life, though not to experience it. She
found experience impossible, when "a pain—so
utter" dominated her soul (Poem 599:1). Choosing
to live "as one within a Swoon" (6), she knew
that a confrontation with reality would have
"drop[ped her]—Bone by Bone" (8). Numbness acted
as a balm capable of convering her pain tempo-
rarily, but incapable of providing a cure.

   Dickinson's life was a quest for love,
recognition, and human understanding. One of her
biggest fears was of dying "noteless" (Poem
486:17), without her poetic ability ever having
been recognized. Although she declined to publish, her poetry was her attempt to communicate
with the world. She longed for someone to empathize with her, for someone to acknowledge her
as "'Emily'" (Poem 227:9) instead of merely ca-
tegorizing her as "woman." She never married—
perhaps by choice, perhaps from chance, perhaps
out of fear—and she seems never to have received
romantic attention from a man. The only deep
bond with a male that she experienced was with
her brother Austin. From her father, she received neither love nor gentleness, a lapse that
had lasting effects on her self-esteem. Never
did Emily Dickinson recover from her childhood
neglect, moving through life externally placid
and internally haunted. Although she yearned for
"The Might of Human love" (Poem 1648:4), her
poetry reveals that she spent her life meditat-
ing on its absence.

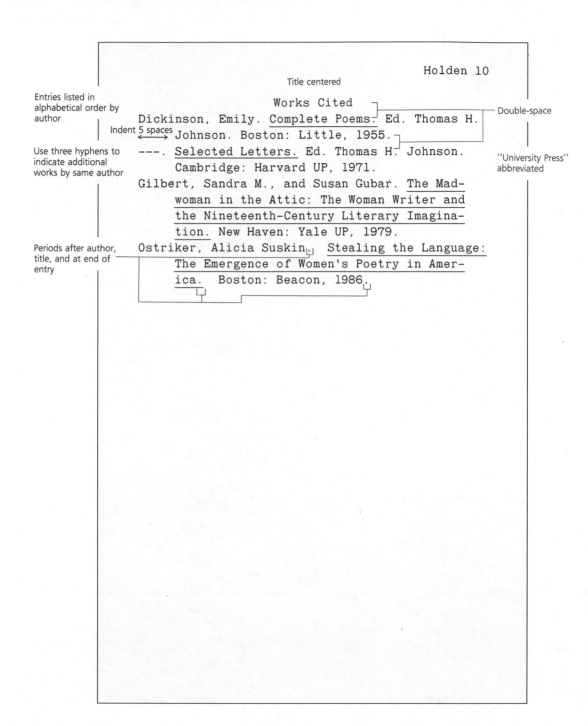

Holden 10

Title centered

Works Cited

Entries listed in alphabetical order by author

Dickinson, Emily. Complete Poems. Ed. Thomas H.

Indent 5 spaces → Johnson. Boston: Little, 1955.

Use three hyphens to indicate additional works by same author

---. Selected Letters. Ed. Thomas H. Johnson. Cambridge: Harvard UP, 1971.

Gilbert, Sandra M., and Susan Gubar. The Madwoman in the Attic: The Woman Writer and the Nineteenth-Century Literary Imagination. New Haven: Yale UP, 1979.

Periods after author, title, and at end of entry

Ostriker, Alicia Suskin. Stealing the Language: The Emergence of Women's Poetry in America. Boston: Beacon, 1986.

Double-space

"University Press" abbreviated

PART FOUR

Writing
under Pressure

E ven though the machine-scorable multiple-choice test has sharply reduced the number of essay exams administered in schools and colleges,
you can be certain that essay exams will continue to play a significant role
in the education of liberal arts students. Many instructors—especially in the
humanities and social sciences—still believe an exam that requires you to
write is the best way to find out what you have learned and, more important,
how you can use what you have learned. Instructors who give essay exams
want to be sure you can sort through the large body of information covered
in a course, identify what is important or significant, and explain your decision. They want to see whether you understand the concepts that provide
the basis for a course and whether you can use those concepts to interpret
specific materials, to make connections on your own, to see relationships, to
draw comparisons and find contrasts, to synthesize diverse information in
support of an original assertion. They may even be interested in your ability
to justify your own evaluations based on appropriate criteria and to argue
your own opinions with convincing evidence. Remember that your instructors hope they are encouraging you to think more critically and analytically
about a subject; they feel therefore that a written exam best allows you to
demonstrate that you are doing so.

As a college student, then, you will be faced with a variety of essay exams,
from short-answer identifications of a few sentences to take-home exams that
may require hours of planning and writing. You will find that the writing
activities and strategies discussed in Parts I and II of this book—particularly
reporting information, illustrating, defining, comparing and contrasting, and
arguing—as well as the mapping strategies in Chapter 11 describe the skills
that will help you do well on all sorts of these exams. This chapter proposes
some more specific guidelines for you to follow in preparing for and writing
essay exams, and analyzes a group of typical exam questions to help you
determine which strategies will be most useful.

But you can also learn a great deal from your experiences with essay
exams in the past, the embarrassment and frustration of doing poorly on one
and the great pleasure and pride of doing well. Do you recall the very best
exam you ever wrote? Do you remember how you wrote it and why you
were able to do so well? How can you be certain to approach such writing
tasks confidently and to complete them successfully? Keep these questions in
mind as you consider the following guidelines.

Essay Examinations 22

PREPARING FOR AN EXAM

First of all, essay exams require a comprehensive understanding of large amounts of information. Since exam questions can reach so widely into the course materials—and in such unpredictable ways—you cannot hope to do well on them if you do not keep up with readings and assignments from the beginning of the course. Do the reading, go to lectures, take careful notes, participate in discussion sections, organize small study groups with classmates to explore and review course materials throughout the semester. Trying to cram weeks of information into a single night of study will never allow you to do your best.

Then, as an exam approaches, find out what you can about the form it will take. There is little that is more irritating to instructors than the pestering inquiry, "Do we need to know this for the exam?"; but it is generally legitimate to ask whether the questions will require short or long answers, how many questions there will be, whether you may choose which questions to answer, and what kinds of thinking and writing will be required of you. Some instructors may hand out study guides for exams, or even lists of potential questions. However, you will often be on your own in determining how best to go about studying.

Try to avoid simply memorizing information aimlessly. As you study, you should be clarifying the important issues of the course and using these issues to focus your understanding of specific facts and particular readings. If the course is a historical survey, distinguish the primary periods and try to see relations among the periods and the works or events that define them. If the course is thematically unified, determine how the particular materials you have been reading express those themes. If the course is a broad introduction to a general topic, concentrate on the central concerns of each study unit and see what connections you can discover among the various units. Try to place all you have learned into perspective, into a meaningful context. How do the pieces fit together? What fundamental ideas have the readings, the lectures, and the discussions seemed to emphasize? How can those ideas help you digest the information the course has covered?

One good way to prepare yourself for an exam is by making up questions you think the instructor might give and then planning answers to them with classmates. Returning to your notes and to assigned readings with specific questions in mind can help enormously in your process of understanding. The important thing to remember is that an essay exam tests more than your memory of specific information; it requires you to use specific information to demonstrate a comprehensive grasp of the topics covered in the course.

READING THE EXAM CAREFULLY

Before you answer a single question, read the entire exam and apportion your time realistically. Pay particular attention to how many points you may earn in different parts of the exam; notice any directions that suggest how long an answer should be or how much space it should take up. As you are doing so, you may wish to make tentative choices of the questions you will answer and decide on the order in which you will answer them. If you have immediate ideas about how you would organize any of your answers, you might also jot down partial scratch outlines. But before you start to complete any answers, write down the actual clock time you expect to be working on each question or set of questions. Careful time management is crucial to your success on essay exams; giving some time to each question is always better than using up your time on only a few and never getting to others.

You will next need to analyze each question carefully before beginning to write your answer. Decide what you are being asked to do. It can be easy at this point to become flustered, to lose concentration, even to go blank, if your immediate impulse is to cast about for ideas indiscriminately. But if you first look closely at what the question is directing you to do and try to understand the sort of writing that will be required, you can begin to recognize the structure your answer will need to take. This tentative structure will help focus your attention on the particular information that will be pertinent to your answer. Consider this question from a sociology final:

> Drawing from lectures on the contradictory aspects of American values, discussions of the "bureaucratic personality" and the type of behavior associated with social mobility, discuss the problems of bettering oneself in a relatively "open," complex, industrial society such as the United States.

Such a question can cause momentary panic, but you nearly always can define the writing task you face. Look first at the words that give you directions: *draw from* and *discuss*. The term *discuss* is fairly vague, of course, but here it probably invites you to list and explain the problems of bettering oneself. The categories of these problems are already identified in the opening phrases: contradictory values, bureaucratic personality, certain behavior. Therefore, you would plan to begin with an assertion (or thesis) that included the key words in the final clause (bettering oneself in an open, complex, industrial society) and then take up each category of problem—and maybe still other problems you can think of—in separate paragraphs.

This question essentially calls for recall, organization, and clear presentation of facts from lectures and readings. Though it looks confusing at first, once it is sorted out, it contains the key terms for the answer's thesis, as well as its main points of development. In the next section are some further examples of the kinds of questions often found on essay exams. Pay particular attention to how the directions and the key words in each case can help you define the writing task involved.

SOME TYPICAL ESSAY EXAM QUESTIONS

Following are nine categories of exam questions, divided according to the sort of writing task involved and illustrated by examples. You will notice that, although the wording of the examples in a category may differ, the essential directions are very much the same.

All of the examples are unedited and were written by instructors in six different departments in the humanities and social sciences at two different state universities. Drawn from short quizzes, mid-terms, and final exams for a variety of freshman and sophomore courses, these questions demonstrate the range of writing you may be expected to do on exams.

Define or Identify Some questions require you to write a few sentences defining or identifying material from readings or lectures. Almost always such questions allow you only a very few minutes to complete your answer.

You may be asked for a brief overview of a large topic, as in Question 22.1. This question, from a twenty-minute quiz in a literature course, could have earned as much as 15 of the 100 points possible on the quiz:

Question 22.1

Name and describe the three stages of African literature.

Answering this question would simply involve following the specific directions. A student would probably *name* the periods in historical order and then *describe* each period in a separate sentence or two.

Other questions, like 22.2, will supply a list of specific items to identify. This example comes from a final exam in a communications course, and the answer to each part was worth as much as 4 points on a 120-point exam.

Question 22.2
Define and state some important facts concerning each of the following:
   A. demographics
   B. instrumental model
   C. RCA
   D. telephone booth of the air
   E. penny press

With no more than three or four minutes for each part, students taking this exam would offer a concise definition (probably in a sentence). Then that definition would be briefly expanded with facts relevant to the main topics in the course.

Sometimes the list of items to be identified can be quite complicated, including quotes, concepts, and specialized terms; it may also be worth a significant number of points. The next example illustrates the first five items in a list of fifteen that opened a literature final. Each item was worth 3 points, for a total of 45 out of a possible 130 points.

Question 22.3

Identify each of the following items:
1. projection
2. "In this vast landscape he had loved so much, he was alone."
3. Balducci
4. *pied noir*
5. the Massif Central

Although the directions do not say so specifically, it is crucial here not only to identify each item but also to explain its significance in terms of the overall subject. In composing a definition or identification, always ask yourself a simple question: Why is this item important enough to be on the exam?

Recall Details of a Specific Source

Sometimes instructors will ask for a straightforward summary or paraphrase of a specific source—a report, for example, or a book or film. Such questions hold the student to recounting details directly from the source and do not encourage interpretation or evaluation. In the following example from a sociology exam, students were allowed about ten minutes and required to complete the answer on one lined page provided with the exam.

Question 22.4

In his article, "Is There a Culture of Poverty?," Oscar Lewis addresses a popular question in the social sciences. What is the "culture of poverty"? How is it able to come into being, according to Lewis? That is, under what conditions does it exist? When does he say a person is no longer a part of the culture of poverty? What does Lewis say is the future of the culture of poverty?

The phrasing here invites a fairly clear-cut structure. Each of the five specific questions can be turned into an assertion and illustrated with evidence from Lewis's book. For example, the first two questions could become assertions like these: "Lewis defines the culture of poverty as _____ ," and "According to Lewis the culture of poverty comes into being through _____ ." The important thing in this case is to stick closely to an accurate summary of what the writer said and not waste time evaluating or criticizing his ideas.

Explain the Importance or Significance

Another kind of essay exam question asks students to explain the importance of something covered in the course. Such questions require you to use specific examples as the basis for a more general discussion of what has been studied. This will often involve interpreting a literary work by concentrating on a particular aspect of it, as in Question 22.5. This question was worth 10 out of 100 points and was to be answered in 75 to 100 words:

Question 22.5

> In the last scene in *The Paths of Glory*, the owner of a cafe brings a young German girl onto a small stage in his cafe to sing for the French troops, while Colonel Dax looks on from outside the cafe. Briefly explain the significance of this scene in relation to the movie as a whole.

In answering this question, a student's first task would be to reconsider the whole movie, looking for ways this one small scene illuminates or explains larger issues or themes. Then, in a paragraph or two, the student would summarize these themes and point out how each element of the specific scene fits into the overall context.

You may also be asked to interpret specific information to show that you understand the fundamental concepts of a course. The following example from a communications mid-term was worth a possible 10 of 100 points and was allotted twenty minutes of exam time.

Question 22.6

> Chukovsky gives many examples of cute expressions and statements uttered by small children. Give an example or two of the kind of statements that he finds interesting. Then state their implications for understanding the nature of language in particular and communications more generally.

Here, the student must start by choosing examples of children's utterances from Chukovsky's book. These examples would then provide the basis for demonstrating one's grasp of the larger subject.

Questions like these are usually more challenging than definition and summary questions because you must decide for yourself the significance or importance or implications of the information. You must also consider how best to organize your answer so that the general ideas you need to communicate are clearly developed.

Apply Concepts

Very often courses in the humanities and social sciences emphasize significant themes, ideologies, or concepts. A common essay exam question asks students to apply the concepts to works studied in the course. Rather than providing specific information to be interpreted more generally, such questions will present you with a general idea and require you to illustrate it with specific examples from your reading.

On a literature final, an instructor posed this writing task. It was worth 50 points out of 100, and students had about an hour to complete it.

Question 22.7

Many American writers have portrayed their characters or their poetic speaker as being engaged in a quest. The quest may be explicit or implicit, external or psychological, and it may end in failure or success. Analyze the quest motif in the work of four of the following writers: Edwards, Franklin, Hawthorne, Thoreau, Douglass, Whitman, Dickinson, James, Twain.

On another literature final, the following question was worth 45 of 130 points. Students had about forty-five minutes to answer it.

Question 22.8

Several works studied in this course depict scapegoat figures. Select two written works and two films and discuss how their authors or directors present and analyze the social conflicts that lead to the creation of scapegoats.

Question 22.7 instructs students to *analyze,* Question 22.8 to *discuss;* yet the answers for each would be structured very similarly. An introductory paragraph would define the concept—the *quest* or a *scapegoat*—and refer to the works to be discussed. Then a paragraph or two would be devoted to each of the works, developing specific evidence to illustrate the concept. A concluding paragraph would probably attempt to bring the concept into clearer focus, which is, after all, the point of answering these questions.

Comment on a Quotation

On essay exams, an instructor will often ask students to comment on quotations they are seeing for the first time. Usually such quotations will express some surprising or controversial opinion that complements or challenges basic principles or ideas in the course. Sometimes the writer being quoted is identified, sometimes not. In fact, it is not unusual for instructors to write the quotation themselves.

A student choosing to answer the following question from a literature final would have risked half the exam—in points and time—on the outcome.

Question 22.9

Argue for or against this thesis: "In *A Clockwork Orange,* both the heightened, poetic language and the almost academic concern with moral and political theories deprive the story of most of its relevance to real life."

The directions here clearly ask for an argument. A student would need to set up a thesis indicating that the novel either is or is not relevant to real life, and then point out how its language and its theoretical concerns can be viewed in light of this thesis.

The next example comes from a mid-term exam in a history course. Students had forty minutes to write their answers, which could earn as much as 70 points on a 100-point exam.

Question 22.10

"Some historians believe that economic hardship and oppression breed social revolt; but the experience of the United States and Mexico between 1900 and 1920 suggests that people may rebel also during times of prosperity."

Comment on this statement. Why did large numbers of Americans and Mexicans wish to change conditions in their countries during the years from 1900 to 1920? How successful were their efforts? Who benefited from the changes that took place?

Although here students are instructed to "comment," the three questions suggest evidence to be used in constructing an argument. Just as in Question 22.9, a successful answer will require a clear thesis stating a position on the views expressed in the quotation, specific reasons to support that thesis, and evidence from readings and lectures to argue for the reasons. In general, such questions don't require a "right" answer: whether you agree or disagree with the quotation is not as important as whether you can argue your case reasonably and convincingly, demonstrating a firm grasp of the subject matter.

Compare and Contrast

It could well be that instructors' most favored essay exam question is one that requires a comparison or contrast of two or three principles, ideas, works, activities, or phenomena. This kind of question requires you to explore fully the relations between things of importance in the course, to analyze each thing separately and then search out specific points of likeness or difference. Students must, thus, show a thorough knowledge of the things being compared, as well as a clear understanding of the basic issues on which comparisons and contrasts can be made.

Often, as in Question 22.11, the basis of comparison will be limited to a particular focus; here, for example, two works are to be compared in terms of their views of colonialism.

Question 22.11

Compare and analyze the views of colonialism presented in Memmi's *The Colonizer and the Colonized* and Pontecorvo's *The Battle of Algiers*. Are there significant differences between these two views?

Sometimes instructors will simply identify what is to be compared, leaving students the task of choosing the basis of the comparison, as in the next three examples from communications, history, and literature exams.

Question 22.12

In what way is the stage of electronic media fundamentally different from all the major stages that preceded it?

Question 22.13

What was the role of the United States in Cuban affairs from 1898 until 1959? How did our role there compare with our role in the rest of Spanish America during the same period?

Question 22.14

Write an essay on one of the following topics:
1. Squire Western and Mr. Knightley
2. Dr. Primrose and Mr. Elton

See Chapter 17 for more on comparing and contrasting.

Whether the point of comparison is stated in the question or left for you to define for yourself, it is important that your answer be limited to those aspects of likeness or difference that are most relevant to the general concepts or themes covered in the course.

Synthesize Information from Various Sources

In a course with several assigned readings, an instructor may give students an essay exam question that requires them to pull together (to synthesize) information from all the readings.

The following example was one of four required questions on a final exam in a course in Third World studies. Students had about thirty minutes to complete their answer.

Question 22.15

On the basis of the articles read on El Salvador, Nicaragua, Peru, Chile, Argentina, and Mexico, what would you say are the major problems confronting Latin America today? Discuss the major types of problems with references to particular countries as examples.

See p. 402 for information on forecasting statements.

This question asks students to do a lot in thirty minutes. They must first decide which major problems to discuss, which countries to include in each discussion, and how to use evidence from many readings to develop their answers. A carefully developed forecasting statement will be essential to developing a coherent essay.

Analyze Causes

In humanities and social science courses much of what students study concerns the causes of trends, actions, and events. Hence, it is not too surprising to find questions about causes on essay exams. In such cases, the instructor expects students to analyze causes from readings and lectures. These examples come from mid-term and final exams in literature, communications, and sociology courses:

Question 22.16

Why do Maurice and Jean not succumb to the intolerable conditions of the prison camp (the Camp of Hell) as most of the others do?

Question 22.17

Given that we occupy several positions in the course of our lives and given that each position has a specific role attached to it, what kinds of problems or dilemmas arise from those multiple roles and how are they handled?

Question 22.18

Explain briefly the relationship between the institution of slavery and the emergence of the blues as a new African-American musical expression.

Question 22.19

Analyze the way in which an uncritical promotion of the new information technology (computers, satellites, etc.) may support, unintentionally, the maintenance of the status quo.

These questions are presented in several ways ("why," "what kind of problem," "explain the relationship," "analyze the way"), but they all require a list of causes in the answer. The causes would be organized under a thesis statement, and each cause would be argued and supported with evidence from lectures or readings.

Chapter 9 presents strategies for analyzing causes.

Criticize or Evaluate

Occasionally instructors will invite students to evaluate a concept or work. Nearly always they want more than opinion: they expect a reasoned, documented judgment based on appropriate criteria. Such questions not only test students' ability to recall and synthesize pertinent information; they also allow instructors to find out whether students can apply criteria taught in the course, whether they understand the standards of judgment that are basic to the subject matter.

On a final exam in a literature course a student might have chosen one of the following questions about novels read in the course. Each would have been worth half the total points, with about an hour to answer it:

Question 22.20

Which has the more effective plot: *The Secret Agent* or *A Passage to India*?

Question 22.21

A Clockwork Orange and *The Comfort of Strangers* both attempt to examine the nature of modern decadence. Which does so more successfully?

To answer these questions successfully, students would obviously have to be very familiar with the novels under discussion. They would also have to establish criteria appropriate to evaluating an effective plot or a successful examination of modern decadence. Students would initially have to make a judgment favoring one novel over the other (although such a judgment need not cast one novel as a "terrible" and the other as a "perfect" illustration). The answer would then give reasons for this judgment, argue each reason with evidence from the novels, and probably use the writing strategies of comparison and contrast to develop the discussion.

This next question was worth 10 of 85 points on a communications midterm. Students were asked to answer "in two paragraphs."

Question 22.22

Eisenstein and Mukerji both argue that moveable print was important to the rise of Protestantism. Cole extends this argument to say that print set off a chain of events that was important to the history of the United States. Summarize this argument, and criticize any part of it if you choose.

Evaluative questions like these involve the same sorts of writing strategies as those discussed in Chapter 8.

Here students are asked to criticize or evaluate an argument in several course readings. The instructor wants to know what students think of this argument and also, even though this is not stated, why they judge it as they do. Answering this unwritten "why" part of the question is the challenge: students must come up with reasons appropriate to evaluating the arguments and with evidence to support their reasons.

PLANNING YOUR ANSWER

The amount of planning you do for a question will depend on how much time it is allotted and how many points it is worth. For short-answer definitions and identifications, a few seconds of thought will probably be sufficient. (Be careful not to puzzle too long over individual items like these. Skip over any you cannot recognize fairly quickly; often, answering other questions will help jog your memory.) For answers that require a paragraph or two, you may want to jot down several ideas and examples to focus your thoughts and give you a basis for organizing your information.

See pp. 383–87 for information on clustering and outlining.

For longer answers, though, you will need to develop a much more definite strategy of organization. You have time for only one draft, so allow a reasonable period—as much as a quarter of the time allotted the question—for making notes, determining a thesis, and developing an outline. Jotting down pertinent ideas is a good way to begin; then you can plan your organization with a scratch outline (just a listing of points or facts) or a cluster.

For questions with several parts (different requests or directions, a sequence of questions), make a list of the parts so that you do not miss or minimize one part. For questions presented as questions (rather than directives) you might want to rephrase each question as a writing topic. These topics will often suggest how you should outline the answer.

You may have to try two or three outlines or clusters before you hit on a workable plan. But be realistic as you outline—you want a plan you can develop within the limited time allotted for your answer. Hence, your outline will have to be selective—not everything you know on the topic, but what you know that can be developed clearly within the time available.

WRITING YOUR ANSWER

As with planning, your strategy for writing depends on the length of your answer. For short identifications and definitions, it is usually best to start with a general identifying statement and then move on to describe specific applications or explanations. Two sentences will almost always suffice, but make sure you write complete sentences.

For longer answers, begin by stating your forecasting statement or thesis clearly and explicitly. An essay exam is not an occasion for indirectness: you want to strive for focus, simplicity, and clarity. In stating your point and developing your answer use key terms from the question; it may look as though you are avoiding the question unless you use key terms (the same key terms) throughout your essay. If the question does not supply any key terms, you will find that you have provided your own by stating your main point. Use these key terms throughout the answer.

If you have devised a promising outline for your answer, then you will be able to forecast your overall plan and its subpoints in your opening sentences. Forecasting always impresses readers and has the very practical advantage of making your answer easier to read. You might also want to use briefer paragraphs than you ordinarily do and signal clear relations between paragraphs with transition phrases or sentences.

Strategies for cueing the reader are presented in Chapter 12.

As you begin writing your answer, freely strike out words or even sentences you want to change by drawing through them neatly with a single line. Do not stop to erase, and try not to be messy. Instructors do not expect flawless writing, but they are put off by unnecessary messiness.

As you move ahead with the writing, you will certainly think of new subpoints and new ideas or facts to include later in the paper. Stop briefly to make a note of these on your original outline. If you find that you want to add a sentence or two to sections you have already completed, write them sideways in the margin or at the top of the page, with a neat arrowed line to show where they fit in your answer.

Do not pad your answer with irrelevancies and repetitions just to fill up space. You may have had one instructor who did not seem to pay much attention to what you wrote, but most instructors read exams carefully and are not impressed by the length of an answer alone. Within the time available, write a comprehensive, specific answer without padding.

Watch the clock carefully to ensure that you do not spend too much time on one answer. You must be realistic about the time constraints of an essay exam, especially if you know the material well and are prepared to write a lot. If you write one dazzling answer on an exam with three required questions, you earn only 33 points, not enough to pass at most colleges. This may seem unfair, but keep in mind that instructors plan exams to be reasonably comprehensive. They want you to write about the course materials in two or three or more ways, not just one way.

If you run out of time when you are writing an answer, jot down the remaining main ideas from your outline, just to show that you know the material and with more time could have continued your exposition.

Write legibly and proofread. Remember that your instructor will likely be reading a large pile of exams. Careless scrawls, misspellings, omitted words, and missing punctuation (especially missing periods needed to mark the ends of sentences) will only make that reading difficult, even exasperating. A few seconds of careful proofreading can improve your grade.

MODEL ANSWERS TO SOME TYPICAL ESSAY EXAM QUESTIONS

Here we will analyze several successful answers and give you an opportunity to analyze one for yourself. These analyses, along with the information we have provided elsewhere in this chapter, should greatly improve your chances of writing successful answers.

Short Answers

A literature mid-term opened with ten items to identify, each worth 3 points. Students had about two minutes for each item. Here are three of freshman Brenda Gossett's answers, each one earning her the full 3 points.

> *Rauffenstein:* He was the German general who was in charge of the castle where Boeldieu, Marical, and Rosenthal were finally sent in *The Grand Illusion*. He along with Boeldieu represented the aristocracy, which was slowly fading out at that time.
>
> *Iges Peninsula:* This peninsula is created by the Meuse River in France. It is there that the Camp of Hell was created in *The Debacle*. The Camp of Hell is where the French army was interned after the Germans defeated them in the Franco-Prussian War.
>
> *Pache:* He was the "religious peasant" in the novel *The Debacle*. It was he who inevitably became a scapegoat when he was murdered by Loubet, LaPoulle, and Chouteau because he wouldn't share his bread with them.

The instructor said only "identify the following" but clearly wanted both identification and significance of the item to the work in which it appeared. Gosset gives both and gets full credit. She mentions particular works, characters, and events. Though she is very rushed, she answers in complete sentences. She does not misspell any words or leave out any commas or periods. Her answers are complete and correct.

Paragraph-length Answers

One question on a weekly literature quiz was worth 20 points of the total of 100. With only a few minutes to answer the question, students were instructed to "answer in a few sentences." Here is the question and Camille Prestera's answer:

> In *Things Fall Apart,* how did Okonkwo's relationship with his father affect his attitude toward his son?

> Okonkwo despised his father, who was lazy, cowardly, and in debt. Okonkwo tried to be everything his father wasn't. He was hard-working, wealthy, and a great warrior and wrestler. Okonkwo treated his son harshly because he was afraid he saw the same weakness in Nwoye that he despised in his father. The result of this harsh treatment was that Nwoye left home.

Prestera begins by describing Okonkwo and his father, contrasting the two sharply. Then she explains Okonkwo's relationship with his son Nwoye. Her answer is coherent and straightforward.

Long Answers

On final exams, at least one question requiring an essay-length answer is not uncommon. John Pixley had an hour to plan and write this essay for a final exam in a literature course.

Question

> Many American writers have portrayed their characters or their poetic speaker as being engaged in a quest. The quest may be explicit or implicit, external or psychological, and it may end in failure or success. Analyze the quest motif in the work of four of the following writers: Edwards, Franklin, Hawthorne, Thoreau, Douglass, Whitman, Dickinson, James, Twain.

John Pixley's Answer

Key term *(quest)* is mentioned in introduction and thesis.

First writer is identified immediately.

> Americans pride themselves on being ambitious and on being able to strive for goals and to tap their potentials. Some say that this is what the "American Dream" is all about. It is important for one to do and be all that one is capable of. This entails a quest or search for identity, experience, and happiness. Hence, the idea of the quest is a vital one in America, and it can be seen as a theme throughout American literature.   1

> In eighteenth-century Colonial America, Jonathan Edwards dealt with this theme in his autobiographical and personal writings. Unlike his fiery and hard-nosed sermons, these autobiographical writings present a sensitive, vulnerable man trying to find himself and his proper, satisfying place in the world. He is concerned with his spir-   2

Edwards's work and the details of his quest are presented.

itual growth, in being free to find and explore religious experience and happiness. For example, in *Personal Narrative,* he very carefully traces the stages of religious beliefs. He tells about periods of abandoned ecstasy, doubts, and rational revelations. He also notes that his best insights and growth came at times when he was alone in the wilderness, in nature. Edwards's efforts to find himself in relation to the world can also be seen in his "Observations of the Natural World," in which he relates various meticulously observed and described natural phenomena to religious precepts and occurrences. Here, he is trying to give the world and life, in which he is a part, some sense of meaning and purpose.

Transition sentence identifies second writer. Key term is repeated.

Contrast with Edwards adds coherence to essay.

Another key term *(external)* from the question is included.

Franklin's particular kind of quest is described.

Although he was a contemporary of Edwards, Benjamin Franklin, who was very involved in the founding of the U.S. as a nation, had a different conception of the quest in his writings. He sees the quest as being one for practical accomplishment, success, and wealth. In his *Autobiography,* he stresses that happiness involves working hard to accomplish things, getting along with others, and establishing a good reputation. Unlike Edwards's, his quest is external and bound up with society. He is concerned with his morals and behavior, but, as seen in Part 2 of the *Autobiography,* he deals with them in an objective, pragmatic, even statistical way, rather than in sensitive pondering. It is also evident in this work that Franklin, unlike Edwards, believes so much in himself and his quest that he is able to laugh at himself. His concern in this society can be seen in *Poor Richard's Almanac,* in which he gives practical advice on how to find success and happiness in the world, how to "be healthy, wealthy, and wise."

3

Transition sentence identifies third writer. Key term is repeated.

Comparison of Whitman to Edwards and Franklin sustains coherence of essay.

Still another version of the quest can be seen in the poetry of Walt Whitman in the mid-nineteenth century. The quest that he portrays blends elements of those of Edwards and Franklin. In "Song of Myself," which clearly is autobiographical, the speaker emphasizes the importance of finding, knowing, and enjoying oneself as part of nature and the human community. He says that one should come to realize that one is lovable, just as are all other people and all of nature and life. This is a quest for sensitivity and awareness, as Edwards advocates, and for great self-confidence, as Franklin advocates. Along with Edwards, Whitman sees that peaceful isolation in nature is important; but he also sees the importance of interacting

4

Whitman's quest is defined.

with people, as Franklin does. Being optimistic and feel-ing good--both in the literal and figurative sense--is the object of this quest. Unfortunately, personal disappoint-ment and national crisis (i.e., the Civil War) shattered Whitman's sense of confidence, and he lost the impetus of this quest in his own life.

Transition: key term is repeated and fourth writer is identified.

Quest of James charac-ter is described.

This theme of the quest can be seen in prose fiction   5
as well as in poetry and autobiography. One interesting example is "The Beast in the Jungle," a short story writ-ten by Henry James around 1903. It is interesting in that the principal character, John Marcher, not only fails in his life-long quest, but his failure comes about in a most subtle and frustrating way. Marcher believes that some-thing momentous is going to happen in his future. He talks about his belief to only one person, a woman named May. May decides to befriend him for life and watch with him for the momentous occurrence to come about, for "the beast in the jungle" to "pounce." As time passes, May seems to know what this occurrence is and eventually even says that it has happened; but John is still in the dark. It is only long after May's death that the beast pounces on him in his recognition that the "beast" was his failure to truly love May, the one woman of his life, even though she gave him all the encouragement that she possibly, decently could. Marcher never defined the terms of his quest until it was too late. By just waiting and watching, he failed to find feeling and passion. This tragic realization, as someone like Whitman would view it, brings John Marcher's ruin.

Conclusion repeats key term.

As seen in these few examples, the theme of the quest   6
is a significant one in American literature. Also obvious is the fact that there are a variety of approaches to, methods used in, and outcomes of the quest. This is an ap-propriate theme for American literature since Americans cherish the right to "the pursuit of happiness."

This is a strong answer for two reasons: (1) Pixley has the information he needs, and (2) he has organized it carefully and presented it coherently.

EXERCISE 22.1

The following essay was written by Don Hepler. He is answering the same essay exam question as his classmate John Pixley. Analyze Hepler's essay to discover whether it meets the criteria of a good essay exam answer. Review the criteria earlier in this chapter under "Writing Your Answer" and in the annotated commentary of John Pixley's answer. Try to identify the features of Hepler's essay that contribute to its success.

Don Hepler's Answer

The quest motif is certainly important in American literature. By considering Franklin, Thoreau, Douglass, and Twain, we can see that the quest may be explicit or implicit, external or psychological, a failure or a success. Tracing the quest motif through these four authors seems to show a developing concern in American literature with transcending materialism to address deeper issues. It also reveals a drift toward ambiguity and pessimism.   1

Benjamin Franklin's quest, as revealed by his *Autobiography,* is for material comfort and outward success. His quest may be considered an explicit one, because he announces clearly what he is trying to do: perfect a systematic approach for living long and happily. The whole *Autobiography* is a road map intended for other people to use as a guide; Franklin apparently meant rather literally for people to imitate his methods. He wrote with the assumption that his success was reproducible. He is possibly the most optimistic author in American literature, because he enjoys life, knows exactly *why* he enjoys life, and believes that anyone else willing to follow his formula may enjoy life as well.   2

By Franklin's standards, his quest is clearly a success. But his *Autobiography* portrays only an external, not a psychological success. This is not to suggest that Franklin was a psychological failure. Indeed, we have every reason to believe the contrary. But the fact remains that Franklin *wrote* only about external success; he never indicated how he really felt, emotionally. Possibly it was part of Franklin's overriding optimism to assume that material comfort leads naturally to emotional fulfillment.   3

Henry David Thoreau presents a more multifaceted quest. His *Walden* is, on the simplest level, the chronicle of Thoreau's physical journey out of town and into the woods. But the moving itself is not the focus of *Walden.* It is really more of a metaphor for some kind of spiritual quest going on within Thoreau's mind. Most of the action in *Walden* is mental, as Thoreau contemplates and philosophizes, always using the lake, the woods, and his own daily actions as symbols of higher, more eternal truths.   4

This spiritual quest is a success, in that Thoreau is able
to appreciate the beauty of nature, and to see through
much of the sham and false assumptions of town life and
blind materialism.

Thoreau does not leave us with nearly as explicit a   5
"blueprint" for success as does Franklin. Even Franklin's
plan is limited to people of high intelligence, personal
discipline, and sound character; Franklin sometimes seems
to forget that many human beings are in fact weak and
evil, and so would stand little chance of success similar
to his own. But at least Franklin's quest could be dupli-
cated by another Franklin. Thoreau's quest is more problematic, for even as great a mystic and naturalist as Thoreau himself could not remain in the woods indefinitely.
This points toward the idea that the real quest is all internal and psychological; Thoreau seems to have gone to
the woods to develop a spiritual strength that he could
keep and take elsewhere on subsequent dealings with the
"real world."

The quest of Frederick Douglass was explicit, in that   6
he needed physically to get north and escape slavery, but
it was also implicit because he sought to discover and redefine himself through his quest, as did Thoreau. Douglass's motives were more sharply focused than either
Franklin's or Thoreau's; his very humanness was at stake,
as well as his physical well-being and possibly even his
life. But Douglass also makes it clear that the most horrible part of slavery was the mental anguish of having no
hope of freedom. His learning to read, and his maintenance
of this skill, seems to have been as important as the
maintenance of his material comforts, of which he had very
few. In a sense, Douglass's quest is the most psychological and abstract so far, because it is for the very essence of freedom and humanity, both of which were mostly
taken for granted by Franklin and Thoreau. Also, Douglass's quest is the most pessimistic of the three; Douglass concludes that physical violence is the only way out,
as he finds with the Covey incident.

Finally, Mark Twain's *Huckleberry Finn* is an example   7
of the full range of meaning that the quest motif may assume. Geographically, Huck's quest is very large. But
again, there is a quest defined implicitly as well as one
defined explicitly, as Huck (without consciously realizing
it) searches for morality, truth, and freedom. Twain's use

of the quest is ambiguous, even more so than the previous
writers, because while he suggests success superficially
(i.e., the "happily-ever-after" scene in the last chapter), he really hints at some sort of ultimate hopeless-
ness inherent in society. Not even Douglass questions the
good or evil of American society as deeply as does Twain;
for Douglass, everything will be fine when slavery is
abolished; but for Twain, the only solution is to "light
out for the territories" altogether--and when Twain wrote,
he knew that the territories were no more.

Twain's implicit sense of spiritual failure stands in   8
marked contrast to Franklin's buoyant confidence in material success. The guiding image of the quest, however, is
central to American values and, consequently, a theme that
these writers and others have adapted to suit their own
vision.

EXERCISE 22.2

Analyze the following essay exam questions in order to decide what kind of
writing task they present. What is being asked of the student as a participant
in the course and as a writer? Given the time constraints of the exam, what
plan would you propose for writing the answer? Following each question
is the number of points it is worth and the amount of time allotted to answer it.

1.   Cortazar is a producer of fantastic literature. Discuss first what fantastic
literature is. Then choose any four stories by Cortazar as examples and discuss
the fantastic elements in these stories. Refer to the structure, techniques, and
narrative styles that he uses in these four stories. If you like, you may refer
to more than four, of course. (Points: 30 of 100. Time: 40 of 150 minutes.)

2.   During the course of the twentieth century, the United States has experienced three significant periods of social reform—the progressive era, the
age of the Great Depression, and the decade of the 1960s. What were the
sources of reform in each period? What were the most significant reform
achievements of each period as well as the largest failings? (Points: 35 of
100. Time: 75 of 180 minutes.)

3.   Since literature is both an artistic and ideological product, each writer
comments on his material context through his writing.

   a.   What is Rulto's perspective of his Mexican reality and how is it portrayed through his stories?

   b.   What particular themes does he deal with, especially in these stories:
"The Burning Plain," "Luvina," "They gave us the land," "Paso del
Norte," and "Tell them not to kill me."

    c. What literary techniques and structures does he use to convey his perspective? Refer to a specific story as an example.

(Points: 30 of 100. Time: 20 of 50 minutes.)

4.   Why is there a special reason to be concerned about the influence of TV watching on kids? In your answer include a statement of:

    a. Your own understanding of the *general communication principles* involved for any TV watcher.

    b. What's special about TV and kids?

    c. How advertisers and producers use this information. (You should draw from the relevant readings as well as lectures.)

(Points: 20 of 90. Time: 25 of 90 minutes.)

5.   Analyze the autobiographical tradition in American literature, focusing on differences and similarities among authors and, if appropriate, changes over time. Discuss four authors in all. In addition to the conscious autobiographers—Edwards, Franklin, Thoreau, Douglass—you may choose one or two figures from among the following fictional or poetic quasi-autobiographers: Hawthorne, Whitman, Dickinson, Twain. (Points: 50 of 120. Time: 60 of 180 minutes.)

6.   How does the system of (media) sponsorship work and what, if any, ideological control do sponsors exert? Be specific and illustrative! (Points: 33 of 100. Time: 60 of 180 minutes.)

7.   Several of the works studied in this course analyze the tension between myth and reality. Select two written works and two films and analyze how their authors or directors present the conflict between myth and reality and how they resolve it—if they resolve it. (Points: 45 of 130. Time: 60 of 180 minutes.)

8.   *Man's Hope* is a novel about the Spanish Civil War written while the war was still going on. *La Guerre est Finie* is a film about Spanish revolutionaries depicting their activities nearly thirty years after the Civil War. Discuss how the temporal relationship of each of these works to the Civil War is reflected in the character of the works themselves and in the differences between them. (Points: 58 of 100. Time: 30 of 50 minutes.)

9.   Write an essay on one of these topics: The role of the narrator in *Tom Jones* and *Pride and Prejudice,* or the characters of Uncle Toby and Miss Bates. (Points: 33 of 100. Time: 60 of 180 minutes.)

Appendix
Writing with a Word Processor

Prepared by the Daedalus Group

Do you compose your essays in longhand and then use a word processor to prepare a clean, nicely printed final copy for your instructor? Then this brief appendix is for you. Even the simplest and least expensive word processor provides many extremely powerful tools for writers. If you learn to use those tools well, you'll find that your word processor can help you with all the stages of the writing process, not just the final editing. This appendix will describe some word-processing techniques you can use for invention, drafting, revising, and editing. The specific techniques you use will depend partly on the particular word-processing software available to you, and partly on your own strategies as a writer. You may want to experiment with various techniques until you find the ones that work best for you.

WORD-PROCESSING BASICS

Composing with a word processor involves a few very basic steps. First you have to write something: in word-processing jargon, this is called "entering text." Once you've entered some text, you can do various things with it.

You can modify your text in various ways. For example, you can add to it. You can also delete part of what you've written. Or you can rearrange it, say by changing the order of your words or sentences or paragraphs. Once the text reads the way you like it, you can work with its format (that is, its physical appearance) and print it. A word processor allows you to do all these things on your screen without having to recopy or retype anything.

Creating Files Whenever you enter text that you want to refer to or work on again—such as invention activities, notes from sources or a rough draft of an essay—you can store or "save" your work in the computer's hard disk or on floppy disks. To do so, you have to tell the computer to save your work in a "file." If you don't do this before you exit your word processor or turn your computer off, you'll lose everything you've written. To save your work, you give the word processor a command, usually the "save" command. The way to give this command varies with different word processors, so you'll need to check your program's manual to see how to do this.

Most word processors ask (or "prompt") you to type in a "file name" for work you want to save. Many word-processing programs ask you to do this after you enter text; a few require you to do so before you start entering text. This is so the computer will know how to identify your work so you can get access to it later.

What should you name your file? Your instructor may ask you to use a specific file name; if not, make up a name you can remember—ideally, one that indicates what's in the file. FILE 1 isn't a good name, for example, because it says nothing about what's in the file. The more information you can get into the file name, the better: the first draft of an essay on Martin Luther King, Jr., for instance, might be named KING 1.

File names are necessarily short. On IBM or IBM-compatible computers, they may have no more than eight letters or numbers. The rules for naming files vary, though, depending on what kind of computer you're using. If you're using an Apple Macintosh, for instance, you can give your files longer, and thus much clearer, names, like "KING ESSAY, DRAFT 1."

Once you've entered a file name, the computer will store what you've written in an electronic file. You need to save your work frequently, every fifteen minutes or so. This is necessary to guard against losing it accidentally—because of a power failure, for example. For work you especially don't want to lose, you might make backup copies on a separate floppy disk.

Entering Text

To enter text, simply start your word processor and, when the "editing screen" appears, begin typing. The cursor—in some programs, a blinking white line; in others, a solid rectangle—will indicate where on the screen the next character will appear. No need to press a carriage return key (or "enter" key) at the end of each line—the only time you'll need the carriage return key is when you want to begin a new paragraph.

Modifying Text

You can add, delete, or reorganize your work with a few simple keystrokes. Every word-processing system has its own strokes for particular commands; check your user's manual to find out which keystrokes to use for your particular program.

To add text, just move the cursor to the spot where you want the new text to go and begin typing. Most word processors will automatically insert the new text where you put it in the existing text.

To delete text, simply press the backspace key, which erases characters to the left of the cursor. On IBM-compatible computers, you can also use the "del," or delete key to remove the character indicated by the cursor.

Working with Blocks of Text

One of the greatest conveniences a word processor offers is the ability to work with and manipulate blocks of text. Simply mark off (or "define") the block of text you want to work on, and you can then do various things with it. For example, you can:

- "cut"—delete it completely

- "cut and paste"—delete it from one place in the text and insert it somewhere else
- "copy"—leave it where it is and also insert a copy of it somewhere else
- "reformat"—boldface or italicize it; adjust its spacing; and so on

The manual for your word processor will tell you the specific commands to use. Most word processors also have an "undelete" or "restore" command in case you make a mistake; be sure you learn how to use it.

Formatting and Printing

Formatting the text means arranging its physical appearance: justifying (or not justifying) the margins; determining the spacing (single, double, triple, etc.); adding page numbers. Some word processors allow for special formats—for setting off quotations, numbering footnotes, keeping bibliographic entries, and so on. It's probably best not to get too fancy; remember that your first obligation is to make your work clear and readable.

Once you think you've got the format right, print out a copy of your text. If your word processor permits it, "preview" the finished document on-screen so that you can make any necessary changes before printing.

SOME USEFUL TECHNIQUES

All word processors offer features that can well serve any writer. Following is a brief catalogue of some of the most useful features, ones you will want to try out if you are writing with a word processor.

Working with a Split Screen

Many word processors have a split-screen capability, allowing you to divide your screen into two (or sometimes more) "windows." You can use the windows for displaying various things—sections of your draft, invention notes, information from outside sources, an outline of your plan, whatever. For instance, you might use one window to display a section you're working on, and put some earlier section in another window. You might, for example, want to keep your introductory paragraph in one window while you work on a later paragraph in another window. Such a two-paragraph view can help you to keep your main point always in mind, and to avoid straying from that point as you draft.

Some word processors allow you to work with a different file in each window, thus letting you keep some of your notes in front of you as you draft. This would facilitate work with source materials—when inserting block quotations, for instance, or even when paraphrasing rather than quoting a source's words.

Cutting and Pasting

Cutting and pasting takes its name from a common method used by writers who work with pen and paper—namely, cutting up a text into little strips, arranging them in some order, and then pasting them down on a piece of paper. Word processors let you cut and paste electronically—that is, you can "cut" a block of text from one place in your text and "paste" it in somewhere else. It is so easy that you can arrange and rearrange your text many different ways before finally settling on any one way. Experienced writers say that this function allows them to revise more easily than ever before, and thus encourages them to do so more ambitiously.

To cut and paste, simply select the block of text you want to move and use the "cut" or "move" commands (depending on your word processor). If at any time you want to go back to your original arrangement, you can easily reverse the procedure, sometimes with a single "undo" command.

With some word processors, you can cut and paste between different windows on your screen, and even between files. Imagine, for example, that you discover a need for some dialogue or for a different example in your draft. If your system allows you to cut and paste between screens, you could, with a few keystrokes, move an anecdote (or an example) from the screen with your invention notes right into your draft.

You can also "copy" text, which means to leave it where it is in your draft or notes and at the same time to insert it elsewhere. This copying feature allows you to experiment with your materials, to try them out here and then there. Say, for instance, that you have one especially powerful quotation to use and you can't decide whether it should go at the beginning of your essay, to draw readers in, or at the end, to leave them with something memorable. Copying allows you to try it out in both places, see where it works better, and then decide.

Highlighting

With a word processor you can highlight portions of your text, either by underscoring or boldfacing. Highlighting can help you to check over your text for various things. You could, for example, decide to highlight all examples, and thus see at a glance whether there are any places in your draft with too many or not enough examples. You could do the same with other important elements—topic sentences, dialogue, anecdotes, whatever. Someone working on a typewriter could of course do the same, but a word processor allows you, with a keystroke or two, to make the highlighting go away once you've checked what you want to see.

Using the Search Function

"Searching" is one of the most useful functions a word processor can offer to a writer. By issuing a single command, you can locate particular words or punctuation marks or even kinds of spacing every time they occur in your text. You could, for instance, use the search function to find every use of the word *I*, perhaps to check that you not overuse it. Or you might want to find every instance of the word *he*, perhaps to check whether it should instead be *he or she*. You can also use the search function to check for consistency—to make sure you spell a word one way throughout, for instance, *theater* or *theatre*, not both.

In addition to making a search, your word processor will allow you to "search and replace"—in other words, to search for one word or other element and automatically replace it with another. Say, for instance, that you've named Shakespeare as the author of a play that was actually written by Ben Jonson. With a search-and-replace function, you simply instruct your word processor to find every occurrence of the word *Shakespeare* in your text and to replace it with the words *Ben Jonson.*

A word of warning, however. The search-and-replace function is merely a tool; *you* must be the one to do the actual checking. It can lead you to various elements; you still have to decide which elements to check and what's appropriate or inappropriate. Like all word-processing features, the search-and-replace function is but a tool. You are still the writer.

Spell-Checkers

Most word processors include a spell checker. Spell checkers are simply functions that compare each word in your text to a list of words stored in the program's memory. It will question any of your words that it can't find on its list. Some spell checkers will also offer alternative spellings to replace the misspelled word, and most allow you to add your own words to the list, thus creating your own personal word list.

Be aware, however, that spell checkers are not human, and they aren't magic; they're simply programs that compare strings of letters without any understanding of what the letters mean. In fact, a spell checker can be wrong, and in various different ways. For instance, it may signal that a correctly spelled word is misspelled when it can't find it in its list of words. On the other hand, there are some spelling errors it will never recognize. For example, a spell checker will not call attention to mistaken usage of the possessive *its* or the contraction *it's.* Both are correct spellings, and the spell checker cannot tell whether you've *used* them correctly or not. You'll have the same difficulty with another often confused pair, *affect* and *effect.* The point is, don't assume that your draft has no spelling errors just because the spell checker doesn't find any.

Usage, Style, and Grammar Checkers

You can also find programs that check for usage, style, and, sometimes, grammar. Like spell checkers, these can be helpful tools that can alert you to some things you may want to check for—*be* verbs, extremely long sentences, instances of the passive voice, and so on. Properly used, such programs can help you to see your writing more critically by pointing out potential problems. But they are even more likely to mislead you than spell checkers because they can catch only some problems, and they sometimes flag nonexistent problems. Be aware of the limits of the programs if you use them; and don't expect miracles from them. Like spell checkers, usage, style, or grammar checkers don't correct with an eye for content. Only you can do that.

USING THE ST. MARTIN'S SOFTWARE

The *St. Martin's Guide to Writing* is accompanied by software for invention and revision, called the *St. Martin's MindWriter/Descant*. It is available for both IBM-compatible and Macintosh computers; simply ask your instructor for your copy.

Designed to be used with the *St. Martin's Guide,* the *MindWriter/Descant* program features many of the writing options presented in the book. The program works around a series of questions, or "prompts," which will help you to generate material and then to analyze and respond to text. For invention, it will help you find a topic and then to define, focus, and discover what you know or can find out about it. For revision, it will help you then to critique and edit text, either your own or someone else's.

This program is designed to accompany the *St. Martin's Guide,* not to replace it. For both detailed explanations and examples, it will refer you to the book. It is also designed to be used with your own word processor. Although the *MindWriter/Descant* program performs basic word-processing functions, it does not provide all the functions you may be used to. You may, therefore, wish to transfer the materials you generate in response to the *MindWriter/Descant* program into a more powerful word processor. And, when you are ready to revise, you can transfer your draft back into *MindWriter/Descant* and follow its prompts for analyzing and responding to text.

Following is a brief description of the program. For specific information about how to use it on your computer, you will need to consult the *St. Martin's MindWriter/Descant* user's manual.

When you first start *MindWriter/Descant,* you will be asked to enter your first and last name in a space provided for that purpose, and then you'll see a new screen with a "menu," or list of chapters (2–10), from the *St. Martin's Guide.* After you select the appropriate chapter, you'll see another, smaller menu listing four choices: *Writing Assignment*; *Invention and Planning*; *Reading and Revising*; *Continue Earlier File.* Choose the first option to view the writing assignment; then choose the second option, Invention and Planning, to begin invention work for the assignment you're beginning.

Invention and Planning

You will then see a menu offering three kinds of invention work: *Choosing a Possible Topic*; *Exploring a Topic*; *Setting Goals and Outlining.* Each menu item leads you to a set of prompts, which appear at the top of your computer screen. Enter any response to the prompts in the "editing box," or "window," in the middle of the screen; then go on to the next one. If at any point you're not sure what to do or what a particular prompt means, you can select Help from a menu bar above the editing box for explanations of prompts or instructions on how to operate the program.

When you've made your way through the prompts, you can save your work in a file, print it out, or do both. If you don't have time to address all the prompts, you can save what you've done to return to later. Once you've worked through the three invention activities, the next step is to load the file containing all your responses into your word processor. *MindWriter/ Descant* saves text such that it can be brought up on most word processors; so load this file as you would any text file (consult your word processor's manual if you have questions). Here you can modify the file as you need to, adding and deleting material as necessary, reorganizing what you've written, and so on, until you're satisfied that your draft is complete. Remember, however, to save your work often.

Reading and Revising

Once you have a draft, you're ready to go on to the reading and writing materials. Start by selecting Reading and Revising for the appropriate chapter from the main *MindWriter/Descant* menu. You'll then see another menu, offering two choices: *Reading with a Critical Eye* and *Identifying Problems*. Whichever option you select, the screen will be divided into three parts. The upper portion of the screen displays a series of prompts designed to help you critique a draft. You can use it for evaluating your own writing or that done by someone else. In the middle of the screen is an editing box, where you can enter your responses to the prompts; and at the bottom of the screen is the text you are analyzing.

You can call up drafts generated in most any word-processing program and evaluate it by using the guidelines in the *MindWriter/Descant* program. The section on Reading with a Critical Eye presents prompts that will help you to analyze how successfully the draft fulfills the writing assignment, and the section on Identifying Problems will help you then to plot strategies for revision.

As with the invention and planning materials, you can save your responses to the reading and revising prompts, print them out, or both. Unless your instructor asks you not to, give a copy to the writer of any draft you evaluate. If you've been analyzing your own work, you can print a copy of your comments to keep beside you as you revise; or if your word processor allows you to display two files simultaneously, you can display the *MindWriter/ Descant* comments in one portion of the screen and your draft in another.

MindWriter/Descant is designed to help you with your writing assignments. Use it however it works best for you. Do not feel compelled to respond to every prompt, and feel free to work out of sequence—beginning in the middle of the invention prompts if you already have a topic, abandoning a topic that isn't working for you and starting over again with more general prompts, moving back and forth between your word processor and the revision prompts to read and respond to very rough drafts as well as final ones. And when you find an activity that works particularly well for you, be sure to see what else the *St. Martin's Guide* has to say about it.

Acknowledgments (continued from page iv)

Robert N. Bellah; et alia. "Mythic Individualism" from *Habits of the Heart,* pages 144–147. Copyright © 1985 The Regents of the University of California.

Jean Brandt. "Calling Home." Reprinted by permission of the author.

California State Department of Education excerpt. Reprinted by permission from the *Handbook for Planning an Effective Literature Program,* copyright 1987, California State Department of Education, P.O. Box 271, Sacramento, CA 95802-0271.

Brian Cable. "The Last Stop." Reprinted by permission of the author.

Forrest Carter. "Willow John" is excerpted from *The Education of Little Tree* by Forrest Carter, published by University of New Mexico Press and reprinted by permission of Eleanor Friede Books, Inc. Copyright © 1976 by Forrest Carter.

K. C. Cole. "Why There Are So Few Women in Science," *The New York Times,* Copyright © 1981 by The New York Times Company. Reprinted by permission.

Kim Dartnell. "Where Will They Sleep Tonight?" Reprinted by permission of the author.

Peter Davis. From *Hometown,* Copyright © 1982 by Peter Davis. Reprinted by permission of Simon & Schuster, Inc.

Annie Dillard. "Handed My Own Life" from *An American Childhood* by Annie Dillard. Copyright © 1987 by Annie Dillard. Reprinted by permission of HarperCollins Publishers Inc.

Annie Dillard. Excerpt from *Teaching a Stone to Talk* by Annie Dillard. Copyright © 1982 by Annie Dillard. Reprinted by permission of HarperCollins Publishers Inc.

Barbara Ehrenreich. "The Wretched of the Hearth," from *The New Republic,* April 2, 1990, pp. 28–31. Reprinted by permission.

Gretel Ehrlich. From "Rules of the Game: Rodeo" from *The Solace of Open Spaces* by Gretel Ehrlich. Copyright © 1985 by Gretel Ehrlich. Reprinted by permission of Viking Penguin, a division of Penguin Books USA, Inc.

Victor Fuchs. Excerpted by permission of the publishers from *How We Live* by Victor Fuchs, Cambridge, Mass.: Harvard University Press, Copyright © 1983 by the President and Fellows of Harvard College.

Kristin A. Goss. "Taking a Stand against Sexism," from *The Harvard Crimson,* March 5, 1986. Copyright © 1986 by the Harvard Crimson. Reprinted by permission.

Stephen Jay Gould. Selections are reprinted from *Ever Since Darwin, Reflections in Natural History,* by Stephen Jay Gould, by permission of W. W. Norton & Company, Inc. Copyright © 1977 by Stephen Jay Gould. Copyright © 1973, 1974, 1975, 1976, 1977 by The American Museum of Natural History.

Jan Gray. "Father." Reprinted by permission of the author.

Suzan Shown Harjo. "Last Rites for Indian Dead," *Los Angeles Times,* September 16, 1989. Copyright © 1989 by Suzan Shown Harjo. Reprinted by permission.

Gerald Haslam. "The Horned Toad" from *New Arts Review.* Copyright © 1983 by Gerald Haslam. Reprinted by permission of the author.

Ernest Hemingway. Reprinted with permission of Charles Scribner's Sons, an imprint of Macmillan Publishing Company, from *Death in the Afternoon* by Ernest Hemingway. Copyright 1932 by Charles Scribner's Sons, renewed 1960 by Ernest Hemingway.

Rachel Richardson Smith. "Abortion, Right and Wrong," from *Newsweek,* March 25, 1985. Reprinted by permission of the author.

Jessica Statsky. "Children Need to Play, Not Compete." Reprinted by permission of the author.

Jason Thornton. "Documenting *Document.*" Reprinted by permission of the author.

Alice Walker. "Everyday Use" from *In Love and Trouble: Stories of Black Women,* copyright © 1973 by Alice Walker. Reprinted by permission of Harcourt Brace Jovanovich, Inc.

Webster's dictionary definition of "brave." By permission. From *Webster's New Dictionary of Synonyms* © 1984 by Merriam-Webster Inc., publisher of the Merriam-Webster® dictionaries.

Adam Paul Weisman. "Birth Control in the Schools," *The New Republic,* March 16, 1987. Reprinted by permission of *The New Republic,* © 1987, The New Republic, Inc.

E. B. White. "Death of a Pig" from *Essays of E. B. White* by E. B. White. Copyright 1947 by E. B. White. Reprinted by permission of HarperCollins Publishers Inc.

William Carlos Williams. From *The Farmer's Daughters.* Copyright 1938 by William Carlos Williams. Reprinted by permission of New Directions Publishing Corporation.

Tobias Wolff. From the book *This Boy's Life,* copyright © 1989 by Tobias Wolff. Used by permission of Atlantic Monthly Press.

Al Young, "Unripened Light" from *A World Unsuspected: Portraits of Southern Childhood,* copyright © 1987 by Al Young. Reprinted by permission of the author.

Gary Zukav. Excerpted from *The Dancing Wu Li Masters* by Gary Zukav. Copyright © 1979 by Gary Zukav. Reprinted by permission of William Morrow & Co., Inc.

Author and Title Index

Subject Index